AMERICAN POLITICAL PATTERNS

Conflict and Consensus

AMERICAN POLITICAL PATTERNS

Conflict and Consensus

DAN NIMMO
University of Houston

THOMAS D. UNGS
Wichita State University

Little, Brown and Company

Boston

Preface

The publication of a new book in a field already crowded with texts risks being met with a caution or cynicism not unlike that which greets an advertising campaign introducing a laundry powder. The claims on the package are often greater than the performance. No single book can hope to satisfy all the demands of teachers who must communicate to students the broad spectrum of American government. Nor can all the needs of a widely varied student population be fulfilled by any text, regardless of its size or scope. With these limitations recognized, we dare to suggest that this is a different kind of textbook.

More and more teachers are decrying the failure of political scientists to incorporate and integrate new findings into introductory texts. Combined with this view has been a growing criticism in the profession of existing texts as lacking a consistent framework and as being too large to permit the use of the great variety of excellent paperback supplementary materials. We have sought to provide a book that integrates within a coherent interpretive context some of the more important findings and insights about American politics. Priorities such as these force hard choices and the sacrifice of some things which others may feel essential. We believe that the majority of beginning students possess more knowledge of the "nuts and bolts" of American government than their predecessors of five or ten years ago. Also, students are more responsive to material that integrates and interprets than to material that inundates with details under the guise of being "comprehensive." This book seeks to provide a basis for inquiry and understanding, and a consistency of framework from beginning to end.

There is little merit in the presentation of data for its own sake; it is useful only when it contributes to understanding. We have been selective in our choices while recognizing that the individual instructor may prefer other data to illustrate or supplement the same point. Also, much attention has been given to avoiding the pitfalls of failing to articulate or inform by over-insistence on brevity or preciseness in choice of words. On the other hand, we have tried to avoid informality or simplicity of language where its use would endanger our meaning. Although we have utilized topical examples where they might illustrate a particularly crucial point, we have deliberately sought to avoid, too, the anecdotal tone for its own sake. The final product, we hope, is neither patronizing nor pretentious.

We know of no way to achieve a consistent and well integrated framework short of a deliberate effort to link each chapter closely with the preceding material. Many otherwise good textbooks have failed by compromising this essential consideration. Instructors can, however, vary the sequence by utilizing related supplementary materials that suit their own needs and orientations to the discipline. The bibliographic notes at the end of each chapter are suggestive only. If we have successfully achieved our goals, students will find the reading stimulating enough to explore further.

The wisdom of only brief treatment of some areas, and exclusion of others, will be questioned by some. Our problem is one of an abundance of riches in a discipline that is experiencing its own explosion of knowledge.

We have tried to incoporate the advice and suggestions of many individuals. They are too numerous to list here but we acknowledge their gracious help. Professor Allan P. Sindler's contribution to whatever is of merit in our efforts is so large as to deserve special acknowledgment. Professor Samuel Krislov also provided many helpful suggestions. We are similarly grateful for the careful editorial assistance of Mrs. Eileen Mason and Mr. David Giele of Little, Brown and Company. Mr. Donald Hammonds, editor in chief of the College Department of Little, Brown, assisted in ways too numerous to mention, not the least of which was his enthusiasm for a text of this type as a publishing venture. What weaknesses exist are here in spite of the named persons' efforts to change the minds of two determined writers.

Finally, one of us expresses grateful appreciation to the research committee of Wichita State University which provided both relief from teaching duties and funds to aid in completion of the manuscript. The other wishes to acknowledge the assistance of the Department of Political Science at the University of Houston for making funds available at a critical juncture.

D. N.
T. D. U.

Contents

POLITICAL COMMUNICATION

PART TWO

POLITICAL POLICY

To Joan and Theresa

POLITICAL
COMMUNITY

PART ONE

Patterns of Conflict and Consensus in American Government

Any description and interpretation of American government rests upon certain underlying assumptions. In order to establish our approach to the subject matter, we present in the following pages our view of the sources, character, and vocabulary of political activity in America. First, we consider politics as a means of balancing the tensions between conflict and consensus in any community. Next we discuss the quality of American political consensus and the character of our liberal-democratic values. Finally, we examine the American Constitution as a factor shaping political patterns in the polity. Hence, we are concerned in Part One with the nature of politics and, more specifically, with the social, doctrinal, and constitutional setting for the conduct of government in America.

CHAPTER
ONE

Political Activity

With passage of the Voting Rights Act of 1965 the Congress of the United States removed a major obstacle thwarting equal political opportunity for all Americans. Among its sweeping provisions the act suspended literacy tests for voting, permitted federal voting examiners to order registration for Negroes in areas where the franchise previously was denied, and authorized exhaustive investigations of instances of voter discrimination. Coming as it did in the wake of the Civil Rights Acts of 1957, 1960, and 1964, many viewed congressional action in 1965 as a culminating step in assuring political equality for the American Negro. Yet by the following summer Americans once more engaged in a civil rights struggle marked by a prolonged march of demonstrators through Mississippi, voter-registration rallies, demands for "Black Power," sporadic retaliatory outbursts of violence, and renewed efforts for congressional action. Underlying the consensus achieved in 1965 remained cleavages later displayed in the courts, legislative halls, and streets.

The civil rights conflict is but one of myriad social disputes that Americans seek to settle through political action. Its development since World War II illustrates how the fabric of our politics consists of recurrent attempts to reconcile the diverse yearnings of individual citizens with a transcendent desire to live together as Americans. The purpose of this

3

book is to describe and interpret the patterns of political activity in America that work to achieve such reconciliations. We maintain that politics provides an environment of creative conflict wherein concerns for human values thrive, mature, and reach fruition. This chapter focuses on the sources and the role of politics in human life, and leads us to a tentative definition of political activity.

POLITICS AND PEOPLE

The universe of global politics consists of more than 120 independent national polities which together regulate the conduct of more than 3 billion persons. Innumerable smaller political units distinct in form and practice operate below the national level. In America alone, there is a plethora of jurisdictions — the federal government, state governments, counties, municipalities, school districts, water districts, sewer authorities, etc. Caught up as we are in the complexity generated by this diversity of governing units, we sometimes lose sight of the common denominator of all government — people. The character of politics is what it is because people act as they do. Although this notion is neither startling nor novel, its implications deserve continuing reexamination and reemphasis.

THE HUMAN SITUATION

The origins of politics lie in the human situation. Man is circumscribed by physical needs and social wants, yet freed by capacities, skills, and resources that make possible the achieving of personal desires.

Man's physical being imposes a limiting factor that must be overcome for human existence, yet the need for food and water has greater political significance than solely as a prerequisite for human survival. Political awareness and community consciousness develop only after men no longer must spend all waking hours searching for enough to stay alive. Until they satisfy basic physical needs, including adequate clothing, shelter, and reproductive opportunities, men remain "an unrelated agglomeration of people living within certain territorial boundaries." [1]

Man demonstrates remarkable capacities for adjusting to changing surroundings and for fulfilling his desires. His manipulative capacities contribute to the invention of instruments, tools, and technology and promote the acquisition of basic necessities. The human capacity for reason makes man a problem-solving creature of the highest order. In turn, the wedding of these manipulative and contemplative capabilities engenders

---

[1] James C. Davies, *Human Nature in Politics* (New York: John Wiley and Sons, 1963), pp. 27–28; see also Graham Wallas, *Human Nature in Politics* (Bison Book; Lincoln: University of Nebraska Press, 1962).

communication, a necessary condition if men are to band together in communities for the satisfaction of physical needs.

Men congregate in communities, a fact with political implications of its own. They find it important not only to satisfy basic needs but also to place values upon relationships with other people. In doing this, they generate desires for self-esteem, self-respect, and equality.[2] All constitute politically relevant factors, as recent movements for civil rights legislation in America indicate.

Within the context of common human needs and wants, however, the diversity of human preferences is a significant source of political activity as well. At the simplest level, all men require food to exist, but they desire different foods to enjoy living.

Different preferences in satisfying needs are paralleled by differences in social wants. Societies contribute to shaping personal values. "Man is not merely *de facto* associated, but he *becomes* a social animal in the make-up of his ideas, sentiments, and deliberate behavior." [3] People identify with, and learn from, their associates. Diverse identifications engender diverse expectations, tastes, temperaments, skills, resources, and beliefs.

Finally, to this dissimilarity in physical needs and social wants, we must add the variety that prevails in individual capacities for achieving desires: differences in manipulative talents, measurable psychological differences of intelligence and of emotional patterns, and divergencies in both personal skills and resources produced by variations in social opportunities. For example, a disparity in the distribution of economic resources among men — between individuals, social groups, and even nations — contributes to those differences in social rank, status, prestige, and power that play so large a role in political experience. So ubiquitous are inequalities that a democratic polity seeks to relieve them through equality of opportunity, in order to prevent them from becoming "a means of oppression of the less gifted." [4]

In sum, men differ both in their physical and social traits and in their personal preferences. In order to secure a safe and stable environment to advance personal preferences, they make demands upon associates. Out of this context emerge contrasting desires reflected in reciprocal demands. Tension arises between men of diverse preferences, particularly when

[2] See particularly Hadley Cantril's conclusions in *The Pattern of Human Concerns* (New Brunswick, N.J.: Rutgers University Press, 1965), pp. 315–22; Hadley Cantril, *Human Nature and Political Systems* (New Brunswick, N.J.: Rutgers University Press, 1961); and Hadley Cantril, "Don't Blame It on Human Nature," *The New York Times Magazine,* July 6, 1947.

[3] John Dewey, *The Public and Its Problems* (Denver: Alan Swallow, 1927), p. 25.

[4] John Dewey, "Democracy and Educational Administration," *School and Society,* April 3, 1937.

insufficient resources exist to satisfy the wishes of everyone. Thus, the human situation is the source of social conflict, the seedbed of politics.

THE UNIVERSALITY OF HUMAN CONFLICT

Depending upon the perspective of the observer, human conflict has been assailed as, at best, a necessary evil; at worst, incontrovertible evidence of the perversity and rascality of man. In recent years, "conflict theorists" have accepted social disputes as normal and universal and have explored their characteristics, functions, and variations.[5]

We propose that two conditions are necessary for a conflict situation to exist: first, participants (individuals or groups) must perceive their desires as different from the desires of others, and the disputants must actively seek to realize these desires; secondly, these desires must be incompatible (that is, the benefits obtained by one participant are denied to the other, because the scarcity of resources in the situation prohibits every member from obtaining absolute fulfillment of his demands).[6] Conflict is the active dimension of desires of achieving diverse physical needs and social wants in a context of differing human capacities and limited resources.

In social conflicts, opposing forces seek to gain (relative to their own values), to advance their own purposes, and to satisfy their own desires — often without regard for the gains or losses of rivals. Although specific goals of these opposing groups are incompatible by definition, there is usually sufficient commonality of outlook among disputants to permit some reconciliation. Victory, then, is measured not by an opponent's defeat but by the partial success of all participants in the dispute. Each side gets some, but not all, of its desires fulfilled. Compromises advancing the wishes of all contenders constitute satisfactory "victories," and "ties" (frequently viewed as odious in sports and humiliating to national pride in wars) are accepted by participants. Hence, a social conflict is neither purely competitive nor cooperative, but possesses elements of both. Dissimilarity of purposes promotes disagreement, while sufficient identity permits compromise.

[5] See Lewis A. Coser, *The Functions of Social Conflict* (Glencoe, Ill.: The Free Press, 1956); Georg Simmel, *Conflict* (Glencoe, Ill.: The Free Press, 1955); International Sociological Association, *The Nature of Conflict* (Paris: UNESCO, 1957); Robert Lee and Martin E. Marty, *Religion and Social Conflict* (Oxford: Oxford University Press, 1964); Raymond W. Mack and Richard C. Snyder, "The Analysis of Social Conflict," *The Journal of Conflict Resolution*, I (June, 1957), 212–48; Quincey Wright, "The Nature of Conflict," *The Western Political Quarterly*, IV (June, 1951), 193–209; Robert C. North *et al.*, "The Integrative Functions of Conflict," *The Journal of Conflict Resolution*, IV (September, 1960), 355–74; Elton B. McNeil (ed.), *The Nature of Human Conflict* (Englewood Cliffs, N.J.: Prentice-Hall, 1965).

[6] Kenneth Boulding, *Conflict and Defense* (New York: Harper and Brothers, 1962).

The degree of social conflict depends in part upon the characteristics of the members of a society. The likelihood of social conflict decreases in a homogeneous society and in a society in which resources are equally distributed. Moreover, social conflict is somewhat more common when disputants are well organized and members are committed to rigid ideological postures. Societies tend to have more enduring internal cleavages when rules for accommodating differences are not generally understood.[7]

Social conflicts vary as to method of reconciliation, visibility, and type of goal. Conflicts may be face-to-face confrontations (between individuals or groups) or may be indirect, occurring through intermediaries and resolved by third persons.[8] In complex societies, procedures of conflict management are normally institutionalized. Formal organizations — legislatures, courts, political parties, bureaucracies — exist for the expressed purpose of dealing with social conflict through bargaining, the application of agreed-upon standards, discussion, and voting. Secondly, the visibility of social disagreements varies. Open, publicized conflict is taken for granted in a democratic polity where popular inquiry into social demands and popular criticism of social policies are fostered. In contrast, a more authoritarian, totalitarian, or otherwise closed regime demonstrates less tolerance for popular conflict in efforts to maintain a façade of harmonious commitment to the ruler, ideology or national goal. Finally, goals provoking disagreement may be specific and material (for example, higher taxes) or less concrete, more symbolic, and ideological ("roll back communism").

Conflict is contagious. Demands are usually met by counter-demands, contrariness, and opposition. In the process, disputants recruit support for their respective claims. As more people become involved in a conflict, the disagreement becomes more publicized, and the prospect for negotiating differences becomes more realistic. Attempts to mobilize support generate efforts to control and influence the behavior of others.

On the surface, conflict divides people into opposing camps resulting in potentially severe cleavages. Paradoxically, cleavage itself can, and often does, promote social integration. If a society possesses a tolerance for internal conflict, people can openly join groups for promotion of personal values. In so doing, they agree to social definitions of what are, and are not, legitimate disagreements. Group standards and objectives are formulated, members recruited, the boundaries of group life demarcated, and social stability advanced. The promotion of such group cohesion strengthens consensus: "Consensus on the norms of tolerance which a

[7] Mack and Snyder, *op. cit.*
[8] Ruth Benedict, *Patterns of Culture* (New York: Mentor, 1946), p. 96.

society or organization accepts has often developed only as a result of basic conflict, and requires the continuation of conflict to sustain it." [9]

Conflict is both catalyst and product of social change. Social diversity implies continued dissatisfaction with the status quo, particularly as new values are prized by groups formerly satisfied with, or perhaps not satisfied with, the existing social arrangement. Both groups seeking new goals and those protecting older ways make claims upon others. Conflict and change are interlocked, each promoting and intensifying the other until accommodations are found. An overly cooperative society may become stagnant; by the same token, a highly competitive society may be crippled unless it discovers some method for adjusting disruptive social disputes.

Although social conflict promotes both social stability and change, it can threaten both. Conflicts can and do intensify; positions harden; goals are dogmatically stated, tenaciously held. Conflict relations grow embittered, and adversaries come to desire one another's downfall, both physical and social. The costs of conflict grow in excess of any rewards if pushed to uncontrolled, competitive extremes. Because social annihilation as well as cooperation inhere in human conflict, societies have evolved means of regulating disputes and preventing internal explosions. Politics is one such means. Before turning to the discussion of politics from that standpoint, let us explore more precisely what it is that people are interested in conserving when they seek to regulate social controversies. This leads us to examine another fact of human existence — human community.

THE UNIVERSALITY OF HUMAN COMMUNITY

Conflict appears with such frequency between human beings that we are able to speak of it as a universal trait of man. No less universal is the collective experience of mankind — that is, the tendency of people to join together and share their experiences as human beings. In defining community we adopt the words of Professor R. M. MacIver: "Wherever any group, small or large, live together in such a way that they share, not this or that particular interest, but the basic conditions of a common life, we call that group a community." [10]

Despite regional, racial, religious, or class differences, despite all align-

[9] Seymour Martin Lipset, *Political Man* (Garden City, N.Y.: Doubleday & Co., 1959), p. 22.

[10] For the characteristics of community see the following: R. M. MacIver, *Society: A Textbook of Sociology* (New York: Farrar and Rinehart, 1937), pp. 8–9; John Dewey, "Communication and Communal Living," in Joseph Ratner (ed.), *Intelligence in the Modern World* (New York: Modern Library, 1939), pp. 385–400; Jessie Bernard, *American Community Behavior* (Rev. ed., New York: Holt, Rinehart, and Winston, 1962); Robert A. Nisbet, *Community and Power* (New York: Oxford University Press, 1962); and Philip E. Jacob and James V. Toscano (eds.), *The Integration of Political Communities* (Philadelphia and New York: J. B. Lippincott Co., 1964).

ments of desires separating social groups, and despite all forms of diversity dividing individuals, a collective disposition cuts across these cleavages. No assurance exists that communities stem simply from the urge to have them; but the desire for collective action is a necessary, if not a sufficient, condition for their emergence. The desire to associate — the "sense of community" — is facilitated by the union of those manipulative and contemplative capacities of man mentioned earlier, a union producing language and effective communication. "A community consists of people who have learned to communicate with each other and to understand each other well beyond the mere interchange of goods and services." [11]

Several forces intensify the sense of community devotion. Men are bound to community by attachment to family, neighbors, friends, jobs, property, and religion. Gradually they come to be increasingly loyal to the idea of being "in the same boat together." [12] The process is frequently advanced if other factors that add impetus for association are present: shared values, beliefs, traditions, and laws; common territory and boundaries. These lend viability to community and are reinforced themselves by collective experience.

Although a community may originate without any unity of purpose among members beyond that of association for its own sake, in time shared values (notions of what is right and wrong, good or bad, desirable or undesirable) and beliefs (notions of what does and does not exist, what can and cannot be expected) develop. The integration of social groups into the community is facilitated when collective values and beliefs are widely held, transmitted, and pursued. When these values and beliefs are absorbed into community traditions and institutions, they serve, as we shall see later, as impersonal mediators in adjusting community disputes.

A desire to share common territory implies that social controversies cannot be settled by driving one set of antagonists from that territory, although movie and television epics about the American West suggest such a simple solution to the struggle between farmers and ranchers. Recent civil rights disputes can not be adjusted by removing either segregationists or integrationists from the United States, although some southern Whites and Black Muslims propose the alternative. When disputants occupy the same territory, other remedies must be discovered.[13]

The sharing of disagreement is no less a characteristic of community

[11] Karl Deutsch, *Nationalism and Social Communication* (Cambridge, Mass.: The M.I.T. Press, 1953), p. 65.
[12] Thomas C. Schelling, *The Strategy of Conflict* (New York: Oxford University Press, 1963), p. 11.
[13] Bernard, *op. cit.*, pp. 3–9.

than a sharing of association, communication, territory, and values. A community is a union of conflicts as well as consensus. If conflict is not tolerated, the desire for association is threatened, and the community may cease. So long as the commitment for association is genuine, social conflict serves as a mechanism for presenting popular demands for community decision. The tacit agreement for collective living implies no contract to forgo disputes; but a sense of community imposes the requirement of managing disputes, of adjusting them before their scope and intensity endanger community survival.

A community possesses several dimensions. In our analysis of the American community, we find three dimensions — the personal, social, and politico-constitutional — that are particularly significant in shaping the patterns of American government.

First, we designate a *personal* dimension consisting of individual responses to community life in the form of attitudes, feelings, or sentiments. Although our focus is upon personal attitudes, we are equally interested in the sharing of common values and beliefs among large numbers of Americans. Shared values and beliefs comprise ideologies or doctrines; examples include liberal democracy, socialism, and fascism. Such doctrines are not restricted to unified sets of ideas, internally consistent or accepted by all members with equal loyalty. Shared personal responses frequently reflect merely a fundamental agreement among individuals of the worth of the community itself; beyond that, members can disagree sharply over other values and beliefs.

Secondly, the *social* dimension consists of community members sharing a "self-sufficient system of action which is capable of existing longer than the life span of single personalities."[14] Here we include both socially relevant attributes of Americans (age, sex, ethnic, racial, and religious affiliations, etc.) and the relations linking people into a social unit (group memberships, status, privileges, occupations, etc.). Thus, aggregates of individuals, rather than the individuals themselves, joined by shared characteristics and activities make up the social dimension.

Finally, given the potential diversity in the social composition of a community and in personal attitudes, disputes over social goals, values, and beliefs are normal. When procedures and rules for settling social disputes are devised and generally accepted as legitimate, the activities performed in conjunction with them constitute the *politico-constitutional* dimension of community. Tentatively we can identify the political aspect of this dimension as the activities of persons involved in conflicts requiring community adjustment; the constitutional portion refers to the written

[14] D. F. Aberle *et al.,* "The Functional Prerequisites of a Society," *Ethics*, LX, No. 2 (January, 1950), 101.

and unwritten conventions that develop in the process of mediating disputes.

POLITICS: THE REGULATION OF SOCIAL CONFLICT

In observing that men act politically because of human traits, we have only hinted at the types of activity that are political. The nature of politics is varied, and no single definition mirrors its many facets. Moreover, political terminology comprises words defined with only modest precision in ordinary discourse, but appropriate concepts can be clarified to assist systematic description and analysis of political behavior.[15] Given the variety of notions that prevail both in politics and in daily discourse about government, any definition of politics is at best a working one — one that aids understanding but does not purport to be final or definitive. What follows is an attempt to construct a vocabulary of politics from terms used in ordinary discourse. As a beginning, we offer the notion that politics is the most inclusive process by which social conflict is regulated in a community.

THE POLITICAL PROCESS AND SOCIAL CONFLICT

What are the implications of labeling politics a "process" concerned with "social conflict"? As a term frequently employed in discussing human affairs, *process* refers to a series of activities related to one another. These activities form distinctive patterns; that is, any single activity "is explained when it is so related to a set of other elements that together they constitute a unified system," and we understand such activity "by identifying it as a specific part in an organized whole."[16] In this sense, we define politics as a series of human activities related to adjusting social disputes, a series manifested in patterned form.

In noting the active nature of politics, we stress that all government consists of people doing things. Normally, we shall use the terms politics and government interchangeably, for when "government" does something, it is people who do it; thus, government is people acting politically. Instead of referring to government as an impersonal agency that acts and to politics as the method by which it acts, we use both terms to denote patterns of activity in conflict regulation.

[15] Sheldon S. Wolin, *Politics and Vision* (Boston: Little, Brown and Co., 1960), p. 14.
[16] Abraham Kaplan, *The Conduct of Inquiry* (San Francisco: Chandler Publishing Co., 1964), p. 333; Samuel H. Beer *et al.*, *Patterns of Government* (2nd ed.; New York: Random House, 1962), p. 6.

By activity we refer both to physical activity (the overt behavior of walking, talking, writing, marking a ballot, etc.) and mental activity (perceiving, reflecting, possessing attitudes, etc.). Relationships between political participants cannot be identified and adequately explained apart from the behavior of other participants in the setting of the action. For example, just as in economics the behavior of neither buyer nor seller can be understood in isolation, in politics there are reciprocal relations between governors and governed. These reciprocal relations constitute political patterns, and we assume that certain factors are associated with shaping them. Subsequently, we identify the personal, social, and politico-constitutional factors normally linked to regularities in American government.

Activities designated as political arise from the presence of social conflict in the community. We said earlier that individuals pursue personal desires in fulfilling physical needs and social wants. Yet no one can pursue all his desires simultaneously and, hence, we must act selectively. By ordering our personal preferences and establishing priorities, we direct our behavior toward particular goals. Our disposition to achieve these specific aims constitutes the goal-oriented activity we designate as politically relevant *interests*.[17]

Conflicts of interest develop within and between individuals, groups, political parties, legislatures, courts, etc. We distinguish three levels of politically important interest conflicts — personal, social, and corporate. First, intrapersonal conflicts involve the cross-pressures encountered when an individual faces incompatible courses of action. As we see later, this type of conflict plays a significant role in voting behavior in America. Secondly, as discussed in Part Two, interest conflicts occur between persons (interpersonal) and groups (intergroup). Finally, conflicts between official, or corporate, interests develop between officials located in differing agencies of government (see Part Three).

THE POLITICAL PROCESS
AND CONFLICT REGULATION

Regulation is "the process by means of which a system attempts to maintain or preserve its identity over time as it adapts to changing conditions."[18] Politics is a process of regulation; it permits a community to

[17] Vernon Van Dyke, "Values and Interests," *The American Political Science Review*, LVI (September, 1962); 567–76; J. D. B. Miller, *The Nature of Politics* (London: Gerald Duckworth & Co., 1962), p. 39; see also Arthur Bentley, *The Process of Government* (Evanston: The Principia Press of Illinois, 1949); Charles B. Hagan, "The Group in a Political Science," in Roland Young (ed.), *Approaches to the Study of Politics* (Evanston, Ill.: Northwestern University Press, 1958), pp. 38–51; and David B. Truman, *The Governmental Process* (New York: Alfred A. Knopf, 1951).

[18] Morton A. Kaplan, *System and Process in International Politics* (New York: John Wiley & Sons, 1957), p. 89.

adapt to changes manifested in interest conflict by adjusting social disputes, thus advancing community viability. As a regulatory process, politics in America possesses two overlapping aspects, each of which appears in several distinctive patterns. First, people cannot derive satisfaction of their desires from the community nor can social disputes be accommodated publicly until popular demands and conflicts are known. The activities by which interests are mobilized, confront one another, and are transmitted to community officials we call *conflict representation*. Secondly, once social conflict is publicized, accommodation occurs at various points in the community; we label activities directed at adjusting interest disputes as *conflict resolution*. Although later in this book we devote separate portions of our discussion to conflict representation (Part Two) and conflict resolution (Part Three), we shall give here a few introductory comments regarding the character of these twin aspects of politics.

Conflict Representation. From our perspective the crucial criterion in defining representation is participation in the communication of social conflict. Representation refers to the activities of any person who publicizes interest disputes for community resolution be he congressman, reporter, voting citizen, lobbyist, administrator, teacher, or student.

Viewed as a method of political communication, conflict representation occurs in any government; but its function as link between governors and governed is highlighted in a representative democracy such as the United States. Where policies are made by relatively few individuals, the effectiveness of democratic control depends in large part on the means devised for transmitting desires from citizens to officials and vice versa.

Unfettered conflict representation facilitates a free exchange of political ideas and debate of issues. We have already noted that politically relevant ideas include both values and beliefs. In either case, the political significance of an idea depends upon the meaning people attribute to it in interest disputes; that is, an individual's subjective interpretation of the worth of an idea is frequently more politically relevant than its intrinsic truth. For example, although it is impossible to define the intrinsic character of "justice," as a vague idea it receives widespread loyalty and has been used as an appeal to generate considerable activity and conflict.[19]

As expressions of human activity, ideas serve as weapons in conflicts of interests. Their meaningfulness to people is used to rationalize interests, mobilize support, and justify or attack the political order. Ideologies, doctrines, and myths are frequently employed in this fashion, as exemplified by the monumental sacrifices made in the Soviet Union in the name of communism or the gargantuan efforts made by the United States

---

[19] Arnold Brecht, *Political Theory* (Princeton: Princeton University Press, 1959), chap. X.

in two world wars as a protector of democracy. As symbolic appeals, frequently in the form of political issues, ideas are manipulated to advance interests; a "higher standard of living," the "Communist menace," and "mongrelization" have served as rallying cries. As indicators and weapons of interest conflict, political ideas are inextricably linked to conflict representation.

Conflict representation takes many forms. In examining American government, we select the following six patterns of popular participation that contribute to the communication of conflicts in the community (see Part Two for detailed discussion of each): *participation* patterns by which Americans express themselves to policy officials; patterns of political *opinion*, or the formation and activation of political attitudes; political *leadership* patterns, or the persuasive elements of politics; patterns of political *choice* through elections; *partisan* patterns, or the role of political parties; and patterns of *pressure* by which political groups contribute to political communication.

Conflict Resolution. In America social conflict is resolved when institutions make binding (legitimate) community policy concerning a dispute. In our community this need not mean definitive settlement of the controversy; rather, conflict resolution implies a method of sufficiently moderating social tensions in order to avoid destructive competition. In the process new conflicts may well be created, if the outcome of policy controversies is disputed (as in our opening illustration of the civil rights movement). Thus, as a means of reconciling opposing forces, politics aims at a *modus vivendi* that keeps social disputes within the boundaries of cooperative-competitive relations.

If conflict resolution is to produce effective community policy, there must be a willingness on the part of citizens to accept community decisions as binding. Legitimate policies are those people feel they should obey. The sources of this feeling of legitimacy are twofold. First, people may obey because they fear that, if they refuse, force will be used against them. Although overt force may never be employed, the threat of severe punishments or deprivations (torture, jailing, death) is frequently sufficient to achieve obedience. Force, however, does not always produce compliance; if the desire to disobey offsets any penalties, force is of limited effectiveness. Civil disobedience and nonviolent protests attest to the fact that neither imprisonment nor brutality always promote obedience. Moreover, compliance frequently emerges where force is neither employed nor threatened, suggesting a second source of political legitimacy — consent. Derived from an understanding between citizens and officials, consent is given when people agree to being governed under specified rules and conditions. To gain obedience, the possibility of personal reward is substituted for the threat of personal deprivation.

The agreement between governors and governed on which government by consent rests consists of both written and unwritten rules and procedures for regulating social conflicts. It is manifested in traditions, habitual compliance, political doctrines, institutions, and ceremonies. Its existence signifies a tacit treaty between disputing interests to preserve community association despite pursuit of less inclusive claims. This is not to say that all such rules and procedures are beyond change; many become the subject of hot dispute. When constitutional conflicts do occur, they normally reflect the efforts of newly emergent interests to obtain advantages in politics formerly reserved to others.

Within the framework of legitimacy provided by accepted constitutional arrangements for adjusting disputes, interests influence community policy-making. By influence we mean the reciprocal relations that exist when an individual or group, in accordance with his interests, induces another to modify his behavior despite desires to the contrary. At the simplest level, in a family a parent influences his child to the extent that he gets the child to do something the child ordinarily does not wish to do. As with legitimacy, influence may be produced either by threat of deprivation or promise of reward; that is, by coercion or persuasion, about which we shall say more in Chapter Seven.[20]

The resolution of social conflict that emerges as social interests influence community decisions we designate public policy. Policy encompasses not only what appears in written statutes and what is "on the books" but conventions as well. For example, the unwritten two-term tradition in the Presidency was accepted policy until 1940, then formalized by Constitutional amendment in 1953. No statute calls for quadrennial party conventions to nominate candidates for President, yet it is policy to do so. Conversely, laws on the books are not always practiced policy; the Volstead Act forbidding manufacture of intoxicating liquor was the written law of the land in the 1920's, but actual policy on prohibition was another matter. Moreover, since written statutes alone do not describe actual policy, it should be clear that policy-making itself is a continuous process that does not stop with a congressional vote or presidential signature.

Conflict resolution touches not only the participants in social disputes; it also affects bystanders — the audience to the conflict. When policies affect the dominant membership of the community, directly or indirectly, we speak of that policy as public in character.[21] Whether it originates

---

[20] Robert Dahl, *Modern Political Analysis* (Englewood Cliffs, N.J.: Prentice-Hall, 1963), p. 50; Talcott Parsons, "On the Concept of Influence," *The Public Opinion Quarterly*, XXVII, No. 1 (Spring, 1963), 37–62; Karl W. Deutsch, *The Nerves of Government* (New York: The Free Press of Glencoe, 1963), pp. 110–27.

[21] Dewey, *The Public and Its Problems*, p. 27.

from decisions of private individuals or groups, or community agencies, public policy has consequences for the whole of the community. Such community-wide consequences permit us to distinguish between politics in a family, school, church, business, trade union, club or fraternity and the politics of the whole community. It is in this sense that we are concerned with politics as the most inclusive process of conflict regulation in the community; we will be interested in forms of "private government" only insofar as they have consequences affecting the bulk of the community rather than exclusive segments.

Finally, the character of public policy is shaped by the nature of the conflicts that stimulate its formulation. In American government we can designate four major areas of social conflict contributing to significant policy-making since the origin of the republic. In our discussion we shall cite examples of each of the following policy areas: (1) political economy (fiscal, resource, agrarian, business, and labor policies); (2) political liberty (civil rights, citizenship, immigration, voting and suffrage, etc.); (3) political equality (legislative apportionment, social policies of health, education, and welfare, etc.); and (4) political security (foreign, military, and scientific-technological policies).

The areas of public policy, the interest conflicts underlying each, and the process of decision itself are so intertwined that it is difficult to understand particular policies in isolation from one another. The interrelations of policies are clearly manifested in the operation of political institutions where policies are formulated. An institution has been defined as a "cluster of ideas and beliefs, usages and ways of behavior, and material things . . . which form a co-ordinated and organized whole." [22] For our purposes we focus attention upon one aspect of this definition, the recognition that institutions consist in part of co-ordinated clusters of behavior, and speak of them as patterns of interest activity. Such patterns possess a particularly stable character associated as they are with clusters of ideas and beliefs, traditions, conventions, and laws popularly accepted as legitimate. A community's political institutions, however, are not necessarily limited to those prescribed by written constitutions or statutes. For example, in the Middle Ages public policy was often church-made policy; even today military cabals or tribal clans constitute politically relevant institutions in many communities. And although Americans take great pains to differentiate through written prescriptions the institutions authorized to serve as conflict regulators, others such as the mass media, business and labor organizations, academic establishments, and religious bodies frequently make decisions with community-wide repercussions.

[22] Maurice Duverger, *An Introduction to the Social Sciences* (New York: Frederick A. Praeger, 1964), p. 233.

Therefore, in examining American government we are interested in any institution that contributes noticeably to social-conflict regulation for the entire community. These normally include the Presidency, Congress, the courts, bureaucratic arrangements, political parties, and elections, but are not restricted to them.

American political institutions are staffed by persons authorized to bind community members in accordance with constituted and conventional rules and procedures. These officials make choices between alternative actions, the consequences of which extend beyond immediate interests to the whole community. In regulating conflict, officials negotiate with one another for mutual advantage, compete with one another before the electorate, persuade followers and fellow policy-makers to adopt preferred courses of action, and command subordinates to accept political decisions. These four patterns of conflict regulation are distinctive styles of bargaining, competition, persuasion, and command. Each characterizes a particular area of American government; each will be explored in detail in Part Three.

In summary, since governmental policy originates in human activity, we share the view that "Law is activity . . . a forming, a systematization, a struggle, and adaptation, of group interests, just as government is." [23] The character of conflict resolution stems from the activity entering into the formulation of policy, the personal attitudes that give rise to feelings of legitimacy, and the reciprocal consequences of policy on human behavior that contribute to community viability. Although conflict resolution possesses an overall continuity, we find it useful to select five patterns from that seamless activity for discussion in separate chapters of Part Three: policy *formulation,* or the activities by which policy choices are initiated and defined; policy *leadership,* or the stimulation of conflict resolution; policy *adoption,* or the acceptance of policy choices as legitimate; policy *application,* which consists of decisions rendering general policies effective in specific instances; and policy *adjudication* by which challenges to community policy are adjusted.

AMERICAN POLITICAL PATTERNS

We now can recapitulate our working definition and the justifications for it. In analyzing government, it is useful to think of politics as human activity concerned with regulation of social conflict. This usage is appropriate to our view of the human situation, of people who (1) are physical beings living in societies; (2) possess differing needs, wants, capacities,

[23] Bentley, *op. cit.*

and resources; (3) pursue conflicting values resulting from the diversity; (4) associate in order to achieve values that come from sharing human experience in community; (5) seek to balance conflicting interests with that of community preservation; and, consequently, (6) utilize politics as a method of regulating social conflict.

In America conflict regulation consists of patterns of behavior by which social conflict is represented and resolved. Representation is a process of communication that makes the conflict known through patterns of participation, opinion, leadership, choice, partisanship, and pressure. Resolution is a process of accommodation that keeps conflict within manageable limits through policy-making. Officials make binding public policy with acts of formulation, leadership, adoption, application, and adjudication. Politics occurs within a community marked by social diversity, variable doctrinal and politico-constitutional consensus, and policy disagreement. The style of conflict regulation is a blend of competition, persuasion, bargaining, and command. The precise mixture contributes to the democratic character of the political community. In short, politics is what it is because the community is what it is. Bearing these points in mind, we now turn to a closer look at the nature of the American political community.

BIBLIOGRAPHICAL NOTE

Several recent works now available in paperback editions focus on the conflict-regulating functions of politics. In *The Semisovereign People* (New York: Holt, Rinehart and Winston, 1960) E. E. Schattschneider presents a very readable account of the role of American political parties and groups in representing social conflicts to decision-makers. More general treatments of the relationship between politics and conflict are J. D. B. Miller, *The Nature of Politics* (London: Gerald Duckworth & Co. Ltd., 1962) which stresses the impact of human diversity on the development of political interests, and Bernard Crick, *In Defense of Politics* (Chicago: The University of Chicago Press, 1962), which poses a much narrower definition of politically relevant conflicts than those cited in other works. Somewhat more sophisticated discussions of the nature of human conflict in both national and international policy-making are found in Kenneth Boulding's *Conflict and Defense: A General Theory* (New York: Harper & Row, Publishers, Torchbook Edition, 1963), and Thomas C. Schelling's *The Strategy of Conflict* (New York: Oxford University Press, 1963).

For accounts concerning the sources, consequences, and functions of conflict in human affairs, the following merit attention: Lewis Coser, *The Functions of Social Conflict* (London: The Free Press of Glencoe, Paperback Edition, 1964); Georg Simmel, *Conflict and The Web of Group-Affiliations* (London: The Free Press of Glencoe, Paperback Edition, 1964); and Edmund Stillman and William

Pfaff, *The Politics of Hysteria* (New York: Harper and Row, Publishers, 1964). The most useful work on the dimensions of human conflict relevant to political activity is Elton B. McNeil, *The Nature of Human Conflict* (Englewood Cliffs, N.J.: Prentice-Hall, Inc., 1965), available in hardbound edition. Concerning the sources of human conflict one should consult James C. Davies, *Human Nature in Politics* (New York: John Wiley and Sons, Inc., 1963), also in hardbound edition, and Hadley Cantril, *Human Nature and Political Systems* (New Brunswick, N.J.: Rutgers University Press, 1961). Finally, in this review of major works dealing with conflict theory one should not ignore the classic presentation by Thomas Hobbes, *The Leviathan*, available in several editions.

Treatises on the nature of human community are also abundant. After Aristotle's *Politics* the following are noteworthy: Robert A. Nisbet's *Community and Power* (formerly entitled *The Quest for Community*), now available in paperback edition (New York: Oxford University Press, 1962); the difficult, but significant work by Ferdinand Tönnies, *Community and Society: Gemeinschaft und Gesellschaft* (New York: Harper & Row, Publishers, Paperback Edition, 1963); Sebastian de Grazia's analysis of the sources of community in widely shared beliefs, *The Political Community: A Study of Anomie* (Chicago: The University of Chicago Press, Phoenix Edition, 1963); Karl W. Deutsch's *Political Community at the International Level* (Garden City, New York: Doubleday & Company, Inc., 1954); Philip E. Jacob and James V. Toscano, *The Integration of Political Communities* (New York: J. B. Lippincott Company, 1964); and, the related classic of John Dewey, *The Public and Its Problems* (Denver: Alan Swallow, 1927). A useful textbook introduction to the sources and dimensions of American community is Jessie Bernard's *American Community Behavior* (New York: Holt, Rinehart and Winston, Revised Edition, 1962). R. M. MacIver devoted several works to interpreting the community bases of American social interaction including *The Web of Government* (New York: The Free Press, Paperback Edition, 1965), and *The Modern State* (London: Oxford University Press, Paperback Edition, 1964). An abstract, but comprehensive, discussion of the relationship between political activity and human community is presented by Carl J. Friedrich in his *Man and His Government* (New York: McGraw-Hill Book Company, Inc., 1963).

The standard treatment of the essential functions of political concepts is T. D. Weldon's *The Vocabulary of Politics* (Baltimore: Penguin Books, Inc., 1953). Also useful is Thomas Landon Thorson, *The Logic of Democracy* (New York: Holt, Rinehart and Winston, 1962). If the student desires to sample the myriad definitions suggested for political activity he may start with the following: Harold Lasswell, *Politics: Who Gets What, When, How* (New York: Meridian Books, Inc., 1958), relating politics and influence; Alfred de Grazia's definition of the politically relevant and his ensuing discussion of political ideas institutions, and behavior in *Political Behavior* (New York: The Free Press, Revised Edition, 1962); Francis J. Sorauf, *Political Science: An Informal Overview* (Columbus, Ohio: Charles E. Merrill Books, Inc., 1963); Robert A. Dahl, *Modern Political Analysis* (Englewood Cliffs, N.J.: Prentice-Hall, Inc., 1963); Joseph Tussman, *Obligation and the Body Politic* (New York: Oxford University Press, 1960); and Heinz Eulau, *The Behavioral Persuasion in Politics* (New York: Random House, 1963).

Finally, for attempts to suggest theories intended to explain political activity the reader should consult the following paperback publications, each of varying quality and degree of difficulty, currently available: Lewis Froman's succinct description of the American polity in *People and Politics* (Englewood Cliffs, N.J.: Prentice-Hall, Inc., 1962); Karl W. Deutsch's related complex volumes, *Nationalism and Social Communication* (Cambridge, Massachusetts: The M.I.T. Press, Paperback Edition, 1965) and *The Nerves of Government* (London: The Free Press of Glencoe, Free Press Paperback, 1966); Pendleton Herring's timeless and useful account of American political parties in a pluralist framework, *The Politics of Democracy* (New York: W. W. Norton & Company, Inc., Paperback Edition, 1965); and Richard R. Fagan's discussion of political communication relevant to the principal patterns of conflict representation in any polity, *Politics and Communication* (Boston: Little, Brown and Company, 1966). Currently available in standard editions are the volumes in David Easton's trilogy on the nature of political systems: *The Political System* (New York: Alfred A. Knopf, 1953), *A Framework for Political Analysis* (Englewood Cliffs, N.J.: Prentice-Hall, Inc., 1965), and *A Systems Analysis of Political Life* (New York: John Wiley & Sons, Inc., 1965). William C. Mitchell's *The American Polity* (New York: The Free Press of Glencoe, 1962) demonstrates the use of systems analysis in interpreting American political patterns.

CHAPTER TWO

Political Consensus

Politics, the process of social-conflict regulation, is inseparable from human association. The form and behavior of the political process, however, vary considerably from community to community. These differences are traceable to variations in social relations, constitutional arrangements, and personal orientations. In this chapter we explore the social background of American government and the ideological patterns associated with American convictions.

CONFLICT, COMMUNITY, AND CONSENSUS

A PLURALIST AMERICA

Recognizing the pluralistic character of our society facilitates discussion of American political patterns. First it is helpful to distinguish between *pluralism* as a social doctrine and the use of the term *pluralist* in a descriptive sense. The former was expounded primarily by English thinkers at the beginning of this century to counter the theory of state sovereignty, which holds that the state exists as *the* preeminent institution of society and determines values and commands personal loyalty. Pluralists urge instead that any society is composed of a multiplicity of independent groups, each of which should be permitted to contribute to the formation of individual values and social policy. The state, viewed as only one group among many, has no right to the final word on personal or social preferences. The pluralists' concern with the existence of a variety of social groups emphasizes the fact that multiple affiliations contribute to the basis for our politics. A society designated as pluralistic is marked by the existence and social acceptance of many "autonomous centers of decision-making authority," [1] reflecting a diversity of desires that promote varied interests and social conflicts. In this sense, America may be viewed as pluralistic.

In America pluralist arrangements characterize both social and constitutional dimensions of community life. For example, the organization of popular demands upon governmental officials is markedly pluralistic. The noted journalist Walter Lippmann has asserted that democracy works in America because "outside the government and outside the party system, there have existed independent institutions and independent men." "Because the courts, the churches, the press, the schools, and private property have existed independently of government," he insists, "the nation has remained the master, . . . has not become the servant of its government." [2]

Pluralistic societies possess an intermediate layer of stable, organized group life lying between the family and community authority; people find comfort in voluntary associations, schools, and churches. These independent groups constitute the backbone of a socially diverse America and give rise both to complementary and incompatible interests. Tension among groups renders it difficult for any single association to control the whole policy-making apparatus. Like planets mutually attracting and repelling one another, it is improbable that any one social group will dominate the universe of politics. The fact that one person may belong to many groups limits any one group's influence. Thus groups compete for an individual's loyalties, but encounter trouble in influencing more than a limited area of an individual's behavior. Groups thereby have difficulty dominating not only the governmental process of the community but even the behavior of their own membership. Union members who vote against the candidate supported by their local, Democrats who voted for Dwight Eisenhower, doctors who support "socialized" medi-

[1] For the nature of pluralism and a pluralist society see the Rockefeller Brothers Fund Special Studies Project, *The Power of the Democratic Idea* (Garden City: Doubleday & Co., 1960), pp. 34–36; William Kornhauser, *The Politics of Mass Society* (Glencoe, Ill.: The Free Press, 1959).

[2] Walter Lippmann, "The Deepest Issue of Our Time," *Vital Speeches*, II (1936), 603.

cine — all indicate multiple affiliations and cross-pressures limiting a group's influence.

Matching the plurality of social demands in America is a pluralistic governmental pattern that divides conflict regulation among multiple and often conflicting centers of policy-making. The presence of semi-autonomous clusters of community officials makes it possible for groups to travel a variety of routes in attempts to influence policy. If one set of governing officials is inaccessible, perhaps another may be open to presentation of interest demands. We will deal with this phenomenon in Chapter Eleven, but an example here suggests what can occur. In the summer of 1964 the U.S. Secretary of Defense, Robert McNamara, announced far-reaching plans for consolidating portions of the National Guard and the reserve components of the U.S. Army and Air Force. Distressed by the prospect of loss of prestige, money, rank, defense capability, and of other potential deprivations, members of the Reserve Officers Association immediately protested the proposed action. Although the reorganization could have been accomplished through executive channels, threatened interests were successful in convincing Members of Congress to hold hearings on the matter. Several congressmen were eager to investigate, for their concern for military preparedness was aroused by the fact that they held reserve commands in various military units. The result was a delay in the execution of the deed — a delay produced by playing congressmen, executive officials, and local areas possessing reserve units against one another. Finally, Secretary McNamara had to resolve the issue by utilizing an executive order for modified reorganization. Thus we see the multiple lines of access to policy-makers available to threatened interests.

In a pluralistic society many groups are so specialized that they cannot spread their influence over all policy-makers. There is no positive assurance, for example, that a labor interest can produce a bill to raise the minimum wage and one to curtail steel imports, plus an administrative restriction on foreign automobile advertising, and a corporation decision favoring profit-sharing plans. Moreover, specialization may make it easier for officials to possess autonomy in their own policy areas; the fact that the Federal Bureau of Investigation has long maintained a base of popular support outside of Congress or the Presidency has resulted in its semi-independent jurisdiction over policy-matters. This "checks and balances" scheme was formalized in the Constitution by separating policy-makers into institutions possessing overlapping jurisdictions, yet not dependent upon one another for their authority. A pluralistic society was equipped with a pluralistic constitutional character to match.

This duality of pluralistic arrangements, both social and political, means that individuals are seldom totally dependent either upon particular social groups or political officials for the advancement of interests. Citizens have options and they retain choice in how best to pursue their desires. Furthermore, since multiple affiliations contribute to, as well as reflect, multiple interests, people seldom put "all their eggs in one basket." Consequently, there is less tendency to invest any single issue of public policy with an extreme degree of emotional attachment. In a pluralistic society there is a tendency to "spread interests so that few defeats need be final disasters." [3] Single-interest politics, single-issue campaigns, and single-principle parties are rare in pluralistic communities; rather broad policies emerging from a process of bargaining and compromise between diverse interests are characteristic.

Because a pluralistic polity is characterized by diversity of purpose, the meaning of *the* community interest is confounded. The notions of public interest, national interest, or common good symbolize ideals of common purpose and striving but are frequently employed to rationalize narrower stands. Occasionally, a single interest may even attempt to elevate its own interest to the level of an entire community. Karl Marx, for example, argued that two major interests exist in modern society — the class interests of bourgeoisie and proletariat. In conflict the latter would prevail, classes would thereby disappear, class struggles would vanish, and the state — the instrument for exploiting the proletariat — would wither away. The public interest then could be defined as the proletariat interest. Adolph Hitler rejected any diversity of interest in Nazi society, even the duality of class interests, and identified Germany's public interest with that of a single "race." In both examples a public interest was viewed as a unifying community purpose overriding diverse popular wishes. But in the pluralistic American environment the legitimacy of multiple, conflicting desires is generally taken for granted. Definition of the public interest in this disharmonious collectivity is contingent upon open conflict. In pluralistic polities the notion of the public interest serves as a term of interest rationalization and as a goal binding community members together.

Diversity of experience in religious, educational, and other intermediate groups which lie between the family and government precludes a consistent social value system. The learning of group loyalties, the origins and intensity of social conflicts, the relations among rulers and ruled, the style of conflict regulation, and the perspective taken on the community will are all affected by such pluralism. The fact of plural purposes also affects the character of community ideals and procedures, thus shaping American political doctrine and constitutional arrangements. We will examine this relationship in Chapters Three and Four; first let

[3] *The Power of the Democratic Idea*, p. 35.

us look at the effects of plural purposes on political community and consensus.

POLITICAL COMMUNITY AND CONSENSUS

We noted earlier that communities are a universal aspect of human living that exist because people commit themselves to associate in order to derive the benefits of shared human experience. Yet conflict appears in virtually every pattern of human association. When interests of association override desires to press for potentially disruptive advantages, we say there is *political community*. Political community reflects the active desire to preserve the collectivity. Professor David Easton has phrased it this way: "We only ask whether the members of the group that we are examining are sufficiently oriented toward each other to want to contribute their collective energies toward pacific settlement of their varying demands. . . ." People show "some minimal readiness or ability to continue working together to solve their political problems." [4]

But may the commitment to preserve collective effort at the expense of full realization of personal group demands not erode the pluralist base of society? Is the multiplicity of associations, purposes, affiliations, and loyalties characteristic of America not sacrificed for a higher order — the community? That danger surely exists, but there is no incompatibility, in logic or experience, in the co-existence of political community and pluralistic diversity. The presence of political community need not imply any single interest for all members other than that of preserving association; the multiplicity of groups can remain and the plurality of social demands continue. Indeed, pluralistic politics becomes the shaping force of the political community.

Our response to "What is it that makes a group of people a community?" is simply: the desire to share experience; the purposive activity consummating that desire by settling disputes we label *political community*. Others, however, respond as follows: "The answer is — . . . religious and political beliefs. And these beliefs fulfill a need common to man everywhere. Never mind their variety. There are many lands and diverse customs, but it is the same need in all men that brings them together." [5] Perhaps the "need" to share religious and political beliefs is as basic to man as those of food, clothing, and shelter. And perhaps the basis of community is not only the desire to associate, but a desire to satisfy these other fundamental needs. In any event, we prefer to view a political community as existing when people preserve their association

[4] David Easton, "An Approach to the Analysis of Political Systems," *World Politics*, IX, No. 3 (April, 1957), 383–400.

[5] Sebastian De Grazia, *The Political Community* (Chicago: The University of Chicago Press, 1948), pp. ix–x, 189.

through conflict regulation. While the reasons for people associating and acting to preserve that association should be explored, we take the existence of the American political community as given.

Consistent with our definition of community, an integrated doctrine accepted by all members with the same degree of loyalty is not a requisite of political community. Yet over time distinctive sets of political ideas tend to develop, even though they need not be rigidly doctrinaire. These ideas constitute a portion of the community consensus. Community consensus may be thought of, as suggested earlier, as a sharing of values (incorporating attitudes about the correctness of human goals and conduct) and beliefs. Such a consensus is variable in content, particularly in its political aspects.

First, the values and beliefs on which agreement prevails cover a wide range. They can encompass ideas about the legitimacy of policy-makers; constitutional arrangements; fundamental judgments regarding the desirability of (for example) free speech, majority rule, political equality, or popular control of policy-makers; and such policy appraisals as the appropriateness of free medical care. Second, the matters in question may seem to have no political relevance whatsoever; for example, Americans get worked up over such items as the desirability of smoking cigarettes, females wearing topless bathing suits, or infant thumb-sucking. Third, each item of consensus may be agreed to by differing numbers of people: there may be universal agreement on the ideal of free speech, fewer may agree to abide by the wishes of the majority, and only a handful may approve of the protection against self-incrimination. Fourth, there is a variation in the intensity of agreement: some may believe in the ideal of political equality so strongly that they participate in voter-registration drives; others protest taxes of a particular nature so much that they, like Thoreau, go to jail; others merely accept the ideal of a free vote, yet do nothing to preserve it; and some people simply acquiesce to the rule of law out of simple expediency. Fifth, the items upon which there is agreement may be consistent with one another, or they may not: people agree that political equality is a "good thing," yet some insist that it is best to prevent women, juveniles, Negroes, or others from voting. Finally, the consequences of political consensus vary considerably: consensus may actively support the continuance of a given set of activities, procedures, and policies, such as Social Security programs; it may passively permit a particular action in a given area without popular objection, as allowing Federal aid for school construction; or it may be decisive in inhibiting any political activity at all, as when popular sentiment limited our involvement in World War II prior to Pearl Harbor.[6]

[6] V. O. Key, Jr., *Public Opinion and American Democracy* (New York: Alfred A. Knopf, 1961), p. 29.

In sum, community consensus refers to a state of agreement in personal orientations toward a variety of matters. We employ the narrower notion of *political consensus* to speak of personal agreement — acceptance or acquiesence — with public officials, rules and procedures, democratic values, and policy choices; and we refer to these areas of political consensus as *official, constitutional, doctrinal,* and *policy* consensus. Political consensus does not "cause" a particular pattern of political behavior and may not be consistent with a particular pattern of political behavior. Instead, political consensus is shaped by social and constitutional patterns, as well as by a consensus of personal convictions. It is thus a "working" consensus in the sense that — like the community interest — it is tentative, filled with contingency, and subject to modification. This working consensus helps define the issues that must be resolved and the effective limits of political conflict at any given time. "Disagreements, often fundamental ones, arise within it; and citizens who stand outside the prevailing consensus often make precious contributions to democracy precisely because they do so." [7]

AMERICAN POLITICAL CONSENSUS

AN AMERICAN IDEOLOGY?

References to something called "Americanism" imply that our citizens either do — or should — share a common set of ideals. "Americanism" is manifested by, and reinforced through, symbolic references to our forefathers, great moments in our history, "The Star Spangled Banner," pageants, and other reminders of our communal attachment. The absence of conflicting value symbols within the community leads us to suspect general agreement on democratic "fundamentals." Alexis de Tocqueville, in his classic work, *Democracy in America,* offered the observation that Americans were not interested in philosophy but that they, nevertheless, were "in possession of one, common to the whole people." [8] Writers since De Tocqueville have continued to point out the existence of an "underlying consensus" within the American polity that enables it to survive continuing and serious disputes over policy alternatives.[9] The obvious fact that the federal community has, with the one major exception of the Civil War, managed to accommodate peacefully serious differences over policy, strongly supports the existence of some kind of basic agreement over values and political processes within which differences are settled.

[7] *The Power of the Democratic Idea,* p. 20.

[8] Alexis de Tocqueville, *Democracy in America* (Galaxy ed.; New York: Oxford University Press, 1947), p. 251.

[9] Robert A. Dahl, *A Preface to Democratic Theory* (Chicago: The University of Chicago Press, 1956), pp. 132–33; Bernard Berelsen *et al., Voting* (Chicago: The University of Chicago Press, 1954), p. 313; and Sebastian De Grazia, *op. cit.,* p. ix.

That at least some form of agreement exists is obvious to any reader of political news. For example, whenever Americans engage in presidential campaigns, debate is heated, invective is common, and at some point each side accuses the other of "selling America short." Candidates seem to grasp for uncomplimentary charges that will, hopefully, devastate the opposition. At such times the likelihood that there will ever again be consensus on who shall govern seems remote. Then on election eve both sides urge all Americans to exercise their right to vote and remind them of their obligation to participate in a free election. Votes are cast, ballots are counted, and — seemingly in miraculous fashion — the winner is accepted without fear of violence or other manifestations of refusal to acquiesce in the electoral verdict.

Americans take for granted this peaceful determination of who shall occupy political office. Even though election campaigns are bitterly contested, it is expected that they will be fought within bounds of generally held ideas about what is fair and unfair, honest and dishonest. Consensus on who shall rule, in short, is tied to the fact of a prior consensus on how governors shall be chosen, reflecting even a deeper constitutional consensus. There seems to be some, although less clear-cut, consensus on issues of policy as well. It would be surprising indeed for presidential candidates seriously to debate the proposition that an official church should be established in the United States; yet, the decision of the United States Supreme Court in 1962 to reject the reading of officially sanctioned prayers in public schools invoked serious controversy over the meaning of the First Amendment to the Constitution of the United States. Suddenly, the legitimate offices of the Justices, the phraseology of the First Amendment, and the interpretation of "freedom of religion" were questioned.

To illustrate further, the New Deal era in American history precipitated a major debate over the role and function of government in social and economic matters. In 1934 former President Hoover declared that the continuance of New Deal programs would mark "a vast casualty to Liberty." President Franklin Roosevelt conceived the New Deal as the extension of liberty within the context of the vastly changed social and economic circumstances of the Twentieth Century. A reporter asked Roosevelt a series of questions aimed at revealing his political philosophy. Frances Perkins, Secretary of Labor during the New Deal years, reported the following exchange:

"Mr. President, are you a Communist?"
"No."
"Are you a capitalist?"
"No."

"Are you a Socialist?"

"No," he said, with a look of surprise, as if he were wondering what he
was being cross-examined about.

The young man said, "Well, what is your philosophy then?"

"Philosophy?" asked the President, puzzled. "Philosophy? I am a Christian
and a Democrat — that's all." [10]

Both Roosevelt and Hoover were clearly committed to the preservation
of the American free-enterprise economic system; both placed emphasis
on the value of the individual. Yet they were in obvious disagreement
over the best means to preserve these commitments in the face of major
economic dislocations. For Hoover, New Deal social and economic policies threatened the democratic values of economic and individual freedom; for Roosevelt, these same policies were a necessary means for
preserving these values. The debate over the New Deal took place within
the context of a general agreement on certain matters. As in the case of
the debate over prayers in the public schools, the methods by which
long-range values were to be secured and preserved, not the values
themselves, posed disagreement.

Such illustrations suggest areas of agreement concerning legitimacy of
officials, constitutional procedures, values to be sought, and policies to be
adopted; they also suggest areas of conflict. Our concern here, however,
is the extent of the consensus. To assure community stability, must *all*
or nearly all men hold these values, or is it sufficient for only certain
groups to accept them? Systematic research that might provide complete
answers to this question is absent, yet the past decade has produced an
increasing amount of significant inquiry into the nature of American
political consensus. Despite frequent references to a fundamental consensus or "ideology," provisional findings tend to justify doubts over the
extent to which particular political values are held by the vast majority
of Americans.

We noted before that the explicit body of general and abstract values
and beliefs which constitute the American ideological consensus are
reasonably clear, integrated, and elaborate. Over time they tend to
provide a framework for determining the legitimate exercise of power,
proper relationships between politics and other spheres of activity, and
distinctions between a political right and a political wrong. The elements
of liberal democracy constitute a series of propositions, values, and guides
for action that have found expression in the Constitution, other famous
political documents, court decisions, and public addresses. The average
American has heard of such expressions, but usually takes them for

[10] Frances Perkins, *The Roosevelt I Knew* (New York: The Viking Press, 1946), p.
330.

granted rather than explores their meaning. The National Opinion Research Center, for example, discovered in 1946 that 79 per cent of the Americans surveyed could not correctly explain the meaning of the "Bill of Rights," even though they had heard of it.[11] Moreover, familiarity does not imply that all Americans agree with these fundamentals when stated in the form of specific application of abstractions. A man whose political choices *are* consciously influenced to a substantial degree by a body of doctrine that constitutes an ideology is termed an *ideologue*. The following discussion considers the question of how many Americans can be classified as ideologues.[12]

AMERICAN POLITICAL VALUES: THE AMBIVALENT MAJORITY AND ACTIVE MINORITY

The value Americans place on political activity itself — the popular image of politics — is part of the climate of American values that conditions the response of citizens to official actions, constitutional procedures, fundamental ideals, and policy choices. Ideas regarding right and wrong in politics are influenced by the esteem of politicians in the eyes of community members. Moreover, opinions about politics imply views of the political community. Is there a consensus among Americans regarding politics itself? It has been said that when Americans "talk politics," they do so less with reverence and awe than with invective and cynicism. Perhaps the national pastime is not baseball but "damning politicians up hill and down dale . . . as rogues and vagabonds, frauds and scoundrels. . . ." [13] Historian Carl Becker has written that Americans approach government as a "friendly enemy, a neighbor who will probably do well enough if you keep your eye on him." [14] Is this characterization of a quasi-hostile American sentiment toward government an accurate one?

One way to find out what Americans think about politics is to look at the verdict of popular literature. Two themes emphasized by the successful political novelist tell us something about American political attitudes. The first emphasizes the style manifested in obtaining public office: the buying and selling of influence. Organized politics is frequently identified with machine activity, persuasion is seen as coercion, and the rewards of office bear the mark of spoils. And when politicians themselves

[11] Compare this with findings assembled by Hadley Cantril and Mildred Strunk (eds.), *Public Opinion: 1935–1946* (Princeton: Princeton University Press, 1951).

[12] For the nature of ideologue behavior see Angus Campbell *et al.*, *The American Voter* (New York: John Wiley & Sons, 1960).

[13] H. L. Mencken, *A Mencken Chrestomathy* (New York: Alfred A. Knopf, 1956), p. 148.

[14] Carl L. Becker, *Freedom and Responsibility in the American Way of Life* (New York: Vintage Books, 1960), p. 7.

are not sinful, they are featured as well-intentioned Pollyannas falling victim to the depravity of the beast in efforts to accomplish beneficial ends. A second theme focuses on what the politician must do to retain office and execute his program. Allen Drury's President in *Advise and Consent*, for example, is forced to resort to character assassination in order to secure Senatorial confirmation of a Cabinet appointee. Politicians frequently are viewed as sacrificing the public interest for purposes of personal` aggrandizement. Political novels, in short, often intertwine a curiously romantic admiration of the politician's capacity to act with an implied condemnation of his actions.[15]

Although some political journalists, historians, and novelists view Americans as negatively disposed toward politics, systematic examination reveals changing perspectives. In 1944 the National Opinion Research Center reported that 69 per cent of Americans interviewed in a nationwide survey were opposed to their sons' entering politics "as a life's work." Negative responses emphasized "dishonest" and "dirty" aspects of politics; a few even felt that, at best, it was a "useless occupation." More recent surveys, however, reveal a decline in percentage of negative responses. George Gallup reported that in 1965 more than one out of every three Americans desired to see his son undertake a political career although a majority of 54 per cent still felt that there was too much corruption in politics and that the career lacked prestige, opportunity, and security.[16]

Despite its tarnished image politics as a profession has been gaining in public acceptance over the past two decades. Americans are growing more sensitive to the contributions of politicians toward individual happiness and the preservation of society. One crude indicator is the finding that 85 per cent of Americans cite their government and political tradition as one of the aspects about the United States of which they are "most proud." This figure contrasts sharply with responses in four other nations. Only 3 per cent of Italians cited political or governmental traditions as aspects of their government of which they were "most proud" — as compared to 7 per cent for Germans, 30 per cent for Mexicans and 46 per cent for British.[17]

John Conway has pointed out that the politician's lifework is no longer viewed as a mere craft applying customs and conventions developed by

[15] Irving Howe, *Politics and the Novel* (New York: Horizons Press, 1957); Allen Drury, *Advise and Consent* (Garden City: Doubleday & Co., 1959); for a recent· example of the first theme see Edwin O'Connor, *The Last Hurrah* (Boston: Little, Brown & Co., 1956).

[16] News Release, American Institute of Public Opinion, March 3, 1965.

[17] Gabriel A. Almond and Sidney Verba, *The Civic Culture* (Princeton: Princeton University Press, 1963), p. 102.

individual trial and error. It is increasingly viewed as a professional undertaking in which actions are based upon systematic analysis of tasks
to be performed. Whereas the NORC survey revealed that negative attitudes toward politics were highest among the better educated, Conway
points to the increasing number of educated and distinguished citizens
now entering politics as a challenging career channeling creative energies.
Whereas sixty years ago men with high talent turned attention to the
challenges of business and industry, their sons and grandsons have
devoted their lives to public service. Given the same negative attitude
toward politics as a career that prevailed before the turn of the century
it would have been unlikely that men of the calibre and background of
Nelson Rockefeller, Adlai Stevenson, and John F. Kennedy would have
entered upon political careers. Crises produced by depression and war, and
an expansion of the U.S. role in world affairs have left a residue of a more
positive popular view of government as a "channel for necessary change,
not its obstacle." [18] Although Conway's assertions are not documented
with systematic data, they present an interesting contrast to the attitudes
discussed previously. Politics in American life is no longer viewed as
the activity of slick wheelers and dealers but is increasingly regarded as
a necessary requisite for civility and a polity of free discussion.

In summary, the verdicts of popular literature and popular surveys are
ambiguous; we cannot conclude that politics is regarded either as a
positive good or a necessary evil by American citizens. American attitudes toward politics combine reverence and skepticism, awe and fear,
respect and dismay. While one writer can insist that there has been a
rise of the "profession of politics to a level of prestige" never known before, it is still possible for a businessman turned candidate for U.S.
Senator to solicit votes of those who "are sick of politicians who offer
momentary advantages . . . and are for businessmen with some horse
sense." [19]

The ambiguity of the popular verdict can be explained in several ways.
The prestige of any activity, or of any individual, is a relative thing. The
criteria used by Americans to evaluate occupations are vague. An occupation that carries with it status in one era may not in another; the eu-
phemistic redesignation of janitors as "custodial engineers" is a case in
point. And when attitudes reflect ambivalence, there is good reason. The
same government providing a citizen's protection also calls for sacrifice;
payment of income tax is both a privilege and a burden.

Attitudes toward and involvement in political affairs result from the

---

[18] John Conway, "Politics as a Profession in the United States," *Daedalus*, 92, No.
4 (Fall, 1963), 845.
[19] From a campaign brochure of Gordon McClendon, candidate for nomination to
the United States Senate, 1964.

interrelationship of many factors, and differ among nations. Hadley Cantril's research on the interaction of personal aspirations and worries with the "hopes and fears for their country" among the same people revealed wide variation among national groups. (1) In nations where radical political changes have recently occurred — Cuba and Dominican Republic — personal involvement with national affairs is high. In the United States, the most economically advanced nation in the world and a nation of great democratic political stability, there is relatively little personal involvement in public affairs with the exception of international matters. (2) In a nation which is economically underdeveloped and in the process of gaining national independence — Nigeria — personal political involvement is high in national affairs but very low in regard to international matters. On the other hand, the people of India, a nation which achieved independence some years ago but which is still underdeveloped economically, show little personal involvement in national affairs. (3) In Brazil — long unified into a nation but underdeveloped economically and politically unstable — personal involvement in national problems is very low. (4) Among people, such as in Yugoslavia, who were recently united after centuries of division into nationality groups and who have strong central leadership, there is a high degree of personal involvement in national affairs. Israel, another recently created nation, but unified along religious lines, also shows a high degree of involvement. (5) In nations which have experienced direct involvement in war — Yugoslavia, West Germany, Israel, the Philippines — or where the consequences of another war are recognized — as in the United States — there exists a high degree of involvement in problems faced by the nation in international affairs. (6) Generally speaking, people with higher education display greater concern in areas relating to international affairs, social problems, and political independence. The correlation between higher education and personal concern regarding economic matters is no higher than among the less well educated.[20]

The high political and economic stability of the American system has apparently resulted in less personal involvement and provides another dimension in seeking to understand American attitudes toward politics. One more dimension in this pattern is the historical setting which has conditioned prevailing political values.

Daniel Boorstin has written that Americans are living in "one of the most spectacularly lopsided cultures in all history."[21] They have experienced amazing success and vitality in the operation of their govern-

[20] Hadley Cantril, *The Pattern of Human Concerns* (New Brunswick: Rutgers University Press, 1965), pp. 252–54.
[21] Daniel J. Boorstin, *The Genius of American Politics* (Phoenix Books; Chicago: The University of Chicago Press, 1960).

mental system and have a firm belief in the superiority of democracy as the "best form of government." Yet they are distinctly uninterested in reflecting, speculating, and theorizing about politics. Furthermore, argues Boorstin, Americans have never felt the need for an explicit political theory. Our ideas have been "given" us and thus are automatically defined. They are "given by certain facts of geography or history peculiar to us."

Three factors, says Boorstin, account for the lack of interest in theory. First, the Founding Fathers equipped Americans with a framework for answering all future questions. Our values were "pre-formed"; the Constitution represents a gift of the past which is useful in solving the problems of the present. Americans credit the Founding Fathers with amazing vision. Constitutional consensus is high, and the Constitution is viewed as virtually the final word in the debate over political institutions and arrangements. Although Americans have recognized change as necessary and desirable, they have always justified changes on the ground that they should occur within the general context of principles established in 1789. Boorstin contends that because of pre-formed values, Americans are not interested in debating the questions as to whether the particular philosophy inherited ought to be re-examined in the light of change and contemporary conditions.

Secondly, "givenness" results from the belief that American values are implicit in our institutions. American soil, social arrangements, and cultural climate are considered unique. The "American way of life" is something special since it emerges out of a particular atmosphere found nowhere else in the world. This concept of the "American way" complements the "pre-formation theory" in the sense that "Americanism" is being constantly given anew to each generation born in America or migrated to the community. On the one hand, argues Boorstin, Americans look upon the Founding Fathers as having provided a permanent theoretical framework. On the other hand, they see these same values emerging out of the *land* of America itself, to be given to each new generation.

Finally, Boorstin maintains that "givenness" is the product of the unique continuity of American History. Europe has been racked with revolutions, with divisive ideological debates, and with other types of cataclysmic change. Americans, on the other hand, see their history as a continuous pattern of similar events so that past and present are really very much the same. Our political history is marked by unity and cohesion in political values. Even our Civil War has been blamed on ideologies or values imported from abroad. For those who are searching for an explicit American democratic philosophy, or who attempt to build one, Boorstin advises that the American mind is really found in the political institutions by which Americans have lived. Our institutional forms have remained virtually unchanged since the nation was founded; and while the operation of these institutions — Congress, Supreme Court, and the Presidency, among others — has been altered, they continue to reflect the "general truths" that describe American democracy.[22]

Other serious scholars have similarly assessed the general American attitude toward both politics and political ideas as ambiguous and non-reflective. Robert G. McCloskey has characterized such an American ideology as "ambivalent." American ideologues "hold contradictory ideas simultaneously without bothering to resolve the political conflict between them." Illustrating his view that ideologues themselves are uncertain about the nature of democratic values, McCloskey examined three areas of American politics: the literature of our political thought, the American institutional structure, and the way Americans behave politically.[23]

In the first instance, a reading of the statements of American leaders from Jefferson onward reveals ambivalence in attitudes toward the canons of the democratic ideology and value structure. Jefferson can with little difficulty be quoted to support positions diametrically opposed to each other; quotations of Alexander Hamilton establish both his commitment to government by the people and his hostility to republican government. Consistency on the part of the great political leaders in American history is more atypical than it is normal.

A pattern of ambivalency also emerges in the operation of American political institutions. The Presidency has been expected by some to reflect public opinion; others have viewed the presidential function as one of molding and creating opinion. We expect, on the one hand, that the legislative branch should determine policy by majority rule; yet, on the other, there are those who strongly support procedural rules, such as the Senate filibuster and the power of standing committees in the legislative process, that give special advantage or control to the minority position. Americans will attribute to the Supreme Court the power of final arbiter in Constitutional disputes, but at the same time insist that Congress control the court through its impeachment and legislative powers. The Constitution itself contributes to this quality of ambivalence. It has been interpreted as an instrument which created a unified national government but is also a document that was written with "states rights" as a foremost consideration in the minds of the Framers.

[22] *Ibid.*
[23] Robert G. McCloskey, "The American Ideology," in *Continuing Crisis in American Politics,* ed. Marian D. Irish (Englewood Cliffs, N.J.: Prentice-Hall, 1963), pp. 10–25.

Finally, McCloskey sees a basic ambivalence in American attitudes toward specific policy issues and political phenomena. Despite strong insistence that all should have the opportunity for education to the limit of their ability, there is an accompanying suspicion and sometimes contempt for the "egghead" in society. The time-honored assertion that "experience is the best teacher" rests uncomfortably in its place beside advice that "books unlock new worlds." Although virtually none of our political leaders would fail to emphasize the security and necessity of the "rule of law," the nation during the past decade or more has witnessed Southern governors in actual defiance of the "law of the land" as interpreted by federal courts. "No other nation," McCloskey remarks, "has had a record of lynching and mob violence comparable to ours." He concludes with the suggestion that "it may be idle to seek for 'the' American tradition, for a 'consensus' in any usual sense of the word. Perhaps our only really basic quality of mind is the pragmatic spirit that can tolerate such a state of affairs and build an enduring polity upon it." [24]

Does our knowledge of the distribution of American attitudes toward fundamental goals and ideals warrant such assertions as have been made up to this point? Is the American as a political thinker ambivalent toward politics, non-reflective in political thinking, and contradictory in his political values? Partial answers to these questions can be derived empirically. We could select values pertaining to our areas of consensus, question people about them, and measure the intensity of agreement and disagreement. Those who assert the existence of an American ideology would expect empirical measurements of attitudes to show a vast majority of Americans in agreement with statements asserting liberal-democratic points of view and in disagreement with those opposing these views. Unfortunately, survey data revealing the nature of American political consensus are too scattered and incomplete to justify any concrete or precise statement of American beliefs. A leading student in this area of research, V. O. Key, Jr., remarked that "the identification of those elements of national character that constitute the basic American consensus, or that permit the government to operate as if there were a basic consensus, can be accomplished only by educated intuition." [25] What evidence does exist, however, casts doubt on unqualified assertions about the existence of a fundamental American ideology beyond simple agreement on general statements about the values of liberal democracy.

A survey conducted by James W. Prothro and Charles M. Grigg among a sample of registered voters in two locales — Ann Arbor, Michigan and Tallahassee, Florida — revealed substantial consensus on abstract postu-

---

[24] *Ibid.*, p. 24.
[25] Key, *op. cit.*, p. 42.

lates about democratic precepts but little agreement on concrete application of these same principles.[26] For example, support for statements
about the principle of democracy itself ("Democracy is the best form of
government"), majority rule ("Public officials should be chosen by majority vote"), and minority rights ("The minority should be free to criticize") ranged from 94.7 to 98.0 per cent. In contrast, agreement failed to
reach 90 per cent on propositions relating to specific application of
these general principles. On about half of these propositions a majority
indicated "undemocratic" attitudes; that is, there was more disagreement
than agreement. Significantly, however, this study found that agreement
with statements that reflected specific applications of democratic values
was more evident among better-educated and higher-income groups
within the sample.

Other studies on the extent of value consensus in America tend to
support these findings. A more extensive study in 1958, directed by
Herbert McClosky, examined the range of agreement on democratic
values among two groups: one termed "political influentials," the other
the "general electorate." [27] The influentials were made up of 3020 delegates and alternates to the 1956 Republican and Democratic national
conventions who responded to a series of items aimed at determining the
level of agreement with democratic values and their application. A representative sample of 1484 adults in the general population were asked to
indicate agreement or disagreement with the same statements. McClosky
concluded that "a large proportion of the electorate has failed to grasp
certain underlying ideas and principles on which the American political
system rests." Defining consensus as existing where 75 per cent or more
of the respondents agreed with a "pro-democratic" proposition or where
75 per cent disagreed with an "anti-democratic" statement, the study revealed that political influentials reached consensus on seven of twelve
items expressing democratic "rules of the game" — fair play in political
life and elections, respect for the processes of law, and rights of minorities. This level of approval was significantly greater than among the
general electorate. Levels of agreement on items indicating commitment
to specific application of the democratic values of free speech, procedural
rights, and the belief in equality failed to produce consensus in either
group. Political influentials reached consensus on four of nine free-speech
and procedural-rights items, while the general electorate displayed con-

[26] James W. Prothro and Charles M. Grigg, "Fundamental Principles of Democracy; Bases of Agreement and Disagreement," *The Journal of Politics*, XXII (Spring,
1960), 276–94.
[27] Herbert McClosky, "Consensus and Ideology in American Politics," *The American Political Science Review*, LVIII, No. 2 (June, 1964), 361–82.

sensus on none. On fifteen statements reflecting belief in political, social, and economic equality, the general electorate again failed to give a "pro-democratic" response. On these items the influentials found consensus on only two of the fifteen items, both involving economic equality.

McClosky's findings reveal similar patterns to those which emerged in Prothro and Grigg's research. Political influentials and the electorate gave equally overwhelming support to abstract statements about democracy and freedom; but, as indicated above, the political activists who stand relatively high on the educational, social, and economic ladders, supported the maxims of democratic ideology to a significantly greater extent than the general electorate. Although McClosky's data indicate that the more articulate and more politically involved groups lend greater support to substantive liberal democratic values, "consensus and democratic ideology are poorly developed among the electorate and only imperfectly realized among the political influentials."

Other research reveals equally important and similar findings. In a study based upon a series of in-depth conversations with fifteen "urban common" men in the Atlantic seaboard area, Robert E. Lane found little evidence of familiarity or agreement with democratic principles of liberty and justice ("government of laws and not of men," "due process of law," etc.). "In short," Lane concluded, "the defense of any philosophic notion of freedom or of any abstract plan of freedom is, if present, an unreliable shelter for the open system; and when the implications of generalized advocacy for the Bill of Rights is shown to mean even a limited tolerance of Communists and atheists, this modest defense seems to fall away." [28] This probable lack of commitment to democratic values emphasizing toleration of minority views was uncovered earlier in Samuel A. Stouffer's study of attitudes toward communism and civil liberties. He reached the similar conclusion that support for these values lies largely within the better-educated and higher social-economic urban groups who also comprise the majority of the politically active element in American society.[29]

Apparently political attitudes on specific issues are not generally shaped for Americans by conscious reference to a unified body of inter-related political ideas. Voters, for example, seldom respond to policy issues on the basis of a "liberal-conservative" ideological framework. The University of Michigan's Survey Research Center data reveal that voter response to domestic issues is considerably more influenced by factors

---

[28] Robert E. Lane, *Political Ideology* (New York: The Free Press of Glencoe, 1962), 461.

[29] Samuel A. Stouffer, *Communism, Conformity and Civil Liberties* (New York: Doubleday Co., 1955).

relating to self-interest than by conservative-liberal ideological constructs. Lower socio-economic groups tend to support Democratic domestic positions while their Republican counterparts are drawn from the better-educated, higher-income groups. Exceptions to this pattern (well-educated voter chooses the Democratic position; less well-educated voter supports Republican policies) seem to be accounted for on the basis of higher political involvement, indifference to issues, or lack of political awareness.[30] As the voter becomes more sophisticated through education and political activity, the tendency to view issues and develop political attitudes in ideological terms is more evident. The Survey Research Center's study of the 1956 presidential election found that about 85 per cent of the American electorate did not look on issues in an "ideological" sense. Furthermore, the study concludes that only 3½ per cent of voters in 1956 could be designated as ideologues — "persons whose comments imply the kinds of conception of politics assumed by ideological interpretation of political behavior and political change."

While the bulk of the American public accepts the democratic ideology when it is offered in general, abstract statements, there is no marked agreement on these principles when they are put in the form of specific statements. There appears to exist only a small group in the American public who tend to be "carriers of the creed" in the sense that their political behavior is influenced substantially by ideological considerations. The group — in V. O. Key, Jr.'s terms, the "political subculture" [31] — marked by a greater degree of political involvement and generally higher socio-economic status, goes beyond mere lip-service commitment to democratic values. Activists also show a much higher degree of political efficaciousness — a feeling that the individual can exert influence on government through his vote and other political activity — than does the population. Herbert McClosky reported that in response to the statement, "I feel that my political leaders hardly care what people like myself think or want," 39 per cent of the general electorate agreed, as compared with 10.9 per cent of the political influentials. For the most part, less than one-fourth of the influentials display attitudes of "political futility," as compared to a much higher portion of the general electorate.[32] Although agreement upon democratic values among the activist sub-community is by no means universal, acceptance and application of the precepts of liberal democracy lie primarily within the confines of this small core in the population.

[30] Angus Campbell *et al.*, *The American Voter* (New York: John Wiley & Sons, 1960), pp. 205–08; see also Robert McCloskey, "Conservatism and Personality," *The American Political Science Review*, LII (March, 1958), 27–45.

[31] Key, *op. cit.*, p. 51.

[32] McClosky, *op. cit.*, pp. 370–71.

POLITICAL CONSENSUS:
NECESSARY OR EXPENDABLE?

We have been speaking of several separate, but related, matters: (1) the ambivalent image Americans have of politics and politicians, a point related to questions of official consensus; (2) the relatively small percentage of the total population possessing ideological conceptions of politics, a point related to doctrinal consensus; and (3) the relative lack of consensus on specific applications of pervasive democratic values among Americans in general, a point related to both doctrinal and constitutional consensus. It should be evident that the research of social scientists substantiates (although it does not prove) the contentions that Americans find ideological consensus on general "principles" only; that what consensus does exist on application of these values lies within the "political sub-culture" or leadership group; that even this leadership group is ambivalent in what it defines as "fundamental" in the application of such principles; and, finally, that voters are seldom ideologically motivated but are inclined to respond to issues on the basis of self-interest or other non-ideological grounds. Consensus on particular policy issues (legislative, executive, and judicial decisions in the normal operation of the polity), while crucially important to community stability, is considered of less importance than the need for agreement on the "basics" of the democratic value system. Presumably, a democratic polity cannot survive an absence of substantial acquiescence on propositions which stand as cornerstones for the entire community. Much of what has been said here is not easily reconcilable with the classical theory of democracy or the long-held assumption that stability in American political processes has been the product of universal acceptance of fundamental values.

We should not be too surprised to find such patterns in American political thinking. Plural forms and purposes in community social and politico-constitutional arrangements partially condition community beliefs. A diversity of group memberships frees the individual from dependence upon any single association within the community; as a consequence, "he is likely to see things a little from the outside and to rehearse the larger social issue in his own mind." [33] A pluralist society nurtures an ideal of its own — the autonomy of the individual: "The autonomous man respects himself as an individual, experiencing himself as the bearer of his own power and as having the capacity to determine his life and to affect the lives of his fellows." [34] The pursuit of that ideal affects the character of pluralist political consensus. A ready-made agree-

[33] *The Power of the Democratic Idea*, p. 35.
[34] Kornhauser, *op. cit.*, p. 10.

ment upon values exists in the abstract, but an emphasis on a "me" viewpoint (rather than "you") frequently renders these principles non-operational in practice. Hence, the American capacity to tolerate in personal beliefs inconsistencies between abstract ideals and their concrete realization can be accounted for. It was this seeming inconsistency between the American "conscience" and practice that Gunnar Myrdal characterized as an "American Dilemma" in his famous critiques of race relations. In pointing out that "the status accorded the Negro in America represents nothing more than a century-long lag of public morals" Myrdal argued that the dilemma could not continue unaltered.[35] Recent civil rights legislation and demonstrations support his conclusions. But how much of a dilemma carries over to community consensus?

The widespread absence of agreement on specific application of fundamentals certainly raises questions about the stability of a political community in which much of the electorate does not share a commitment to ideological values generally identified with "America." Perhaps stability of the political community is possible even in the absence of general consensus. A number of writers have decried what they describe as "mass democracy": a breakdown of the traditional relationships, personal and institutional, which give life and sustenance to any polity. To illustrate, Edward H. Carr, writing in the early 1950's, described mass democracy as "a new phenomenon — a creation of the last half-century — which it is inappropriate and misleading to consider in terms of the philosophy of Locke or of the liberal democracy of the nineteenth century." Carr charges that "the new democratic society consists no longer of a homogeneous closed society of equal and economically secure individuals mutually recognizing one another's rights, but of ill-coordinated, highly stratified masses of people of whom a large majority are primarily occupied with the daily struggle of existence." [36]

Although there is no test that life in the nineteenth century was generally marked by a mutual recognition of "one another's rights," one might seriously doubt if the nineteenth century witnessed a more extensive consensus on fundamentals than does the latter half of the twentieth. It is reasonable to assume, and much history would support it, that American society has at no time been marked by a high level of value consensus. A "political sub-culture" carrying the democratic faith and applying its maxims has probably always existed jointly with a non-ideologically inclined mass electorate. Apathy and indifference among the American electorate are clearly demonstrated phenomena; voters of this type also

---

[35] Gunnar Myrdal, *An American Dilemma* (New York: Harper & Brothers, 1944), p. 24.

[36] Edward H. Carr, *The New Society* (Boston: Beacon Press, 1957), pp. 74–75.

display low levels of political awareness and are rarely involved in political life. The question is not whether all Americans equally share intense commitment to fundamentals; evidence shows they do not. Discussion is better focused on the extent, location, and content of consensus necessary to sustain the democratic polity. The polity has been fairly stable. There must be explanations for this stability, it would seem, other than mere assumptions about universal consensus, either within the population as a whole or within the carriers of the creed.

An American political theorist, Carl J. Friedrich, dismisses fears about the absence of conscious commitment to basic values by pointing out that democracy is sustained by habitual patterns of behavior rather than conscious and articulate acceptance of the creed.[37] Behavior patterns, political and otherwise, are learned and may not necessarily be conscious in the sense that their explanation is rooted in acceptance and understanding of an ideological construct. Americans do give lip service to democratic values; and while they sometimes fail to support them when offered in terms of specifics, overt defiance of law, contempt for due process of law, and hostility toward the rights of others is the exception and not the rule. In short, despite individual ambivalence the collective polity operates *as if* a general consensus did exist.

Some students have observed that if the general electorate were to take a more active role in politics, democracy itself would be endangered. The thrust of this argument is that an open society is seriously endangered where the fundamental values of cultural and political diversity do not significantly condition political activity. Commitment in the abstract to democratic values, without extensive and intensive commitment to their specific application, does characterize the political attitudes of the general population. Yet the absence of commitment to specific application does not mean hostility to the values themselves; absence of consensus may only indicate indifference. The continued presence of stability, marked by peaceful transitions of power in the American political community, lends credence to the assertion that "the ideology is non-controversial" and its elaborations are "in the direction of ceremonialization and glorification, not explanation and justification." [38]

American political consensus then, is not decisive in the sense that it — and it alone — renders governing actions legitimate. Rather, American lip-service consensus is supportive of the political community, liberal democratic ideals, and constitutional procedures so long as people behave as if they *accept* the principles of each even though they may not actively

[37] Carl J. Friedrich, *The New Belief in the Common Man* (Boston: Little, Brown & Co., 1942).
[38] *Ibid.*

believe in them. Furthermore, it is a permissive consensus to the extent that policy decisions are at least widely accepted rather than opposed and violated. And, finally, the apparent higher consensus on liberal democratic tenets among political activists is decisive in shaping the context of limitations and taboos within which leaders accept the responsibility to govern.

Such generalizations are tentative at best and contingent upon more thorough research into American consensus and conflict, but they do raise other questions, to be dealt with in following chapters: (1) What is the nature of the liberal democratic creed that some Americans are indifferent to, others accept, and others actively believe in, and how well do the principles of that creed fit American political behavior? (2) What is the nature of constitutional procedures that shape and are modified by the pursuit of political values?

BIBLIOGRAPHICAL NOTE

The most widely-known statement of the pluralistic model of American politics is David A. Truman's *The Governmental Process* (New York: Alfred A. Knopf, 1951).

Works available in paperback editions which deal with decision-making patterns in the American Community include: Robert A. Dahl's *Who Governs?* (New Haven: Yale University Press, 1961), which demonstrates a pluralistic pattern of power in one American community; C. Wright Mills's *The Power Elite* (New York: Oxford University Press, 1956), which argues the existence of a decision-making pattern dominated by a small hierarchy at the top of the power structure; and Nelson W. Polsby's *Community Power and Political Theory* (New Haven: Yale University Press, 1963), which examines a number of community power studies from a point of view highly sympathetic to Dahl's method.

There are numerous works addressed to an exposition and discussion of American character and political values. The following are among those available in paperback editions: Louis M. Hartz's *The Liberal Tradition in America* (New York: Harcourt, Brace & World, 1955), examines the historical development and meaning of American liberal-democratic ideology; Joseph Tussman's *Obligation and the Body Politic* (New York: Oxford University Press, 1960) approaches from a philosophic perspective the role and responsibilities of the citizen in a democratic society; Joseph L. Blatner, *The Political Novel* (New York: Random House, 1955) examines the novel as an instrument of expression and a shaping factor of American political values; Daniel J. Boorstin, *The Genius of American Politics* (Chicago: University of Chicago Press, 1960); Max Lerner, *America as a Civilization* (New York: Simon & Schuster, 1957) analizes American pluralism and culture in the 1950's; David Riesman, *The Lonely Crowd* (Abridged: New York: Doubleday & Co., 1955) presents a sociologist's view of an American people changed from "inner-directed" to "other-directed" personalities; and Michael McGiffert (ed.), *The Character of Americans* (Homewood, Ill.: The Dorsey Press, 1964), a collection of essays by historians and social scientists dealing with American values and culture from both historical and contemporary points of view.

For those interested in empirical measurement and data on political attitudes and consensual norms, the following are highly useful sources of information. Gabriel A. Almond and Sidney Verba, *The Civic Culture* (Boston: Little, Brown and Company, 1965) is available in paperback; Angus Campbell *et al.*, *The American Voter* (New York: John Wiley & Sons, 1960); and Robert E. Lane, *Political Ideology* (New York: The Free Press, 1962), also available in an abridged paperback edition; Samuel Stouffer, *Communism, Conformity and Civil Liberties* (New York: John Wiley & Sons, Science Editions, 1966).

The gap between belief and practice in America is illustrated in Gunnar Myrdal's *An American Dilemma* (New York: Harper & Bros., 1944), a classic study in American attitudes toward the Negro minority. Sebastian de Grazia, *The Political Community* (Chicago: University of Chicago Press, 1948), discusses the close association of a system of beliefs to the maintenance of political community, and is available in a paperback edition. Also available in paperback, Carl Becker's *Freedom and Responsibility in the American Way of Life* (New York: Vintage Books, 1960) represents an eminent historian's view of citizens' responsibilities and examines American attitudes toward government. E. E. Schattschneider's *The Semisovereign People* (New York: Holt, Rinehart and Winston, 1960), argues the existence of a public interest as opposed to a series of individual pressure groups seeking purely private interests. Finally, V. O. Key, Jr.'s *Public Opinion and American Democracy* (New York: Alfred A. Knopf, 1961) contains an insightful discussion of the gap between theory and practice in American democratic values.

CHAPTER THREE

Liberal Democracy

In discussing political consensus, we observed that Americans generally are reluctant to agree to specific applications of democratic principles even though the abstract postulates themselves are widely held by citizens. Policy conflicts occur within a context of broad acquiescence to vague principles of democratic doctrine and constitutional procedure. Few of us expect to read in our morning paper of a Gallup Poll reporting on efforts to determine the degree of popular support for the proposition that "democracy is the best form of government." Nor would we expect that Americans generally conceive of their government as anything other than democratic; in fact, in one survey 88 per cent of Americans interviewed characterized the United States as a "democracy."[1] Both the superiority and presence of democracy are largely taken for granted.

This popular acceptance of, perhaps faith in, the desirability of democracy raises the question: What is it that is so good? What is a "democratic" political community? Certainly "liberty" and "equality" are characteristics, but the meaning conveyed by these terms is by no means unambiguous. Does, for example, the word liberty include free economic choice? Is that choice violated by a centrally planned and controlled

---

[1] Herbert H. Hyman and Paul B. Sheatsley, "The Current Status of American Public Opinion," in Daniel Katz *et al.* (eds.), *Public Opinion and Propaganda* (New York: Henry Holt and Co., 1954), p. 41.

45

economy or even by a regulated economy? Is "capitalism" essential to democracy? Is belief in the Judeo-Christian religious tradition and Greco-Roman cultural heritage part of the democratic creed? Are particular political arrangements — separation of powers, checks and balances, federalism, political parties — requisites of democratic government? To what extent can democracy be qualified before it is sacrificed? Such questions are not easily answered. Americans have struggled with them for generations. In this chapter we explore the principles of democracy traditionally associated with American political doctrine and practice.

THE DOCTRINE OF LIBERAL DEMOCRACY IN AMERICA

THE NATURE OF LIBERAL DEMOCRATIC THEORY

In Chapter One we noted that a developed community consists of overlapping patterns of social action, conflict regulation, and beliefs. As with the politically relevant portions of any belief system, the American political doctrine of liberal democracy constitutes a theory that helps both to describe political life in the community and to prescribe standards of social conflict regulation. In its prescriptive aspects American liberal democracy shares certain ethical postulates with earlier democratic theories. Democratic theory has always provided guidelines for persons seeking a better life than has ever been realized in any political community. Classic democratic principles have been modified by the American historical experience and now comprise a set of distinctive community ideals. As ideals they do not purport to describe accurately how people actually behave in politics. They serve instead as the stars by which men chart their course to better horizons; by following such markers, it is assumed that individuals can reach their ultimate destinations.

To assert on the one hand that many Americans do not embrace democratic values and yet also to argue that these values serve an important function in the American political system seems a contradiction. In fact it is not. Despite only lip-service acquiescence from many Americans, liberal democratic values serve as the abstract aspirations passed from generation to generation and symbolized as the "American way." As such they tend to set the boundaries within which citizens define goals, pursue desires, and make claims on society for recognition of their interests.

The central tenet in any set of democratic ideals rests upon the desirability of giving to every individual a maximum opportunity for self-development. His perfectability consists of development of his knowledge, his intelligence, his personality, his freedom of choice, and his dignity.

This perfection is to be accomplished by allowing the individual full participation in the regulation of his own conduct. John Dewey summed it up well: "The key-note of democracy as a way of life may be expressed, it seems to me, as the necessity for the participation of every mature human being in formation of the values that regulate the living of men together." [2] Out of joint participation in the making of social choices is to emerge a genuine sense of community, a sharing of human experience worth preserving. So conceived, democratic politics possesses a distinctive purpose. It is "the education of an entire people to the point where their intellectual, emotional, and moral capacities have reached their full potential and they are joined, freely and actively, in the genuine community." [3] Politics as a distinctly human endeavor is to be judged on the basis of its contribution to human perfection. In the democratic polity, conflict is to be so regulated as to render it creative. Political institutions and procedures (legislatures, periodic elections, etc.) can be designated democratic only to the extent that they contribute to the substantive democratic value of individual dignity by providing creative tension.

In its *prescriptive* tenets liberal democracy asserts certain *substantive values* for all citizens. Democracy is viewed in terms of an overriding ideal of human dignity; the political community is democratic to the extent that this ideal transcends particularized interests and charts the behavior of members.

Contrasted to this perspective is one defining democracy not as a set of substantive ideals but as a body of *operating principles* employed in regulating social conflict. Thus, a political community is democratic to the extent that (1) popular control of policy-makers is broadly based, (2) open discussion and criticism of policy is tolerated, (3) political liberties are protected, and (4) political equality is recognized.[4] The focus of this definition is upon the working criteria of liberal democratic politics and the tone is *procedural*.

The two conceptions are not totally divorced; American liberal democracy contains both elements: a series of ethical postulates concerning the rationality of man, individual dignity, the desirability of liberty, equality, etc.; and a series of procedural and institutional criteria which attempt to establish the operating principles of self-government, such as popular control, majority rule, minority rights, and due process of law.

[2] John Dewey, "Democracy and Educational Administration," *School and Society*, April 3, 1937.
[3] Lane Davis, "The Cost of Realism: Contemporary Restatements of Democracy," *Western Political Quarterly*, XVII, 1 (March, 1964), 40.
[4] See Henry B. Mayo, *An Introduction to Democratic Theory* (New York: Oxford University Press), 1960.

LIBERAL DEMOCRACY IN THE
AMERICAN POLITICAL TRADITION

Political activity in the American community is shaped by both past and present. The fact that the ideals of liberal democracy are not considered as bases for legitimate social conflict, even though we may disagree on the application of those ideals in policy struggles, is a vital "given" in the political community. How it developed can be examined profitably by considering the ideals of liberal democracy in their historical context as well as by summarizing them as they exist in the present era. With an understanding of the nature of liberal democratic doctrine, we can then explore the relationship of the theory to political conflict and note what, if any, contrast exists between doctrine and behavior.

In 1840 the Frenchman Alexis de Tocqueville attributed American liberalism to the fact that Americans were "born free." A century later the same theme was expounded by Louis M. Hartz as he undertook to explore the origins of our "natural liberalism." [5] Whereas the struggle for liberal democracy in Europe was fought against a social and political system based upon feudal class lines and privilege, Americans never faced the problem of such an *ancien regime*. American liberalism has been "middle class" from the start. Hartz points out that neither a privileged group based on class ("aristocracy") nor an underprivileged one favoring a radical political movement ("proletariat") has played a significant political role. From colonial beginnings onward there was fundamental agreement on the right of every American to possess private property, a value which was distinctly middle class in origin. Even slavery was conceived by many, including the United States Supreme Court in the Dred Scott Case, as more of an extension of the "right" than its negation.

Despite inconsistencies the absence of a political and social creed other than middle-class liberalism resulted in what Hartz identifies as the "moral unanimity of a liberal society." He characterizes American doctrine as consisting of two major themes. First, from its beginnings it has reflected the political theory of John Locke. Political dissension has revolved around techniques of decision-making, not the Lockian ideals underlying political doctrine and procedures. The power of judicial review by American courts, for example, might never have developed without fundamental agreement among *leaders* on which principles the courts should apply in interpreting the constitutionality of actions performed by the executive or legislative branches. Secondly, because Lockian liberalism has been pervasive, the American political creed has historically been

[5] Louis Hartz, *The Liberal Tradition in America* (Harvest Book; New York: Brace & World, 1955).

a "fixed dogmatic liberalism of a liberal way of life." [6] In short, deviations from the normal pattern have been neither tolerated nor really possible. We can obtain a somewhat clearer picture of the nature of American political doctrine if we examine briefly the liberal Lockian background from which it emerged and the democratizing influences of the American experience.

To say that the United States came into existence as a result of the Revolution of 1776 is true, yet that event alone did not mark the origins of "Americanism." The political ideas of the American Revolution reflect in fact, English liberal thinking and institutions as much or more than an indigenous American development. The French Revolution of 1790 was a major surgery on French political institutions. It was radical in that its avowed purpose was the destruction of the monarchy and the creation of a political arrangement totally new to French experience. The American Revolution, on the other hand, was couched in demands for the "rights of Englishmen," demands offered in the form of petitions to Parliament and legally-oriented arguments against English claims of colonial empire. It also was motivated and justified by appeals to natural rights and social contract. James Otis, a major figure in revolutionary thought, combined appeals to the "law of nature" with legal arguments that the British Constitution was being violated by the Crown in its relations with the colonies. "Every British Subject," Otis argued in the *Rights of the British Colonies* (1764), "born on the Continent of America, or in any other of the British dominions, is by the law of God and nature, by the common law, and by act of Parliament (exclusive of all charters from the Crown), entitled to all the natural, essential, inherent and inseparable rights of our fellow subjects in Great Britain." [7] Beginning around 1765 and ending with the outbreak of the Revolution, colonial sentiment regarding relations with the British Crown moved from initial assertions that taxation without representation was illegal, to denial of Parliamentary authority to govern the colonies (although allegiance to the King was recognized), and ultimately to outright assertion of independence.[8] British actions were no longer regarded as simply illegal or unconstitutional, they were now cited as fundamentally immoral — as against the laws of Nature and nature's God. But, the "proof" of that immorality depended on borrowed politicial ideas, specifically those of John Locke developed in an earlier era of "Glorious Revolution."

---

[6] *Ibid.*, Chap. I.

[7] See Alpheus Thomas Mason, *Free Government in the Making* (New York: Oxford University Press, 1965), p. 93.

[8] Clinton Rossiter, *Seedtime of the Republic* (New York: Harcourt, Brace and Co.), 1953.

Locke founded his political thought upon the concept of a state of nature, a condition that preceded civil society as we know it. Within the state of nature, where all men are "free, equal, and independent," man is governed by no law except the natural law, the author of which is God. Man attains knowledge of natural law through use of his reason. This natural law is the basis of the fundamental and inalienable right to life, liberty, and property. These natural rights reside with every man by virtue of his being born. Since they do not originate with man, it follows that no man or group of men may usurp them and they cannot be given up.

Locke described man's life in the state of nature as quite inconvenient (if not completely insecure), a condition resulting from the tendency of man to violate the fundamental moral law. In the state of nature none is obligated to obey man-made rules of authority; hence, the only means of enforcement of the laws of nature was through action taken by each individual suffering injury. This "want of a common judge" to protect individual rights created insecurity and brought man to recognize the need for creation of a civil society authorized to make laws and enforce obedience to them. Since the individual is largely free in the state of nature (he is *morally* obligated to respect others' natural rights), any provision under which his liberty is qualified or given up requires his consent.

The social contract was Locke's means to bring man from the state of nature into civil society. Each individual agrees with every other individual to a contract under which he forfeits some of his natural freedom in return for the benefits derived from man-made rules governing relationships between individuals. In short, the rights of the natural state from which men come are replaced by those of community to which they aspire. Locke held, however, that the rights of life, liberty, and property were universal and inalienable; thus they could never be taken away. The civil society or government created by the contract was, therefore, prohibited from violating these rights. Its authority was limited to activities serving the common good. But who was to decide which rules are to be made? Locke recognized that unanimous consensus would be impossible and suggested rule by majority as the only practical decision-making device.

Government exists then only as a trustee of the people who have agreed to the contract. It has no authority independent of that granted by the people. Locke's ultimate weapon to prevent abuse of this arrangement by political officials is the right of revolution. Whenever governors violate the natural rights of the governed, they forfeit the authority placed in them under the social contract. Disobedience and rebellion is justified, and the individual is freed of any obligation to obey civil law.

Such action returns man to the state of nature until such time as he agrees to the creation of another government by contract.

Few documents in American political thought so well reflect the wedding of the Lockian background and the American experience as does the *Declaration of Independence,* penned by Thomas Jefferson. In fact, Jefferson was accused of copying the Declaration from Locke's *Treatise on Government.* The content of the Declaration indicates that the concepts of natural law, natural right, and social contract were thoroughly ingrained in the political thought of the American revolutionists. Carl Becker concludes that "the strength of the Declaration was precisely that it said what everyone was thinking. . . . Where Jefferson got his ideas is hardly so much a question as where he could have got away from them." [9] Jefferson admitted that the ideas of the Declaration were not novel but were precisely intended to reflect common thoughts. As a concise statement of the position of the colonists, the document reflected a basic agreement on fundamental concepts among those committed to separation. As a revolutionary instrument, it served as a justification for resistance to any claims of British sovereignty over the American colonies. It thus answered the British, American Tory malcontents, and the "proper opinions of mankind." Its philosophy is the broad philosophy of liberal democracy. It later became the basis for innumerable academic addresses, election sermons, and Fourth of July orations by which Americans reaffirmed their belief in its principles.

The Declaration tells us something about how Americans use political ideas as guides to action and as instruments in both the pursuit of community goals and rationalization of specialized interests. Because American political thinkers have been politicians first and philosophers second, they have "made the American government both with their thoughts and with their hands." [10] Caught up in the pressures of conflict regulation, American political theorists frequently have utilized political ideals as tools of persuasion in efforts to appeal for the widest possible support for policy stands. As a result any such set of ideas as those in the Declaration provides a reflection of the types of thinking current and fashionable among political leaders. Specifically the Declaration mirrors the Lockian political ideals present among community leaders at the time of the Revolution. It also reveals what symbolic appeals political leaders thought useful to win support and furnish guidelines of liberal democ-

[9] Carl L. Becker, *The Declaration of Independence* (New York: Harcourt, Brace and World, 1922), pp. 24, 26.

[10] On this feature of American political ideas see Robert G. McCloskey, "American Political Thought and the Study of Politics," in Roland Young (ed.), *Approaches to the Study of Politics* (Evanston, Ill.: Northwestern University Press, 1958), pp. 155–71.

racy acceptable to colonial Americans. The Declaration marks a turning point in the clash of ideas leading to the American Revolution, a clash of ideas that mirrors a far more intense conflict of interests between colonists themselves concerning what groups could best be served by independence rather than remaining in the Empire. The *Declaration of Independence* reflects in part the resolution of that conflict on behalf of those favoring severance.

What, then, is the theory reflected in the *Declaration of Independence?* It can be reduced to the two basic propositions of individual dignity and republican government. Each has been expanded upon and incorporated into American institutions and beliefs during the course of our history.

First, man is a rational creature capable of governing himself. The emphasis is upon an individual who possesses inalienable rights, who is politically equal to all other men, and who is capable of rational choice between alternative courses of action. As the core value in the liberal creed, the individual lays claim to the right to make his own political, economic, and social choices and to have the right respected and defended. In the words of the *Declaration of Independence*, government exists "to secure these rights," and "whenever any Form of Government becomes destructive of these ends, it is the Right of the People to alter or to abolish it. . . ." The notion of individual dignity, founded upon natural rights, carries with it the implication that the standard of judgment in evaluating the individual is *not* to be his economic class, social position, race, or creed. Individuals are to be judged as individuals. The concept of "equality before the law" is a clear expression of the individualistic ethic of liberal democracy. Justice is to be rendered on the basis of equal treatment to all, notwithstanding the circumstances of the accused. So, too, the assertion of equality of opportunity is derived from the individualistic content of liberal democracy. In this sense, equality refers to the condition under which the individual can fairly compete for economic, social, or political benefits. It does not argue that all men are necessarily, or ought to be, equal in intelligence, ability, economic wealth, or social status. It does insist that individual choices ought to be left free and that arbitrary limitations imposed on the expression of these individual rights are illegitimate.

Such is the moral basis of the liberal ideology. Its propositions are a series of ethical rules that ought to guide the actions of men in their political relationships. The fact that countless instances may be found that contradict the moral postulates are irrelevant to the value of the aspirations of the doctrinal ideals themselves. Where natural rights are denied, government is, by virtue of its failure to preserve these rights, illegitimate. Neither the notion of natural rights nor its corollary concept of individualism can be demonstrated empirically. To say that all men are endowed with the rights of life, liberty, and happiness is to assert that there are valid and unchangeable rules which take precedence over conflicting man-made rules. Locke, in holding these propositions as self-evident to rational man, provided a highly credible, if inexact, yardstick by which political institutions can be judged. New England colonists and succeeding generations of Americans have employed the standard to deny the proposition that any political system which flouts individual rights has a right to exist.[11]

A second basic element in the Declaration's statement of Lockian liberal democracy is the concept of representative government and majority rule. Given the equality of all men, and given the assertion that community authority exists only as an instrument to achieve the aims of the governed, the people must have a way of making their voices heard. A system under which all men may participate directly in the making of laws is impossible. The closest alternative to direct democracy is an arrangement under which the people choose policy-makers to act in their behalf. These officials must, however, be kept responsible to citizens, an end which is achieved through periodic, fixed elections. Moreover, unanimous agreement among representatives is unlikely, since all men do not have the same interests nor do they conceive general social goals in the same way. It follows that the only practical way for a democratic polity to operate is through representative government acting under majority rule. The greater number, limited by several considerations regarding the rights of the minority, should obtain its wishes in preference to the lesser. Clearly implied in liberal theory is the proposition that the minority may not be coerced by a majority whose desire, if implemented, would violate basic human freedoms and rights. The "rule of law" carries with it the conviction that individual and minority rights may be qualified only within the framework of fair and impartial procedures. Arbitrary actions by individuals or by the majority are controlled by safeguards built into the institutional processes. The concept of "due process of law" in the Fifth and Fourteenth Amendments, for example, is a major Constitutional restriction on governmental action.

Liberal democratic ideals proclaim a theory of human rights superior to any commands made by policy-makers acting through majority sanction; yet majority rule is defended as the practical implementation of rule by the governed. To the extent that the majority acts tyrannically, liberal democracy is sacrificed. But to the extent it cannot operate at all, liberal democracy is endangered also. Can majority rule and the concept of individual (minority) rights be made compatible propositions? Liberal

[11] Hartz, *op. cit.*

political theory has from Locke onward struggled with this dilemma. Accepting the concept of majority rule, what limits are to be imposed on its decision-making prerogatives? Jefferson, in his Inaugural Address in 1801, spoke of a basis for reconciliation when he argued that "though the will of the majority is in all cases to prevail, that will, to be rightful, must be reasonable; that the minority possess their equal rights, which equal laws must protect and to violate which would be oppression." [12] Liberal democratic doctrine illustrated by Jefferson's remarks rests upon the assertion that legitimate rule of the majority is that of the rule of reason. Majority action may not be the "right" choice, but the action must be rational in the sense that individuals weigh alternatives and make a choice based upon recognition of and respect for individual rights such as free inquiry, freedom of dissent, etc. — in short the inviolability of certain minority rights.

Ultimately, majority rule rests on the ethical-moral assertion that purely private interests ought not to prevail over considerations of the "public good," "community interest," or the "national interest." Where the rational basis for defending majority rule is absent, majority rule becomes a very vulnerable, if not indefensible, proposition. Under such circumstances the will of a majority becomes morally illegitimate because it is arbitrary and irrational. To the extent that any given majority of the people acting directly or through its chosen representatives violates the moral imperative of rational choice (which includes recognition of minority rights), its decisions are illegitimate.

The Lockian tradition is perhaps the most pervasive and persistent factor contributing to the origins and development of American political doctrine. There have been others. For many of the revolutionary leaders the ideas of Thomas Hobbes were converted into a respect for centralized authority. Moreover, the thesis of James Harrington that political stability is dependent upon the actual distribution of property had a profound influence. And the tradition of balanced authority from Montesquieu may have inspired the thinking of many colonial politicians. Regardless of the ideas that made their way to American shores, however, all had to be modified in light of the uniqueness of American experience. Notions of liberty, authority, property, and balance had been developed in a European culture marked by feudal traditions, class distinctions, and limited opportunity for individual improvement. Out of reactions against such conditions America was founded; on the new continent were factors that significantly transformed the values held by colonists fleeing from feudal and clerical oppression.

[12] Adrienne Koch and William Peden, *The Life and Selected Writings of Thomas Jefferson* (New York: The Modern Library, 1944), p. 371.

In attempting to identify the major forces helping to shape American political doctrine, historians have provided an extensive inventory. For example, in 1893 Frederick Jackson Turner presented what has become one of the more venerable explanations of the growth of liberal democracy. He emphasized factors regarded as indigenous to the American environment — the democratizing and nationalizing influences of the frontier. As the New England colonist pushed westward across the continent, he found a unique environment separate and apart from America's European origins. The untamed wilderness conditioned social life. It threatened the safety of settlers and led them into close cooperation with one another in conquering the continent. As each new frontier was occupied and towns and manufacturers grew, the westward movement toward cheaper land and better opportunities continued. Although the frontier ended about 1890 when the Pacific Ocean was reached and the coastal regions settled, its alleged impact on American ideas and political development was permanent. "The most important effect of the frontier," Turner argued, "has been . . . the promotion of democracy here and in Europe." [13] Relatively cheap land furthered the principle of democratic opportunity. It called forth an independent and individualistic citizen insistent on political equality. A democracy oriented toward the well-being of the common man spread across frontier communities.

The frontier also developed a sense of nationalism, a term used by Turner to express the growth of unity, a growing nationalization of politics, and a conscious sense of community identity. He illustrated his point by reference to national legislation — railroad legislation, internal improvements, homesteading acts, and tariffs protecting frontier interests — in response to frontier needs. The mobility of the American population reduced the effects of localism by mixing people of varied ethnic and sectional backgrounds. The result was the growth of intellectual traits, social patterns, and economic arrangements uniquely American.

How much is explained by such an interpretation is open to question. That frontier conditions influenced the adaptation of liberal democratic ideals to American experience is clear, but democracy was challenged as well as nurtured by the American frontier. Critics have pointed out that frontier "individualism" sometimes masked an orthodoxy of outlook not altogether tolerant of diverse views. Tar and feathers, lynch mobs, and vigilantes were never too far in the background of frontier democracy. Encroachments upon free speech, press, and inquiry are modern-day reversions found in some pockets of lingering frontierism. Still other critics hold that the theory is not applicable to frontier areas other than

[13] Frederick Jackson Turner, "The West and American Ideals," in *The Frontier in American History* (New York: Henry Holt and Co., 1921).

perhaps the Middle West, and Turner is charged with failing to present evidence that the frontier actually reshaped the institutions of democracy.[14]

Along with frontier expansion other factors have certainly conditioned the descent of liberal democracy from its Lockian origins. A geographical isolation from Europe and the vast expanse of an unsettled continent with seemingly unlimited natural resources promoted individual autonomy. The unsuccessful man could move on burying his failures, perhaps even his enemies, behind him. Moreover, V. L. Parrington has traced the development of democratic values as a reflection of the agrarian tradition struggling against wealth and centralized authority.[15]

A variety of religious beliefs contributed their share to doctrinal statements. Protestant views emphasized the importance of individual salvation through work, the value of free choice, and the sanctity of private property. Catholics regarded private property as a God-given right. In later years Protestant, Catholic, and Jewish churches stressed the necessity of social welfare programs to relieve the burdens of the underprivileged. The Protestant Ethic and the Social Gospel combined to highlight the place of rights to both "property" and the "pursuit of happiness" in liberal democracy.[16]

Migration to America also left its mark. Since beginning its enumerations in 1820, the Bureau of the Census has estimated that forty-three million immigrants have come to America. More than thirty-five million have come from Europe with Germany, Italy, Ireland, Austria-Hungary, Russia, England, and Scandanavia contributing from one to six million immigrants each. In addition, other European countries, Latin America, Canada, Asia, and Africa have witnessed sizable emigrations to our shores. Each immigrant grouping has contributed to the diversity of our social composition and produced pressures for freedom of participation, dissent, uniqueness, and nonconformity. Conversely, however, the tendency of these groups to cluster together in large cities or sections of the nation produced pressures for conformity to social, religious, and cultural patterns associated with each particular group. Nevertheless, the chronicle of the development of liberal democratic doctrine includes geographi-

---

[14] George Rogers Taylor (ed.), *The Turner Thesis* (rev. ed.; Boston: D. C. Heath & Co., 1956), pp. 34–75. Ray Allen Billington (ed.), *The Frontier Thesis: Valid Interpretation of American History?* (New York: Holt, Rinehart & Winston, 1966).

[15] Vernon Louis Parrington, *Main Currents in American Thought* (New York: Harcourt, Brace and Co., 1927.)

[16] R. H. Tawney, *Religion and the Rise of Capitalism* (New York: Harcourt, Brace and World, 1926); Marquis W. Childs and Douglass Cater, *Ethics in a Business Society* (New York: Harper & Row, 1954).

cal, economic, religious, and social influences operating in conjunction with inherited Lockian ideals.

THE PATTERN OF LIBERAL DEMOCRACY IN AMERICA

THE POLITICS OF LIBERAL DEMOCRACY

Up to this point we have been concerned primarily with the substantive aspects of liberal democratic theory — the set of ideals related to the dignity and development of the human personality. We noted, though, that these ideals were to be pursued through the operation of procedures of representative government, particularly those connected with majority rule and minority rights. Thus from a Lockian background come both substantive and procedural dimensions of liberal democracy.

Politics, we have said, is the most inclusive set of human activities concerned with the regulation of social conflict. Defined from the perspective of its characteristic procedures, democracy is a distinctive style of conflict regulation marked by efforts to maximize personal choice through the maintenance of *open* conflict. Although this is not a complex notion, the specific procedures by which social conflict is revealed and resolved in the democratic political community — the institutional imperatives of liberal democracy — need to be considered in some detail. These imperatives may be subsumed under five general principles, which, if they actually operate in processes of conflict regulation, designate the political community as democratic: *popular control, popular consultation, political leadership, political equality,* and *political liberty.* In political patterns each is interwoven with all others.

Popular Control. We noted that the keynote of substantive democracy was sounded by John Dewey; the keynote of procedural democracy was suitably stated by Joseph Schumpeter as "that institutional arrangement for arriving at political decisions in which individuals acquire power to decide by means of a competitive struggle for the people's vote." [17] Schumpeter also stressed the "vital fact of leadership" in arguing that without effective leadership to articulate and translate the people's will into public policy democratic theory becomes an unrealistic ideal. In short, the heart of democracy is the conversion of social conflict into institutionalized competition. For popular control of conflict regulation to exist, the governed need not participate actively in the making of community decisions; rather they need to possess the right to participate in the choice of

[17] Joseph Schumpeter, *Capitalism, Socialism and Democracy* (Second Edition; New York and London: Harper and Row, 1942), p. 269.

governors at the ballot box. Elections are declarations whereby authority is made legitimate as people consent to being governed by chosen officials.

As the institution of popular control, elections must be characterized by universal right of suffrage, be held at reasonably regular intervals, and present meaningful alternatives to the electorate. By meaningful alternatives we mean competing sets of individuals — not necessarily competing programs of action — appealing for support in their efforts to be chosen as authoritative officials. From this perspective elections may be viewed as interest conflicts concerning the question of who shall govern, conflicts which are taken to the wider audience of the electorate for decision. Elections are periodic expansions in the scope of interest conflict, expansions which take the form of peaceful competition. Although popular influence over chosen officials may continue between elections through a variety of formal and informal channels, such political participation differs from the ideal called for in doctrinal interpretations of liberal democracy. In the latter individual dignity is advanced through participation in "formation of the values that regulate the living of men together." Procedural interpretations view recurring elections as expedients offering the closest approximation to the broad participation called for by the liberal democratic idea.

Popular Consultation. Popular consultation is the procedural requirement established to shape the manner by which conflicts are represented to policy makers. In attempting to bring conflicts out into the open and discuss them, popular consultation is embodied in those institutional safeguards that assume free communication of conflict to policy-makers. To the extent that this principle operates successfully, it contributes to the maintenance of what is termed an "open society." The defining characteristic of such an arrangement is the fact that nothing in the political community is immune to criticism; there are no sacred cows that cannot be examined. So conceived, popular consultation is essentially a process by which all members of the community are given the opportunity to compare political reality with their conception of how things ought to be. This process rests on the assertion that it is desirable for information to be dispersed freely and fully. Furthermore, the rationale underlying the desirability of self-examination is the assumption that human beings are fallible creatures. Since they may err in their relationships, full information and examination provide a safety valve assuring that mistakes will be detected, improvements made, and the human personality developed.

A distinguishing feature of open consultation among community members is the willingness to tolerate the consequences of individual diversity, such as the acceptance of social disagreement as legitimate in human life. Former Justice Robert A. Jackson, for example, in an opinion of the

U.S. Supreme Court striking down a state rule compelling the pledge of allegiance to the flag by all public school students, termed the right of political unorthodoxy a "fixed star in our constitutional constellation." [18] Such toleration of conflict contributes to the development of an environment where moderation of disputes is possible and compromise becomes a preferred way of resolving differences. Bargaining is to popular consultation what electoral competition is to popular control. Authoritarian procedures demanding conformity of individual values to all community norms — whether they flow from doctrines of communism, fascism, or whatever — are basically inimical to the environment of open conflict characteristic of liberal democracy.

A variety of institutions in modern liberal democracies are vehicles for popular consultation. Many such arrangements publicize social conflict, although they may not have been conceived specifically for that purpose. Periodic elections stimulate conflicts between partisan groups seeking authority to govern. Political parties in campaign efforts directed at mobilizing popular support, indoctrinating prospective followers, and activating sympathizers publicize both similarities and differences of outlook. In later chapters we will take note of how parties, pressure groups, mass movements, and policy officials often depend upon their ability to control the publicizing of interest conflict in order to realize their goals. One institution justifies its existence in a liberal democracy on the grounds of unique service in the revelation of conflict and transmission of information — the news media. "Where the press is free," said Thomas Jefferson, "and every man able to read, all is safe." [19] In liberal democratic theory the legitimate function for the news media is the communication of information as an aid to popular discovery of truth. The maintenance of an open community ultimately depends upon both a free press for unencumbered distribution of ideas and an educational system capable of inculcating individuals with the values of free inquiry and self-examination. School and press are thus the ultimate institutional requisites of popular consultation.

Political Leadership. Although the American commitment to substantive democratic ideas is generally weak in political practice, certain critical groups possess a higher commitment than the population at large. The democratic beliefs of this political subculture of activists and leaders, combined with institutional safeguards mentioned above, contribute to the survival of liberal democratic values. Such political leadership is itself

---

[18] *West Virginia Board of Education* v. *Barnette,* 319 U.S. 624 (1943).
[19] Letter to Colonel Charles Yancy, 1816, quoted in Saul K. Padover, *Thomas Jefferson on Democracy* (Mentor Books; New York: The New American Library, 1946), p. 89.

a requisite of an operating democracy. If the function of democratic politics is to render conflict creative, the extent to which it does so depends largely upon the quality of political leadership. Political leaders mobilize electoral majorities and aid in making popular control effective; political leaders make popular consultation operational by injecting issues into the community for criticism and discussion. Indeed, we may argue that it is conflict between political leaders that preserves free choice in a liberal democracy, for differences within the leadership corps promote alternative policy choices and the formation of a variety of groups seeking responsibility to govern. If conflict within the leadership cadre is to be maintained, leaders in a liberal democracy must be recruited from a variety of social classes, must exhibit a diversity of social interests, and all must have some access to policy-making institutions. The presence of a pluralist social system and a decentralized and fragmented politico-constitutional system within the American community contribute to the likelihood of these conditions, but they do not alone assure them. There must also be a pervasive commitment among political leaders to certain procedural rules by which conflict is represented and resolved, including taboos upon overly demagogic appeals for support from potential followers. There must be, asserted V. O. Key, Jr., "certain restraints on political competition" that "help keep competition within tolerable limits." [20] To assure the existence of an active minority opposition there must be respect for the fundamental rights of speech, press, assembly, and property, and leaders must not exploit public opinion by unscrupulous tactics and appeals that endanger the democratic order. Leaders must be willing to accept the electoral verdict if defeated; the victors must, on the other hand, not seek to resolve conflict with opponents by resorting to either physical or character assassination.

Political Equality. Political leaders in a liberal democracy must also be willing to abide by other procedural norms, particularly those involving the working principles of political equality. The procedural perspective on liberal democratic theory defines political equality as the recognition that each individual should possess an equal opportunity to influence decisions of policy-makers. Essentially this refers to universal adult suffrage whereby every adult should possess the franchise, each voter should cast only one vote per office in question, and each vote cast should be counted equally. Although equality in liberal democratic doctrine is viewed as the equal opportunity of all persons to develop individual capacities, the procedural interpretation does not go so far. Political

[20] V. O. Key, Jr., *Public Opinion and American Democracy* (New York: Alfred A. Knopf, 1961), p. 539; see also Andrew Hacker, "Liberal Democracy and Social Control," in Joseph Fiszman, *The American Political Arena* (Boston: Little, Brown and Co., 1962), p. 94.

equality is conceived rather as primarily a prerequisite for decision-making. If the principle of "one man, one vote" operates, it leads to the corollary that a majority of votes should count for more in the final decision than does a minority. Hence, majority rule is a subsidiary working principle of liberal democracy that says, in effect, that legitimate community decisions have majority support. But majority rule possesses its own proviso: regardless of majority backing, no policy action is legitimate if it deprives the minority of its political freedoms. This introduces the fifth working standard of liberal democracy, political liberty.

Political Liberty. The rationale underlying the working principle of political liberty stresses the freedom of individual participation. Specifically each person is to be free to exercise political choice, criticize existing policies (and perhaps the existing politico-constitutional system), organize groups, parties, and associations, for purposes of proselytizing opposing views, and follow alternative political leadership. Herein lies the essential contribution of political liberties — freedom of speech, press, and assembly. Each of these freedoms is an attempt to assure: (1) that the opportunity of no community member to participate at some point in the conflict regulation will be blocked by majority or minority decision, (2) that community followers will not be the pawns of leaders, (3) that political leaders will not have legal opportunity to destroy the loyal opposition, and (4) that self-examination will not suffer from artificial limitations placed upon free inquiry.

We noted that the very preservation of majority rule requires respect for tolerance of minorities. Majorities rarely need protection of their freedoms to speak or write. Justice Douglas, defending these rights of the minority, offered the eloquent argument that "freedom to differ is not limited to things that do not matter much. That would be a mere shadow of freedom. The test of its substance is the right to differ as to things that touch the heart of the existing order." [21] Truly, the minority of today can never hope to become tomorrow's majority unless it has the opportunity to argue its cause in the marketplace of ideas. Commitment to "government by the people" requires, therefore, accompanying commitment to the procedures through which minorities can act in a meaningful fashion. It is true that many voters do cast their vote without weighing alternatives or without making use of available sources of information. Yet this fact does not vitiate the *necessity* of protecting these freedoms. Without them there can be no democracy at all.

From the procedural perspective each political liberty constitutes a method of safeguarding freedom of choice, particularly electoral choice. Substantive interpretations of liberal democracy see political liberty in a much broader framework. In such doctrine the ultimate political liberty

[21] *Beilan v. Board of Education* 356 U.S. 399 (1958).

is not the guarantee of certain political procedures, but the assurance of self-development through self-inquiry. John Dewey, for example, defined the democratic idea of freedom as something more than the simple right of the individual to *do* as he pleases, "even if it be qualified by adding 'provided he does not interfere with the same freedom on the part of others.'" Instead Dewey insisted, "While the idea is not always, not often enough, expressed in words, the basic freedom is that of freedom of mind and of whatever degree of freedom of action and experience is necessary to produce freedom of intelligence."

Conflict over application of governmental limitations of political and personal liberties has always existed. How much protection against government is necessary to maintain political and social diversity and autonomy? Are there areas of activity that require greater protection than others? The crucial nature of the "first freedoms" — speech, press, and assembly — to the preservation of an open society is clear. In addition to these substantive rights, there are others that less directly involve, but are no less basic to, the viability of a pluralistic democracy. These are the procedural rights that protect the individual against arbitrary police action and insure him a fair "day in court" when his life, liberty, and property are at stake.

First Amendment Freedoms: Search for a Balancing Formula. Statements to the effect that freedom is not absolute do not go very far in resolving the crucial question of *how much* freedom may constitutionally be restricted. For example: should books that shock prevailing moral standards be banned from sale and distribution, or is the right of free press too precious to ever permit such action? Should government be permitted to prohibit spoken or written words that call for the overthrow of government even though the words may not call for taking immediate steps to implement achievement of the goal? Should peaceful "freedom marches" be banned where local police fear that demonstrators may be seriously harmed?

All of these questions lie at the heart of the continuing effort of the Supreme Court to achieve a balance between what are often viewed as competing values — individual rights *versus* societal interests. In a sense, the issue as stated here is misleading since it suggests an unbridgeable dichotomy between individuals and social values. Pluralism rests upon the desirability of maintaining a large degree of individual autonomy. Collective interests in an open society are also served by individual freedom since restriction of one man's freedom might ultimately lead to the sacrifice of the rights of the many. Nevertheless, the problems of coping with individual expression without sacrificing what are considered the legitimate prerogatives of the larger number is generally well understood.

How, then, has the Supreme Court dealt with such problems? Justice Holmes in *Schenck* v. *United States* (1919) laid down the "clear and present danger" test as a judicial formula for dealing with First Amendment cases. "The question in every case is whether the words are used in such circumstances and are of such a nature as to create a clear and present danger that they will bring about the substantive evils that Congress has a right to prevent." In *Abrams* v. *United States,* also decided in 1919, Holmes gave a more precise definition to the test. His dissenting opinion in that case defined a "present" danger as one that "imminently threatens immediate interference with the lawful and pressing purposes of the law." Thus, danger would have to be imminent before the legitimate instruments of the state could move in to prevent it. Where applied, the clear-and-present-danger test would permit judicial scrutiny of governmental claims that interference with free expression is clearly necessary. At the same time, however, the Holmes formula recognizes that there are limits to the use of these freedoms; "substantive" evils can be prevented.

Until the mid-1930's advocates of the clear-and-present-danger test could not command a majority on the Supreme Court. Where violations of the First Amendment rights were claimed and were upheld by the Court, the majority relied on other tests as a basis for decision. For example, the Court struck down a Minnesota statute used to bar a newspaper from further publication on grounds that it was guilty of publishing "malicious, scandalous, and defamatory" attacks. The Court ruled that freedom of the press prohibits prior censorship as to what is published.[22]

Even though it was not consistently supported by more than four justices, the clear-and-present-danger test found its way into majority opinions. West Virginia's compulsory flag salute was struck down in 1943 as a violation of the First Amendment. The freedoms of that amendment, said Justice Jackson, "are susceptible of restriction only to prevent grave and immediate danger," a situation held not to be present in failure to salute the flag.[23] A 1940 ruling, *Thornhill* v. *Alabama,* found a state law that forbade peaceful picketing unconstitutional on grounds that the law violated freedom of speech. Picketing posed no "clear danger of substantive evils." *Thomas* v. *Collins* (1945) declared invalid a Texas law requiring a permit before a union could solicit members for the organization. One authority suggests that this decision may have been "the high watermark in the use of clear-and-present-danger."[24]

[22] *Near* v. *Minnesota* 283 U.S. 697 (1931).
[23] *West Virginia Board of Education* v. *Barnette* 319 U.S. 624 (1943).
[24] Alpheus T. Mason and William M. Beany, *American Constitutional Law* (Englewood Cliffs, N.J.: Prentice-Hall, 1964), p. 480.

In 1938, Justice Harlan F. Stone suggested that First Amendment rights should be accorded a special place in the framework of Constitutional values. This test, known as the "preferred position" argument, holds that since the freedoms of speech, press, assembly, and religion are crucial to democratic government, they must be accorded special treatment.[25] This doctrine strengthened the position of the advocates of the clear-and-present-danger test by adding another element to their argument. If speech, press, assembly, and religion occupy a preferred place in constitutional values, the presumption that governmental restrictions are constitutional need not be granted. In assessing restrictions on these rights, the Court, as guardian of the Constitution, must decide if a clear and present danger exists.

Clear-and-present-danger is not solely used to uphold the claims of defendants. Without discarding the Holmes doctrine, the Court has found some actions undeserving of protection. *Chaplinsky* v. *New Hampshire* (1942) declared that freedom of speech did not extend to protection of "fighting" or "offensive" words that threaten breach of the peace. Chaplinsky was arrested after publicly proclaiming religion a "racket" and after calling a policeman "a God damned racketeer" and "a damned Fascist." Justice Murphy, speaking for the Court, found no "special value" in protecting such utterances.

By the end of World War II new problems arose to challenge the clear-and-present-danger test. Justice Frankfurter repeatedly attacked both the test and the preferred-position doctrine and called for the Court to assume a more restrained position in dealing with First Amendment cases. Two especially difficult areas of law confronted the justices: the "hostile audience" and the "cold war" problem of dealing with groups that, according to Congress and the states, threatened national security.

The "hostile audience" problem was dramatically illustrated by the issue raised in *Feiner* v. *New York* (1951). In the course of a street-corner speech, Feiner employed derogatory language about the President of the United States, other public officials, and the American Legion. He was arrested when members of the crowd became unruly and threatened him. For the first time the Supreme Court directly used the clear-and-present-danger test to *uphold* the action of government. Feiner's conviction for disorderly conduct was sustained on grounds that "a clear danger of disorder" existed. He could deliver the speech, but not if the danger of his inciting a riot existed. The Court was severely criticized for its decision on grounds that those who threatened the speaker — and not the speaker, who had not advocated violence — should have been punished. Perhaps, in the words of one critic, "the speaker went to jail in a situation where

[25] *United States* v. *Carolene Products Co.* 304 U.S. 144 (1938).

the threat of riot was a patently trumped up device for shutting up a 'radical.' " [26]

In cases arising out of congressional efforts to regulate subversive activity, the Supreme Court moved toward a new position in evaluating First Amendment claims. The culmination of this change was reached in *Dennis* v. *United States* (1951) when the Court upheld the conviction, under the Smith Act, of eleven top leaders of the Communist party charged with teaching and advocating overthrow of the government. The defendants were also charged with conspiring to organize the United States Communist party for the purpose of overthrowing the government by force and violence. None of the government's charges included overt activity with the immediate intention of revolution. In rejecting the contention that immediate and clear danger must be established to justify any abridgement of the rights of free expression, Chief Justice Vinson laid down a new test: "Whether the gravity of the 'evil,' discounted by its improbability, justifies such invasion of free speech as necessary to avoid the danger."

Dissatisfaction with Vinson's balancing test in the Dennis case led the activist element on the Court to assert the position that the First Amendment is an absolute that bars governmental infringement of any kind. The grave-and-probable-danger test was qualified in *Yates* v. *United States* (1957) when the Warren Court drew a distinction between the instruction of mere abstract doctrine and actual incitement to dangerous action. Nevertheless, the clear-and-present-danger test has not been restored to its former eminence. In recent years the Court has again moved toward that test in defending the right of association of civil rights groups against state attempts to limit their effectiveness. In such cases it has upheld these groups on grounds that the state failed to show overriding cause for regulatory activities. Freedom of association is of greater importance.[27] The fact that these cases involved civil rights organizations and not members of a highly suspect and unpopular left-wing party may have facilitated the Court's movement back toward clear and present danger; certainly it was more palatable to the American public.

As changes in membership occur, the activists may succeed in swinging the balance back toward the more restrictive elements in the Holmes criteria. Whatever test — new or old — may be employed, the problem of finding a balance between the rights of the individual and the need to maintain social order will be a continuing one.

---

[26] Martin Shapiro, *Freedom of Speech: The Supreme Court and Judicial Review* (Englewood Cliffs, N.J.: Prentice-Hall, 1966), p. 61.

[27] See, for example, *NAACP* v. *Alabama* 357 U.S. 449 (1958); *Louisana ex. rel. Gremillion* v. *NAACP* 366 U.S. 293 (1961).

It should be kept in mind that in their difficulties of balancing social and individual interests, courts are not insulated from the pressures of the political system. Professor Martin Shapiro has pointed out that argument over the proper course of judicial action basically involves neither the question of what the framers of the First Amendment really intended nor dispute over abstract theories of individual liberty. He sees the basic issue as "the political one of what a certain governmental institution ought to do about a certain set of demands." [28]

The Nationalization of the Bill of Rights. The Bill of Rights — more exactly, the first eight of the ten amendments that constitute it — directly limits the authority of the national government in relation to individual citizens. State constitutions contain similar prohibitions against state activity, either in the form of a separate Bill of Rights or through other provisions. Presumably, therefore, the citizen is protected against actions of both units of government. In fact, there have traditionally existed wide variations among the states as to the extent and interpretation of state-guaranteed substantive and procedural rights.

Before the Fourteenth Amendment was adopted, the Supreme Court took the position that the Bill of Rights protects the citizen against actions of the national government only.[29] Following the Civil War the question arose as to whether the privileges-and-immunities clause or the due-process clause of the Fourteenth Amendment applied the guarantees of the Bill of Rights against state governments. Legal controversy early became centered on the due-process clause, which provides that "no state shall deprive any person of life, liberty, or property without due process of law." Until 1890 the Supreme Court held to its prewar view that the Bill of Rights limited national action only, but in 1890 it interpreted the Fourteenth Amendment's due-process clause as protecting property rights against state action. In other cases, the Court held to the position that the Fourteenth Amendment did not protect other guarantees of the Bill of Rights against the actions of state governments.

The first major break in this stand came in 1925 when the Court agreed that the First Amendment guarantees of speech and press were among the "liberties" protected by the due-process clause of the Fourteenth Amendment.[30] Further "nationalization" of the Bill of Rights followed. In 1937 the right to peaceably assemble was incorporated, and in 1940 the Court extended protection against state action abridging the free exercise of religion.[31] In 1947 the First Amendment prohibition against

[28] Shapiro, *op. cit.,* p. 5.
[29] *Barron* v. *Baltimore* 7 Pet. 243 (1833).
[30] *Gitlow* v. *New York* 268 U.S. 652 (1925).
[31] *De Jonge* v. *Oregon* 299 U.S. 353 (1937); *Cantwell* v. *Connecticut* 310 U.S. 196 (1940).

governmental establishment of religion was applied against the states when the Court ruled that a "wall of separation" must exist between church and state.[32]

Other provisions of the Bill of Rights remained outside the scope of the Fourteenth Amendment. Faced with the very important question of which, if any, of these guarantees were to be applied against states, the Court responded in *Palko* v. *Connecticut* (1937). Palko had been convicted of second-degree murder and given a life sentence. On appeal by the state, he was tried a second time, convicted of first-degree murder, and sentenced to death. He appealed on grounds that the due-process clause of the Fourteenth Amendment, which protected individuals against action of state governments, guaranteed the Fifth Amendment prohibition against double jeopardy (no person shall "be subject for the same offense to be twice put in jeopardy of life or limb"). Although Palko's appeal was denied, the Court, speaking through Justice Cardozo, laid down a general formula — known as the "fair trial rule," or "selective incorporation" — for determining which of the guarantees contained in the first eight amendments applied against the states through the due-process clause. State actions that violated "fundamental principles of liberty and justice" were prohibited by the Fourteenth Amendment. This "natural law" doctrine of selection stands in opposition to the belief of Justice Black and others that all of the Bill of Rights were incorporated in the Fourteenth Amendment.

Many of the guarantees of the Bill of Rights have been read into the Fourteenth Amendment. As the Court has moved toward further general application of these provisions against the states, it has also laid down more specific prescriptions in guiding state law-enforcement officers. In *Gideon* v. *Wainwright* (1963) the Court overturned the conviction of Clarence E. Gideon, sentenced by a Florida court for breaking and entering. Gideon had been convicted four times previously and had served prison sentences for felonies. A five-page, hand-written petition, drafted in prison and accompanied by a pauper's affidavit, represented his appeal to the Supreme Court. Gideon asked the Court to overturn his conviction on grounds that his request that the state provide him counsel should not have been denied by the Florida courts. Specifically, he was urging that the Sixth Amendment provision of right to counsel is a "fundamental right" and therefore applies against the states. Gideon won his appeal. A unanimous Court ruled that an accused must be allowed counsel — either his own or, if unable to afford his own, court-appointed — in all criminal cases.[33]

---

[32] *Everson* v. *Board of Education* 330 U.S. 1 (1947).

[33] For an excellent and fascinating account of the *Gideon* case and the issues it raised, see Anthony Lewis, *Gideon's Trumpet* (New York: Vintage Books, 1964).

One year later, after state and federal courts had received thousands of petitions similar to Gideon's, the Supreme Court took another step in specifying what is required by states to assure a fair trial. In *Escobedo* v. *Illinois* (1964) a five-to-four majority ruled that a confession obtained by police was not admissible during trial because the defendant had been denied his right to consult his attorney and had not been informed of his right to remain silent.

In June, 1966 the Court went considerably beyond the Escobedo decision. In *Miranda* v. *Arizona* (1966) and three other cases decided at the same time another five-to-four majority ruled that (1) a suspect taken into custody must be informed of his right to remain silent; (2) a suspect has the right to have a lawyer present during interrogation; (3) a court-appointed lawyer must be provided if the suspect requests one but is unable to pay for counsel; (4) a suspect may waive the right to counsel, but the prosecution must prove that the suspect knew his rights; and (5) if a suspect initially waives the right of counsel or starts to talk, but later requests counsel or chooses to remain silent, his wishes must be complied with. Perhaps mindful of the thousands of petitions from inmates of prisons throughout the country who had not been accorded these protections, the Court ruled one week later that the Miranda decision would not apply retroactively.

Whether, in the face of severe criticism among members of the bar, congressmen, and law enforcement officers, the present Court will further extend its conception of what constitutes a "fair trial" is a conjectural question. But the trend is clearly in the direction of stricter and more detailed prescriptions governing the rights of the accused.

In its doctrinal aspects liberal democracy focuses upon the individual. It is a set of substantive ideals fostering the destiny of individual dignity — active participation in decision-making, active debate of policy, initiation of ideas rather than response to leadership, equality of opportunity for personal development, and freedom of intelligence. In its procedural aspects, however, liberal democracy focuses not on the individual but upon the collective political community. It is a set of institutionalized principles designed to promote community stability by achieving consent of the governed — popular control, popular consultation, political leadership, political equality, and political liberty. Neither focus can be ignored in seeking understanding of the democratic political process; both the ideals and procedures of conflict regulation contribute to the overall pattern that distinguishes one political community from another. With this observation in mind, we can now reconsider the point raised at the close of the last chapter: the contrast in American ideology between the generalized commitment to abstract values of liberal democracy and the con-

FIGURE 3-1

Nationalization of the Bill of Rights

PROVISION	APPLIED TO STATES?	IMPORTANT DECISIONS
First Amendment		
speech, press	Yes	*Gitlow* v. *New York* (1925)
assembly and petition	Yes	*De Jonge* v. *Oregon* (1937)
free exercise of religion	Yes	*Cantwell* v. *Connecticut* (1940)
no establishment of religion	Yes	*Everson* v. *Board of Education* (1947)
Second Amendment		
right to keep and bear arms	No	
Third Amendment		
quartering of troops in private homes without consent of owner	No	
Fourth Amendment ·		
no unreasonable searches		*Wolf* v. *Colorado* (1949)
and seizures	Yes	*Mapp* v. *Ohio* (1964)
Fifth Amendment		
indictment by grand jury for serious offenses	No	
no double jeopardy	No	
no self-incrimination	Yes	*Malloy* v. *Hogan* (1964)
no denial of life, liberty or property without due process of law	Yes *	
Sixth Amendment		
right to counsel in criminal prosecutions	Yes	*Powell* v. *Alabama* (1932)
right of accused to confront		*Gideon* v. *Wainwright* (1963)
witnesses against him	Yes	*Douglas* v. *Alabama* (1965)
right to speedy and public trial	Yes	
trial in district where crime was committed	No	
trial by impartial jury	Yes **	
Seventh Amendment		
trial by jury in civil suits	No	
Eighth Amendment		
no excessive bail	No	
no excessive or cruel and unusual punishment	Yes	*Louisiana ex. rel. Francis* v. *Resweber* (1947) — Supreme Court assumed application against states

* Same specific restriction in Fourteenth Amendment.
** Jury trial not required, but must be impartial where used.

current reluctance of Americans to agree to the consequences of their specific application.

THE AMERICAN IDEOLOGY REVISITED

In 1962 at Okanogan, Washington, Mr. and Mrs. John Goldmark brought a libel suit in a Washington court against a newspaper publisher, a former state legislator, and two members of the John Birch Society. Goldmark brought the suit after he was defeated for renomination as a candidate for the state legislature. He and his wife charged that the defendants had libeled them as "being Communist sympathizers," and members of Communist-front organizations. Goldmark, an active and prominent member of the American Civil Liberties Union, charged that these accusations were absolutely false. A jury awarded the Goldmarks $40,000 in damages on grounds that the attacks upon them and the American Civil Liberties Union constituted slander and exposed them to public contempt.[34]

The fact that an accusation of association with, or support of, Communist causes may constitute libel illustrates a point made at the beginning of this chapter and lends support to the previously discussed position of Professors Hartz and Boorstin. Communism is left to the realm of academic discussion; few see it as a realistic alternative to the "American system." Persons falsely accused of association with Communist groups can seek legal redress on grounds of character assassination. It is not, in Boorstin's terms, part of the "givenness" in American values.

Some writers have suggested that an American ideology is more easily understood by taking note of what it opposes rather than by identifying concise, logical, non-contradictory liberal-democratic values. Communism is a clear example of what the American creed is not; Americans reject it as inimical to the basic values of individual liberty and representative government. A Hitler or a Stalin pursues policies that are seen as clearly in violation of democratic methods. In domestic affairs, the suggestion of an established state church, or a law banning criticism of welfare legislation would be perceived as a clear violation of democratic values and procedures.

Commentators have frequently pointed to the "pragmatic mood" of Americans as indicative of a people more interested in practical solution, experiment, and "common sense" than in theories or doctrines.[35] Since their political ideas are "given" rather than the result of ideological debate, there is no need to be highly conscious of a democratic ideology.

---

[34] For a resume of some of the problems connected with the communist threat and civil liberties see John P. Roche, *The Quest for the Dream* (New York: The Macmillan Co., 1963).

[35] Key, *op. cit.*, p. 49.

This pragmatic orientation toward political controversy is complemented by the translation of liberal ideology into a host of *symbols* that reflect, but do not define in concrete — or necessarily logical — terms, the content of liberal democracy. Political symbols are the vehicles through which we as Americans express abstract notions and values such as "freedom" or the "rule of law." They reflect the attachment or meaning that such ideas have for us. As such, we can develop great devotion for the symbols, even though we may never be in agreement with the reality supposedly represented by them. In this sense the dilemma analyzed by Gunnar Myrdal which was discussed earlier can perhaps be better understood. We acquiesce to the substantive and procedural values of liberal democracy through its symbols, not necessarily through its content.

The American·flag, for example, stirs an emotional response that represents attachment to the values associated with America and what "America stands for." Observance of national holidays such as Veterans' Day and the Fourth of July provide occasion for speeches, editorials, and other expressions that emphasize attachment to American democracy. Similarly, folk heroes have played a significant role. Lincoln, Washington, and Jefferson represent the highest virtues of the American democrat, as illustrated by the frequent reference that competing interest groups make to these heroes. The principles of political and social equality have been symbolized in the "log cabin to White House" concept; and although that symbol may no longer play so important a role in electing presidents as it once did, a reverse kind of symbolism may be operating in the use of the term "egg-head" to describe candidates who are too intellectual to represent the common man. Probably the greatest symbolic representation of American beliefs is the Constitution itself. Politicians, lecturers, and group spokesmen have identified the Constitution as the great symbol of the American liberal democratic faith. Whether the object is to support or to oppose governmental action, the Constitution has frequently been pointed to as symbolic of the great wisdom of the Founding Fathers and as the instrument which reflects the meaning of democracy, freedom, and individual liberty.

For many Americans then, symbolic loyalty alone is sufficient to promote contentment within the community. Despite deprivations and recurrent policy conflicts, most Americans are at least loyal to liberal democratic values in their symbolic form. Indeed, democratic symbols become ends in themselves, ends which contribute to community viability. Symbolic gratification may serve as a sufficient reward for the dissatisfied to assure that they do not bolt the community; and for those who disapprove of actual application of democratic ideals, attachment to the symbols serves as a demonstration both to themselves and other members of the community that we are all "Americans" and "democrats" despite our disputes.

Sociologist Scott Greer answers the question, how can we reconcile the apparent stability of the American political community with the fact that Americans generally are not committed to specific application of liberal democratic ideals and procedures, in another way. He concludes that "it is apparent that in a society with a democratic political structure and ideology, democratic processes are relatively rare . . . by and large [the average man] does not participate. . . . Produced by the struggles between various professionally directed interest groups, largely quite undemocratic in their control processes, freedom of choice for the individual is something of a by-product. It exists, perhaps, through the balance of 'countervailing forces.'" [36] Countervailing forces in our community would be the sub-community of political activists. There is a higher degree of commitment to liberal democratic ideals among the element of political leadership — the group conducting the day-to-day activity in political decision-making. The general public is not involved, but neither does it question the legitimacy of the regime.[37] Americans generally accept the role of the relatively small leadership corps. And although 100 per cent agreement on fundamental values is absent even among activists, neither leaders nor followers divide along ideological lines. Ideological harmony is taken for granted. Social conflict in America is not a clash of ideologies, but one of interests.

We suggest that the framework constituted by an ambivalent majority, an activist minority, and the promise of symbolic gratifications functions to promote stability in the American political community. And despite some harsh and abrasive evidence to the contrary, there is a liberal democratic tone to it as well. To these elements at least one other should be added at this point: the institutional restraints on popular conflict. For example, the American arrangement of "checks and balances" is something of a built-in life preserver of the American political community. But by checks and balances we refer to more than just the politico-constitutional arrangement of authority whereby officials counter officials. We speak also of the system of social checks and balances in pluralist America that permits influence and access to constituted authority to be widely distributed among diverse interests. In fact, the constitutional system is it-

---

[36] Scott Greer, "Individual Participation in Mass Society," in Roland Young (ed.), *Approaches to the Study of Politics* (Evanston, Ill.: Northwestern University Press, 1958), pp. 340–41.

[37] Key, *op. cit.*, p. 50.

self a reflection of the compromise necessary within a pluralist society in order to insure the distribution of liberal democratic ideals and procedures. Why this is so comprises the subject matter of the next chapter.

BIBLIOGRAPHICAL NOTE

Democratic theory has had a long development. Leslie Lipson's *The Democratic Civilization* (New York: Oxford University Press, 1964) contains a good review of this historical growth. There are many editions of John Locke, the most influential of the architects of democratic theory. Thomas P. Peardon has edited and written a helpful introduction to Locke's *The Second Treatise of Government* (New York: Liberal Arts Press, 1952).

Universal agreement on the meaning and essential elements of democracy is distinctly absent. The following sources, all available in paperback editions, present different views and approaches: H. B. Mayo, *An Introduction to Democratic Theory* (New York: Oxford University Press, 1960) represents a scholarly effort to identify major features while drawing comparisons to other points of view. A. D. Lindsay's *The Modern Democratic State* (New York: Oxford University Press, 1962) presents an historical review of democracy and discusses the "operative ideals" of the modern democratic state. Robert A. Dahl, *A Preface to Democratic Theory* (Chicago: University of Chicago Press, 1956) examines two prevailing "model" theories of democracy and constructs his own model of modern democracy. Thomas L. Thorson, *The Logic of Democracy* (New York: Holt, Rinehart & Winston, 1962) argues the validity of democracy by employing the methods of logic. Willmoore Kendall, *John Locke and the Doctrine of Majority-Rule* (Urbana: University of Illinois Press, 1965) is a provocative argument that Lockean theory is majoritarian and not individualistic in its emphasis. Also now available in paperback, Joseph A. Schumpeter's *Capitalism, Socialism, and Democracy* (New York: Harper & Row, Torchbook Edition, 1962) is an outstanding contribution to the discussion of the compatibility of democracy and socialism. William Ebenstein, *Today's Isms*, 4th edition (Englewood Cliffs, N.J.: Prentice-Hall, 1964) is a good elementary introduction to comparison of communism, fascism, capitalism, and socialism.

The development and interpretation of American democratic values comprises a sizeable array of literature. Alexis de Tocqueville's classic study, *Democracy in America*, is available in several paperback editions. Another classic study by a nineteenth-century foreign observer, James Bryce, *The American Commonwealth*, 2 vols. (New York: G. P. Putnam's Sons, 1960), is less analytical than de Tocqueville's work. A more recent view of American democratic politics by a foreigner is D. W. Brogan, *Politics in America* (Garden City, N.Y.: Doubleday & Co., 1960), which concentrates on the development and role of political parties. Walter Lippmann's *The Public Philosophy* (New York: New American Library, 1955), available in paperback, is a critical and controversial interpretation of contemporary western democracies. Also available in paperback, Eric Hoffer, *The True Believer* (New York: New American

Library, 1951), is a brilliant essay on the psychology of mass movements and their threat to democratic freedom. For an analysis and defense of democratic values from the perspective of one of the great philosophers of the twentieth century see John Dewey, *The Public and Its Problems* (Denver: Alan Swallow, 1954).

For those interested in analyses of American values based on empirical data, the following are highly useful: William Kornhauser, *The Politics of Mass Society* (Glencoe, Ill.: The Free Press, 1959); Seymour M. Lipset, *Political Man* (Garden City, N.Y.: Doubleday & Co., 1960); and Gabriel A. Almond and Sidney Verba, *The Civic Culture* (Boston: Little, Brown and Company, 1965). The latter two works cited are available in paperback editions.

There is a wealth of material in the area of civil rights and liberties. The classic statement on the question of balancing individual rights and social interests is John Stuart Mill's *On Liberty* (1859), available in many editions, including paperback. The following represent a sampling of more recent works dealing with the same problem: F. E. Oppenheim, *Dimensions of Freedom* (New York: St. Martin's Press, 1961); Zechariah Chafee, Jr., *Free Speech in the United States* (Cambridge: Harvard University Press, 1946), a celebrated exposition of the free speech doctrine in American law; Carl L. Becker, *Freedom and Responsibility in the American Way of Life* (New York: Vintage Books, 1960) traces the history and analyzes American concepts of civil liberties; and Alexander Meiklejohn, *Free Speech and Its Relation to Self-Government* (New York: Harper & Bros., 1948), a provocative exposition of the position that free speech is an "absolute" right; and Walter Lippmann, *The Public Philosophy,* cited previously, which argues the reponsible as opposed to an unrestricted use of freedom.

An indispensable source in developing knowledge and insight into civil liberties questions is the reading of Supreme Court decisions. Wallace Mendelson, *The Constitution and the Supreme Court,* 2nd edition (New York: Dodd, Mead and Co., 1965) contains leading cases and valuable commentary. Edmond Cahn, ed., *The Great Rights* (New York: The Macmillan Co., 1963) presents the views of four justices of the Supreme Court on the meaning of the Bill of Rights. The following works, all in paperback editions, treat both specific and general aspects of civil liberties: For an exposition and analysis of Supreme Court tests in deciding freedom of speech cases see Martin Shapiro, *Freedom of Speech: The Supreme Court and Judicial Review* (Englewood Cliffs: N.J., Prentice-Hall, 1966); Harold J. Spaeth, *The Warren Court* (San Francisco: Chandler Publishing Co., 1966) examines and evaluates the Warren Court's record; John P. Roche, *Courts and Rights* (New York: Random House, 1961) is a short but excellent treatment of the role of the judiciary and general trends in judicial activity in the area of civil rights and liberties; Benjamin M. Ziegler, *The Supreme Court and American Economic Life* (Evanston, Ill.: Row, Peterson & Co., 1962) shows the development of the Supreme Court's changing views in the area of economic rights.

One of the best means of "getting the feel" of the human factors in civil liberties cases is to follow a case from its beginnings to final court action. C. Herman Pritchett and Alan F. Westin, ed., *The Third Branch of Government* (New York: Harcourt, Brace & World, 1963) contains eight such case studies and an excellent introduction by the editors; Anthony Lewis, *Gideon's Trumpet*

(New York: Vintage Books, 1966) is a fascinating account of a landmark case in the area of right to counsel; Lucius J. Barker and Twiley W. Barker, Jr., *Freedoms, Courts, and Politics* (Englewood Cliffs, N.J.: Prentice-Hall, 1965) combines the case-study technique with excellent commentary on the political, legal, and moral aspects of civil liberties problems.

CHAPTER
FOUR

Constitutional Politics

The Constitution of the United States is probably the most revered document of its kind in the world. More than any other fundamental law, it symbolizes the unity of a political community. It is the Bible of American democracy, and, as the Bible is for some the ultimate source of theological legitimacy, the Constitution represents the ultimate legitimizing force for competing groups and interests. The comment of one student of constitutional law that "in a real sense America's history is the American Constitution" [1] is indicative of the profound importance to conflict regulation of its background, formulation, interpretation, and development. Virtually all of the great issues in the political community have been argued as constitutional questions of one kind or another. The continuing and growing vitality of the document represents our attachment to the "rule of law."

Liberal-democratic doctrine embodied in the Constitution of the United States constitutes one element of American political consensus. The "spirit" of the Constitution, like democratic ideals, is invoked periodically by conflicting groups in pursuit of incompatible goals; but rarely

[1] C. Herman Pritchett, *The American Constitution* (New York: McGraw-Hill Book Co., 1959), p. viii.

is the basic law itself in danger of rejection. The principles of the Constitution are regarded as fundamental in the sense that they must not be tampered with, even though they are subject to changing interpretation. This chapter explores the nature of American constitutionalism, emphasizing its origins and development in social-conflict regulation.

AMERICAN CONSTITUTIONALISM: SYMBOL AND INSTRUMENT OF GOVERNANCE

We have emphasized that a sense of community exists wherever people desire to take common action. The rules under which their association is conducted — a basic agreement upon the procedures recognized as legitimate in social-conflict regulation — comprise the constitutional system of the community. Constitutions both institute and reflect stable relationships of authority among policy-makers and between officials and other community members. The nature of American constitutional politics depends upon the community's pluralist social composition, the conflicts requiring regulation, and popular attitudes rendering instituted authority, rules, and procedures legitimate. The reciprocal influence of these social, politico-constitutional, and personal forces continuously work to "re-constitute" constitutional democracy in America.

Liberal democracy as part of the American value system has at least two dimensions: the doctrinal and the procedural. By the same token, there are two aspects to American constitutionalism. To grasp the dynamic nature of constitutional government, it is useful to draw a distinction between the "written," "literal," or "documentary" Constitution and the "working," "living," or "dynamic" constitution. In its broadest sense a constitution consists of all agreements that together provide the basis for political community. These include rules, customs, traditions, ideas, myths, attitudes — anything that establishes and preserves stable relationships of authority between community members. In this sense the "constitution" of the community is distinct from its "Constitution" — the document bearing a series of formalized restraints and rules of procedure — albeit that the latter is a portion of the former. Whether we speak of Great Britain's Constitution as "unwritten" because it includes more than explicitly written rules or the American or French Constitutions consisting of single documents, we refer to the basic statement of the formal institutions and rules of government. As thus defined, a Constitution outlines *constituted authority* in the polity including procedures, the relationship between political officials and institutions, and legal authority and limitations, as distinct from the informal arrangements that also play a part in conflict regulation. The particular provisions provide standards for political action — a fundamental law by which right or wrong, the legitimacy or illegitimacy of conflict regulation, is judged.[2]

Men lend substance to the phrase "a government of laws" (or, of course, deny it) by actively accepting (or rejecting) the restraints upon their behavior that laws imply. In this sense the American Constitution is a great deal more than hallowed parchment written upon by the Constitutional Framers at Philadelphia in 1787. It is, in fact, an instrument for regulating social conflict as well as a symbol of the constitutional consensus. That instrument is not limited simply to the original document and its twenty-four amendments; rather it is a "living document," and many factors have gone into shaping the meaning of its words. Time and experience have altered the nature of American political institutions; moreover, our rights and liberties (and their limits) have been given meaning by different men facing problems peculiar to their own eras. Actions of leaders such as Abraham Lincoln and Franklin Roosevelt, the rise of extra-Constitutional agencies (political parties, for example), court decisions, and the atrophy of other institutions (the Electoral College) have all shared in shaping the content of the basic "law of the land." Sometimes bitter battles have arisen over proposed amendments; other changes have come so subtly and smoothly that they were part of our constitutional life before their implications had been fully perceived.

The American Constitution, as both a symbol of consensus and instrument of governance, obtains its life and meaning from the activities of people. American constitutionalism is not a series of fixed propositions but the product of continuing conflict and accommodation. Let us look then, at some of these that have molded our Constitution.

PATTERNS OF CONSTITUTION-MAKING

THE CONSTITUTIONAL BACKGROUND

During our most severe crisis over the nature of the American federal community, supporters of the Confederacy marshalled arguments to "prove" the legitimacy of their claim that no permanent, indissoluble union was created by the Constitution written in 1787.[3] To the contrary, they asserted, the federal union comprised a league of autonomous states. The Constitution was viewed as a compact of states under a single fundamental law; maintenance of the compact rested upon continued balance between national prerogatives and "states rights." In contrast, Lincoln's

---

[2] Herman Finer, *Theory and Practice of Modern Government* (New York: Henry Holt and Co., 1949), chap. 8.

[3] One of the major contributions to the literature of political theory by an American was evoked, and itself provoked, by this crisis: John C. Calhoun's *Disquisition on Government* (1853).

defense of the Union rested upon the conviction that the Constitution of 1787 created a community of people within a federal framework that could not be dissolved by the action of any single state or group of states. His supporters cited the language of the Constitution under which states agreed to a strong central authority operating directly on individual citizens. Contrary to both views was another: the political community came into existence long before the Convention of 1787 or the Articles of Confederation. It was an "organic" community, a term designating a people unified through the gradual assimilation of diverse traditions, habits, and beliefs. Orestes Brownson, a leading journalist during the 1830's asserted, "The Union is in each of the states, and each of the states is the Union." [4]

The great debate during the nineteenth century indicated the failure of the Framers of the Constitution to specify the nature of the political community. They had papered over a fissure that changing interest patterns during the next half century parted again. The Civil War was the testimony of failure to breach the gap — the major instance in American political experience when peaceful accommodation of competing interests proved impossible.

It would be a mistake to assume that political stability derives solely from a document created by constitution-makers in the late eighteenth century. Rather, it was the pervading sense of community that made possible the accommodations of conflicting interests represented by delegates attending the convention. For example, our discussion of the roots of American liberal-democratic doctrine described the *Declaration of Independence* as the major expression of the ideals of Lockian liberalism. This instrument, with its precepts of individual rights, limited government, and popular control, has had "a decisive impact on the development of our governmental system." [5] Following independence, its principles were clearly reflected in the constitutions of the individual states. Seven of the states adopted Bills of Rights containing the guarantees included in the Declaration. Moreover, all of the new state constitutions incorporated to varying degrees concepts of popular rule, limited government, separation of powers, and checks and balances. These provisions reflected a common Lockian heritage, common disquieting experiences under the British monarchy, and common traditions of the rule of law, articulated and developed in England and transported to the colonies. All were deep in the intellectual soil of the American community.

[4] Henry F. Brownson, *The Works of Orestes A. Brownson* (Detroit: Thorndike Nourse, 1882–87), XVIII, 114.

[5] Edward S. Corwin and Jack W. Peltason, *Understanding the Constitution* (3rd ed.; New York: Holt, Rinehart & Winston, 1964), p. 1

A pre-convention desire for a common political community was reflected in certain political arrangements from 1774 onward that kept the colonies (later states) united in a common endeavor. The first of these, the Continental Congress, came into existence in 1774 and adopted the *Declaration of Independence,* financed and prosecuted the war with England, carried on foreign relations, and submitted the Articles of Confederation to the thirteen states for ratification. Although this "first American experiment in reconciling unity with localism" [6] did not produce a "perpetual Union" as provided for in the Preamble, it did a remarkably good job during the eight years of its existence (1781–89) despite its inability to solve what proved to be insurmountable problems.

The story of this "union of states," under which "each state retains its sovereignty, freedom, and independence," is a familiar one. Representation in a single-house Congress was based on equality of states — that is, one vote per state — and legislative, executive, and judicial functions were united in this single body. Control over taxation, commerce, and individuals was retained by each of the thirteen autonomous states. Foreign affairs, postal matters, settlement of disputes between states, the power to borrow money, control of armed forces, and the regulation of coinage, weights, and measures were vested in the central government. Lacking discretion to tax, regulate commerce, and enforce its mandates, the Congress struggled through eight years of economic difficulties, grave problems in foreign affairs, and the refusal of the states to amend (unanimous consent was required) the Articles in order to provide the central government with adequate enforcing authority.[7]

The Confederation succeeded in keeping alive a minimal sense of community. But "it took time and bitter experience to convince men of the folly of particularism. . . . The ultimate breakdown of the Confederation . . . was due not so much to the defects of the Articles as to the psychological unreadiness of Americans to submit to any outside control, and to the 'hard times' which made any government an adventure." [8] A recent work on the background and writing of the Constitution evaluates the period in similar terms. Stressing the disharmony of Americans of the 1780's, the Mitchells write:

> The colonies were differently founded and governed, had different products and habits of life, and, with poor means of travel and transport, were

[6] Samuel Eliot Morison and Henry Steele Commager, *The Growth of the American Republic* (New York: Oxford University Press, 1950), I, 257.

[7] Disagreeing with a large amount of the historical evaluation of the Confederacy, Professor Merrill Jensen has depicted the period as one of general optimism, economic progress and stability. See Merrill Jensen, *The New Nation* (New York: Alfred A. Knopf, 1950).

[8] Morison and Commager, *op. cit.,* p. 259.

distant from each other. They had little experience of self-government. Their knowledge of jurisprudence was theoretical. They were insistent on "the rights of Englishmen," but did not grasp their responsibilities to themselves. Freed of irksome parental oversight, they rejoiced in liberty without much thought of how to preserve it. They fought a war of Independence, but did not trouble to organize a nation as a result of it.[9]

The America of the constitutional fathers was homogeneous "not only in blood and background but in pursuits," yet "disharmonious" in that potential for interest conflict was pervasive.[10] Sectional cleavages, post-Revolution animosities, lack of effective communications — all contributed to the expansion of potentially destructive conflict. Within this community shaped by common experiences and incompatible desires, the Constitutional Framers were able to accommodate wide diversities of interest and confine conflict within manageable bounds. The nature of this accommodation is reflected in the provisions of the Constitution.

THE CONSTITUTIONAL CONVENTION:
CONSENSUS AND CONFLICT

A conference of states met at Annapolis in September, 1786 to work out solutions for state problems involving commercial transactions. It adjourned quickly after approving a resolution requesting a convention of all states to consider general revision of the Articles of Confederation. Congress responded by approving a convention "for the sole and express purpose of revising the Articles of Confederation." The fifty-five delegates who convened in Philadelphia in May, 1787 were the elite of American politics. Seven had been governors of their states, forty-one had served in Congress, and eight were active in writing their state constitutions. Together they constituted a nucleus of the influential men of their time — merchants, bankers, gentlemen farmers, lawyers, and investors. Some commentators have made much of the fact that the "common man" — the small farmer, the worker, the resident of the back-country rural areas — was absent, a fact supposedly resulting in the creation of a document that reflected the interests of an aristocratic, propertied minority as opposed to a democratic majority.[11] Certainly those who met at Philadelphia were the political leaders of the era. They comprised the inner

[9] Broadus and Louise Mitchell, *A Biography of the Constitution of the United States* (New York: Oxford University press, 1964), p. 7.

[10] *Ibid.*, p. 21; David G. Smith, *The Convention and the Constitution* (New York: St. Martin's Press), 1965.

[11] See, for example, V. L. Parrington, *Main Currents in American Thought* (New York: Harcourt, Brace & Co., 1930), pp. 279–91. "In short," he states, "in this war of ideas the democrats were provided with little ammunition and fought at great disadvantage."

group of political activists that made the decisions and generally dominated post-Revolutionary America. But, certainly, their purpose in writing the Constitution was to establish a democratic system of government.

John P. Roche has described the Founding Fathers as "first and foremost superb democratic politicians": political leaders accustomed to heeding the opinions of constituent groups and "committed (perhaps willy-nilly) to working within the democratic framework, within a universe of public approval." [12] Joint aims as politicians tended to override lesser differences between delegates as spokesmen of "large" or "small" states, of yeomen or gentry, of merchant or agrarian interests. There were several common political objectives among them, but pre-eminent was the desire to establish a government for the entire American community. They sought a polity that could regulate conflicts among all Americans, that could not be limited by the parochial and partial jurisdictions possessed by each state. Their conception of community was as expansive as the continent, and their vision of the public interest transcended the private interests of their localities.

There was also unity of outlook regarding the shape politics should take; that is, the pattern would be one of a representative democracy — a republic — not a direct democracy implying policies made by popular majorities. Richard Hofstadter described the Framers as "realists" whose political attitudes were shaped by a generally pessimistic view of the nature of man, a view of "reality" that they believed should be translated into the legal framework of government. Uncontrolled by law, man would be unable to provide either stable government or protection of property. Although some delegates (George Mason, for example) did insist that "the genius of the people must be consulted," Edmund Randolph, among others, was more concerned about "the turbulence and follies of democracy." Committed to representative democracy, the delegates nevertheless viewed an unencumbered majority as destructive of stability and liberty. In Hofstadter's opinion, the framers' concept of liberty "was linked not to democracy but to property," and the liberties they were attempting to protect were "chiefly negative." He urges that "they wanted freedom from fiscal uncertainty and irregularities in the currency, from trade wars among the states, from economic discrimination by more powerful foreign governments, from attacks on the creditor class or on property, from popular insurrection." [13] United in their desire for a stronger continental government and united in their opposition to ex-

---

[12] John P. Roche, "The Founding Fathers: A Reform Caucus in Action," *The American Political Science Review*, LV, No. 4 (December, 1961), 799.

[13] Richard Hofstadter, *The American Political Tradition* (New York: Vintage Books, 1958), p. 11.

tremes on either the right (autocratic government) or left ("mob rule"), the delegates sought to devise techniques of conflict regulation that would lead to neither extreme and still be acceptable to Americans.

As has generally been true in the pattern of American politics, convention politicians were also united in ideological outlook. Such doctrinal precepts as balanced government, limited government, the federal principle, and separation of powers, did not comprise the items for disagreement on the convention agenda but did arise later as principal matters for discussion in the political maneuvering directed at gaining support for ratification of the Constitution. The conflicts that did emerge in the chosen secrecy of the Convention revolved about the appropriate design of a political community that would fulfill the goals of authority, be national in scope, republican in pattern, and most acceptable to those in the states who would have to agree to it.

The decision of American leaders to strengthen the bonds of union was deliberate and calculated. This unity of purpose carried over into the framing of the Constitution. But agreement upon procedural details was not as easily achieved. Hence, the convention was marked less by detached reflections of democratic philosophers than a combined sense of urgency, expediency, and cooperation characteristic of democratic but practical-minded men of affairs. The plan of union that came forth was an unexpected one, a product of political craftsmanship rather than a victory of philosophic conviction. The document later put up for adoption by a somewhat disappointed Madison emphasized principles of federalism, balance, and diversification of authority and social interest, all of which are in both the literal and living instrument of conflict regulation we now possess.

Constitutional historians agree that the working plan of the Convention was the Virginia Plan.[14] Conceived primarily by James Madison, it called for a national legislature of two houses, the lower to be elected directly by the people and the upper chosen by the lower from persons nominated by state legislatures. A national executive was to be chosen by the national legislature. The crux of the plan was in its relegation of authority:

> [T]he National Legislature ought to be impowered to enjoy the Legislative Rights vested in Congress by the Confederation and moreover to legislate in all cases to which the separate States are incompetent, or in which the harmony of the United States may be interrupted by the exercise of individual Legislation; to negative all laws passed by the several States, contravening in the opinion of the National Legislature the articles of

---

[14] See *Documents Illustrative of the Formation of the Union of the American States* (Washington, D.C.: U.S. Government Printing Office, 1927), pp. 953–56.

Union; and to call forth the force of the Union against any member of the
Union failing to fulfill its duty under the articles thereof.

This scheme would have freed the American political community from
dependence upon localized regulation of conflict in a "disharmonious"
society. It has been called the utopia of convention delegates. It was, in
fact, agreed to in principle early in deliberations. Conflicts then developed over how much modification was necessary to make the plan acceptable to Americans in their respective states. Blending features of the
Virginia Plan with those of the New Jersey Plan — a proposal that
emerged as a "palatable alternative to the folks at home" [15] — produced
an acceptable compromise.

The New Jersey Plan did not seek dramatic restriction in the scope of
community authority but rather a redefinition of which interests should
have preference in the exercise of that authority. It included a proposal
for a single-house legislature representing states as units that opened up a
conflict over what groups would be given privileged access to influence
national policy-making — those in the more populous states favored by
the Virginia Plan or those in the less populated states that would benefit
by the New Jersey Plan. Faced with the possibility of a destructive impasse over the nature of the distribution of interest access, the delegates
eventually accepted the Connecticut Compromise, which provided for a
two-house national legislature, one house with representation apportioned
by population and the other recognizing equality of states — two Senators
per state, regardless of population. That they had not, however, compromised their political objective of effective community authority is
revealed by the fact that the delegates also voted to include a provision
of the New Jersey Plan that is a major feature of the federal arrangement
— the "supremacy clause." Article VI of the Constitution provides that
"this Constitution, and the Laws of the United States, shall be the supreme Law of the Land." In effect, this provision establishes the primacy
of the Constitution, treaties, and *valid* acts of Congress whenever state
law conflicts.

The political pattern shaped by the Connecticut Compromise deals primarily with Congress. A bicameral legislature — one house chosen directly
by the people and representative of numbers, the other (Senate) to be
elected by the legislatures in each state on the principle of equality of
states — achieves a balance between control of legislators by the people
and control by the "aristocracy." In Madison's words, the indirectly chosen
Senate would serve as a check against the "fickleness and passion" of the
people and would, consequently, protect minorities by its veto over the

[15] Roche, *op. cit.*, p. 806.

"excesses of the first branch." Not all delegates were convinced that such a bicameral arrangement provided the necessary safeguards against reckless majorities; they fought hard to write a property qualification for suffrage into the Constitution. Strong opposition forced a compromise leaving the setting of voting qualifications to individual states. As one student puts it, "Property and principle, property and wisdom, were pretty generally equated." [16]

The dispute over representation was not the only one resolved by bargained compromises. A worry that commercial interests might be threatened in a Senate sympathetic to agrarians helped to produce an arrangement whereby all money bills would be introduced in the House of Representatives. An underlying disagreement concerning slavery contributed to provisions that slaves would be counted three-fifths for purposes of direct taxation and representation; there also would be a twenty-year moratorium on congressional regulation of the slave trade. And provisions regarding federal courts helped to insulate the judiciary from the republican principle. Appointed by an indirectly chosen President and approved by the indirectly elected Senate, federal judges were to enjoy life tenure.[17]

The Electoral College, for which members were to be chosen in each state as its legislature provided, marked at the time an ingenious way of placating seemingly conflicting interests desiring that the President be selected by Congress, by the states, and by the direct election of the populace. First, a four-year term was settled on as long enough to reduce the effects of popular pressure. Second, Congress would be working with an indirectly elected executive and thus could not be forced into obedience to the wishes of a popularly elected leader. But the crux of the compromise resided in the expectation that the President would normally be chosen by the House of Representatives. This expectation was premised on the belief that following George Washington — everyone's candidate for the first President — no one could have such a primacy in the hearts of his countrymen as to be selected President by the Electoral College without opposition. Generally it was thought that any election would probably involve more than two candidates; hence the Electoral College would find it difficult to provide anyone with a majority. In that event, the House of Representatives could choose a President from among the three highest candidates, each state delegation casting one vote. After the choice of President, the person having the highest number of electoral votes would become Vice-President. In the event of a tie, the

---

[16] Alpheus T. Mason and Richard H. Leach, *In Quest of Freedom* (Englewood Cliffs, N.J.: Prentice-Hall, 1959), p. 126.

[17] Smith, *op. cit.*, p. 85.

Senate was to choose the Vice-President, each senator possessing one vote. That these expectations were not met was less the fault of the bargain than of the development of political parties, which functioned as filters in the selection process. The breakdown of the procedure in 1800 led to a revision of the process as stated in the Twelfth Amendment.

Thus the Constitution was a product of political bargaining carried on in an atmosphere of consensus on the need for change and of conflict over form and procedure. Our understanding of the meaning of the Constitution in the twentieth century can be advanced if we keep in mind Roche's assertion about its origins in the eighteenth: "The Constitution, then, was not an apotheosis of 'constitutionalism,' a triumph of architectonic genius; it was a patch-work sewn together under the pressure of both time and events by a group of extremely talented democratic politicians." [18]

As a makeshift framework for social-conflict regulation in the American political community, the Constitution has required constant reinterpretation of its major operating principles. Those principles — the concepts of balance and federalism — were the products of conflict regulation within the Convention itself. They were not achieved through the automatic application of settled maxims of political theory, yet they were elevated to the level of theoretical discourse in later years. As working principles, the concepts of balance and federalism provide the link between liberal democracy and constitutional politics in America.

THE CONSTITUTIONAL DOCUMENT: DOCTRINAL PRINCIPLES AND CONSTITUTIONAL CONSENSUS

Such tenets as balanced government, separation of powers, checks and balances, and federalism did not enter into the process of constitution-making until the struggle for ratification, when they were employed as convenient ideological terms to describe and justify what had been done at the Convention. Such appeals were convenient for two reasons: (1) there remained a general predisposition against unbridled authority from Revolutionary days, and (2) concepts of limited government formed the working vocabulary of political leaders whose support would have to be won for ratification of the Constitution.

Fear of over-centralized control and the consequent desire to place limits upon its exercise were rooted in the English constitutional system. The principle of limited monarchy and the development of an independent judiciary were accepted expressions of the concept of the rule of law. Baron de Montesquieu, the French political theorist, as well as John Locke, had emphasized the utility of the principle of separated powers in

[18] Roche, *op. cit.,* p. 815.

limiting the dangers inherent in the exercise of governmental authority.[19] To varying degrees, all post-Revolutionary state constitutions incorporated the concept of separate institutions and the corollary operation of checks and balances. The delegates to the Constitutional Convention had available the first volume of John Adams, *The Defense of the Constitutions of United States of America* (1787–88). This major work refuted foreign observers who criticized the new nation for its non-centralized power structure, or confederation. Considered by many as the father of American conservatism, Adams feared that the rights of property, the liberties of the people, and the welfare of all could be maintained only under a system of "balanced powers." He observed:

> The majority has eternally, and without one exception, usurped over the rights of minority. . . . Self-interest, private avidity, ambition, and avarice will exist in every state of society, and under every form of government . . . The only remedy is to take away the power, by controlling the selfish avidity of the governor, by the senate and house; and of the house, by the governor and senate.[20]

The strongest and most articulate effort to explain and justify the Constitution as the very embodiment of the concept of balance is *The Federalist,* a series of eighty-five letters written by James Madison, Alexander Hamilton, and John Jay. *The Federalist* provides a forceful, practical, and theoretical defense of the major features of the Constitution and clearly illustrates how the authors appealed to broad doctrinal principles and "the common sense of the situation" to build support for an accomplished fact.

Papers *No. 10* and *No. 51* argued that the balance provided in the constitutional structure was the most practical guarantee for the maintenance of liberty and republican government.[21] Madison's presentation in *No. 10* is premised upon the existence of what he considered a universal manifestation of social interests — "factions . . . sewn into the nature of man." Madison used the term to refer to a people united for some purpose or cause "adverse to the rights of other citizens, or to the permanent and aggregate interests of the community." In *No. 51* the authors make clear their conviction as to the dangers to liberty and stability arising from the very nature of man: "But what is government itself, but the greatest of all reflections on human nature? If men were angels, no government would be necessary." Says Madison, "In framing a government which is to be

[19] Smith, *op. cit.,* p. 54.
[20] Quoted in Andrew M. Scott, *Political Thought in America* (New York: Holt, Rinehart & Winston, 1959), p. 109.
[21] James Madison, Alexander Hamilton, and John Jay, *The Federalist* (New York: The Modern Library, 1937).

administered by men over men, the great difficulty lies in this; you must first enable the government to control the governed; and in the next place oblige it to control itself." The problem, then, is to balance the Lockian concept of representative government with the recognized tendencies of men to abuse power.

Since factions are universal they cannot be removed. Perhaps, however, they can be prevented by removing their cause. But the cause can be removed only by (1) stifling the freedom of action facilitating factional dissent or by (2) developing a society in which all opinions, interests, and goals would be identical. Such means of eliminating factions would be worse than the malady itself: "Liberty is to faction what air is to fire; but to abolish liberty would be to destroy free government itself." As for the second remedy, said Madison, it is "impracticable" because "as the reason of man continues fallible, and he is at liberty to exercise it, different opinions will be formed." How then to achieve the balance between the protection of liberties of all, especially the rights of "property," and the necessity to control the natural frailties of men? Majorities can always, by numbers, control the minority factions; but the majority itself is dangerous to the liberties of the minority and the "permanent interests" of the community. Madison's view that factions were not "curable" forced the conclusion that "relief is only to be sought in the means of controlling *effects.*" Since "neither moral nor religious motives" provide control, the answer lies in the mechanics of governmental organization. Two such organizational principles are to be found in the Constitution: the provision of republican, or representative, government and the division of policy-making authority through the operation of federalism and separated branches of government.

"Pure democracy," defined as direct rule by an assembly of citizens who "administer the government in person," provides no protection against unreasonable majorities. Representative democracy, and more particularly a republic within the confines of a large society, is the institutional arrangement most suitable for controlling factions. Representative democracy prevents arbitrary majority rule by enlarging, filtering, and refining popular views through representatives "whose wisdom may best discern the true interest of their country." But Madison, recognizing that the elected representatives may themselves "betray the interests of the people," extends his argument by claiming that a large republic lessens such danger. A large republic not only has within it a larger number of "fit characters" to serve as representatives, but large republics also make more difficult control of elections, thus enabling the people to select the most qualified candidates. The larger the area to be governed, the more difficult it is for a majority to comprise the whole; or, as Madison writes in

No. 10, "If such a common motive exists, it will be more difficult for all who feel it to discover their own strength, and to act in unison with each other."

Essays *No. 10* and *No. 51* both view the principle of division of policy authority between states and nation as an added safeguard against the destruction of liberty through majority faction. The argument is explicit in *No. 51:* "In the compound republic of America, the power surrendered by the people is first divided between two distinct governments, and then the portion allotted to each subdivided among distinct and separate departments. Hence, a double security arises to the rights of the people. The different governments will control each other, at the same time that each will be controlled by itself." Thus federalism and separated powers were to complement one another in preserving republican arrangements.

Federalism as an organizing convention was a compromise directed at achieving not only "a more perfect union" as the Framers wanted but also a practicable one from the viewpoint of state leaders. Experience under the Articles had convinced the Framers — some more than others, to be sure — that a continental polity with a stronger authority was a necessity if the problems of the new nation were to be solved. The cardinal principle of a federal system of government is the arrangement under which the functions of the political community are divided between a central policy authority and the subpolities that together compose the whole. Each level exercises authority in its own sphere of action. Martin Diamond, in his study of the meaning attached to the word "federalism" by the Framers, concluded that the Framers "like all other men at this time . . . regarded federalism, not as a kind of government, but as a voluntary association of states who sought certain advantages from that association." Division among the delegates was over the practicalities of the federal arrangement. Diamond asserts that compromise of conflicting positions would have been impossible had not James Madison succeeded in convincing federalists that a large-scale republic acting directly on the people in each state would not subvert the integrity of the separate states.[22]

Agreement upon the definition of a federal republic in America came with the Connecticut Compromise. But the very language of it, necessary under the circumstances, assured that the issue was not settled by the Framers. Both the supremacy clause and the later Tenth Amendment provided a basis for continuing dispute over the nature of the relationship between central and state policy jurisdictions. The question of "states rights" versus "national power" emerged as a great issue even before the

---

[22] Martin Diamond, "What the Framers Meant by Federalism," *A Nation of States,* Robert A. Goldwin (ed.) (Chicago: Rand McNally & Co., 1963), pp. 24–41.

dawn of the nineteenth century, erupted in Civil War in mid-century, and remains today a basis for national debate. What is the "spirit of the Constitution" in regard to this question? What did the constitutional Fathers intend as the demarcation line between legitimate and illegitimate exercise of either state or national authority? There is no certainty as to the Framers' intent; moreover, later interpretations of congressional power have only served to compound the problem. The compromise over federalism in the convention was like that of balanced government, an ambiguous one. It was, almost certainly, the only way in which the competing interests could be accommodated.

The separation of governing institutions was also justified by the federalists as necessary to the preservation of republican government. In theory, placing the functions of government into separate and distinct institutions would protect against the danger of power falling into the hands of a single interest. Moreover, the operation of checks and balances supposedly could reinforce separation. Authority was thus assigned to each of the three institutions restraining exercise of powers by any of the others. In effect, in certain areas each branch was given authority to intrude upon the activities of the remaining two. To illustrate: the presidential veto is a restraint on the legislative powers; the power of the purse limits presidential action; and jurisdiction rests with the courts to review the constitutionality of laws or executive actions when called upon to do so. The provision for a bicameral legislature, under which each house may veto the actions of the other, is another reflection of the same principle. Further, federalism is itself a mechanism to achieve checks and balances by its division of authority between nation and states.

According to *The Federalist* these provisions were placed in the Constitution to control the exercise of policy-making in general, regardless of which interests could most influence it. A few delegates also sought restraint on the power of the people, more specifically the popular majority. Yet the Framers were fully aware that a constitution that smacked too much of an attempt to permit control by a minority of the social, economic, and political elite would not win approval in many of the states. George Mason's warning that in their zeal to insulate the national government from the people, the Framers "should not incautiously run into the opposite stream," indicated that a balance between popular rule and the minority had to be struck.[23] *The Federalist* urged that such had been accomplished.

The Federalist argument is not totally convincing. Certainly, placing the functions of government into separate and distinct institutions to protect against power falling into the hands of a single minority or majority

[23] For the position of George Mason see Smith, *op. cit., passim.*

sounds plausible enough; but, by the same token, separation of powers and checks and balances can be quite unworkable. Given total independence from the other two branches, the third, by refusing to take action, can block the operations of policy-making. Hence, a minority in control of one set of policy-making positions (presidency, legislature, or courts) may effectively tyrannize the community through obstruction without ever capturing the whole apparatus. Suppose, for example, that the executive refused to enforce the policy pronouncements of the legislature? Furthermore, if a majority faction did capture all policy-making positions, thereby allowing the three branches to act in concert, the simple device of separation would not serve as a safeguard against majority tyranny.

Logic, however, is not necessarily the determining factor in judging the influence of works of political theory. It is likely that the Framers did not know precisely what they intended in their specific document; of political relevance in this age is that the working principle of balance has come to symbolize one feature of the living constitution. It does, as we shall note later, continue to fragment policy authority, contribute to the growth of subgovernments, and make possible minority rule. One of the authors of *The Federalist*, Alexander Hamilton, envisioned the difficulty of living with this "bundle of contradictions" and moved quickly to overcome them by forming a majority faction in control of all three branches, the Federalist party.

The Framers recognized that after having designed the document through bargaining, they would have to use persuasive techniques in order to get it ratified, and then they would have to make it work. Its success depended on inventiveness of community politicians. Although *The Federalist* constitutes the principal effort to rationalize in doctrinal terms the makeshift accomplishments of 1787, we should keep in mind that what is propaganda in one era often becomes political theory in succeeding generations. Furthermore, in at least one aspect the Federalist argument reflects a clear motivation of the founders. In his expressed concern for the mischievous nature of faction, Madison spoke for most of the Founding Fathers. They hoped that by expanding the community of conflict regulation to continental proportions, the tyranny of parochial majorities could be avoided. *The Federalist* underscores the primary goal of "withdrawing particular objects of contention from local majorities." [24] It so happens that the federal form of government combined with separate institutions sharing policy authority proved the most harmonious method of achieving this goal. But it is worth noting that Madison's essays were not totally optimistic regarding the ability of Americans to

[24] Smith, *op. cit.*, p. 31.

maintain a continental community; for in his adroit defense of the Constitution in *No. 10,* Madison recognizes that "the influence of factious leaders may kindle a flame within their particular states. . . ." He hoped that they would "be unable to spread a general conflagration through the other states . . . ," but he foresaw the distinct possibility that the fires of majority and minority tyranny might burn out of control within individual states. In their own fashion, state segregation laws, loyalty oaths, censorship ordinances, and the like provide abundant testimony to the reasonableness of Madison's concern.

PATTERNS OF CONSTITUTIONAL CONFLICT

By adroit appeals to the doctrinal currency of the period — limited government, balance, representative democracy, and federalism — continental-minded politicians proved sufficiently persuasive to build consensus in ratification of the Constitution. That ratification did not come easy. Opponents attacked the Constitution as a sacrifice of state autonomy, as failing to secure the rights of Americans, as an "anti-republican" arrangement, and as going considerably further than necessary in order to strengthen the Articles of Confederation. Some convention delegates returned home to fight against ratification. By June, 1788 nine states had ratified thus permitting the new Constitution to go into effect. This number did not, however, include New York and Virginia, large and influential states whose approval was crucial to the success of the new government. Within a month both states ratified and new patterns of conflict regulation began to emerge.

Since ratification the constitutional principles discussed above have become symbols of American unity. But interestingly enough, as working principles of politics, those same precepts of balance, separation, and federalism have produced conflict as well as consensus; for the constitutional arrangement dispersing policy-making authority among separate sets of officials at both the federal and subcommunity levels builds tension into virtually all American political patterns. We have already suggested how separation of powers and checks and balances constitute potential obstructions as well as safeguards in limited government. We shall see in Chapter Eleven that a series of independent and autonomous clusters of authority often possessing incompatible interests in policy-making, both enrich and complicate patterns of conflict regulation in America.

There are other ways that constitutional procedures modify the context of interest conflict within which politics operates. Constitutions are designed as instruments of political action. By providing the institutional ground rules through which formal changes may occur — that is, amendment procedures — the Constitution provides certain procedural advantages and disadvantages for conflicting interests. The American Constitution, by virtue of its symbolic status, has been the supporting instrument for many interests in each era of our history. It has, for example, been a bastion of property rights at one time and the instrument for subordination of property rights at another. Time, technology, ideas, events, and personalities — all have operated to expand, contract, and redefine its meaning. An examination of the patterns of change in the Constitution illustrates the relationships between social conflict and constitutional politics.

PATTERNS OF CONSTITUTIONAL CHANGE

A brief glance at the formal amendments to the Constitution reveals that Article V, the amending clause, has been used infrequently and that some of the twenty-five amendments are of little significance as they affect conflict regulation in the modern American political community. The first ten amendments — the Bill of Rights — can be virtually considered as a part of the original document since they were added shortly after ratification. Of the remaining fifteen, less than half have had a significant effect on the basic governmental structure or major clauses of the document. The Eleventh and Twelfth were added as quick remedies for disruptive situations not foreseen by the Framers. The Eleventh removed from federal courts jurisdiction in suits brought against states by private individuals. The Twelfth was aimed at eliminating the possibility of a tie in electoral votes for President, a situation that had arisen in the election of 1800. The Eighteenth ("prohibition") was the result of the determined effort of well-organized interests but was repealed (Twenty-first Amendment) after fourteen years of frustrated attempts to enforce its legislation against other unwilling groups. The Twentieth abolished "lame duck" sessions of Congress, so designated because congressmen defeated in the November elections continued to serve in the short session of Congress running from December to the following March. The Twenty-third abolished payment of a state poll tax as a voting qualification in federal elections at the time when only five states still imposed the requirement. Finally, the Twenty-fourth Amendment, which granted residents of the District of Columbia a voice in presidential elections, hardly qualifies as a major alteration of the electoral system.

Three of the remaining seven amendments (Thirteenth, Fourteenth, and Fifteenth) are labeled the Civil War Amendments since they were aimed at the abolition of slavery and at guaranteeing the newly-won rights of the Negro. Amendments Sixteen (permitting a direct tax on incomes),

Seventeen (providing for direct election of Senators), and Nineteen (women's suffrage), ratified between 1913 and 1920, reflected the Progressive movement with its emphasis on extension of democratic participation by all citizens. The Twenty-second Amendment limited the period that any person can serve as President. The Twenty-fifth, ratified in 1967, provides for succession to a vacancy in the Vice-Presidency and also sets up procedures under which the Vice-President becomes acting President in case of Presidential disability.

Despite changes in the American Constitution the striking fact is that only twenty-five amendments have been approved, although in excess of five thousand amendments have been proposed in Congress since 1789. Relatively difficult procedural hurdles for amendments account in part for this low rate of acceptance. The greatest barriers have been in obtaining favorable congressional committee hearing action and achieving the necessary two-third vote in each house of Congress to *propose* amendments. A minority can, therefore, block proposals in either house. The alternative method of proposal through constitutional convention has not developed into a practical one. Such a convention, which would be called by Congress at the request of two-thirds of the states, could presumably propose extensive changes. Right-wing organizations have sought such a convention in recent years but with little support outside their own circles. The additional requirement that at least three-fourths of the states must *ratify* a proposed amendment further enhances the position of the minority in blocking change. Winning ratification of amendments in three-fourths of the states has not been easy. All states except Nebraska have two-house legislatures; since both houses must approve amendments, a minority needs only succeed in convincing a single chamber not to ratify. Despite this obstacle states have accepted all but six of thirty-one proposed amendments. Only one, the Twenty-first, has been ratified by the alternative method of three fourths of state ratifying conventions.

Amendments have tended to come in clusters. Twelve were added during the first fifteen years of the nation's existence. No formal changes were approved between 1804 and 1865; but as a result of the slavery issue, three won acceptance in the succeeding five years. Another forty-three years passed before the Sixteenth and Seventeenth Amendments became part of the fundamental law in 1913. The last eight amendments have been adopted within the last forty-eight years, but four of these came in a fourteen-year period (1919–33), and the last four since 1950.

The political temper of the American electorate may explain in part this clustering tendency. The amendments added to the Constitution between 1913 and 1933 reflected dissatisfaction articulated during the height of the Progressive movement. One student of the American Con-

FIGURE 4-1

Constitutional Amendments

1967	XXV
1965	XXIV
1964	XXIII

| 1951 | XXII |

| 1933 | XX   XXI |

1920	XIX
1919	XVIII	PROGRESSIVE ERA AMENDMENTS
1913	XVI XVII

1870	XV
1868	XIV	CIVIL WAR AMENDMENTS
1865	XIII

| 1804 | XII |
| 1798 | XI |

| 1791 | I   II   III   IV   V   VI   VII   VIII   IX   X | BILL OF RIGHTS |

stitution has pointed out that the change in the source of proposed amendments since 1933 is largely explained by the fact that control of the policy-making branches of government has passed from conservative to liberal spokesmen. Congress has been more willing to enact legislation expanding federal activities based on a broad construction of legislative powers; the Presidency has grown in functions and status; and the Supreme Court has refrained from narrow interpretation of the Constitutional powers of either branch while at the same time it has handed down a number of far-reaching decisions in the areas of civil rights and liberties generally reflecting liberal preferences. Failing to halt tendencies considered undesirable or destructive of important values, entrenched interests have resorted to the formal amendment process as a means of protection. Proposals to limit presidential power in foreign affairs; proposals to fix a ceiling on the level of the progressive income tax; and a proposal to ease the formal process of amendment are among measures supported by conservative groups seeking to reverse the trend begun during the New Deal era.[25] The Twenty-second Amendment, for example, may be viewed as an avenue to check the power of the President in the sense that it was largely aimed at preventing the continued re-election of a dominant President such as Franklin D. Roosevelt.

The vitality of the Constitution as an instrument for adjusting disputes rests in its capacity to respond to changed environment by accommodating new demands resulting from such change. To define constitutional change solely in terms of the use of the formal amending process is a distortion of the shifting constitutional situation. Changes in behavior patterns — in shifting social, political, economic, and technological patterns in the community — often subvert the most rigid of institutional forms. Thus significant modification has come through other means.

CONSTITUTIONAL CHANGE
AND CONSTITUTIONAL BALANCE

Separation of powers and checks and balances are expressed in the Constitution as: (1) limits and checks on the powers granted to the three major institutions of government, and (2) provisions confining the operation of the principle of majority rule. With the exception of the Twenty-second, there has been no amendment which has significantly altered the first of these arrangements; the second has been partially altered through amendments extending the suffrage and providing for direct election of Senators. Other kinds of changes have, nevertheless, marked the development of balance as a working principle. These include, for example, the assertion and development of the concept of judicial review, the growth of the presidential role in policy-leadership, the emergence of independent regulatory agencies in conflict resolution, and the rise and development of political parties.

Nothing in the Constitution explicitly provides for court determination of the legitimacy of actions of Congress or the President. Article VI declares that the Constitution, laws of Congress, and treaties of the United States must be enforced by all courts, state or federal, as the "supreme law of the land." No specific designation clarifies which branch should decide what constitutes conflict between the documentary authority and official actions. Asserting that the Supreme Court could exercise the function of reviewing legislative acts to determine their consistency with the Constitution, Chief Justice John Marshall clarified which branch would decide. In the case of *Marbury* v. *Madison*, the Court, under Marshall's

[25] Clement C. Vose, "Conservatism by Amendment," *Yale Review*, 46 (September, 1956), 176–90.

leadership, held that since the Constitution was paramount, any action contrary to its provisions must be null and void. Marshall argued that courts by nature of their peculiar historical and constitutional role are charged with the responsibility of reviewing challenged acts of Congress to determine legitimacy. Marshall's decision, coming at a time when his own Federalist party had lost control of both presidential and legislative offices, countered the emerging dominance of Jeffersonian Republicans.

The subsequent history of the principle of judicial review as employed by the Supreme Court reveals a significant impact on the working notion of balanced policy authority. The Court has declared a very small number (83) of federal actions unconstitutional, but these actions include major pieces of legislation as well as presidential actions. The bulk of these decisions (74) were made between 1865–1936, marking a steady expansion of the Court's influence in policy-making. The peak was reached during the New Deal when the Court under Chief Justice Hughes invalidated twelve New Deal measures within four years (1933–37). During the same period three presidential actions were also declared unconstitutional.[26] The frequent use of the judicial veto in the mid-1930's, often on the basis of narrow majorities, led to President Roosevelt's attempt to "pack" the Court — to pass legislation under which new justices were to be added in order to produce a majority of votes in favor of New Deal measures. Congress refused to approve the proposal. Since 1937 the Court has not been active in invalidating congressional action.

To what extent has judicial review served as an effective check on the other two policy-making branches of the American community? Although the authority has been used sparingly to strike down policies, the fact that the Court *can* render invalidating decisions is a limiting factor in itself. Congress or the President may hesitate to act in the face of a strong expectation that the Court would find policy unconstitutional. A potentially adverse decision does not, however, always prevent action. Behavior frequently depends upon the permanency of adverse Court decisions; that is, can the Court make its decision stick? Robert A. Dahl's study of the incidence of "reversal" led him to conclude that "there is . . . no case on record where a persistent law-making majority has not, sooner or later, achieved its purposes." Dahl found that one-third of Supreme Court cases holding congressional legislation unconstitutional were ultimately overridden by amendment or subsequent Court decisions. Many of the remaining two-thirds involved minor legislation, temporary measures, or trivial sections of statutes.[27] We may conclude that the Court can (and has) exercised a check on other branches. Even in the absence of

---

[26] See Schubert, *op. cit.*, pp. 188–90.
[27] Robert A. Dahl, *A Preface to Democratic Theory* (Chicago: The University of Chicago Press, 1956), p. 110.

frequent declarations of unconstitutionality, the potentiality of the power plays an important, if not precisely determinable, role. In the long run, however, the Court has not been able to prevent ultimate achievement of original goals by determined legislative and popular majorities.[28]

A recent book on the Presidency points out that presidential history is marked by "inexorable though occasionally interrupted expansion of power and influence by the Chief executive . . ."[29] Although the Framers designed the selection process through a compromise that produced insulation of executive authority from direct popular control, the rise of political parties transformed the Electoral College into an agency that simply reflects the popular choice in each of the states. The result is that the President is the only popularly chosen official whose constituency is the whole of the American political community. His policy role has varied depending upon the man who occupied the office, but the trend has been in the direction of increased policy leadership. The President is leader of his party, prodder of Congress, and spokesman for the "national interest" as opposed to the narrower interests of congressional constituencies. In his study of the growth and development of the Presidency, Edward S. Corwin remarked: "The dogma of popular sovereignty had to adapt itself to the comparative rigidity of the national constitution, which it did by exalting and consolidating the power of the one national official who is — in a sense — elected by the people as a whole. The claim set up by Jackson to be the 'People's Choice' has been reiterated, in effect, by his successors many times, and with decisive results for the presidential office."[30]

Article II of the Constitution is addressed to the "executive power," a power which "is still indefinite as to *function* and retains, particularly when it is exercised by a single individual, much of its original plasticity as regards method."[31] Professor Corwin's point highlights the fact that a very short Article II almost certainly would be molded by the pressures of personality, events, and demands. The presidential role has consistently grown in scope and importance until it has cut across the technical limitations which underlie precepts of separate powers and checks and balances. The extent to which the judicial and legislative policy-making effectively checks the President is a concern to students of the American polity. These and other considerations on the nature of presidential powers are discussed at length in later chapters.

[28] *Ibid.*, pp. 108–10.
[29] Donald B. Johnson and Jack L. Walker, *The Dynamics of the American Presidency* (New York: John Wiley & Sons, 1964), p. 1.
[30] Edward S. Corwin, *The President: Office and Powers* (New York: New York University Press, 1948), p. 38.
[31] *Ibid.*, p. 1.

The creation of the President's Cabinet, an agency not even mentioned in the Constitution but which developed during Washington's Administration, is a clear example of Constitutional change without amendment. Further, the proliferation of executive agencies, especially in this century, has created in a sense a whole new level of policy-making not envisioned by the Framers. Of special importance are those agencies created by Congress and empowered to reach decisions that are partly legislative and partly judicial in nature, agencies not responsible to the President nor considered as either distinctively legislative or judicial. A mechanical definition of separation of powers is inadequate in fixing their place within the constitutional structure.

Although Madison in *The Federalist, No. 10* cautioned against the dangers of disputing factions, the very substance of politics is conflict. The Framers were fully aware through their own experiences that groups join together in more or less common cause seeking to achieve their interests. The Constitution, nevertheless, says nothing about political parties; and although the Jefferson-Hamilton split within Washington's Administration was looked on with disfavor by Washington, this division represented the first partisan split under the new government. Contests for control of both executive and legislative branches — and ultimately, the judiciary — are major devices in making operational a governmental system based on the separation of functions into three distinct institutions. That parties have sometimes played a coordinating role is evident. Control of both executive and legislative branches has rested in the same party through most of our history, and Presidents have made appointments to the federal courts with clear partisan considerations in mind. Occasionally the effect of this pattern of party control has been to alleviate — but by no means eliminate — the incidence of conflict between the three branches. Parties are organizations through and between which competition for policy authority occurs. Despite the fact that there are strong differences of opinion within parties and that at times different parties have controlled the three branches during the same period of years, it is generally true that informal modification of the principle of balanced government has been accomplished through the operation of the American party system.

CONSTITUTIONAL CHANGE
AND CONSTITUTIONAL FEDERALISM

Many writers have addressed themselves to the "crisis" of the federal system, a term generally designating the problems created by an enlarged central authority that has encroached upon areas once believed to be the sole province of the states. The range of central activities runs from subsidizing public education to enforcement of civil rights against recalcitrant state governments. Many factors have contributed to increased central policy-making: the enlargement of the electorate through removal of restrictions on the suffrage; the increasing complexity of America in terms of geography, economics, and technology; the growth and persistence of problems that overlap state boundaries; the failure, refusal, or inability of states to solve problems within their own borders; the historically conditioned and sustained growth of a sense of national community; the development of common cultural patterns; the high mobility of the American population tending to reduce the pull of parochialism in shaping attitudes and values; and the growth of the Presidency as representative of the national constituency. Formally, the Constitution has undergone few changes reflecting these forces. The language of the Tenth Amendment, reserving to states or the people "powers not delegated to the United States by the Constitution, nor prohibited by it to the States," has gone unchanged since adoption in 1791. What has occurred is a continuing reinterpretation of the nature of federalism as originally constituted.

When Congress created a national bank during Washington's Administration and a second one in 1816 — both in spite of bitter argument that such action went beyond the delegated powers of Congress — a number of states laid heavy taxes on branches of the bank within their borders. The refusal of James McCulloch, cashier of the Baltimore branch, to pay such a tax precipitated a constitutional issue over the extent of central jurisdiction under the federal arrangement. When the issue reached the Supreme Court, Chief Justice Marshall faced two major constitutional questions: the authority of a state to levy a tax on a national agency and thus, by implication, threaten its very existence; and, secondly, the legitimacy of Congress to create a bank when the Constitution did not specify its authority to do so.

The first was answered by Marshall's assertion that "the power to tax involved the power to destroy." States could not levy a tax on a legitimate instrumentality of the national government. But was the bank a legitimate agency? In answer to this question, Marshall cited the principle of "implied powers." The "government of the Union, though limited in its powers, is supreme within its sphere of action," wrote the Chief Justice. Under the supremacy clause, state laws in conflict with authorized policies of Congress must give way. Was, then, Congress within its "sphere of action" in chartering a national bank? Yes, argued Marshall, even though nothing in the Constitution specifically authorizes a national bank. Following the enumeration of the powers of Congress in Article I, Section 8 of the Constitution is the clause authorizing Congress "to make all Laws which shall be necessary and proper for carrying into Ex-.

ecution the Foregoing Powers. . . ." The constitutionality of the bank hinged on how narrow or broad an interpretation was to be given to the words "necessary and proper." The Framers, argued Marshall, had deliberately written a Constitution that only broadly outlined congressional jurisdiction. A constitution that contained a detailed listing of all powers flowing from generally granted powers could "scarcely be embraced by the human mind." "We must never forget," Marshall cautioned, "that it is a *constitution* we are expounding." The criterion for interpretation established by the Chief Justice was: "Let the end be legitimate, let it be within the scope of the Constitution, and all means which are plainly adapted to that end, which are not prohibited, but consist with the letter and spirit of the Constitution, are constitutional. . . ." In the case at hand, the enumerated powers to coin and borrow money and to regulate its value implied — made "necessary and proper" — the legitimacy of a national bank.[32]

Marshall's concept of a continental political community rested upon the belief that the Constitution must, if it was to endure, be adapted to fit the needs of each generation. Except for the period running generally from the last decade of the nineteenth century to the mid 1930's, the Supreme Court has used the implied-powers criterion to uphold the extension of community-wide authority into many new areas. Moreover, it has overturned a number of *state* statutes found inconsistent with the Constitution, in order to preserve community-wide authority under the federal principle. Three specific grants of power to Congress have formed the base from which these activities have proceeded: the power to regulate interstate and foreign commerce, the power to declare war, and the power to tax and spend for the general welfare.

"Commerce . . . among the several states" has been interpreted to include not only the movement of goods but matters that "affect" commerce. Thus where certain interstate activity applies, it is a crime under federal law to transport stolen automobiles across state lines; to kidnap; to sell adulterated goods; or to discriminate in employment or the use of public accommodations. Laws establishing minimum wages, prohibiting child labor, regulating labor-management relations, and controlling the production and marketing of agricultural commodities are justified as being "necessary and proper" to carrying out congressional responsibility in regulating commerce. In time of war, if national resources must be totally mobilized, congressional jurisdiction assumes almost absolute proportions. Military conscription, rationing of goods, control over production and consumption, and price control, are "necessary and proper"

---

[32] *McCulloch* v. *Maryland,* 4 Wheaton 316 (1819).

in a concerted war effort. Finally, "to tax and spend for the general welfare" has been interpreted to include laws providing for social security,
unemployment compensation, subsidization of agriculture, grants to
states for highway construction, and support of education. The power
to tax may be used in regulating or eliminating activities deemed harmful or undesirable. High taxes on the sale of sawed-off shot guns and narcotics, for example, are aimed not at producing revenue but at driving
these activities out of existence.

A full listing of the regulatory and welfare statutes passed by Congress
during this century, especially since 1930, would clearly reveal the impact
of implied powers upon the federal-state relationship. Debate over passage of this legislation has been marked by references to "states rights"
under the Tenth Amendment allegedly usurped by a loose interpretation
of the powers of Congress under the "necessary and proper" clause. Underlying the constitutional dispute are conflicts of interests as well as
principle that represent perhaps more mundane and practical considerations. To business interests, for example, an extension of governmental
regulation of labor-management relations may be viewed as an undesirable limitation upon practices considered as useful or necessary for
economic success. A labor union official might, on the other hand, view
federal activity as enhancing his bargaining with employers on behalf of
members. One side may employ the rhetoric of "states rights," the other
that of "national needs"; yet in both cases the constitutional argument is
often a surface justification for achieving more immediate goals.

CONSTITUTIONAL POLITICS
AND LIBERAL DEMOCRACY

The Constitution of the United States was first designed and later modified by political leaders generally committed to tenets of liberal democracy. In effect, within the American perspective the distinction
between substantive and procedural ideals of liberal democracy could
really be summed up as one between liberal democracy and what Americans conceive of as "constitutional democracy." The latter is something
less than the full realization of the working principles of democracy that we
described in Chapter Three. Partially by intent and partially by circumstance constituted authority in American government restrains the full
operation of popular control and consultation, political leadership, equality, and liberty. What operate are constitutional procedures of separated authority, balance, and federalism in such a fashion that we must
always recognize the "qualified" nature of our liberal democracy. For
example: Majority rule, the corollary to political equality, is checked in

the operation of the Electoral College, and could be checked by court discretion, by state actions, etc. Or political liberty, conceived of as the right to participate, has been limited because the states in the federal union may determine voting qualifications.

But this modified version of the procedural ideals of liberal democracy is not the final framework for conflict regulation in America. Indeed, Americans have never accepted the permanency of our constitutional democracy at any time. Many instances of constitutional change discussed in this chapter have been directed at bringing the institutions and ideals of constitutional and liberal democracy closer together. In short, ideals need not always be the captives of practice; political behavior can be shaped in the direction of greater liberty and equality.

But what of substantive values of liberal democracy; how well are they reflected through constitutional democracy? To the extent that constitutional restraints can be exploited to *liberate* the individual, then constitutional democracy is a stepping stone on the road to the realization of democratic ideals. The procedures underlying constitutional democracy can increase respect for human dignity, the potential for human development, and the freedom of intelligence. But when used, instead, as an instrument to restrict the development of individual potential — whether by local, state, national or *any* level of the political community — then constitutional government is a guise for bondage, not liberation. To which of these ends our liberal-democratic procedures will be put depends less upon the institutions themselves than the active dedication of Americans to the ideals to which they give quick lip-service.

Cleavage within the American community is contained by the limits of a basic political consensus marked by acquiescence to liberal-democratic ideals and procedures. Debate over policy choices and goals is seldom cast in terms of whether the basic features and values of the constitutional system should be retained. But the implementation and specific application of our beliefs and constitutional systems are subject to continuing controversy. Underlying such controversy are diverse and conflicting interests. Our political community is the product of at least a partially open society which, by definition, encourages differences as well as agreement. Neither the number nor status of groups remains static: powerful interests lose their power (for example, prohibition forces); relatively weak groups become stronger (labor unions, NAACP); new groups enter the political scene (John Birch Society, National Farmers Organization); and some, such as the Whig Party, disappear entirely. These changes are reflected in, and are in turn affected by, a pattern of constituted authority and thus vitally influence the determination of policy, the resolution of conflict. Such an overlapping system of funda-

mental values and rules can remain viable in a democracy only so long
as potentially destructive conflict is exposed and adjusted.

BIBLIOGRAPHICAL NOTE

Colonial ideas, experience, and institutions played a crucial role in the decisions
reached in the Constitutional Convention. The following represent a sample
of important works dealing with the period prior to 1787: Daniel J. Boorstin,
The Americans: The Colonial Experience (New York: Random House, 1958)
traces the influence of the colonial period on American character and political
ideas; the importance of Puritan influences on American political ideas and
society are analyzed in Ralph Barton Perry, *Puritanism and Democracy* (New
York: Harper & Row, 1944), and Thomas J. Wertenbaker, *The Puritan Oli-
garchy* (New York: Grosset and Dunlap, 1947). Both are in paperback editions.
Carl L. Becker, *The Declaration of Independence* (New York: Harcourt, Brace
& Co., 1922) is a classic study of the formation and meaning of this important
document. Clinton Rossiter, *Seedtime of the Republic* (New York: Harcourt,
Brace & Co., 1953) analyzes American political history from the colonial period
to 1776. Alpheus T. Mason, *Free Government in the Making*, 3rd ed. (New
York: Oxford University Press, 1965) is an excellent source of readings in the
ideas of the colonial and revolutionary periods.

Interpretation of the work of the Framers is abundant. Charles A. Beard's
*An Economic Interpretation of the Constitution of the United States With New
Introduction* (New York: Macmillan Co., 1954) — first published in 1913 —
has been a highly influential interpretation of the motives of the Founding Fa-
thers. For a critical view of Beard's thesis see Robert E. Brown, *Charles Beard
and the Constitution* (Princeton: Princeton University Press, 1956). V. L. Par-
rington, *Main Currents in American Thought: The Colonial Mind 1620–1800*
(New York: Harcourt, Brace & Co., 1927) also interprets the motives of the
Framers from the perspective of the Progressive era of the era 1900's. Alan
P. Grimes, *American Political Thought*, rev. ed. (New York: Holt, Rinehart and
Winston, 1960) provides good background narrative to the era and contains
an excellent bibliography. David W. Minar, *Ideas and Politics* (Homewood,
Ill.: The Dorsey Press, 1964) analyzes American experience and its relationship
to changing institutions and ideas.

Among the original sources on the debates in the Constitutional convention
is Max Farrand's outstanding work, *The Records of the Federal Convention of
1787*, 4 vols. (New Haven: Yale University Press, 1937). Arthur E. Sutherland,
Constitutionalism in America (New York: Blaisdell Publishing Co., 1965) traces
the origins and growth of five major constitutional ideas. A paperback edition,
A Biography of the Constitution of the United States (New York: Oxford University Press, 1964) is an outstanding "life story of the Constitution."

The Federalist is essential reading for a full understanding of the theory
and political considerations behind the Constitution. For a very helpful and
important analysis of this major work in American political thought see Gott-
fried Dietze, *The Federalist* (Baltimore: The Johns Hopkins Press, 1960). It is

now available in a paperback edition. Anti-federalist thought from its early beginnings through the fight over adoption is excellently treated in another paperback, Alpheus T. Mason, *The States Rights Debate: Antifederalism and the Constitution* (Englewood Cliffs, N.J.: Prentice-Hall, 1964). Another paperback, Robert A. Goldwin, ed., *A Nation of States* (Chicago: Rand McNally, 1963) contains some excellent essays illustrating the continuing debate over the meaning and purpose of American federalism.

The judicial role in constitutional change has been widely written upon. The following paperback editions are valuable sources of information and analysis: Carl Brent Swisher, *The Growth of Constitutional Power in the United States* (Chicago: University of Chicago Press, 1963); Robert G. McCloskey, *The American Supreme Court* (Chicago: University of Chicago Press, 1960); Loren P. Beth (Evanston, Ill.: Row, Peterson & Co., 1962); and Howard Dean, *Judicial Review and Democracy* (New York: Random House, 1966).

Edward S. Corwin's *The Doctrine of Judicial Review* (Princeton: Princeton University Press, 1914) contains a classic essay on *Marbury* v. *Madison.* John P. Frank's study, *Marble Palace: The Supreme Court in American Life* (New York: Alfred A. Knopf, 1958) provides insight into the relationship of the Supreme Court to changing American social and economic patterns. For other relevant works in this area see the bibliographical note at the end of Chapter Fifteen.

Finally, those interested in explanations of specific phrases in the Constitution should consult Edward M. Dumbauld, *The Constitution of the United States* (Norman: University of Oklahoma Press, 1964) and Edward S. Corwin, *The Constitution and What It Means Today,* 12th edition (New York: Atheneum, 1963). The latter is in paperback edition.

POLITICAL
COMMUNICATION

PART TWO

Patterns of Conflict
Representation in
American Government

*We have talked about three dimensions of the American
pluralistic community: social diversity, which generates
points of tension; contrasting personal values and beliefs
within the overall doctrinal framework of liberal democracy;
and a fragmented institutional context produced by constitutional bargains and growth. Our concerns in Part Two center
about one question: How are patterns of conflict representation affected by social, personal, and politico-constitutional
pluralism? Let us examine, then, the methods for making conflicts known to policy-makers — political communication — and
whether they reflect the pluralistic American setting.*

CHAPTER
FIVE

Political Participation

We have designated as political any pattern of human activity concerned
with public management of social disputes. Since the regulation of interest conflict consists of its representation as well as resolution, it is appropriate to turn to the more significant ways by which disagreements are
transmitted to policy officials. Because our polity shares with "all new
nations of the world the belief that the ordinary man is politically relevant
— that he ought to be an involved participant in the political system," [1]
it is useful to begin our discussion with the most inclusive pattern of
conflict representation — political participation. Other representative patterns — opinion, leadership, choice, partisanship, and pressure — can
then be viewed as specific modes of participation. In this chapter we are
concerned with the nature of political participation, the plural forms of
American participation, and the degree of citizen involvement associated
with constitutional, social, and personal dimensions of community life.

[1] Gabriel A. Almond and Sidney Verba, *The Civic Culture* (Princeton: Princeton
University Press, 1963), p. 4.

109

POLITICAL PARTICIPATION IN AMERICA

THE NATURE OF POLITICAL PARTICIPATION

Since public insurrections are infrequent, we can say that a substantial number of Americans support their political community in at least a passive fashion through a willingness to be obligated by community decisions. Despite this willingness, however, relatively few actively engage in altering the course of governmental affairs. Many take no part in selecting public officials and display no cognizance of the diverse interests that vie for community recognition of exclusive goals. In a study of popular responses to government in five nations, including the United States, Professors Gabriel Almond and Sidney Verba refer to persons who support public decisions but do not seek to modify them as *subjects* in the polity rather than *participants*.[2] It is a distinction worth maintaining in our account of American participation. Viewed within the context of our discussion of politics as conflict regulation, it is convenient to designate political participation as "taking part in making the basic decisions as to what are the common goals of one's society and as to the best ways to move toward these goals." [3]

The participant is actively concerned with community affairs and his conduct makes a difference in the outcome of social disputes. First, by his votes, opinions, partisanship, and urgings he discloses his interests. The aggregate behavior of citizen-participants thus serves as a principal manifestation of social diversity and conflict in pluralist America. Secondly, his activity induces others to take account of his presence and, perhaps infinitesimally, to modify their behavior while adjusting to his. In this fashion the participant accrues influence in governmental affairs, an influence which liberal-democratic communities seek to extend by increasing citizen involvement in public decision-making.

The import of political participation is emphasized in both procedural and substantive views of liberal democracy. We noted earlier that democracy requires, at some point, that "all those who are affected by social institutions must have a share in producing and managing them." [4] In the American polity protections and procedures for popular control, popular consultation, political equality, and political liberty are formalized in the Constitution: First Amendment protections of free speech, press, religion,

---

[2] Almond and Verba, *op. cit.*, pp. 17–29.

[3] James C. Davies, *Human Nature in Politics* (New York: John Wiley and Sons, 1963), p. 23.

[4] John Dewey, "Democracy and Educational Administration," *School and Society,* April 3, 1937.

assembly, and petition guarantee rights of participation; voting clauses in the Fifteenth, Nineteenth, Twenty-second and Twenty-fourth Amendments are explicitly concerned with the qualifications for participation. Under current interpretation the Constitution is an instrument protecting, fostering, and urging civic participation.

Political participation is a distinguishing feature of substantive liberal democracy as well. It is not stressed simply for its own sake but because of its contribution to the full development of the individual personality. Liberal-democratic doctrine provides a profile of the creative citizen fostered by free participation: a high personal motivation, an open mind committed to the discovery of truth and free of limiting predispositions, a rational self-assessment as well as appraisal of reality, and a sense of altruism to the extent that community welfare is placed above selfish private interests. To reach this ideal, participants must seek to be informed, maintain interest, and strive to act upon the basis of reasoned principles rather than emotional appeals.[5]

As we take a closer look at the character of political participation in America, it is well to keep in mind the criteria established for such activity in a liberal democracy. In this fashion we can compare the nature of American participation with our conception of the ideal, a necessary prelude to political judgment.

THE PLURALIST CHARACTER
OF AMERICAN PARTICIPATION

Although Americans can participate in politics in a number of ways, a majority choose not to involve themselves in political activity. Professor Hugh Bone has estimated that the proportion of Americans that could be classified as intense political activists probably does not exceed 1 per cent of the adult population and may be as low as ¼ per cent.[6] Even in presidential elections where we would expect broad participation, the rate of nonvoting is currently around 40 per cent of the potential electorate.

To obtain some idea of how Americans do participate beyond the passive acquiescence of the subject, we examine specific, but overlapping, forms of citizen activity: opinion-holding, political leadership, voting, partisan activity, and group membership (see Table 5-1). Since each is a separate pattern of conflict representation discussed in following chapters, we confine ourselves here to estimating the proportion of Americans

[5] Bernard Berelson, Paul Lazarsfeld, and William McPhee, *Voting* (Chicago: The University of Chicago Press, 1954).
[6] Hugh A. Bone, *American Politics and the Party System* (3rd ed.; New York: McGraw-Hill Book Co., 1965), p. 533.

TABLE 5-1

A Profile of American Political Participation

MODE OF POLITICAL PARTICIPATION	ESTIMATED PROPORTION OF AMERICANS AS PARTICIPANTS
Opinion Participation:	
Normally express political opinions when asked	70–90%
Normally express informed political opinions when asked	30–50%
Possess basic "textbook" information of politics	15–40%
Leadership Participation:	
Personal Leadership (attempts to influence political views of others through discussion)	50–70%
Voluntary leadership in political campaigns	3–5%
Partisan precinct leadership	.25–1%
Voter Participation:	
Infrequent participants (vote occasionally in elections)	30–40%
Regular participants (vote consistently in all elections — national, state, local)	25–30%
Apoliticals (no voting in elections)	3–7%
Partisan Participation:	
Party identifiers (consider themselves as Republicans or Democrats)	65–75%
Attend political meetings, rallies, dinners, etc.	5–7%
Support financially campaigns of parties or candidates	4–10%
Actual membership in a political club or organization	2–3%
Voluntary Organized Participation:	
Membership in organization of any kind	60–65%
Membership in organizations that sometimes take stands on political issues	30–35%

so involved and to assessing the political relevancy, frequency, and intensity of the activity. We are interested in noting whether the activity is directly or indirectly related to politics, is performed regularly or sporadically, and involves the citizen personally or vicariously.

Opinion Participation. The most effortless way to participate in politics is by voicing opinions on current political issues and personalities. Americans do this with marked frequency; however, the intensity of their general political involvement is so low that they tend to read, view, and listen to political information much more sporadically and thereby possess a relatively meager fund of political knowledge.

Professors Hyman and Sheatsley reported in 1950 that in published surveys of public opinion fewer than 15 per cent of Americans generally express "no opinion" on issues in question; "Americans," they concluded, "are an articulate people and they express opinions on virtually every conceivable issue." [7] Other available evidence underscores this American tendency toward holding an opinion. Exploring the distribution of opinions on a variety of foreign and domestic issues in 1956, the Michigan Survey Research Center reported that "no opinion" responses ranged from 10 per cent (on the issue of federal aid for school construction) to 30 per cent (on the proposition "the government ought to leave things like electric power and housing for private businessmen to handle").[8]

Although the average American is more likely to have an opinion about a political issue or personality than not, his opinion will not necessarily be an informed one. Democratic theory generally prescribes that every citizen should be sufficiently aware of political matters to make policy and electoral judgments. But for most Americans, politics is at best only an avocation; and political awareness must be purchased at the price of forgoing activities of greater interest. In budgeting his leisure time, the citizen devotes comparatively little attention to reading about politics, listening to political news, or viewing political programs. Moreover, when he does, topics of political interest are normally those emphasized by the popular communications media as newsworthy. In reciprocal fashion, citizen interest helps to shape news to the extent that reporters, editors, and columnists, acting as political participants, select stories of interest to their audience. Perhaps the highest levels of this type of participation came in 1960 when as many as 80 million persons viewed a debate between presidential candidates; in 1963 even greater numbers shared in mourning President Kennedy's death by watching the televised funeral. Generally, for reasons of time, the American is likely to be uninformed about political issues; but if informed, he is likely to be more knowledgeable about emotionally charged events than abstract questions of popular control, equality, and liberty.

There is ample indication that supportive evidence is not a necessary condition for holding opinions. Professors Hyman and Sheatsley estimate that over 10 per cent of opinion-holders "will answer 'don't know' when the interviewer asks them why they feel that way." Similarly the Michigan Survey Research Center revealed in a 1956 study that on the average

[7] Herbert H. Hyman and Paul B. Sheatsley, "The Current Status of American Public Opinion," in Daniel Katz *et al.* (eds.), *Public Opinion and Propaganda* (New York: Henry Holt and Company, 1954), pp. 36–37.

[8] Angus Campbell, Philip E. Converse, Warren E. Miller, and Donald E. Stokes, *The American Voter* (New York: John Wiley & Sons, 1960), pp. 171–76.

about one respondent out of three could not be classified as familiar with public issues; individuals were so listed if they both possessed an opinion *and* knew what "government is doing about it." [9]

If we extend our investigation to see how many Americans participate by seeking political knowledge of even a more general nature, we find even a more marked lack of information. For example: the "textbook" knowledge most Americans have of politics is quite low; the American Institute of Public Opinion reported in 1954 that only 19 per cent of Americans could correctly name the "three branches of the Federal Government." In 1945 only 55 per cent knew that there are two United States senators from their own state, and only 40 per cent could identify correctly the number of United States Supreme Court justices. In the area of current events the disparity of political information is also apparent; the Survey Research Center estimated that not more than 50 per cent of Americans were informed regarding which political party controlled Congress during the 1950's.[10]

Opinion participation is fairly evenly spread throughout various social groupings in the community. The comparative ignorance of political institutions and events, however, differs among groupings in the population. There is an apparent sub-community of the political knowledgeable composed of more younger than older people, more men than women, more urban than rural residents, and the better educated.[11]

Leadership Participation. A person need not commit himself strongly to the political life to have an opinion; the acquisition of political information demands more involvement. Efforts to persuade others to one's own view require even more enthusiasm for governmental affairs. Yet there are Americans who participate by providing political leadership through electioneering, financial contributions, political discussion, and writing political letters.

The most intense and visible manifestation of leadership participation occurs in American elections. Running for political office is the most obvious form of electoral activity, but there are a variety of other participants caught up in any campaign. Much of the organization of support falls to volunteers hosting coffee klatches and teas, typing addresses, licking envelopes, displaying bumper stickers, and speaking at precinct meetings. Such activity demands that the American engaging in it take a public stand; because of social and personal factors (discussed later) many

---

[9] Hyman and Sheatsley *op. cit.*, p. 37; Campbell *et al., op. cit.*, p. 174.

[10] Donald E. Stokes and Warren E. Miller, "Party Government and the Saliency of Congress," *The Public Opinion Quarterly*, XXVI (Winter, 1962), 531–46.

[11] Robert E. Lane and David O. Sears, *Public Opinion* (Englewood Cliffs, N.J.: Prentice-Hall, 1964), p. 62.

Americans are unwilling to display their loyalties so openly. The proportion of Americans participating in grass-roots politics is never large; one estimate is that only 5 per cent of the electorate in 1955 had served in the capacity of volunteer workers.[12]

Political campaigns require not only the time and energy of candidates, leaders, and workers but also financing by those willing to sacrifice money, often in what is deemed a losing cause. An individual is more likely to participate in this fashion as (1) his income increases, (2) his personal interests become more clearly affected by electoral results, and (3) he exerts influence in general community policy-making. Although various incentives have been proposed in order to increase participation in the financing of political campaigns, including tax rebates for contributions, only one has been adopted. Under this plan (approved in 1966) taxpayers could choose each year to have $1 of their income tax (or $2 for joint returns) allocated for expenses of the next presidential campaign. Should a large number of citizens choose such an option, political funding may become an activity shared by more than the current minority of Americans who contribute to political campaigns.[13]

Political discussion serves as the vehicle for leadership participation for many Americans. Studies consistently reveal that seven of every ten Americans engage in political conversation both during and between election campaigns. Moreover, 54 per cent of Americans in 1952 reported that they influenced the opinions of their friends in discussions. The relative proportion of such informal "opinion leaders," or self-designated persuaders, is generally somewhat lower, ranging from 21–27 per cent of the adult population.[14] Robert Lane reports in his study of political life that people tend to talk more about political personalities than issues, concrete matters than vague abstractions, and the sensational aspects of government (scandal) than day-to-day political events.[15]

Americans also write letters to officials. Letter-writing campaigns are stimulated primarily at the behest of organized groups. As a form of participation, letter-writing is undertaken by people who are more literate, of upper occupational and educational status, those with a relatively strong sense of their own political effectiveness, and those perceiving certain issues as highly salient to their interests. A study undertaken of the letter-writing proclivities of Americans in 1964 revealed that only 15 per cent of a national sample could recall having written a letter to a

[12] See Robert E. Lane, *Political Life* (Glencoe, Ill.: The Free Press, 1959), p. 53.
[13] *Ibid.*, pp. 56–62.
[14] See Lester W. Milbrath, *Political Participation* (Chicago: Rand McNally & Co., 1965), p. 23.
[15] Lane, *op. cit.*, pp. 86–92.

public official, and two-thirds of those letters were initiated by a hard core of 3 per cent of Americans. Only 3 per cent, moreover, could recall writing letters to newspapers or magazines, and two-thirds of these letters were written by ½ per cent of Americans.[16]

The product of campaigns is the selection of leaders to govern for limited periods of time. Governing in all its dimensions constitutes a form of direct, regular, and personal participation. Since we are concerned in this chapter with the forms of participation related primarily to the representation of social conflict rather than its resolution, we postpone consideration of policy participation until Part Three. It should be borne in mind, however, that there is a link between the citizen-participant and the policy-participant in our community, a link formed primarily by the methods of representation discussed in this and following chapters.

Voter Participation. Perhaps the most prized form of citizen participation in a republic is the casting of votes in the election of officials. So long as Americans cannot themselves make policy decisions, voting comes closest to a method of directly shaping public policy, as provided for in the Constitution. Yet only 25–30 per cent of the adult population vote with any distinguishable degree of regularity in American elections — federal, state, and local. Another 30–40 per cent cast votes so infrequently and sporadically that it is fair to label them as "nonvoters." Finally, another 3–7 per cent are so apolitical that they find no meaning in political experience — elections or otherwise — and decline to participate in community affairs. Hence, although we expect voting to be one of the more direct, regular, and intensely pursued forms of American participation, we find it is not.[17]

It is possible to classify voter participants on the basis of the factors that stimulate their interest in an election: those who find elections personally meaningful, those deriving vicarious satisfaction from the political game, and those virtually detached from the political community.

In the first category we can differentiate ways in which participants approach the voting act. First, there are voters who utilize the franchise as a means of advancing personal interests. They feel competent to identify their goals, can find alternative means for self-advancement, attempt to select the most effective means, and make their voting choice accordingly. Distinguished from this self-interested participant is the partisan who employs his vote primarily to promote the interests of a candidate or party, with secondary reference to personal gain. He too possesses a sense of competence, efficacy, and obligation to vote. Finally,

[16] Philip E. Converse et al., "Electoral Myth and Reality: The 1964 Election," *The American Political Science Review*, LIX, No. 2 (June, 1965), 333.

[17] Lane, *op. cit.*, pp. 45–62.

there is a third class of personally involved voters — the independents. The latter are conceived of as rational and open-minded citizens interested not in self, cause, candidate, or party, but in the promotion of the civic good, public interest, or common will. Hence, to personally committed participants the vote may be viewed as a tool for satisfaction of self, partisan, or community interests.

Americans only vicariously involved in election campaigns are consumers of political information, not activists. Participation is manifested by following political combat rather than actually voting. Politics is conceived of as a spectator, not a participant, sport. The spectator, substituting second-hand reporting of political reality for the reality itself, is particularly prone to thrill to the entertainment content of the communication media.

Finally, there is the citizen who places politics far down on his list of preferred activities. His sense of civic obligation is as low as his participation. For personal and social reasons he simply withdraws from politics and does not vote at all. Perhaps his nonparticipation stems from lack of opportunities produced by low status, low income, or limited education. Or apathy may reflect a conscious choice to turn attention to obligations perceived as more pressing — to business, home, leisure, etc. For many the source of inactivity is a lack of self-competence and esteem and a sense of political inefficacy. Americans alienated from the political community because they feel powerless to change the course of political events or view politicians as corrupt, power-grabbing, and high-handed, may withdraw from voter participation as a method of escape.

Partisan Participation. Mention of the partisan voter suggests another of the general modes of American participation in politics — membership and service in one of the major political parties, Republican or Democrat. We are not speaking here of the three-fourths of Americans (discussed in Chapter Eight) who feel a loyalty or attachment to a particular party, but rather of the individuals who, working as precinct leaders, party chairmen, secretaries, fund raisers, or professional organizers, occupy a niche in the party hierarchy. Although estimates of the proportion of citizens participating in partisan activity run as high as 5 per cent, only about ¼ per cent of the potential electorate comprise the core of precinct leaders in America.[18]

The effect of organized party activity on elections is more noticeable when gauging the work of the minority party in an area. The majority needs only to activate its supporters rather than win new adherents, a task less apparent on the surface than minority efforts at conversion. The impact of partisan activity also varies with the type of election. The in-

[18] Hugh A. Bone, *Grass Roots Party Leadership* (Seattle: University of Washington, 1952).

dependent effects of campaign activity by precinct activists are reduced in elections between well-known public figures or in campaigns involving clear-cut cleavages between the two parties. But in elections where personalities or issues are unknown, such as party nominations, or those involving long ballots, school board races, or charter revisions, precinct organizers may supply the margin of victory.

Voluntary Participation. Americans are afforded opportunities for indirect political participation through membership in voluntary organizations. Depending upon the nature of the group, the activities of members may have considerable political relevance. Some voluntary organizations, notably the Southern Christian Leadership Conference or the Students for a Democratic Society, participate in public protests and demonstrations against policies they find offensive. Others, such as the League of Women Voters, direct their efforts at stimulating greater citizen concern in public affairs. Moreover, any voluntary activity, such as working in a United Fund drive, stimulates greater interest in community affairs and increases the likelihood of more direct political participation in the future. It was estimated in 1952 that at least 64 per cent of Americans belonged to formal organizations of some type and that half that percentage were members of groups that take stands on political questions.[19]

THE CONTEXT OF POLITICAL
PARTICIPATION PATTERNS

Each activity within the above categories varies in the frequency and intensity of its performance according to the politico-constitutional, social, and personal features of our community. In general we can say that the degree to which people are willing to devote time, energy, and attention to political participation depends upon the extent to which (1) there are no legal restraints preventing them from doing so; (2) they are stimulated to participate by interest conflicts, especially in political campaigns; (3) they perceive their social and economic interests as related to political choice; and (4) they define political behavior as personally meaningful and efficacious. Exploring the relation of these factors primarily to voter turnout gives us a better idea of who participates in American politics and why.

THE POLITICO-CONSTITUTIONAL DIMENSION

The provisions of our written constitution, associated statutes, and unwritten political practices and traditions help define the universe of

[19] See Angus Campbell et al., The Voter Decides (Evanston, Ill.: Row, Peterson, 1954).

eligible political participants in the community. Once eligibility has been established, the amount of voter participation tends to vary with such politically relevant factors as historical circumstances, type of election, and variety of interest conflict.

Constitutional and Statutory Prescriptions for Participation. We have designated the politically active member of the community as a citizen-participant. This is particularly necessary in discussing American participation because the notion of citizenship is one that carries both legal and psychological implications. In the first instance, community policy distinguishes between the legal status of the citizen and the noncitizen, or in the terminology of the Constitution, between "citizens" and "persons." Noncitizens may be required to register annually with the Government of the United States, restricted in wartime, deported for sufficient cause, or may suffer other personal restrictions not commonly the lot of the citizen.

Specific paths to American citizenship are defined in Article XIV, Section 1, of the Constitution and in federal statutes. These include birth, naturalization, or congressional action. Citizenship is automatic for persons born in the republic, under its territorial jurisdiction, or of American parentage. Naturalization is a process whereby individuals born outside of the United States, after following certain procedures, receive the rights of citizenship. Finally, Congress can award citizenship by collective grant as it did with the American Indian in 1924.

Citizenship is also a personally meaningful notion carrying a sense of civic obligation. One of the primary purposes of many academic courses in civics or "citizenship training" is to transmit a sense of citizen duty. In their cross-cultural survey of five nations, Gabriel Almond and Sidney Verba pinpointed the nature of obligations perceived by individual citizens. They found that Americans possess a variety of ideas on what role the "ordinary man should play in his local community." For example: 21 per cent felt he should take an active part in local government, only 6 per cent perceived an obligation to be active in political parties, and 32 per cent felt he should participate in nongovernmental civil activity or "organizations interested in local affairs." Among more passive forms of participation, 21 per cent felt men should try to understand politics and keep informed, and 40 per cent felt that they should vote. In all, more than eight out of every ten felt some type of civic obligation to participate, a proportion in excess of that of other polities surveyed (Table 5-2).

The greater the citizen's sense of civic duty, the more likely he will be to involve himself in community politics. As a legally defined citizen he is eligible to participate; his feeling of obligation stimulates him to do so. This sense of obligation currently is the strongest among citizens of

TABLE 5-2

The Obligation to Participate

| | PERCENTAGE WHO CHOOSE IN: | | | | |
FORM OF PARTICIPATION	UNITED STATES	UNITED KINGDOM	GERMANY	ITALY	MEXICO
Active Participation in Local Community:					
Take part in activities of local government	21	22	13	5	11
Take part in activities of political parties	6	4	4	1	5
Take part in nongovernmental activity and in organizations interested in local affairs	32	17	9	5	10
More Passive Community Activities:					
Try to understand and keep informed	21	11	24	6	29
Vote	40	18	15	2	1
Take interest in what is going on	3	13	6	15	4
Participation in Some Form of Politically Related Activity	83	72	61	32	59
NUMBER OF CASES	970	963	955	995	1007

Source: Adapted from Gabriel A. Almond and Sidney Verba, *The Civic Culture* (Princeton: Princeton University Press, 1963), p. 171.

higher socio-economic status, the better educated, residents of urban areas, persons living outside the South, and Whites.[20]

Although the population of eligible citizen-participants is determined by federal constitutional and statutory arrangements, not all citizens are automatically allowed to vote in elections. Under terms of Article I of the Constitution, states establish voting requirements within limits contained in other articles. In an earlier era the major restrictions upon voting were property requirements. Gradually these were replaced by demands that individuals give proof of economic standing as a voting prerequisite, normally through payment of poll taxes as evidence of nonpauper status. Ironically the poll tax was originally substituted for property requirements as a liberalizing measure but ultimately grew so discriminatory to Negroes and impoverished Americans that the need for adopting an amendment to the Constitution (the Twenty-fourth) abolishing poll tax requirements in elections for federal officials was felt. Moreover, litigation produced Supreme Court decisions declaring state poll taxes, notably

[20] Almond and Verba, *op. cit.*, chap. 6.

in Texas and Alabama, unconstitutional. Property and tax restrictions for local voting — in school board elections or bond elections — are continuing reminders that the franchise frequently is limited to citizens with an economic "stake" in the community.[21]

Individual states have periodically disfranchised particular groups. In the South the Negro has been the target; in the Southwest the American Indian was enfranchised only after a long struggle by the Association of American Indian Affairs. Amendments to the federal Constitution have restricted states from denying suffrage rights to groups on grounds of race, color, sex, servitude, or place of residence (the presidential franchise being extended to District of Columbia residents as recently as 1961). As a result, disfranchisement now occurs within a less expansive framework; states use citizenship, residency, age, registration, and literacy as voting requirements.

In a community with a mobile population, such as the United States, requirements demanding a given period of residence within a state, county, or precinct prior to voting frequently disfranchise large portions of the electorate. Restrictions vary, but required periods of residence range from six months to two years in a state and from one month to a full year in a county or precinct. It has been estimated that 5 million Americans in the 1952 presidential election failed to meet state, county, or precinct residence requirements.[22] All states restrict the franchise to citizens of a specified age. Generally twenty-one years is the age requirement. Georgia and Kentucky, with eighteen as the minimum, and Alaska (nineteen) and Hawaii (twenty) are exceptions.

Registration refers to the requirement of many states that an individual must, in advance of election day, provide evidence that he possesses the requisite qualifications for voting; get his name on a registration list; and on voting day establish that he has conformed to local election rules. Registration procedures vary considerably: permanent registration systems require that the voter establish his credentials only once, when he meets citizenship, age, and residency qualifications; periodic registration asks voters to reestablish qualifications at selected periods throughout their lives. As important as the type of system employed is the administration of it; registration rolls may be administered centrally in a county or in separate voting districts. As a general rule, the more complex the administrative detail, the greater the opportunities for manipulation by privileged interests.

[21] Chilton Williamson, *American Suffrage: From Property to Democracy,* 1760–1860 (Princeton: Princeton University Press, 1960).

[22] Clinton Rossiter, *Parties and Politics in America* (Ithaca: Cornell University Press, 1960), p. 31.

The rationale for voting requirements is to assure that qualified voters each cast but one ballot and that those ballots count equally. Frequently, however, methods are used either to disfranchise qualified voters or give preference to some votes over others. Literacy tests have been one method for disqualifying voters: each applicant is required to read and explain a passage of a state constitution, statute, or other document to the satisfaction of an election judge. Dual standards of administration in the past have converted literacy tests into instruments of selective discrimination, particularly against Negroes in the South. Through passage of the Voting Rights Act of 1965, along with civil rights legislation in 1957, 1960, and 1964, the way was opened to limit the effectiveness of literacy tests as tools of selective disfranchisement (See Figure 5-1).

A more veiled approach to limiting the franchise in many areas has been to permit universal suffrage but to reduce the proportionate value of individual votes through devices of nonreapportionment, malapportionment, or gerrymandering. Although not directed at the franchise *per se*, such techniques shape the pattern of interest representation. We shall consider them in greater detail in our discussion of Congress.

Finally, in all states there are persons who lose their franchise in particular elections because they are incarcerated in prisons, are too ill to go to the polls, even though qualified, have their ballots thrown out by election judges due to improper marking, or are away from home on election day and cannot take advantage of often complicated procedures for absentee voting. Restrictions on absentee voting are particularly troublesome for members of the armed forces. In one fashion or another, each of these circumstances reflects a legal restriction on citizen participation.

The Political Impetus for Participation. Legal criteria designate the potential electorate but give no clue as to the frequency with which qualified voters exercise their options. Despite a relative drop following Reconstruction, "the proportion of the population voting has increased almost continuously from the period of the Revolution to the present." [23] This long-term tendency, however, has not been matched in all historical periods, electoral levels, and election campaigns. Historically, for example, there have been variations in voter turnout associated with periods of prewar politics, which attract citizen attention, as opposed to postwar declines in partisan sensitivities; eras of sectional conflict, which tend to promote higher turnout; and times of economic upheaval, which stimulate political interest. Moreover, within a given era, the nature of the election itself, the complexity of the voter's task, and the intensity of conflict govern differences in voting participation.

[23] Lane, *op. cit.*, p. 26.

FIGURE 5-1

The Post-World War II Evolution of Voting Rights

1957 CIVIL RIGHTS ACT

1. Affirmed citizen's right to seek court injunctions to protect voting rights.
2. Authorized Federal Government to seek court injunctions to remove violations of voting rights.
3. Created Federal Civil Rights Commission to investigate violations of voting rights.
4. Created Civil Rights Division in Department of Justice.

1960 CIVIL RIGHTS ACT

1. Authorized Attorney General to request court findings of patterns or practice of denial of Negro voting rights when violations warranted this.
2. Authorized courts to issue orders that Negroes were qualified to vote if voter discrimination was proved.
3. Authorized courts to appoint referees to aid Negroes in registration and voting.

1964 TWENTY-FOURTH AMENDMENT

Outlawed poll tax as voting requirement in federal elections.

1964 CIVIL RIGHTS ACT

1. Prohibited oral literacy tests in federal elections; prohibited unequal application of registration requirements; prohibited denial of right to vote because of voting-record errors or omissions where records were immaterial to qualification.
2. Required presumption of literacy where persons were educated in schools with instruction primarily in English.
3. Established special three-judge federal courts to hear voting-rights suits.

1965 VOTING RIGHTS ACT

1. Suspended literacy tests.
2. Appointed federal voting examiners to administer registration in states and counties using literacy tests in 1964 with voter participation below standards established by the act. (Registration or turnout of less than 50 per cent of its population.)
3. Authorized Attorney General to seek federal court findings of voter discrimination.
4. Authorized Attorney General to proceed against discriminatory state poll taxes.

Nature of Election. Patterns of electoral participation vary considerably with the level and regularity of elections. Normally, federal elections produce higher turnouts than local elections. Enthusiasm for voting drops consistently as the election gets nearer the American's front porch. Presidential elections are especially attractive to voters. Not since the 1920's has one failed to draw a turnout of at least half of those of voting age in the community. The same cannot be said of the congressional elections held between presidential elections. The fact of substantial falloff (as high as one-fifth) from the presidential election frequently is attributed to the lack of a commanding personality in the election; it seems equally probable that the type of communication saturation that characterizes campaigns in presidential elections is missing. Congressional candidates find it more difficult to break through the wall of voter indifference without the community-wide controversy stimulated by a struggle for the Presidency. Participation in state and local elections is usually less than in federal elections. Although elections for executive officials at all levels (Presidents, governors, mayors, etc.) draw more voters than do those for legislative and judicial officers, mayoral elections seldom attract voters to the extent that presidential and gubernatorial elections do.

Differences in voter turnout are associated with the type of election involved as well as its level. Nonpartisan elections draw fewer voters than those permitting party designations for candidates and appeals. Special elections to fill vacancies, special bond elections, and sundry others attract few voters, normally fewer than regular elections. A similar contrast exists between primary and general elections. Despite urgings of Populists that the direct primary would bring forth voters eager to express their choice in the selection of candidates, the expected throng did not appear; even in Southern one-party states where primaries are traditionally "the election" no such high rate is observed, and turnout is about equal to that of two-party states holding primaries. General elections attract higher voter interest.[24]

Election Procedure. Voters tend to go to the polls so long as the decisions to be made are relatively simple. Anything that complicates the choice tends to cut participation — a long or intricate ballot (especially if marked by hand) listing so many offices that the voter tires of the whole business, burdensome registration or voting rules, lengthy delays at the polls, or a series of candidates or issues unknown to the citizen. State and local governments are particularly prone to pile elections on top of one another with amazing frequency; primary, general, and special elections are staggered throughout the year. One result is that voters find it both

[24] V. O. Key, Jr., *American State Politics* (New York: Alfred A. Knopf, 1956), pp. 133–68.

burdensome and impossible to maintain interest in consistent electoral participation.

Electoral Conflict. E. E. Schattschneider asserts that nonvoting reflects the tendency in American politics for elections to be held on meaningless matters.[25] The conflict involved may not be of sufficient salience to move the citizen to the polls. It is a fundamental task of political leadership to expose matters of citizen concern; apathy frequently is produced by inept appraisals of what is on the voter's mind rather than by an insensitive electorate. So long as it holds true that "the more stimuli about politics a person receives, the greater the likelihood that he will participate in politics, and the greater the depth of his participation," political leaders cannot avoid responsibility for promoting voter turnout.[26]

Schattschneider argues that low participation levels will prevail so long as our two major parties fail to offer different partisan programs to the electorate and to follow through effectively on them once elected. Whether or not this is true, there are indications that the mere presence of parties in elections substantially affects turnout rates. In partisan elections precinct activity through personal contact with voters promotes turnout somewhat more than in elections where party designations and appeals are forbidden. As a reference symbol, party is associated with turnout to the extent that citizens with strong party loyalties are far more likely to be regular voters than are independents or party leaners. Republicans vote in greater proportions than Democrats; hence, a potentially larger Democratic electorate is balanced by relatively greater Republican voting, producing close interparty competition for some federal elections. There is evidence that anticipation of a close vote between competing parties itself influences participation. Actual margins are perhaps less important in conditioning turnout than the expectation of close elections. Such an assessment increases citizen concern and the hope that the vote "will count for something." This seems particularly true of persons with intense partisan preferences who go to the polls in greater proportions if the election outcome is doubtful (Table 5-3). For this reason many candidates "run scared" in order to motivate supporters to cast ballots rather than stay at home and assume the attitude that "one more vote won't make any difference."

THE SOCIAL DIMENSION

Certain features of a citizen's social background are related to the frequency and intensity of his political participation. Among those deserving

---

[25] E. E. Schattschneider, *The Semisovereign People* (New York: Holt, Rinehart & Winston, 1960), and *Party Government* (New York: Holt, Rinehart & Winston, 1942).
[26] Milbrath, *op. cit.*, p. 39.

TABLE 5-3

Relation of Perceived Closeness of Election and Intensity
of Partisan Preference to Voting Turnout, 1956

	ELECTION PERCEIVED TO BE					
	ONE SIDED			CLOSE		
	INTENSITY OF PREFERENCE			INTENSITY OF PREFERENCE		
	WEAK	MEDIUM	STRONG	WEAK	MEDIUM	STRONG
Voted	70%	71%	73%	71%	79%	89%
Did not vote	30	29	27	29	21	11
	100%	100%	100%	100%	100%	100%
NUMBER OF CASES	130	170	88	301	360	226

Source: Angus Campbell et al., The American Voter (New York: John Wiley & Sons, 1960), p. 99.

individual consideration are social class, demographic characteristics, and group memberships, including family background. Although there are tendencies for participation rates to be higher among certain social groupings than others, participation patterns are not monopolized by a single political elite.

Social Class. The notion of social class is common in political analysis, but usage varies considerably. For Professor Robert Lane "class status" is indicated by "objective criteria (such as income, occupation, and education), plus a network of social relations, plus a person's conception of his own place in society"; we adopt this definition. Generally lower-class status is associated with reduced political participation, while "it has long been known that political participation in the United States increases with increasing status." [27] There are several factors accounting for variations in participation between classes: differences between persons in the amount of leisure time available for participation, their awareness of the stakes involved, the extent to which differing group expectations emphasize political action, and different skills acquired for reflecting about abstract and remote political matters. In each case the opportunities for political activity are greater for upper- and middle-class Americans.

Education. It is useful to consider the relation between participation and the objective criteria that aids in determining class status. For example: education tends to promote a sense of political awareness, civic obligation, and a faith in one's ability to affect government decisions. It also increases the likelihood of exposure to political information, which

[27] Lane, op. cit., pp. 220–21.

provides added stimulus to vote. Table 5-4 illustrates the relation between educational levels and voter turnout. Note in particular that college graduates vote in consistently greater proportions than do those with only high school diplomas. This fact from tabular data was reinforced by turnout figures in 1964 when more than 80 per cent of persons 21 years old and over who had completed one or more years of college voted in the presidential election, contrasted with 69 per cent of *all* persons 21 years old and over, and only 51 per cent of citizens with less than an eighth grade education.

TABLE 5-4

Relation of Education Levels to Voter Participation in Presidential Elections, 1948–1960

| | PER CENT VOTING IN ELECTION YEAR | | | |
EDUCATION LEVEL	1948	1952	1956	1960
Grade School	55	62	60	67
High School	67	80	74	81
College	79	90	90	90

Source: Based upon data released by the Survey Research Center, University of Michigan. See *Voting Research and the Businessman in Politics* (Ann Arbor, Michigan: Foundation or Research on Human Behavior, 1960), p. 33; and Fred I. Greenstein, *The American Party System and the American People* (Englewood Cliffs, N.J.: Prentice-Hall, 1963), p. 19.

Occupation. Occupational status is directly associated with aggregate increases in participation. The likelihood of political activity is highest among the professionally employed and managerial, business, and technically skilled occupations. The consistency of these relative differences is illustrated by Figure 5-2.

Income. Income, usually a function of occupation, also is linked to participation rates. Those with higher earnings tend to vote, publicize favorite candidates with lapel buttons and bumper stickers, and contribute to campaign financing in greater proportions than those of low and moderate means. In his survey of research on American participation, Lester Milbrath reports that only those earning seventy-five hundred dollars or more per year are likely to work in party organizations or political clubs. However, as we move from lower- to higher-income groupings, there is not a proportionate increase in voter participation; "for each thousand-dollar increment in income, the absolute increase and the rate of increase in turnout declined." [28] Consequently, both education

[28] Milbrath, *op. cit.,* pp. 120–21.

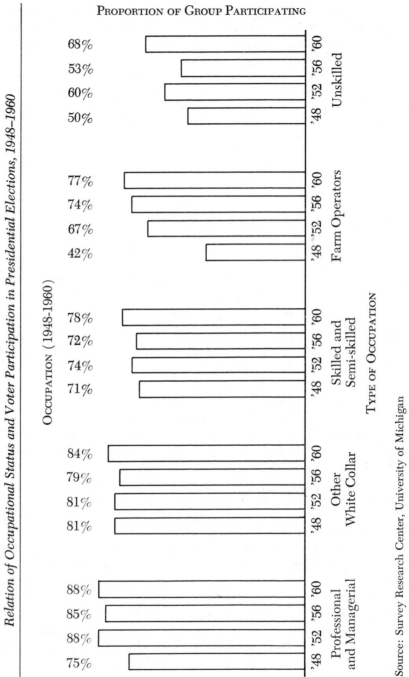

FIGURE 5–2

Relation of Occupational Status and Voter Participation in Presidential Elections, 1948–1960

PROPORTION OF GROUP PARTICIPATING

OCCUPATION (1948-1960)

TYPE OF OCCUPATION

Unskilled

68%
53%
60%
50%

Farm Operators

77%
74%
67%
42%

Skilled and Semi-skilled

78%
72%
74%
71%

Other White Collar

84%
79%
81%
81%

Professional and Managerial

88%
85%
88%
75%

'60 '56 '52 '48

Source: Survey Research Center, University of Michigan

and occupation are somewhat better indicators of the association between social class and voter participation than relative income.

Socio-Demographic Considerations. Aside from demographic factors linked to social class, there are those of age, sex, ethnic background, religion, and residence associated with the variable frequency of political activity.

Age. Among various age groupings voting rates have been higher for persons in the thirty to fifty-five age bracket than for those just entering the voting population or for the elderly. Young adults (particularly those unmarried) and the less prosperous elderly tend to vote in relatively fewer numbers than the middle-aged, apparently because the latter perceive a greater material stake in election outcomes. Youth from minority groupings try to use politics as a means of personal and social advancement and participate with somewhat higher frequency. On the whole, participation increases with maturity through the mid-forties and fifties, then tapers off markedly.

Sex. If women voted with the frequency and consistency of men, their total vote could outnumber males, given the approximate fifty-two to forty-eight predominance of women in the adult population. This, however, has never been the case; in presidential elections since 1948, for example, the turnout rate of men exceeded that of women by 5 to 13 per cent. Males have averaged 10 per cent greater voting participation over that period. We will explore some of the reasons for this difference in Chapters Six and Eight. Although men tend to participate more frequently and in a greater variety of ways, participation rates among women are increasing. Moreover, as Table 5-5 indicates, participation rates for men and women tend to converge as the educational level of the latter increases.

Ethnicity. Differences in participation among members of ethnic groupings, especially among Negroes, is closely associated with the relatively low social standing of many ethnic minorities. Rates of Negro activity are much lower than for Whites; from 1948–56 little more than one-third of Negroes voted in presidential elections. Efforts of Negro groups to rectify this have had noticeable effects, and one-half to two-thirds of Negroes surveyed in 1960 and 1964 had voted in contrast with voting rates of approximately 75 per cent for Whites. In the case of the Southern Negro there appears to be a moderate association between the enthusiasm of Negro organizations and the rate of voter registration; political organizations have stimulated a rising sense of political competence among Negroes. Levels of Negro participation in the South are affected somewhat by the percentage of Negroes living in a given locale; as Negro concentration increases, the intransigence of controlling interests also in-

TABLE 5-5

*Relation of Education to Level
of Political Participation, by Sex*

| | LEVEL OF EDUCATION | | | | | |
| | GRADE SCHOOL | | HIGH SCHOOL | | COLLEGE | |
MODE OF PARTICIPATION	M	F	M	F	M	F
Voted and participated in one of the following: attempted to influence through discussion, supported campaign financially, attended political meetings or rallies, belonged to political club, wore a campaign button or used campaign sticker, or did other work for party or candidate.	30%	11%	37%	23%	50%	41%
Only Voted	40	41	43	48	41	47
Failed to vote but participated in some other fashion as above.	4	4	5	5	5	6
No participation of any variety	26	44	15	24	4	6
	100%	100%	100%	100%	100%	100%
NUMBER OF CASES	253	289	353	531	177	153

Source: Adapted from V. O. Key, Jr., *Public Opinion and American Democracy* (New York: Alfred A Knopf, 1961), p. 331 from data of the Survey Research Center, University of Michigan, 1956.

creases, and steps frequently have been taken to decrease registration rates.[29]

Religion. As is the case with ethnicity, it is difficult to assess the independent influence of religious affiliation upon participation. Both are closely linked to other class and status factors. Generally, Protestants have lowest participation rates (with Episcopalians and Presbyterians slightly more active than Baptists), Catholics are more frequent participants, and Jews are the most active. The percentage of each grouping that voted in the presidential election of 1964, for example, was 62, 71,

[29] See Donald R. Matthews and James W. Prothro, "Social and Economic Factors and Negro Voter Registration in the South," *The American Political Science Review*, LVII, No. 1 (March, 1963), 38–39.

and 81 per cent respectively. Professor Milbrath has suggested that such differences are partly attributable to greater cohesion among the more active religious denominations and that politics may be used by them as a means of forestalling discrimination.[30] There is also evidence that regularity of church attendance is roughly associated with voting; that is, regular attenders are more likely to vote. In the South there is some relation between Negro registration rates and the religious affiliations of the White majority; "the larger the proportion of Roman Catholics in a county, the higher the rate of Negro registration regardless of what other factors are controlled." [31] This does not, however, mean that any single religion is the vehicle of the Negro registration rate.

Residence and Region. Political participation tends to increase in more industrial, commercialized areas; but again the character of residential surroundings is closely tied to those factors of social class, income, education and population groupings already mentioned. Generally, people residing in a rural setting have not displayed the frequency of political activity common to urban dwellers. Studies of voting behavior of rural residents suggest that voting turnout in rural areas fluctuates considerably more than in urban regions. For example: the Michigan Survey Research Center found that 43–46 per cent of rural residents surveyed in 1956 voted "in some past presidential elections, not in others," as contrasted with 39 per cent of urban dwellers who, once having become voters in presidential elections, were more inclined to participate regularly thereafter. The lower voting participation of rural persons is particularly highlighted in the South, where voter turnout for all social groupings is lower than in other regions.[32]

Group Memberships. A social factor of critical importance in shaping the varying pattern of political participation is the group-joining proclivities of the citizen. Superficially a willingness to join any group, no matter how nonpolitical its purposes, indicates a degree of participation to the extent that all group life consists of some internal conflict regulation. Beyond this, membership in face-to-face groups has other effects on participation.

A group of principal influence is the family. Children from politically attuned families tend to participate in politics more frequently once they grow older. The treatment of the child and the degree of parental attention and harmony contributes to the child's future political interest, his sense of political efficacy, his partisan loyalty, and his sense of civic obligation. If public affairs are ignored in the home or if their discussion

[30] Milbrath, *op. cit.*, p. 137.
[31] Matthews and Prothro, *op. cit.*, p. 42.
[32] Campbell, *et al., The American Voter*, pp. 404–8.

stimulates parental bickering, the child may prefer to avoid political matters that threaten his security.[33]

Group members with high political awareness, sensitivity, and activity are likely to expand their political participation outside the group. This is especially true of labor-union members. Their attention encompasses a broader range of political affairs than nonmembers, and they tend to be more firmly issue oriented. Joiners, such as union members, are more likely to participate in politics if they feel that group aims are relevant to their respective definitions of personal interest.

Finally, the degree of homogeneity within the group and the consistency of a citizen's group memberships are associated with the frequency of his participation. More diversified groups tend to have members with relatively little interest in politics, whereas homogeneity frequently breeds political activity. This is partially due to the fact that the unified group gives the participant a single cause to pursue. Moreover, it is generally the case that participation is higher for persons who experience no conflict between their multiple group memberships (no cross-pressuring) or between leading spokesmen within a single group to which they belong.

THE PERSONAL DIMENSION

In attaining provisional understanding of factors linked with participation patterns, it helps to take into account one other aspect — the meaning attributed by a person to political acts. Constitutional and social factors demarcate the boundaries within which a citizen views politics; his assessment necessarily governs a decision to act or remain passive.

Generally we can say that citizens undertake political activity if (1) they derive personal benefits of an economic, social, psychic, or intellectual nature; and (2) their sense of personal commitment, efficacy, and competence leads them to conclude that politics is a useful means of satisfying needs and wants.

The citizen's assessment of the significance of the election determines his interest in it. If he feels important decisions are being made, if the offices he is being asked to vote on are respected and regarded as powerful ones, or if the election is perceived as critical to his own interest or sense of community purpose, then he is more likely to participate. The longer a person lives in any community — national, state, local, organizational — the greater his sense of community identification. In a highly mobile society it appears that many Americans no longer put down roots very deeply; they fail to identify with state or local events, personalities, or issues. National politics, however, holds their interests; their national

[33] Lane, *op. cit.*, pp. 204–9.

community identity transcends their shift from residence to residence. Despite the myth of intense concern over what goes on in the courthouse or statehouse, few local elections generate excitement and drama. Moreover, the individual often feels he can do more with his vote in national elections than if he uses it in feeble protest against the "courthouse gang."

Many Americans see a direct link between politics and their economic interests; they are motivated toward participation in efforts to secure material gain. A vote may be viewed as a method of promoting tax reduction; a campaign contribution might be converted into favorable treatment in contract negotiations. And politics can be an instrument for improving the community economy, promoting social welfare, and achieving the "good life." By the same token, direct participation may be regarded as destructive to personal economic interests. Citizens frequently withdraw from political controversy for fear of losing jobs, driving off prospective clients, or alienating customers.

Political activity is often congenial to social interests. Through politics, citizens associate with particular groups to which they aspire, promote friendships with respected neighbors, and obtain the coveted admiration of others. Here again, however, a desire to fulfill social aspirations can depress political participation. Individuals shy away from political controversy that threatens rejection from social peers. They avoid political discussions because they fear social ostracism for expressing their true feelings. Married couples, for example, have been known to avoid voting in preference to casting contrary ballots.

Some Americans are politically active because they find it exhilarating. Politics can bolster the ego, yielding a feeling of importance at being in the center of things. There is a certain thrill attached to involvement in momentous decisions. Yet political activity requires a commitment to groups, persons, and causes; and many citizens find such involvement uncongenial to their private lives. Unwilling to endure political criticism, failure, and the pangs of impotence resulting from the defeat of dearly held causes, they withdraw into a world of neutral observation and contemplation.

The satisfaction of intellectual curiosity frequently serves as sufficient inducement to political activity. For many, both the promise of a better world and a better understanding of it stimulates participation. A sophisticated notion of how politics can contribute to personal and social betterment tends to promote politically relevant behavior. But there are also those who come away from political discussion, campaigning, and learning more confused and harassed than they wish.[34]

Politics, then, can be a means of relieving personal frustrations or pro-

[34] *Ibid.*, pp. 101–32.

moting anxieties. The assessment a citizen makes of politics contributes to his depth of emotional commitment (involvement), the value he attaches to his participation (efficacy), and what difference he thinks he can make by acting (competence). Research indicates that Americans possessing strong feelings of involvement, efficacy, and competence are more likely than others to hold political opinions and vote. Moreover, their sense of civic obligation is deeper, and they are less inclined toward political cynicism. A cynical response to politics — the feeling that it is useless to vote — renders participation unlikely.[35] Yet there are instances in which voting frustration is the trigger that stimulates citizens to partisan activity as a way of improving election options.

Finally, citizen-participants are normally persons who feel they are capable of dealing with all aspects of their social environment. Professor Milbrath observes, "They feel personally competent; they know themselves and feel confident of their knowledge and skills; their ego is strong enough to withstand blows; they are not burdened by a load of anxiety and internal conflict; they can control their impulses; they are astute, sociable, self-expressive, and responsible." [36] In short, they have taken to heart Socrates' classic dictum that "the unexamined life is not worth living." They have examined political life and set out to live it.

POLITICAL PARTICIPATION
AND LIBERAL DEMOCRACY

Interest conflict in America is revealed to policy-makers in the variety of ways citizens participate in politics. Although liberal-democratic theory prescribes a high level of direct, frequent, and personal participation as a necessary condition of human development in a democracy, Americans do not as yet measure up to the ideal. In this chapter we have tried to pinpoint a few of the features of our polity — constitutional and statutory provisions, the intensity of campaign conflict, socio-demographic characteristics, and personal motives — that seem to have a direct bearing on varying levels of participation.

What remains is the question of how variable patterns of political participation affect the overall process of conflict regulation. We have said that interest conflict has its source in the diverse activities of Americans pursuing incompatible goals. As a principal manifestation of that conflict, political participation is the crux of conflict representation.

[35] Morris Rosenberg, "Some Determinants of Political Apathy," *The Public Opinion Quarterly,* XVIII (Winter, 1954), 349–66; Robert E. Agger, Marshall N. Goldstein, and Stanley A. Pearl, "Political Cynicism: Measurement and Meaning," *The Journal of Politics,* XXIII, 477–506.
[36] Milbrath, *op. cit.,* p. 89.

So long as participation patterns are distorted by certain community features, those disputes that are transmitted for public regulation through the normal channels of representation tend to be those of highest relevance to regular citizen-participants. The upshot is that even in the absence of elitist domination of political activity, serious social tensions frequently are not revealed within the community until such time as they impinge upon the interests of citizens permitted, capable of, and willing to participate. And in such emerging social crises the concerns expressed to policy officials reflect the interests of citizens who can and do participate, not necessarily those most directly caught up in the crises.

A control over participation is one way (but not the sole method) of dominating interest struggles. Deciding who may participate and thereby controlling access to representative channels by statutory definitions of the franchise facilitates the selection of conflicts to be disclosed and interests heard. But that same control can contract representative channels and render them useless in the communication of conflict. In more recent disputes over civil rights and Viet Nam policy and in earlier struggles concerning slavery or labor-management relations, normal devices were insufficient for voicing grievances. Protests, demonstrations, strikes, picketing, boycotts, and other means of participation had to be used.

By political design, social chance, and personal choice the community possesses a host of potentially unrepresented citizens. A test of any polity's stability is its capacity to adjust to, or merely allay, pressing controversies. And a test of its democratic character lies in its willingness to disclose and tolerate differences through political participation. It can do so by removing discriminatory constitutional restrictions, supporting adequate living standards, and fostering the growth of creative and responsible citizens. In such a way it may maintain its pluralist character yet fashion a working consensus arrived at through citizen initiative rather than imposed without active sanction of the citizen-participant.

BIBLIOGRAPHICAL NOTE

There are two standard works describing in detail the ways Americans involve themselves in politics and the reasons for their doing so. The first, Lester W. Milbrath's paperback edition of *Political Participation* (Chicago: Rand McNally & Company, 1965) provides a compilation of the communications, personal, social, political, and constitutional factors associated with citizen participation; it also includes a useful, annotated listing of basic research reports on modes of participation. Milbrath seeks to integrate and update the research summarized in Robert E. Lane's *Political Life* (Glencoe, Ill.: The Free Press, 1959), which

PETH

remains the best single source of current hypotheses concerning the actions and motives of political man. For purposes of comparing American participation patterns with those of other polities, *The Civic Culture* (Boston: Little, Brown and Company, 1965), by Gabriel A. Almond and Sidney Verba, is an indispensable report of research conducted in five nations at varying stages of democratic development. For a general description of the ways Americans participate in politics, relying less upon reports of individual researchers, see Howard Penniman, *The American Political Process* (Princeton, New Jersey: D. Van Nostrand Company, Inc., 1962).

The significance of unfettered participation in the democratic polity is described and interpreted in the following: Henry B. Mayo *An Introduction to Democratic Theory* (New York: Oxford University Press, 1960); Anthony Downs, *An Economic Theory of Democracy* (New York: Harper & Row, Publishers, 1957); and Robert A. Dahl, *A Preface to Democratic Theory* (Chicago: The University of Chicago Press, Phoenix Books, 1963). The reader will find Alan P. Grimes, *Equality in America* (New York: Oxford University Press, 1964) a handy guide to current legislative and judicial policies expanding the universe of potential political participants. The relationship of political participation to fulfillment of basic human needs is discussed in James C. Davies, *Human Nature in Politics* (New York: John Wiley and Sons, Inc., 1963).

For each mode of political participation discussed in Chapter Five, and the personal, social, and politico-constitutional factors associated with its patterning, a variety of publications are available. Those interested, for example, in the degree and variety of opinion participation should note Gabriel A. Almond, *The American People and Foreign Policy* (New York: Frederick A. Praeger Paperbacks, 1960), Samuel A. Stouffer, *Communism, Conformity, and Civil Liberties* (New York: John Wiley & Sons, Inc., Science Editions, 1966), and Robert E. Lane and David O. Sears, *Public Opinion* (Englewood Cliffs, N.J.: Prentice-Hall, Inc., 1964). An excellent discussion of leadership at the personal level is Elihu Katz and Paul F. Lazarsfeld, *Personal Influence* (New York: The Free Press of Glencoe, Paperback Edition, 1964). For works describing partisan and voluntary participation respectively, consult the bibliographic notes to Chapters Nine and Ten.

For an introduction to the research concerning voter participation the reader should consult the abridged edition of *The American Voter* (New York: John Wiley & Sons, Inc., 1964) by Angus Campbell, Philip E. Converse, Warren E. Miller, and Donald E. Stokes. Also useful is Hugh A. Bone and Austin Ranney, *Politics and Voters* (New York: McGraw-Hill Book Company, Inc., 1963), as well as selections from Edward C. Dreyer and Walter A. Rosenbaum, *Political Opinion and Electoral Behavior* (Belmont, California: Wadsworth Publishing Company, 1966) and Joseph R. Fiszman, *The American Political Arena*, 2nd edition (Boston: Little, Brown and Company, 1966). Factors impinging on voter turnout are inventoried by both Lane and Milbrath cited above. In addition, more specialized treatments of personal factors can be found in Hadley Cantril, *The Pattern of Human Concerns* (New Brunswick, New Jersey: Rutgers University Press, 1965); Murray B. Levin, *The Alienated Voter* (New York: Holt, Rinehart and Winston, Inc., 1960); Robert E. Lane, *Political Ideology* (New York: The Free Press of Glencoe, 1962); and Maurice Stein, *et al.*, *Identity and Anxiety* (New York: The Free Press of Glencoe, 1960). Social factors are discussed in William Peterson (ed.), *American Social*

Patterns (Garden City, New York: Doubleday & Company, Inc., 1956); Bernard Berelson, *Voting: A Study of Opinion Formation* (Chicago: The University of Chicago Press, Phoenix Edition, 1966); and Samuel Lubell, *The Future of American Politics* (Garden City, New York: Doubleday & Company, 1956). For a discussion of political and constitutional factors associated with voting participation, in addition to those discussed in *The American Voter,* consult Henry M. Bain and Donald S. Hecock, *Ballot Position and Voter's Choice* (Detroit, Mich.: Wayne State University Press, 1960).

CHAPTER
SIX

Political Opinion

We noted in discussing political participation that Americans are quicker to hold politically relevant opinions than engage in any other single political activity. Few questions have generated such universal speculation among philosophers and politicians alike as those concerned with the proper role of public opinion in government. Controversy persists among both thinkers and practitioners over whether there can be "government by public opinion." Democratic optimists praise the potential for popular rule; skeptics view the notion as illusory or decry the evils of mobocracy. In recent years scholarly concern has focused on the task of clarifying the nature of public opinion, its formation, and distribution. In the following pages we examine the relationship between public opinion and conflict representation in pluralist America. We explore the character of American opinion, community influences on the formation of politically relevant attitudes, and how the American opinion process represents and generates conflict and consensus in our liberal-democratic community.

138

THE POLITICAL OPINION PROCESS

POLITICAL ATTITUDES, OPINIONS, AND COMMUNICATION

Public opinion has been defined in a variety of ways. One view refers to a group of people confronted by an issue, divided in their ideas, and engaged in open discussion.[1] Another asserts that public opinion consists of "speculative views held by the masses of the people as to alteration or improvement of their institutions." [2] Yet another regards public opinion as more than a mere aggregate of individual judgments; rather, as an "organization" of sentiments produced by communication and reciprocal influence.[3] In formulating our definition it helps to distinguish between attitudes, interests, and opinions. We can then more easily explore the nature of political opinion, as contrasted with public opinion, and define the boundaries of the opinion process, its function in a liberal democracy, and its principal participants.

In an early account of the nature of public opinion, George Carslake Thompson distinguished between three classes of personal views "according to their definiteness with regard to practical action." The first he labeled a "general preference," to refer to any vague personal sentiment concerning individual desires. A second level he called "a wish for a particular end or course of action," to speak of preferences for more specific personal goals. Finally, he wrote of "a belief as to the best practical means for achieving those particular ends which are desires" — views about specific policies designed to advance goals originating in vague desires but now focused on concrete ends.[4]

These three levels of preference correspond to personal attitudes, interests, and opinions. We conceive of attitudes as long-term predispositions, vague in content and diffuse in structure, concerning matters of a general, abstract, and inclusive nature. They are acquired gradually throughout life and are fairly stable and enduring. A feeling of pride for America, anxieties over possibilities of war, a concern for personal health, a yearning for a better way of life — all are personal attitudes of potential political significance. Attitudes are "that broad, and necessarily im-

---

[1] Herbert Blummer, "The Mass, the Public, and Public Opinion," in Bernard Berelson and Morris Janowitz (eds.), *Reader in Public Opinion and Communication* (Rev. ed.; New York: The Free Press, 1966), pp. 43–50.

[2] A. V. Dicey, "The Relation between Law and Public Opinion," in Bernard Berelson and Morris Janowitz (eds.), *Reader in Public Opinion and Communication* (Glencoe, Ill.: The Free Press, 1950), p. 118.

[3] Charles H. Cooley, *Social Organization* (New York: Charles Scribners, 1910), p. 121.

[4] George Carslake Thompson, *Public Opinion and Lord Beaconsfield* (New York: Macmillan Co., 1886), pp. 22–27.

precise, combination of psychological factors within a person that in part determine how that person shall react to any given situation." [5]

Our personal attitudes constitute mental images of what each of us deems desirable or undesirable. As vital components of our perspectives on life, they define our needs and wants relative to those of others in society. When such general preferences direct us toward active pursuit of fairly specific goals, we are said to possess interests. For example: if our yearning for a higher standard of living disposes us to seek a college education, we have, in Thompson's phrase, "a wish for a particular course of action" beyond mere predispositions. As we noted in Chapter One, disputes between interests constitute the bulk of social conflict regulated by political means.

Finally, when in response to a given situation we sharpen and express our preferences "as to the best practical means for achieving those particular ends which are desired," we have opinions. To illustrate: suppose that while pursuing our goal of a college education in conjunction with our concern for a higher living standard, our view on the merit of federally financed scholarships is solicited. Our reply will take the form of a short-term preference on a matter specific, topical, and immediate in impact. Emanating as they do from an "arousal of pre-existing, related attitudes," [6] opinions are expressions (verbal, written, or gestural) of attitudes that have been sharpened under the influence of concrete stimuli; their character is a function of the reciprocal impact of our personal predispositions and the external conditions we perceive as relevant to our interests.

In this context we can define public opinion as the distribution of individual opinions about public matters; that is, all issues which have, or could have, consequences affecting the entire community. This broad usage, however, does not help us to distinguish between curbstone thoughts about the proper marital status of movie stars and opinions regarding favorites in a race for the American Presidency. Consequently, rather than employ the broad concept of public opinion, it is preferable to confine our discussion to those opinions especially relevant to the affairs of the political community. By *political opinion,* then, we refer to the distribution of sharpened and expressed personal attitudes in response to issues generated by social conflict of sufficient scope to stimulate regulatory activities affecting the entire community.[7] The opinion process

[5] Terence H. Qualter, *Propaganda and Psychological Warfare* (New York: Random House, 1962), pp. 11–12; Bernard Berelson and Gary A. Steiner, *Human Behavior* (New York: Harcourt, Brace & World, 1964), p. 558.

[6] L. W. Doob, *Propaganda, Its Psychology and Techniques* (New York: Henry Holt and Co., 1935), pp. 29–35.

[7] See also V. O. Key, Jr., *Public Opinion and American Democracy* (New York:

serves as a principal mode of political participation linking personal attitudes and public policy. It fosters a mutual exchange between citizens and officials that is critical to political communication in a democracy.

We stressed earlier that a democratic community takes the legitimacy of open conflict for granted as a proper means for exposing error, stimulating change, and contributing to human perfectability. Peaceful accommodation of these disagreements is facilitated by political dialogue in at least two ways. First, open debate exposes acquired predispositions to both public and self-scrutiny, thus facilitating self-clarification and self-knowledge, prerequisites for the development of free intelligence in a liberal democracy. Secondly, an unfettered exchange of views is designed to assure all citizen-participants that their interests receive a fair and impartial hearing. Open consultation promotes a spirit of compromise if, through discussion, people can modify their demands and agree to partial, not total, satisfaction of desires. In this fashion the opinion process is a principal vehicle in our pluralist community for adjusting as well as representing social disputes and molding the community consensus. In his study of American consensus, for example, Herbert McClosky notes that one of the reasons that support for liberal democratic values is stronger among the more politically active citizens than the general electorate is that activists, through the communications process, are "unavoidably exposed to the liberal democratic values which form the main current of our political heritage" and, as a result, are united "more firmly behind the values of the American tradition." [8]

This view of the opinion process as one of open political communication directs our attention to its specific participants. Here we are interested in the holders of opinions who express views on community matters and how their politically relevant attitudes are acquired. In the following chapter we will be concerned with leaders and channels of opinion.

CONFIGURATIONS OF AMERICAN OPINION

In America we encounter three modes of opinion expression: opinion consensus, opinion clusters, and opinion groupings. Although there is considerable overlap, each has its distinctive features. From previous discussion we recall that consensus consists of widely shared convictions concerning the legitimacy of the political community, its fundamental

---

Alfred A. Knopf, 1961), p. 14, which holds that public opinion refers to "those opinions held by private persons which governments find it prudent to heed"; and Bernard C. Hennessy's distinction between public opinion and "effective" opinion, and the distortions occurring in the former: *Public Opinion* (Belmont, Cal.: Wadsworth Publishing Co., 1965), pp. 30–31, 122.

[8] Herbert McClosky, "Consensus and Ideology in American Politics," *The American Political Science Review*, LVIII, No. 2 (June, 1964) 375.

values, procedures, leaders, or policies. From research findings we learned that Americans agree upon few specific ideals, and those few exist either as vaguely defined concepts ("justice," "liberty") or as products of habitual compliance with constitutional rules of the game. However, leaders frequently act as if consensus did exist and employ the term "public opinion" as evidence of this broad agreement in justifying more narrow interest behavior.

Where controversy persists, we can anticipate opposing clusters of individual opinions on specific political questions. The common pattern of opinion-clustering consists of expressions on each of two sides of an issue, but there may be as many clusters as there are possible stances on an issue. For example, one of the continuing issues in President John F. Kennedy's Administration was his foreign policy toward Cuba. When asked whether they were satisfied with the handling of the Cuban situation in early 1963, 52 per cent of a cross-section of Americans expressed approval, 33 per cent disapproval, and 15 per cent had "no opinion." [9] Such a two-sided clustering (excluding those with no opinions) is likely to develop as debate progresses, as positions harden, and as the alternative courses of action are pared down. Controversies involving three or more policy options stimulate a greater number of opinion clusters. When asked on March 4, 1964 whether they thought the Johnson Administration was "pushing integration too fast, or not fast enough," Americans sampled answered as follows: 30 per cent thought "too fast," 15 per cent thought "not fast enough," 39 per cent thought the pace "about right," and 16 per cent had "no opinion." [10] V. O. Key, Jr., has suggested that these "multimodal" distributions (as opposed to two-sided or "bimodal" alignments) are more likely among highly informed persons than in the community at large where most questions elicit a "pro" or "con" response. [11]

Opinion clusters reflect patterns of individual opinions without reference to the group affiliations or social characteristics of persons involved. In contrast, opinion groupings are patterns associated with stands taken by organized groups or with identifiable segments of the population. Some theorists have urged that all political opinions are the weighted products of group stands rather than the sum of individual preferences. Both James Madison's account of factions and John C. Calhoun's view of concurrent majorities expressed the notion that community opinion springs primarily from the interaction of group interests. Certainly groups enter the opinion process at all points, but certain

[9] Hazel Gaudet Erskine, "The Polls: Kennedy as President," *The Public Opinion Quarterly*, XXVIII, No. 2 (Summer, 1964), 338.
[10] *Ibid.*, p. 340.
[11] Key, *op. cit.*, pp. 53–60.

qualifications are pertinent to their role. First, group stands are products of bargaining within the group situation as leaders strive for internal harmony before contending with other interests. Secondly, when group cohesion disintegrates, intragroup cleavages and inter-factional alliances between dissidents of formerly opposing groups frequently form. Hence, organized opinion sometimes fails to reveal factional or coalitional views. Finally, although many individual opinions correlate with group stands, there are countless instances when individual preferences fail to conform to group positions. We return to a detailed discussion of organized groups in Chapter Ten.

The other variety of opinion groupings involves patterns unique to identifiable segments of the population. These include groupings in geographical sections (South, West, etc.); persons divided by residential areas (urban, suburban, and rural alignments); social-class groupings (upper, middle, working classes, etc.); religious categories (Baptists, Catholics, etc.); and ethnic groupings (Negroes, Puerto Ricans, etc.). Potentially there are as many such opinion groupings as there are segments of the American population. In actuality, however, the congruence between opinion distributions and social groupings is never a perfect one; for example, not all urban consumers agree that farm subsidies should be abandoned, nor do all farmers agree that such payments are desirable. As in the case of organized stands, intra-group conflict and inter-group consensus render it hazardous to generalize about the predominant opinion of a given social grouping. This will become more apparent in our discussion of voting opinions in Chapter Eight.

PROPERTIES OF AMERICAN OPINION

Political opinions vary considerably in basic properties; for example, in direction, intensity, concentration, stability, and saliency. Direction simply refers to whether an opinion on an issue is favorable, unfavorable, or qualified. To illustrate: some Americans in 1966 favored unconditional bombing of industrial centers in North Viet Nam; others preferred immediate cessation to all aerial bombardment; a third cluster desired bomb attacks, but only to produce negotiations for a settlement of the conflict.

The direction of a person's opinion is frequently influenced more by his personality needs, partisan affiliation, or cultural background than subtleties of the issue in question; that is, "there are tendencies to give mostly pro or mostly con answers regardless of the content of the question." [12] A well-adjusted person, for example, seems more likely to react to novel ideas without hostility, to be a "yeasayer." Moreover, Lester

[12] Robert E. Lane and David O. Sears, *Public Opinion* (Englewood Cliffs, N.J.: Prentice-Hall, 1964), p. 7.

Milbrath found that under certain conditions, Democrats are slightly more prone than Republicans to react positively to assorted cues.[13] Finally, Americans as a people tend to respond more positively to issues independently of content than is the case in other cultures. In any event, we can say generally that the more evenly matched "pro" and "con" opinion clusters are, approaching a fifty-fifty split, the more intense the conflict situation will be regardless of reaction proclivities of citizens. Qualified expressions, suggest Professors Lane and Sears, are more likely to come from educated persons, those with relatively little intensity of feeling upon issues, and individuals giving oral rather than written responses to questions.

Intensity denotes the resolve with which citizens hold opinions. For example: some cling passionately to stated views, and virtually no degree of persuasion can shake their stand; slogans such as "Better Dead than Red" reflect this intensity. Others feel strongly about few issues and are either fickle or open-minded; their opinions are subject to change in the course of political debate. In general Americans hold intensely opinions on matters touching the public morality of political leaders, events threatening the security of the homeland (such as the attack on Pearl Harbor in 1941), or actions perceived as a threat to long-term policy traditions (such as occasional proposals that the United States extend diplomatic recognition to Communist China). Less emotionally charged and more routine policy questions, such as the annual request of the President to Congress to raise the legal limit on the national debt, stir intense feelings among relatively few Americans.

Concentration refers to the distribution of complementary opinions within a single sector of the population rather than throughout all segments of the community. We have already noted, for example, that democratic ideals are more widely supported among political activists than other groupings. Frequently shifts in public policy owe their origins to the fact that highly intense views on a question of social importance are concentrated in a minority, then spread to other groupings in the community. Intense minorities, for example, helped to provoke sit-ins, protest marches, and other demonstrations in the 1950's and 1960's that eventually led to civil rights legislation.

When we say that opinions are stable we mean that both the distribution and intensity of opposing views are fairly constant. The distribution of partisan loyalties among Americans, for example, has remained remarkably stable in recent decades. So long as the bulk of political

---

[13] Lester W. Milbrath, "Latent Origins of Liberalism-Conservatism and Party Identification: A Research Note," *The Journal of Politics*, XXIV, No. 4 (November, 1962), 679–88.

opinions is stable, the opportunities for political leaders to capitalize on major opinion shifts are minimized. V. O. Key, Jr., asserted that, "Irresponsible centers of leadership enjoy their greatest opportunities under circumstances of fluid opinion." "A policy most urgent in the national interest, unless it rests on stable opinion, may be scuttled because those who seek individual or group advantage can manipulate a fluid opinion or an opinion not grounded in firmly fixed beliefs or standards." [14] The degree of opinion stability, of course, depends upon the degree that persons will shift their preferences because of either changes in their long-term attitudes or in the conditions impinging upon their lives. We shall consider this aspect of opinion stability and change in Chapter Eight when we discuss shifts of electoral choices in political campaigns.

Finally, citizens are more apt to express political opinions when the issues involved are salient to them; that is, when the issues concern matters that people find personally meaningful. Thus, whether an issue arouses salient responses or not depends in part on what concerns people in America. In studying American political opinions, Hadley Cantril sought to discover "the concerns of the American people for themselves and for America." His national sample indicated that health, living standards, children, housing, and happiness are principal concerns Americans have about their own lives, while questions of peace and war are focal points of their concern for the community.[15] These areas, then, are likely to be particularly salient in generating political opinions, and Americans are likely to be relatively more informed about public issues in these areas. Partial confirmation of this expectation is revealed in Table 6-1, although it is interesting to note that no politically related issue was as familiar to Americans as the nonpolitical question of the length of women's skirts.

We can better understand opinion distributions and properties by generalizing about the pattern *normally* approximated in conflict representation. Let us assume, for example, that Americans are asked to answer the following question: "In general, how do you feel about foreign aid — are you for or against it?" First, there will be few Americans (12 per cent when such a question was asked in a national survey in 1963) [16] with no response to the question, the "no opinions" or *nonparticipants*. This leaves two sets of Americans who do possess opinions. The first is composed of citizens (frequently a majority) who hold an opinion but

---

[14] Key, *op. cit.*, p. 261.

[15] Hadley Cantril, *The Pattern of Human Concerns* (New Brunswick, N.J.: Rutgers University Press, 1965), pp. 34–44.

[16] Hazel Gaudet Erskine, "The Polls: Some Gauges of Conservatism," *The Public Opinion Quarterly*, XXVIII, No. 1 (Spring, 1964), 168.

TABLE 6-1

Exposure of Americans to Selected Community Topics

ISSUE	PERCENTAGE OF NATIONAL SAMPLE WHO HAD HEARD OR READ ANYTHING ABOUT THE ISSUE
War Related:	
Civil War in China (1948)	70%
Civil War in China (1949)	76
Trouble in Formosa Straits (1955)	77
War in Indochina (1953)	71
Crisis in Berlin (1959)	78
Crisis in Berlin (1961)	
July	76
September	89
Miscellaneous Foreign Relations:	
The Marshall Plan (1947)	64
Truman's Point Four (1950)	23
Foreign Aid Bill (1958)	51
The Peace Corps (1962)	71
European Common Market (1961)	22
Foreign Trade Proposals:	
1948	32
1953	32
1954	45
1955	52
1959	37
1962	52
Domestic Questions:	
House Un-American Activities Committee (1949)	64
Hoover Commission Reports on Governmental Reorganization (1949)	41
Corruption in Washington (1952)	86
Tidelands Oil (1953)	39
Dixon-Yates Controversy (1954)	37
Taft Hartley Labor Law:	
1947	61
1948	72
1949	83
1950	79
1952	74
Truman's Seizure of Steel Industry (1952)	82
Kennedy Plan for Medical Care to Aged (1962)	81
Water Fluoridation:	
1952	56
1953	68
Discovery of Polio Vaccine (1954)	90
Length of Women's Skirts (1947)	92
Flying Saucers (1950)	94

Source: Hazel Gaudet Erskine, "The Polls: Exposure to Domestic Information," *The Public Opinion Quarterly*, XXVII, No. 3 (Fall, 1963), 491–500, and "The Polls: Exposure to International Information," *The Public Opinion Quarterly*, XXVII, No. 4 (Winter, 1963), 658–62.

are largely indifferent about the outcome of the matter. The views of this *indifferent majority* are likely to be uninformed, of low intensity, unstable, diffuse, and stimulated by an issue of low salience to them. There will be another set of opinion-holders who take the issue more seriously. This *informed minority* consists of two types. A particularly intense group will give a definite affirmative or negative response; namely, "Yes, foreign aid is a good thing, and I am writing my congressman to say so," or "No, foreign aid should be abandoned, and I am a member of 'America First, Last, and Always,' a group sworn to end it." The preferences of this intense set of "yeasayers" and "naysayers" are likely to be passionate, informed, stable, concentrated, and salient. Yet there will also be those with less passionate resolve who qualify their replies; they might respond: "I favor foreign aid, but only so long as the money benefits the people of a nation rather than its rulers," or "I oppose foreign aid generally, but I'm willing to see it extended to those nations supporting our foreign policy." This qualified minority, by reaching a definite viewpoint at the time of decision, frequently plays a significant role as the conflict develops.

THE GENERATION OF POLITICAL OPINION PATTERNS

To understand how opinions are generated in the American community we must look at two overlapping phases of the process. First, since opinions are basically expressions of sharpened personal attitudes, we need to know more about how attitudes are acquired, including the functions attitudes perform for individuals and the agencies from which citizens learn politically relevant predispositions. Secondly, we must investigate how these vague preferences are focused into more precise opinions, the opinion-forming phase. In exploring these aspects of the opinion process, we see that the same sets of community forces shaping configurations of political participation — human personality, social environment, and political controversy — mold opinion patterns as well.

PERSONAL ATTITUDES: THE BASES OF POLITICAL OPINIONS

The relative lack of political involvement and knowledge among Americans is disquieting to anyone who feels that democratic viability depends upon an informed citizenry. The fact remains that opinion participation is a widespread, even if not informed, method of making social conflicts known to policy officials. That American opinions are not always anchored in evidence is one thing; that they are grounded in deep-seated and politically relevant attitudes is another.

Professor Daniel Katz points to four significant functions that personal attitudes perform for individuals possessing them: (1) the instrumental, adjustive, or utilitarian; (2) the ego-defensive; (3) the value-expressive; and (4) the knowledge function.[17] The first function, by helping an individual to mediate between his inner desires and conflicts and the demands of the outer world, facilitates his adjustment to physical and social surroundings. As stated in Chapter One, in striving for satisfaction of his needs and wants, an individual is frequently frustrated by the counter-desires of others. In the process he tends to acquire positive attitudes toward the features of his immediate environment that assist him in fulfilling his desires and negative sentiments regarding perceived obstacles. When compelled to choose between conflicting desires and manifold pressures impinging upon him, his acquired attitudes frequently aid him in ordering his preferences and deciding upon a course of action. In short, personal attitudes aid him in articulating his interests and expressing relevant opinions. This is true, for example, of a citizen's partisan sentiments, a particularly important cluster of attitudes influencing American elections. By viewing events as Republicans or Democrats, many Americans are able to reconcile the advice of their personal friends, opposing candidates, news editorials, reference groups, and miscellaneous campaign propagandists in reaching difficult voting decisions.

Attitudes also act as a buffer between the individual and an unfriendly world. In performing the ego-defensive function, attitudes serve as mechanisms by which we defend ourselves against hostile criticism and rationalize our pursuit of interests, particularly those not generally having social sanction. One of the frequent reasons for a lack of political information among Americans is that many citizens shun evidence about political realities that runs counter to their fundamental sentiments and beliefs. Although not able to justify a political opinion on the basis of evidence, uninformed or misinformed opinion participants persist in doing so as a matter of self-defense.

Linked to the defense of ego is the value-expressive function — an expression of inner-most beliefs and yearnings. This kind of attitude is more than a protective device; it assists a person in "establishing his self-identity and confirming his notion of the sort of person he sees himself to be." [18]

Finally, in performing the knowledge function, attitudes aid individuals in understanding experienced reality by providing guidelines for

[17] Daniel Katz, "The Functional Approach to the Study of Attitudes," *The Public Opinion Quarterly*, XXIV (Summer, 1960), pp. 163–76. See also Avery Leiserson, "Notes on the Theory of Political Opinion Formation," *The American Political Science Review*, XLVII, No. 1 (March, 1953), 171–77; M. Brewster Smith *et al.*, *Opinions and Personality* (New York: John Wiley & Sons, 1956).

[18] Katz, *op. cit.*, p. 172.

the organization of perceptions. For example, the doctrinaire Marxist committed to the view that the history of society is one of class struggle possesses a convenient frame within which he can fit and interpret information regarding famines, depressions, and wars. Everything can be interpreted as anchored in the economic dislocations of men regardless of its actual origins.

To the extent that attitudes perform a knowledge function for the individual, he may find it more convenient to cling to long-term predispositions in assessing reality in preference to acquiring additional information that threatens predilections. It is not surprising, therefore, that Americans hold political opinions supported more by vague attitudes than cold facts. Political information frequently implies shades of gray that render unqualified convictions unrealistic. At these times one feels more secure maintaining intense opinions than being caught up in intolerable ambiguities.[19] Political information may transmit more about harsh realities than the citizen cares to know; consequently, opinion holders are inclined to be influenced more by political symbols and slogans than discriminating data.

Thus, in assessing the personal functions of attitudes, we encounter a partial explanation for the degree of political ignorance in the formation of opinions. Variable political knowledge is not simply a result of differing life chances associated with social class, age, education, sex, residence, etc. People choose to be ignorant about some matters and informed about others. They are likely to avoid information that threatens stable attitudes, is dramatically at odds with current political understanding, disrupts social camaraderie, interferes with the pursuit of personal ambitions, or muddies clear-cut alternatives with intolerable ambiguity. Small wonder, therefore, that "the attention of most people to most political communications . . . is marginal or peripheral," and the bulk of Americans manifest indifference.[20] Political attitudes outrank political information in the personal priorities of a large percentage of Americans; we shall see momentarily that the learning of such attitudes frequently precedes chronologically the acquisition of information as well.

POLITICIZATION: THE LEARNING
OF POLITICAL ATTITUDES

Since opinion formation in the polity is a product of the reciprocal influence of personal attitudes and political stimuli, knowing something about

[19] Else Frenkel-Brunswik, "Intolerance of Ambiguity as an Emotional and Personality Variable," *Journal of Personality*, XVIII (1949), 108–43.

[20] Lewis A. Dexter, "Marginal Attention, Pressure Politics, Political Campaigning, and Political Realities," *International Review of History and Political Science*, 1964, pp. 115–23; Robert E. Lane, *Political Life* (Glencoe, Ill.: The Free Press, 1959), pp. 101–32.

the way in which personal attitudes are acquired will help us to understand American political opinion. Political attitudes are acquired as we
make, or fail to make, personality adjustments; as we conform to social
norms and institutions; as products of an overarching influence of per-
petuated culture; and as we strive to satisfy physical and social requirements. They may even have origins in the inherited capacities of
individuals.[21] While human personality, society, culture, nature, and
biology doubtlessly are contributing forces, we confine our discussion to
politically relevant attitudes gained through the learning process. That
process we can call politicization.

Socialization has been defined as the "learning of social patterns cor-
responding to an individual's societal position as mediated through
various agencies of society." Within that context, political socialization
— what we call politicization — refers specifically to "the process of induc-
tion into the political culture." The "end product is a set of attitudes —
cognitions, value standards, and feelings — toward the political system,
its various roles, and role incumbents." [22]

As related to American government, we regard politicization as a learning process by which attitudes are acquired about our political community, its doctrinal values, structure of constitutional authority and
procedures, and officials. So conceived, American politicization produces
consensus and cleavage. On the one hand, children are inculcated with
attitudes of community loyalty through acculturation. Those convictions
normally transcend conflicting group identifications. By the same token,
children also acquire interest attachments that produce disagreement
with other community members. Therefore, an examination of patterns
of politicization should advance our understanding of how the underlying
tension between community and conflict is rendered manageable through
politics. First, let us illustrate the types of consensus-dissensus attitudes
that are acquired; then we shall examine in detail the important agencies
of American political socialization.

An excellent example of how community identification is learned appears in David Easton and Robert Hess's study of the "child's political
world." Through a survey of several hundred school children, they found
that Americans are imbued at a very early age with a positive faith in the
political community. Prior to their teens they invest the very word
"America" with emotional feeling; it tends to symbolize for them all that
is good, worthwhile, and trustworthy about their society. This early, in-

[21] Ashley Montague, *The Biosocial Nature of Man* (New York: Grove Press, 1956).
[22] See Orville G. Brim, Jr., "Socialization through the Life Cycle," *Items*, XVIII,
No. 1 (March, 1964), 1–5; Herbert Hyman, *Political Socialization* (Glencoe, Ill.: The
Free Press, 1959); Gabriel A. Almond and James S. Coleman, *The Politics of the
Developing Areas* (Princeton: Princeton University Press, 1960).

tensely forged link between child and community is an enduring one, eroded only infrequently by the frustrations and responsibilities of adult citizenship.[23]

We noted in Chapter Two that Americans traditionally have expressed ambivalent views regarding the merit of politics. This ambivalence is more characteristic of adults than children. David Easton and Jack Dennis reported from studying predominantly white, public-school children in large metropolitan areas that over 90 per cent had formulated a fairly clear idea of what the word "government" meant by the time they were in the eighth grade. Moreover, they found children generally support the notion that government can guide and care for people. For example: among children surveyed in grades three through eight in the Chicago area, 77–91 per cent expressed agreement with the statement, "The government usually knows what is best for people." Easton and Dennis concluded: "The child's early contentment with government is fairly complete, and it is one which exhibits the characteristics of a high acceptance of government as a given, necessary part of the natural environment. If the child is to develop discontent and a desire for change, it is undoubtedly yet to be learned. It thus will be overlaid upon an early base of high regard for the government." [24]

A learning of positive attitudes toward the political community and government is also paralleled by the acquisition of supportive sentiments toward certain community leaders, particularly the President. In a separate study complementing the one discussed above, Hess and Easton found that the President is consistently viewed by American children in positive terms, an appraisal that continues well into the later years of adolescence and even adulthood. They found, for example, that a substantial majority of respondents in grades two through eight viewed the President as a harder worker, more honest, more friendly, and more knowledgeable than most men. Moreover, children expressed beliefs that the President is a "good person," and 61 per cent of second-graders thought him the "best in the world." A similar study undertaken in New Haven, Connecticut revealed that children tended to be markedly more sympathetic and enthusiastic than adults in their response to political leaders.[25]

[23] David Easton and Robert D. Hess, "The Child's Political World," *Midwest Journal of Political Science,* VI (1962), 236–37.

[24] David Easton and Jack Dennis, "The Child's Image of Government," in Roberta Sigel (ed.), "Political Socialization: Its Role in the Political Process," *The Annals of the American Academy of Political and Social Science,* CCCLXI (September, 1965), 40–57.

[25] Robert D. Hess and David Easton, "The Child's Changing Image of the President," *The Public Opinion Quarterly,* XXIV (1960), 632–44; Fred I. Greenstein, "More on Children's Images of the President," *The Public Opinion Quarterly,* XXV

We observed earlier that the American system of public education places high priority upon citizenship training; courses are offered for purposes of instilling a sense of obligation and civic competence in students. Whether the message gets across solely in the classroom is uncertain, but evidence indicates that it is learned somewhere. For example: Gabriel Almond and Sidney Verba reported from a cross-cultural study that a majority of Americans (51 per cent) feel that "the ordinary man should be active in his local community" and that as the degree of formal education increases, the tendency to feel such obligation increases also. But they point out that civic ideals and civic behavior are not always in accord: fewer do participate than feel they should do so. Americans also learn a sense of civic competence to the extent that three out of four responded that they *believed* their influence could bring about a change in an "unjust" community-wide regulation.[26]

That not all groupings in America acquire similar attitudes of competence is revealed in studies of the learning of racial identification. At least as early as at the age of four, some children have acquired a recognition for racial differences along with a sense of the social and political consequences frequently linked to those differences. For example, Goodman quotes one child with an acute sensitivity for the implications of racial distinctions: "The people that are white, they can go up. The people that are brown, they have to go down." [27]

Put briefly, citizens learn respect for their political community, selected leaders, and perhaps their own political potential. That learning continues beyond childhood throughout the life cycle. Since "it is apparent that the socialization experienced by a person in childhood cannot prepare him for all the roles he will be expected to fill in later years," [28] we need to know more about the socializing agencies — "the actual or imagined set of people one uses as a model, usually those one wants to be approved by" [29] — that influence politicization at all stages. The general pattern is clear. The family sets politicization in motion. Then, as the child grows older, parental influence decreases. The family is gradually supplanted by a complex of forces that include schooling, membership in voluntary associations, social aspirations, religion, and aging. In some instances, these new experiences and reference groups reinforce the politically

---

(1961), 648–54, and *Children and Politics* (New Haven: Yale University Press, 1965), p. 42.

[26] Gabriel A. Almond and Sidney Verba, *The Civic Culture* (Princeton: Princeton University Press, 1963), p. 185.

[27] M. E. Goodman, *Race Awareness in Young Children* (Cambridge, Mass.: Addison-Wesley, 1952), p. 28.

[28] Brim, *op. cit.*, p. 1.

[29] Berelson and Steiner, *op. cit.*, p. 558.

relevant convictions acquired in formative years; but, as contacts with the social environment expand, conflicting views will be encountered.

The Family. With the development of many stable attitudes during childhood and the family serving as "the primary social institution in all lands," it is to be expected that the family is the most influential of all politicizing agencies.[30] Parents occupy a central role in molding attitudes in the early years. These attitudes may not be political *per se* but are politically relevant. Thus, as parental guardians filter influences from the community at large, politics are transmitted to the offspring. Seldom are political attitudes formed in rebellion against parents; rather, they are molded in conformity with parental sentiments. As a result, the likelihood of generational differences in political outlook is diminished.[31] We are interested in two particular sets of politically relevant attitudes acquired in the family environment: (1) a sense of political awareness; and (2) partisan loyalty along with its complementary religious, ideological, and class perspectives.

The first opportunity that most Americans have to become politically attuned is in the family circle. Political awareness, it has been said, is "contagious from one family member to another. . . ."[32] The sources of this contagion are twofold. First, in its role as socializer the American family transmits cultural norms of individual freedom and responsibility. On the one hand, the child's sense of personal effectiveness is heightened when his demands are given consideration. "The more the family treats a child's needs and demands with seriousness appropriate to his age," writes Robert Lane, in summarizing numerous studies of politically relevant behavior in the family, "the more he is, as an adult, likely to believe that his political efforts will be rewarded."[33] On the other hand, parental training introduces the child to social duties and obligations. Working in conjunction with the school, the family introduces children to prescribed standards of behavior, accepted views of their culture, and a certain sense of citizen duty. In America the content of civic obligation transmitted to the child varies considerably. For example: the child reared in a Southern locale has been less likely to acquire a sense of civic duty than one who has grown up in another section.

Children also tend to observe and later imitate the explicit political behavior of parents. This is a second source of political awareness in the family. The more active American political participants are products of

[30] J. Gillespie and G. Allport, *Youth's Outlook on the Future* (New York: Doubleday & Co., 1955), p. 8.

[31] Hyman, *op. cit.*, pp. 123–53.

[32] See particularly Paul Lazarsfeld *et al.*, *The People's Choice* (New York: Columbia University Press, 1948).

[33] Lane, *op. cit.*, pp. 208–9.

families in which parents voted regularly, discussed politics, listened to
political news, read about governmental affairs, and attempted to exert
political influence. By focusing attention on politics, the family can communicate to the child that political participation, along with earning a
living, recreation, and other activities, should be a meaningful experience
in life.

Herbert Hyman, in an inventory of research findings concerning political socialization, points to the crucial role the family plays in orienting
the child toward a preferred political party. A study based upon a national
sampling of political opinion in 1952 revealed the following clusters: 82
per cent of children with Democratic partisan convictions were members
of families in which both parents were Democrats; 73 per cent of Republican loyalists came from families in which both parents were Republican
identifiers.[34] The dominant tendency in America is for parents to agree in
partisan loyalties; the cumulative influence normally results in children's
adopting the political affiliation of their parents (see Table 6-2). When
parents contradict one another, identification of the dominant influence
is difficult; but the child is somewhat more apt to communicate with, and
be influenced on political matters by, the father. If parental conflict is
intense or if both parents exhibit political indifference, no clear-cut partisan symbols are transmitted; and the child is likely to become "independent."

TABLE 6-2

*Resemblance in Party Identification
between Parents and Children, 1958*

	PARTY IDENTIFICATION OF PARENTS		
PARTY IDENTIFICATION OF OFFSPRING	BOTH PARENTS WERE DEMOCRATS	BOTH PARENTS WERE REPUBLICANS	PARENTS HAD NO CONSISTENT PARTY IDENTIFICATION
Democrat	76%	16%	40%
Republican	8	67	29
Independent	15	15	26
Apolitical	1	2	5
	100%	100%	100%
NUMBER OF CASES	641	381	334

Source: This is a modified version of Table 7-1 reported in Angus Campbell *et al.,
The American Voter* (New York: John Wiley & Sons, 1960), p. 147.

[34] See Angus Campbell *et al., The Voter Decides* (Evanston, Ill.: Row Peterson,
1954), p. 99; Hyman, *op. cit.,* pp. 69–72.

Partisan loyalties are formed relatively early; they have been found in a majority of children between ages seven through fourteen.[35] Religious preferences are also normally acquired early. Partisan and religious identifications frequently complement one another throughout life. Consequently, church groups tend less to shape politically relevant attitudes independently than to reinforce the stable bond between partisan and religious preferences. As we shall see in our discussion of voting choice, however, the two loyalties may conflict, and the less intense loyalty may be modified.

American children seldom acquire a strong sense of either political ideology or class status in the family. Hyman has argued that a partisan, rather than an ideological, attitude is more serviceable to the individual in later life. Partisanship provides "an organizing principle for handling the new issues, on which specific socialization has not been possible"; but the inflexible nature of many ideologies renders them less useful in adapting to unanticipated political situations.[36] Class loyalties, as political attitudes, also perform fewer instrumental or knowledge functions. The major political relevance of the class factor in the American family is twofold. First, class position relates to political awareness; for example, upper-class children are more interested in politics than lower-class children are.[37] Secondly, since the class, social status, and partisan affiliations of a family are likely to be complementary, the learning of party loyalties is frequently influenced by social-class position.

The School. Formal agencies of education intervene between parent and child very early. The politicizing effects of formal education are difficult to gauge because schools operate in tandem with family, friends, and other community influences. Although the primary grades broaden the child's horizons considerably, his experiences are still tied to the home environment. The high school years are a different matter. First, maturation from childhood to adolescence is accompanied by a developing capacity for integrating diverse attitudes into consistent outlooks. Secondly, textbook knowledge and current-events information begin to intrude upon previously formed political attitudes. Thirdly, a systematic effort at citizenship training is likely to be encountered. Finally, newly acquired friends are likely to possess differing views from those taught by the family.

Studies indicate that two sets of politically relevant attitudes are generally formed in the high school environment: a greater appreciation for democratic values and a heightened sense of partisan loyalty. Illustrating

35 Easton and Hess, *op. cit.*, p. 245.
36 Hyman, *op. cit.*, p. 75.
37 Lane, *op. cit.*, pp. 220–34.

the former, Edgar Litt investigated in three localities the influence of high school citizenship courses on (1) inculcating democratic values, (2) breaking down political chauvinism, (3) increasing sensitivity to the importance of politics, and (4) creating an understanding of politics as a means of resolving social disputes. He found that regardless of social background, "agreement with the maxims of the democratic creed and rejection of political chauvinism are increased in the civic education programs. . . ." In a predominantly working-class locality, however, there was no increase in the belief that a citizen could "influence government action through political participation," and only students in an upper-class school learned to appreciate the conflict-resolving function of politics.[38] In sum, secondary education may prepare Americans more for passive obedience in the community than for active citizen participation.

The "climate of opinion" in the high school complements that of its surroundings, and the student who comes to it without a consistent party preference tends to acquire the preference most prevalent in the school. In a study of the politicizing effects of the high school, Martin Levin points out that there is an influence on students to "choose the political party that *had already been chosen*" by the preponderant number of adults in the area "regardless of the party preferences of their own parents." [39]

College attendance affects the politicization process by increasing a person's tolerance for social nonconformity and conflict, his sense of civic obligation and political efficacy, the likelihood that he will have political opinions, and the probability that he will vote. Moreover, as with any form of education, it shapes "the kinds of influences to which a person is subjected throughout his life." [40] The college-educated citizen-participant is more apt than others to have group memberships and social aspirations that produce attitude changes in later years.

Group Associations. Group memberships normally reinforce prevailing attitudes and related behavior to the extent that they expose a person to a homogeneous, rather than a conflicting, climate of opinion. However, when group attitudes run contrary to personal attitudes, the individual tends to adjust his outlook to that of the group if he (1) feels strongly about being accepted as an equal, (2) increases his personal contact with members, (3) finds group stands salient, (4) has no other way of obtaining political information and defining political positions, and (5) is impressed

---

[38] Edgar Litt, "Civic Education, Community Norms, and Political Indoctrination," *American Sociological Review*, XXVIII, No. 1 (February, 1963), 69–75.

[39] Martin L. Levin, "Social Climates and Political Socialization," *The Public Opinion Quarterly*, XXV, No. 4 (Winter, 1961), 600.

[40] Key, *op. cit.*, p. 341.

by the persuasive qualities of group leaders. Among the most influential groups in attitude development are occupational colleagues and social friends.[41]

In adulthood an individual's growing class consciousness (produced by family responsibilities, occupational surroundings, and income) affects the content of his political attitudes. Social mobility — at least upward mobility — is a case in point. The citizen on the rise socially tends to adopt the attitudes of his new reference groups; those moving down the social ladder, however, cling to the attitudes of their former, more prestigious peers. Moreover, attitudinal differences are roughly associated with various levels of social stratification. Working and lower classes are more favorable to government policies aimed at promoting social and economic equality; upper classes, although more generally opposed to welfare policies, are far more likely than members of lower classes to support values implied in democratic procedures, civil rights legislation, and constitutional arrangements. Class differences in political attitudes, however, have not been hardened into divergent ideological alignments and do not foreshadow the onset of intense class warfare.[42]

The Church. In surveys conducted by the National Opinion Research Center between 1951–64, fewer than 6 per cent of Americans failed to think of themselves as members of one of the three major religious groupings in the community — Protestant, Catholic, or Jewish.[43] Although the rate of church attendance is considerably less, the high percentage of identifiers suggests that organized religion can play an important part in the politicization of Americans. Politically relevant attitudes are by-products of many religious teachings. Emphasis on individual dignity and worth yields a sense of political efficacy as well as a set of standards for judging governmental actions. Moreover, Bernard Hennessy has pointed to the conservative influence within many churches that helps shape political attitudes of members. This conservative influence flows from acceptance of absolutist doctrines not always congenial to the give-and-take relativism of democratic politics and from a preference for the status quo sometimes exhibited in successful churches. To the extent that any social and political perspective, be it conservatism or whatever, does characterize religious bodies, attitudes learned by members will influence their assessment of political issues of the day.[44] Evaluations of community

[41] Berelson and Steiner, *op. cit.*, pp. 566–70.

[42] See Arthur Kornhauser, "Public Opinion and Social Class," *American Journal of Sociology,* LV (January, 1950), 333–45.

[43] Hazel Gaudet Erskine, "The Polls: Organized Religion," *The Public Opinion Quarterly,* XXIX, No. 2 (Summer, 1965), 327.

[44] Hennessy, *op. cit.*, pp. 206–15.

policies toward crime, alcoholism, gambling, divorce, birth control, communism, education, and numerous other matters are continually colored by religious leanings as well as other predispositions.

Aging. Aging has a twofold influence on changes that take place in attitudes acquired during childhood, adolescence, and adulthood. First, maturity brings with it some change in the ability to assimilate new information and modify old attitudes. Apparently this ability increases markedly through adolescence, gradually decreasing in its acceleration thereafter, with intellectual growth continuing at least to age fifty.[45] Secondly, there is evidence that aging contributes to a growing desire to preserve the status quo no matter what policy is necessary to do so. For example, Gergen and Back have utilized surveys of George Gallup and Elmo Roper to study the relation between aging and policy attitudes. They found that "the aged person tends to prefer those solutions which would terminate problems as rapidly as possible." Moreover, "this evidence was consistent with the notion that the aged tend to have a more constricted orientation to future time." The elderly were more likely to forbid a troublesome activity, such as billboard advertising or boxing, rather than regulate it. They also were more likely to go to war with "slight provocation" and more favorable to UN bombing of Communist China during the Korean War than were younger groups.[46] One other clue that aging has an effect on politicization is Crittenden's finding that Republicanism increased among the aged between 1946 and 1959 despite the predominant partisan trend during that period in America toward the Democratic party.[47]

POLITICAL INFLUENCE: THE FORMATION
OF POLITICAL OPINIONS

Two observations that have been discussed previously are useful in pinpointing the contributions of the overall political setting to the shaping of opinion patterns. First, although significant and politically relevant attitudes are acquired early in life (images of the community and its leaders, party loyalty, religious preference, political awareness, etc.), the child is not the sole father of the political man. Attitude changes occur, and no person is destined to continue through life viewing government in ways preordained by youth. Secondly, attitudes do not dictate political opinions; they are but one element in the opinion-forming matrix that includes

[45] Nancy Bayley, "On the Growth of Intelligence," *American Psychologist,* X (1955), 805–18.

[46] Kenneth J. Gergen and Kurt W. Back, "Aging, Time Perspective and Preferred Solutions to International Conflicts," *The Journal of Conflict Resolution,* IX, No. 2 (June, 1965), 176–86.

[47] John Crittenden, "Aging and Party Affliation," *The Public Opinion Quarterly,* XXVI (Winter, 1962), 648–57.

diverse and frequently contradictory stimuli as well as predilections. Attitudes are tendencies to action rather than the actions themselves.

Opinion formation is a process of influence. Opinion-holding marks a personal adjustment to a changed environment as personal attitudes are aroused in the face of new knowledge, new stimuli, and new feelings. Viewed from the leader's perspective, the molding of opinion involves the subtle wedding of intimidation and salesmanship. He must convince his audience that there is something to lose by failure to comply with his desires and much to gain by doing so. Whether this combined promise of deprivation and gratification stimulates the desired opinion depends partly on the skills and techniques of the leader, which are discussed in the next chapter. But opinion influence also depends upon the audience's perception of the leader, which is, in turn, governed by the follower's attitudes, his estimation of the leader, and his understanding of the leader's purposes.

Opinion formation can be a prelude to attitude change. One of the most interesting aspects of an opinion-influencing situation is the tendency for nonleaders to coordinate their opinions with their perceptions of the positions of leaders. Lane and Sears have commented about this tendency of people "to agree with people they like and . . . to like people they agree with." [48] By so doing, the individual reduces conflict between his own preferences and the opposing desires of respected leaders. This coordinating tendency may lead to misperceptions of a revered leader's otherwise distasteful position. Refusing to believe the leader proposed what he did, the individual does not change his attitude toward the leader. In sum, the source of a communication governs the way an appeal is perceived and reacted to. Citizens frequently assimilate a previously undesirable stand into their own attitudes and gradually "come around" to new positions. In such a situation, a person is especially likely to qualify or change conflicting sentiments that seem less crucial to individual identity while holding on to more personally functional, intense, and salient attitudes. In sum, efforts to remain consistent in orientations toward political leaders, issue stands, groups, parties, and friends can produce modifications in attitudes as opinions are formed. This is particularly true in making electoral choices, a point we return to in Chapter Eight.

POLITICAL OPINION AND LIBERAL DEMOCRACY

As with participation patterns generally, the opinion process does not provide an accurate representation of interest conflict to policy officials. Distortions occur because (1) expressed opinions are only imperfectly drawn samples of underlying attitudes and interests; (2) once expressed,

[48] Lane and Sears, *op. cit.*, p. 44.

opinions are funneled into a number of representative channels (including elections, newspaper editorials, party platforms, group stands, and a host of opinion surveys ranging from haphazard guesses to systematic samplings), where there is ample opportunity for misinterpreting the direction and intensity of these views; (3) it is not easy to distinguish between the opinions of indifferent majorities and intense minorities, measure them, and decide which (if any) should be given greater weight; and (4) once made public, there is no assurance that all opinions will be entertained or effective in policy formation. Hence, the opinion process is a selective one that considers many conflicts but overlooks and ignores many others.

It is apparent that a person's stock of politically relevant attitudes is normally acquired in advance of his political information and knowledge. To the extent that his attitudes govern his observation of governmental affairs, both the cues that arouse his attitudes and the evidence for his political judgments are filtered through a perceptual screen of personal predispositions. This raises doubt as to whether the opinion process reflects a steady movement toward the development of the free human intelligence, which is the cornerstone of substantive democracy, or serves only as an imperfect procedural safeguard against covert policy-making on behalf of privileged interests.

Paradoxically, despite the fact that unconsciously and tenaciously held attitudes may impede the development of reasoned democratic politics, by fostering judgments based upon acquired predispositions rather than free human intelligence, it is partially through the learning of those attitudes that the individual acquires personal independence. As long as he possesses his own predispositions to act, he is something more than a product of the immediate social pressures surrounding him. His acquired convictions contribute to the distinctive purposes underlying his behavior; that is, to the interests manifested through his activity, particularly his political choices. Attitude-learning is a contribution to personal autonomy, one that makes for greater freedom of choice with respect to immediate options.

Politicization contributes both to community consensus and conflict. In learning to identify with community traditions and respect democratic procedures, citizens acquire attitudes that transcend their more specific and narrower interests. Frequently, however, the process of attitude formation yields desires and loyalties dictating a conflict of interests. People can grow so autonomous that they push their demands beyond the limits of community. Robert Alford has suggested this possibility in his comparative study of voting behavior in Anglo-American democracies. In Great Britain, he points out, consensus tends to be "built into individ-

uals," presumably through socialization processes, "with values of deference and accommodation being strongly held." But in America the "levels
of individual tolerance of differences are lower." In short, a working
consensus of liberal democracy is weak. Consensus-building through
politicization is not the distinctive pattern. But loyalty to institutional
arrangements, including those learned attachments to parties and procedures, provide the necessary safety valve: the absence of strong majority parties combined with the presence of a system of checks and
balances on majority rule "force moderation upon the political system;
institutional devices reinforcing consensus are required because consensual values are probably not deeply internalized." [49] For such a political consensus to persevere, constitutional loyalty is required both of
opinion participants and opinion leaders. Just how opinion leaders fit into
conflict representation is our next concern.

BIBLIOGRAPHICAL NOTE

There are several conveniently available paperbacks that can be used to
supplement previous discussion of the relation between attitudes, opinions,
and communication and both configurations and properties of American
opinion. One of the best is Robert Lane and David O. Sears, *Public Opinion*
(Englewood Cliffs, N.J.: Prentice-Hall, Inc., 1964). James N. Rosenau presents
an overall appraisal of the opinion process in his *Public Opinion and Foreign
Policy* (New York: Random House, 1961). Still very useful is Walter Lippmann's classic presentation, *Public Opinion* (New York: The Macmillan Company, Paperback Edition, 1960). Gabriel A. Almond, *The American People and
Foreign Policy* (New York: Frederick A. Praeger, Publisher, 1960) is highly
recommended for a view of psychological and sociological factors molding
opinion patterns. Among the better texts that should be consulted for reference
are Bernard C. Hennessy, *Public Opinion* (Belmont, California: Wadsworth
Publishing Company, Inc., 1965) and V. O. Key, Jr., *Public Opinion and
American Democracy* (New York: Alfred A. Knopf, 1961).

The results of opinion surveys focusing on American reactions to a host of
public issues are summarized conveniently in current issues of the *Public
Opinion Quarterly*. In addition the student should consult Samuel A. Stouffer,
Communism, Conformity, and Civil Liberties (New York: John Wiley & Sons,
Inc., Science Editions, 1966); John M. Fenton, *In Your Opinion* (Boston:
Little, Brown and Company, 1960); Bruno Bettelheim and Morris Janowitz,
Social Change and Prejudice (New York: The Free Press of Glencoe, 1964);
Hadley Cantril (ed.), *Public Opinion 1935–1946* (Princeton, N.J.: Princeton
University Press, 1951); and the work of V. O. Key, Jr., cited above. For sur-

[49] Robert R. Alford, *Party and Society* (Chicago: Rand McNally & Co., 1963),
p. 4.

veys of opinion undertaken in connection with voting studies see the bibliographic note at the end of Chapter Eight.

Various aspects of the relation between personality and political attitudes are detailed in M. Brewster Smith, Jerome S. Bruner, and Robert W. White, *Opinions and Personality* (New York: John Wiley & Sons, Inc., Science Editions, 1956); T. W. Adorno *et al.*, *The Authoritarian Personality* (New York: John Wiley & Sons, Inc., Science Editions, 1964); and Christie R. Jahoda and Marie Jahoda, eds., *Studies in the Scope of "The Authoritarian Personality"* (New York: The Free Press of Glencoe, 1954). See also Harold D. Lasswell, *Psychopathology and Politics* (New York: The Viking Press, 1960); Hadley Cantril, *The Psychology of Social Movements* (New York: John Wiley & Sons, Inc., Science Editions, 1963); and Leon Festinger, Henry W. Riecken, and Stanley Schachter, *When Prophecy Fails* (New York: Harper & Row, Publishers, Torchbook Edition, 1964).

The ways by which people acquire politically relevant attitudes are treated in several works. The most useful compilation of such studies attempting to integrate research findings is Herbert Hyman's *Political Socialization* (Glencoe, Illinois: The Free Press, 1959). The performance of various socializing agencies in transmitting politics to the child are treated in Roberta Sigel, ed., "Political Socialization: Its Role in the Political Process," *The Annals of the American Academy of Political and Social Science*, Volume 361 (September, 1965); Fred I. Greenstein, *Children and Politics* (New Haven: Yale University Press, 1965); and selections from Joseph R. Fiszman, *The American Political Arena*, 2nd edition (Boston: Little, Brown and Company, 1966). For reference the works of Charles E. Merriam should be consulted, *Civic Education in the United States* (New York: Scribner's, 1934) and *The Making of Citizens* (Chicago: The University of Chicago Press, 1931).

CHAPTER
SEVEN

Political Leadership

The distinction between leaders and followers is fundamental in any
governing arrangement. In the regulation of social conflict not everyone
is a regulator. Whether the polity is democratic or authoritarian, relatively few serve as key functionaries in communicating and adjusting
interest differences. The behavior of political leaders distinguishes them
from other participants and from nonparticipants. As molders of opinion
they help shape principal patterns of conflict representation; as makers of
policy they contribute to the persistent resolution of conflict. In Chapter
Twelve we shall discuss the policy-making aspects of political leadership;
here we are concerned with the intrusion of political leadership into
opinion-forming processes. Specifically, we explore the nature and character of American political leadership; the community bases of leadership
patterns; the nature and techniques of persuasion employed by opinion
leaders, including the use of opinion channels to influence political
choices; and the significance of political leadership in a liberal democracy.

163

LEADERSHIP IN THE AMERICAN POLITY

A DEFINITION OF POLITICAL LEADERSHIP

Recent research concerning the nature of leadership dispels the myth that some are born to lead, others to follow. Leadership is not so much a "capacity" imparted to superior persons by birth or social upbringing as a complex set of relationships of leaders and followers. The thrust of contemporary thinking is summed up concisely by Lester Seligman, a long-time student of presidential leadership: "The current view is that leadership is an interactional relationship, involving the acceptance by followers of the cues and direction of a leader." [1] Leadership occurs whenever someone coordinates the activities of others in pursuit of collective goals; in America it is a behavioral pattern marked by three attributes — reciprocity, a specific setting, and influence.

Reciprocity is crucial to any meaningful definition of political leadership; "influence may be exerted by the leader but it is also exerted by the followers." [2] Obviously there can be no leaders without followers. Through their obedience, followers bestow legitimacy upon their leaders; but that legitimacy is only as strong as the bonds of mutual obligations linking leaders and nonleaders. In exchange for active support, leaders accept the responsibility to govern, humanize the governing process, and endeavor to maintain compliance.

Paradoxically freedom to do as one chooses springs from the willingness of a few persons to perform governing tasks for all. Even in the American republic high rates of participation are common among only a small portion of citizens. Indeed, "the first step in political understanding consists in recognizing that a remarkably small number of persons take an active personal interest in the work of political organization." [3] In allotting our time to other pursuits, few of us develop the skills or opportunities for political leadership. Our attention to politics peaks during presidential elections, but falls off markedly as we turn to occupational, family, and recreational activities. By default, if for no other reason, a minority accepts responsibility to govern; the indifferent majority responds to leadership out of conviction, fear, a promise of personal gain, and mostly mere habit.

By transmitting a feeling to citizens that someone "cares," leaders

---

[1] Lester G. Seligman, "Developments in the Presidency and the Conception of Political Leadership," in Joseph Fiszman (ed.), *The American Political Arena* (Boston: Little, Brown and Co., 1962), pp. 146–53.

[2] *Ibid.*

[3] Avery Leiserson, *Parties and Politics* (New York: Alfred A. Knopf, 1958), p. 180.

also provide a "human side" to what commonly seems an impersonal government. Through identification with the personalities of leaders, an emotional and cognitive bond is forged between rulers and ruled. In Franklin Roosevelt's fireside chats, Harry Truman's "give 'em hell" oratory, and Lyndon Johnson's narrations of his boyhood on the Pedernales River, we catch glimpses of the human side to policy appeals. Faith in presidential leadership, particularly in periods of crisis, may be as much a result of personal impressions of the leader's human qualities as a rational assessment of his proposals.

The humanizing aspect of leadership is bound up with efforts to mobilize citizen compliance. Individual styles for securing compliance differ: the authoritarian leader seeks to persuade by playing upon followers' fears, neuroses, frustrations, and illusions; the democrat endeavors to build support by appealing to positive aspirations of citizens, their self-respect and well-being; the charismatic leader possesses a religious aura that elicits passionate followership; and the traditional leader identifies legitimate stewardship with customs and conventions of the community. A leader frequently combines styles in a given situation. For example: in mobilizing support for his Viet Nam policies in 1965–66, President Lyndon Johnson appealed to American fears of communism by urging repulsion of aggression before all Southeast Asia was lost, to democratic aspirations by giving as the rationale for the war the right of self-determination, and to custom by emphasizing peaceful aims in the American tradition.

There is evidence that charismatic appeals are less intrinsic to American political leadership than combinations of other styles. The charismatic style relies upon the leader's ability to appear "infallible, omniscient, and incorruptible" in order to secure legitimacy. James C. Davies sought to determine the appeal of charisma in the voting behavior of participants in the 1952 presidential election. Drawing upon responses of a random sample of the adult population, he found that only 2 per cent possessed a charismatic orientation to Eisenhower and none to Stevenson. The bulk of citizens reacted to less mystical personal attributes, issue stands and partisan appeals.[4]

The character of the relationship between leaders and followers is in part a function of the setting within which leadership occurs. American political history illustrates that opportunities for presidential influence appear greatest in times of community crisis — in times of war (as exemplified by the posture of Abraham Lincoln in the Civil War), periods of economic depression (as shown by Franklin Roosevelt's power), or

[4] James C. Davies, "Charisma in the 1952 Campaign," *The American Political Science Review*, XLVIII (December, 1954), 1083–1102.

upon occasions when public confidence is shaken (illustrated by the days following the assassination of John F. Kennedy). Conditions of the times provide the problems with which potential leaders try to cope, an important factor shaping the character of political leadership.

The contextual nature of leadership also carries implications for the type of attributes required to exert influence; in different settings the roles of leader and follower may be interchanged, with the follower in one situation becoming a leader in another. We frequently endeavor to recruit officials from persons with demonstrated competence in other leadership settings. Businessmen, engineers, military men, and lawyers have all moved to the U.S. Senate, the White House, and a variety of Cabinet positions. Their success depends in part upon whether the behavioral characteristics that produced effective leadership in one endeavor also do so in politics, a profession with its own specialization of skills and responsibilities. Persons with limited political experience occasionally find it difficult to adjust to governmental service where their activities are circumscribed by demands for public disclosure, criticism, and a variety of constitutional restraints. Since behavior patterns appropriate to the situation rather than personal traits are frequently the crucial determinants in achieving influence, political leaders may perform effectively whether honest or dishonest, calculating or altruistic, rich or moderately endowed, articulate or tongue-tied.

Finally, influence is a necessary attribute of political leadership. From the perspective of the opinion process, a leader is "one who, in the course of interacting with others, influences their attitudes and behavior more than they influence his." [5] Leadership demands mutual adjustment between participants, but in the process the leader modifies citizen behavior in conformity with his own somewhat more autonomous interests. It is this act of modification that defines leadership as an influence relationship. The degree of influence exerted by the leader depends upon his successful adjustment both to his followers' interests and the political situation.

POLITICAL LEADERS IN AMERICA

The universe of political leaders is ever changing as are the characteristics that distinguish leaders from nonleaders. Neither leaders nor followers whirl in fixed orbits. Studies of political activists, influentials, and carriers of the creed all hint at the identity of our most "prestigious givers of cues." [6] Drawing upon the working distinction between authority as

---

[5] W. Phillips Davison, "The Public Opinion Process," *The Public Opinion Quarterly*, XXII, No. 2 (Summer, 1958), 91–106.

[6] *Ibid.*

given by the U.S. Constitution and by extra-constitutional practice, we can speak of three categories of political leaders.

First, we can designate "official" leaders, who occupy positions authorized by the Constitution, congressional legislation, or state and local constitutions and statutes. Among leaders in this category are the President, Cabinet members, congressmen, bureaucratic officials, judges, ambassadors, governors, state legislators, and military commanders.

A second category includes "nonofficial" leaders — persons who represent interest conflicts to policy officials even though not always explicitly designated to do so by formal procedures. Local, state, and national party leaders; leaders of pressure organizations; lobbyists; members of the communications media, including reporters, columnists, and commentators; or organizers of mass demonstrations — all are included in this category of political leadership.

Finally, there are "personal" leaders — the host of individuals who lead opinion because they have the trust and respect of colleagues, friends, neighbors, clients, and others. These persons are exposed to political communications more frequently than other citizens and are consulted by their associates for information and counsel; they are "likely to influence other persons in their immediate environment."[7] They may be teachers, employers, barbers, bowling-team members, drinking buddies, ministers, doctors, coffee-klatch informants, etc. They lead opinion, not because they possess constitutional authority, but because of personal influence flowing from mutual feelings of interpersonal faith.

American political leaders differ from nonleaders in several *general* respects. We stated earlier that leaders tend to be more active politically, more committed to community ideals, somewhat more ideological in outlook, and more partisan in their approach to community affairs. Moreover, they communicate more with one another, with other group leaders, and initiate communications with nonleaders more than followers do.

Professor Lewis Froman has suggested other behavioral characteristics setting leaders apart from nonleaders. For one thing, leaders hold attitudes more intensely than do nonleaders. Moreover, their preferences are more resistant to change and are more likely to serve as the basis for political behavior. Opinions of leaders are governed more by acquired predispositions than attitude-arousing cues. The most relevant cues for leaders revolve about political issues and events rather than personalities. Finally, meaningful issues to leaders tend to be of a material rather than symbolic character. In all these respects nonleaders differ markedly. They possess a narrower range of values held less intensely, have rela-

---

[7] See Elihu Katz and Paul F. Lazarsfeld, *Personal Influence* (Glencoe, Ill.: The Free Press, 1955).

tively little knowledge or interest in political issues or events, are more likely to be assuaged by symbolic gratifications, and are more subject to leadership cues in styling their opinion behavior.[8]

THE BASES OF AMERICAN POLITICAL LEADERSHIP

We have described political leadership as a relationship involving reciprocal influence. Moreover, that relationship is contextual in nature; that is, both leaders and followers are affected by certain factors that shape the setting of political leadership. As in our accounts of participation and opinion patterns, we classify these factors in accordance with three dimensions of community — personal, social, and politico-constitutional.

PERSONAL ATTITUDES TOWARD POLITICAL LEADERS

In any opinion-forming situation, the extent of a leader's influence is governed in part by the esteem with which he is held by his followers. His reputation, in turn, is affected by the fact that he is engaged in a political enterprise, by the position he holds, the decisions he makes, and his ability to satisfy his followers' desires.

We observed earlier that American views of politicians are neither wholly positive nor negative. Although there is a gradual increase in the prestige of politics as a career, the American culture has generally accorded a lower esteem to public service than to careers in business, the military, the clergy, etc. Moreover, our political folklore has emphasized that we won our independence as a nation by rebelling against the authority of political leaders, a point reinforced by restraints placed on leaders through state constitutions following the Revolutionary War and much later in the Populist Era. The result is a curious mixture of permissiveness and hostility toward political leaders in our community. Aside from their relatively high prestige among children, persons with little formal education, and lower-status citizens, politicians are still regarded with a certain suspicion that hinders them in obtaining a positive popular response.

The degree of confidence placed in official leaders varies with governmental position occupied. For example: the Presidency as an institution of leadership is respected in its own right; anyone assuming the office is heir to a long-term tradition of devotion, which enhances his ability to strike a desired responsive cord among followers during his term in

[8] Lewis A. Froman, Jr., *People and Politics* (Englewood Cliffs, N.J.: Prentice-Hall, 1962), pp. 38–48.

office. That respect for the office, however, is not converted automatically into approval of the incumbent, as illustrated by the fluctuation in personal popularity of Presidents Roosevelt, Truman, Eisenhower, Kennedy and Johnson during portions of their tenure (Table 7-1). Although a general "pro-incumbent" sentiment has prevailed since the 1930's (as evidenced by the fact that only one of the Presidents fell dramatically below 50 per cent in popular approval), it has not been sufficient to transcend political events, partisanship, and periodical revelations of "wrongdoing" among presidential subordinates.

TABLE 7-1

Personal Popularity of American Presidents, 1933–1966

PRESIDENT *	LOWEST PERCENTAGE OF NATIONAL SAMPLE APPROVING CONDUCT OF PRESIDENTIAL OFFICE BY INCUMBENT	HIGHEST PERCENTAGE OF NATIONAL SAMPLE APPROVING CONDUCT OF PRESIDENTIAL OFFICE BY INCUMBENT
Franklin D. Roosevelt [1] (1933–1945)	50%	84%
Harry S. Truman [2] (1945–1953)	36%	87%
Dwight D. Eisenhower [3] (1953–1955)	60%	79%
John F. Kennedy [4] (1961–1962)	71%	83%
Lyndon B. Johnson [5] (1964–1966)	44%	83%

Data reported only for selected years in which questions soliciting approval-disapproval responses are comparable and available.
Sources:
[1] John M. Fenton, *In Your Opinion* (Boston: Little, Brown and Co., 1960), pp. 44–74.
[2] *Ibid.*
[3] Elmo Roper, *You and Your Leaders* (New York: William Morrow & Co., 1957), pp. 264–70.
[4] Hazel Gaudet Erskine (ed.), "The Quarterly's Polls," *The Public Opinion Quarterly*, XXV, No. 4 (Winter, 1961), 663.
[5] American Institute of Public Opinion.

This suggests that leadership images are traceable to the courses of action the politician chooses in regulating conflicts. There are at least two levels of choice involved. The more obvious is the choice of one policy from among several options to which followers react directly in a positive or negative fashion. Thus, Americans either actively supported our intervention in Korea in 1950 or grudgingly accepted "Truman's War." A second choice lies in the leader's selection of the type of role he wishes to play in relation to his followers. Does he as President, for example, desire to be regarded as steward of all the people, as guardian of the Constitution, as leader of the Free World, or what? In making this decision, a President, like any political leader, shapes indirectly the types of problems he will most often face, the variety of communications posed to him, the interests most often seeking his attention, and the conduct both he and his followers will expect of him. In this respect, the general image of Harry Truman shifted periodically between poles of "skilled statesman" and "mere politician" as his actions conformed (or failed to) to the image he projected as final decision-maker in the governing process.

Along with the general respect afforded politicians, either individually or in the abstract, a leader's influence in molding opinions will depend upon his ability to appeal to salient needs and wants of citizens. If he can adjust and project a helpful image, his influence is increased. In a study of the public response to Franklin Roosevelt, F. H. Sanford observed that citizen views of their leader were influenced by the degree that they felt dependent upon him. In the reciprocal relation between Roosevelt and his constituents, the latter relieved certain desires to submit to authority, felt some sense of material gain, and perceived that they were winning the approval of a respected personage.[9]

If the leader is to personify the deeply felt aspirations of his followers, he must have some skill in selecting and manipulating appealing symbols in varying political contexts. W. Phillips Davison has pointed out, "The leader leads not because he is entirely different from others, but because he is much like the others and may symbolize and fuse their aspirations and desires."[10] Through the ability to identify with symbolically stated popular causes ("anti-communism," a "balanced budget," or "more spending power"), a leader may convert approval of the cause into approval of the leader. There are indications that President Eisenhower's popularity came in part from his ability to personify an American preference for "nonpartisanship." Attracting citizens of all traditional partisan affiliations, he seemed to "rise above politics." He was less successful in transferring his own positive image to the Republican presidential candidate in 1960, Richard Nixon, who did not possess this reputation.

THE SOCIAL CHARACTERISTICS
OF AMERICAN POLITICAL LEADERS

The social background of political leaders is one clue to the type of life experiences that go into the formation of their political attitudes and

[9] F. H. Sanford, "Public Orientation to Roosevelt," *The Public Opinion Quarterly*, XV (Summer, 1951), 189–216.
[10] Davison, *op. cit.*

interests. Elitist theories of politics postulate that similarity of background produces a sense of common interest in a leadership corps and welds the elite into a dominant group dedicated to the control of public affairs on its own behalf. If this is the case, meaningful popular choice may be negated; public dispute between elites may be nothing more than a façade behind which entrenched leaders govern in their own behalf, and "political power, properly so called, . . . merely the organized power of one class for oppressing another." [11] Is this true of American leadership?

Evidence indicates that official leaders tend generally to come from middle and upper classes. Yet, on the whole, there is a sufficient distribution of official, nonofficial, and personal leaders throughout the social structure to assure minimum representation of diverse social interests. From an extensive survey of the social characteristics of public leadership, Professor Wendell Bell and his colleagues concluded that official leaders normally come from families of better than average socio-economic status. Most have more formal education than the average American, are professionally trained, and have backgrounds as lawyers.[12] A more specific study of the social backgrounds of selected American governing officials reveals that occupations of the fathers of political leaders tend to be of higher status. Professional, proprietary, and governing backgrounds contributed a majority of American presidents, Vice-Presidents, and Cabinet members from 1789–1934. Similarly a majority of civil servants (1940), U.S. senators (1949–51), and members of the House of Representatives (1941–43) possessed such a heritage. Yet those same types of occupations constituted only a little more than 10 per cent of the labor force in America as late as 1890. A middle- and upper-class predominance in the backgrounds of official leaders is even more pronounced for judicial officers; research reveals that movement into a judicial career frequently is from a prominent professional family.[13]

Analyses of other characteristics of official leaders reveal a similar disproportion in social ties. Native-born white Protestants dominate positions of community authority in American politics, frequently excluding sizable minorities. Official leadership in America is almost the private preserve of males; and, if in elected positions, these men are normally

[11] See Karl Marx and Friedrich Engles, *The Communist Manifesto*, ed. Samuel H. Beer (New York: Appleton Century-Crofts, 1955).

[12] For a review of studies dealing with such leaders see Wendell Bell, Richard J. Hill, and Charles R. Wright, *Public Leadership* (San Francisco: Chandler Press, 1961).

[13] Donald R. Matthews, *The Social Background of Political Decision-Makers* (Garden City, N.Y.: Doubleday & Co., 1954); Bancroft C. Henderson and T. C. Sinclair, *The Selection of Judges in Texas* (Houston: Public Affairs Research Center, 1965).

from fifty to sixty years of age. Due to constitutional limitations upon their participation, office-holding is not common for the younger members of our society.

In their social backgrounds, nonofficial leaders are somewhat more representative of the composition of the American community; but again no perfect correspondence prevails. In particular, the local organizational leaders of our two major political parties have varied backgrounds. The proportion of specific social groupings in the upper echelons of party leadership varies from locality to locality depending upon what type of coalition of interests is suited to electoral victory. A recent study of partisan organization in Wayne County (Detroit), Michigan serves as an illustration. Dividing the hierarchies of Democratic and Republican parties into the "top elite" (district chairmen and executive board members) and "precinct leaders," Samuel Eldersveld found that among Democrats the elite structure disproportionately represented the Irish, business and professional groups, and unionized labor. Republicans overrepresented the business-managerial groups, members of predominantly White labor unions, and Negroes. Recruitment gaps appeared for certain subgroups in the area — the very young, unskilled workers, those with only elementary school education, and smaller nationality groupings — whose voting strength seemed less crucial to success. In similar fashion, leadership in many locales reflects the dominance of particular racial, ethnic, religious, and socio-economic interests in each county and precinct.[14]

The social composition of communications leadership — reporters, editors, television commentators, etc. — is difficult to gauge. If we confine ourselves to correspondents in Washington, D.C., we find that in the 1960's 93 per cent had attended college, the most sizable proportion hailed from the Northeast and Midwest, and their median salary was $11,579 — significantly above the national average.[15] Since, however, the Washington Press Corps is considered to be the elite of the political reporters, we might expect political journalists in the nation as a whole to be somewhat more representative, in social characteristics, of other members of the community.

So long as it is possible for social interests to organize freely into voluntary organizations, we can expect that many minorities unrepresented by official or partisan leadership will have spokesmen within their own associations. Negro leaders, for example, have represented a variety of points of view in such organizations as the National Association for

---

[14] Samuel J. Eldersveld, *Political Parties* (Chicago: Rand McNally & Co., 1964), chap. 4.

[15] William L. Rivers, "The Correspondents after 25 Years," *Columbia Journalism Review*, I, No. 1 (Spring, 1961), 4–10.

the Advancement of Colored People, the Congress on Racial Equality, and the Southern Christian Leadership Conference. Even within voluntary associations, however, not all underprivileged, indifferent, or passive Americans have their interests represented by group leadership. In the summer of 1966, for example, a major rift developed between leaders of major Negro civil rights organizations and those of the Student Nonviolent Coordinating Committee; the latter charged older Negro groups with being too modest in their demands and not representative of oppressed Negroes in the South seeking "Black Power."

In examining opinion patterns during the 1940 presidential election campaign in an Ohio county, Paul Lazarsfeld found only minor differences in the percentages of various occupational groupings contributing personal influentials (Table 7-2). Although the table indicates that analysis in a later election underscored this broad distribution of opinion leaders among occupational groupings, a relation between other components of class-status and personal leadership exists. For example: those with more formal education — and, consequently, those more likely to be in professional or managerial capacities — are more likely to be opinion leaders. To the extent that formal education produces an image

TABLE 7-2

Occupational Distribution of Personal Leaders,
1940 and 1948

ERIE COUNTY, OHIO, 1940		ELMIRA, NEW YORK, 1948	
OCCUPATION	PER CENT PERSONAL LEADERS	OCCUPATION	PER CENT PERSONAL LEADERS
Professional	35	Professional and	
Proprietary,		Managerial	31
Managerial	25	White Collar	18
Clerical	33	Skilled Workers	27
Commercial, Sales	44	Semi- and	
Skilled Workers	35	Unskilled	
Semi-skilled		Workers	22
Workers	32		
Unskilled Workers	23		
Farmers	15		
Housewives	13		
Unemployed	15		
Retired	35		

Source: This is a modified version of Table 6.1 in Robert Lane, *Political Life* (Glencoe, Ill.: The Free Press, 1959), p. 91; and is based on data from Paul F. Lazarsfeld, *et al.*, *The People's Choice* (New York: Columbia University Press, 1948), p. 50, and Bernard Berelson *et al.*, *Voting* (Chicago: The University of Chicago Press, 1954), p. 377. Reprinted with permission of The Free Press from *Political Life* by Robert E. Lane. Copyright © 1959 by The Free Press, a Corporation.

of knowledgeability and expertise, it is more probable that the school-trained will be consulted for information and advice in political affairs. Moreover, people are more influenced by personal leaders perceived to be of the same or higher social status than by those below them on the social ladder.

By definition, personal leaders influence opinion formation within their immediate group environment. It is not surprising that these influentials are distributed throughout all adult age groups, religious denominations, and racial and ethnic groupings. Males, however, tend to be dominant as personal leaders in political affairs. But to what degree do personal leaders within various groupings transcend them and influence the opinion behavior of those belonging to other groups? How often, for example, does a twenty-year-old modify the opinions of middle-aged people? Apparently not very often. In their study of the 1948 presidential election, Bernard Berelson and his colleagues concluded that people in particular age groups tend to rely upon people of the same age for political counseling; and, furthermore, "youth seems to have much more respect for elders' opinions than the elders do for youth's." By the same token, women tend to influence women more than men, Protestants influence Protestants, etc. With cross-sectional opinion leadership — for example, White to Negro — class and status are more influential factors than age, sex, race, religion, or ethnic background.[16]

In sum, empirical research has established the general overrepresentation of middle- and upper-class backgrounds in leadership ranks. Social advantage facilitates both the pursuit of a political career and a devotion to political affairs as an avocation. Higher social status, income, education, and politically related occupations make it easier to obtain coin of the political realm — money, proper social contacts, experience in dealing with a variety of social problems, leisure time for politics, respect, and a general image of success in all endeavors.

Based upon such findings as those cited, combined with the view that politicians must always follow the dictates of the wealthy, some observers have argued that the American polity is governed by a single economic elite. Labeled variously as a "ruling elite," a "power elite," an "establishment," a "corporate elite," or an "invisible government," the argument has been that a single group of entrenched, modern-day aristocrats make puppets of the President, Congress, bureaucrats, and judicial officials.[17]

[16] Bernard Berelson *et al.*, *Voting* (Chicago: The University of Chicago Press, 1954).

[17] For example: see C. Wright Mills, *The Power Elite* (New York: Oxford University Press, 1957); Richard H. Rovere, *The American Establishment* (New York: Harcourt, Brace & World, 1961). For an opposing perspective, see Douglass Cater, *Power in Washington* (New York: Random House, 1964).

That such economic interests play a crucial role in policy-making in America is unquestioned. We discuss their participation in policy formulation in Chapter Eleven. However, it is much harder to say that a single elite rules the community in its own self-interest. It is difficult to identify a single interest among leaders of diverse corporations beyond a sharing of the vague view that capitalism is a preferred way of ordering the economy. Business leaders possess no inherent group interest; they must define it in give-and-take among themselves. Within that framework, interest conflict generates between and among corporate managers, bank presidents, union leaders, board chairmen, and other economic titans. They encounter hardships in imposing their views on political leaders when they can neither agree among themselves nor articulate unequivocal individual demands.[18]

We find, then, that the disproportion of middle- and upper-class representation in leadership echelons does not yield a government exclusively *for* these groups as well as *of* and *by* them. There is, in fact, less of a concentration of influence in a leadership elite than a dispersion of opinion leadership among a plurality of groups, parties, and individuals. Several factors mitigate the effects of elitist control of leadership in American government. First, the relatively large size of the middle class (as compared to upper and lower classes) minimizes sharp cleavages between the affluent and the impoverished. Secondly, there is sufficient diversity within overrepresented classes to produce multiple centers of influence, division of interest, and competition between political leaders. Finally, competition engenders different appeals not normally based upon narrow class lines for support; these persistent efforts at political persuasion arouse conflicting sentiments and divide American political opinion into a plurality of clusters and alignments. Hence, although the deck of political leadership is stacked to the advantage of certain social groups, the distribution of opinions need not, nor does it normally, coincide with that arrangement of privilege.

POLITICAL PERSUASION AND LEADERSHIP

In preceding chapters we observed that Americans place a relatively low priority on acquiring information about governmental affairs. Since political attention is marginal, leaders are frequently thwarted in their efforts to build support. Their chances for success are enhanced if they are skilled in articulating salient issues and employing persuasive tech-

---

[18] For an account that raises serious questions about the existence of an articulated self-interest among the business community, see Raymond A. Bauer, Ithiel de Sola Pool, and Lewis Anthony Dexter, *American Business and Public Policy* (New York: Atherton Press, 1963), pp. 105–242.

niques. In the process of exerting influence, opinion leaders are affected by several political and constitutional factors: (1) methods of coercion and persuasion available to them; (2) events and issues; (3) processes of leadership selection; (4) relevant groups (parties, pressure organizations, official agencies, and the communications media) and their structure, position on issues, and opinion-forming activities; and (5) constitutional restraints. A discussion of political persuasion enables us to get an impression of the aggregate effects of these factors on opinion leadership.

Nature of Political Persuasion. Of all political communities in the world, the American polity selects the greatest number of its official leaders through elections. Even political leaders serving in appointive federal positions — Cabinet members, agency heads, ambassadors, information officers, judges, etc. — are chosen by elected leaders and thus affected to some degree by the accepted practice of popular leadership selection. In the federal community, competition for office is vigorous; and the man seeks the office, not the office the man. To a remarkable degree, patterns of opinion leadership are shaped by the constitutional requirement that leaders must win popular electoral support both to obtain and retain office. Thus, a premium is placed on skills of political persuasion; and coercion, as a legitimate means of influencing political opinion, is minimized.

Coercion and persuasion are differing, albeit overlapping, dimensions of influence. Coercion, here, refers to the use of force to get people to do what they otherwise would prefer not to do; persuasion uses promised benefits to achieve active consent while minimizing threats of deprivations. Coercion succeeds where people change their behavior because of fear of reprisal; persuasion results in behavioral shifts due more to prospects of rewards. Realistically, of course, coercive and persuasive tactics are intermingled in American elections; voters sometimes have been intimidated or kept from the polls as well as promised benefits for voting a particular way. Despite infrequent reversions to coercive tactics, political leaders, hoping to engineer active consent rather than reluctant compliance, generally prefer to influence opinion through persuasive techniques.

Techniques of Political Persuasion. An examination of our most publicized form of leadership selection — the presidential campaign — will help to illustrate some of the techniques of political persuasion. In later chapters we will consider in detail the manifold factors that enter into nominations.

Charles O. Jones has written that a presidential campaign may be divided into three phases for purposes of description — planning, testing, and critical phases. Aside from such problems as coordinating party factions, scheduling appearances, or lining up a staff of lieutenants, campaign-planning involves designing appropriate persuasive appeals. Campaign communications share much in common with all messages of propaganda in that they constitute deliberate efforts by some interest to form, control, or alter attitudes of other groups by use of the instruments of communication, with the intention that in any given campaign the opinion of those so influenced will be that desired by the candidate.[19] They are directed at activating loyal supporters, converting the wavering, and neutralizing the opposition.

Campaign planning is a joint endeavor of specialists in public relations and mass persuasion, skilled surveyors of popular attitudes, and experienced party leaders. Each brings a different skill to the task, and each plans to reach the voter in different ways. The public-relations expert attempts to influence the voter as a member of a mass audience. To this end he employs tactics based upon the following assumptions: (1) a mass audience, composed of individuals who have certain personal attitudes and social characteristics in common, exists; (2) individual behavior consists of making selections between alternative products, candidates, or policies and can be influenced by direct mass advertising appeals; (3) an effective persuasive message must be symbolized to please personal predispositions (for example, if audiences are predisposed to relish succulent fruits, then prunes must be advertised as juicy rather than dry); (4) the symbol must be not only appealing but of sufficient salience to *activate* the potential buyer, voter, or follower; and (5) sensational presentations, repetition, and saturation can ultimately wear down sales resistance and penetrate the citizen's marginal attention to politics.

To make a pleasing presentation, a candidate requires some idea of what is on the voter's mind. It is the job of the political-opinion analyst to reach the citizen as a member of an opinion cluster rather than a unified mass. His function in campaign-planning is to sample popular attitudes, assess responses to the candidate, and perhaps suggest issues the candidate should emphasize. For him election outcome is dependent less upon the mass convergence of individual selections than the decisions of persons in politically significant social categories — the middle-class worker, the Negro, the urban dweller, the party loyalist, the female voter, etc.

The experienced politician also has a role to play. His target is the voter in his home precinct, and his technique that of personal contact. He hopes to mobilize a vigorous grass-roots organization that will com-

[19] Charles O. Jones, "The 1964 Presidential Election — Further Adventures in Wonderland," in Donald G. Herzberg (ed.), *American Government Annual, 1965–1966* (New York: Holt, Rinehart & Winston, 1965), pp. 1–30.

plement the candidate's impersonal efforts. Studies of political persuasion reveal that mass appeals are most effective when filtered through an intermediate layer of personal leaders who stand between channels of mass communications and the prospective voter. Normally these personal opinion leaders consist of the candidate's friends, neighbors, and colleagues. A major task of grass-roots party organization is to put precinct leaders into positions of personal leadership and thus increase the chances for favorable citizen response to campaign appeals.

In studying the joint impact of political parties and television on voter participation in Wayne County, Michigan, in 1956, Professor Samuel Eldersveld found that "the role of both party contact and television in getting out the vote is striking." Citizens with high exposure to both party contacts and television were much more likely to be interested in foreign and domestic affairs, discuss politics with friends, and to vote than those with low exposure to either or both.[20] In earlier days the party was the primary tool of the political leader in mobilizing electoral support. Now it appears that mass persuasion and personal contact through party must be combined in a political leader's campaign appeals.

The testing phase of the campaign involves the application of the stratagems planned by the candidate and his staff. It calls for an assessment of their reliability in achieving desired results and a continuing adaptation to the changing campaign setting. In this phase it is even more apparent that the selection of appealing issues is crucial to successful political leadership. At this point the normal marginal attention of Americans to political communications must be converted to active interest. Skill is required along with a congenial, or at least not a hostile, atmosphere in which to influence behavior.

Charles O. Jones's interpretation of the 1964 presidential election, for example, indicates that Republican candidate Barry Goldwater was continually thwarted in his efforts to find issues that would engender popular support. The magnitude of the difficulty was compounded by the fact that, throughout the campaign, opinion samplings consistently showed President Johnson to have a commanding lead of nearly two to one. Republicans experimented with a variety of issues: foreign policy (Viet Nam, Cuba, the threat of communism); domestic affairs (Big Government, civil rights, violence in the streets); and personalities (Johnson's wealth and Humphrey's connections with the Americans for Democratic Action). None touched off sufficient support to counter Democratic claims of "moderation," "peace," and "prosperity." Within the context of the campaign, Goldwater's selection of issues was dictated by the need to challenge the Democratic lead; opposition choices, however, were made

[20] Eldersveld, op. cit., pp. 512–23.

in the more comfortable realization that victory would come if no one "rocked the boat." [21]

A more successful example of the adaptation of persuasive techniques to unexpected changes in the campaign setting appears in Theodore White's account of *The Making of the President, 1960*. It also illustrates the tenor of decision-making in the critical campaign phase. On October 19 of that election year, Martin Luther King, certainly the most prominent Negro leader in the movement for civil liberties in the last decade, was arrested in Atlanta for using "sit-in" techniques while attempting to integrate a restaurant. On the suggestion of a campaign adviser, Senator and candidate John Kennedy placed a long-distance call to the wife of the incarcerated Negro leader. When news of the dramatic call reached the press and then the world, its impact was immediate and effective. Writes Mr. White, "One cannot identify in the narrowness of American voting of 1960 any one particular episode or decision as being more important than any other in the final tallies . . ."; yet, "when one reflects that Illinois was carried by only 9,000 votes and that 250,000 Negroes are estimated to have voted for Kennedy, that Michigan was carried by 67,000 votes and that an estimated 250,000 Negroes voted for Kennedy; that South Carolina was carried by 10,000 votes and that an estimated 40,000 Negroes there voted for Kennedy, the candidate's instinctive decision must be ranked among the most crucial of the last few weeks." [22]

These examples from the testing and critical phases of two presidential campaigns highlight the principal problem of facing the political persuader. He must constantly adjust his treatment of salient issues to popular responses to his positions on them. Since issues generally serve as the stimuli around which attitudes coalesce and opinions form, it is through issues that politicians can activate large bodies of people. But the existence of issues reflects the presence of social conflict, of interests vying with one another for advantage. In order to mobilize support among diverse *and* conflicting interests, the political leader reduces complex social disputes to familiar, easily grasped symbols, sufficiently salient to capture the marginal attention of the citizen and yet vague enough to recruit broad support. A "Return to Normalcy," "New Frontiers," or a "Great Society" — all were born of efforts to establish sympathetic rapport between candidates and a pluralist public following.

Channels of Political Persuasion. The political candidate defines issues to run on, tests their effectiveness, and makes tactical changes in their presentation as necessary. Thus campaign issues are "ideas that are

[21] Jones, *op. cit.*
[22] Theodore H. White, *The Making of the President, 1960* (New York: Atheneum Publishers, 1961), p. 323.

agitating small, face-to-face groups . . . taken up by men . . . concerned with mass manipulation . . . who have at their disposal the means of organization and publicity." [23] To render his appeals on these issues effective to large numbers of diverse social interests, the campaigner selects appropriate means of publicity. In part he relies on the personal contact of his agents in counties and precincts to carry his message to citizens at the grass roots. But the bulk of his publicizing efforts are centered upon the use of mass communications as a conduit to voters. Hence, most issues in American presidential elections reach us either in the form of a candidate's appearances at rallies, on television or on radio, or as news about those activities. Newsgathering thus serves as a political activity as vital in opinion leadership in a free polity as the candidate's efforts to adapt controversy to his own ends. The reporter, in transmitting informative and persuasive cues, is an opinion channel; in selecting newsworthy items for public exposure, he is an opinion leader.

Charles Wright has provided a useful and concise listing of the distinguishing features of the mass media: (1) mass communications are directed "toward relatively large, heterogeneous, and anonymous audiences"; (2) communications are open and public, "often timed to reach most audience members simultaneously, and are transient in character"; and (3) the opinion leaders using mass communications rely upon "a complex organization that may involve great expense," including a variety of communication channels — newspapers, television, radio, magazines, journals, movies, etc.[24]

As politically functioning institutions in a liberal democracy, the mass media expose controversy and provide an open forum for conflicting interests and criticism of the actions of officials. Ideally this function is performed on behalf of all citizens, and "the press" is the citizen's agent in American government. Moreover, a "free press" is considered a citizen's right and is protected by constitutional guarantees, statutory regulation, and gentleman's agreement. Hence, the protection of a free press guaranteed by the First Amendment limits interference in the activities of communications media. Only relatively minor restrictions are placed on that freedom; for example, television cameras are barred from courtrooms in the interest of impartial litigation, individuals may seek redress for libelous utterances in the press, or movies may be censored in the "public interest." In exchange for this protection, the media are to supply unfettered channels for political information, persuasion,

[23] Davison, op. cit.; Murray Edelman, "Symbols and Political Quiescence," The American Political Science Review, LIV, No. 3 (September, 1960), 695–704.
[24] Charles R. Wright, Mass Communication (New York: Random House, 1959).

and entertainment. Deliberate distortion of news is frowned upon, but news organizations are free to interpret and comment as they see fit.

The ideal of a socially responsible communications process is tempered by economic and political realities. The sheer cost of media operation, particularly television, restricts access to the more affluent. Economic considerations also limit the ability of the press to raise all significant conflicts to the level of open discussion. Newspapers caught up in efforts to sell advertising by increasing circulation are constrained to publicize conflicts that meet standards of newsworthiness — those of interest and importance to readers. Thus, political interests within the news audience condition the types of conflicts that political communicators choose to report; minority interests may get passed over in efforts to attract a large readership.[25]

In a study of the means used by national leaders for mobilizing public support, James N. Rosenau reasons that the opinion-making capacity of a political leader is in part a function of his access to communications channels. Rosenau examined the opinion-making potential of 1,067 community leaders who attended a White House Conference regarding the 1958 foreign-aid program. He found that occupational role was the primary determinant of opinion-making potential; that is, when an individual occupies a prestigious position, he is more likely to become an opinion leader because his position gives him entrée to opinion channels. Leaders in labor and communications fields were found to possess high opinion-making potential; those in teaching-research occupations were of lowest potential. Businessmen had only moderate access to the general public through communications channels; "business leaders may have a high degree of access to policy-makers and other opinion-makers, but their capacity to circulate opinions to the general public would appear to be considerably less than that possessed by leaders of several other fields." Party leaders (district or state chairmen) also possessed low opinion-making potential; this may reflect their tendency to concentrate on personal contacts, leaving "broad public appeals to the governmental representatives of . . . party." [26]

For decades, access to communications channels has been the chief factor in making the President of the United States an effective opinion leader. Virtually any action of the President is news. Presidential news conferences constitute the most obvious channel to the public; a Presi-

[25] See Fred S. Siebert, Theodore Peterson, and Wilbur Schramm, *Four Theories of the Press* (Urbana: University of Illinois Press, 1956); Dan D. Nimmo, *Newsgathering in Washington* (New York: Atherton Press, 1964).

[26] James N. Rosenau, *National Leadership and Foreign Policy* (Princeton: Princeton University Press, 1963), p. 154.

dent skilled in its use publicizes his stands on controversial issues, thus forcing recalcitrant administrative subordinants into line. For example, military officials within the Pentagon frequently have opposed presidential policy supporting greater unification of the armed forces. In the face of the President's monopoly of the mass media, colonels, generals, and chiefs of staff have found it necessary to resort to more covert ways of arguing for autonomy of their particular branches. When John Kennedy was President, attempts to "crack down" on leaks of policy controversies to the press from Pentagon officials produced a variety of charges of "news management" and "governmental secrecy," some substantiated and some not.

In efforts to facilitate access to communications channels, other official leaders have relied upon a variety of techniques. Congressmen, for example, regularly supply filmed presentations of reports from Washington to television stations in their home constituencies. Bureaucratic agencies have established offices of public information in efforts to control the release of information from the agency and to give reporters a convenient place for securing prepared releases covering agency events. Information officers serve as points of access between government officials and reporters: they provide the news media with news about officials and reportorial access to policy-makers.

In efforts to secure information for public consumption, reporters and parent news organizations are social interests in their own right. As pressure groups they make claims upon official agencies of policy-making. These claims include demands for information, unencumbered access to policy-makers for interviews, and freedom from official control. Often the result is a conflict of media and official interests fought on the abstract level of the requirements for "orderly administration" versus the "people's right to know." Tension between official and press is almost inevitable in a democratic community built upon public disclosure of conflict. Whether out of conviction, principle, or attempts at economic gain, the communications industry in America is continuously at odds with policy-makers as newsgatherers publicize controversies that officials and private interests might prefer to keep secret. One measure of the extent to which the democratic function of a free press has been compromised lies in how much "official information" is reported without critical efforts to secure all evidence relevant to the political issue. The degree to which the communications media function autonomously reflects the open, democratic nature of the society. In serving as passive conduits and active participants, opinion channels create conflict as they try to expose and represent it.

The effectiveness of mass communications in political persuasion is difficult to assess. Bernard Berelson has said, "Some kinds of *communication* on some kinds of *issues,* brought to the attention of some kinds of *people* under some kinds of *conditions* have some kinds of *effects.*" [27] Since mass communications media do not operate in isolation, they must be evaluated as contributory agents that compliment, supplement, or counter the impact of personal contacts, family discussions, and other opinion channels.

Students of communication note three kinds of effects that mass communications have upon opinion. First, if a citizen forms an opinion as a result of a message from the mass media and does something about it (for example, votes), he has been *activated.* From studies cited in this chapter and Chapter Five, we know that a person is more likely to participate politically if stimulated through mass communications channels.

Secondly, mass communications frequently *reinforce* existing opinions. Loyal Democrats or Republicans normally find in mass communications reasons for voting in accordance with their partisan preference. Citizens predisposed to favor a candidate perceive his messages in a favorable light and look with displeasure upon his opponent. Our attitudes tend to shape the types of communications we expose ourselves to, perceive, and remember. Moreover, our friends and family also guide our reading, listening, and viewing habits. Consequently, we expose ourselves to what we want and expect to read, hear, or see; and the messages that filter through are not likely to pose views contrary to our preferences.

Finally, a relative minority change their opinions as a result of messages communicated through the mass media. Although one study indicates that as many as 5 per cent of Erie County, Ohio voters changed their opinions in the 1948 presidential election as a result of mass communications, *conversion* is the most infrequent of the types of effects discussed. For example, in isolating Iowa counties, where television was viewed with both high and low frequencies in the 1952 presidential election, researchers found no substantial independent effect of television as a factor influencing the party division of the vote.[28] This conversion effect is most likely to occur among persons with no clear-cut preferences between candidates, those with unstable preferences, or citizens faced with persuasive pressures that dictate contradictory choices. A clearly per-

---

[27] Bernard Berelson, "Communications and Public Opinion," in Wilbur Schramm (ed.), *Mass Communications* (Urbana: University of Illinois Press, 1949), p. 500. Joseph T. Klapper, *The Effects of Mass Communication* (Glencoe, Ill.: The Free Press, 1960).

[28] Paul F. Lazarsfeld *et al., The People's Choice* (New York: Duell, Sloan & Pearce, 1944); Katz and Lazarsfeld, *op. cit.;* Herbert A. Simon and Frederick Stern, "The Effect of Television upon Voting Behavior in Iowa in the 1952 Presidential Election," *The American Political Science Review,* XXXXIX (June, 1955), 470–77.

ceived communication might be just the cue to trigger an opinion change in this setting.

POLITICAL LEADERSHIP
AND LIBERAL DEMOCRACY

Professor Sidney Verba has observed that political behavior is "not determined solely by the predispositions that an individual brings into the political process from his experiences and training in primary groups." It is "also affected by the way in which the political system interacts with these dispositions." [29] In this chapter we have discussed leadership as a principal mode of behavior in the political system that stimulates learned predispositions and produces opinions, votes, and other forms of citizen participation. The opinions that count in a democracy are those that are counted; that is, opinions represented to policy officials. The democratic politician's life is consumed in counting opinions. Since he is so attuned to opinions, it is not surprising that he wants to shape them. He does so, not by coercion, but by persuasion and by adjusting his behavior to the demands of the citizens he leads.

In the reciprocal relationship between leader and follower, American political leaders, with rare exceptions, uphold the rules that make possible a democratic representation and resolution of interest differences. By practicing fair play — accepting defeat without violent protest and tolerating each other — political leaders make possible an environment of relatively free politics. Their disputes provide nonleaders with an opportunity to choose between competing sets of would-be rulers. But these rules of fair play extend beyond the leadership corps; they also condition the relationship of leaders to followers. More particularly, they limit the effectiveness of leaders in shaping political opinion. V. O. Key, Jr., observed that despite the proclivity of American politicians to "humbug the people," it is characteristic that "admonitions ever recur against arousing class against class, against stirring the animosities of religious groups, and against demagoguery in its more extreme forms." [30]

Constitutional and conventional restraints are not the only factors conditioning the relations of leaders and led. We have suggested others along the way: the repository of semi-fixed attitudes that political communicators must take into account in influencing opinions; the lack of attention given by Americans to political communications in the first place; the distribution of political leaders throughout many social cate-

[29] Sidney Verba, *Small Groups and Political Behavior* (Princeton: Princeton University Press, 1961), p. 37.

[30] V. O. Key, Jr., *Public Opinion and American Democracy* (New York: Alfred A. Knopf, 1961), p. 539.

gories despite a relative concentration of those of middle- and upper-class backgrounds among the leadership corps; the variable distribution of access to channels of mass communications; and the conflicting leadership roles of officials and newsgatherers in a democratic community.

But perhaps the greatest restriction upon the ability of political leaders to shape broad bodies of opinion in America is the fact of the dispersion of political leadership itself. The setting of political leadership is a crucial determinant of the effectiveness with which leaders influence opinions. The overall setting of American political leadership is one of dispersed authority, dispersed power, dispersed resources for influence, and dispersed political opinions. A concentration of political leadership in a small band of influentials is hardly to be expected in pluralist America despite continuing warnings that precisely such a concentration is taking place. To a large degree, the character of this dispersion is inherent in the processes by which we recruit and select our leaders, institutionalize conflicts for public office, and seek to pressure officials to do our bidding. All are distinctive patterns of conflict representation bound to American political opinion and leadership. We turn to the first of these patterns, one involving the critical fact of voter participation in government, in the next chapter.

BIBLIOGRAPHICAL NOTE

The study of political leadership has concerned social scientists for some time. At first they limited themselves primarily to the life histories of notable leaders. In more recent decades studies have emerged that focus on the characteristics, skills, and styles of political leaders. Many of these are summarized and their findings integrated into a consistent framework in Wendell Bell, Richard J. Hill, and Charles R. Wright, *Public Leadership* (San Francisco: Chandler Publishing Company, 1961). The situational aspects of leadership are covered in such works as E. S. Borgardus, *Leaders and Leadership* (New York: Appleton-Century-Crofts, Inc., 1954); A. W. Gouldner, *Studies in Leadership* (New York: Harper & Row Publishers, 1950); and selections from Louis Petrullo and B. M. Bass, *Leadership and Inter-personal Behavior* (New York: Holt, Rinehart and Winston, Inc., 1961). A useful study of the social characteristics of American political leaders is Donald R. Matthews, *The Social Background of Political Decision-Makers* (New York: Random House, 1954). James D. Barber in his *Political Leadership in American Government* (Boston: Little, Brown and Company, 1964) includes selections illustrating the nature of leadership patterns. In the area of personal leadership one should consult Elihu Katz and Paul F. Lazarsfeld, *Personal Influence* (New York: The Free Press of Glencoe, Paperback Edition, 1964). Elmo Roper's *You and Your Leaders* (New York:

William Morrow and Co., 1957) is a useful account of American responses to political leadership.

Various facets concerning the nature and techniques of political persuasion are explored in works dealing with propaganda, public relations, opinion-formation, and campaigning. Among the most conveniently available of these are: Terence H. Qualter, *Propaganda and Psychological Warfare* (New York: Random House, 1962); Martin Mayer, *Madison Avenue, U.S.A.* (New York: Pocket Books, Inc., 1959); Stanley Kelley, *Professional Public Relations and Political Power* (Baltimore: The Johns Hopkins Press, 1956) and *Political Campaigning* (Washington, D.C.: The Brookings Institution, 1960); James N. Rosenau, *National Leadership and Foreign Policy* (Princeton, New Jersey: Princeton University Press, 1963); Murray B. Levin, *The Compleat Politician* (Indianapolis: The Bobbs-Merrill Company, Inc., 1962); Nelson W. Polsby and Aaron B. Wildavsky, *Presidential Elections* (New York: Charles Scribner's Sons, 1964); and Theodore H. White's narratives of two presidential elections, *The Making of the President 1960* (New York: Atheneum Publishers, 1961) and *The Making of the President 1964* (New York: Atheneum Publishers, 1965).

The use of the mass media as a persuasive channel is discussed in a general fashion in Charles R. Wright, *Mass Communication* (New York: Random House, 1959). The function of the press in a liberal democracy, as well as other political systems, is explored in Fred S. Siebert, Theodore Peterson, and Wilbur Schramm, *Four Theories of the Press* (Urbana: University of Illinois Press, Paperback Edition, 1963). Also very useful is Douglass Cater, *The Fourth Branch of Government* (Boston: Houghton Mifflin Company, 1959). Studies of the effects of mass communication for activating, changing, and reinforcing political attitudes are surveyed in Joseph T. Klapper, *The Effects of Mass Communication* (Glencoe, Illinois: The Free Press, 1960).

CHAPTER
EIGHT

Political Choice

Americans declare their political choices by casting votes in community-wide elections. Recalling our earlier discussion of political opinion, we can view voting choices as expressions of political preference espoused when politically relevant attitudes are stimulated by campaign appeals; that is, each act of choice — each vote — is a statement of opinion under specific conditions. In the following pages we will examine: (1) the electoral setting of political choice; (2) the methods undertaken to discover electoral choice patterns; (3) the constitutional, socio-demographic, personal, and campaign factors associated with normal patterns of partisan voting; and (4) the impact of those patterns upon liberal democracy in America.

THE ELECTORAL CONTEXT
OF POLITICAL CHOICE

The primary, but not sole, purpose for holding elections in the American polity is to select individuals to occupy governing positions for limited, specific terms of office. True, in local areas Americans also go to the polls to accept or reject city charters, approve or refuse constitutional amendments, grant authority to increase taxes, vote revenue bonds, create special governing districts, etc. Here, however, we will confine our discussion to the regular federal elections held for selecting the President of the United States, senators, and members of Congress. Holding such elections helps to regulate social conflict in America in three major ways — by providing for citizen entry into the policy process in an indirect fashion thus reinforcing bonds of community consensus, by establishing a method for popular selection of governing officials, and by expressing political opinion to policy-makers.

Elections exist as one acceptable democratic mechanism for citizen participation in community policy-making. A principal feature of democratic doctrine prescribes that citizens possess equal shares in the popular control over policy processes. In a direct democracy this normally means that each community member casts one vote, either in popular assembly or through referendum, to determine policies. However, our constitutional arrangement, prescribing the policy procedures of a representative democracy, dictates that federal decisions be made by popularly accountable officials. In the absence of provisions for direct participation in policy-making, then, elections held under conditions of universal adult suffrage provide a feasible alternative yielding an indirect voice in community government on a relatively equal basis. Moreover, through their periodic activity as voters and their willingness to abide by electoral verdicts, Americans tacitly accept the legitimacy of this constituted arrangement, despite frequent distortions of political equality resulting from suffrage restrictions, malapportionments, gerrymanders, etc.

Furthermore, by transforming social conflict into electoral competition, elections provide a device for solving one of the most ticklish problems faced by any political community, i.e., who shall rule. During election campaigns disputants hope to win authority so that they can convert group demands into community policy. In the process, they expose conflicts that divide elective policy officials to a broad audience, the electorate, for adjustment.[1] Thus, policy conflicts, and the deeper social differences that lie at their source, yield to electoral competition: an open and peaceful (albeit loud) struggle among candidates seeking public offices. Once the competition for office is decided on behalf of winning candidates, interest conflicts are renewed in policy-making circles as a variety of partisan, group, and constituency elements take issue with proposals of both the victorious President and any congressional majority.

[1] E. E. Schattschneider, *The Semisovereign People* (New York: Holt, Rinehart & Winston, 1960), pp. 62–77; Seymour Martin Lipset, *Political Man* (Garden City, N.Y.: Doubleday & Co., 1959), pp. 30–35.

Finally, American elections provide policy officials with an indication, although imperfect, of public concerns, satisfactions, and irritations. In mobilizing voters, political leaders endeavor to define attractive goals for potential followers. Candidates and supporters define issues symbolizing major areas of social disagreement — the role of federal government in the economy, American foreign relations, civil rights, etc. As efforts to increase voter support among a broad aggregate of diverse interests intensify, these policy issues grow clouded. Consequently, voter choices frequently are but vague, fuzzy, and ambiguous declarations of policy preferences. Election mandates are difficult, if not impossible to ascertain. The social cleavages marking the election assist policy-makers in noting public *concerns,* but seldom reveal policy expressions that can be readily translated into policy *decisions.*

THE STUDY OF POLITICAL CHOICE

Students of politics possess various techniques for compiling the constitutional, social-demographic, personal, and electoral factors associated with collective voter preferences. Although none provides a single key to mysteries of American voting behavior, we can describe the two most frequently employed — aggregate data studies and surveys of voter preferences.

Analysis of aggregate data provides a picture of mass voter habits over extended time periods within particular geographic areas — precincts, counties, congressional constituencies, states, or regions of the United States. Data employed come from official election returns. The precinct is the primary vote-recording level in American politics. From it, returns for candidates, parties, and issues are reported to higher levels for purposes of official tabulation. Studies based upon aggregate figures interpret the recurring voting behavior of an electorate by comparing the proportion of popular vote cast for parties and candidates in a voting district with the social composition of that district. Reports of the United States Bureau of the Census, for example, provide such data as general level of income, education, ethnic background, housing conditions, age structure, types of occupations, etc. in a given area.

Statistical analyses have produced indecisive correlations of general social variables and voting patterns: Republican strength in suburbia, Democratic strength associated with the concentration of ethnic groups in precincts of larger cities, etc. However, the political "meaning" attributed to an individual's being a midwestern farmer, for example, is not revealed in such findings; indeed, from aggregate analysis it is impossible to say anything concrete about how any individual farmer voted. By their very nature, aggregate analyses deal not with individuals but categoric groupings; personal perceptions, feelings, and motivations are uncharted.[2]

The limits of aggregate analysis in explaining electoral choice suggest the utility of questioning people directly about personal motives for political actions. Despite frequent jests and outbursts of alarm during political campaigns regarding the use of sample surveys as measures of public sentiment, opinion polls have now joined aggregate analysis as part of political and scholarly activity. By providing candidates with helpful information, polls increasingly affect political strategy. Few politicians undertake major campaigns without some appraisal of voter dispositions. Some may conduct their own samplings; many contract with polling firms for an assessment. Moreover, as employed by social scientists, survey research has supplied much of the data upon which is based current knowledge of American voting patterns.

The use of opinion surveys assumes the feasibility of selecting a *representative* sample of the population of potential American voters. In such a sample the individuals questioned possess specified politically relevant characteristics in the same proportions as those characteristics are distributed throughout all members of the polity. For example; if 10 per cent of American voters are of Irish extraction and this is a politically relevant fact, then that characteristic should be represented in the same proportion in a national survey. One way of providing such a cross-section of the voting population is through the selection of a stratified sample. By this procedure vital statistics, such as United States Census data, are employed to estimate the proportions of Americans with particular characteristics. The sample is then so drawn as to represent each strata proportionately. Often the very purpose of a survey is to extract politically relevant factors; in such cases pollsters may make up a stratified sample on the basis of characteristics that have proved helpful in obtaining representativeness in the past. Or, they may employ the technique of *random* sampling which assures an equal probability for each individual in the population to be chosen for the sample.

The art of sampling has improved with experience and now combines various sampling techniques in pursuit of increasingly representative cross-sections. One of the most normal procedures in nationwide sampling today is to select at random areas of the country (precincts, census areas, city blocks, etc.) and then systematically select particular dwelling units in those areas. Interviewers are given specific instructions for choosing individuals in particular households for interviewing thus avoiding inter-

---

[2] Austin Ranney, "The Utility and Limitations of Aggregate Data in the Study of Electoral Behavior," in Austin Ranney (ed.), *Essays on the Behavioral Study of Politics* (Urbana: University of Illinois Press, 1962), pp. 91–102.

viewer bias in the selection process. The potential of survey research has been increased in a few studies by employing a panel technique. A panel consists of a sample of voters, chosen by one of the above methods, that is interviewed on several separate occasions during the course of a campaign. This permits an assessment of opinion change as the campaign develops.[3]

Whether responses regarding voter attitudes, intentions, and past behavior are reliable or not depends upon more than the procedure for sample selection. Questions must be phrased to elicit meaningful responses; interviewers must be trained in sophisticated techniques for ferreting out appropriate information. A variety of interviewing procedures are usually employed, including mail questionnaires, face-to-face interviews, and telephone interviews. Although there is no assurance that survey techniques can ever be rendered foolproof, continuous improvements have been made in the last three decades. Table 8-1 illustrates that the Gallup Poll, for example, has since 1936 been able to gauge fairly accurately the voting intentions of the American electorate. On only three occasions was there a discrepancy of more than 2 percentage points in predicted intentions and the actual vote outcome, well within accepted limits of error.

TABLE 8-1

Accuracy Record of Surveys by American Institute of Public Opinion: Presidential and Congressional Elections: 1936–1964 (Gallup Poll)

YEAR	PREDICTED PERCENTAGE OF MARGIN PARTY VOTE	ACTUAL PERCENTAGE OF MARGIN PARTY VOTE	DEVIATION
1936	53.8 (Roosevelt)	60.2	−6.4
1940	55.0 (Roosevelt)	54.7	+ .3
1944	55.3 (Roosevelt)	53.8	−1.5
1946	47.0 (Democrat)	45.7	+1.3
1948	44.5 (Truman)	49.4	−4.9
1950	51.0 (Democrat)	50.3	+0.7
1952	51.0 (Eisenhower)	55.4	−4.4
1954	51.5 (Democrat)	52.7	−1.2
1956	59.5 (Eisenhower)	57.8	+1.7
1958	57.0 (Democrat)	56.5	+0.5
1960	51.0 (Kennedy)	50.1	+0.9
1964	64.0 (Johnson)	62.0	+2.0

Source: Published releases of the American Institute of Public Opinion.

[3] Useful introductions to survey research include Frederick J. Stephan and Philip J. McCarthy, *Sampling Opinions* (New York: John Wiley & Sons, 1958); and Charles H. Backstrom and Gerald D. Hursh, *Survey Research* (Evanston, Ill.: Northwestern University Press, 1963).

A published survey can be a tool of political propaganda as well as understanding; hence, some surveys may distort, rather than reflect, the status of a candidate's appeal at a given point. However, the political candidate himself is interested in obtaining accurate information. The candidate may publish findings favorable to him, but he will also work to correct the defects in his campaign revealed by other studies.

Aggregate analysis and sample surveys generate vast quantities of data about voter characteristics, preferences, intentions, and recorded behavior. The management of complex arrays of statistical data was once a forbidding task. The development of high-speed computers has facilitated rapid analysis of combined aggregate and survey data gathered in a series of studies extending over several decades on a variety of issues. Quick retrieval and manipulation of such data has led to computer simulations of elections. The relative potential effect on voter opinions of such factors as campaign issues, candidate personalities and appeals, long-term partisan loyalties, variable turnout rates among segments of the population, etc., are rapidly computed and then considered under a variety of hypothesized campaign conditions in order to predict election outcomes.[4]

COMMUNITY INFLUENCES ON POLITICAL CHOICE PATTERNS

Aggregate and survey analyses reveal patterns of political choice under a variety of conditions associated primarily with federal elections. A review of the constitutional, socio-demographic, personal, and campaign factors provides us with a picture of the major community influences shaping expressed preferences.

CONSTITUTED INFLUENCES

The constitutional aspect of American elections is threefold. Electoral preferences are regulated by a highly formalized setting of statutes; by features of the written Constitution, notably federalism; and by operating constitutional conventions consisting of customs and habits, particularly the partisan tradition.

Statutory Features. Statutory regulation of American elections is extensive. Among regulatory devices are control of absentee voting, residence and registration requirements, provisions for tabulating "legal"

---

[4] See William McPhee, "Note on a Campaign Simulator," *The Public Opinion Quarterly*, XXV, No. 2 (Summer, 1961), 184–93; Ithiel de Sola Pool and Robert P. Abelson, "The Simulmatics Project," *The Public Opinion Quarterly*, XXV, No. 2 (Summer, 1961), 167–83; and James Coleman *et al.*, "Computers and Election Analysis: The *New York Times* Project," *The Public Opinion Quarterly*, XXVIII, No. 3 (Fall, 1964), 418–46.

votes, placement and position of candidate names on the ballot, provisions for write-in voting, and ballot length. State statutes are seldom impartial in their effects upon electoral competition. Each distributes advantages or disadvantages to interests jockeying for electoral advantage; each may be manipulated to the profit or detriment of disputants. By way of illustration, we cite here how the type of ballot form used, the scheduling of elections, and the nature of constituencies can affect voter options and conduct.

Two major ballot forms are utilized in American elections; the party-column and office-column ballots. The former, employed in over 50 per cent of the states, facilitates "straight-ticket" voting for one party's entire slate. All Democratic, Republican, or other party candidates appear in a single column with partisan designation at the top. The office-column ballot groups candidates by the office sought; partisan affiliation is indicated next to each office-seeker's name. Survey research in 1956 revealed that where ballots facilitated straight-ticket voting, six out of ten Republicans voted straight ticket. But in the absence of the party-column ballot, one-half of Republican voters selected Eisenhower for President and crossed party lines to vote for one or more Democrats for other positions. Stevenson voters chose all Democratic candidates in seven of every ten cases when the ballot facilitated doing so but voted a straight ticket in only six of every ten instances using the office-column ballot.[5] The prescription of ballot type is a statutory decision that helps foretell the nature of elections in the state. Party-column ballots promote elections of partisan competition by providing voters with opportunities to choose between alternative sets of candidates; the office-column ballot tends to produce elections waged as conflicts between candidates supported by more narrow interests.

Federal elections are often held in conjunction with local and statewide contests. The greater the number of elective offices to be voted upon, the less citizens seem to know of the positions, backgrounds, and loyalties of candidates for each. Consequently, choice patterns frequently are conditioned by any symbol that simplifies the voter's selection from among numerous candidates for several offices. The partisan attachment of the candidate normally provides such a symbol. When federal, state, and local elections are staggered, voters can rely less upon such a "sorting" device and must base their preference upon known characteristics of the candidate — his stand, his personal character, his sectional background, or perhaps a prestigious name.

[5] Angus Campbell, Philip E. Converse, Warren E. Miller, and Donald E. Stokes, *The American Voter* (New York: John Wiley & Sons, 1960), pp. 266–89; Warren E. Miller, "Presidential Coattails: A Study in Political Myth and Methodology," *The Public Opinion Quarterly*, XIX, No. 1 (Spring, 1955) 26–39.

Moreover, when federal, state, and local elections are simultaneously scheduled, the forces that produce triumph for a given slate of candidates at one level frequently carry over into races for other offices., For example, where ballot forms facilitate straight-ticket voting and federal elections coincide with state and local contests, "coattail" voting may occur: several party candidates ride to victory on the coattails of the strongest vote-getter on the ticket. Aggregate studies have suggested that an attractive candidate for the Presidency may draw votes to lesser-known party candidates for congressional and state offices, as evidenced in some key races in elections of 1952 and 1956. Yet in those same elections Democratic dominance at the congressional level was not seriously eroded by Eisenhower's popularity, for particularly in 1956 the Democrats reinforced their congressional majority. In some federal elections, patterns of choice reflect the voting strength of candidates for gubernatorial offices. There is evidence, for example, that President Harry S. Truman's slim margin of victory in competition for Illinois' electoral votes in 1948 owed much to the substantial majority received by Adlai E. Stevenson as gubneratorial candidate on the Democratic ticket. Hence, federal patterns can be shaped by the tenor of state politics as well as the reverse.

But the patterns revealed in aggregate studies may be products of something other than coattail voting. Surveying opinions in the 1952 presidential election, for example, Professor Warren E. Miller reported that among possible "coattail voters" only 3 per cent of Stevenson voters and 15 per cent of Eisenhower voters cast votes only on the basis of the attractiveness of the candidate. For all others, both long-term partisan preference and issue stands had an equal, if not greater, influence upon their choices. In short, coattail voting may stem from the attractiveness of candidates at particular levels; but the same pattern may be produced by factors extraneous to candidate appeal. This raises the question of the personal motivations underlying choice patterns, a point we shall discuss in detail later.[6]

Whatever the reason for the straight-ticket phenomenon, politicians put some stock in the coattail theory. In his 1966 proposal for a constitutional amendment changing the terms of members of the House of Representatives to four years, President Lyndon Johnson urged that House and presidential terms coincide. A House candidate, then, could always appear on a ballot headed by his party's candidate for President; and congressional campaigns, and perhaps victories, would be tied more closely to the simultaneously held presidential campaign. Regardless of

---

[6] For analyses of split-ticket voting see Angus Campbell and Warren E. Miller, "The Motivational Basis of Straight and Split Ticket Voting," *The American Political Science Review*, LI, No. 2 (June, 1957), 293–312; and Malcom Moos, *Politics, Presidents and Coattails* (Baltimore: The Johns Hopkins Press, 1952).

reasons for straight-ticket voting (candidate appeal, party loyalty, or issue stands), the change in election scheduling could be expected to produce greater coincidences in choice patterns for the two offices.

Statutes regulating constituency boundaries, size, and composition affect preference patterns in two ways. First, choices for members of the U.S. House of Representatives are clearly tied to the characteristics of constituency voters — whether Republican or Democratic in voting habits; rural, urban or suburban in temperament; etc. Congressional apportionment may serve to divide some constituent interests and assuage others. Constituency lines can be drawn to split a dominant interest normally capable of mustering sufficient votes to elect a congressman. This has long been true for minority groups in metropolitan areas that find their "ghettos" divided in sections by constituency boundaries in order to prevent control of election competition. Professor Avery Leiserson points to another link between constituency type and choice patterns. Voters in different size constituencies have differing perspectives on the nature of a given election. The participant voting in a 350,000-voter congressional district, for example, feels that his vote is more efficacious than if voting as a member of the President's multi-interest constituency of 60–70 million voters. In sum, "the electoral system may condition the voter to take a larger or a narrower view of his own and the public's interests, and this will be reflected in the elective office-holder's conception of the political principle to which he feels accountable." [7]

Federal Features. As an operating feature of the American polity, federalism distributes political authority throughout several governing levels. As a result, each layer of the polity elects public officials to manage affairs peculiar to the level involved; that is, we choose a President, senators, and congressmen for national office, each state selects its own governors, legislatures, and judges, etc. In the process of mobilizing support for his own election, each official directs his appeals and promises his loyalties to the members of his particular national, state, or local constituency. In turn patterns of partisan support have tended to develop around these local candidacies over the years. Thus, a by-product of the federal arrangement has been reinforcement of variations in partisan voting between sections as regions, states, and local areas.

Sectional variations in partisan voting are among the most enduring patterns of American voting behavior. Regional loyalties to a single party have prevailed throughout American political history. Democratic dominance in Southern sections and Republican ascendency in Northeastern areas was taken for granted for decades. Alignments in recent presidential elections indicate modifications in these historical regional patterns,

[7] Avery Leiserson, *Parties and Politics* (New York: Alfred A. Knopf, 1958), pp. 285–86.

but Republican or Democratic dominance in certain sections is still common in the selection of locally-elected members of the Senate and House of Representatives.

Regional patterns of partisan choice are paralleled by traditional state loyalties. Under the federal arrangement whereby states elect their own governing officials, a party can establish itself as the major force in state politics even though its nationwide strength is less imposing. There are clear-cut examples of one-party dominance in particular states, a dominance that makes it possible for those states to deliver partisan majorities in presidential and congressional elections as well. For example; 1964 marked the first time in American history when Vermont gave its electoral votes to a Democratic candidate for President, a fact reflecting the long Republican domination of that state's politics. Similar one-party dominant states exist throughout the polity — South Carolina, Mississippi, and Alabama for Democrats, and Maine or Kansas for Republicans.

A number of these states demonstrate less consistency in presidential voting patterns than in former years. Changes in preferences within the states may be caused by several factors: critical issues such as desegregation in Alabama or Mississippi; the migration of partisans of the opposition party into a state such as the movement of Republicans to Florida and Arizona; the Republican surge in metropolitan areas of individual states of the South, particularly in presidential elections; and some tendency for national parties to identify with distinctive stands in policy conflicts, thus reinforcing motivations for ticket splitting between state and federal elective officials.[8]

Configurations of partisan choice vary from one locale of residence to another, a point of considerable importance in a federal polity that chooses its President through an Electoral College and its representative assemblies from local constituencies. The fact that urban or metropolitan America, outside the South and Southwest, has traditionally been a center of Democratic support has had considerable import in presidential elections. Urban majorities have facilitated Democratic efforts to capture electoral votes in populous states — New York, California, Pennsylvania, Illinois, Ohio, and Michigan. Republican-dominated urban areas are less likely to contribute to the building of a majority in the Electoral College since they are concentrated in less populous states of the Midwest and South. Outside the South, rural areas frequently supply Republican support, although agrarian voting has tended to vary with economic trends affecting farm prices.

Suburban America is neither predominantly Republican nor Demo-

[8] See, for example, Donald S. Strong, *Urban Republicanism in the South* (University, Alabama: Bureau of Public Administration, University of Alabama, 1960).

cratic in voting patterns. In the period immediately following World War II, migrations of urbanites to the suburban areas consisted primarily of upper-middle-class citizens with Republican preferences. Consequently, the elections of that era reflected Democratic strength in central cities, but suburbia was Republican territory. However, with rising incomes and pressures brought about by Negroes moving into formerly all White, urban areas, middle- and lower-class citizens also sought suburban residence. Hence, suburban precincts now manifest mixed vote patterns; that is, some suburbs reflect Republican dominance, others are Democratic. From an aggregate analysis of voting patterns in selected American suburbs, Professor Fred Wirt concluded that although "there is a more Republican than Democratic cast to suburbia as a whole," data indicates "we also have working class, elegant and mixed salad suburbs whose constituents are revealed with differing socio-economic characteristics, whose ecology reveals other differences, and whose politics question severely the notion of suburbia as a 'political Jordan' from whose waters Democrats emerge in the image of the compleat Republican." [9]

Partisan Features. Constitutions are sets of habits as well as collections of statutes and written principles. Few patterns of political choice are as apparent as that of the two-party tradition in American federal elections. There is a remarkable stability in the distribution of votes between the two parties over extended time periods. Republican majorities in presidential elections typified the period from 1864–1932. Thereafter Democratic majorities have prevailed. There have been exceptions to both patterns; for example, Democratic victories in 1876, 1884, 1892, 1912, and 1916; Republican breakthroughs in 1952 and 1956.

The Republican and Democratic parties have also alternated in their control over Congress with some consistency, despite the fact that in some districts and states congressional seats have been under the proprietorship of the traditionally dominant party without serious challenge from the opposition. To some extent these locales of one-party dominance, have provided "safe" districts from which a party could continue to thrive in the face of a national landslide against it. In this fashion they have helped to preserve a two-party competition in eras of one-party trends. For example, even in the wake of a sizable defeat suffered in the presidential election of 1928, the Democratic party was able to retain its congressional seats in the South as a base from which to continue the role of an opposition party; by the same token, Republicans in 1936 found solace in the fact that they could retain control of areas such as Maine and

[9] Frederick M. Wirt, "The Political Sociology of American Suburbia: A Reinterpretation," *The Journal of Politics*, XXVII, No. 3 (August, 1965), 666.

Vermont even though Franklin Roosevelt had achieved an overwhelming victory at the expense of Alf Landon nationally.

Long-term shifts in party fortunes at all levels are associated with the extent to which voters think of themselves as Republicans or Democrats. It is possible to classify presidential elections according to the extent that they reflect, for example, current patterns of dominant partisan leanings in the political community. Based upon survey analysis of American voting behavior, the Michigan Survey Research Center has attempted a fourfold classification of elections — maintaining, deviating, reinstating, and realigning elections. Each reflects a variation of Democratic or Republican strength, but within the context of a two-party tradition.

If the party of the dominant number of partisan identifiers wins (a maintaining election) it indicates that campaign cues may have reinforced prevailing partisan leanings and stimulated loyalists to turn out in sufficient numbers for victory. Or those campaign appeals may not have had sufficient salience to influence voters away from basic predispositions. A deviating election occurs if issues, candidates, and other influences produce sufficient temporary defection among majority party identifiers in an election for the minority party to win. Democrats voting for Eisenhower in 1952 and 1956 are cases of such electoral deviation. An election following a deviation may restore the party of majority identifiers and, thus, reinstate the dominant party. Finally, over a period of years the distribution of identifiers can shift; the majority sinks to minority status, and a specific election reveals a realignment in basic party preferences among citizens. Sometimes realigning elections follow crises in American social life that cause personal defections from one party to the other, as in the period of economic turmoil from 1929–32. Some realigning is, perhaps, always taking place through gradual changes in identifications, but it is seldom of sufficient magnitude to shift the majority party to minority status. Moreover, changes in identification can reinforce the dominant party position, as did the popular grief following the assassination of John F. Kennedy in 1963.[10]

SOCIAL INFLUENCES

Effects of economic and social crises on partisan realignments suggest another dimension of the context of American federal elections: the social features of the polity linked to broad shifts in voting patterns. As a political pattern, voter opinion is shaped by two aspects of this social

---

[10] See Angus Campbell, et al., op. cit., pp. 531–38; Donald E. Stokes, "Party Loyalty and the Likelihood of Deviating Elections," The Journal of Politics, XXIV, No. 4 (November, 1962), 689–702; and V. O. Key, Jr., "A Theory of Critical Elections," The Journal of Politics, XVII (February, 1955), 3–18.

dimension of community elections: a person's membership both in socio-demographic groupings and social groups. Both provide points of reference for individual behavior. Our political guides are often those who are either like ourselves in some respect or are our social intimates.

Socio-Demographic Groupings. Americans respond differently to federal elections depending upon their sex, age, education, ethnic background, religion, locale of residence, occupation, and class status. Table 8-2 provides an indication of the proportions of different social groupings associated with partisan choice in recent presidential elections.

Sex. We have already seen that men are more active politically in the American polity than women; they participate more, vote more, and are

TABLE 8-2

Partisan Presence of Social Groupings
in Presidential Years 1948–1964 *

SOCIAL GROUPING	PER CENT FAVORING DEMOCRATIC PARTY				
	1948	1952	1956	1960	1964
Men	52	43	45	51	60
Women	49	41	39	49	62
Age 21–29	—	—	43	54	64
Age 21–34	57	46	—	—	—
Age 30–49	—	—	45	54	63
Age 35–44	57	45	—	—	—
Age 45–54	44	42	—	—	—
Age 55 and over	43	35	—	—	—
Age 50 and over	—	—	39	45	59
Grade School Education	63	48	50	55	66
High School Education	51	42	42	52	62
College Education	22	27	31	39	52
Protestants	43	36	37	38	55
Roman Catholics	62	51	51	78	76
Jews	—	77	75	81	—
Whites	50	39	41	49	59
Negroes	50	63	61	68	94
Professional and Executive	20	31	32	42	54
White Collar	47	34	37	48	57
Manual	—	—	50	60	71
Farmers	60	36	46	48	53

* Compiled from data released by the American Institute of Public Opinion and the Michigan Survey Research Center. Data reflects percentage favoring Democrat as opposed to Republican, Independent, or other parties (Progressives, Dixiecrats, etc.).

overrepresented in leadership positions. In recent decades, however, the female population has taken a more active interest in politics. The rate of voting among women has increased gradually since their enfranchisement in 1919. As voters in presidential elections, women, shifting their support from one party to another more frequently, appear slightly more fickle in their party affiliations than men do. An overall comparison of partisan predispositions prior to the 1960's revealed that women were 3–5 per cent more Republican than men, a difference so slight that it could be produced by other social characteristics (age, residence) rather than any intrinsic political differences between males and females.[11]

Age. Although no single age grouping in America indicates a consistent partisan preference, age is related to political choice in at least two ways. First, maturity brings with it opportunities for greater political involvement and participation; in the past, older age groupings have been more likely than the younger to vote in federal elections. Secondly, party loyalties tend to intensify with age. The longer one gives his support to a given party, the more inclined he is to continue doing so. There are exceptions, of course, for with maturity also come more social and economic reasons for shifting party loyalties. For example, an individual in his thirties with a record of lukewarm support for Democratic candidates may, as a result of possible upward social mobility, acquire a preference for the Republican party.

We noted earlier that a majority of young people entering the voting population for the first time in any given election bring with them the partisan loyalties inculcated by family, church, and school. The remainder of younger voters are more likely to manifest political independence, switching partisan preferences from one election to another. For these new voters issues and candidate personalities frequently provide the cues shaping their political opinions. However, their greater involvement in community affairs in later years frequently tempers independence and produces both higher participation and more consistent partisanship.

A study of younger voters conducted in Cambridge, Massachusetts, after the presidential elections of 1952, indicates the types of influences that combine with age to shape partisan loyalties in the early years. In their preferences, people age twenty-one to twenty-four tended to agree more with their parents or spouse than with close friends, and least with fellow workers. Work groups apparently stimulated little change in the party dispositions inherited from the family. Among youth from lower socio-economic groups, change from the family partisan affiliation appeared to be roughly associated with the degree of discipline in the home; the more disciplined the child was, the greater the likelihood of

[11] Angus Campbell *et al., op. cit.,* pp. 483–93.

rejection of parental political values. Education also was linked to partisan leanings among younger voters. The well-educated exhibited greater proclivity for change than did the more poorly-educated.[12] In sum, the factor of age does not shape political preferences independently; strength and length of party attachment, changing social characteristics, and the degree of political involvement associated with maturity are more direct in influencing voter opinions.

Education. Surveys indicate that consistent Republican voters frequently come from the ranks of voters with more formal education. Since education is at least one component of class status, there tends to be an overall pattern of upper-status Republicanism. Republicans tend primarily to come from those having postgraduate training as lawyers, medical doctors, and engineers. Voters with graduate degrees in the sciences, humanities, and social sciences, particularly academicians, are more frequently Democrats.

Ethnicity. Although deep ethnic cleavages do not characterize either policy or electoral controversies to the extent that they have in European nations, there are stable patterns of partisan preference among different ethnic groups. Democrats have drawn strength in federal elections from voters of Irish, Polish, Italian, and Slavic background more often than have Republicans. The latter have been able to count more upon Americans of English, Scottish, Welsh, German, and Scandinavian ancestry. In recent years, Negro voters have shifted dramatically away from the party of Abraham Lincoln to the Democrats. As Table 8-2 indicates, Negroes have demonstrated a consistent preference for the Democratic party and Democratic candidates in presidential elections since at least 1948.

Religion. The precise effect of religious background upon voting is difficult to gauge. Although there are both Catholic Republicans and Protestant Democrats, the overall pattern is one of greater affiliation of Protestants with Republicanism. Jews have more consistently favored Democratic candidates; Catholics have done so to a slightly lesser degree than Jews. The religious factor has been more apparent in some campaigns than others; for example, the candidacy of John F. Kennedy triggered both pro- and anti-Catholic sentiments among many Americans. The Michigan Survey Research Center, in its study of the 1960 campaign, estimated that, in the nation as a whole, Kennedy's religion provided him with 4.3 per cent more support from Catholics than would have been expected if people had voted primarily on the basis of partisan affiliation.

[12] Eleanor E. Maccoby, Richard E. Matthews, and Anton S. Morton, "Youth and Political Change," in John R. Owens and P. J. Staudenraus (eds.), *The American Party System* (New York: The Macmillan Co., 1965), pp. 305–18.

Yet losses from Protestant Democrats and Independents were of the magnitude of 6.5 per cent. The overall effect of the religious issue was a loss of 2.2 per cent of "normal" Democratic support.[13] However, this loss was more than offset by the peculiarities of voting in the Electoral College. The Catholic shift to Kennedy occurred in populous states and was sufficient to carry the electoral votes of those states for the Democratic candidate. Defections by Protestant Democrats developed in states with fewer electoral votes. In sum, being a Catholic cost Kennedy 2.2 per cent of the popular vote nationally but provided a windfall of ten electoral votes that he might not otherwise have received.[14]

Occupation. In general, occupational groupings account for some differences in partisan support. Businessmen, both large and small, have tended to furnish support to the Republican cause, although there is considerable variation with type of business, locale, etc. Republican strength is commonly drawn from white collar, business, managerial, professional, and executive classes. Workers, whether unskilled, organized or unorganized, lean considerably more toward Democratic partisanship.

Class Status. Membership in primary groups and secondary groupings including partisan attachments, contributes to a person's subjective appraisal of his standing in the community — his class status. We noted in Chapter Five that class status is associated with patterns of political participation; to the extent that it contributes to political interest, class status is tied also to patterns of partisan choice in federal elections.

The relation of class status and partisan preference is at least twofold. First, the class status of parents is a factor influencing the type of partisanship the child is exposed to in the family circle. Throughout politicization, a subjective feeling that the child belongs to a particular social class frequently is learned concurrently with partisanship. We noted earlier that for most Americans the learning of party identification is of greater political salience than the learning of class identification. Nevertheless, both affiliations are a joint product of the maturing process, and a change in one is sometimes related to shifts in the other. For instance: in the study mentioned earlier, Eleanor Maccoby and her associates found that, among youths of ages twenty-one to twenty-four, upward social mobility generally marked increasing affiliations with Republican partisanship; yet those moving down the social ladder and already disposed to the Republican party did not surrender that commitment.[15]

---

[13] Philip E. Conserve *et al.*, "Stability and Change in 1960: A Reinstating Election," *The American Political Science Review*, LV, No. 2 (June, 1961), 269–89.

[14] Ithiel de Sola Pool, Robert P. Abelson, and Samuel Popkin, *Candidates, Issues and Strategies* (Cambridge, Mass.: The M.I.T. Press, 1964), p. 117.

[15] Eleanor E. Maccoby *et al.*, *op. cit.*, p. 318.

The second aspect of class status — a citizen's social standing as indicated by occupation, income, and education — is associated more directly with political choice. In comparing class voting in four Anglo-American political communities (Great Britain, the United States, Canada, and Australia), Robert Alford found that occupational categories of Americans are associated with the partisan direction of voting choice. Using a series of opinion surveys covering the period of 1936–62, Alford developed an "index of class voting" based upon the percentage of persons in manual and non-manual occupations voting for the "left" party (in American elections this was the Democratic party). Although class and partisanship were not as strongly associated in America as in Great Britain, the index of class voting was sufficiently high to warrant including class along with regional and religious influences as significant factors explaining variations in the distribution of popular votes between our two major parties.[16]

Fewer than one-third of Americans refuse, when asked in interviews, to classify themselves as members of a particular socio-economic category — upper class, middle class, working class, etc. This penchant for self-classification, however, cannot be equated with an intense sense of class awareness fostering serious conflicts between distinguishable class interests in specific elections. Nor has class conflict formed a consistent framework for partisan competition. Speaking primarily of perceived status, as opposed to the class voting explored by Alford, the authors of *The American Voter* have observed that no intensification of class consciousness among Americans in recent decades has produced partisan cleavages based on basic social divisions.[17]

Occasionally, however, political parties have made distinct appeals to class consciousness, and analysis of gross voting patterns do indicate moderate class cleavages. In some periods, class considerations in large measure shaped electoral outcome. For example, V. O. Key, Jr., found that as federal measures for the relief of the unemployed came into existence in the 1930's they provided salient political issues to destitute classes and attracted citizens of all partisan persuasions to the Democratic cause. However, as the New Deal progressed, "persons at all economic levels at each election moved away from the Democratic party but at rates varying with level of economic status." Thus, upper-class Republicans resumed their partisan loyalties more quickly than did working- and lower-class Republicans benefiting from policies of the Democratic

[16] Robert R. Alford, *Party and Society* (Chicago: Rand McNally & Co., 1963), pp. 219–49.

[17] Angus Campbell *et al., op. cit.,* p. 347; Heinz Eulau, *Class and Party in the Eisenhower Years* (New York: The Free Press of Glencoe, 1962).

administration.[18] In other eras, class and status factors were less relevant in explaining the apparent consensus of voters in all socio-economic categories on a particular candidate or party, as in the Eisenhower victory of 1952 or the Johnson landslide of 1964. In sum, it is unlikely that an American consistently votes Republican or Democrat because he identifies his interest as upper, middle, or working class. Research findings have not determined whether an individual perceives a party's position from a class-status perspective or judges his class position in a partisan frame of reference. There is a complex mingling of party, class, and status affiliation among Americans which shapes choice patterns in federal elections.

We can recapitulate these tendencies among social groupings by noting that Democratic support commonly is greater among lower-income groupings, Southerners, dwellers in central cities of metropolitan areas, organized and unskilled laborers, first- and second-generation Americans, Negroes and other ethnic minorities, Catholics and Jews, farm operators, and both the relatively unschooled and those with graduate training. On the other hand, Protestants, prosperous farmers, managerial and professional types, the college-educated, residents of upper-class suburbs, Northerners and Midwesterners, and middle-aged, middle- and upper-income groupings, and an increasing number of Southern dissidents from the Democratic party tend to align themselves with the Republicans.

Of the socio-demographic groupings listed in Table 8-2 it is noteworthy that only one — the Negro — has consistently contributed a majority support in recent elections to one of the two parties. Clearly both parties have drawn substantial support from all socio-demographic groupings in the community. Moreover, each grouping has shifted proportions of support from one party to another between elections. This lends credence to the point made earlier that American elections are manifestations of social consensus as well as conflict. Partisan competitive appeals do not normally correspond to deep-seated disputes between categoric interests — rich versus poor, educated versus uneducated, Protestant versus Catholic, men versus women, etc. In turn the lack of consistent loyalty to either major party from specific social groupings suggests that we must look beyond categoric interests for factors contributing to the shaping of voting patterns.

Social Groups. Demographic categories such as religion, age, etc, are secondary social groupings distinguishable from what students of politics label as "primary groups." Generally both face-to-face primary

[18] V. O. Key, Jr., *The Responsible Electorate* (Cambridge, Mass.: The Belknap Press of Harvard University Press, 1966), p. 35.

influences and impersonal secondary influences on choice patterns tend to complement one another. People with similar social characteristics and backgrounds are more likely to mingle with one another socially; for example, those in a particular age grouping usually have friends of similar age, workers associate with workers, etc. Amorphous categoric interests are defined and sharpened through more intimate group membership. The Negro protest, for example, took much of its impetus in the late 1950's and early 1960's from feelings of discontent voiced in Negro churches, schools, and neighborhoods. But if primary and secondary forces do not coincide, which has greater impact upon voting behavior? Evidence is inconclusive but warrants a general proposition that social groups are of more immediate significance for choices made in specific elections, whereas demographic groupings leave their mark upon more enduring political attitudes and sentiments.

Primary groups influence voting choices at two levels. Group life, particularly family upbringing, molds politicization. Identifications and attitudes promoting both interest conflict and community consensus are learned in intimate family and friendship circles. Having explored this relation earlier, we turn to a second level: how group memberships are linked to voting acts. We can get some idea of the relation by noting the general influence of family and friends on the American voter. In the American family, husbands and wives demonstrate remarkable consensus in voting opinions. Surveys of voting behavior indicate that fewer than 10 per cent of married couples disagree in candidate preferences in presidential elections. Where husband-wife conflict does take place, the wife frequently chooses to accept the husband's view. A wife that does not accede to her husband's preference tends to resolve the family dispute by not voting at all. In reviewing several studies of the influence of the family upon the political choices of the child, Professor Robert Lane concludes that where intra-family consensus prevails, the parent-child pairing is also likely to be one of agreement.[19] The American family emerges as a relatively homogeneous political unit compared with other social groups.

Evidence regarding the precise impact on voting choice of membership in other face-to-face groups is fragmentary. In a study of voting patterns in Elmira, New York in the 1948 presidential election, an explicit attempt was made to delineate the relation between individual choice and social group membership. It was found that a person's circle of immediate friends tends to reinforce his existing political preferences. Where conflict prevails between individual and group sentiments, the

[19] Robert E. Lane, *Political Life* (Glencoe, Ill.: The Free Press, 1959), pp. 208–9.

former appeared to yield as the campaign progressed.[20] In any election, close associates and co-workers are focal points for the type of political discussion and personal leadership described in Chapter Six.

ATTITUDINAL INFLUENCES

Popular votes are opinions expressing personal reactions to alternative candidates, parties, issues, and groups in specific elections. It is helpful to think of the personal factors underlying political choices as including both how an individual views politics in general — his political *perspectives* or predispositions — and what he views as important in a given election, what activates his politically relevant attitudes on behalf of respective disputants — his political *perceptions*. The campaign setting helps shape the appeals that a voter may find salient to his interests; we take this into account in discussing the campaign influence later. In this section we focus on three factors related to shaping voter perspectives on campaigns in federal elections — partisan identification, ideological commitment, and personal consistency.

Party Identification. One way to conceive of federal electoral competition is to regard it as a contest between rival sets of prospective policy-makers. To facilitate the mobilization of votes on their behalf, candidates organize into competing sets and run as the nominees of our traditional political parties. They may or may not advocate particular features of party platforms or actively support individual candidates of their own party. In any event, they have traditionally identified themselves with party labels — Republican or Democrat — in federal elections and have limited voter options for President, congressman, or senator, to two.

By paring down the multiplicity of conflicting social interests to competing sets of candidates, partisanship provides points of reference for personal political attitudes. Studies conducted by the Survey Research Center of the University of Michigan and by the American Institute of Public Opinion coincide in finding that Americans demonstrate fairly consistent partisan loyalties. The Survey Research Center reveals that "three Americans out of four freely classify themselves as Democrats or Republicans, and most of those who call themselves Independents grant that they are closer to one party than they are to the other."[21] The Gallup Poll's surveys indicate approximately four out of five making a partisan declaration.

Whatever the source of these commitments — emotional satisfaction,

[20] Bernard R. Berelson, Paul F. Lazarsfeld, and William N. McPhee, *Voting* (Chicago: The University of Chicago Press), 1954.

[21] Angus Campbell, "Some Findings of Voting Research," *Voting Research and the Businessman in Politics* (Ann Arbor, Mich.: The Foundation for Research on Human Behavior, 1960), p. 3.

habit, conscious reflection, family, etc. — partisan identifications constitute personally meaningful symbols that simplify the task of choosing between competing candidates. The psychological attachment a person feels toward either party does much to shape his long-term political perspective. To the extent that such predispositions guide political perceptions, partisan loyalty is a major, but not the sole, factor associated with patterns of political choice in the community. It has been estimated that if Americans were to cast votes in keeping with abiding partisan sentiments in presidential elections, the distribution of the two-party vote between Democrats and Republicans would be 54–46 per cent.[22] This figure is adjusted to compensate for the fact that Republicans are more likely to vote than Democrats in American elections. That such a distribution is not ordinarily obtained, however, suggests that factors other than partisan attachment shape voter opinions and produce variations.

There are at least three variables that may inhibit Americans from voting in accordance with their party loyalties: the compatibility of their partisan sentiments with other political desires, the intensity of their party loyalties, and the possibility of shifts in partisan leanings. Partisan attachment is but one attitude — one element in a broader set of personal attitudes shaped by group loyalties, personal idiosyncracies, and the social-demographic attributes discussed above — that mold a voter's perspective on a political campaign. So long as partisan sentiments are compatible with other personally defined interests and with what the voter perceives in the campaign, there is a likelihood that partisan attachment will determine voter opinions. This was apparently so in 1964 when 87 per cent of Democratic identifiers cast their vote for the Johnson-Humphrey ticket. However, this was not the case in 1952 and 1956 when many Democrats felt the stronger pull of Eisenhower's candidacy or in 1960 when many Democrats voted for Richard Nixon because of religion or issue stands. Taking such instances into account, Professor Philip E. Converse and his associates assessed the relative impact of partisan loyalty on the vote by asserting that it is useful to "think of election results as reflecting the interplay of two sets of forces: stable, long-term partisan dispositions and short-term forces specific to the immediate election situation." [23]

Americans also vary in the intensity with which they hold to their party loyalties. This too produces variations from the expected 54–46 per cent distribution. The Survey Research Center has found it useful to distinguish between strong, weak, and independent partisans and out-

---

[22] Philip E. Converse *et al., op. cit.*
[23] *Ibid.*

right Independents. Strong partisans are likely to be unswerving in their support of party candidates, year in and year out. Weak partisans, Democrat or Republican, may yield to pressures and appeals that produce defections from their long-term partisan attachments. An "independent" Democrat or Republican is a "leaner"; that is, one who feels himself somewhat closer to one or the other party but whose loyalties are not rigid. The true Independent prefers neither party.

Party identification is, as any attitude, fairly stable; and the distribution of Republican-Democratic identifiers in the community is even a more stable factor (see Table 8-3). Both, however, are subject to change. If identifiers begin to feel that their party no longer stands for what they desire and their partisanship is unsatisfying, they may change that identification in keeping with what may be a more favorable stand attributed to the opposing party.[24] If they do not change their identifications, they may at least change their voting support in one election. Some 20 per cent of Republicans voted for Mr. Johnson in 1964; this represented a substantial increase from the 5 per cent supporting the Democratic ticket in 1960.

TABLE 8-3

*The Distribution of Partisanship
in the American Political Community*

YEAR	SURVEY	PER CENT DEMOCRATS	PER CENT REPUBLICANS	PER CENT INDEPENDENTS
1940	Gallup	42	38	20
1950	Gallup	45	33	22
1952	SRC	47	27	22
1953	SRC	47	30	18
1954	SRC	47	27	22
1956	SRC	44	29	24
1957	SRC	47	26	21
1958	SRC	47	29	19
1960	SRC	46	27	23
1960	Gallup	47	30	23
1961	SRC	47	24	24
1962	SRC	47	26	23
1964	Gallup	53	25	22

Source: Gallup Surveys are taken from published releases of the American Institute of Public Opinion; Michigan Survey Research Center results are taken from Donald E. Stokes, "Party Loyalty and the Likelihood of Deviating Elections," *The Journal of Politics*, XXIV (November, 1962), p. 692.

[24] Donald R. Matthews and James W. Prothro, "Southern Images of Political Parties: An Analysis of White and Negro Attitudes," *The Journal of Politics*, XXVI, No. 1 (February, 1964), 82–111.

Ideology. The political outlook of a small number of Americans can be traced to basic ideological commitments. For these citizens, federal elections serve as a competition between candidates intent upon obtaining mandates for initiating liberal or conservative programs. Earlier, however, in discussing American political consensus, we noted that only 15–16 per cent sampled in 1960 possessed "reasonable" knowledge of the differences between liberal and conservative ideology.[25]

Yet ideological considerations influence choice patterns in other ways. As intense minorities, the ideologically disposed shape political alternatives with an impact out of proportion to numbers. The Populists of an earlier era are but one example. In a later period, definite ideological disputes were found among Republicans in the pre-convention maneuverings of 1964. The victorious conservative faction carried its doctrinaire appeal into competition with rival Democrats. To the extent that there were relatively few ideologically oriented voters, party strategy based upon the assumption of a wider distribution of these voters contributed to electoral defeat in the Republican cause of 1964.

Personal Consistency. From what has been said, it is easy to theorize that individual political choices are largely foreordained by personal perspectives. Relatively stable partisan, socio-economic, and even ideological interests do predispose many voters to examine parties, candidates, and issues in a light most congenial to personal values. This tendency is particularly evident among strongly identified partisans, the more intensely class conscious, and the ideologically aroused. If all voter choices were so governed, then variations in electoral outcome could be explained as reflections of differences in levels of participation within an electorate possessing relatively hardened attitudes. Thus, the thrust of any campaign would be to reinforce acquired attitudes and increase turnout of partisan supporters. In fact, much of current opinion and attitude research underscores the feasibility of such a view of voter behavior. For many Americans, personal consistency reflects campaign judgments and choices made in conformity with fixed personal perspectives. But there is another view, supported by sufficient evidence to place it on a par with that just described, that may provide partial explanation for choice patterns: that personal consistency may be a product of changed perspectives as well as distorted perceptions.[26]

[25] Angus Campbell *et al.*, *op. cit.*, p. 249.

[26] For a discussion of these contrasting views see: Robert E. Agger, "Panel Studies of Comparative Community Political Decision-Making," in M. Kent Jennings and L. Harmon Zeigler (eds.), *The Electoral Process* (Englewood Cliffs, N.J.: Prentice-Hall, 1965), p. 271; Marshall N. Goldstein and Robert S. Cahill, "Mass Media and Community Politics" in Robert S. Cahill and Stephen P. Hencley (eds.), *The Politics of Education in Local Government* (Danville, Ill.: The Interstate Printers & Publishers, 1964), pp. 163–88.

To be sure, a voter may bring a host of partisan, class, ideological, and group loyalties into focus during an election. In the campaign he may perceive information about the positions of his favored candidate, the views of friends, or appeals from respected opinion leaders that fail to conform with his personal preferences. Such was the case among some Protestant Democrats in 1960 who were torn between Kennedy, the Democrat but Catholic candidate, and Nixon, the Republican but Protestant contender. What are the implications for political choice when an individual faces such conflict between his perspectives and perceptions and, consequently, is cross-pressured?

Students of political opinion have hypothesized that when confronted by multiple and contradictory influences, people strive to order their predispositions and perceptions into a consistent perspective on the political universe. This effort at intellectual and emotional tidiness has been labeled a "strain toward consistency" or "drive toward congruity"; it aims at yielding a consistent cluster of politically relevant personal attitudes.[27] In the process, personal values are modified, particularly among persons with unstable and fluid attitudes toward political matters. This is often true of the less formally educated or persons with little interest in politics. Such voters are especially prone to be swayed by political persuasion. For a voter, the extent of attitude change, if any, depends largely on the intensity and direction of previously held attitudes, their consistency, and the degree of harmony or discrepancy perceived by the voter between his political preference and those of his friends, favored candidates, parties, groups, etc.

The cross-pressured voter may preserve personal consistency in politics by changing a previously held attitude. For example: he may change the intensity of his allegiance to a formally held attachment, despite the fact that he continues to adhere to it; the Protestant Democrat may vote for a party Catholic but think less of his party and grow weaker in Democratic loyalty or, alternately, feel less committed to his Protestant sentiments. Again, a person may allow intensely held attitudes to drive out weaker preferences completely; some Southern segregationists foreswore long-term Democratic loyalties rather than vote for a presidential nominee and stay in a national party pledged to removal of segregation.

For the voter deeply committed to a given preference, however, a perceptual shift may prove easier than an attitude change. The voter who finds that his preferred candidate says things with which he does

[27] See Carolyn W. Sherif, Muzafer Sherif, and Roger E. Nebergall, *Attitude and Attitude Change* (Philadelphia and London: W. B. Saunders Co., 1965); and Denis G. Sullivan, "Psychological Balance and Reactions to the Presidential Nominations in 1960," in M. Kent Jennings and L. Harmon Zeigler (eds.), *The Electoral Process*, (Englewood Cliffs, N.J.: Prentice-Hall, 1965), pp. 238–64.

not agree, for example, may start to misperceive the position of the candidate in a more personally acceptable light; some isolationists adjusted to the Eisenhower candidacy in 1952 by convincing themselves that he was devoted to increasing withdrawal of the United States from foreign affairs. Finally, however, the resolution of personal conflict produced by cross-pressuring may be impossible. For many the attractive course of action is to withdraw temporarily from the political community through nonparticipation and to make no choice whatsoever between competing interests.

In sum, we can say that at the personal level voter choices are influenced (1) by stable political attitudes comprising personal perspectives; (2) by efforts to balance those perspectives with compatible and conflicting perceptions, efforts often yielding changes in both perspectives and perceptions; and (3) by the persuasive elements that are perceived by the voter in the political campaign. With this in mind, we can now take a closer look at the impact of campaigns on political choice.

CAMPAIGN INFLUENCES

In a large sense our political predispositions serve as eyeglasses through which we discern the most salient features of the campaign setting. Of these, three are particularly noteworthy — campaign communications, the candidates, and the issues. Campaign information penetrates the voter's awareness from several sources including mass communications, group discussions, and local party activity. We discussed the effect of mass and group communication on conflict representation in Chapter Seven; we shall consider precinct activity in the following chapter. Keeping in mind that campaign communications help determine the candidates and issues that voters grow sensitive to in the election, we limit our discussion here to perceptions of candidates and issues in election campaigns.

Political Candidates. In federal elections the styles and personalities of presidential candidates must not diverge too far from popular predispositions regarding how a candidate "should act" in the election and what a President "should be." Candidate style and voter predisposition combine to structure "images" in the minds of voters of candidates for public office. The popular and reassuring image of Dwight Eisenhower; the peppery image of a Harry Truman employing outspoken, rapid-fire rhetoric; the image of the "calculating manipulator" acquired by Lyndon Johnson; the "intellectual grace" of John F. Kennedy; and the "sincere but impetuous" image that dogged the Goldwater candidacy — all are ways in which voters perceive candidates. Voters develop a picture of a presidential, senatorial, or congressional candidate that tends to stick.

A candidate's image may have significant impact on presidential elections. Although a candidate of the minority party in 1952 and 1956, General Eisenhower leaped to victory by capturing Democratic votes. Both campaigns reflected less a conflict of partisan, group, or ideologically defined interests than a victory of a commanding personality. There is reason to believe that a community with a fragmented process of representing and resolving conflict, such as the American community, must place heavy emphasis on a conflict of personalities in an election campaign. Candidate images normally have more personal meaning for Americans than abstract discussions of doctrinal programs, complex treatises defining community interests, or explanations of shifting patterns of authority and power.[28] Moreover, so long as parties do not present voters with clear-cut policy alternatives, voters are forced to choose between personalities.

For all his efforts to pass as a conservative candidate for President of the United States in 1964, there is evidence that Barry Goldwater was not regarded as one by a majority of the electorate. One survey revealed in early September that 40 per cent of Americans sampled perceived the political position of the Republican candidate to be "conservative"; 45 per cent viewed the Senator as holding a "radical" position. Only 8 per cent described his position as "middle of the road" and 7 per cent as "liberal." His opponent was perceived by 25 per cent of respondents as holding a "conservative" position, by 42 per cent as "middle of the road," and by 30 and 3 per cent respectively as either "liberal" or "radical." Two out of every three Americans queried saw Mr. Johnson's position as one evidencing greater "responsibility." [29] Another survey of the national electorate revealed only 35 per cent of Americans responding favorably to Goldwater when given the opportunity to say what they liked or disliked about the two candidates. This was the lowest percentage of favorable responses since Adlai Stevenson's 52 per cent in 1956.[30]

Voters respond in different ways to what they perceive as the personal qualities of candidates as well as to political philosophy. Again surveys of the 1964 presidential campaign are instructive. In a nationwide survey of 2,271 Americans prior to the election, the Opinion Research Corporation (the firm contracted by Goldwater forces to assess popular sentiment) reported that Lyndon Johnson was perceived to have the following favorable qualities: "warm and friendly personality" (55 per cent), "shows

[28] V. O. Key, Jr., *Public Opinion and American Democracy* (New York: Alfred A. Knopf, 1961), p. 250.

[29] See Charles O. Jones, "The 1964 Presidential Election — Further Adventures in Wonderland," in Donald G. Herzberg (ed.), *American Government Annual, 1965–1966* (New York: Holt, Rinehart & Winston, 1965), p. 17.

[30] Philip E. Converse *et al.*, "Electoral Myth and Reality: The 1964 Election," *The American Political Science Review*, LIX, No. 2 (June, 1965), 321–37.

good judgment" (49 per cent), and "honest and truthful" (40 per cent). The percentage of voters perceiving such favorable qualities far exceeded those who saw Johnson with unfavorable qualities, such as "too much of a politician," "too liberal," or "promises anything to get votes." Although Goldwater was regarded by 60 per cent of respondents as a man who "speaks his own mind," 47 per cent also thought he "acts without thinking." [31] Apparently perception of the latter trait caused many weak Republican identifiers to shift to the Democratic column. There is considerable evidence to indicate, however, that Johnson's positive image was buttressed more by policy stands than by features of his personality. Goldwater's personality was projected favorably, but his issue positions aroused an antagonism that offset such gains. Even in the South his policy stands received favorable responses almost entirely on civil rights issues.

Images of opposing candidates are among the most salient features of presidential elections; however, this is not true of congressional campaigns. A study of the 1958 congressional campaign revealed that in districts pitting candidates against one another, a majority of those interviewed were relatively unaware of the identity of the contenders. In congressional races the image of the incumbent is generally more pervasive than that of his opponent. And if the incumbent is of the voter's party, the likelihood that he is known by his party's identifiers is considerably greater. Findings from the 1958 study reveal the interplay between party preference, candidate awareness, and political choice in congressional elections; 92 per cent of respondent voters chose their own party's candidate if they had not heard of either contender; but, of those aware of both candidates, 83 per cent voted for their party's candidate.[32]

Political Issues. Obviously, in some campaigns, issues are more significant short-term forces shaping political choices than in others. The issue-oriented voter responds to statements that simplify the various interest conflicts marking electoral competition. In fact, though, current proposals for resolving social conflicts are more salient campaign features for considerably fewer voters than are candidate personalities, party labels, or ideological disputes.

We can get an idea of how partisanship, issues, personalities, and participation interact by looking at a successful simulation of the 1964 presidential election. Researchers at the Massachusetts Institute of Tech-

[31] Thomas W. Benham, "Polling for a Presidential Candidate: Some Observations on the 1964 Campaign," *The Public Opinion Quarterly*, XXIX, No. 2 (Summer, 1965), 185–99.

[32] Donald Stokes and Warren Miller, "Party Government and the Saliency of Congress," *The Public Opinion Quarterly*, XXVII, No. 4 (Winter, 1962), 541.

nology developed a simulation based upon certain assumptions and certain factors relevant to the campaign. Those factors included party identification, voter turnout, and issues of civil rights, nuclear responsibility, and social welfare legislation. That there were publicized differences between Mr. Johnson and Mr. Goldwater on these three issues requires no documentation. The study assumed that all Democrats except those strongly in opposition to civil rights would vote for Johnson; that is, they would vote in accordance with their party identification unless cross-pressured dramatically because of this one issue. Secondly, it was assumed that Republicans would stick with Goldwater unless they favored the Democratic stand on at least two of three salient campaign issues. Finally, it was assumed that Independents would divide on the basis of issue stands; those with a clear position on civil rights would vote in accordance with stands taken on that issue, and those without it would vote according to views on the other two sets of issues. In short, partisan identification would be the significant factor in voting choice for a person unless cross-pressures produced through perceptions of issues could outweigh partisan loyalty. These assumptions produced a simulation with a median error of only 3.4 per cent between predicted vote for Johnson and actual vote. From their findings, the researchers concluded "the most dramatic aspect of the 1964 election was the extent to which it was genuinely dominated by issues rather than by social stratification or by personality." [33]

Generally voters in national elections seem to care little about most issues; many are not familiar with what the issues are. This is even more correct for congressional elections than presidential. The fact that voters in congressional elections are unaware of issues as well as candidates suggests the likelihood that partisan preference plays a central role in choice patterns in congressional contests.

The more general and symbolic the issue, the more likely the electorate as a whole perceives it; the more material and specific the issue, the less the public will know about it. Often the voter is unaware of the issue orientation of candidate or party, or if aware, ignores any seeming contradiction between his party predisposition, issue preference, and candidate choice. Issues that have a particular impact upon political choice in federal elections are those directly tied to partisan competition rather than a conflict of less inclusive group interests. The voter tends to perceive the issue stands of his party and candidate within the framework of his party preference; the extent to which he can accept the candidate

[33] Ithiel de Sola Pool, Robert P. Abelson, and Samuel L. Popkin, "A Postscript on the 1964 Election," *The American Behavioral Scientist*, VIII, No. 9 (May, 1965), 39–44.

of his party as the *legitimate* one for him depends upon how strongly he feels about what his party traditionally stands for and how the candidate's position conforms to that definition. For example, data from the American Institute of Public Opinion indicate that in 1948 many Southern Democrats bolted to the Dixiecrat party because of anger at "Harry Truman's civil rights program" rather than out of dissatisfaction with the Democratic party generally. Indeed, in October, 1947, 60 per cent of Southerners questioned had expressed satisfaction with Truman as President but in April, 1948 — after his sponsorship of civil rights proposals — virtually "the same percentage of Southerners were dissatisfied with Truman's performance." The incident helped "confirm the fact that the Dixiecrats . . . were protesting much more about the policies of President Truman than about the policies of the Democratic party." [34]

Finally, when there are several issues in a campaign, voters may be in sympathy with a candidate on one or more matters, but the candidate's position on others can offset any gains obtained. In the presidential campaign in 1964, for example, a large proportion of the voters detected no differences between the foreign-policy stands of the two parties; but those who did favored the Johnson approach by a two to one margin. This was true despite the fact that only eight years previously the position of the Eisenhower Administration in foreign matters was supported by more than five to one over the challenge of Adlai Stevenson.[35]

There is one way in which voters respond to political issues without being particularly concerned with issues specific to the election campaign itself. The major issue for these voters (24 per cent of those surveyed by the Michigan Survey Research Center in 1952) is whether things, in general, are going "good" or "bad." Their appraisal of the goodness or badness of the times then helps shape their evaluation of the performance of the incumbent President or Congress. For example, in 1952 there were indications that former supporters of the New Deal and Fair Deal Democratic administrations registered their growing disenchantment, brought about by an uneasiness over the war in Korea and inflationary trends, by voting for the "outs," the Republicans. In analyzing voting patterns in presidential elections of 1936–60, V. O. Key, Jr., suggested that shifts in party fortunes could be attributed largely to a tendency for many "switchers" to support the "outs" when they appraise the general policy performance of the "ins" as inadequate. Such switchers are normally weak partisan identifiers or independents who suffer no discomfort in shifting their support between parties; "standpatters,"

[34] John M. Fenton, *In Your Opinion* (Boston: Little, Brown and Company, 1960), p. 68.
[35] Philip E. Converse *et al.*, "Electoral Myth and Reality," *op. cit.*, pp. 331–32.

wrote Key, are those with strong partisan convictions likely to support their party despite the fact that they may actually disagree with its performance in, or out, of power. In sum, voters reacting to the policy performance of a President or Congress formulate a general impression of the way affairs of state are conducted and vote accordingly, an impression shaped in varying degrees by the strength of their partisan loyalties.[36]

POLITICAL CHOICE
AND LIBERAL DEMOCRACY

Choices in American federal elections demonstrate the effects of four overlapping sets of forces. First, constitutional provisions, statutory regulations, and American traditions are institutional factors shaping the boundaries of voting behavior. Secondly, a variety of social and demographic forces are associated with shifts in political choice. Thirdly, personal perspectives reflect psychological needs and wants met through identification with partisan, socio-economic, and ideological frames of reference. Finally, impinging upon this context of fairly stable boundaries, backgrounds, and preferences, are the issues, candidates, and communications perceived in specific elections.

Americans exhibit few of the characteristics generally expected of those making political choices in a functioning democracy. Electoral participation is particularly sparse below the level of a presidential election. Choices demonstrate little of the rationality, principle, and altruism traditionally associated with democratic citizenship. More often perspectives are colored, perceptions distorted, and information meager. It is difficult to reconcile this set of circumstances with ideal democratic doctrines and procedures.

One way to surmount the difficulty is to accept the possibility that successfully operating democracy requires none of the substantive attributes suggested in democratic theory, only the procedural characteristics. The requisites of democratic viability would then be what exists: moderate to light participation levels, an open communications system to which participants hearken in only marginal fashion, an open leadership corps with a tendency towards upper-class recruitment, and a relatively stable two-party arrangement yielding personally meaningful identifications with candidates, groups, and issues. If we are willing to accept the goal of democratic government as community stability and preservation, this listing is apparently sufficient. Any distortions in

[36] V. O. Key, Jr., *The Responsible Electorate, op. cit.;* Angus Campbell, *et al., op. cit.,* pp. 240–44.

conflict representation could thus be accepted as both normal and desirable. This, however, denies the overarching purpose of democracy as conceived in conventional political theory. Passive participation, conditioned perspectives, and selective perceptions do not suffice for the full development of a free intelligence. Judged by this criterion, American patterns of political opinion, leadership, participation, and choice do not measure up very well. If the liberal-democratic conception of how things should be is our goal, then we have far to go in reaching it. Some would revise the ideal, others the reality that falls short of it. Professor Lane Davis described the problem well: "Translating the *descriptive principles* of present democratic reality into *prescriptive terms* . . . indicates the main features of the status quo and provides a model for tidying up loose ends. Democracy becomes a system to be preserved not an end to be sought. Those who wish a guide to the future must look elsewhere." [37]

BIBLIOGRAPHICAL NOTE

In recent years excellent handbooks have appeared explaining polling procedures currently used to study voter behavior. One such introductory account is Charles H. Backstom and Gerald D. Hursh, *Survey Research* (Evanston, Ill.: Northwestern University Press, 1963). A more elaborate treatment is contained in Frederick J. Stephan and Phillip J. McCarthy, *Sampling Opinions* (New York: John Wiley & Sons, Inc., Science Editions, 1963). Methods of aggregate analysis are explained for the beginner in E. E. Schattschneider and Victor Jones, *Local Political Surveys* (New York: Holt, Rinehart and Winston, Inc., 1962). See also Louis H. Bean, *How to Predict Elections* (New York: Alfred A. Knopf, 1948). A compilation of related techniques of social research is Maurice Duverger's *An Introduction to the Social Sciences* (New York: Frederick A. Praeger, Publisher, 1964).

Many of the voter studies utilized in the preparation of our discussion of political choice are now in paperback editions. Among these Angus Campbell, Philip E. Converse, Warren E. Miller, and Donald E. Stokes, *The American Voter* (New York: John Wiley & Sons, Inc., 1964) is indispensable. For results of computer simulations of the 1960 and 1964 presidential elections see Ithiel de Sola Pool, Robert P. Abelson, and Samuel Popkin, *Candidates, Issues*

[37] Lane Davis, "The Cost of Realism: Contemporary Restatements of Democracy," *Western Political Quarterly*, XVII, No. 1 (March, 1964), 46; for an attempt to revise the conception in light of political realities, see Lester W. Milbrath, *Political Participation* (Chicago: Rand McNally & Co., 1965), pp. 153–54; for a recent statement contrasting several points of view on the nature of modern democratic theory see Jack L. Walker, "A Critique of the Elitist Theory of Democracy," *American Political Science Review*, LX, No. 2 (June, 1966), 285–95.

and Strategies (Cambridge, Massachusetts: The M.I.T. Press, rev. ed., 1965). Other analyses of voting behavior conveniently available are Hugh A. Bone and Austin Ranney, *Politics and Voters* (New York: McGraw-Hill Book Company, 1963); Alvin Boskoff and Harmon Zeigler, *Voting Patterns in a Local Election* (Philadelphia: J. B. Lippincott Company, 1964); and the popular accounts by Samuel Lubbell, *The Future of American Politics* (Garden City, New York: Doubleday & Company, Anchor Books, 1960) and *Revolt of the Moderates* (New York: Harper & Row, Publishers, 1956).

For detailed discussion of personal, social, constitutional, and campaign influences on voting the following deserve examination: Paul F. Lazarsfeld *et al.*, *The People's Choice: How the Voter Makes Up His Mind* (New York: Columbia University Press, Second Edition, 1948); Bernard Berelson *et al.*, *Voting: A Study of Opinion Formation in a Presidential Campaign* (Chicago: The University of Chicago Press, Phoenix Edition, 1966); Angus Campbell *et al.*, *The Voter Decides* (New York: Harper & Row, Publishers, 1954); the compilation of previously published articles by the authors of *The American Voter* entitled *Elections and the Political Order* (New York: John Wiley and Sons, Inc., 1966); William N. McPhee and William A. Glaser, eds., *Public Opinion and Congressional Elections* (New York: The Free Press of Glencoe, 1962); M. Kent Jennings and L. Harmon Zeigler (eds.), *The Electoral Process* (Englewood Cliffs, N.J.: Prentice-Hall, Inc., 1966); Robert R. Alford, *Party and Society* (Chicago: Rand McNally & Company, 1963); Seymour Martin Lipset, *Political Man* (Garden City, New York: Doubleday & Company, Inc., 1959); Heinz Eulau, *Class and Party in the Eisenhower Years* (New York: The Free Press of Glencoe, 1962); V. O. Key, Jr., *The Responsible Electorate* (Cambridge, Massachusetts: The Belknap Press of Harvard University Press, 1966); Eugene Burdick and Arthur J. Brodbeck (eds.), *American Voting Behavior* (Glencoe, Illinois: The Free Press, 1959); and Malcolm Moos, *Politics, Presidents and Coattails* (Baltimore: The Johns Hopkins Press, 1952).

Questions of personal consistency in voting behavior are explored in Carolyn W. Sherif, Muzafer Sherif, and Roger E. Nebergall, *Attitude and Attitude Change* (Philadelphia: W. B. Saunders Company, 1965). See also Muzafer Sherif and Carl I. Hovland, *Social Judgment* (New Haven: Yale University Press, 1961).

CHAPTER
NINE

Political Partisanship

In his now classic description of American democracy, Professor Pendleton Herring wrote that the task of political leadership is "to bring the diversity of our society into working harmony" and that "our system of political parties is designed to implement this purpose." [1] Partisan patterns contribute to conflict regulation in a two-fold manner: first, by competing for control of community authority in popular elections, partisans publicize social disagreements; secondly, by occupying crucial positions of official leadership, partisans formulate policies directed at adjusting social disputes. Given this central role of the partisan politician in our government, it is useful to examine the following aspects of American partisanship: (1) the types of political participation labeled partisan, (2) the definition of political party, (3) the general characteristics of American parties as shaped by personal, social, and constitutional dimensions of the polity, and (4) the specific functions served by partisan performance.

[1] Pendleton Herring, *The Politics of Democracy* (New York: W. W. Norton & Co., 1940), p. 64.

219

PARTISANSHIP AND THE
AMERICAN PARTY PATTERN

THE PARTISAN PARTICIPANT

Traditionally the partisan is a follower of any political cause or faction. In this broad sense, social conflict implies partisanship and vice versa; all political participants are partisans be they party members, group affiliates, or candidates for public office.

Within the framework of this traditional notion of partisanship, we restrict the term to a narrower usage. In talking about the American polity, we shall refer to the partisan as directly concerned with the cause of an organized party. But it should not be inferred that nonpartisan is a synonym for nonpolitical. The notion of nonpartisanship commonly distinguishes between the interests of political parties and other political groups in governmental affairs. The separation is formalized in nonpartisan elections for some local or state offices wherein political parties are legally excluded from participation; the nonpartisan ballot bears no party designations for candidates. Nonetheless, since all elections imply some ordering of interest conflict, even nonpartisanship has a distinctive political quality.

We can distinguish between four overlapping types of partisans — policy, organization, identified, and infrequent partisans. The first category denotes members of a political party who are elected or appointed to official governing positions. Their policy behavior may or may not be motivated by solely partisan considerations; the complicating factors of pressure-group influence, the image of social servants they attempt to convey, their overall perspectives as policy-makers — all contribute to their policy performance.

We distinguish the partisan-in-office from political participants who devote their efforts to advancing what they consider to be primarily exclusive party interests. Organizational partisans staff and manage positions as county chairmen, members of the national committee, etc. The very term party organization designates the transactions between partisans who make a career out of partisan service.

Identified partisans most persistently support their party's candidates for public office. Whatever the source of their affiliation — politicization, rational conviction, regional traditions, habit — these loyalists view the political party as a meaningful demand channel for communicating needs and wants to policy officials.[2] As political participants, they

---

[2] Samuel J. Eldersveld, *Political Parties* (Chicago: Rand McNally & Co., 1964), pp. 1–23.

display more involvement, more interest, more knowledge, and more active belief in community values than non-identifiers. Several studies illustrate these characteristics of identified partisans. The Michigan Survey Research Center reported greater interest in the 1956 presidential campaign among the more intensely partisan of those sampled (Table 9-1). Moreover, partisans cared more about election outcomes: 82 per cent of strong identifiers and 62 per cent of weak identifiers were classified as caring "very much" or "pretty much," but only a bare majority (51 per cent) of Independents were so concerned. Lester Milbrath, in surveying studies of political participation, hypothesized that strong partisanship correlates positively with greater knowledge of politics: *"Gladiators generally have more knowledge about politics than spectators who, in turn, have more knowledge than apathetics."* Finally, in his study of American political consensus, Herbert McClosky found that partisanship is characteristic of those portions of the population most committed to liberal-democratic values. As carriers of the creed, partisans represent diverse social interests within an overall framework of constitutional and doctrinal consensus.[3]

TABLE 9-1

Relation of Strength of Partisan Identification to Campaign Interest, 1956

DEGREE OF INTEREST	STRONG PARTY IDENTIFIERS	WEAK PARTY IDENTIFIERS	INDEPENDENTS
Very much interested	42%	23%	25%
Somewhat interested	38%	42%	43%
Not much interested	20%	35%	32%
Total	100%	100%	100%
NUMBER OF CASES	624	651	415

Source: Angus Campbell, *et al., The American Voter* (New York: John Wiley & Sons, 1960), p. 144.

Although three of every four Americans are estimated as identified with the Republican or Democratic party, there remains that 25 per cent not so committed. These infrequent partisans lend active, but sporadic, support to a given party. Some seldom vote or otherwise participate in the political community only as spectators. Others are Independents, dividing loyalties to parties over time or regularly splitting their ballots.

[3] Angus Campbell, Philip E. Converse, Warren E. Miller, and Donald E. Stokes, *The American Voter* (New York: John Wiley & Sons, 1960), pp. 143–44; Lester W. Milbrath, *Political Participation* (Chicago: Rand McNally & Co., 1965), p. 66; Eldersveld, *op. cit.,* p. 456; Herbert McClosky, "Consensus and Ideology in American Politics," *The American Political Science Review,* LVIII, No. 2 (June, 1964), 361–82.

In close contests the support of these infrequent partisans can produce the slim margin required for victory.

Overall, the greater the personal meaning attached to partisanship, the more likely an individual is to hold political opinions and vote. The relationship of participation and partisanship is reciprocal: partisanship intensifies an involvement and emotional commitment to community affairs that is assuaged by participation. Party people are the most visible of participants and, over the years, have been the most viable of social disputants. Keeping in mind that parties are the organizers of partisanship, we turn to a definition of party activity in our polity.

A DEFINITION OF POLITICAL PARTY

An American political party may be defined as a coalition of fairly stable, viable (and frequently conflicting) interests, organized to mobilize support in competitive elections for political leaders bent upon winning public office and, hence, control of community policy-making. Three elements in this definition merit closer scrutiny.

First, by emphasizing the coalitional nature of American parties, we recognize that in performing their competitive electoral function, our two dominant parties attract support from all major social interests. Since the desires of partisans to capture public offices and assume governing responsibility must be assuaged through electoral victories, a premium is placed upon a party's capacity to recruit, represent, and exploit a broad and diverse interest following. Thus, American parties are inclusive, or multi-interest, organizations as contrasted with exclusive, limited-interest groups such as factions. As a matter of fact, there are normally several factions within each of our two parties. Because of the presence of divided factions in each, fellow partisans seem frequently to agree on nothing beyond the unifying goals of winning public office. Intra-party cleavages over platforms, programs, and candidates (as mirrored in liberal Republican dismay over Barry Goldwater's nomination and the party's civil rights stand in 1964) are often more bitter than the campaign competition between parties.

Secondly, as stable organizations our parties "exist for politics on a full-time, overt, and continuous basis."[4] Unlike pressure groups (discussed in the following chapter) that display concern with governmental affairs sporadically and only then because of specific issues, parties are always politically involved. Whereas, for example, the National Association of Real Estate Boards limits itself to "politiking" for or against those policies of crucial interest to its members (as in its 1966 campaign con-

[4] Allan P. Sindler, *Political Parties in the United States* (New York: St. Martin's Press, 1966), p. 6.

cerning housing provisions of civil rights legislation pending in Congress), a political party cannot afford to be so selective. In mobilizing diverse electoral support a party remains continuously active on a variety of fronts, both between and during successive election campaigns. Through unrelenting political activity, the party achieves a dual status beyond the reach of most pressure groups: first, it molds a durable organization contributing directly to the management of popular elections; second, it builds a sense of enduring loyalty predisposing followers to accept party appeals and candidates with warm support.

Finally, parties seek to control the authoritative policy-making institutions of the community by occupying key offices within them. To achieve this they nominate and rally support around candidates in competitive elections. Here again they differ markedly from pressure groups in purpose and tactics. The latter are concerned with influencing governing officials, but refrain from entering into direct electoral competition with political parties or other groups to do so. They rarely seek to place their own spokesmen in positions of public responsibility. And, whereas parties openly request that citizens give them the opportunity to govern, pressure groups restrict their electoral activity primarily to contributions of financial and voting support.

GENERAL CHARACTERISTICS OF
AMERICAN POLITICAL PARTIES

Patterns of duocracy, dispersion, and diversity characterize partisan politics in America. Each reflects the aggregate influence of the major features of the American community alluded to in Part One — constitutional pluralism, social diversity, and doctrinal inconsistency. The result is a socially and ideologically diverse two-party arrangement with power fragmented throughout all organizational levels.

Partisan Duocracy. Party development in America reveals the slow emergence of a duocratic pattern; that is, an electoral competition for community power controlled by two major parties that have "adhered to the same basic values and sought the same basic goals in a virtually 'bipartisan' fashion even though they often differed in detail over the best means of achieving those goals." [5]

Origins. After ratification of the Constitution, American politicians faced the problem of putting their scheme to work. That problem was accentuated by three factors. First, the design divided policy authority among separate institutions, states, and localities. Secondly, this constitu-

[5] Harvey Wheeler, " 'Duocracy' or the Imperfect Competition in Our Party System," in Joseph R. Fiszman (ed.), *The American Political Arena* (Boston: Little, Brown and Co., 1962), pp. 302–6.

tional arrangement had to operate in a pluralist society. Finally, democratic habits and traditions produced mounting popular desires for broadened suffrage and representation of diverse interests. The task was to build and integrate a political community of continental proportions within a framework complicated by the terms of the constitutional bargain, social realities, and democratic expectations.[6]

In this pluralist setting a two-party arrangement grew out of a conjunction of necessities. Alexander Hamilton and his colleagues required support in Congress for enacting centralizing programs in the Washington and Adams administrations. The Federalist party that resulted, by closing the gap between President and Congress and altering the relationship with the judiciary, gave birth to policy partisanship. To oppose the Federalists effectively, Jeffersonian and Madisonian adherents recruited partisan support within the states, thus giving rise to the Democratic-Republican party.

Because of the eclipse of the Federalists, repeated two-party competition in federal elections did not develop until after 1832. But the groundwork had been laid in the Democratic-Federalist era. The idea that coalitions of interests legitimately could differ over policy aims and compete for authority to advance those aims, under restraints imposed by the Constitution, was accepted early. Victorious partisans did not destroy the vanquished with far-reaching reprisals, despite the Federalist-enacted Alien and Sedition Acts and Jefferson's attempted purge of federal judicial offices. Conflict over the acceptability of the Constitution was displaced by a consensus that recognized the legitimacy of policy and electoral differences under that Constitution. The duocracy that evolved, particularly after 1865, reflected a bipartisan sanctification of the Constitution but produced sharp disagreements over who should govern and for what purposes.

Partisan trends following the period of one-party dominance by the Democratic-Republicans can be divided into three eras: the Democratic-Whig era of 1828–60, the Republican domination of 1860–1932, and the Democratic ascendency from 1932 to the present. Each has been characterized by long periods of one-party control of the Presidency and Congress in which the other party has been in opposition. Yet each has also witnessed elections marked by vigorous competition between two parties; control of Congress, for example, was open to both parties for periods of more than a decade following both the end of Reconstruction and the close of World War II.

[6] Joseph Charles, *The Origins of the American Party System* (Torchback ed.; New York: Harper & Bros., 1961); William Nisbet Chambers, *Political Parties in a New Nation* (New York: Oxford University Press, 1963).

One-Party Variations. The duocratic pattern in national politics has not been matched by equivalent two-party competition in all regions and states. More states are marked by interparty competition in presidential politics than in contests for control of Congress, governorships, or state legislatures. The degree of interparty competition is indicated by several factors: the proportion of popular votes received by respective parties, the number of congressional and state offices won by each party, the proportion of time that control of these offices is divided between the parties, and the duration of one-party dominance of these offices. Applying such criteria, political scientists have found, in addition to two-party states, two varieties of state one-partyism: one-party dominant states and modified one-party states.[7]

TABLE 9-2
Patterns of Partisan Competition in the Fifty States

ONE-PARTY DOMINANT (DEMOCRATIC)	MODIFIED ONE-PARTY (DEMOCRATIC)	TWO-PARTY (DEMOCRATIC TENDENCY)	(REPUBLICAN TENDENCY)	MODIFIED ONE-PARTY (REPUBLICAN)
Alabama	Arizona	Alaska	California	Iowa
Arkansas	Kentucky	Colorado	Idaho	Kansas
Florida	Maryland	Connecticut	Illinois	Maine
Georgia	North Carolina	Delaware	Indiana	New Hampshire
Louisiana	New Mexico	Hawaii	Michigan	North Dakota
Mississippi	Oklahoma	Massachusetts	Nebraska	South Dakota
South Carolina	Tennessee	Minnesota	New Jersey	Vermont
Texas	Virginia	Missouri	New York	Wisconsin
	West Virginia	Montana	Ohio	
		Nevada	Oregon	
		Rhode Island	Pennsylvania	
		Utah	Wyoming	
		Washington		

Source: Adapted from Austin Ranney, "Parties in State Politics," in Herbert Jacob and Kenneth N. Vines (eds.), *Politics in the American States* (Boston: Little, Brown and Co., 1965), p. 65.

In one-party dominant states a single party holds virtual and seemingly permanent monopoly control of local, state, and congressional elections. Such states are all Democratic, as illustrated by South Carolina, Mississippi, Alabama, and Arkansas; Vermont, once a stronghold of the Republican party, now is more accurately classified as a modified one-party state. In one-party dominant states and districts, voters may display

[7] See, for example, Austin Ranney, "Parties in State Politics," in Herbert Jacob and Kenneth N. Vines (eds.), *Politics in the American States* (Boston: Little, Brown and Co., 1965), pp. 61–101.

different partisan preferences in voting for different offices, thus voting a split ticket. For example, although Texans gave the Republican Presidential candidate, Dwight Eisenhower, popular majorities of 53.1 and 55.3 per cent in 1952 and 1956, Democrats were not seriously challenged in efforts to retain control of twenty-one of twenty-two congressional seats. Moreover since the single dominant party in the past bore either the Democratic or Republican label, one-party dominance has, as we noted in Chapter Eight, contributed to the preservation of a national duocracy. By providing "safe" districts for Republican and Democratic candidates for Congress, one-partyism has yielded a locally-based congressional opposition in eras of Republican or Democratic control of the Presidency. In this respect it is noteworthy that as Republican one-party areas have declined, it has tended to reinforce the minority status assumed by the Republican party in Congress after 1930.

Partisanship in some states, as in the nation, is cyclical; extended periods of one-party dominance are marked by occasional victories for the opposition or gradual shifts of partisan preference. These are the modified one-party states. Examples are Arizona, Virginia, or Oklahoma for Democrats, and Wisconsin or Kansas for Republicans. Local elections in modified one-party areas are touched more strongly by forces shaping the outcome of presidential contests; a presidential election may provide the opportunity for the minority party to win control of state offices. Senatorial elections in Arizona and Maryland in 1952 are cases in point. In both of these traditionally modified one-party Democratic states, Eisenhower received a majority of the popular votes; moreover, Republican candidates were successful in winning senate seats formerly occupied by Democrats. In the case of Arizona, 1952 marked a victory for Barry Goldwater over the Democratic incumbent, thus launching his career in national politics. Modified one-party regions are particularly subject to forces in national politics that erode one-partyism generally — population migrations, economic changes, urbanization, and the gradual diminishing of loyalties produced by the Civil War and its aftermath. In the future it is likely that both modified and dominant one-party states will be marked by greater competition, as exemplified by Democratic inroads in Maine and Vermont and Republican intrusions into Southern politics.

Multi-Party Variations. Minor, splinter, or third parties have occasionally marred the tidiness of the duocratic pattern. By minor parties we refer to those with sufficient viability to retain a separate identity and organization for several generations. Generally, their presence reflects the claims of community interests that feel themselves unrepresented in two-party politics. The character of these interests varies considerably.

Some are concerned with a single cause, as are the Prohibitionists with the manufacture and sale of alcoholic beverages. Others devote efforts to advancing a broader social doctrine. A few, including the Socialist Labor (not to be confused with the Socialist party), Communist, and Nazi parties, do not regard elections as the best way of pursuing revolutionary aims. They advance agitation, infiltration, and violent overthrow as possible alternatives. In this regard it is noteworthy that in its 1966 convention, the Communist Party urged that leftist forces in the United States unite around a single candidate for President in 1968. Other doctrinal parties, including the Socialist party, accept liberal-democratic procedures and seek economic, political, and social reforms through propaganda, public discussion, education, and by running candidates for office. Prior to a decision not to offer candidates in presidential elections in 1960, the Socialist party had attracted broad electoral support in elections in which neither major party responded effectively to discontent among segments of the community, particularly in 1912 when the Socialist party received 6 per cent of the total presidential vote in its appeal to Populists, progressives, and reformers disillusioned with the lack of innovative programs in Republican and Democratic parties. Generally, however, doctrinal parties have not prospered in the American social and ideological setting.

Splinter parties such as the Bull Moose party of 1912 and the Dixiecrats of 1948 originate as dissident factions of a major party; their appearance indicates an unbridged or unresolved internal partisan conflict. The Bull Moose, or Progressive, party was led by Theodore Roosevelt; having failed to obtain the Republican nomination in 1912, Roosevelt expressed his dismay with the candidacy of William Howard Taft by uniting friends, former supporters, politicians suspicious of Taft's candidacy, and others into a party contesting for control of the Presidency. Although the Bull Moose party polled a larger popular vote than did the Taft Republicans, the Democratic party won the Presidency behind Woodrow Wilson. The splinter variety of third party ultimately returns to its parent organization or crosses to the opposition as its members seek a voice within the duocratic structure, particularly in Congress, rather than outside it.

A third party is one that springs to prominence in an election by advocating a program it feels is appropriate to the times or by protesting the status quo. The Populists, for example, reflected agrarian and labor discontent and advocated remedies to the economic dislocations suffered by these groups in the post Civil War era. The party was organized in 1891 and advocated a variety of economic and political reforms: public ownership of railroads, telegraphs and telephones; return of lands formerly granted to railroads to farmers or public ownership; a graduated income tax; free and unlimited coinage of silver; direct election of United States Senators; a direct primary system for nominating party candidates; women's suffrage; and methods whereby popular votes would determine whether certain types of legislation should be adopted or rejected (initiative and referendum). Electoral successes in Southern and Midwestern states prompted the Populists to nominate a candidate for the Presidency in 1892; in that election the party received 22 electoral votes. In 1896 the Populist William Jennings Bryan won the Democratic presidential nomination; the Populist party gradually merged with the Democratic as the latter began to advocate progressive programs. By 1908 the Populists had ceased to be a separate party.

Another example, the Progressive party of 1948 nominated former Vice-President Henry A. Wallace as its candidate for President; it advocated a reduction in world tensions through negotiation and favored extension of national welfare programs. Such third parties of protest and program generally seek to persuade one or both major parties to adopt new policies; either success or failure in these efforts facilitates their passage into political obscurity.

Two-Party Persistence. Duocracy implies more than two-party competition for community offices within a context of bipartisan consensus on constitutional values. There must be some disagreement over policy goals. The American party process meets this criterion. Studies of roll-call votes in Congress consistently reveal policy differences principally over issues of social welfare, federal regulation of the economy, and foreign affairs. Despite intraparty divisions between Southern and Northern Democrats, taking Congress as a whole, Democrats have supported programs for greater federal spending on welfare measures, a more active role for the national government in the economy, and internationalist postures in foreign affairs. Republicans more often have voted to reduce federal spending in domestic and foreign programs. To some extent, these differences reflect a response to proposals of the incumbent President, issues likely to produce partisan alignments. However, during the Eisenhower Administration congressional Democrats often came to the support of the President's domestic and foreign policies when his proposals upheld or advocated greater federal initiative; it was Eisenhower's fellow partisans who wavered in support of such legislation.[8]

Policy differences exist between organization partisans as well as

---

[8] Among studies of legislative conflict see Julius Turner, *Party and Constituency: Pressures on Congress* (Baltimore: The Johns Hopkins Press, 1951); David B. Truman, *The Congressional Party* (New York: John Wiley & Sons, 1959); and Lewis A. Froman, Jr., *Congressmen and Their Constituencies* (Chicago: Rand McNally & Co., 1963).

elected spokesmen. McClosky's survey of delegates to both Republican and Democratic presidential nominating conventions revealed that Democrats were considerably more favorably disposed than Republicans to supporting policies that would produce federal regulation of public utilities and increase ownership of natural resources, federal aid to education, the corporate income tax, and regulation of business enterprise. A similar survey conducted among identified partisans indicated comparable policy differences between Republican and Democratic voters but to a lesser extent than existed between organizational partisans.[9]

It is difficult to ascertain what features of the American polity produced our relatively stable duocracy. It is easier to suggest that it persisted because of the nature of our constitutional arrangement, social structure, and popular attitudes.

Two aspects of constitutional procedure reinforce a duocratic dominance. For one, states by law make it difficult for new parties to enter into electoral competition. By requiring either that parties show electoral strength in past elections or have the support of petition signers before being eligible to enter electoral contests, states demonstrate a bias against new entries. Secondly, these parties find it difficult to elect nominees so long as the arrangement calls for the candidate with a plurality to win a congressional seat or all of a state's electoral votes for President. Either of the two major parties has a sufficient edge on identified adherents to cut down on the success of an intruder. Thus, despite influence in state politics — notably the Nonpartisan League in North Dakota or the Farmer-Labor partisans in Minnesota — most new entries have been squeezed out of federal elections by the major parties.

The absence of bitter and enduring social cleavages has worked against the rise of new parties and reinforced the older duocracy. The two major parties have won adherents from all social groupings; no new party has been able to compete effectively in federal elections by appealing to a single-interest clientele.

Finally, over the course of the last century the Republican and Democratic parties have become personally meaningful symbols to large numbers of Americans and have provided satisfying partisan attachments not easily eroded. Apparently Americans are so wedded to the two-party tradition that popular attitudes have accepted the duocracy as a fundamental feature of constitutional consensus.

Partisan Dispersion. One of the singular features of party organization in America is the dispersion of partisan power. The capacity to control

[9] Herbert McClosky, Paul J. Hoffmann, and Rosemary O'Hara, "Issue Conflict and Consensus among Party Leaders and Followers," *The American Political Science Review,* LIV, No. 2 (June, 1960), 406–27.

the decisions and behavior of party members is lodged in clusters of leaders at local levels. Organization is not merely decentralized; it is non-centralized to the extent that no central power cluster consistently delegates authority to subordinate units. In understanding this partisan dispersion, it helps to compare the formal structure of American parties with the centrifugal forces that militate against centralization.

Centralized Forms and Decentralized Realities. A variety of partisan forms exist at all levels of the American polity — national, state, and local — but their similarities for both major parties permit us to describe them briefly. Normally the local constituency — the ward or county — is divided into voting precincts. The party functionary at this level is the precinct committeeman, captain, or leader. He obtains his position either by election in the party primary, choice of precinct party members assembled in convention, or appointment by county leaders. The precinct leader seldom makes vital party policy decisions on his own. He performs the necessary task of assuring a high level of registration and a respectable turnout of party supporters on election day. Moreover, he spreads party doctrine, attempts to educate his followers politically, and performs a variety of social and economic services. The social characteristics of these functionaries quite often mirror those of the members of the precinct served.

Immediately above the precinct stands the ward, county, or legislative district committee (and in many states a congressional district committee). We call this the constituency level to indicate that it is the lowest level from which a public official is actually elected. County and ward committees are normally composed of precinct leaders in the constituency. The committee kingpin is the county or ward chairman, chosen either by the committee or in the party primary. He is charged with seeing that precinct leaders mobilize majorities in their precincts and that the party as a whole carries the constituency for local, legislative, congressional, senatorial, gubernatorial, and presidential candidates.

Above the voting precinct and electoral constituency is a coordinating level, usually the state central, or executive, committee which is composed of representatives from constituency committees. Normally the state chairman is either the leader of a dominant party faction, the hand-picked spokesman of the governor or both. Party integration of internal partisan differences is made more complicated by the fact that controlling factions desire to retain dominance over dissident elements. Local organizations are represented in regularly scheduled state conventions. State conventions perform tasks ranging from mere ratification of decisions made at other levels to nominating candidates for state-wide office and preparing platforms.

Democrats and Republicans at the national level are organized in essentially the same fashion. Each has a national committee composed of a man and a woman from every state; the national party chairman is normally selected by the presidential nominee although formal approval is given by the national committee. In the event of electoral defeat, a new chairman may be chosen by dominant party interests in an effort to reintegrate and unify the party. A quadrennial national convention of delegates from states and congressional districts meets to nominate a presidential candidate, formulate a platform, bridge internal conflicts, and instill a sense of anticipated victory.

On paper this organization of committees, conventions, and chairmen constitutes a hierarchy linking local precincts to national headquarters. Implicit in this hierarchy is a tight-knit pattern of superior-subordinate relations between highly motivated and involved partisans. In fact, the relations are far more reciprocal, discontinuous, loosely coordinated, and sporadic. The dispersion of partisan control comprises at best a modified hierarchy, or the "American hybrid." [10] There is a diffusion of authority and privilege at all layers, and there is no general expectation among Americans that a lower level should be responsible to those above it in the structure. Leadership, authority, and influence are often splintered among local party organizations; and these organizations form alliances among themselves with both higher-level organizations and non-party forces in opposition to organizations at the same and other levels. The product and stimulus of such coalitions is horizontal and vertical conflict among party interests at all layers.

Several features of the American polity are associated with this partisan dispersion. We single out constitutional pluralism, the electoral system, partisan incentives, and statutory regulation for particular attention. Social diversity also plays a role, as noted in the next section.

Constitutional Pluralism. Since American parties organize for electoral purposes, parties strive to win as many elections as possible by focusing organized efforts upon the individual electoral constituencies from which officials are chosen. By terms of the American constitutional bargain — federalism — this has meant state and local constituencies rather than a national one. The only "national" elections are quadrennial campaigns for President and Vice-President, and even in these elections the national constituency is comprised of the fifty-one constituencies having votes in the Electoral College.

The multiplicity of elective offices in America has prompted a parallel proliferation of largely autonomous partisan units. These organizations

---

[10] Frank J. Sorauf, *Political Parties in the American System* (Boston: Little, Brown and Co., 1964), pp. 44–48.

FIGURE 9-1
*Linkages between Organized, Official, and
Voting Partisans in the American Polity*

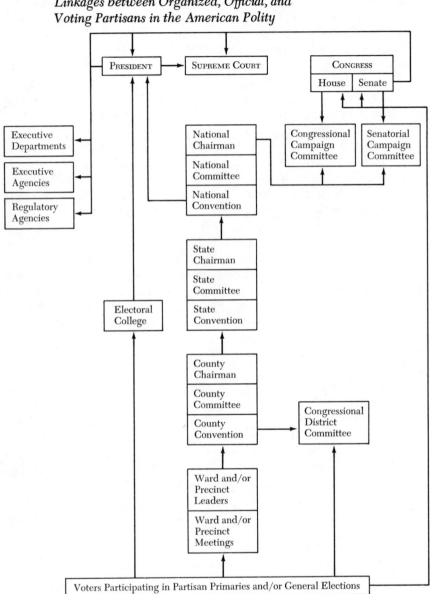

Note: Solid linking lines with arrows indicate participation
in the selection of leaders through direct election,
nominating, appointing, or approving persons for positions.

wage campaigns in separate, but overlapping, constituencies for mayors, councilmen, county judges, state legislative seats, governors, congressmen, etc. The upshot is constituency organizations with sometimes compatible, but frequently conflicting functions, memberships, and authority. Each organization feels that it can most effectively compete for electoral victory by maintaining its autonomy.

The proliferation of semi-permanent constituency organizations is matched by the creation of a host of affiliated groups. Some of these are adjuncts to the party organization and take on many of the characteristic conflicts that divide the parent Republican or Democratic party. These include both Young Republicans and Young Democrats. Volunteer organizations spring up temporarily to handle specific problems in a campaign, such as finances, broadening the base of support, preparation of policy statements, etc. The stimulus for their organization often comes from the major parties. Among such recent groups have been Volunteers for Stevenson, Independents for Eisenhower, Democrats for Goldwater, and Scientists and Engineers for Johnson. No matter what the rationale for their formation is, each adds another element that must be coordinated for partisan effectiveness.

In creating constituency organizations for each electoral unit, party leaders hope to maximize chances for victory. They respond to what Professor David Truman has cited as a basic political fact of federalism; namely, that federalism "creates separate, self-sustaining centers of power, privilege, and profit which may be sought and defended as desirable in themselves, as means of leverage upon elements in the political structure above and below, and as bases from which individuals may move to places of greater influence and prestige in and out of government." [11] But, in shaping their organization in the image of the federal pattern, partisans deprive the national party of a crucial means for demanding party discipline. In the face of the local autonomy of state, county, and district party organizations, national party leaders — the President included — find that the fate of policy decisions rests in the hands of locally responsible governors, mayors, county commissioners, congressmen, etc. who are largely independent of central control. Rather than serving as a tool for disciplining these often recalcitrant officials, as might be the case if the partisan pattern were one of the hierarchical commands from superiors to subordinate elements, partisan dispersion reinforces the autonomy of state, local, and county governments. The upshot is what Professor William Riker suggests in his analysis of the federal arrange-

---

[11] David B. Truman, "Federalism and the Party System," in Nelson W. Polsby, Robert A. Dentler, and Paul A. Smith (eds.), *Politics and Social Life* (Boston: Houghton Mifflin Co., 1963), pp. 518–19.

ment: "This decentralized party system is the main protector of the integrity of states in our federalism." [12]

One of the clearest examples of this tension between partisan levels appeared in the relationship between President Lyndon Johnson and John Connally, Governor of the President's home state of Texas and long-time political advisor and protégé. Both Mr. Johnson's war on poverty and his attempts to repeal Section 14b of the Taft-Hartley Act, permitting states to enact "right to work" legislation, ran afoul of the Governor's position. Connally was particularly adamant in his demand that state governors have the option to veto certain aspects of congressional poverty legislation, a point he justified on the basis of state preservation under the federal principle.

In the absence of rigid party discipline exercised by national leaders over local organizations, revolts by state and local partisans against the parent party are common. Many are prompted by pressure groups. Realizing that party fragmentation provides few central points upon which popular control of party as a political institution can be focused, they find a most effective way to thwart policies at the national level is through appeals to the more influential local organizations. Particularly if these local parties depend upon such pressure groups for financial and electoral support, parochial interests have a voice in partisan affairs out of proportion to their limited scope. Thus, the existence of several strata and clusters of partisan authority, each with a considerable degree of autonomy, affects the total pattern of social-conflict representation in America by channeling disputes and demands through local organizations. As a result, democratic responsibility is often so diffused that the responsiveness of partisan politics to broad social changes is minimized. For example, although civil rights problems existed in the 1930's and 1940's, Southern opponents to civil rights statements in Democratic platforms were able to prevent their inclusion by controlling local party organizations and threatening to bolt the national party. Following the election of President Harry Truman in 1948 despite a Southern defection, this particular pressure tactic lost some of its effectiveness but remained in vogue through 1966.

Electoral System. Coordination problems are intensified by two aspects of the electoral system itself: staggered elections and single-member districts. Under terms of the federal system we select officials to manage public affairs at a variety of governing levels; moreover, through the creation of separate institutions at each level — executive, legislative, judicial — there are numerous officials to be chosen. Added to this is the fact that we assure these separate offices will be even more "independent"

12 William H. Riker, *Federalism* (Boston: Little, Brown and Co., 1964), pp. 91–101.

of one another by providing that these same officials shall serve non-concurrent terms of office; i.e., the President has a four year term, Representatives serve two years, and Senators six; state governors serve either two or four years depending on the state; state legislators serve two or four year terms; the terms of mayors, city councilmen, county commissioners, and other officials vary in similar fashion. Thus, in addition to "mid-term" elections for the House of Representatives and one-third of U.S. senators, elections for governors, mayors, state assemblymen, etc., are sprinkled throughout a four-year presidential term. The device of staggered elections permits local elections to respond to forces and interests in each area; but, by the same token, local party organizations seldom mobilize a unified effort in a single election held in all parts of the country.

When elections are decided by a plurality of votes in single-member districts, parties tend to concentrate efforts on electing officials in regions wherein their strength lies. They are not eager to spread resources too thin by expanding them in districts where, although they might have substantial support, they can at best come in second. This has long hampered Republican organization at the state and local level in the South. Hence, although the national committee might insist upon a high level of partisan activity throughout America, the likelihood is that organization will be stronger where it can be most effective in deciding races. In sum, the mode of election tends to restrict strong partisan organization primarily to districts where the party is in either a dominant or competitive position.

Partisan Incentives. Central coordination is rendered even more difficult by attitudes of partisans. Locally elected community officials, particularly Congressmen, feel that their continued success lies not in the hands of a distant national organization but with the constituency partisans that recruited, nominated, financed, and supported them. For House and Senate members, the incentive is to reward local supporters rather than acquiesce to the wishes of national leadership. In turn, the rewards increase the tendencies of local political leaders to go all out for their constituency officials rather than the national organization.

State Regulation. Partisan dispersion is reinforced by the fact that states, not the federal government, have been most active in regulating parties. Major parties tailor their organizations to fit state requirements rather than central dictates. For example, almost three fourths of the states require that parties hold regular conventions — city and county — of precinct representatives. Thus statutes attempt to substitute broad participation in party affairs for tight-knit control by party leaders but, in so doing, render parties less autonomous as effective competitors in elections. The upshot is both an anti-organization and anti-party bias. In addition, states have laid down the rules for recognizing a party's existence, defining party membership, controlling the nominating process, establishing procedures for the selection of party leaders, formalizing the internal party structure, and regulating campaign finances.

Such policies have had profound consequences on partisan composition and structure. Definitions of party membership, for example, extend to requirements limiting party participation to registrants, those willing to submit to an oath of party loyalty, or both. Fairly open party membership is the result. Both oaths and registration are often perfunctory exercises facilitating switches in formal party membership and, consequently, a lessening of party discipline.

The use of the primary election as a device for selecting a party's nominees for political offices *and* selecting party officials by the total membership (loosely defined) has made its own contributions to what V. O. Key, Jr., called the "atrophy" of party organizations — the weakening and deadening of organizational effectiveness.[13] The comparative ease with which party lines may be crossed in primary contests (for example, in some states voters are given ballots of both parties with no test of party membership required and in one state all primary contests are on a single ballot) tends to disrupt organization efforts to endorse particular candidates who might, if chosen, give a "team" character to the party slate. More critical, however, is the effect on partisan control of nominations. The primary forces the party to open that process to political participants other than organization partisans.

Centralizing Features. In emphasizing the dispersion of partisan power, we are not saying that there is no integration of party loyalties for the whole community. Rather, partisans tend to define party interests in keeping with their more immediate tangible desires for local electoral victories. Much of what they do as members of the national party depends upon narrowly defined ties to constituency organizations. Every four years the highly decentralized organization, composed of loose, sometimes discontinuous and sometimes over-lapping, coalitions of state and local factions, is brought together in convention for the common cause of victory in a presidential election. Yet only when the party's presidential candidate is seeking re-election is there anything that could be termed the "national committee's slate." Otherwise, even the nomination of a President is controlled by either a coalition of state and local leaders in temporary alliance or a dominant faction.

When a group of party leaders refuse to accept the national convention's choice for a presidential candidate and demonstrate open defiance of the party's slate, very minor disciplinary action may be taken. How-

---

[13] V. O. Key, Jr., *American State Politics* (New York: Alfred A. Knopf, 1956), pp. 169 ff.

ever, two contrasting examples reflect possible changes in the American party scene. In 1948, when Southern delegates nominated their own Dixiecrat candidate for President rather than accept Harry Truman as the party choice, there was little in the way of retribution taken against dissident members. The candidate who opposed Truman in the 1948 election, J. Strom Thurmond, entered the Senate in 1955 as a full-fledged Democrat. In 1964 the same senator again bolted the Democratic party and took up Republican identification in the Senate; this time he had to sacrifice his Democratic seniority. Meanwhile, two Southern Democratic congressmen who had supported the Republican presidential candidate in 1964 were deprived of their Democratic seniority. These latter instances testify to the fact that American parties are not wholly without means of retaliation.

Partisan Diversity. We have only partly explained the underlying reasons for dispersion of partisan power in America. The constitutional dimension of our community — its formalized political arrangement, election procedures, and regulatory statutes — helps shape electoral parties in the federal mold. Certain attitudinal traits in the polity, such as partisan incentives and parochial loyalties, reinforce fragmenting tendencies. In conjunction with these forces, the social character of America produces parties that are pluralist in nature, a factor that contributes in its own way to partisan dispersion. Partisan diversity extends to the social composition of our two parties, the motivations behind party membership, and the non-ideological appeals of American parties.

In performing their competitive electoral function, the two American parties attract support from all major interests. To be sure, as noted in Chapter Seven, there are differences in the social composition of each; but these are general tendencies. Since issues of class, region, religion, ethnicity, etc., have not been employed to hammer permanent wedges into the partisan preferences of American voters, both parties have competed with broad platform appeals for the support of large blocks of the uncommitted. In diversifying their clientele, however, parties have complicated the task of achieving organizational unity; "a political party is constantly plagued by the needs to reconcile two divergent essentials: group solidarity (conscious selection of members) and broad social representation (unrestricted entry into the organization)." [14]

The price paid for a pluralist interest following, thus, is occasional internal partisan disputes. In mobilizing frequently incompatible interests, the party opens itself to many of the same social conflicts occurring in the community as a whole. The more inclusive the organization of an American party is, the more likely that its internal struggles will reflect interest disputes occurring in the polity. In this fashion, the parties serve as

[14] Eldersveld, *op. cit.*, 73–97.

channels in the reciprocal communication of disputes and decisions between governed and governors. Common cause is served by bridging and avoiding direct confrontations within the party, thus passing the task of conflict resolution on to official policy-makers.

Not all internal wrangles can be ignored quietly in the name of electoral triumph. Republican and Democratic factions have been commonplace in American political history. For many it has been insufficient merely to be Republican or Democrat; there have been Eisenhower, moderate, conservative, or Eastern Republicans and Jeffersonian, Bourbon, Southern, and Big City Democrats as well. Party cohesion is threatened periodically by groups so dissatisfied with organization decisions that they demand adjustments to suit their interpretation of partisan aims. In response party leaders sometimes work for internal peace, as did both followers of Barry Goldwater and the more "moderate" Republicans, when, after electoral defeat in 1964, they agreed to replace the Goldwater-appointed Chairman of the Republican National Committee with a compromise candidate. Or dissident factions may split away, as in the case of the Dixiecrat revolt of 1948 within the Democratic Party. The political party in America is viable so long as it is able to avoid, adjust, or overcome serious separatist tendencies and prevent crippling party schisms that frequently reflect its diverse following.

The social dimension of partisan diversity, however, extends beyond that fact that each party is a heterogenous grouping of participants with checkered social backgrounds. There is evidence to suggest, notably in Eldersveld's study of partisanship in Wayne County, Michigan and Wolfinger's analysis of ethnic politics, that each party contains diverse, self-conscious interests. Each possesses groups whose members think of themselves as having common goals that set them apart. Eldersveld found that local Republicans were of a business-managerial class and a white-collar Anglo-Saxon subgroup while Democrats consisted of nine identifiable subgroups including Negroes, Poles, the Irish, Southern blue-collar migrants, and a business-professional class. Professor Wolfinger has demonstrated that, particularly in large cities, ethnic minorities have not been assimilated into the social milieu but retain their own ethnic identity, customs, and perspectives. Moreover, they persistently are mobilized in support of political parties, especially the Democratic. It should be emphasized that both parties compete to coalesce diverse interest groups and that support for a given party by any single interest represents a tendency rather than irrevocable loyalty.[15]

---

[15] *Ibid.*, pp. 73–97; Raymond E. Wolfinger, "The Development and Persistence of Ethnic Voting," *The American Political Science Review*, LIX, No. 4 (December, 1965), 896–908.

Nor does either party draw support exclusively from individuals with any particular type of personal motivations. Both Democrats and Republicans possess members who seek to enlarge their circle of social friends, obtain material rewards, and derive emotional satisfaction from partisan participation. In studying responses from 281 precinct leaders in the Detroit, Michigan, area, Samuel Eldersveld did find that the "satisfactions" derived from party activity differ somewhat between Republicans and Democrats. As illustrated in Table 9-3, Democrats were more prone to find party activity personally rewarding because of the social contacts and sheer enjoyment involved than Republicans.[16] In general, however, the incentives for membership are similar for both parties — patronage, privileged administrative treatment, financial inducements, career opportunities, or personal gratification.

TABLE 9-3
Satisfactions from Partisan Work
Among Precinct Leaders, Wayne County, 1956

TYPE SATISFACTION	DEMOCRATS	REPUBLICANS
Personally instrumental satisfactions:		
Social contacts	63%	47%
Political fun (and inside information)	12	8
Business, economic, and political gain	1	1
Group and socially-related satisfactions:		
Moral and philosophical satisfactions	4	3
Ideological or issue satisfactions	3	17
No satisfactions received	15	22
Unclassified	2	2
Total	100%	100%

Source: Adapted by permission of the publisher from data reported in Table 11.1 in Samuel J. Eldersveld, *Political Parties* (Chicago: Rand McNally & Co., 1964), p. 278.

Earlier we noted broad ideological differences between Republicans and Democrats in legislative voting. Here, again, general tendencies rarely harden into direct ideological appeals to the electorate, perhaps because ideological considerations prove meaningless to more than 90 per cent of voters. There is evidence that to a certain extent there is an ideological gap between the doctrinal stands of party leaders and the postures of even the more ideologically attuned Americans. The precise nature of this gap, however, is not clearly indicated by scholarly research. For example, in his study of party behavior in a single metropolitan county, Professor Samuel Eldersveld found that Republican leaders tended to be more conservative than their rank-and-file and on certain

[16] Eldersveld, *op. cit.*, p. 278.

issues, such as civil rights, foreign policy, and government aid to the needy, Democratic leaders were far more liberal than many followers. Ideological diversity, not homogeneity, characterized all levels of organization; but in general the upper echelons of partisans were more likely to be sensitive to ideological considerations. Yet, in examining the liberal inclinations of party leaders and followers, by comparing positions of national-convention delegates for both parties in 1956 with a cross-section of each party's leadership, Professor Herbert McClosky discovered that both Republican and Democratic party leaders generally tend to be more liberal than precinct-level members. The apparent contradiction between the two studies could reflect the differences in utilizing a national as opposed to a local sample of partisans, differing measurements of conservatism and liberalism, differing research designs, etc. In any event these studies indicate that generalizations about the ideological orientations of partisans must be tentative. Both do underscore the fact that abstract ideological appeals are received with greater enthusiasm by party activists than rank-and-file voters.[17]

By couching campaign oratory in symbolic gestures, party leaders normally compensate for the ideological gap between themselves and followers; for example, in presidential campaigns where appeals are directed to a socially and ideologically diverse clientele. When interest coalitions are formed in hopes of electoral gain, party platforms that equivocate or ignore issues threatening party unity are often produced. We commented earlier that the election of 1964 was somewhat of an exception. The exclusive appeal of the Goldwater candidacy reflected a far more concerted effort to appeal to a narrow segment of the electorate than Americans had seen for some time. From the partisan perspective, it demonstrated how a faction can win control of party structure but either make little effort to placate dissidents or fail to capture the loyalty and support of fellow partisans. Whether the phenomenon was an aberration or a forerunner of more doctrinaire partisan appeals in future elections is open to question.

The heterogeneous, flexible, and unsophisticated approach of Americans toward political ideology further reinforces dispersion of partisan power. When and if an ideology does exist a systematically formulated and consistent party doctrine can serve as a tool of organizational control. Committed partisans can be asked to put aside parochial concerns, shun internal interest conflicts, and dedicate themselves to fulfilling higher ideological aims. American Presidents, including Jefferson, Jackson, Lincoln, and both Roosevelts, have had limited success in such appeals. But, in the absence of deep ideological commitment of party members

[17] McClosky, et al., op. cit.

and representative voters, the tool has little coordinating value. The incentive for partisan loyalty is not ideological fulfillment but the promised satisfaction of parochial concerns.

PATTERNS OF PARTISAN PERFORMANCE

As the visible agency of partisanship, the American political party performs a distinctive electoral service — mobilizing community interests in support of claims to govern. Implied in that performance are several specific tasks undertaken by parties, three of which we shall discuss here — selecting community leaders, defining voter options, and shaping public policy.

PARTISAN LEADERSHIP SELECTION

Although American parties play a vital role in recruiting and selecting the community's policy leaders, they do not monopolize the process. There are several factors militating against party domination of leadership selection. Civil service procedures, by relying upon competitive merit appointments, remove partisan influence from selection of administrative personnel. Even with popular elections leadership selection does not necessarily result from partisan competition. The nonpartisan ballot is one method employed at state and local levels to shut parties out of the selection process. Where elections are held on a partisan basis, there is no assurance that the state, district, or local party organization will possess the capacity to create or recruit potential candidates. Prospective candidates frequently develop personal organizations apart from party agencies. Professor Allan P. Sindler has noted that this is particularly true in the case of candidates for Congress. The organizations of congressional candidates frequently tend to be poorly integrated into the local party structure. The result is but another impetus for the diffusion of partisan control.[18] Moreover, although we might expect partisan influence over leadership selection to be greatest in one-party states and regions, elections — particularly general elections — frequently reflect the resolution of intraparty factional tensions rather than two-party competition. Finally, in some areas partisan power is so dispersed that there is hardly a party worthy of the name, let alone partisan influence in recruiting leaders.

Where party activity counts most in staffing public offices is in nominating candidates, organizing campaigns, and publicizing partisan agreements and disputes. To contribute to leadership selection in its critical phases, parties must control nominations. Several considerations under-

[18] Sindler, *op. cit.*, pp. 83–4.

score this necessity; for example, control of patronage is facilitated, responsiveness of elected officials to party programs is promoted, the party's image before the populace is less subject to the whims of the candidate's personality, and harmony can be promoted by rewarding dissident factions with nominations to lesser offices.

Historically three methods of nominating candidates have been utilized. The earliest employed the party caucus; a meeting of select party leaders (often dominated by legislative leaders) who chose the candidates to bear the party label in the upcoming election. In the annals of American political folklore, "King Caucus" expired on the national level following the election triumph of Andrew Jackson over John Quincy Adams in 1828; the latter had been nominated as the official party candidate in the caucus, but Jackson obtained convention endorsement. Although Jackson's nomination by convention marked a turning point in the nominating process, the "smoke-filled room" existed as a variation upon the caucus for some time. The convention expanded the scope of partisan conflict by opening the nominating process to a larger number of party factions than had participated under the unwritten rules of the caucus. Legislative leaders now shared influence with factional leaders within the states. Nominations still resulted from bargains, but the number and interests of the bargainers were changed.

The scope of the nominating conflict was expanded once more with the adoption of primary elections. Candidates were chosen in elections theoretically open to all legally defined party members. Opening the nominating process to statutory partisans was justified by Populists and Progressives on grounds that it would make party leaders responsive to all members and public officials responsible to all citizens. Responsiveness and responsibility were to be assured by converting the nominating process from one of bargaining between "bosses" to electoral competition for partisan votes.

The effort to democratize the nominating process produced unanticipated consequences. Although organized partisans no longer had control of the nominations, neither did the full party membership. A general apathy exhibited by party clientele facilitated domination of nominations by small bands of highly involved partisans. In surveying voter turnout percentages in gubernatorial primaries in 21 states over approximately a forty year period, V. O. Key, Jr. found that a relatively high proportion (28–41 per cent of Republican nominations and 6–44 per cent of Democratic nominations) of primary nominations were made by less than 50 per cent of the primary vote. Interestingly enough, although we might expect control by a relatively few partisans to contribute to a narrowness of outlook that would not necessarily assure broad partisan support for the party's nominee in the general election, let alone broad voter appeal, Key found that the general election fortunes of plurality and majority nominees did not differ sharply. Indeed, "the Democratic nominees by a plurality in the strong Republican states, few though they were, won far more frequently than did majority nominees." [19] Moreover, in many instances potential nominees achieved primary victory because of their ability to mobilize nonpartisans — friends, neighbors, associates, and the generally uninformed primary voter — or succeeded because of a tested political family name (as the Longs of Louisiana or the Blairs of Missouri) or an attractive personality. In any event, they did not owe their nomination to the regular party organization.

There is evidence that primaries contribute to the dispersion of partisan power. Of necessity they publicize internal differences between factions; party leaders find it difficult to avoid open conflict by accommodation through private bargaining. Primary competition frequently forces a public contest with disgruntled losing factions refusing to support the primary victor and party nominee.

Certain tactics have been employed to restore a modicum of bargaining to the nominating process. Half a dozen states hold some form of pre-primary to endorse a candidate in the primary election. This bestows financial support and the aid of precinct organization. In some areas local party organizations use screening committees of faction leaders who meet in caucus, sort the desirable candidates from among those having filed (this normally follows a concerted effort to get desirable candidates to file in the first place), and announce support of a party slate. Efforts to control the nominating process by controlling the primary are only partially successful. There is always the possibility that interests may grow disenchanted with the promises obtained in pre-primary bargaining; if so, they can appeal for some form of redress by forcing a primary fight but must accept the consequences of publicized division.

The general election campaign provides the opportunity for parties to activate the favorably disposed, neutralize the unfavorable, and win new adherents. Since the strongly identified Republican or Democrat is predisposed to support his party's nominee, the campaign is designed to assure that he votes in accordance with his partisan preference. Those strongly predisposed to support the competing party, it is assumed, cannot easily be won over; efforts at conversion are of lesser importance. Voters not so strongly committed — weak Republicans, weak Democrats, and Independents — are fair game for both parties in the campaign.

---

[19] Key, *op. cit.*, p. 143.

They serve as principal targets for speeches, party propaganda, etc. Thus, a premium is placed on the ability of organized partisans at all levels — national, state, constituency, and precinct — to select issues and present their stands in an attractive fashion. In essence, the "campaign should reinforce those voters for whom the party is a major political reference group, but for those segments of the population less inclined to party, it must emphasize the party's program or the appeal and attractiveness of the candidate." [20]

In all elections the precinct leader is an important figure in mobilizing loyalists and securing the faith of the wavering. But, to his traditional campaign involving door-to-door canvassing of voters, new dimensions have been added. Particularly in the competition for important national and statewide offices that warrant the expenditure of vast funds, party leaders and candidates have solicited the services of the mass media, the advertising man, the pollster, and the computer specialist. Instead of guessing at the identity of strong and weak partisans and uncommitted independents, survey research has been used to pinpoint them. Rather than trust the impressions of old-time party leaders regarding the selection of salient issues and the proper form for their presentation, computer simulation has been employed to demonstrate the relative effect of alternative issues. Finally, tested advertising formulas are frequently relied upon for packaging salient appeals.

Recent campaigns for the presidency have offered dramatic testimony to the significant role played by these specialists in popular elections. Candidates such as Richard Nixon, John Kennedy, Nelson Rockefeller, Lyndon Johnson, and Barry Goldwater have all relied upon public relations firms and polling organizations for campaign advice. In 1960, for example, Senator John F. Kennedy was particularly troubled over how to handle the ticklish question of his Catholicism. Among the forces he and Democratic advisers marshalled to assess the relative impact of the religious issue on the electorate were the polling service of Louis Harris and Associates, a variety of public relations firms, and the Simulmatics Corporation. The last-named consisted of a group of businessmen and academic researchers. Their purpose was to devise a simulation of the 1960 campaign relying upon public opinion data gathered between 1952–1960. Through extensive analysis the project was able to furnish the presidential candidate with what later proved to be a remarkably accurate prediction of the aggregate impact of the religious issue on his chances. From a host of such independent sources of information and advice, combined with his own counsel, Senator Kennedy chose to meet

[20] Sorauf, *op. cit.,* p. 112.

the religious issue squarely rather than avoid discussion of his Catholicism.[21]

Campaign innovations raise new problems of organizational control and financing for political parties. For one, a candidate capable of employing such methods successfully and independently of party in either primary or general election can challenge the party for control of the campaign. The party becomes a personal tool of the candidate rather than the candidate serving as the public spokesman of organized partisans. For example, in his 1966 campaign for the Republican nomination for Governor of California, Ronald Reagan relied heavily upon modern campaign techniques. By his victory he was able to inject himself as a force in the Republican party over the protests of his primary opponent George Christopher of San Francisco, a professional politician with a record of both elective and party service.

Traditionally a major task of American parties has been to raise campaign funds. Aside from the costs of election administration, the expenses of elections have been borne by the parties and not by national, state, or local governmental units. With the venerable and locally-based organizational campaign styles of previous years, election costs could be carried largely by the volunteer efforts of precinct workers, constituency organizers, and wealthy patrons. But mass communications, surveys, simulations and packaging are costly services less easily financed. Increased emphasis is placed upon choosing nominees who can pay their own way — both within and through circumvention of the limits placed by law — or who have the support of prosperous nonparty groups interested in the selection of political officials. Moreover, rising campaign costs contribute to the proliferation of separate organizations and committees aimed at supplying individual candidates, not the party, with needed revenue. The upshot is but another obstacle placed in the path of partisan coordination. The conjunction of techniques applied by the behavioral sciences and the rising cost of campaigning erodes party control over the conduct of elections, which, in turn, raises questions concerning the future role of political parties in our democracy. In democratic theory, parties provide the populace with a method for controlling policymakers; but officials who do not rely upon party for electoral success need not be responsive to popular standards of responsible conduct.

PARTISAN CHOICE

In attempting to persuade the electorate of the wisdom of party candidates and platforms, organized partisans define salient issues and sim-

---

[21] See Ithiel de Sola Pool, Robert P. Abelson, and Samuel Popkin, *Candidates, Issues and Strategies* (Cambridge, Massachusetts: The M.I.T. Press, 1964).

plify the alternatives presented to both identified and infrequent partisans. Although tasks of informing and persuading are now increasingly preempted by the politically oriented news media, parties still communicate their messages through personal contacts at the precinct level, politicization, and social gatherings of members.

Canvassing is the form of campaign activity traditionally associated with precinct-level organization. It constitutes all efforts of the precinct leader to increase the turnout of favorably disposed partisans and includes a listing and tabulation of party members, distribution of literature, and doorbell-ringing. There are few studies of the impact of precinct activity upon electoral outcome, but those in existence point to common general conclusions.[22] Grass-roots efforts do produce higher voter turnout than would generally be expected in the absence of active precinct leadership. Reporting on a study of precinct activity in Wayne County, Michigan, Professors Daniel Katz and Samuel J. Eldersveld asserted that "political parties, by increasing their local activity in areas where they have not been active before, do increase the turnout of their party." They found one Michigan township in which the minority party had increased its support for the state ticket "from 23 to 40 per cent of the total vote," after establishing an active local organization. Overall, Katz and Eldersveld concluded that a minority party in the county might increase its votes by as much as 5 per cent through grass-roots activity. The impact of minority party activity appears greater than that of the majority, apparently because the latter has the support of other party functionaries in the area and, hence, the visible effect of precinct leaders alone is lessened.[23]

Over long periods of time, partisan communication has a politicizing effect not easily replaced by the efforts of party competitors. We saw earlier that, once acquired, partisan attachment provides a uniquely experienced feeling of political reality. It helps the voter filter seemingly inconsistent campaign information and transcend contradictory demands placed upon him by his diverse group memberships. There is some evidence that in precincts with relatively strong party organization the intensity of partisan identification rises. For example: Katz and Eldersveld found in their study that Republicans living in precincts with strong Republican organizations possessed a stronger commitment to the party than did Republican partisans in other areas. Although the party is

[22] See Eldersveld, op. cit.; Daniel Katz and Samuel J. Eldersveld, "The Impact of Local Party Activity upon the Electorate," The Public Opinion Quarterly, XXV, No. 1 (Spring, 1961), 1–24; Peter H. Rossi and Phillips H. Cutright, "The Impact of Party Organization in an Industrial Setting," in Morris Janowitz (ed.), Community Political Systems (New York: The Free Press of Glencoe, 1961), pp. 81–116.

[23] Katz and Eldersveld, op. cit.

challenged in its politicizing efforts by the education system, the media, neighborhood groups, and other forces, it remains to be seen whether competitors can provide the personally meaningful reference symbol that equips one for making political choices as effectively as does partisanship.

The days are virtually gone when precinct leaders helped feed and clothe newly arrived immigrants, kept partisans out of jail and off the streets by finding legal support and counsel for them, provided coffee for inebriated party loyalists, and gave political appointments to the unemployed. But the party, by offering its own social rewards of status, attractive career aspirations, congenial friendships, and influence, still retains its critical socializing role.

The political-club movement in America, for example, provides an opportunity for partisans to share cocktails, beer, and political conversation. These clubs exist in several states, notably in California, in order to encourage political discussion, education, and participation. They strive for an existence separate from the regular party organization. In California both the Republican Assembly and Democratic Council, coordinating agencies for such clubs, have had success in endorsing candidates prior to primaries. In some states the club movement — for example, among Texas Liberal Democrats — is divided by a lingering tension between proponents of particular doctrines and more practically minded politicians.[24]

PARTISAN PUBLIC POLICY

Although the primary function of political parties in the American political community is to represent conflict, parties also contribute to the formulation of community policy. Partisanship is exhibited clearly in at least three phases of conflict resolution — policy leadership, adoption, and application. It is less apparent, but still present, in policy adjudication.

In the past, political parties have exerted policy leadership during and between elections. In publicizing selected social conflicts for purposes of winning office, parties have suggested public policies that extend beyond the interests of any single group. When, for example, as leader of his party in 1948–49 President Truman proposed legislation providing for expanded federal programs in areas of social security, slum clearance, public housing, farm improvements, agricultural subsidization, health care, civil rights, and the American economy, he articulated the social

---

[24] Francis Carney, *The Rise of the Democratic Clubs in California*, Eagleton Cases in Practical Politics (New York: McGraw-Hill Book Co., 1960); James Q. Wilson, *The Amateur Democrats* (Chicago: The University of Chicago Press, 1962).

concerns that became the source of the major political issues in the 1950's and 1960's. Despite generalities, party platforms demonstrate an enduring partisan concern in particular areas of social conflict — civil rights, economic well-being, foreign relations, national security, etc. Moreover, by asserting initiative in proposing more specific policy options — as in the case of the Peace Corps idea in 1960 — political parties have exercised additional policy leadership.

The party has provided a major base of support for the American Presidency, one from which the President has been able to increase his total influence in policy leadership. Despite difficulties encountered in disciplining members, the party has provided the President with a tool with which popular approval, respect, and faith can be used to persuade executive agents and congressmen. During the rise of his personal popularity prior to and following the presidential election of 1964, Lyndon Johnson was able to obtain congressional approval for an impressive number of his Administration's programs. This included 1965 passage of voting rights legislation, a medical care for the aged bill, federal aid to education legislation, the establishment of a departmental level agency for urban affairs, a foreign aid authorization and other measures hitherto stalled in Congress. During the period many Democratic congressmen chose to support the program of the President in exchange for his good will as well as the immediate benefits to be derived from party patronage and presidential approval of pet projects for their constituencies. Especially, for a popular President, the political party serves as both the symbol and the reality of a large share of presidential power.

In turn, the Presidency can be used to achieve some degree of party unity despite normal partisan dispersion. The absence of such a centralizing force for the opposition party substantially decreases its effectiveness in policy leadership. The "outs" comprise many oppositions rather than one, and disagreement is as much internal as directed at the governing party. Opposition goals are defined at four levels. First, party members in Congress define legislative aims, although they are not always in agreement among themselves. Secondly, state governors and a few key state legislative leaders seek to furnish personally or parochially based conceptions of national party purposes. Thirdly, leaders of party organizations in major areas of partisan strength (metropolitan areas for Democrats and Midwestern regions for Republicans) provide added factional definitions of party goals. Finally, for either party in opposition there are always retired or defeated leaders of national prominence, including former Presidents, Vice-Presidents, ambassadors, Cabinet members, etc. Each can be counted on to express his own diagnosis and prescription for party ills. The case of the Republican party's preparing for 1966 congressional and gubernatorial elections serves as an example of how partisan leadership is dispersed for the party of the opposition. Differing (sometimes conflicting and sometimes compatible) policy statements on such diverse problems as war in Viet Nam, racial unrest in metropolitan areas, and the proposal for nation-wide daylight saving time could be obtained from such "spokesmen" as: former Vice-President Richard Nixon, California Gubernatorial candidate Ronald Reagan, Senate Minority Leader Everett Dirksen, House Minority Leader Gerald Ford, Michigan Governor George Romney, Barry Goldwater, and former President Dwight Eisenhower, to name but the most prominent. It is difficult enough to generate party unity behind presidential leadership; without it, a community-wide partisan outlook is almost inconceivable.

Party influence is strongest in the initiation of proposals; it is much weaker in converting those proposals into policies adopted by legislative bodies. Nonetheless partisanship intrudes into the legislative process at several points. Parties bear the responsibility for organizing most American legislative bodies; the organization of Congress is controlled by the majority party. Beyond this, as we note in Chapter Thirteen, the extent that party influences policy adoption depends upon the degree of parochialism in Congress, the pressures exacted by the President, and the extent that group pressures and partisan interests in the community coincide.

Where the president has discretion in the appointment of administrative officials and appoints partisans to those posts, his party plays a significant role in the application of public policy. But there are limits to the partisan role in bureaucratic policy-making. Presidential discretion in filling appointments extends only to top administrative posts; below these the norms of career service dictate selection procedures. Moreover, in combination with the tradition of past policy programs, careerism sets definite limits upon the degree of policy modification that can take place during a given administration. Career officials frequently tend to develop loyalties to their agency and its established programs; in such instances both partisan and presidential appeals for support of policy innovations fall on deaf ears. Furthermore legislative oversight (the process by which Congress exercises its responsibility to see that agencies created under its jurisdiction operate as intended, carry out congressionally approved programs, and spend funds as authorized) may modify the degree of presidential control over partisans and nonpartisans in his own administration.

Partisanship is unquestionably a major consideration in staffing judicial posts at various levels. In states that elect judicial officials, partisan considerations weigh heavily in the selection process. In appointing persons to federal judgeships, particularly in federal district courts (see Chapter Fifteen), the President normally selects qualified individuals of his own party. For example, of recent Presidents, John Kennedy appointed the largest number of opposition party members to federal judgeships, but of 122 appointments, only 11 went to Republicans; between 1933–65, a scant 5 per cent of federal circuit and district judgeships were filled with appointments from the opposition party by the incumbent president. This does not, however, mean that a President can automatically appoint party members favorable to him to such positions. The tradition of senatorial courtesy, which permits a Senator of the majority party to reject an appointment made by the President to the bench in his state if the appointee is objectionable to the Senator, results in the President's seeking out Senators for their recommendations concerning federal judgeships. Thus, any presidential attempt to develop a party "machine" in the federal judiciary is restricted, a fact that again illustrates how partisan control is dispersed throughout various levels.

Occasionally a President can be embarrassed by following the advice of a Senator in making a judicial appointment. In 1965, apparently on the advice of Senator Edward M. Kennedy, President Johnson announced his intention to appoint Francis X. Morrissey to a federal district judgeship in Massachusetts. Morrissey had been instrumental in Senator Kennedy's successful senate campaign of 1962. However, a controversy broke out in the Senate over Morrissey's qualifications and competence to sit on the federal bench. His fitness for the appointment was questioned by a committee of the American Bar Association on grounds that he lacked experience as a trial lawyer, had never served as a judge in a court handling jury or equity trials, and had failed to display significant legal competence in his training as a lawyer. Although the Johnson Administration continued to support the nomination, Senator Kennedy finally requested the Senate to recommit the nomination to its Judiciary Committee, thus effectively preventing confirmation.

One of the reasons such controversies arise over partisan appointments to the federal judiciary lies in the wide-spread belief that judges should be "non-political"; that is, partisan considerations should not enter into their judicial decisions. For example, President Franklin Roosevelt proposed in 1937 that he be allowed to appoint additional justices to the Supreme Court for each judge then serving over the age of seventy who did not retire after ten years service. The maximum number of justices for the Court would be raised from nine to fifteen. This was interpreted as an attempt to "pack" the Court with judges amenable to presidential programs previously declared unconstitutional by the Justices. The proposal was criticized in many quarters as a violation of the non-partisan tradition of the judiciary. The incident reflected a general expectation that Americans hold regarding the court system; that is, "once the federal bench has served its patronage function the party has done with it."[25]

In sum, parties originate policy proposals, borrow and modify proposals from other groups, propagandize them, win elections, and organize their newly won authority by staffing the major policy-making positions in the community. Although partisanship plays less of an influential role in leading, adopting, applying, and interpreting policy than in representing social conflict, these functions should not be minimized. We will spell them out, and the limits placed upon their partisan performance, at greater length in Part Three.

POLITICAL PARTISANSHIP AND LIBERAL DEMOCRACY

It is apparent that political parties are vital constitutional institutions in a democracy, that the performance of party functions in America is largely circumscribed by the non-centralized and diverse nature of the duocracy, and that parties are increasingly forced to share the representation of social conflict with other social agencies. Ideally the task of a political party in a democracy is to organize conflict in such a way that political officials are subject to popular control and the entire political process open to popular consultation. Professor Clinton Rossiter has asserted that the "political process in a free country is essentially a conflict, limited and regularized but nonetheless relentless, among groups of men who have contradictory interests and more or less mutually exclusive hopes of securing them."[26] If this be realistic, then liberal-democratic parties can serve the republic by providing officials responsive to the conflict and responsible to the community; that is, parties can help secure the political community for its members.

The consequences of partisan duocracy, dispersion and diversity for American government are noteworthy. As federalistic and pluralistic entities, our two major parties appeal to interests in conflict and, although buffeted by internal cleavages, absorb the more serious social disputes sufficiently to permit peaceful selection of community leadership. As legitimate competitors for political authority, parties are not so much victimized by the conflicts of component interests as energized and even justified by them. Partisanship exists to manage conflict, not by resolving it, but by representing it; and its rationale in America lies in the fact that duocratic structuring of social conflict is an expedient by which com-

[25] Sorauf, *op. cit.*, p. 123.

[26] Clinton Rossiter, *Parties and Politics in America* (Ithaca: Cornell University Press, 1960), p. 39.

munity disagreements are sorted, simplified, and transmitted. Parties exploit diversity of interest, help maintain the integrity of discrete demands, coalesce interests momentarily to win governance, and channel their demands to officialdom. The result is maintenance of a low and hopefully creative level of community tension.

By varying the motto *e pluribus unum,* we might say that partisanship in the American democratic community reflects an effort to obtain "out of many, two"; and the two continually divide in order to unite. Democratic and Republican parties in America have become symbols of the overriding consensus without which no political community could exist. These two structures of partisanship are posited on the assumption that Americans are sufficiently desirous of sharing both their agreements and disagreements to tolerate peaceful party warfare. The American duocracy is as much a part of the constitutional consensus of the community as the U.S. Constitution itself. And to the extent that partisans are carriers of the liberal-democratic creed, the parties bind Americans to substantive, as well as procedural, values of liberal democracy. By publicizing selected social conflicts, partisanship throws open policy-making to the whole of the polity; by avoiding other disputes, parties mitigate the seriousness of cleavage. Through selective representation, partisanship promotes a continuing readaptation between constitution and society.

Despite a challenge to the performance of its functions from many competitors — pressure groups, the mass media, administrative agencies and programs — and the anti-party bias reflected in many state statutes, American parties remain the only large-scale, continuously active, open, and inclusive organizations encompassing a highly diverse clientele and performing numerous complementary functions in securing political office. The partisan process remains the broadest and most enduring mode of political activity whereby conflict is represented, leaders are selected, and choices urged upon us. In short, "the party as a political force, ineffective and inadequate as much of its leadership and organization is, has not been superseded by other political influences or institutions." [27]

BIBLIOGRAPHICAL NOTE

As a result of the paperback explosion of recent years a number of detailed descriptions, analyses, and interpretations of American political parties are now available. Each defines party politics (albeit in slightly different ways), spells

[27] Eldersveld, *op. cit.,* p. 523.

out the characteristics of American parties, and includes examples and anecdotes illustrating the function of partisan politics. Among the best of these are the following: Frank J. Sorauf, *Political Parties in the American System* (Boston: Little, Brown and Company, 1964); Allan P. Sindler, *Political Parties in the United States* (New York: St. Martin's Press, 1966); Fred I. Greenstein, *The American Party System and the American People* (Englewood Cliffs, N.J.: Prentice-Hall, Inc., 1963); Clinton Rossiter, *Parties and Politics in America* (Ithaca, New York: Cornell University Press, 1960); William J. Crotty, Donald M. Freeman, and Douglas S. Gatlin, *Political Parties and Political Behavior* (Boston: Allyn & Bacon, Inc., 1966); and Neil A. McDonald, *The Study of Political Parties* (New York: Random House, 1955).

Moreover, several of the earlier perceptive treatments of partisanship are now also conveniently available in paperbound editions including Pendleton Herring's *The Politics of Democracy* (New York: W. W. Norton & Company, Publishers, 1965), detailing the consequences of American pluralism for party organization; E. E. Schattschneider's account of the problems of party decentralization, in *Party Government* (New York: Holt, Rinehart and Winston, 1942); V. O. Key's study of party politics in the American South, *Southern Politics* (New York: Random House, Vintage Books, 1949); Robert Michels, *Political Parties* (New York: Collier Books, 1962); M. Ostrogorski's *Democracy and the Organization of Political Parties* (Garden City, New York: Doubleday & Company, Inc., Anchor Books 1964); and Austin Ranney, *The Doctrine of Responsible Party Government* (Urbana: The University of Illinois Press, 1962).

Two recent and succinct publications have directed attention to the origins of the American duocracy: William Nisbet Chambers, *Political Parties in a New Nation* (New York: Oxford University Press, 1963) and Joseph Charles, *The Origins of the American Party System* (New York: Harper and Brothers, Torchbook Edition, 1961). Present day aspects of each of the two major parties are treated in Ralph M. Goldman, *The Democratic Party in American Politics* (New York: The Macmillan Company, 1966) and Charles O. Jones, *The Republican Party in American Politics* (New York: The Macmillan Company, 1965).

Among the standard works available for reference one should certainly consult Samuel J. Eldersveld's combined text and report of research in Wayne County, Michigan, *Political Parties: A Behavioral Analysis* (Chicago: Rand McNally & Company, 1964). Other excellent references are Avery Leiserson, *Parties and Politics: An Institutional and Behavioral Approach* (New York: Alfred A. Knopf, 1958); Maurice Duverger, *Political Parties* (New York: John Wiley & Sons, Inc., 1954); V. O. Key, Jr., *Politics, Parties,. and Pressure Groups* (New York: Thomas Y. Crowell Company, Fifth Edition, 1964); and Hugh A. Bone, *American Politics and the Party System* (New York: McGraw-Hill Book Company, Third Edition, 1965).

Additionally, several compendiums of essays concerning American partisan patterns are noteworthy: Demetrios Caraley, *Party Politics and National Elections* (Boston: Little, Brown and Company, 1966); John R. Owens and P. J. Staudenraus, *The American Party System* (New York: The Macmillan Company, 1965); Frank Munger and Douglas Price, *Political Parties and Pressure Groups* (New York: Thomas Y. Crowell Company, 1964) and, Robert A. Goldwin, *Political Parties, U.S.A.* (Chicago: Rand McNally & Company, 1964).

CHAPTER
TEN

Political Pressure

One of the more frequent forms of citizen involvement as stated in our discussion of American participation patterns, is membership in voluntary associations. Alexis de Tocqueville wrote in the early nineteenth century that "the principle of association" differentiated the American community from all others; even earlier Madison fretted over the "mischievousness of faction." Both were emphasizing a fact true today, that Americans attach themselves to sundry organizations to express their interests, contest with one another, and assert influence over public policy. Their collective behavior constitutes patterns of political pressure. As political parties are the visible agencies of partisan activity in America, so political groups are the visible agencies of pressure activity. In the following pages we focus upon the nature of pressure activity in America, what it is that pressure groups contribute to the political process, and how personal, constitutional, and social dimensions of our community limit their scope.

254

THE ORGANIZATION OF POLITICAL PRESSURE

TYPES OF PRESSURE GROUPS

Given our pluralist society, it is not surprising that pressure groups come in all shapes, sizes, and varieties. It is impossible to estimate the number of such diversified organizations that play a part in American government. More than one thousand are represented in Washington by registered lobbyists. The names of a few such pressure organizations yield a clue as to the variety of concerns shaping pressure politics: United States Brewers Association, International Brotherhood of Bookbinders, Tuna Research Foundation, American Federation of Labor, National Cheese Institute, Committee on Free Trade Education, John Birch Society, White Citizens Councils, American Dental Association, and so forth. Since it is obviously not feasible to describe every pressure organization in America, we can get a better picture of the scope of pressure activity by looking at the general types of pressure organizations that exist and the forms of personal, reciprocal, and official pressure they exert. Then, in Chapter Eleven, we can see how these pressure groups interact in policy conflicts.

Ultimately, any social group may exert pressure by seeking to coordinate and promote its interests. It is convenient to distinguish between primary, secondary, and official groups and note the types of pressure normally exerted by each. Primary groups seek to achieve group unity by influencing the personal choices of citizens rather than promote their cause by pressuring public officials. Here we can include (1) kinship groups (the family), which promote conformity in voting behavior, entertainment values, even standards of dress; (2) semi-permanent special interest groups (partisan clubs or neighborhood improvement groups); and (3) the temporary face-to-face groups of which we are all members (committees, classroom gatherings, discussion groups, etc.). Primary groups are important in the pressure politics because they are points of reference for personal conduct and they exert *personal* pressure on members to achieve unity in pursuit of goals. Since we discussed the role of personal pressure in politicization and the shaping of choice patterns, we will concern ourselves in the balance of this chapter with pressures exerted by private secondary and official groups.

Secondary groups also try to influence members, but political energies are directed mainly at advancing their interests over other groups and at winning the support of public officials. Each goal generates a distinctive type of pressure. In a complex pluralist society, individuals can participate in several secondary groups. In his study of public opinion, Bernard

Hennessy has suggested a typology of such groups that includes not only groups with explicit political aims but: (1) economic, including occupational groups such as unions, business, and professional organizations; (2) moralistic-ritualistic, concerned with ethical, spiritual, or philosophic matters such as churches or service organizations; and (3) artistic-recreational, dealing with "creativeness, beauty, [or] physical exercise." [1] One needs only list a few pieces of legislation acted upon by Congress in recent years to recognize that these secondary groups participate in the pressure process. For example: proposals to revise labor legislation stimulate the activity of economic groups; proposals to give federal support to private and parochial schools activate moralistic-ritualistic groups; and such measures as the bill creating a National Council on the Arts and a National Council on Arts and Humanities caught the attention of various artistic-recreational groups.

When citizens are in regular contact with a variety of primary and secondary groups overlapping memberships link the organizations themselves. Associations are groups formed around those overlapping relations.[2] For example, as a wife a woman is a member of a family group; as a mother she is in contact with another group of which her child is a member — the school. Through her child she may associate with school administrators, teachers, etc. It was out of just such overlapping linkages to family and school that the Parent Teachers Association originated, a pressure organization of some note in local and federal politics. Associations are particularly important because, in expanding the perspectives of group members, they help broaden the exclusive interest base of political groups. By exerting *reciprocal* pressure on each other, groups also contribute to the give-and-take that shapes the policy compromises that merge conflicting interests into temporary alliances for common gain (see Chapter Eleven).

Finally, we can add to primary and secondary groups those generating official pressure. Pressure groups exist within, as well as outside of, governmental office. Policy officials often comprise politically relevant groups with more exclusive aims than simple promotion of the "community welfare." Congressional committees, executive bureaus, district courts, and other sets of policy officials exert pressures upon other policy-makers and private political groups. Examples of such official groups are common. For instance: the Special Subcommittee on Government Information (House Committee on Government Operations) has for more

---

[1] Bernard Hennessy, *Public Opinion* (Belmont, Cal.: Wadsworth Publishing Co., 1965), pp. 117–18.
[2] David B. Truman, *The Governmental Process* (New York: Alfred A. Knopf, 1951), pp. 40–41.

than a decade urged executive agencies to release information to the press and public. The subcommittee's permanent administrative staff is the nucleus of a pressure group within the halls of Congress. In alliance with various interests outside Congress, including news organizations, this official pressure group brought about a passage of a "Freedom of Information" bill in 1966 setting standards for what types of information can and cannot be withheld from the public by administrative agencies. Similarly the widely publicized Permanent Subcommittee on Investigations of Senator Joseph McCarthy sought in the 1950's not only to formulate policy but to influence all governmental decisions concerning hiring, firing and promotions of personnel. Virtually all of the sub-governments (about which we shall say more in the next chapter) that constitute American political institutions act as official pressure groups.

ATTRIBUTES OF PRESSURE POLITICS

The workings of pressure groups long have been a central concern of students of American government. We discuss here three major attributes common to all pressure groups. They must (1) reflect organized and regularized efforts to coordinate sets of interests, (2) maintain exclusive purposes, and (3) seek to influence the formulation of public policy.

Recall that in our preceding account of political-choice patterns we distinguished between social groups and socio-demographic groupings. The latter consist of individuals sharing a common characteristic — age, ethnic background, sex, etc. — that places them in the same grouping. Although citizens in particular socio-demographic groupings frequently display similarities in voting behavior, categoric groupings ordinarily lack political significance in the pressure process. Shoppers at the supermarket, picknickers in the park, all guys named Joe, or teenagers on the beach seldom fight with one another or request the community to recognize the primacy of their demands. In rare instances when their behavior assumes political proportions (as when a peaceful and law-abiding assemblage of sunbathers becomes a bottle-throwing mob), they lack organization in their sporadic attempts to intimidate law enforcement officers. For our purposes, organization *plus* regular efforts to influence governmental policy distinguishes a pressure group from these categoric groupings, social gatherings, or unruly crowds. Pressure groups have always been "organized minorities which seek to influence decisions concerning issues of public policy and administration," [3] as opposed to the consensual and clustered manifestations of individual preferences (discussed earlier) that transcend group memberships.

[3] See, for example, Thomas C. Cocharan (ed.), *Concise Dictionary of American History* (New York: Charles Scribner's Sons, 1962), p. 762.

In emphasizing the organized and regularized aspects of pressure politics, we need to remember that organization is not the same thing as unity of purpose. As with a political party, each pressure group consists of sets of interests striving to define, as well as achieve, organizational goals. Tension among both organized sub-groups and individuals yields conflicts within pressure groups as significant in shaping pressure patterns as disputes between political organizations. Because unity frequently gives strength to a group confronting other segments of society, pressure leaders develop formal organizational hierarchies and procedures to reconcile the diverse and conflicting interests within their memberships. But, the tidiness of organization is disrupted in two ways.

First, sub-groups vie for positions of group leadership from which to command the aspirations and efforts of followers. Coalitions of interests in temporary alliance seek to direct group policy. When the American Federation of Labor (AFL) and Congress of Industrial Organizations (CIO) merged into a single labor organization in the 1950's (following a much earlier split between the two), it was necessary to reach agreement on which union should control policy. The solution was to elect George Meany (AFL leader) as President and Walter Reuther (CIO leader) as Executive Secretary of the newly-formed organization. Periodic factional conflicts indicate that the bargain has been only partially successful.

Secondly, the interests of individual group members are not always in harmony with the stated goals of the parent organization. For example: the American Medical Association reflects the goals of many, but certainly not all, doctors. A quick and unconscious conformity to collective goals and standards, frequently labeled by critics of pressure groups as "group-think," is less common than supposed. Citizens may be attracted to particular groups by their publicized positions on certain issues; but it is not unusual for members to disagree with other goals of their respective organizations. Witness, for example, that not all AFL-CIO members vote for the candidates endorsed by their organization's political-action arm, the Committee on Political Education.

The exclusive character of the goals sought by pressure groups is the second attribute we discuss here. E. E. Schattschneider has remarked that pressure politics is essentially that of small groups; that is, the organizations that participate in pressure activity have specialized goals and pursue exclusive interests.[4] Interests are exclusive in the sense that normally only a small segment of the community initiates their pursuit and derives immediate and direct benefits if group aims are obtained.

[4] E. E. Schattschneider, The Semisovereign People (New York: Holt, Rinehart and Winston, 1960), pp. 23–24.

For example: a high tariff placed upon the importation of transistor radios manufactured in Japan directly benefits a relatively small proportion of citizens — the American manufacturers of the product — although secondary rewards may accrue to domestic steel producers, plastics firms, retailers, etc. There are, of course, exceptions to Schattschneider's generalization. By way of illustration, among the legislative proposals pushed through the 89th Congress by the Administration of Lyndon Johnson in 1965 were bills aimed at advancing urban beautification, the establishment of new national park areas, regulation of highway billboards, eradication of unsightly highway junkyards, and prevention of air and water pollution. Although such proposals were advanced by a variety of specialized groups interested in preservation and restoration of natural beauty resources — for which Mrs. Lyndon Johnson provided symbolic leadership — the measures were designed to benefit all Americans. The same might be said of other policies originated as exclusive demands by minority interests, particularly those items of welfare legislation such as social security, medical care for the aged, minimum wage legislation, etc. Hence, pressure groups are "organized minorities" pursuing "exclusive interests" in the sense that they seek to fashion community consent to demands that originate as concerns limited primarily to group members but which may be of ultimate benefit to larger sectors of the population.[5]

There are several implications associated with the exclusive character of pressure groups. First, since the aims of one group frequently run counter to others, pressure tends to generate counterpressure; and reciprocal pressure results. Secondly, the special concerns of pressure groups are not necessarily in harmony with current conceptions of broader community purposes; that is, the goals pursued by *private* interests may not parallel the *public* interests defined by policy officials. To protect the public interest, then, official pressure is often exerted. Moreover, in order to win community approval for their private interests, pressure groups find it expedient either to recruit support from outsiders (becoming more inclusive organizations and compromising their exclusive aims to integrate diverse internal elements) or rationalize their narrow demands in terms of a more vaguely defined public interest (permitting themselves to be bound by current consensus on abstract goals such as liberty, equality, or justice). In either event, the exclusive

---

[5] Note how the exclusive character of pressure groups differs from James Madison's notion of factions: "A number of citizens, whether amounting to a majority or minority of the whole, who are united and actuated by some common impulse of passion, or of interest, adverse to the rights of other citizens, or to the permanent and aggregate interests of the community." Alexander Hamilton, James Madison, and John Jay, *The Federalist* (Modern Library ed.; New York: Random House, 1937), p. 54.

goals of pressure groups are constantly modified in the face of the current social, politico-constitutional, and doctrinal environment. Finally, in governmental affairs, narrow and specialized interest disputes often move into the arena of community conflict regulation; and, pressure activity becomes a public manifestation of private disagreements. Through pressure politics, interest differences are disclosed; publicity replaces the comparative secrecy characteristic of private arguments that do not involve community policy-makers as mediators.

As we define them, pressure groups have a third distinguishing attribute; e.g., a pressure group "seeks to influence the content of governmental decisions without attempting to place its members in formal governmental capacities." [6] Two qualifications are in order. First, persons with extensive experience in pressure politics are frequently appointed to governmental positions. Before his service in the Kennedy Administration as Secretary of the Department of Labor, for example, Arthur Goldberg was a legal counsel for the United Steelworkers Union; Robert Mc-Namara, Secretary of the Department of Defense under both Presidents John F. Kennedy and Lyndon Johnson, moved to his position from the presidency of Ford Motor Company. In noting the frequency of such appointments, however, we should keep in mind that these officials no longer serve as the spokesmen of their pressure organizations after selection. Moreover, although their former experiences and contacts undoubtedly impinge upon their policy decisions, it does not follow that they merely register as law the demands of their former affiliates. As we shall see in Chapter Eleven, policy formulation is considerably more complex involving as it does the intermingling of both unofficial and official pressures.

Secondly, pressure groups seek to influence the elected rather than win elections for themselves, but this does not mean that their spokesmen are divorced from electoral politics. Pressure groups certainly endeavor to influence the selection of party nominees, as did key segments of organized labor in unsuccessful efforts to nominate former Vice-President Alben Barkley as the Democratic candidate for President in 1952. If party control is diffused or party leaders divided, pressure groups have a significant impact on party decisions, perhaps even winning nominations for their own members. But, if a pressure group spokesman receives a party nomination, he runs as a Republican or Democrat, not as leader of the Audubon Society, the Hardwood Plywood Institute, or the Marble Industry of America. Popular consensus on the appropriateness of a two-party arrangement restricts a pressure group from capturing public office in

[6] Harmon Zeigler, *Interest Groups in American Society* (Englewood Cliffs, N.J.: Prentice-Hall, 1964), p. 30.

direct competition with the major parties; hence, the preference for working through party organizations rather than in direct confrontation.

Pressure patterns thus differ from partisan alignments with respect to goals and methods of participants. The goal of the American party is control of governing authority; its method is to mobilize support behind candidates for office. The goal of the American pressure group is to influence policy in a specific area; its methods include identifying with dominant community values, seeking support of allied groups, lobbying with officials, endorsing and financing party candidates — all techniques short of offering group spokesmen for office. In effect, the inclusive character of partisan composition makes parties better suited to represent conflict by bridging interest differences; pressure groups perform the representative function by exclusive recruitment, reconciling internal disputes, and exploiting persuasive techniques in order to unite group members behind policy goals and rationalize private interests in public terms.

FREQUENCY OF PRESSURE PARTICIPATION

In 1952 it was estimated that approximately two of every three Americans belonged to formal organizations of some type. Half of these organized citizens were members of groups that took stands on political issues. That there is some stability in this frequency of group participation is illustrated by data in Table 10-1, despite the increase in percentages of persons who claimed no group memberships between 1952 and 1959 (a difference that could lie in changes in sampling design, statement of questions, etc.).

TABLE 10-1

Frequency of Group Participation in America, 1952 and 1959

PER CENT BELONGING TO:	1952 [a]	1959 [b]
No Organizations	36%	43%
One Organization	33	25
Two or More Organizations	31	32
	100%	100%
NUMBER OF CASES	542	970

Sources:

[a] Survey Research Center, University of Michigan, 1952.
[b] Gabriel A. Almond and Sidney Verba, *The Civic Culture* (Princeton, N.J.: Princeton University Press, 1963), p. 320.

Using data from the Michigan Survey Research Center, V. O. Key, Jr., observed that the frequency of group membership varies with a person's income, occupation, education and other indicators of class status. Of those surveyed in 1952, over 50 per cent in households of professional workers held memberships in three or more groups; only 5 per cent of members of households of unskilled workers belonged to groups. Of six occupational categories, the unskilled and farmer groups had relatively few memberships. Professional and business occupations were roughly correlated with high frequency of memberships; clerical and skilled workers rounded out the picture with a moderate number of memberships.[7] Moreover, Professor Milbrath found that Washington lobbyists for pressure organizations generally have middle- and upper-class backgrounds.[8]

Other surveys underscore the proposition that joiners are recruited primarily from the educated, more politically alert, and more well-to-do portions of the community. However, group participation does not simply mirror the pattern of political participation generally. There are interesting exceptions. Robert Lane reports that joining political clubs (neighborhood organizations performing both social and political functions) bears little relation to one's income. Membership in organizations that "sometimes" take stands on public issues is more common for Negroes than Whites. Finally, there is little difference between the proclivities of men and women for joining groups.[9]

The same data that reveal well over a majority of Americans as joiners also disclose that more than a third belong to no organization of any type. The motives underlying a person's decision to join a group are never clear to us. Being a joiner calls for sacrifice of time, energy, and finances; but the fact that certain status indicators are correlated with frequency of group memberships does not warrant a generalization that high status produces group participation or vice-versa. Finding causes for group membership is also complicated by the varying frequency and intensity with which people actually take part in their groups. Certainly group membership offers an opportunity for political expression and meaningful camaraderie, even though the political purpose of the group itself sometimes has little bearing on an individual's decision to join or retain membership. Personal purpose and membership in a given group are not always identical.

The prevailing "class bias" of pressure politics means that many social interests are not represented in the pressure process. Although pressure patterns are by no means monopolized by the upper social strata, those with middle- and upper-class perspectives do exert more *continuing*

[7] V. O. Key, Jr., *Public Opinion and American Democracy* (New York: Alfred A. Knopf, 1961), pp. 504–7; Schattschneider, *op. cit.*, pp. 20–46.

[8] Lester W. Milbrath, *The Washington Lobbyists* (Chicago: Rand McNally & Co., 1963), pp. 90–96.

[9] Robert Lane, *Political Life* (Glencoe, Ill.: The Free Press, 1959), p. 79.

pressure upon policy officials. Pressure patterns distort the overall picture of American social interests in the same way that participation and leadership patterns are distorted.[10] The more alienated of the unorganized — the dispossessed and the disillusioned — are scarcely represented in pressure politics; consequently, they sometimes seek more sensational methods of publicizing their grievances, including lynchings, assassinations, mob violence, and suicides. Others not represented in pressure politics may take a more peaceful form of mass protest.

SOURCES OF PRESSURE ACTIVITY

It is much easier to cite the broad social changes stimulating the organization of pressure activity than to establish the personal motivations that make joiners of Americans. Students of pressure politics generally share the view that "organized groups begin in response to changes in the relationships between individuals when existing institutions are inadequate to provide a means for the re-establishment of stability."[11] Groups come into being as collective efforts to cope with a variety of social disturbances. They seek governmental decisions that correspond to the hopes and aspirations of members. A good example is the agrarian movement that developed in nineteenth-century America. Southern and midwestern farmers were squeezed between falling prices for produce and increasing marketing costs, particularly in the Plains States where depression followed a post-Civil War agricultural boom. In attempts to obtain public aid for relief of their plight, agrarians resorted to several stratagems. One was a new political orientation for existing social organizations. The National Grange, for example, served as a spearhead for the discontent of farmers in many sections of the community.

Similar attempts to alleviate immediate problems by resorting to political action mark the whole of American history. When segments of the community are denied full access to normal channels of conflict representation (such as elections or legislative representation), organized response to social disruptions becomes particularly pronounced. Any chronicle of the Negro protest of the last two decades would be incomplete without a recounting of the activities of the pressure groups linked to it: the National Association for the Advancement of Colored People, the Urban League, the Southern Christian Leadership Conference, the Southern Regional Council, the Congress of Racial Equality, and scores of lesser known organizations. Similarly, whenever human beings find it impossible to satisfy physical needs and social wants through private means,

[10] Schattschneider, *op. cit.*, pp. 34–35.
[11] Zeigler, *op. cit.*, p. 73.

they frequently turn to political organization in order to gain public support.

THE REPRESENTATIVE FUNCTION
OF PRESSURE PERFORMANCE

It is part of American political tradition to curse the "special interests" for producing conditions that citizens find undesirable in the community. The tone was set long ago by Vernon L. Parrington in his classic account of how Congress divided the riches of America among business and commercial interests toward the close of the nineteenth century: "A huge barbeque was spread to which all presumably were invited. Not quite all, to be sure; inconspicuous persons, those who were at home on the farm or at work in the mills and offices were overlooked; a good many indeed out of the total number of the American people. But all the important persons, leading bankers and promoters and businessmen received invitations." [12] Unto this day whenever Americans are sorely discontent with the management of governmental affairs there are special groups on which to heap the blame — "monied interests," "farmers and sodbusters," the "Easterners," the "pushy minorities," and others. Despite this view, a more dispassionate look at the activities of American pressure groups is possible.[13] When we take it, we find that pressure organizations make a crucial contribution by representing social conflict to community officials. In performing their representative function, pressure groups employ a variety of methods; moreover as mobilizers of interest conflict and molders of public policy they feel the impact of shaping forces in the community impinging on all patterns of conflict representation.

Techniques of Organized Representation and Influence. Considering the plurality of American interests, it is difficult to conceive how popular demands could be correctly reflected without the contributions made by organized groups. As channels of political communication they supplement parties, officials, opinion surveys, journalists, opinion leaders, and elections in transmitting social disputes to policy-makers. In articulating group interests and bringing them to the attention of policy-makers, pressure organizations employ numerous techniques; among them are efforts to organize opinions by adjusting intragroup disputes, politicization, electioneering, coercion, persuasion, securing access to policy officials through lobbying, and official action.

Opinion Organization. Before groups can recruit outside aid in pursuit of their goals, they must first define their aims and mobilize internal

[12] Vernon Louis Parrington, *Main Currents in American Thought* (New York: Harcourt, Brace & Co., 1927), III, p. 23.
[13] See particularly Truman, *op. cit., passim.*

agreement upon them. Of course, if individuals sharing particular sentiments have united as a group because of their common aims, then we
can expect internal differences to center on means rather than ends. But,
given the multi-interest composition of large-scale pressure organizations
that have existed for some time (such as the United States Chamber of
Commerce or large labor unions), frequent efforts at reconciling divergent
views are necessary. The procedures for achieving these adjustments instruct members in how to resolve disputes in the community as a whole.
For example: when citizens encounter democratic procedures within
their organizations, they are more likely to support democratic ways of
settling disputes within the polity. By the same token, it has been asserted
that authoritarian practices in adjusting intragroup cleavages contribute
to such procedures in managing community affairs. The philosopher John
Dewey thought the experience with such "private government" so important that he argued, "To be realized democracy must affect all modes
of human association, the family, the school, industry, religion." [14]

The wish for internal democracy in private political organizations,
however, has been achieved only partially. Private government in trade
unions, business corporations, professional groups, party organizations
and even academic institutions frequently is practiced with authoritarian
overtones — dictated policies, oligarchical controls, and relatively little
participation of members in making group decisions.[15] The differences
between democratic and authoritarian styles of group life illustrate once
again the contrast between substantive ideals and procedural realities of
liberal democracy. The latter make no demands that intragroup disputes
be adjusted in accordance with democratic tenets of popular control and
consultation. So long as intergroup conflict resolution meets those criteria, the political community is labeled democratic regardless of union,
business, religious, professional, or educational authoritarianism. Substantive ideals, however, are more stringent on this point. The development of the full potential of individual talent requires free participation
in all decisions affecting community life, whether in adjusting conflicting
interests within or between groups. Measured by individual (substantive)
standards rather than collective (procedural) criteria, pressure activity is a
necessary, but not sufficient, condition for liberal democracy.

Politicization. As agencies of politicization, pressure groups shape attitudes and opinions of their rank-and-file with only limited success. We
noted earlier that group effectiveness depends in large degree upon the

[14] Joseph Ratner (ed.), *Intelligence in the Modern World* (The Modern Library;
New York: Random House, 1939), pp. 716–19.
[15] Seymour Martin Lipset, *Political Man* (Garden City, N.Y.: Doubleday & Co.,
1959), pp. 358–99.

closeness of identification that members feel toward the group. Data from the Survey Research Center's study of the 1956 presidential election reveal that loyal union members were more likely to give pro-union responses to a variety of political propositions than members with less intense union commitments. Highly intense identifiers were more willing to restrict the influence of business corporations on government decisions, less willing to restrict unions, more willing to have the federal government help people find jobs, and more willing to accept governmental support in obtaining medical and hospital care.[16]

Electoral Activity. Pressure groups advance their aims between and during election campaigns primarily with contributions of money and organizational efforts. The AFL-CIO, for example, delegates to its Committee on Political Education the task of choosing candidates of both parties for financial support. Contributions go into campaign chests, printing propaganda leaflets, purchasing advertising, lending secretarial and administrative staffs, providing private planes for candidate travel, etc. On election day pressure groups help mobilize both the concerned and disinterested by providing car pools and baby-sitting services or taking telephone messages. The significant feature of these campaign tactics is that they are normally channeled through the two major parties. Choosing as they do to concentrate on influencing policy, pressure groups are "fellow travelers" rather than organizers of election campaigns. Moreover, just as the looseness of partisan organization militates against parties commanding the loyal support of particular organizations, the pluralist character of pressure groups renders it necessary for them to "hedge their bets" by supporting candidates of both parties in campaigns rather than allying themselves permanently with either party. Businessmen within the National Association of Manufacturers divide contributions between Democratic and Republican presidential candidates, despite the fact that their support predominantly goes to the latter. Similarly Democratic candidates generally expect greater union support, but Republicans congenial to union interests are not denied contributions.

Coercion and Persuasion. Pressure groups may attempt to influence government decisions by using either coercive or persuasive techniques. Private groups lack a monopoly over the use of legitimate force, which characterizes constituted authority in the political community. Thus, pressure groups rarely deem violence or intimidation desirable ways of publicizing demands. Yet bombings, assassinations, and looting have been employed by some disgruntled groups. For example: in the era of Al Capone, force was threatened and used by "outlaw" interests, and or-

[16] Key, *op. cit.,* p. 507.

ganized crime operated as pressure groups within and outside of the law. Although it would be premature to suggest that coercive methods are things of the past in pressure politics, there has been a tendency in more recent decades for organized groups to utilize accepted techniques of political persuasion. Several legitimate sources of political power are reserved to private groups in the community. The strike is one example of a lawful means employed by labor organizations to publicize their dissatisfactions and induce opposing groups to recognize their claims. Institutional advertising, propagandistic publications, boycotts, collective bargaining — all are methods of political persuasion employed by pressure groups.

Lobbying. One of the most frequently employed techniques in pressure politics is lobbying. In observing the behavior of Washington lobbyists, Professor Lester Milbrath emphasized that lobbying is *"the stimulation and transmission of a communication, by someone other than a citizen acting on his own behalf, directed to a governmental decision-maker with the hope of influencing his decision."* [17] So conceived, the lobbyist is a useful link in the communication chain between pressure groups and public officials. To open the channels, lobbyists seek to establish an environment of mutual respect between themselves and policy-makers. For this reason they provide information on specialized topics to officials, counter the pressures of opposing groups on the policy-maker, contribute money and energy to campaigns, apply pressure selectively rather than saturate officials with demands, and endeavor to project an image of personal honesty, knowledgeability, and painstaking labor. Although these techniques are accepted by one and all as legitimate, less innocuous methods of influence are frowned upon. Both lobbyists and congressmen surveyed by Milbrath condemned bribery as a method of securing influence. Officials, however, distinguish between the more flagrant forms of bribery (direct payoffs) and indirect tactics, including offers to speak at conventions in exchange for an honorarium, weekend cruises, invitations to tour company facilities, etc. The latter are employed primarily to keep communications lines open rather than influence immediate decisions; yet their frequency contributes to the image of the lobbyist as a buyer and seller of influence rather than a necessary functionary in an open polity.

In a broad-ranging account of pressure politics in the formulation of foreign-trade policy, Raymond Bauer, Ithiel de Sola Pool, and Lewis Dexter describe the type of relationship that exists between lobbyists and policy-makers. Staffs of pressure organizations find it both useful and

[17] Milbrath, *op. cit.*, p. 8.

convenient to seek contacts with officials with interests similar or identical to their own. In cementing liaison with congenial officials, lobbyists provide aid and assistance to the very persons they alledgedly pressure; consequently, emphasize the authors, *"the lobbyist becomes in effect a service bureau for those congressmen already agreeing with him, rather than an agent of direct persuasion."* [18] So long as lobbyists serve and support officials, the stereotype of special interests dictating terms to policy officials is misleading. It is not always easy to tell who is doing the pressuring and who the yielding.

Official Action. For those pressure groups that have official status as policy-making agencies (such as the congressional subcommittees mentioned earlier), there is an additional technique of influence not available to non-official groups. This consists of exercising a legally designated capacity to recommend courses of action to fellow policy officials from positions within administrative and legislative institutions of government. As our discussion of policy formulation in Chapter Eleven describes, governing agencies frequently advance narrow interests for official approval. In many cases they do so in alliance with private pressure organizations. We make preliminary mention of it here in order to emphasize an important point: it is a misconception to think of "pressure politics" as confined to the activities of private groups endeavoring to move public officials. Officials themselves bring pressures both upon their colleagues and private interests; this is precisely why pressure politics is a vital activity linking social conflict with its public resolution.[19]

Given the variety of techniques at the disposal of political groups, it is easy to overestimate the political potency of pressure organizations. To the casual observer the policy process appears as a disruptive tug of war between pressure groups, with the victor dictating terms of policy to lawmakers. From this perspective, the public official is a harassed victim of selfish forces, which are intent upon depleting community resources to their own benefit. Without discounting the significance of pressure activities discussed above, it is helpful to turn to the community forces that limit the effectiveness of pressure politics in America.

Community Limitations on Pressure Mobilization. In mobilizing support for policy demands, pressure organizations are constrained by personal attitudes comprising the community consensus, challenges from other groups that spring up in a pluralist society, and features of constitutional authority.

---

[18] Raymond A. Bauer, Ithiel de Sola Pool, and Lewis Anthony Dexter, *American Business and Public Policy* (New York: Atherton Press, 1963), p. 353.

[19] Earl Latham, "The Group Basis of Politics: Notes for a Theory," *The American Political Science Review*, XLVI (June, 1952), 376–97.

Community Consensus. Community consensus limits pressure groups by defining the boundaries and procedures within which interests may make legitimate claims upon the community and by focusing community attention upon some matters but ignoring others.

The number and variety of pressure groups in America is determined in part by our willingness to recognize them as legitimate agents of political representation. Popular attitudes generally accept as legitimate the formation of organizations designed to promote specific interests. It is almost as though Americans refuse to admit the existence of a problem, desire, or activity unless it has taken on organized form. We organize everything from Little League baseball to peaceful picketing, from floating-dice games to crime syndicates. The scope of pressure politics is promoted by pro-organizing attitudes and habits; the legitimacy of particular pressure groups within the overall process is then determined by the sentiments of members and nonmembers concerning appropriateness of goals. For instance; a variety of civil rights groups were able in the first half of this decade to play a significant role in American politics because they gradually became widely recognized as acceptable agencies of protest. On the other hand, Black Muslims, American Nazis, the Women's Christian Temperance Union and the Flat Earth Society (a group devoted to the proposition that the earth is not globular) are examples of organizations that have encountered relative degrees of difficulty in advancing their respective causes. The popular responses concerning the legitimacy of political relevance of their claims have been unfavorable.

Consensus on the procedural ideals of liberal democracy (particularly free speech and association) facilitate the organization of groups; moreover, the right of petition stands as a protection for lobbying techniques. Other "rules of the game," however, restrict group activities. A widespread popular aversion to "dirty politics" cuts down upon opportunities for a free-swinging bartering for influence. Furthermore, the mere existence of community consensus inhibits organizations from pushing advantage beyond the margins established by current concepts of the "public interest." Proposals for diplomatic recognition of the Communist-dominated People's Republic of China, for example, have been consistently viewed in many quarters as counter to the "national interest" and relegated to a state of dormancy.

Community consensus on specific policies is not as frequent in America as fundamental agreement on procedures and long-term goals; but, when it does exist, it helps determine the arenas where pressure groups can make their demands: "a broad consensus on major policies – the sort of policies usually made by cabinets and legislatures – will tend to shift the major arena of political conflict, hence the major efforts of pressure groups, toward the administrative departments."[20] Some of the more noteworthy examples are the shift of conflict over trade policies from Congress to the Presidency; disputes over commerce regulation from Congress to regulatory commissions; and the continual shifting of the civil rights struggle from Congress, to Courts, to Department of Justice, and back to Congress. In each case, a general consensus in one political institution on policy ends has dictated that opposing interests exert pressure where cleavage is still likely.

Finally, a general lack of concern with political issues among citizens affects the efforts of groups in enlisting popular support. Since Americans pay only marginal attention to political communications, as much of our evidence suggests, the problems of arousing support are sometimes insurmountable. Joiners of political groups are likely to be politically active people anyway with views of their own — they read, they discuss, and they vote. In the face of political apathy, it is difficult to raise finances, stimulate letter-writing campaigns, and promote participation at the grass roots, which elective officials allegedly hold in high regard. Pressure groups are limited to appeals for support to an already participating and intense minority. Hence, representation of opinion through the pressure process is at best imperfect and reflects a series of discrete minorities rather than popular majorities.

The Multiplicity of Social Groups. Pressure activity channels the demands of several minorities rather than dominant majorities because of social diversity as well as popular consensus and apathy. We saw in Chapter Four that James Madison argued that the more diversified the society, the larger the number and variety of politically relevant groups and the less the likelihood of any single group dominating policy decisions. The semi-independence of a plurality of groups in America reduces the chances of control by any single group or by groups acting collectively. What we have referred to before as our "social checks and balances" limits the capacity of groups to mobilize support by forcing them to compete with one another for citizen loyalties and resources.

Pressure groups in America are restricted in this competition by the fact that few exist for engaging in purely political activities. Most are concerned with a variety of matters, and they resort to political action only when it is appropriate to group goals. The American Tobacco Growers Association, the American Legion, or the National Association of Retail Druggists are active politically as needs dictate; the major portion of their resources goes toward promoting interests through research, in-

---

[20] Harry Eckstein, "The Determinants of Pressure Group Politics," in Harry Eckstein and David E. Apter (eds.), *Comparative Politics* (London: The Free Press of Glencoe, 1963), p. 409.

formation-dispensing, and other means. Since political action is not neces-sarily appropriate to promotion of all group goals, the intensity of a group's political fervor varies accordingly. As political participants, pres-sure groups are restricted by their other concerns from concentrating to-tal efforts, finances, and energies on the passage of a particular measure. Consequently, they are highly selective in choosing issues on which to concentrate attention. Groups frequently avoid direct confrontation ex-cept upon those issues most crucial to their interests. Chances for success are increased when groups budget their political energies closely. Pro-fessor Schattschneider has emphasized that groups get results by being selective in concerns and biased in membership; *"if everybody got into the act the unique advantages of this form of organization would be destroyed, for it is possible that if all interests could be mobilized the result would be stalemate."* [21]

Because there are so many of them and relatively few resources to share among themselves, specialized pressure groups characteristically lack adequate financing, skilled personnel, information, and time to do an effective job of pressuring policy-makers. Although the total sum spent in a policy campaign is considerable, the overall expenditure is divided among uncoordinated, even conflicting, organizations. Any one organization normally places a lower priority on political activities in budgeting costs than upon other matters. Swiss watch manufacturers, for example, budget more than 2 million dollars annually for advertising and public relations of which only about one-eighth can be spent campaigning against tariff increases.[22]

Constitutional Factors. Beyond social diversity and personal attitudes, the mobilizing capacity of pressure groups also is shaped by constitu-tional arrangements. As with partisan patterns, those of pressure are affected by the operation of separated powers, checks and balances, and federalism. The principal effects lie in (1) determining access of pressure-group leaders to policy officials and (2) forcing adjustments in pressure organization. The first point may be obvious, but it warrants explicit statement: "Governmental structure affects the scope and intensity of pressure-group activity chiefly because expectations of success govern the political mobilization of groups, and whether or not a group can be suc-cessfully influential is determined at least partly by the structure of the government on which it acts." [23]

The opportunities for success depend in part on whether pressure or-ganizations desire to prevent the passage of policies or secure it. The

---

[21] Schattschneider, *op. cit.,* p. 35.
[22] Bauer, *et al., op. cit.,* p. 344.
[23] Eckstein, *op. cit.,* p. 414.

former course is relatively easy in the American political community primarily because of the proliferation of clusters of policy-making authority. In operation, balanced government multiplies the number of semi-autonomous policy agencies throughout the federal level and between federal, state, and local layers of government. Each is virtually an autonomous center of decision at which an interest can be advanced or, if not advanced, then at least protected. Chances for vetoing onerous proposals increase in direct proportion to the number of official groups that must agree before a policy is considered authoritative.[24] Although the chances of preventing detrimental policy decisions is increased, the difficulties faced by a pressure group in obtaining passage of favorable legislation are intensified. The forging of agreement dictates alliances for common action between groups; but common interest may mean watered down positions, bargaining, and a possibility of defection by more demanding group members.

Federalism frequently sharpens conflict between particular interests. Those with favorable access to state leaders seek support there; those that can obtain favor through federal action concentrate energies at that level. The result is manifested in a dispute between those professing loyalties to "states' rights" and "national authority." The contemporary struggle between segregationist and Negro groups reflects differences in access possessed by contending forces. Segregationist forces have frequently had a sympathetic hearing from state and local officials, local courts, and school boards thus making it possible to forestall school desegregation, removal of literacy tests for voting, etc. Negro groups have taken their case to federal officials, particularly the President and Congress, in order to obtain passage of a series of civil rights acts (outlined in Chapter Five). Moreover, they have been able to request investigations by the Department of Justice of cases of discrimination as well as appeal judicial decisions of state courts into the federal judicial system. Thus, for segregationist elements "states rights" have implied favorable policies; for integrationists the tactic has been to circumnavigate state policies through access to federal policy-makers.

In sum, the structure of constituted authority in the American polity necessitates that pressure groups engage in common action in order to convert overlapping interests into policy. The chances of individual groups translating exclusive demands into official action are decreased. They increase for groups having privileged access to officials or those willing to modify more extreme goals. Constitutional government in

---

[24] David Riesman *et al.*, *The Lonely Crowd* (Garden City, N.Y.: Doubleday & Co., 1955), pp. 246–51.

America facilitates the growth of pressure activity, limits more exclusive interests, and is impartial to none.

Constitutional structure shapes internal organization of pressure groups (as it does political parties) as "pressure groups tend somehow to resemble the organizations they seek to influence." [25] Pressure leaders do not force demands on policy-makers; they seek instead to attract attention and recruit aid. Just as they are selective in policy matters, so are they selective in where they apply pressure. In choosing their pressure points, they adjust their internal group organization. For example: a decision to pressure congressmen means not only lobbying in Washington but also influencing home constituents and, hopefully, through them the congressmen themselves. The result is organizational fragmentation into separate congressional districts. But if a group is worried about such an item of policy as the merger of two airlines, the more efficient strategy may call for concentrating appeals on those few officials on the Civil Aeronautics Board who rule on mergers.

Since it is sometimes difficult to know just who the key decision-makers are for particular policies, pressure groups may disperse attentions over a broad grouping of policy officials. Constitutional definitions alone are not reliable; "in the competition for influence [pressure groups] cannot afford to be deceived by political myths." [26] Moreover, insofar as constitutional politics does dictate points of pressure, the non-centralization of governing authority, produced by mechanisms of federalism and separated powers, still generates a fragmentation of organizational energies. As groups spread their efforts, problems of finance and organizational control mount accordingly.

The Effectiveness of Policy Pressure. Although the environment of pressure mobilization is not hostile, neither is it totally congenial. Moreover, combined with the internal characteristics of such groups, patterns of public policy, and official attitudes toward pressure politics, the community factors limiting the capacity of groups to engender broad support also restrict the effectiveness of pressure organizations in influencing policy officials.

Group Characteristics. The features of groups that condition their ability to influence policy include size, motivations, patterns of leadership, and availability of politically relevant resources. Group size and effectiveness are related in two ways. First, sheer numbers mean a great deal in a democracy. Assuming organizational agreement, the spokesman for 16 million union members receives more deference in federal affairs than the president of a neighborhood civic club. But, the advantage of size may

[25] Eckstein, *op. cit.*, p. 414.
[26] *Ibid.*, p. 409.

be offset by the difficulties at achieving organizational cohesiveness. The smaller the membership, the more likely that agreement can be generated among relatively homogeneous interests; an increase in size is frequently accompanied by increasing diversity and internal dispute. For example: persistent disputes within the AFL-CIO or U.S. Chamber of Commerce arise from large memberships scattered over a broad geographical expanse and dispersed among a variety of occupations. Certainly factional cleavages develop within groups that number only two persons (divorce occurs in political, as well as marital, relations), but cohesiveness is more difficult to obtain in mass organizations.

Intense commitment from group participants sometimes overcomes limitations of size. Communist organizations originated as intense minorities with limited resources, but absolute dedication to the group cause produced success in some nations. Few American groups command such devotion, although some seek to do so. The "paper membership" of many mass pressure organizations usually exceeds the number of adherents that can actually be depended upon to support the group line through monetary donations or expenditure of time and energy.

Moreover, group effectiveness is in part a function of organizational flexibility in defining goals. Efforts to achieve internal cohesiveness by building motivational and ideological purity among members can inhibit bargaining and compromise with opposing groups. If groups are overly doctrinaire they tend to lose some of their popular appeal. The zeal of the Ku Klux Klan for white supremacy tends to insulate the Klan from the realities of social change in the American South. An over-conformity to original group goals creates conditions that decrease the appeal of the group, and membership is recruited from the more frustrated and marginal elements of society. Moreover, members feel "boxed in" and isolated; and ultimately turn to violence as a preferred alternative to the politics of bargaining, persuasion, and open debate.[27]

Although pressure groups originate as minorities with shared goals in common, once in existence, changes occur within the organization and its community environment that produce modifications in group aims. Unless some elements accept responsibility for defining group goals, mobilizing support for them, and relating those concerns to the decisions of policy officials, the effectiveness of policy pressure is compromised severely. This task falls to group leaders. For example: if the group is successful in achieving its original aims, new goals must be established or the network of pressure activity may be dissipated. Union leaders have faced this type of problem. Once having obtained minimum-wage legis-

[27] See, for example, James W. Vander Zanden, "The Klan Revival," *American Journal of Sociology*, LXV (March, 1960), 456–62.

lation, higher salaries for members, maximum hours standards, etc., they did not disband union organization. Instead they sought new goals aimed at advancing laboring interests — shorter work weeks, hospitalization plans, corporate stock-sharing schemes, and protections against automation.

Thus, pressure-group leadership, like political leadership generally, consists of defining social goals and coordinating energies in their pursuit. Group leaders perform their tasks by accommodating conflicting factions in the name of unity, forging coalitions of major internal interests, or exploiting internal conflict to strengthen their own bargaining positions. In the process they are likely to develop interests *as leaders* that set them apart from group members; they push exclusive goals within, and in the name of, their respective organizations. Hence, in measuring the political response to a particular policy proposal, it is always necessary to be wary of identifying organized opinion with political opinion generally. Organized opinion may reflect only the interests of group leaders, of dominant factions, or the accommodation of incompatible sentiments in the group.

A group's politically relevant resources also shape policy effectiveness. Material resources include money, manpower, permanent office space near legislative and administrative halls, facilities for regular meetings both *en masse* and individually with key personnel, and perhaps even ownership of a popular newspaper affording access to the reading public. Less tangible resources have their value. Personal "contacts" and friendships with public officials sometimes save both time and energy. Knowledge of the workings of the decision-making machinery is invaluable to efforts of leaders, lobbyists, and the rank-and-file. Finally, any group is better off in a policy struggle if it possesses public respectability. The American Medical Association has used the positive image of the profession (aspects of which were deliberately manufactured, including the bucolic appeal of the personalized "doctor-patient" relationship) as a weapon in combatting a variety of legislative proposals in the field of medical care.[28] Official pressure groups also strive for popular admiration; the Federal Bureau of Investigation and the United States Marine Corps are cases in point.

Policy Patterns. We have seen that by defining lines of access, the pattern of community policy shapes the capacity of groups to mobilize support. In similar fashion it shapes the effectiveness of policy pressure. Some federal policies are designed specifically to control pressure activities. As part of the Legislative Reorganization Act of 1946, the Federal Regula-

---

[28] See Stanley Kelley, Jr., *Professional Public Relations and Political Power* (Baltimore: The Johns Hopkins Press, 1956).

tion of Lobbying Act requires registration of hired lobbyists, periodic reporting of means of publicity, and a listing of legislative measures of
concern to parent organizations. Beyond these requirements for public
disclosure, few formal restrictions limit the range of pressure activity.

Community policies, however, do affect pressure effectiveness in less
formal ways. As buffers between pressure organizers and officials, policies
set the limits of an official's decision-making authority thus permitting
policy-makers to refuse some pressure demands they are not authorized
to fulfill. The official who can "pass the buck" or complain that his "hands
are tied" is in a position to resist interest claims. Hence, one general aim
of pressure politics is to blunt threatening legislation by persuading congressmen to adopt policies that only vaguely outline the discretion of
administrators. The groups then endeavor to work through the most
sympathetic of several officials possessing diffuse, complementary, and
overlapping authority.

Policies also define the legitimate channels of access between group
leaders and officials. To the extent that policies specify precise procedures to be used in making group appeals, they restrict pressure organizations from more congenial informal contacts. For example: the owner
of a television station who seeks access to Federal Communications Commissioners by offering private yacht trips as forums wherein to plead his
case may find himself without the license he hoped to retain through
such tactics. Pressure groups are vitally interested in any change of procedure or authority that might alter carefully arranged access advantages to congressional, administrative, or judicial officials. As we shall see
in Part Three, conflicts over legislative reapportionment or executive
reorganization involve interests that perceive themselves as privileged or
underprivileged because of present policies.

Finally, the pattern of policy shapes the effective influence of pressure
groups in another less obvious way. Policies specify key officials responsible for making decisions pertinent to particular interests. Thus, the
pattern of policy is a roadmap, not only informing groups of access
routes, but more importantly where key officials might reside. This makes
it easier to concentrate pressure rather than disperse it as mentioned
earlier. For example: in bidding for federal contracts (running into mil-
lions of dollars) awarded to aircraft, electronic, and assorted other firms,
a potential contractor may be asked to submit a design of the missile
guiding device he plans to develop. Since other firms are also seeking
such contracts, he is interested in receiving support from such officials
as are authorized to recommend particular projects. In this particular
area more than a dozen agencies, departments, and administrative bureaus play a role in such decisions, each with a specialized function and

each with numerous personnel dealing with particular facets of that function. To a potential contractor it is not feasible to secure access to each responsible official; instead he must be selective. Knowledge of precisely where decision-making authority lies — obtained from familiarity with authorizing legislation *plus* experience in negotiating the administrative labyrinth in Washington — is thus essential.

Official Attitudes. There has been a rapid growth in this century of bureaucratic agencies charged with initiating, adopting, and applying policies. Some operate with a minimum of legislative oversight. This administrative pluralism complements the social pluralism manifested in diverse exclusive and restricted interests. Agencies at all levels of American government have developed close relations with constituent pressure groups, the very interests they have been established to regulate. The nature of this pressure group–public official relation is explored in detail in the following chapter. Here we note that groups have adjusted to established policies by endeavoring to associate themselves more closely with agencies designed to administer those policies.

The attitudes of public officials themselves toward such relations with pressure groups contributes to the ability of groups to influence policy. In their account of relations between congressmen and pressure leaders, Raymond Bauer and his associates found that "the most important part of the legislative decision process was the decision about which decisions to consider"; [29] that is, when the congressman, or any other official, defines the nature of his job, he makes a choice which necessarily affects his later behavior toward policy pressures. Who he will listen to, the pressures he feels, the persons he consults, his perspective on policy-making routine and crises — all are shaped by his own attitudes as a policy-maker. His perspective on his responsibilities conditions the pressures he is attuned to and the pressures that will influence his behavior. By defining his own responsibilities, the policy-maker retains a certain autonomy in the face of pressure politics. Although his freedom of choice is not absolute, neither is his activity the mere sum of all the demands made upon him by the variety of pressure groups. The freedom of the policy-maker remains one of the principal limits upon the effectiveness of policy pressures.

POLITICAL PRESSURE
AND LIBERAL DEMOCRACY

Having described the characteristics of pressure politics, it is appropriate to raise the question, "Is pressure politics democratic politics?" Judged by the tenets of procedural democracy discussed in Chapter Three, we must

[29] Bauer *et al., op. cit.,* p. 405.

conclude that it is. If democracy consists of a series of methods fostering community stability by permitting periodic expressions of popular opinions, then pressure groups perform a democratic service. Moreover, so long as the larger numbers of citizens of our political community have little interest in matters on which governing officials act, it can be argued that the only thing that can count for much in conflict regulation is the opinion expressed by special groups. Hence, by procedural standards, the actual task "of government, and hence democracy as a form of government, is not to express an imaginary popular will, but to *effect adjustments among the various special wills and purposes* [of particular interest groups] which at any given time are pressing for realization." [30]

If, however, the more demanding standard of substantive democracy be applied to pressure politics (whereby we judge the democratic quality of an activity in accordance with the contribution it makes to the development of individual dignity), the verdict is not so clear. To the extent that group welfare is placed above individual worth, pressure groups can inhibit the realization of personal potential. Moreover, we know from past experience that some segments of American society have not fared well in the give-and-take of pressure politics. Recall, for example, our earlier data that the politically organized are predominantly the better educated, upper- and middle-class elements. Although not monopolized by them, pressure politics in the past has been the mechanism employed to improve the lot of those without the greatest need for governmental support. Yet, the use of pressure politics in recent years by Negroes struggling for civil rights, the elderly pursuing fulfillment of medical needs, and the laborer interested in higher living standards indicate that pressure for change can rise from previously unrepresented groups. On balance, pressure politics holds an opportunity for political participation and, despite its flaws, must be an integral part of conflict regulation in the highly pluralist American setting.

Citizens who want to change the course of governmental affairs are told by political experts to "organize." Nothing presented in this chapter should be interpreted as contradicting the wisdom of that prescription. But enough has been said of the limits of pressure activity to make it clear that pressure politics (a corollary of the recommendation to organize) is only an imperfect indication of the variety of social interests in pluralist America and that pressure organization alone is not sufficient to control the course of American policy-making. However, since the same generalization also holds true for other patterns of conflict representation

[30] John Dickinson, "Democratic Realities and Democratic Dogma," *The American Political Science Review*, XXIX (March, 1930), 291–3.

discussed throughout Part Two, it is convenient to pause at this juncture and assess the overall performance of popular representation in America.

BIBLIOGRAPHICAL NOTE

There is an abundant literature on the types, attributes, frequency, and sources of political pressure in the American polity. Convenient descriptions include the paperbound editions of Abraham Holtzman, *Interest Groups and Lobbying* (New York: The Macmillan Company, 1966) and E. E. Schattschneider, *The Semisovereign People* (New York: Holt, Rinehart and Winston, 1960). The study of interest groups by political scientists is surveyed by Harmon Zeigler in *Interest Groups in American Society* (Englewood Cliffs, N.J.: Prentice-Hall, 1964) and by Donald C. Blaisdell, *American Democracy Under Pressure* (New York: The Ronald Press Company, 1957) and Harry R. Mahood, *Pressure Groups in American Politics* (New York: Charles Scribner's Sons, 1966).

Theories of the function of pressure organizations in representing social interests are presented in the following: Arthur F. Bentley, *The Process of Government* (Chicago: The University of Chicago Press, 1908); John Dewey, *The Public and Its Problems* (Denver: Alan Swallow, 1927); David B. Truman, *The Governmental Process* (New York: Alfred A. Knopf, 1958); and J. D. B. Miller, *The Nature of Politics* (London: Gerald Duckworth and Company, Ltd., 1962). The problems posed for liberal democratic politics and for decision-making by pressure organizations are raised in Henry S. Kariel, *The Decline of American Pluralism* (Stanford, California: Stanford University Press, 1961) and Robert A. Dahl, *A Preface to Democratic Theory* (Chicago: The University of Chicago Press, Phoenix Edition, 1963). See also William Riker, *The Theory of Political Coalitions* (New Haven: Yale University Press, 1962).

Contrasting views of the effectiveness of pressure politics in shaping policy decisions are contained in Raymond A. Bauer, Ithiel de Sola Pool, and Lewis Anthony Dexter, *American Business and Public Policy* (New York: Atherton Press, 1963); Lester W. Milbrath, *The Washington Lobbyists* (Chicago: Rand McNally & Company, 1963); Aaron Wildavsky, *Dixon-Yates* (New Haven: Yale University Press, 1962); E. Pendleton Herring, *Group Representation before Congress* (Baltimore: The Johns Hopkins Press, 1929); and, Earl Latham, *The Group Basis of Politics* (Ithaca, New York: Cornell University Press, 1952).

Selectivity and
Distortion in
American Conflict
Representation:
A Postscript

Our interpretation of the expanse and boundaries of conflict representation in the polity illustrates the effects of the great shaping forces surrounding politics in the community — social diversity, fragmented constitutional authority, and a doctrinal consensus of acquiesence. The nature of the social base contributes to the learning of politically relevant attitudes, the chances for political leadership, the probability of participation, and the intensity of partisan feeling. Constitutional practices, habits, and authority distribute advantages and disadvantages to interests sometimes with neutrality, often with partiality. And, our political consensus works to define the matters about which we feel we can safely disagree.

As products of the joint operation of our social desires, constitutional restraints, and political attitudes, patterns of conflict representation fluctuate a great deal. Lines of communication sometimes are broken, others overlap: "Much of the time, indeed, the important processes of democratic politics may paradoxically consist of a discontinuous continuum." [1] That is, there is no single representative link that binds the citizen-participant and community official in a continuous exchange of views. Instead the representative process is a selective one whereby only a few of many social disputes stimulate community regulation. Although this selectivity in communicating conflicts fails to reflect accurately the plurality of American interests, the filtering process does help keep the policy-maker's task of reconciling differences within manageable proportions.

But the character of our representative patterns raises a question touched on at previous points, one that we will want to deal with again in our conclusion; e.g., at what point does selectivity in conflict representation turn to distortion, a distortion so serious that policy-makers are appraised only of minor conflicts and insulated from the most serious of social cleavages until they have passed the point of accommodation? The problem is inherent in the distortions apparent in our political participation. Only a small percentage of Americans who participate regularly and intensely in politics, hold informed political opinions, exert political leadership, render meaningful political choices, and engage in partisan and pressure activities comprise the community's political activists. Thus far the American polity has been able to reconcile limited participation with pluralist aspirations.

[1] Oliver Garceau, "Research in the Political Process," *The American Political Science Review*, XLV (March, 1951), 69–85.

POLITICAL
POLICY

PART THREE

Patterns of Conflict
Resolution in
American Government

*The product of conflict representation is a series of social dis-
putes communicated to governing officials. Complementing
and overlapping this process are official actions directed at
adjusting community differences, an aspect of American politics constituting conflict resolution. As with political communication, the personal, social, and politico-constitutional
dimensions of our pluralist community shape patterns of
policy-making. The result is a style of politics that emphasizes
only a few of the many disputes that originate in society for
official consideration and even a fewer number for official
resolution. In Part Three we examine the policy process as
manifested in the activities of executive, legislative, and
judicial officials. That examination will direct us toward a
final, albeit tentative, assessment of the crucial impact American pluralism has upon the liberal democratic features of
community government.*

CHAPTER ELEVEN

Policy Formulation

In April, 1962, Mr. Roger M. Blough, Chairman of the Board of United States Steel Corporation, informed the President of the United States that his corporation intended to initiate an immediate increase in the general level of steel prices. As a management decision, the increase was prompted by considerations of high labor costs, foreign competition, and the gradual displacement of steel by other metals. Because the steel industry stands at the center of the American economy, any increase in prices could easily lead to similar actions from defense and missile contractors, car manufacturers, and a host of other major industries dependent upon steel resources. To the President and his advisers, the possible results of a steel-price increase appeared awesome, extending to matters of employment levels, inflation, national defense, etc. In short, the decision to increase steel prices was not one affecting merely corporation and clientele; all Americans were involved.

The techniques of persuasion used by President Kennedy to counter corporate action — and eventually to thwart it — are now a familiar story. Personal consultations and appeals to steel executives, a public radio and television appearance aimed at mustering support from all segments of the community, and contacts with a variety of business and industrial leaders who pressured steel magnates to comply were

285

employed. Coercive measures were available if needed — threats of congressional investigations, possibilities of antitrust legislation, and investigations of corporate practices. For example: the F.B.I. was ordered to get the exact words of a statement made by the president of Bethlehem Steel regarding the steel price increase. An Associated Press reporter who had quoted the statement was awakened by F.B.I. agents at 3:00 A.M., an incident that led to criticism of so-called "police state" methods. The result was a monumental joust between policy-makers, each seeking to define appropriate community action, which was finally settled to the President's satisfaction.[1]

The steel case of 1962 illustrates a distribution of officials throughout all levels of governing authority ready, willing, and able to make decisions on behalf of the entire community and involved in the policy process. Some persons within the community must accept the responsibility for making decisions. Thus, policy-making refers to any act connected with the making of social choices that in some way or another touch all members of the community — the formulation, adoption, application, and interpretation of public law.

POLICY FORMULATION
AND PUBLIC POLICY-MAKING

In a liberal democracy public policy-making is a task normally restricted to freely chosen individuals authorized to act for the community. But there are exceptions to this. Political officials fail to monopolize the policy process, especially in a pluralistic society like ours, in which there are several clusters of decision-making authority. Corporation executives, for example, are involved daily in a number of decisions that affect the American economy; the location of industrial plants, the setting of prices, distribution of purchases and sales, and fulfillment of defense contracts are but a few.

Sometimes public officials must compete with nonofficial leaders for the authority to make public policy decisions. The steel case cited above demonstrates how blurred the margin is between private and public authority. It also illustrates a contrast in perspectives underlying the making of policy decisions. In decision-making, businessmen must take into account economic motives, including certainly the desire for profit — a desire that is both socially acceptable and beneficial to most Americans. The politician, however, has another kind of profit motive in mind.

[1] Grant McConnell, *Steel and the Presidency, 1962* (New York: W. W. Norton & Co., 1963).

Prospective votes are his attraction, and they vitally affect the course of the policy process in a liberal democracy. This is not to say that each political leader calculates his policy stands in direct proportion to the number of votes they will bring. But out of a necessity to maximize votes, the politician does take into account the interests of a constituency, which encompasses more than a single corporation, academic institution, labor union, or other private organization. His perspective on community affairs is inclusive and sweeping, his role as a politician forces upon him a broader sense of "public interest" than is normally possessed by another member of the community. Although he does not surrender his private aims and group loyalties, neither consideration normally dominates the policy official's broader outlook. In a community where responsibility to govern is borne by only a few, policy-makers coordinate the special desires of conflicting groups with a rough approximation of community gain.

Finally, we note that public policies emerge as the product of coalitions of diverse interests. As with any social decision, a policy choice reflects the fact that a group has been formed. In this instance, the group consists of a loose alliance of persons who have something to gain from their temporary association. That alliance may take the form of a legislative majority, close agency-clientele relations, majority opinion of a court of judges, or some other. In pluralist America the membership of policy coalitions is a shifting one; sometimes it seems as though each decision requires the forging of a new collectivity. Partners in one policy transaction may be opponents in another. Moreover, different policy questions draw the attention of different interests. The farm bloc in Congress, for example, composed of southern and mid-western spokesmen — both Democrats and Republicans — is hardly the same as a civil rights coalition. These shifting alignments on shifting issues make unlikely the presence of a ruling elite that is intensely interested in all policy issues and shares common views on all matters. From this standpoint, the policy process consists of negotiating treaties between a plurality of conflicting interests.

Policy-making involves the making of social choices, the perspectives and behavior of politicians, and the formation of coalitions. We can speak of this process in terms of five overlapping stages. First, in response to social conflicts, various official and non-official groups (such as those discussed in Chapter Ten) endeavor to fix the terms of policy proposals offered to community officials as acceptable ways for adjusting such disputes. We label such activity as policy *formulation*. Secondly, various politicians take the lead in the continuing adjustment of disputing interests. We call their actions policy *leadership*. Then, in America, the normal course is for policies to be accepted as legitimate by elected legislative officials. This is the pattern of policy *adoption*. But general policies must always be adjusted to individual cases through policy *application*. Finally, controversies arise between established policies and the interests of individual citizens and groups. The disputes normally demand interpretation of the appropriateness, legitimacy, and adequacy of individual laws. This activity is policy *adjudication*.

In this chapter we are concerned with the factors underlying policy formulation — the context of policy decision, the style of policy behavior, policy traditions, and policy values.

THE CONTEXT OF POLICY FORMULATION

For every policy decision that is made, there is a unique setting and a unique set of participants. The participants include the parties to the dispute and the policy-makers seeking to accommodate the disagreement. The access of disputants to the appropriate policy officials also helps shape the decisions that are made. In the last chapter we discussed how social pluralism and the constitutional structure limits the capacity of pressure groups to influence policy. We now want to see how these two factors shape general patterns of policy formulation.

Social Pluralism. A pluralist social base affects the policy process in several ways. The presence of a variety of partially autonomous groups makes for many leaders with different affiliations competing in the policy process. Seldom can any single leader get all he wants for his supporters; compromise is likely. The fact that citizens are members of a variety of groups suggests that when a leader moves against his opponents, he may also be moving against his own allies. Such problems have long plagued spokesmen of pressure organizations advocating high tariff rates on raw materials, industrial goods, and agricultural products into this country. Group leaders, hoping to promote protective rates, frequently attempt to give the impression that all major economic interests in America can benefit from tariff policies. But, in overcoming opposition to protective tariffs by promises of universal benefits, organizational leaders quickly create internal rancor. Although a steel manufacturer may be eager to have protection against his competitors in Europe, his ally in the Chamber of Commerce, perhaps a building contractor, who can increase profits by purchasing inexpensive steel from abroad is not likely to favor such protections. Quite often the successful policy leaders are those possessing the capacity to negotiate such differences; fanaticism or an unrelenting dogmatic policy position may cost the leader needed support. Because he cannot afford to alienate either his own followers or prospective allies in the camp of the opposition, interest demands may have to be tempered.

Social pluralism also effects policy negotiations by providing alternative sources of information for policy formulators. Groups compete for the attention of the official. As a result, the politician has some discretion in choosing the groups to which he listens. A congressman, for example, considering the nuances of a proposal to regulate the sale and licensing of firearms can draw his information from a variety of opponents and proponents of such legislation including local law enforcement agencies, the National Rifleman's Association, firearm manufacturers, his congressional colleagues, and others. The fact that there are many groups seeking his vote provides him with an opportunity to take a more independent stance toward each; he can hear one, two, or "all sides of the story."

Since group leaders are the focal points through which organization claims are channeled, the policy process emphasizes the importance of contacts between official and nonofficial leaders. In this way, a pluralistic social context generates a policy pattern in which influence is broadly distributed among a variety of leaders who occupy positions both inside and outside of formal governmental office. Robert A. Dahl and Charles E. Lindblom have designated this arrangement a "polyarchy," a way in which "ordinary citizens control their immediate leaders and are controlled by them" and, "these leaders in turn control other leaders and are controlled by them." The result is "a society of reciprocal relationships" that "exists to control government policy." [2] In short, citizens have an indirect control over policy leaders, particularly policy officials. It is a popular control exerted through group leaders over governing officials. Any policy choice normally reflects the interplay of all social interests even remotely concerned with the conflict that stimulated the policy action. As long as there is a complex distribution of influence among social groups, any policy decision will usually flow from a "social separation of powers."

Politico-Constitutional Features: Federalism. In an incisive account of the nature of federal government, Professor William Riker has described federalism as a "bargain between prospective national leaders and officials of constituent governments for the purpose of aggregating territory, the better to lay taxes and raise armies." That bargain exists so long as two levels of authority govern the same land and people, each level is autonomous in at least one sphere, and there is formalized guarantee of that autonomy. [3] In a strict sense, the peculiar American federal bargain

---

[2] Robert A. Dahl and Charles E. Lindblom, *Politics, Economics, and Welfare* (Torchback ed.; New York: Harper & Row, Publishers, 1963), p. 306.

[3] William H. Riker, *Federalism* (Boston: Little, Brown and Co., 1964), pp. 11–12.

was for a non-centralized form. Central government was to possess no absolute authority over the states yet was to be supreme in its own sphere; state governments were to share responsibility with the center.

On the surface, such an arrangement is fertile ground for the development of conflicts between governing officials at different levels who seek to extend control over either constituent or central authority. Certainly tension is built into the relationships between governing levels under a federal pattern. In the American community, however, corporate conflict — conflict between state and national governments — has been much less a result of federalism than the host of social problems that, reinforced by a federalist structure of authority, have been manifested in the American polity. Over the years there has been a tendency for central authority to grow stronger, to some extent, at the expense of the states. Response by the federal government to social demands for regulation of business, for alleviation of social and economic ills resulting from unemployment, and for improvement in education at all levels are examples of the extended influence of the federal government in areas once considered outside the scope of federal activity. Professor Riker has suggested that although we are not sure that "the federal executive and legislative are more influential in the society as a whole than the sum of the states together," it is possible to affirm that the center is stronger than a coalition of as many as half the states.

Despite centralizing tendencies, there are still guarantees of state autonomy in both the party system (see Chapter Nine) and the formal Constitution that help to promote the independence of the states from central authority. The fact that the states dictate voting regulations and procedures serves as a brake upon centralist influence. Moreover, the various States of the Union have frequently been beneficiaries, rather than victims, of the growing dominance of the federal polity. Although the impact of Washington policy-making on American society has obviously increased through taxation measures and federal control of interstate commerce, programs of "cooperative federalism," such as grants-in-aid, have enabled the states to share in the increased governmental activity and to prosper accordingly. One such instance in which state prosperity has been aided by federal financing developed through passage of the Federal Highway Act of 1956. The act, aimed at creating a network of interstate highways for rapid transit throughout the country, authorized the federal government to pay 90 per cent of the cost of constructing superhighways even though the states would retain authority to plan and build them. State compliance has made it possible for the federal government to initiate construction of networks of roads beneficial to interstate commerce and national defense; in return states have benefited from the money poured into local economies, increased tourist travel, etc. Moreover, of course, various private groups including the automobile industry, tire-manufacturers, petroleum companies, trucking firms, motel and restaurant concerns, and sundry others have reaped a harvest of increased revenue.

Although the federal arrangement has changed somewhat since 1789 due to the increased role played by the national government and the development of federal-state programs, federalism remains a central feature of the context of policy formulation. By providing separate governing authorities at national and state levels of the political community, federalism yields different points at which interests seek to influence policy-making. Failing to gain satisfaction of its demands locally, a social interest can turn to Washington for assistance, or if unhappy over federal policies, a group can attempt to block them by appealing to state and local officials. For example, in the 1820's Southern dissatisfaction with the "tariff of Abominations" of 1828 (which placed duties on woolens, molasses, and other goods imported into the South) was manifested through arguments that the national government had no authority to force states to accept legislation viewed as hostile to state interests. Moreover, some state leaders, following John C. Calhoun, argued that a state could suspend, within its own territorial jurisdiction, a federal law when the passage of such law exceeded the powers delegated to the national government by the Constitution. Again, in the mid-1800's interests desirous of maintaining slavery held privileged access to southern state officials long after they had suffered defeats in Congress. The conflict between pro-slavery and free-soil forces was gradually converted into one of state's rights vs. national authority as each set of contending interests obtained control of these separate units of government. More recently, the civil rights movement reflects the efforts of a group virtually prohibited from participation in state politics (the southern Negro) to realize their demands through federal action. As in the past the ability to appeal to policy-makers at various governing levels in a dispute over social values has produced a direct confrontation of state and national authorities.

Politico-Constitutional Features: Separated Powers. Such examples suggest that federal-state disputes are primarily conflicts between social interests capable of engaging various governing units to represent their exclusive aims. The federal arrangement channels disputes over social values through both official and non-official leaders at all levels of government. Thus, both state and national officials are faced with tasks of negotiating policies on behalf of the interests they represent. Not all conflicts between governing units, however, are embedded solely in disputes between social interests. In the American polity, the mere presence of "separated powers" (with separate governing institutions sharing policy-making authority) and attempts to achieve "checks and balances" provide for a form of corporate conflict (that is, conflict between specific governing units or official groups rather than between non-official groups that generate the bulk of social disputes outside formal agencies of government). Corporate conflicts are inherent in the tension that develops between separate governing branches provided for by the Constitution and between the subunits attached to them; moreover, to mediate these conflicts policy coalitions are forged that perform crucial functions in policy formulation.

Corporate Conflict. Whether intentional or not, the Framers guaranteed that official conflict would occur when they provided for three primary governmental institutions and divided up the functions of government among them. Tension mounts as Congress seeks to intrude upon presidential responsibility for appointments and budgeting. The Framers assured such rivalry by giving President and Congress joint authority over decision-making in both areas. If it deems necessary, each can project itself into the affairs of the other. That both President and Congress have done so with some frequency needs little documentation. The chief executive must win legislative approval of his program, prevent emasculation of budget requests by economy-minded congressmen or inflation of them by pork barrel-minded congressmen, or block passage of measures deemed harmful to presidential interests. Except for the Eighty-third Congress and Lyndon Johnson's first full year in office, congressional acceptance of presidential programs was less than 50 per cent in each of the years between 1953 and 1964.[4] President Harry S. Truman turned conflict into an asset in 1948 when he ran for re-election as much against the "do-nothing Eightieth Congress" as against his opponent Thomas E. Dewey. Both the overlapping authority provided for by constitutional edict and the fact that each branch represents different social, economic, and political constituencies provide the background for institutional conflict. That context increases the likelihood that policies emerging from the struggle will be forged through negotiation and conciliation.

Policy contests have not been limited to those between President and Congress. Although they are not as common, there have been controversies between the courts and either President or Congress. One needs only recall President Roosevelt's dissatisfaction (discussed in Chapter Nine) with the Supreme Court in the 1930's for an instance of executive-judicial conflict. In 1965 Senator Everett Dirksen's desire to override the Supreme Court's verdict that both houses of state legislative bodies be apportioned on the basis of population reflected disagreement with

[4] *Congressional Quarterly Weekly Report,* XXXI (October 23, 1964), 2569.

the courts from another branch. More recently judicial-congressional conflict broke out over the authority of a committee of the House of Representatives to conduct investigations. The committee in question, the House Un-American Activities Committee, set out in the summer of 1966 to inquire into the nature of groups protesting United States involvement in the Viet Namese War. Operating under the view that protests might have harmful effects upon the American war effort, and mindful of allegations that the "peace movement" had been infiltrated by subversive forces, the committee sought to question leaders of protest movements, such as the United States Committee to Aid the National Liberation Front, regarding their intentions, backgrounds, and affiliations. In response to the inquiry the American Civil Liberties Union sought an injunction in a federal court to restrain the committee on the grounds that Congress has no constitutional authority to conduct the inquiry. The acting chairman of the committee, Democratic Congressman Joe Pool of Texas, announced his decision to proceed regardless of any court decision, arguing that the legislative branch retains ultimate authority in our constitutional system and cannot be restrained by the judiciary when conducting investigations pursuant to legislative purposes.

Subunit Autonomy. Separation of powers as a working principle increases the likelihood of official conflict in another way. By separating the major institutions of government, the Founding Fathers made it possible for subunits — executive bureaus, committees, etc. — that developed as adjuncts of each branch to have a large measure of autonomy from one another. To have some idea of the bewildering array of the extent of the growth of such subunits we need only glance at Figure 11-1. However, even it fails to mirror the degree of fragmentation within the executive, legislative, and judicial branches for it ignores the existence of the subunits that exist within each house of our bicameral Congress and within each of the dozens of administrative agencies. Policy decisions often emerge from the clash of these units.

Earl Latham has written that the major function of official groups is "to provide various levels of compromises in the writing of the rules, all within the body of agreed principles that forms the consensus upon which the political community rests," and that each of the three principal branches of government has a special role in performing this function. He goes on to point out that the legislature "ratifies the victories of the successful coalitions." [5] Thus, its major function is to adopt policies formulated and initiated at other points in the community. We speak

[5] Earl Latham, "The Group Basis of Politics: Notes for a Theory," *The American Political Science Review,* XLVI (June, 1952), 390.

FIGURE 11-1

Governmental Organization of the United States *

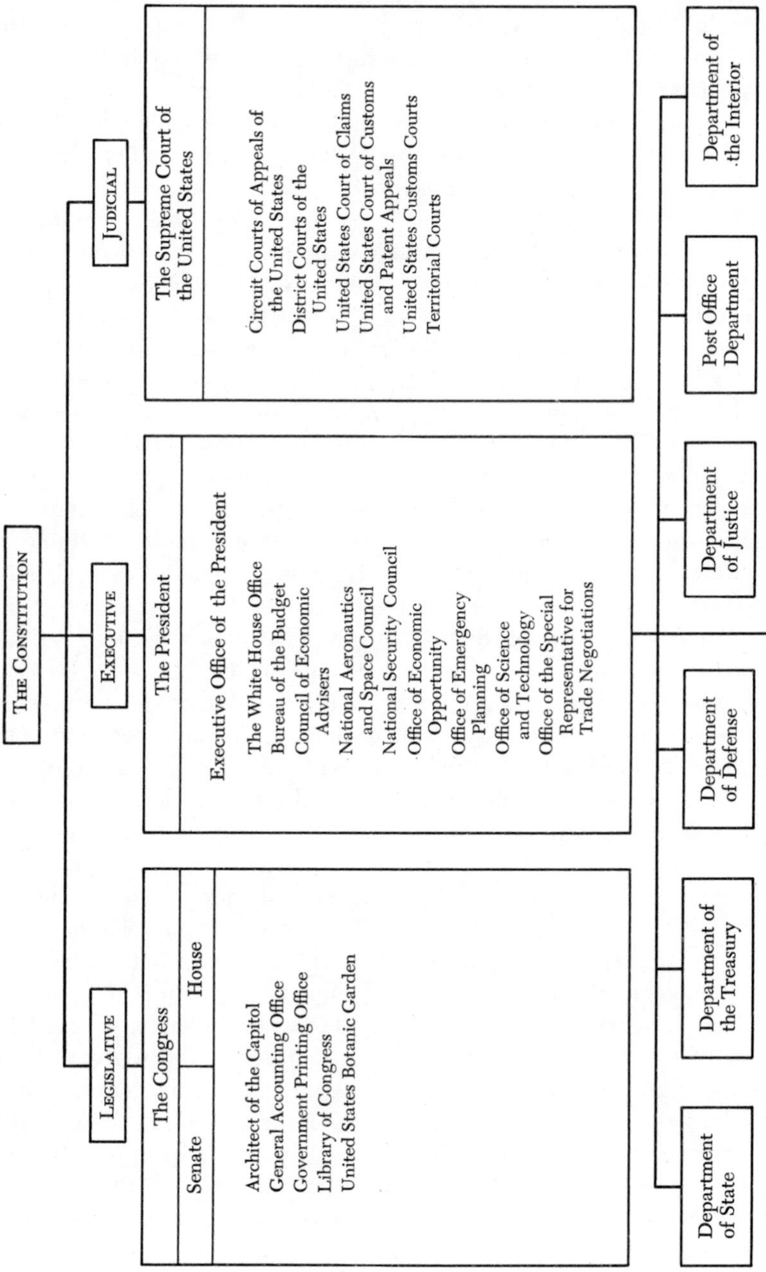

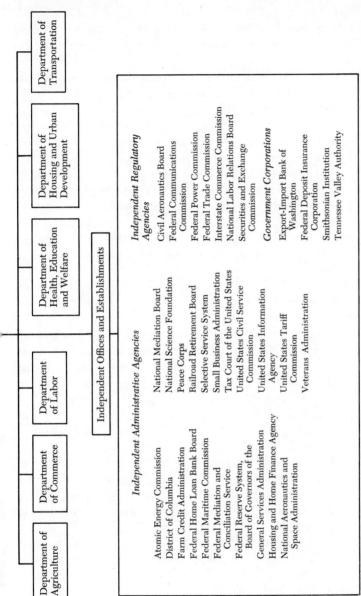

Department of Agriculture

Department of Commerce

Department of Labor

Department of Health, Education and Welfare

Department of Housing and Urban Development

Department of Transportation

Independent Offices and Establishments

Independent Administrative Agencies

Atomic Energy Commission
District of Columbia
Farm Credit Administration
Federal Home Loan Bank Board
Federal Maritime Commission
Federal Mediation and Conciliation Service
Federal Reserve System, Board of Governors of the
General Services Administration
Housing and Home Finance Agency
National Aeronautics and Space Administration
National Mediation Board
National Science Foundation
Peace Corps
Railroad Retirement Board
Selective Service System
Small Business Administration
Tax Court of the United States
United States Civil Service Commission
United States Information Agency
United States Tariff Commission
Veterans Administration

Independent Regulatory Agencies

Civil Aeronautics Board
Federal Communications Commission
Federal Power Commission
Federal Trade Commission
Interstate Commerce Commission
National Labor Relations Board
Securities and Exchange Commission

Government Corporations

Export-Import Bank of Washington
Federal Deposit Insurance Corporation
Smithsonian Institution
Tennessee Valley Authority

°Adapted from *United States Government Organization Manual, 1965-1966*, Washington, D.C. Government Printing Office, 1965

here of the legislature as a whole. Within any legislative body are a series of groups — committees, subcommittees, and constituency blocs — that unofficial policy leaders must contend with in the struggle for favorable decisions.

Each legislative body tends to generate its own "house" interest (that is, governing prerogatives its members desire to protect against encroachment from the President, courts, or the other legislative body), as Latham has referred to it. The expression of these official interests takes several forms — the notion that the congressman can be disciplined only by his colleagues and possesses immunity from many forms of legal action symbolizes mutual feelings among legislators that they perform a function in life apart from that of other governing officials; members of the United States Senate form a closely knit group viewing itself as a prestigious "club" that bands together to protect Senate prerogatives.

Further diversification of interest in Congress arises as committees and subcommittees within each chamber develop concerns of their own. Moreover, on routine legislative matters either chamber may acquiesce to the recommendation of one of its committees or subcommittees on the assumption that committee members possess an expertise in specialized areas and can give advice that should be heeded. Tenure and seniority on committees (see Chapter Thirteen) automatically confer status and respect for the subject-matter competence of members; as legislators remain with their respective committees despite changes in house majorities the image of competence is reinforced. The result of this combination of longevity, specialization, and public authority is the development of a semi-autonomous policy-making group — committee or subcommittee — advancing interests frequently at odds with others represented in the legislature: "Thus in Congress there is a seesaw between the politics of the congressional majority leadership and the politics of the committees in which the influence of special interests and seniority are concentrated. Here committee leaders are often fulcrums in the balance." [6] Such congressional leaders serve as key personnel in initiating or blocking policy acted upon by the legislature. This was the case, for example, in the 1960's when the House of Representatives was considering adoption of a bill to provide medical care programs for the aged under the Social Security system. Chairman of the House Ways and Means Committee, Wilbur Mills (Democrat of Arkansas) effectively opposed the measure against efforts of Democratic party leaders in Congress directed at passage. It was not until 1964 that he relented, primarily in response to the widely held view that the results of that year's presidential election

[6] J. Leiper Freeman, *The Political Process* (Rev. ed.; New York: Random House, 1965), pp. 26–27.

made it apparent that his congressional support might leave him if he remained opposed. He then supported a broader measure than proposed by the Johnson Administration, but was able to obtain limiting features in the bill in exchange for his support.

In theory the administrative arm of government functions to apply and enforce the agreements that legislators and other officials have negotiated and adopted as law. Administrative application, however, is a task possessing considerable discretion. The precise intent of Congress in passing a specific rule is seldom clear; there is room for administrative interpretation as to the law's meaning. When, for example, a particular expense constitutes a legitimate deduction in computing an income tax return is frequently an open question; the interpretation given the regulation covering deductible expenditures by the internal revenue agent is, therefore, as crucial to the pocketbook as the "letter of the law." Or, to cite a more familiar example: in many cases it is the policeman's discretion as to whether a driver has or has not violated a 35 mile per hour speed limit, the motorist's disclaimers to the contrary notwithstanding.

The exercise of administrative discretion contributes to a continuing reshaping of policies, especially in the case of regulatory agencies charged with responsibilities for making, applying, and interpreting rules. A quasi-judicial regulatory agency, for example, is thus a sub-government in the sense that it combines executive, legislative, and judicial tasks. One such agency, the Interstate Commerce Commission, performs an important function in setting railroad rates, seeing that they are enforced, and deciding when rules have been violated by railroad companies. Likewise the National Labor Relations Board not only applies labor legislation aimed at eliminating unfair labor practices but investigates complaints from labor and management, promotes collective bargaining, and may prescribe rules and regulations advancing the purposes of major labor statutes.

Similarly the exercise of discretion in policy application by other administrative departments and agencies engages them in the formulation of policy as semi-independent entities. When administrative departments, such as the Department of Health, Education, and Welfare are further broken down into administrative bureaus, yet another level of autonomy is maintained. If this is the case, bureau leaders seldom find it necessary to work through departmental heads. Their liaison with Congress is more direct, and both technical expertise and protected career status tend to insulate them from efforts at presidential or departmental control. Their semi-autonomy, derived from longevity and expertise, as in the case of the legislative committee, is combined with an independence that results from the difficulties of integration inherent in large-scale organizations.

Often a major controversy develops between the bureaucratic expert and the demands for loyalty to partisan policy, as represented in the program of the President. The bureau leaders emerge as significant shapers of policy.

Policy Clusters. Separated authority also contributes to the origins of policy clusters and the struggles that ensue between incompatible clusters. By such clusters we refer specifically to coalitions of officials and non-officials — alliances normally composed of leaders from relevant executive bureaus, congressional committees, and pressure organizations — who decide the final terms of policy in specialized areas. Policy coalitions comprise what Professor J. Leiper Freeman has called the "subsystems" of government or what reporter and presidential adviser Douglass Cater terms the "subgovernments of Washington." Each cluster develops an exclusive self-interest in its own sphere and strives to perform autonomously in that sphere.[7]

The appearance of policy clusters is part of a continuing effort in a technologically developed America to adjust eighteenth-century policy-making organs to twentieth-century interests. Binding policies are made in ever narrowing sectors of public concern. Although all members of the community are at least indirectly affected by defense policy, only a relatively small segment of the population is informed about policies made in this area. Few have the expertise to be so interested. Others have no time. Thus, policy clusters ally "the expert, the interested, and the engaged" in coalitions that transcend the separate authorities of President, Congress, and the courts. These coalitions arise in response to the need to coordinate the efforts of legislative, administrative, and subject-area experts in a particular area of policy-making. Among examples of such policy tandems are the following: The House Subcommittee on Government Information, administrative information officers, and Washington reporters cluster for securing information from government officials; the House Agriculture Committee, the Sugar Division of the Agriculture Department, and leaders of the sugar industry are allied in their concern with sugar prices and quotas of imported sugar; the Bureau of Indian Affairs, the House and Senate Committees on Indian Affairs, and the Association on American Indian Affairs once clustered their concerns around policies toward the American Indian.[8]

Only particular policy leaders in each agency, committee, or group are members of the policy cluster; for example, the chairman of a committee may be capable of acting on behalf of the entire committee in

[7] *Ibid.*, p. 11; Douglass Cater, *Power in Washington* (New York: Random House, 1964), pp. 3–48.

[8] See, for example, Freeman, *op. cit.*; Cater, *op. cit.*, pp. 17–20.

negotiating with agency and private leaders. Hence, the policy coalition is normally restricted to a small number of influential group leaders representing the most intensely interested of clients. The clustering of policy leaders represents a desire to negotiate differences or push common interests that transcend separate branches. So long as they operate under joint agreements to "live and let live," there is little difficulty. Yet they sometimes attempt to encroach upon one another's informal prerogatives and jurisdictions.

An example should help to illustrate how policy clusters operate. Interests within the Department of the Treasury and the Foreign Relations Committee of the U.S. Senate have for some time been bent on inducing American business firms to invest in construction of plants in other nations. Profits to American firms engaging in such transactions could conceivably slow the gold outflow from the U.S. Treasury. Having American interests abroad, particularly in some of the "leaning" Communist satellite nations, might ease the strain of negotiating foreign policy between East and West. In 1965 a policy coalition of such interests supported the building of a synthetic rubber plant in Communist Roumania by the Firestone Tire and Rubber Company. Apparently this particular policy decision encroached upon the concerns of other business and political groups for when the Firestone Company cancelled its plans, Senator William Fulbright, Chairman of the Senate Foreign Relations Committee, charged that undue pressure had been brought to bear on the company by various groups, including some characterized by him as "extremist right wing." He argued that the Young Americans for Freedom and the Goodyear Tire and Rubber Company, a Firestone competitor, had organized boycotts, distributed handbills, and made other attempts to force Firestone to abandon the project. He also charged that the State Department had been "strangely reluctant" in its support of Firestone's negotiations. In effect, two policy coalitions may have been pitted against one another: one made up of Firestone, the Treasury Department, and Senator Fulbright; the other, such strange bedfellows as Goodyear, the Young Americans, and the State Department. The upshot was a policy decision that President Lyndon Johnson considered sufficiently detrimental to his program to demand a State Department investigation of the entire matter.

We have already seen that any pressure organization is made up of a bundle of conflicting interests. Pressure leaders articulate and represent the views of a winning coalition within their organization at any given time. Congress and the administration also represent assemblages of conflicting interests. In sum, there is partial autonomy of subcommittees and committees of Congress, of bureaus within agencies, and of factions within groups. Diversification of policy interests at every level of authority generates a policy process that reflects the give-and-take of conflicting policy leaders. Professors Dahl and Lindblom put it more clearly when they write that "social pluralism is so great in the United States that, combined with the constitutional structure, the extent of bargaining among diverse social groups in making government policy is a dominant feature of our political system."[9] This brings us to another force that shapes the pattern of American policy formulation — the styles of policy decision. We are interested here particularly in the bargaining style, which is most characteristic of policy formulation in the American polity.

STYLES OF POLICY FORMULATION

We refer to policy style as the general method employed by policymakers in reaching a decision and obtaining compliance. The most pervasive policy style in American government is bargaining. In addition, three other styles can be distinguished — persuasion, command, and competition. Each helps to determine the type of resolutions that emerge through the policy process.

Bargaining is the method by which policy decisions are reached when leaders explore and accept mutually beneficial adjustments of their differences. Bargaining is carried out under conditions of reciprocity. Indeed political bargaining is so stable a pattern of American policymaking that it constitutes an institution promoting, as well as based upon reciprocal relations among leaders. Through bargaining, attempts are made to regulate conflict by modifying the goals of participants. Each policy leader seeks to change the demands of others and finds that his own requests are modified in the process.[10]

Certain characteristics of the American community make bargaining a crucial commodity in the political process. One has already been mentioned: The existence of a plurality of social interests within the community makes it necessary for leaders to resolve their disputes; a fundamental agreement on the worth of the community itself makes it possible for them to negotiate those differences. Thus bargaining is possible so long as the interests dividing political leaders are not preceived as irreconcilable. If differences are fundamental, it is difficult to find acceptable compromises.

In America the need for mutual adjustment through bargaining is rendered inescapable by constitutional features as well as social pluralism. Under conditions of separated authority the only way that major policy decisions can be legitimized in a final sense is to receive approval of all branches concerned — executive, legislative, and judicial; then it must

[9] Dahl and Lindblom, *op. cit.*, p. 307.
[10] Dahl and Lindblom, *op. cit.*, pp. 324–65.

secure obedience from the citizens themselves. Political leaders are forced to be interdependent if anything is ever to be accomplished at all. Obstruction, stalemate, and the avoidance of choice may work well in some instances; but it does not suffice for very long. Although our constitutional arrangement makes it difficult to coordinate the actions of three separate branches, it is still flexible enough to permit bargaining between leaders of each. The constitutional pattern contributes to disharmony and makes bargaining indispensable. The anomaly of legal separation but policy interdependence characterizes all political bargaining in the community.

In most bargaining situations participants enter negotiations with unequal advantages; that is, there is an uneven distribution of resources that strengthens the hands of some leaders. What a participant has to offer in the mutual exchange with fellow bargainers is one such vital resource. Of course, he must have something that others want, or negotiations would probably not have been undertaken in the first place. But unless one participant can be convinced that the opposition's offer is sufficiently attractive to make up for the costs incurred, then negotiations may break down. This relates to a second set of resources: the skill of the political leader as a negotiator. The opposition must be assured of the merit of his opponent's offer, the sincerity behind it, the capability to deliver, and his willingness to listen to alternatives. Whether the bargainer is able to explore mutually beneficial adjustments depends in part upon the intensity of his desires, the commitment he has made to his followers, and the flexibility exhibited by fellow negotiators. Another resource is the prestige that a political leader brings to the bargaining situation. The President of the United States or the Speaker of the House of Representatives usually has an advantage in bargaining; the famous dictum attributed to the late House Speaker Sam Rayburn that in Congress a legislator must "go along to get along" illustrates the premium he placed upon the capacity of House leadership to induce members to comply in exchange for better committee assignments, help in supporting legislation, etc. Such leaders can command support from others; consequently, they are able to make attractive and effective offers to those involved in negotiations. They also can make veiled threats such as refusing to support a congressman's bill or withholding patronage. With positions of political prestige go the power to promise and cajole.

We can distinguish between types of bargaining. One such form is the *explicit* contract between group leaders.[11] In explicit bargaining the

[11] Lewis A. Froman, Jr., *People and Politics* (Englewood Cliffs, N.J.: Prentice-Hall, 1962), pp. 53–58; Thomas C. Schelling, *The Strategy of Conflict* (New York: Oxford University Press, 1963), pp. 21–52; William C. Mitchell, *The American Polity* (New York: The Free Press of Glencoe, 1962), pp. 291–307.

participants attempt to reduce the chances of misunderstanding to a minimum by formalizing their agreement in clear terms. Communication between bargainers is usually facilitated as much as possible in order that each is aware of the other's expectations and demands. In international politics, treaties are examples of explicit bargains; in domestic affairs, wage contracts, government defense contracts, etc., are illustrations. Perhaps the most famous example of this explicit type of arrangement was the framing of the Constitution of the United States. Here the terms of the contract were formalized but in a fashion that was often ambiguous. Explicit bargaining also took place in the 1960 Republican convention. Richard Nixon, apparently feeling that he needed the support of Governor Nelson Rockefeller of New York, rushed to confer with the Governor in order to head off a revolt against the platform pending before convention delegates. Rockefeller had criticized the platform as lacking in strength and specifics. The result was the famous "Compact of Fifth Avenue," an arrangement negotiated between Mr. Nixon and Mr. Rockefeller that provided for Mr. Nixon to support stronger platform planks on civil rights and foreign affairs and Mr. Rockefeller to support Mr. Nixon and the platform.

More significant for most American policy-making is the *implicit* or *tacit* bargain. Ambiguity of terms is common and often approved. Moreover, the responsibilities of participants to one another are purposely left vague and couched in such notions as "future support," "good will," or "favorable disposition." In implicit bargaining the communication between leaders is less open and may comprise nothing more than persons "feeling each other out" on an issue. Intuition tends to replace the spoken word. The most common example of the implicit bargain in America is the exchange of support for legislative measures whereby one congressman agrees to "go along" with another in voting for a particular piece of legislation in exchange for tacit cooperation at some future time. The extent to which leaders can cash in on their gentlemen's agreements and tacit understanding depends more upon their interpersonal respect than upon the terms of the agreement. When implicit bargaining reaches the point where the bargainers are not sure of the terms agreed upon, we have a situation which William Mitchell has labeled *conjectural* bargaining. Where there is little direct communication, each party is forced to guess what the behavior of others will be.[12] The accuracy of such intuitive rapport is difficult to gauge; politicians may act on the assumption that an agreement has been made when none has at all.

The heart of political bargaining is the gradual exploration of mutual advantages; bargains are made because everyone can be pleased to some

12 Froman, *op. cit.,* p. 55; Mitchell, *op. cit.,* pp. 295–96.

degree. Through bargaining differences between people can be settled directly. Such activity is socially beneficial. In sum, people adjust their behavior to each other rather than to some overall plan of community action, a notion of the public interest, or the dictates of popular majorities. The criterion for judging the success of a policy decision is the contribution it makes to mutual toleration. But there are weaknesses in this method of policy formulation. Professors Dahl and Lindblom insist that the strategic consequence has been that *"no unified, cohesive, acknowledged, and legitimate representative-leaders of the 'national majority' exist in the United States."* [13]

James Madison and John C. Calhoun both theorized that, given the nature of the American polity, it is unlikely that national majorities of sufficient stability could be generated to control either the formulation of public policy or the policy-makers themselves. Madison, writing in *Federalist Paper No. 10* pointed to separation of powers and social diversity as limitations on majority control; the first, by dividing governing authority among separate agencies would render it difficult for a single interest — majority or minority — to control policy-making without first obtaining control of all governing units and the second, by fashioning diverse and frequently incompatible purposes would decrease the likelihood that majority coalitions could be formed. Calhoun, some years later in his *Disquisition on Government* argued that given the difficulty in generating popular majorities (and given the lack of wisdom underlying actions) ruling majorities should be constituted of coalitions of minorities, or concurrent majorities, as a safeguard for social diversity in America. In any event, the difficulties surrounding the formation of both popular and legislative majorities makes it necessary to forge support for particular policies in other ways than through appeals to the "majority interest." The creation of policy clusters linking official and nonofficial leaders with compatible interests and the formation of effective majorities through bargaining between semi-independent policy coalitions is the characteristic style of policy formulation in the American polity.

Each bargained coalition between policy clusters speaks for those fractions of the community represented by the allied leaders. Thus, formulated policies reflect a series of adjustments that group leaders find mutually beneficial. Dahl and Lindblom spell out the consequences of this feature of the policy process in detail: Proposals emanating from one policy cluster may effectively be obstructed by an opposing alliance; to avoid such minority vetoes, the assent of all significant leaders involved in the issue under discussion must be obtained; thus public policy must have the widespread acceptance of all major political leaders (presidential

---

[13] Dahl and Lindblom, *op. cit.*, p. 336.

confidants, committee and subcommittee chairmen, bureau chiefs, pressure organization leaders, etc.); to win that widespread support, normally there must be promises and assurances of beneficial gains to strategically placed leaders; and, although seldom will all parties to the policy conflict be completely satisfied, the demands of the more effectively organized will prevail. In essence, then, policies are formulated at two levels: first, in specialized areas — such as regulating sugar imports, appropriations for particular projects including construction of dams, waterways, and highways in local areas, etc. — policies are formulated by clusters of strategically located interest spokesmen; secondly, for more general policy questions — labor legislation, welfare legislation, foreign aid spending, etc. — requiring the formation of larger alliances, policies are hammered out in negotiations between leaders of separate policy clusters. The result is a combination of rule by minorities and by concurrent majorities.

There are also other side effects of bargaining: it is difficult for elected leaders to control bureaucratic appointees who are perfectly capable of bargaining from independent sources of support provided by the very groups the administrative official is regulating; the time it takes to make policy decisions is virtually interminable; it is impossible to fix responsibility for public policy in the American community on any single individual, party, or legislative body; and the costs of policy-making tend to be high when measured in terms of wasted efforts, resources, and time. One other supposed result of bargaining — the likelihood of irrational social choices — will be examined in some detail later.

We suggest, then, that policy formulation in American government is marked more by efforts to avoid choices than to make them. Because of the complexities involved in forging agreements, it is sometimes easier for leaders to flee from conflicts rather than define and adjust them. To the extent that this is true, there is perhaps a gap in the political process. Social conflict is represented continuously to policy-makers through voting, partisanship, pressure groups, etc. But so much emphasis must be placed upon conserving bargaining resources for situations involving crucial stakes that policy leaders tend to be highly selective in choosing the issues on which to take a stand. No President, for example, girds himself to fight every conceivable battle. Each must decide when it is appropriate to make policy choices and when it is not wise to do so. In this day and age, a President budgets his resources of public opinion, patronage, and economic beneficence. He may fight for a civil rights bill but feel only lukewarm about prevention of air pollution. He may channel his forces for a foreign aid bill but give only token support to legislation aimed at restricting cigarette advertising. In short, because policy-makers must be prepared to bargain, they can ill afford to waste their energies on causes they deem insignificant or dangerous to their own interests. Hence, they must not only negotiate policy decisions but also avoid many of the opportunities that present themselves for bargaining.

Selectivity exercised by political leaders, candidates, reporters, partisans, and pressure organizers reveals some social disputes but conceals others. Political bargaining further distorts the overall process of conflict regulation in America. From the perspective of community viability, of course, the success of the process must be judged by its contribution to regulation of the most critical of social disagreements. But from the standpoint of individual development, the distorted pattern of politics falls short of democratic doctrine.

Many people regard politics as the art of compromise. Compromise is one way that bargained agreements can be reached, generally by both parties to a dispute surrendering some of their demands. It is often recognized that if disputants hold to their claims, no participant will profit. If all sides decide to give in a little, the result is that none are completely satisfied but, by the same token, neither are they unhappy with the product of the bargaining. Most bargaining situations call either for an exchange of support or compromise. In these respects, bargaining differs from the other styles of policy decision: persuasion, command, and competition.

We have already learned that persuasion refers to efforts to change a person's behavior by holding out the promise of gratifications and rewards. But unlike bargaining, persuasion does not necessarily imply that the policy leader must himself surrender any of his gains in order to secure support. Persuasion involves reciprocity, but the costs to the persuader are relatively lower than those paid by the leader who employs the method of political bargaining. The used-car salesman who sets a definite price for an automobile and then convinces the customer of its appropriateness rather than haggling with the prospective buyer over that price persuades rather than bargains. Normally persuasion is a means by which leaders convince non-leaders to support a policy decision; in the formulation of policy itself, persuasion is a means by which leaders of greater prestige, respect, and resources sell their policy choices to those leaders of lesser status. Recent Presidents, for example, have made a practice of holding occasional "White House breakfasts" for Congressional leaders. In some instances, these are negotiation sessions for purposes of forging policies. More often they are meetings that permit the President to outline his program, to overcome opposition to his policy choices, and plan the most expedient course of action for securing passage.

If a policy leader can threaten reprisal, as well as promise rewards to those who find his policy choices acceptable, and he does so with regularity, then his style is that of command rather than bargaining or persuasion. Using the analogy of the used-car salesman, we might liken command to a situation in which a person must have transportation, there is only one dealer in town, and as a result the salesman can name his price. Leaders often use this method in seeking the compliance of nonleaders. As a control relationship, it is much less reciprocal in nature.

In a command situation, it is normally assumed that all superiors and subordinates are generally agreed upon achieving well-defined goals. The extent to which a policy leader can command support depends largely on the number and variety of techniques of control at his disposal. In Chapter Twelve we expore the President's degree of hierarchical control over his subordinates in administrative agencies. Some of the more formalized sanctions that he may use include review of budget requests, discretion over appointment of upper-echelon personnel, review and clearance of legislative proposals from agencies, the authority to reorganize agencies, and the ability to limit the release of certain information from such agencies. The authority to review and cut agency budget requests is of particular import. Since agencies and bureaus cannot *formally* request more funds from Congress than are authorized in the President's budget, bureau autonomy is perceptibly limited. However, bureau leaders before congressional committees, having been questioned by sympathetic legislators, sometimes have been able to circumvent such formal restrictions.

For example, during the administration of President Dwight Eisenhower some military leaders particularly Air Force officers, grew alarmed at presidential proposals to cut back spending for heavy bombers. Although instructed to support the President's policy publicly, a few were able to voice their discontent in congressional hearings when questioned by legislators who also opposed the budget cut. As a result, Congress ultimately budgeted more for a heavy bomber program than the President had requested. The ability of the President to command compliance from his subordinates is in some measure limited by the presence of informal policy clusters mentioned earlier. Likewise, within a particular administrative agency, there may be a continuing tussle between the administrative superior who seeks to command support and the subunits who manage to obtain outside help by bargaining their way into policy coalitions.

A final policy style — competition — refers to the institutionalizing of conflict.[14] In American government the political choice that normally flows from this style is not a policy choice at all but the selection of policy-makers, which we label elections. Applicants for civil service posi-

[14] See, for example, Mitchell, *op. cit.*, pp. 288–90.

tions also compete with one another, but the rules of the contest are normally more formalized than those for election of officials.

As a method for arriving at policy decisions, competition is used less frequently than the other means we have outlined. To some degree, judicial action can be viewed as a competition between interests that is often resolved to the total satisfaction of only one of the disputants. What one side wins, the other loses or at least perceives that it has lost. The forces upholding segregation or the losing interests in reapportionment cases, antitrust decisions, and cases involving New Deal legislation in the 1930's came away with little satisfaction. Indeed, it is because the Supreme Court is often called upon to decide winners and losers between competitive interests that it receives the type of criticism it does from many defeated groups. A common observation about the American judiciary is that through adjudication it is often forced to make policy decisions that the processes of bargaining, persuasion, and command have either been unable to make or policy leaders have chosen to avoid.

The various styles of policy leaders condition the types of decisions that are made. Social pluralism and constitutional structures place a premium upon political bargaining as a way to get things done in our democracy. The other styles of policy decision, such as persuasion, command, or competition, are forced to take a back seat. Each is better suited to a society marked by more universal agreement on values and a more tightly integrated system of authority. In some ways, the bargaining process has become the epitome of how policies "should be arrived at" in America. Thus, it has become as much a symbol of the American political process as the Constitution, the two-party system, the Presidency, and the Supreme Court. The bargaining process has been the chief factor shaping the tradition of policy decision in America.

TRADITIONS OF POLICY FORMULATION

The consequences of the bargaining style are not limited to contemporary policy-making; they stretch far back into the history of American government. The tradition of policy decision refers to the accustomed habits, expectations, conventions, and guidelines involved in making policy choices. There are certain taboos that seldom suffer violation in the conciliation of clashing interests. We limit ourselves to considering three of the more significant traditions of policy decision: (1) the tradition of reciprocal influence — referred to by critics of American government as the custom of "you scratch my back and I'll scratch yours"; (2) the tradition of policy incrementation or "muddling through"; and (3) the tradition of the public interest.

In the American community, political bargaining is of such frequency and import that it has become a professional undertaking. Perhaps no activity so distinguishes the role of the politician in our political community as that of bargaining. His life and energies are devoted to the continuous reshaping of coalitions. His selection as a policy-maker (whether through election or appointment) depends upon his negotiating skills; his success as a policy-maker is equally dependent upon the forging of policy alliances. In striking political bargains, the politician often loses all sense of the substantive issues underlying policy formulation; the policy leader seems more concerned with accommodating and adjusting than pursuing rational policy goals. It is this overriding concern with finding working solutions rather than perfect ones that contributes to the tradition of reciprocal influence in policy-making, that is, the premium placed upon compromise, maintenance of communication, renunciation, and face-saving.[15] Policy-makers often have more in common as politicians than divides them as spokesmen of interests. They are willing to adjust to each other's demands rather than push their differences to the margin. They act as friendly adversaries and loyal opponents.

Earlier discussion noted that only recently have Americans begun to respond to the give-and-take of the politician's job positively. Previously Americans tended to look upon reciprocal influence as the shady side of politics. In efforts to focus favorable light upon the actions of the Founding Fathers, for example, we sometimes lose sight of the fact that the republic was born in an environment of reciprocal influence. Except for the framing of the Constitution, probably the most famous political bargain in American history was the one between Alexander Hamilton and Thomas Jefferson that determined the location of the national capital. Accounts vary, but it is commonly held that Jefferson agreed to the payment of the national domestic and foreign debts at par (to the benefit of commercial interests and speculators) in exchange for Hamilton's support in soliciting the necessary votes to place the seat of government on the Potomac.

The tradition of reciprocal influence is a long one. Its results have sometimes been admirable, sometimes disconcerting. Respect for that tradition contributes to the decisive nature of policy clusters that dot the landscape of American government. They possess the capacity for making policy decisions in limited and specialized areas. Professor Freeman has summed it up: "Many of the decisions reached in subsystems, though they may be considered minor or detailed or insignificant when cast individually against a global backdrop, are collectively the stuff of which a large share of our total public policy is made." [16]

15 Dahl and Lindblom, *op. cit.*, p. 306.
16 Freeman, *The Political Process*, pp. 66–67.

Bargaining contributes to "irrational" policy choices; that is, policies result from the reciprocal adjustments of leaders to one another rather than from reference to long-range community goals. Ideally, public policy in a democracy should be formulated only after thorough debate and all policy alternatives have been considered; the choice of policies would then be a process of rational calculation of ends and means. The pervasiveness of political bargaining in American government has contributed to a tradition of policy formulation that differs considerably from this democratic ideal. Charles E. Lindblom distinguishes between the ideal, which he refers to as the "rational-comprehensive" method of policy-making, and the reality, which is labeled the method of "successive limited comparisons." [17] The first consists of five major steps: (1) policy goals are normally clarified prior to the consideration of policy alternatives; (2) means to obtain the policy objectives agreed upon are sought; (3) the criterion for judging "good" policy "is that it can be shown to be the most appropriate means to desired ends"; (4) choice among alternative means is comprehensive, including every factor relevant to every option; and (5) a "theory" of effective policy-making procedures is adhered to at each step.

The systematic procedure for policy formulation outlined above is particularly difficult to follow in the American community. Where social pluralism and constitutional fragmentation exist, disagreement upon policy objectives is normal and conditions the whole of the policy process. We have remarked that there is no dramatic consensus except upon the most vaguely defined and abstract goals. Any analysis of means is necessarily colored by a lack of agreement on ends. On many overall policy objectives we have no idea of what might be the preferences of members of the community. Given the marginal attention of Americans to political matters and the distortions apparent in major patterns of conflict representation, the failure to obtain a community expression on policy values is hardly unexpected. In most instances, policy leaders themselves must articulate such objectives. Conflict among leaders intrudes at all stages of policy decision. Moreover, comprehensive analysis of policy alternatives requires full intelligence of all anticipated consequences of each option. It is certainly open to debate whether policy-makers possess the time, resources, energy, and intellectual capacity to engage in such a demanding operation. Finally, it is questionable whether a body of ac-

[17] See Charles E. Lindblom, "The Science of 'Muddling Through,'" *Public Administration Review*, XIX (Spring, 1959), 79–88; Y. Drer, "Muddling Through — 'Science' or Inertia?" *Public Administration Review*, XXIV (September, 1964), 153–57; Charles E. Lindblom, "Contexts for Change and Strategy: A Reply," *Public Administration Review*, XXIV (September, 1964), 157–58; and Charles E. Lindblom, *The Intelligence of Democracy* (New York: The Free Press, 1965).

cepted canons for policy formulation exists that can provide the guidelines of theory emphasized in the rational-comprehensive method.

Recognizing the problems inherent in the practical application of the rational-comprehensive method, Lindblom describes a procedure more in keeping with the behavior patterns of politicians faced with the day-to-day tasks of making policy. This procedure, which is variously referred to as the method of successive limited comparisons, incremental change, and disjointed incrementalism, includes the following steps: (1) the selection of policy goals and the means for reaching them overlap, and there, the usefulness of means-end analysis is limited; (2) the criterion for judging "good" policy "is typically that various analysts find themselves directly agreeing on a policy"; (3) the analysis of appropriate policy normally neglects both anticipated and unanticipated consequences of a given policy option, many of the potential policies themselves, and the values that conceivably are affected by policies; and (4) canons or theories of policy-making are less significant in the final formulation than the process of comparing each new policy with the pattern of existing rules, procedures, laws, and statutes. In sum, incrementalism amounts to a process of making policies by adding in piecemeal fashion to the body of current policy and adjusting to the demands of all relevant interests. This means a presidential sensitivity to what *can* be gained by pushing certain issues; administrative *modifications* of existing programs, legislative *additions* increment by increment, and judicial *interpretation* of existing statutes and case law.

Creeping incrementalism is a by-product of that political bargaining style generated by conditions of social pluralism and constitutional fragmentation. Pluralism makes intergroup conciliation necessary. Great and dramatic policy shifts are unlikely; each policy innovation is normally preceded by gradual changes in policies extending over decades. Policy *evolution* is more likely than policy revolution. The New Deal followed a slowly mounting body of liberal legislation adopted at both the state and national levels that began in the Populist era and extended through the New Freedom of Wilson, the Progressive movement, and the economic adjustments undertaken by the Hoover Administration. Policy leaders informally recognize the presence and appropriateness of the tradition of incrementation: President Johnson flew to Independence, Missouri in July of 1965 in order to affix his signature to so-called medicare legislation in the presence of former President Harry S. Truman, the man who had initiated the policy struggle almost two decades earlier.

On the surface, this method of policy-making appears relatively chaotic. It reveals no centrally located and deliberate effort to coordinate the disparate efforts of policy leaders. But incrementalist procedures do simplify some of the complexities of the policy process. Instead of considering all policy alternatives in a given conflict situation, leaders limit themselves to those that differ only slightly from the pattern of existing policy. The worth of each policy is measured by what has been accomplished in the past rather than solely by what diverse interests want. In this way, the policy tradition insulates the policy-maker from his more demanding clients. Policy-making is simplified in another way. The best policy is the one on which there is bargained agreement. Rather than focusing on their possible effect on long-range goals, only their effect on immediate policy coalitions are taken into account. Policy-making develops into a search for workable solutions, not "true" ones.

The intermingling of bargaining, reciprocity, and incrementalism has left its mark upon the politician's conception of the "public interest." Throughout American history, political leaders have urged that the guideline of governmental action should be the general interest of all rather than the special interest of the few. The contrast drawn between private and public interests is common in political writings, and "in the literature of the subject the public interest refers to general or common interests shared by all or by substantially all members of the community." [18]

Beyond that claim of general concerns, the notion of the public interest has had a history of being many things to many people. Most frequently it is viewed as a set of substantive ideals against which all policy proposals should be judged; the most obvious example is that we are all supposed to want and need a "better standard of living." The concept is thus recognized as a symbol to which all agree (few people are opposed to "the public interest") and to which special interests appeal in order to rationalize their policy desires. The public interest may also be conceived of as the balancing of group interests involved in the social process at any given moment.

Our purpose here is not to define the nature of the public interest but to note how bargaining has helped shape the traditional view of the American politician toward that vague notion. Superficially it appears that since the method of making policy by increments is not based on the assumption of agreed-upon policy values, there is no overall public interest that can serve as a guide to policy decision. But there is a notion of community interest implied in the operation of bargaining, reciprocal influence, and policy-making by incrementation: that the public interest consists of maintaining the decision-making process of the political community itself. A policy decision is judged to be meaningful on the basis of its contribution to the conciliation of warring interests. To the extent that

[18] E. E. Schattschneider, *The Semisovereign People* (New York: Holt, Rinehart & Winston, 1960), p. 23.

it accomplishes this, it generates a *modus vivendi* for community interests. Furthermore, following this line of thought, it is assumed that any policy thus contributing to community viability advances the democratic cause of individual development despite the fact that the policy itself is the product of bargaining between polity leaders rather than of direct participation in policy-making by the bulk of the citizenry. There is, as Professor Emmette Redford has phrased it, "a public interest in the availability of adequate organization and process, measured by the needs and ideals of society, for representing claims and resolving issues." [19]

The policy traditions of reciprocal influence, incremental change, and the public interest, are offshoots of a pervasive bargaining style. They reflect the underlying expectations, procedures, and standards of American policy-making. They imply that a great portion of policy decisions emerge not from calculated attempts to resolve interest conflict but from efforts to let problems "work themselves out."

We need to underscore once more that in the American community conflict resolution may come through indecision as well as decision, avoidance of choice as well as choosing, and force of circumstance as well as active deliberation. In this sense, the policy process seeks a workable formula, not a satisfying solution. Thus, it is "something between a resolution of conflict and a tabling of issues, with perhaps a little bit of passing the buck involved." [20]

PUBLIC POLICY AND AMERICAN POLITICAL INSTITUTIONS

Public policy is formulated in the American polity within a context of social pluralism and constitutional fragmentation. The American community certainly generates disagreement and makes integration difficult. But the policy process is more than just a mirror image of plural forms. It manages conflict in such a manner that it is possible to build a consensus of a higher order than might otherwise be the case if every group got precisely what it asked from the community. As we shall see in the following four chapters, each of our major policy-making institutions contributes something more to public policy than efforts at mutual adjustment. The Presidency brings to the policy process a voice that transcends the multiplicity of policy clusters. The same is true for Congress, the courts, and administrative agencies; all work to modify fragmentation.

[19] Emmette S. Redford, "The Never-ending Search for the Public Interest," in Emmette S. Redford (ed.), *Ideals and Practice in Public Administration* (Tuscaloosa: University of Alabama Press, 1958), p. 113.

[20] Raymond A. Bauer, Ithiel de Sola Pool, and Lewis Anthony Dexter, *American Business and Public Policy* (New York: Atherton Press, 1963), p. 483.

Perhaps the most fundamental characteristic of policy-making in the modern era in America is the tension that exists between coordination and fragmentation, between centralization and decentralization, and between numerical and concurrent majorities. It is a tension that we have encountered often in our discussion of American government. It is both a product of and a contributor to the divergence between doctrinal and procedural democracy. In our discussion of presidential leadership, congressional adoption, bureaucratic application, and judicial interpretation, we ask the reader to keep in mind the preliminary considerations outlined in this chapter.

BIBLIOGRAPHICAL NOTE

The most valuable account of the consequences for policy-making of social pluralism and constitutional fragmentation in America is Robert A. Dahl and Charles E. Lindblom, *Politics, Economics, and Welfare* (New York: Harper & Row, Publishers, Harper Torchbooks, 1963). The consequences of social pluralism for American politics are also spelled out in Pendleton Herring, *The Politics of Democracy* (New York: W. W. Norton & Company, Inc., 1965). That the seeds of constitutional fragmentation were sewn early in the republic's history is indicated in discussions of our constitutional arrangement, notably David G. Smith, *The Convention And The Constitution* (New York: St. Martin's Press, 1965) and Arthur N. Holcombe, *The Constitutional System* (Chicago: Scott, Foresman and Company, 1964).

Various aspects of federalism as related to policy-making are explored in William H. Riker, *Federalism: Origin, Operation, Significance* (Boston: Little, Brown and Company, 1964); Daniel J. Elazar, *American Federalism: A View from the States* (New York: Thomas Y. Crowell Company 1966); Robert A. Goldwin (ed.), *A Nation of States* (Chicago: Rand McNally & Company, 1963); and Roscoe C. Martin, *The Cities and The Federal System* (New York: Atherton Press, 1965). The relation of constitutional fragmentation to the formation of policy clusters is discussed in J. Leiper Freeman, *The Political Process: Executive Bureau-Legislative Committee Relations* (New York: Random House, Revised Edition, 1965); a more critical view is Douglass Cater's *Power in Washington* (New York: Random House, 1964). In contrast one should consult C. Wright Mills, *The Power Elite* (New York: Oxford University Press, 1957) and Richard H. Rovere, *The American Establishment* (New York: Harcourt, Brace & World, Inc., 1962).

Alternative styles and traditions in policy formulation are described in a number of recent works. Those focusing on bargaining, mutual adjustment, and incremental changes in policy include Charles E. Lindblom, *The Intelligence of Democracy* (New York: The Free Press, 1965) and David Braybrooke and Charles E. Lindblom, *A Strategy of Decision* (New York: The Free Press of Glencoe, 1963). See also James M. Buchanan and Gordon Tullock, *The Calculus of Consent* (Ann Arbor: The University of Michigan Press, Ann Arbor Paperbacks,

1965) for an attempt to construct an elaborate model of decision-making. The nature of the public interest is elaborated in Glendon A. Schubert Jr., *The Public Interest* (New York: The Free Press of Glencoe, 1960), Carl J. Friedrich (ed.), *The Public Interest* (New York: Atherton Press, 1960). A lively account of attempts at mutual adjustment in policy formulation is Aaron Wildavsky's *The Politics of the Budgetary Process* (Boston: Little, Brown and Company, 1964). The value questions implied by American patterns of policy formulation are discussed in Abraham Kaplan, *American Ethics and Public Policy* (New York: Oxford University Press, 1963) and the Rockefeller Brothers Fund Special Studies Project, *The Power of the Democratic Idea* (Garden City, New York: Doubleday & Company, Inc., 1960).

CHAPTER
TWELVE

Policy Leadership

The age-old formula for making public policy is uncomplicated. It states that under an arrangement of separated powers the legislature passes laws, the executive enforces, and the judiciary interprets. It is a recipe for rule-making found in the language and tone of the first three articles of the Constitution of the United States. It has advantages of both simplicity and convenience. But from our discussion thus far, we know that the processes of conflict resolution are not quite that clear-cut. Informal alliances link legislative, administrative, and pressure-group leaders into partially independent policy coalitions. Separate institutions share common law-making functions. Authority and influence are dispersed throughout the constitutional structure. It is never easy to confirm responsibility for policy formulation. In this mosaic of sometimes segmented, sometimes overlapping policy activity, the President is most often looked to as the figure who consolidates the disparate efforts of multiple subgovernments. His capacity to do so constantly fluctuates; his role and influence in policy-making is shaped and altered by varying relationships with the individuals and groups that participate in the policy-making process.

THE PRESIDENCY AND POLICY LEADERSHIP

Earlier we noted that leadership consists of coordinating human activities in the pursuit of collective goals. More specifically, policy leadership involves defining community goals, initiating policy proposals in pursuit of them, and obtaining both official and popular compliance. In America the President takes the lead in forging a continuous reconciliation of diverse interests within the community. In the current era the focus of popular political attention is on the President; in fact, it has been thrust upon him. His every action is subject to adulation, acclaim, complaint, or dismay. Whether he is signing a bill, addressing Congress, traveling abroad, or pulling his dog's ears, he is news. The popular concern that he arouses is a measure of his impact upon American political life.

Although the Presidency seems to dominate the American polity in the mid-twentieth century, this domination was largely unforeseen by the Founding Fathers and was achieved after a long and sometimes bitter tension between the President and other governing institutions. This is not to say that the executive was deemed unimportant. Although the Framers probably saw the legislative branch as the focus of the system, they nevertheless intended an executive of great independence and potential. Presidential selection was made independent of the legislature, and a fixed term of office (subject only to removal by impeachment) was provided. In addition, control over foreign relations was left to the chief executive, he was made chief of the administrative branch, and was provided with a veto over legislation. Basically — as even a cursory glance at Article II will show — the formal powers assigned to the President are unchanged from what they were in 1787. "The executive Power shall be vested in a President of the United States of America" — the opening words of the Article — provide for, but do not define, the extent of such powers. This fact led Professor Corwin to remark that for some the clause produces a "nightmare" and for others it "should be a vision realized." [1] What the Presidency has been and is cannot be explained or understood within the context of the legal status of the office alone. All Presidents have been charged with the constitutional responsibility to "take care that the laws be faithfully executed," yet the meaning attached to this responsibility has differed markedly.

During the administration of Andrew Jackson, Daniel Webster charged that "The President carries on the government; all the rest are subcontractors." After growing steadily in significance prior to 1865, the

[1] Edward S. Corwin, *The President: Office and Powers* (New York: New York University Press, 1948), p. 2.

Presidency was an office in eclipse during the several decades that followed the Civil War. The impeachment trial of President Andrew Johnson marked the zenith of an era of congressional government in America. Congress, not the President, accepted the responsibility for initiating and fixing the final terms of policy; community goals were worked out in a close alliance of private and congressional interests. In 1885 Woodrow Wilson spoke of "the declining prestige of the presidential office." "Its power," Wilson wrote, "has waned because the power of Congress has become predominant."[2] Yet by mid-twentieth century Harry S. Truman depicted presidential power as "the greatest and most important office in the history of the world." A steady, if sometimes interrupted, growth in the power, prestige, and influence of the Presidency is clearly evident.

Given the nature and substance of leadership, the President cannot be a neutral force in interest conflict. Nationalization of politics has occurred within the institutional setting of federalism and separation of powers. That is, problems once deemed to be purely local matters — race relations, urban slums, education — are now among the major concerns of the national government. Increasingly, national politics reflects the clash of nationally-based social and economic interests. Although congressional elections still reflect particularized constituency interests (e.g., agricultural, labor, segregation) the impact of national programs and goals is more clearly felt in these contests. The Presidency has been at the center of the trend toward nationalization. Through his actions the President represents a variety of groups within his national constituency. Because Congress was designed to represent more parochial interests, conflicts between the two branches naturally emerge within the context of this division of policy leadership. Groups seek access at those points in the policy process which further their own goals or give special advantage in blocking undesired alternatives. Over the last six decades some interests — notably civil rights groups and organized labor — have turned toward presidential leadership to achieve more favorable representation of their goals. These developments tend to support Arthur Bentley's view, expressed at the turn of the century, that if groups are not satisfied fairly through the legislature, the executive supplants Congress in performing the task.[3]

Congressmen, as individual representatives, must respond to pressures more localized than those of the national constituency of the President. Further, policy leadership in Congress is dispersed among several officials

---

[2] Woodrow Wilson, *Congressional Government* (Boston: Houghton Mifflin Co., 1885), p. 43.

[3] Arthur Bentley, *The Process of Government* (Evanston, Ill.: The Principia Press of Illinois, 1949).

— the Speaker of the House, the majority and minority leaders of House
and Senate, and key committee chairmen. Each possesses a semi-autonomous standing in specialized areas of policy-making. Legislative policy
goals are cast within a framework of interests, institutional, organization,
and formal powers different from those of the Presidency. But incentives
for cooperation (for example, party ties and loyalty, domestic or foreign
crisis), which stimulate and encourage cooperation between the two
branches, do exist. The keynote of the relations between presidential and
congressional policy leadership is a process of negotiation and accommodation by which leaders in both branches can exert influence on policy.
The aim of policy leadership at all levels is to coordinate rather than
integrate policy goals. A President must, then, shelter the autonomous
interest claims of congressional policy leaders within the overall pattern
of presidential policy.

Presidential leadership is challenged at other points within the governmental structure. A large and sprawling administrative branch contains numerous warriors claiming the right to decide policies in specific
areas. Leadership is made more complicated by the existence of regulatory agencies with policy-making authority distributed among commissioners not directly responsible to the President. Coordination is further
restricted by multiple sublayers of decision-making in executive departments legally responsible to the chief executive. By yielding to or giving
special access to certain groups, administrative bureaus develop support
for their goals outside the executive branch, a situation which weakens
the ability of the President to control the executive hierarchy. For example, an administrative agency seeking goals not desired by the President
may achieve them through active support of sympathetic congressmen or
special interests. The President seeks to meet the administrative challenge
by several strategems: by administrative reorganization to facilitate command, by publicizing major policy demands for public support, by patronage threats and promises, by persuasion, by bargaining, etc. Despite
these controls, the administrative challenge remains an unblunted restriction upon the policy leadership of the Presidency.

Although federal judges are appointed by the President, the judiciary
poses an indirect threat to presidential leadership. As policy is made by
increments (see Chapter Eleven), the judiciary has the option in cases
before it to pass on the constitutionality of each increment. Policy leadership results in the gradual modification of existing policy patterns.
Presidential policy leadership is exerted when he initiates the process of
incrementalism, defines the goals to be obtained with each addition of
policy, and specifies the points at which comparisons are to be made between the old and the new. The judiciary influences presidential leader-

ship through its continuing redefinition of the nature of the policy tradition. For example, the Supreme Court's restrictive interpretation of national power in the area of economic regulation prior to 1937 severely hampered New Deal attempts to meet the problems of the economic depression. A subsequent change in the Court's position opened the way for the initiation of new policy and further extention of federal programs.

Court decisions are also in themselves increments that modify the shape of the policy pattern. In the case of *Brown* v. *Board of Education*, for example, the Supreme Court exercised policy initiative in overturning the traditional policy of segregation in public school systems. In this case, the increment added by the Court was a major one. It was a decision that presented important problems of policy leadership to Presidents Eisenhower, Kennedy, and Johnson in the course of the decade that followed. The decision had to be enforced in areas of the South where both state governments and community sentiment were hostile to integration. Use of federal troops to achieve integration in Little Rock, Arkansas, and at the University of Mississippi were two major instances of executive action enforcing policy initiated by the judiciary.

PRESIDENTIAL PERSPECTIVE
AND POLICY LEADERSHIP

A President's behavior and policy choices are conditioned by factors ranging from formal Constitutional authority to far more subtle and unstructured influences. His perspective on leadership responsibilities will differ from his predecessors. Each sees his tasks, his resources, and his limitations in a different light, yet there are certain features and prerogatives of the Presidency as an institution that transcend the particular incumbency of any President. The office of the Presidency is molded by constituted authority, traditional responsibilities, and popular expectations. Presidential perspective on governmental affairs is shaped in part by these "givens" of the executive office. They force upon any occupant the responsibilities for being a community leader, an administrative leader, a military leader, a diplomatic leader, a legislative leader, and a partisan leader.

The Presidency as the major policy leader in the American political system is discussed in the remainder of this chapter. In this section we explore the traditional roles of the President that shape his perspectives on leadership responsibilities. Next, we will focus more directly on these roles as they are conditioned and altered by pressures emanating from the political system and the executive branch itself.

The President must define his governing responsibilities from many points of view, yet it is but one man who must consolidate the resources available for the fulfillment of each task. Sometimes the responsibilities of the office seem incompatible, and at other times they appear coordinate. It is up to the occupant to consolidate his perspectives into unified action. If he does he upholds the "UNITY of the executive," which Alexander Hamilton envisioned as "the best part of the distinguishing features of our constitution." [4]

A President's perspective on policy leadership is shaped in large part by the multiple jurisdictions and responsibilities distinguished in the Constitution. It is worth reiterating that although the Constitution draws seemingly distinct boundaries between the symbolic, administrative, strategic, international, and legislative dimensions of the President's policy leadership, they are joined whenever the President chooses to act. There is that "seamless unity" uncovered by students of the Presidency in which "distinctions of this sort lose their last shred of meaning." [5]

CONSTITUTED AUTHORITY
AND POLICY LEADERSHIP

Debate in the Constitutional Convention of 1787 over the executive centered around the question of how best to achieve an executive strong enough to enforce national laws but sufficiently limited so that he could not become a threat to republican government. Under the leadership of James Wilson, James Madison, and Alexander Hamilton, the Framers decided upon a single executive rather than a collegiate body. The President was given prerogatives independent of the other branches of government. The intentions of constitutional politicians regarding the scope of presidential authority are not certain. Professor Corwin urged in his analysis of the Presidency that two conceptions of executive power have prevailed since 1787. One is that the executive should be "subordinate to the supreme legislative" and the other that the executive should be "within generous limits, autonomous and self-directing." In sum, it was a confrontation of "the idea that the people are *represented* in the legislature versus the idea that they are *embodied* in the Executive." The vagueness of the Constitutional arrangement is such that the conflict has never truly ended. As Corwin asserts, "Taken by and large, the history of the Presidency has been a history of aggrandizement." [6]

To one observing the contemporary Presidency, the view of an histori-

---

[4] Alexander Hamilton, James Madison, John Jay, *The Federalist* (Modern Library ed.; New York: Random House, 1937), p. 463.

[5] See Clinton Rossiter, *The American Presidency* (New York: The New American Library, 1956); Richard E. Neustadt, *Presidential Power* (New York: John Wiley & Sons, 1961); Donald B. Johnson and Jack L. Walker (eds.), *The Dynamics of the American Presidency* (New York: John Wiley & Sons, 1964).

[6] Corwin, *op. cit.*, p. 38.

cal struggle between two different conceptions of the office seems out of focus. For in this era perhaps more than any other, the Presidency has assumed the character that at least one of the Framers envisioned. Alexander Hamilton in *Federalist, No. 70* foresaw a strong chief executive: "Energy in the executive is a leading character in the definition of good government. . . . A feeble executive implies a feeble execution of the government. A feeble execution is but another phrase for a bad execution; and a government ill executed, whatever it may be in theory, must be, in practice, a bad government." Hamilton believed that the Constitution laid the foundation for the exercise of strong leadership. Article II, he argued, supported the notion "that the *executive power* of the nation is vested in the President; subject only to the *exceptions and qualifications* which are expressed in the instrument." Hamilton urged upon President Washington the vigorous employment of executive action in foreign affairs and in the organization of the administrative branch of the new government. His perception of the office as the fulcrum of leadership in the American system drew its legal foundations from the specific grants of power in the Constitution and its vitality from the individual who would occupy the office and put his powers to use. The twentieth-century Presidency represents the fulfillment of Hamilton's view of the proper role of the executive.

What has the ever-changing constitutional bargain bestowed on the President? For an answer to this question we must look at the Constitution and relevant statutes, interpretations of presidential authority by incumbents and by the courts, and the development of the office by custom and usage.

THE PRESIDENT AND SYMBOLIC LEADERSHIP

President Taft's description of the President as "the personal embodiment and representative of their [the people] dignity and majesty" conveys the meaning attached to the President's tasks as a community leader. Studies of public attitudes toward the President reveal an attachment unlike public attitudes toward other public officials or occupational groups. Fred I. Greenstein classified research findings regarding the "psychological functions of the Presidency" under five headings. First, the President "*simplifies perception* of government and politics" by serving as "the main cognitive 'handle' for providing busy citizens with some sense of what their government is doing." Secondly, the President provides "*an outlet for emotional expression*" through his ceremonial activities and through public interest in his (and his family's) private and public life. Thirdly, the President is a "*symbol of unity*" as evidenced by public reactions to the death of incumbent Presidents. Despite differences of opinion over an incumbent's particular policy choices, the Presidency represents the nation as a unified whole. Death of the man who occupies the office is also the loss, even though only temporary, of the focal point of the system. The shock and grief felt by all groups over the assassination of President Kennedy clearly revealed this factor. Fourthly, the President provides citizens with a *"vicarious means of taking political action."* International crises enable Americans to identify closely with the President in the sense that he may be viewed as acting decisively and effectively for them in an otherwise impersonal world. Finally, the President is a *"symbol of social stability"*; he represents order and security of the "ship of state." [7]

The representation of community goals within the polyarchical context of policy formulation in the American system is not easily achieved. As a symbol of what is most revered in American tradition and institutions, the man who occupies the Presidency is in a strategic position to utilize his status in initiating and formulating specific policy. He, more than any other official, can rationalize policy claims in the name of the "public interest." Likewise, more than any other official, he has continuing access to a broad segment of the political community. A crisis in labor-management relations or in Viet Nam thrusts the President into the role of representing the national interest and articulating national goals. Whatever his response to the problems at hand, he will be listened to closely. Similarly, the State of the Union address or special appeals to Congress or the nation reflect more than a party program or the goals of any particular set of interests within the system. As a symbol of national leadership, the President in effect sets the agenda and the general perimeters of conflict. In this respect, the symbolic nature of the office of President modifies the pluralistic and fragmented nature of policy-making in the American community. His prestigious and exalted position encourages — and sometimes forces — exclusive interests to bow to a larger community interest. Thus, for example, President Kennedy, as symbol and representative of the larger community, forced the steel industry in 1962 to alter its decision to increase prices. Among the resources at his command, and one which played a significant role, was his stature as chief executive of the nation.

THE PRESIDENT AND
ADMINISTRATIVE LEADERSHIP

The constitutional mandate that the President "take care that the laws be faithfully executed" fixes a responsibility that is often difficult to meet.

---

[7] Fred I. Greenstein, "The Psychological Functions of the Presidency for Citizens," in Elmer E. Cornwell, *The American Presidency: Vital Center* (Chicago: Scott, Foresman & Co., 1966), pp. 30–36.

Administrative subordinates whirl with a centrifugal force that keeps throwing them out of the presidential orbit. Many presidential orders fall short of producing obedient response. The lines of command are often tenuous. Professor Louis Koenig distinguishes between the "imagined Presidency" and the "real Presidency." "The imagined Presidency is vested in our minds with more power than the President really has. The real Presidency is what the Presidency effectively is in the present, what it can do in a given situation." [8]

As leader of the administrative bureaucracy, the President must consolidate sprawling clusters of policy activity numbering almost 2½ million persons. Administered programs range from efforts to alleviate poverty to confining criminals in federal prisons. In 1800 nonmilitary federal employees numbered around three thousand; when the Capitol was moved in that year to the District of Columbia, the complete files of the executive branch were shipped in seven packing cases. By 1965 the number of employees in President Johnson's Executive Office alone numbered over twelve hundred persons. The job of directing, controlling, and coordinating this huge branch of government constitutionally falls to the President. So does the responsibility for what goes wrong within it.

The legal basis of the authority of the President to command the administrative branch lies in the Constitution and in statutory authority granted him by Congress. The Constitution does not grant explicit authority both to appoint *and* remove employees in the executive branch, but the power of removal was tacitly recognized by Congress as early as 1789 when it created the Department of State. In 1926 the Supreme Court upheld the President's right to remove an official in a case involving a postmaster who had been dismissed by President Wilson despite the fact that the Tenure of Office Act of 1867 required "the advise and consent of the Senate" before officers of that type could be removed. In *Myers* v. *United States* Chief Justice (and former President) Taft pointed out that the power to remove was directly derived from the constitutional grant of "executive power" and from the mandate to see that the laws are faithfully executed. The *Myers* decision was substantially qualified by a unanimous Supreme Court decision in 1935, which ruled that a member of the Federal Trade Commission — a regulatory body created by Congress whose members were given seven-year terms — could not be removed for political reasons by President Roosevelt. The Court distinguished between officials who perform "purely executive" functions and members of "quasi-judicial or quasi-legislative" agencies who carry out

[8] Louis W. Koenig, *The Chief Executive* (New York: Harcourt, Brace & World, 1964), p. 5.

duties delegated by Congress that are not part of the executive function under the Constitution.[9]

A major supplement to constituted authority over the administrative bureaucracy comes from legislative action. The Budget and Accounting Act of 1921, for example, vested in the President control of the initiation and execution of the federal budget. Financial control is a major weapon in the hands of the President. It means the life or death of an administrative agency.

Even though the President may legally exercise these controls the congressional role in budgeting must be recognized. The objectives of the President in formulating the budget are often quite different from those of congressmen. Budgets can be cut or increased. It is not unusual for Congress to appropriate more than the President requests for an agency or program. When an appropriations bill includes items not requested or supported by the President, the Chief Executive faces the choice of vetoing the entire bill or accepting the undesired item; he does not possess the item veto. Finally, an administrative agency may succeed in by-passing presidential strictures on spending by gaining the support of congressional interests sympathetic to the agency and in a position to satisfy its request.

Congress has also given the President general powers to alter the organization of the administrative branch. To an administrator the prospect of losing his authority through alteration of the organizational structure may be the incentive necessary to bring about compliance with presidential wishes. Finally, because the complexity and scope of congressional responsibility has increased so much (especially in economic matters and in meeting wartime emergencies) much authority previously delegated to the legislature has been given to the President or to designated administrative officials. As early as 1911, Congress authorized the Secretary of Agriculture to make rules and regulations governing the use of federal grazing lands. Other examples of such delegation include wartime controls over prices and rent, agricultural marketing agreements reached between the Secretary of Agriculture and producers of farm commodities, and presidential action under the Taft-Hartley Act of 1947 to prevent strikes from taking place for at least ninety days. Delegations of legislative authority raise questions concerning the sanctity of separation of powers as a working principle in the modern era. The Supreme Court has generally been willing in recent years to accept congressional

[9] *Humphrey's Executor* v. *United States* 295 U.S. 602 (1935); see also *Wiener* v. *United States* 357 U.S. 349 (1958) in which the Supreme Court extended the Humphrey decision to include quasi-judicial officers even though Congress had not provided specific statutory limits to prevent their removal by the President.

delegations of authority that leave wide discretion with the executive officials. Generally, the Court has insisted that Congress may not abdicate its constitutional function to make laws, but the limits of delegation are broad and general in scope.[10] Since the President possesses the power to "hire and fire" heads of administrative departments who are delegated policy-making discretion of this kind, the ultimate responsibility for its exercise lies with the President himself. Yet, as we saw earlier and will in subsequent sections, presidential sanctions are limited by factors which have little or no bearing on the strictly legal relationships between subordinates and the President as administrative leader.

THE PRESIDENT AND
STRATEGIC LEADERSHIP

The Constitution states that the President "shall be Commander in Chief of the Army and Navy . . . and of the Militia of the several States, when called into the actual Service of the United States." Legally, the President may send armed forces wherever he wishes. Although Congress alone is constitutionally empowered to declare war, the President, in using troops, may precipitate armed conflict, leaving Congress no choice but to appropriate funds to bring the conflict to a successful conclusion. In 1907, during a period of strained relations with Japan, Theodore Roosevelt ordered the fleet to sail around the world as a show of both peaceful intentions and the right of the American navy to sail in Pacific waters. Although he lacked funds to finance more than half the trip Congress was forced to appropriate the money necessary to bring the fleet home. President Truman ordered troops to the defense of South Korea in 1950, an action which committed the nation to a conflict that was never officially designated as a "war" by Congress.

As a strategic commander in time of war, the President has authority to do more than issue military orders. Presidents Wilson and Franklin Roosevelt extended wartime controls over the American economy, labor, and transportation facilities, and approved the government's seizure of strike-bound or strike-threatened plants and industries. In February, 1942 the Army, acting in the name of the Commander in Chief, evacuated seventy-thousand Japanese-Americans from the three West Coast states and part of Arizona on grounds that a danger of espionage and sabotage existed. During the Civil War President Lincoln combined the powers of Commander in Chief with his constitutional duty to "take care that the laws be faithfully executed" and derived what he termed the "war power."

[10] See, for example, the discussion in *Yakus* v. *United States* 321 U.S. 414 (1944); for an example in which the Supreme Court has declared congressional delegations as exceeding constitutional bounds see *Schecter Poultry Corporation* v. *United States* 295 U.S. 495 (1935).

He used this power to justify a series of unprecedented measures, including suspension of the writ of habeas corpus in designated areas and expenditure of unauthorized funds from the federal treasury. Moreover, using powers granted under Article II and by congressional statute, Presidents may use force to compel compliance with federal law and to prevent domestic disorder and violence. In 1841 President Tyler ordered federal militia to put down a rebellion against the government of Rhode Island, and in 1894 Grover Cleveland broke the Pullman strike by ordering federal troops to protect the movement of United States mails.

Generally speaking, the courts have recognized and upheld the use of presidential "emergency powers" during wartime, but the Supreme Court in *Youngstown Sheet and Tube Co.* v. *Sawyer* (1952) denied President Truman's assertion that "inherent" emergency powers of the Presidency justified seizure of the steel mills in 1952 in order to avoid a crippling strike. The President, in this instance, decided not to employ the Taft-Hartley Act which provided him with means to temporarily prevent the strike. Despite the Court's denial of the seizure in this case, Professor Joseph Tanenhaus has remarked that the decision advanced a new perspective on presidential authority. He labels it the "relativity of presidential power." Operating under this theory, the Court no longer accepts the position that the Constitution "is one and the same regardless of circumstances." Instead presidential authority possesses a situational dimension. Normally the President can do only what the Constitution and laws specifically authorize. But, under the relativity theory, he "can exercise prerogative in time of grave emergency . . . if Congress acquiesces." [11] The notion of relativity is an attempt to reconcile an eighteenth-century Constitution with twentieth-century realities of cold-war politics. Whether the courts in the future will accept this reading of presidential peacetime emergency powers cannot be known or predicted with any degree of certainty.

THE PRESIDENT AND
INTERNATIONAL LEADERSHIP

The increasing involvement of the United States in world affairs during this century and the grave risks inherent in foreign-policy decisions in the atomic age have combined to make the President's role as an international leader of crucial importance. It is, in fact, a role that he cannot avoid. Although he must in some respects share authority with Congress in the field of foreign affairs, his role in shaping and guiding relations

[11] Joseph Tanenhaus, "The Supreme Court and Presidential Power," *The Annals of the American Academy of Political and Social Science*, CCCVII (September, 1956), 106–13.

with other nations is so paramount that he virtually dominates this function. The Senate must concur in treaties made with foreign nations, but the increasing use of the executive agreement has provided Presidents with a mechanism by which formal concurrence is avoided. An executive agreement — one made by the President with the head of a foreign state — does not require approval of either house of Congress. Executive agreements are entered into on the basis of indirect constitutional powers granted the President as Chief Executive or they may be based on authority granted by Congress. The exchange in 1940 of fifty United States destroyers in return for long-term leases to naval bases on British territory was by executive agreement based on presidential powers. International postal agreements and American participation in a number of international associations are examples of statute-based executive agreements. About 2000 executive agreements have been concluded since 1940.

To cite another area: Since the end of World War II, with the advent of large appropriations for foreign aid and the defense establishment, the power of the purse has assumed even greater importance. The fact that the executive branch exclusively holds much information regarding foreign and defense affairs puts Congress in an awkward position. Congress is often reluctant to cut appropriations in the face of a presidential plea that appropriations requests are "essential" to American foreign policy.

The Constitution specifies that control of foreign affairs is exclusively a function of the national government, yet it is generally silent in regard to the specific locus of control of foreign policy. The President's primacy stems from his role as Commander in Chief and his authority to make treaties, appoint diplomatic representatives, and recognize foreign governments. Confirmation of major presidential appointments and appropriations, and passage of laws that affect foreign policy (for example, tariff regulations, neutrality acts) provide some measure of congressional participation in foreign affairs. Yet the dominance of the President in this field is unquestioned. President Truman gave his opinion on the subject when he said in 1948, "I make American foreign policy." As early as 1799, John Marshall, then a member of the House of Representatives, described the Presidency as "the sole organ of the nation in its external relations, and its sole representative with foreign nations." [12] Marshall's statement has become commonly accepted as the most accurate description of the President's role in this area. The Supreme Court has repeatedly affirmed the primacy of the President in foreign affairs. Justice

[12] Quoted in Edward S. Corwin, *The President: Office and Powers* (New York: New York University Press, 1957), p. 216.

Sutherland once commented that the President possessed not only specific constitutional and statutory authority in these matters but also "the very delicate plenary and exclusive power of the President as the sole organ of the federal government in the field of international relations. . . . ." [13] Historically he alone has exercised the power of recognizing new governments, a power which has sometimes meant the success or failure of a new government. President Wilson brought down the Huerta regime in Mexico in 1915 by refusing recognition. The President also has the sole prerogative in receiving foreign diplomats and in forcing their recall. President Washington demanded the recall of the French minister Edmond Genêt, whose attempt to build public support for the French in their war against England jeopardized the American declaration of neutrality regarding the war.

Although in the field of foreign affairs the relative position of Congress and the President has been subject to serious debate throughout American history, there is no longer serious doubt that the President dominates the scene.

President Truman's remark, "I make foreign policy," is an accurate statement of the presidential role provided that it is understood within the context of the limits of his choices. During the Cuban crisis of 1962 President Kennedy and his advisers weighed a number of alternative ways (bomb the missile sites, invade Cuba, negotiate with the Soviet Union, establish a naval blockade) to meet the threat of Soviet missiles housed in the nearby unfriendly nation. The final decision to assert whatever force became necessary to bring about withdrawal of the missiles had to be made within the context of both a national and international constituency. As leader of the western alliance of nations the President shouldered the responsibility of maintaining the security of other nations as well as the United States.

Kennedy received general support both at home and among western allies during the Cuban crisis. President Johnson's decision to support the South Viet Nam government, on the other hand, has faced serious criticism both within the United States and among other nations. Congressional critics led by Senator Fulbright, chairman of the Senate Foreign Relations Committee, attacked the President's decision to escalate military operations in Viet Nam. Leaders of other nations, such as General De Gaulle of France, have openly opposed American policies in Southeast Asia.

The effectiveness of presidential leadership in foreign affairs, as in other of his leadership roles, is dependent upon receiving and maintaining the support of many interests. Congressional control of appropriations, the

[13] *United States* v. *Curtiss-Wright Export Corporation* 299 U.S. 304 (1936).

power to investigate, and the right to criticize command the respect of the President in his choice of alternatives. Similarly, the opinion of other national leaders — friendly, unfriendly, or neutral — must be weighed in assessing American goals and actions in international matters. The President is the primary manager of international treaty organizations (for example, North Atlantic Treaty Organization, Southeast Asia Treaty Organization, and the United Nations) and he heads a nation with domestic programs closely related to foreign affairs. Economic or social crises at home may shake the confidence of leaders of other nations in the President's ability to lead the free world. Conversely, the actions he takes in exercising his international leadership may well affect his ability to maintain his support at home.

The management of all these interests within the context of a long-range foreign policy is to a greater extent dependent upon the ability of a President to persuade and to bargain than it is to command a course of action. The techniques of each President will differ and the resources at his command will vary with circumstances. President Kennedy, for example, enjoyed wide personal popularity both at home and abroad, an image that President Johnson has not been able to match. Yet the Viet Nam crisis sharpened considerably after Kennedy's death, and one can only speculate as to whether his popularity would have maintained such high levels if he had lived to face the same crises as President Johnson, or whether he would have acted in the same way as has President Johnson. As chief foreign policy-maker a President's choices are affected by circumstances, personalities, and events as well as by constitutional grants of authority.

THE PRESIDENT AND
LEGISLATIVE LEADERSHIP

In the previous chapter the observation was made that Americans must deal with eighteenth-century policy-making organs in a technological twentieth-century. The presidential role in legislative policy-making is a clear illustration of the point. His power in legislative affairs is considerably less a product of constitutional grants than a result of the development of the office itself. Article II enjoins the President to provide Congress with information ("State of the Union" address and special messages), provides the President with authority to call special sessions "on extraordinary occasions," and permits him to set adjournment whenever the two houses cannot agree on a date. A negative power — the veto — was added. Within ten days of receiving a bill, the President may either sign it into law, allow it to become law without his signature, or return it to Congress with a message stating his reasons for vetoing it. In the event that Congress adjourns within the ten-day period, the President may exercise the so-called "pocket veto" by simply failing to sign the bill. With this type of veto, Congress is unable to exercise its option of overriding the President's action by a two-thirds vote of both houses. There is no count of the number of times a presidential *threat* of veto has prevented congressional action on legislation disapproved by the Chief Executive, but there is no question that this threat has served both to prevent undesired action and to induce Congress to comply with presidential wishes.

The presidential role in legislative matters is clearly more extensive than his formal powers. That role has been shaped by factors closely linked to the development of the office, especially during this century. Presidents, speaking and acting as the representatives of a national constituency, have seized the initiative in proposing legislative policy and guiding it through Congress. Policy goals sought by Presidents have been achieved by various means. Woodrow Wilson broke tradition by delivering in person a special message asking for currency-reform legislation. Franklin D. Roosevelt sent a message to Congress in 1942 which in effect said that if Congress did not pass price- and wage-control legislation by a specified date, he himself would establish such controls by executive order. The tact, vigor, and style of a President are crucial factors in obtaining major legislation. For example: President Johnson's proposal for voting rights legislation in 1965 followed on the heals of national shock and outrage over inhumane treatment of civil rights marchers in Selma, Alabama. In this instance, the mood of Congress and the vigor of the President combined to bring about major legislation, which gave further protection to the right to vote.

Techniques used by strong presidents such as Wilson and Franklin Roosevelt are now considered the common stock of their successors. When they are not used, there is concern over the lack of presidential leadership; cries of "dictatorship" are usually taken as political rhetoric rather than responsible and serious criticism. Legislative leadership is not, however, synonymous with dominance of Congress. A president may utilize his prestige, his position as party leader, his peculiar role as representative of the larger community, and his formal powers to achieve his goals. He is, on the other hand, limited by the institutional, social, and constitutional pluralism of the system. Congress possesses the constitutional mandate to legislate, and it is jealous of its prerogatives. Presidents must bargain within these limits, and their success or failure will depend on factors ranging from presidential tactics to the size of the president's party membership in Congress. We turn next to the president's role as party leader.

THE PRESIDENT AND
PARTISAN LEADERSHIP

Unlike the leadership responsibilities sketched briefly above, the President's partisan leadership is not a task bestowed by constitutional edict. Political parties were the conscious creations of policy leaders such as Hamilton, Madison, and Jefferson. They were designed specifically to support presidential efforts of command and persuasion. Over the years partisan loyalties have served as major props for presidential leadership.

It is often remarked that the President is the only elective policy official in America with a community-wide constituency; he and the Vice-President are selected as national leaders by voters in all of the United States. One minor qualification needs to be made. Given the Electoral College method of selection, the populous states figure more prominently in the governing plans of most presidential aspirants or incumbents. The "national constituency" is cut into fifty-one segments of which some are relatively more important than others. Moreover, within any segment there are certain areas — notably the larger urban centers — that by necessity must be given more consideration in planning elections. Finally, we need to repeat that the President is not just a neutral agent of community action. He is a group leader who is elected by a coalition of major interests, and at any given moment he speaks for differing sets of interests. He acts as a community-wide representative primarily in his symbolic role as head-of-state.

The fact that the President is a party affiliate and leader contributes to his outlook on policy formulation in several ways. Certainly the process of his selection as party standard bearer and the election campaign are shaping forces of the pattern of his behavior as President. We have already seen that the presidential campaign is a testing ground for his leadership. His capacities for organization, decision-making, bargaining, command, and persuasion are revealed under pressure; from the campaign we also get a sense of how he perceives the political sentiments of Americans.

The method by which a candidate wins nomination also has consequences for his future as a policy leader. If the party is to be a major tool for persuasion and command, a presidential candidate must be assured that his nomination actually provides him with such an instrument. Either a pre- or post-convention campaign filled with rancor and bitterness may produce partisans who are only lukewarm in their enthusiasm for the chosen President. More often it means that the candidate does not become President at all. For example, the hard and sometimes bitter battle for the Republican nomination in 1964 left some party members lukewarm or unwilling to support Senator Goldwater during the election campaign. Throughout the nominating and election campaign, the presidential aspirant has an opportunity to forge a coalition that will promote his position as policy leader; the success of his administration may depend upon his capacity to do so.

No set formula exists for guaranteeing a presidential nomination. The prescription changes with shifting patterns of social interests. A workable pre-convention campaign technique in one year may lead to disaster four years later. Yet the nominating process always makes certain demands upon the presidential aspirant, and the way in which an aspirant meets these demands may have some bearing on his potential for policy leadership. In the struggle for nomination, the presidential aspirant undergoes the first major test of his ability to define collective goals. In this instance, he must demonstrate that he is the man best qualified to present party aims in terms that organized and loyal partisans can identify with sympathetically. An accurate appraisal of the desires of party activists is mandatory. Professors Polsby and Wildavsky suggest that convention delegates generally share the following goals: "to gain power, to nominate a man who can win the election, to unify the party, to obtain some claim on the nominee, to protect their central core of policy preferences, and to strengthen their state party organizations." [14]

There are several phases of the nominating process in which the aspirant can demonstrate his grasp of organizational demands: The interim period between elections, the primaries, the selection of state and district delegates, and the phase of national-convention bargaining. The interim phase is devoted to mobilizing support among organized partisans within the fifty states. The aspirant must become known and respected. The interim campaign normally begins the day after the presidential election, but it may start even earlier. Following his unsuccessful bid for the vice-presidential nomination in the 1956 Democratic convention, John F. Kennedy began his move toward the Presidency. Senator Barry Goldwater emerged as a contender for the 1964 presidential nomination on the day he withdrew his name as a possible nominee in the 1960 Republican convention and admonished conservatives to "get to work" and recapture control of the party. A candidate serves his cause well in the interim phase by successful forays into the various states during the mid-term congressional elections. Richard Nixon in 1958 and Barry Goldwater in 1962 carefully cultivated contacts with state party leaders; their efforts bore fruits in the nominating conventions that followed two years later. During the interim phase the prospective candidate seeks to convince organized par-

[14] Nelson W. Polsby and Aaron B. Wildavsky, *Presidential Elections* (New York: Charles Scribner's Sons, 1964), p. 64.

tisans that he can unify the party, protect their policy interests, and help their state organizations. Party leaders, in turn, attempt to make their claims upon the aspirant in this phase of the nominating process.

A chief function of the primary phase is that it affords the candidate with an opportunity to convince party organizers that he can win. He does this by securing as many votes as possible from identified partisans. It also enables him to publicize both his candidacy and his policy position. More practically, the primary allows the candidate to enter into the process of selecting delegates to the national nominating convention. Fewer than one-third (fifteen) of the states select convention delegates by primaries. The rules of the primary vary: In some states the results of the primary commit delegates to support the winner in the convention, but in others delegates are merely informed of voter "preference" and have no legal obligation to abide by it; in some states candidates must give their consent before their names can be placed on the ballot, but in two states (New Hampshire and Florida) this is not necessary; finally, in most states participation in primaries is restricted to registered members of the party, but in Wisconsin and Minnesota the primary is "open" and the voter may take his choice of which primary election to participate in.

A major decision facing a presidential aspirant in the primary phase is to enter or not to enter. Some candidates, such as presidents running for reelection, hardly need to enter primaries in order to lay claim on the party nomination. Others, such as Richard Nixon in 1960, believe they have more to gain than lose by entering. Nixon entered all Republican presidential primaries in 1960 even though he ran unopposed in all of them. He viewed the primaries as an opportunity to show that he was not taking the presidential nomination for granted and also as a means to test his campaign organization and tactics prior to the general election.[15] John Kennedy in 1960 used the primary as a springboard to the party nomination. His victory over Senator Hubert Humphrey in West Virginia helped to demonstrate that his religious affiliation should not preclude his nomination and also that he had a capacity for defining and running on issues that were of salient concern to voters.

Primary victories are not easily converted into convention nominations. A single loss among a string of primary successes — for example, Harold Stassen's defeat in Oregon in 1948 — may prevent a candidate from receiving the nomination. Or if a candidate lacks organizational support, his primary victories may be hollow ones, as Estes Kefauver discovered in his attempt to become the Democratic candidate in 1952. In some instances, a candidate who captures the support of key party leaders may

[15] Richard M. Nixon, *Six Crises* (Garden City, N.Y.: Doubleday & Co., 1962), pp. 308–09.

be able to suffer narrow margins of victory and even losses in primaries and yet move easily to the nomination. Barry Goldwater's primary campaigns were dotted with failures, but he marched steadily toward the 1964 Republican nomination without serious difficulty.

The great majority of delegates to national nominating conventions are chosen through state and district conventions. The presidential aspirant, then, must either be able to influence the selection of delegates or persuade chosen delegates to back his candidacy. In either event, key party leaders must be responsive to his campaign for the nomination. Techniques for obtaining that support vary widely. Promises, bargaining, citing a candidate's popularity in opinion polls, and bringing pressure upon delegates from supporters in the local community are a few of the techniques most commonly used. Backers of Wendell Willkie's candidacy in 1940 sought to influence chosen delegates by developing a "grass-roots" campaign in local areas; telegraph messages recording pro-Wilkie local sentiment were sent to the state delegations. A similar technique was employed, but with less positive results, by Governor William Scranton when he belatedly challenged the 1964 candidacy of Senator Goldwater.

The national convention is the culmination of the nominating process. If the nomination is still in doubt, the convention affords the last opportunity to forge a winning coalition. This may mean bridging conflicts between separate partisan interests, reconciling them, or even exploiting factional disputes. Each step of the convention can turn into a struggle between contenders — the report of the Credentials Committee and the seating of delegates, the selection of temporary and permanent convention officers, the report of the Platform Committee, the call for nominations, control of demonstrations, and ultimately the balloting.

Serious contenders must have substantial support from outside their own state delegations. In Republican conventions the normal pattern has been for two such aspirants to emerge; Democratic conventions have been marked by a larger number of serious contenders. In their study of state-delegation voting in national conventions during the years 1940–64, Frank Munger and James Blackhurst uncovered some interesting factional cleavages that recur over the years. Generally Republican conventions have been made up of two factions: a conservative wing with strength in the Midwest and South and a more progressive wing based largely in the Northeast. Moreover, "all the successful candidates for nomination in the contested Republican conventions from 1940 to 1964 have won victory by appealing to one or the other of the poles of the party." Multifactional alignments have been more characteristic of Democratic conventions. Munger and Blackhurst suggest that candidates for the Democratic nomination have built their majorities by differing combinations of left, center, and right factions (roughly the industrial and urban states of the Midwest and West, those of the Northeast, and those of the South respectively). Again, the revealed pattern over the twenty-year period has been fairly consistent: "control of the convention has shifted from the left-center to the center-right, back to the left-center, then to the center, and once more to left-center." Hence, although serious contenders seek to build alliances of various partisan interests, the pattern has been for the successful candidate to base the greatest part of his strength in one faction and move from there.[16] Thus, any President relying upon partisan support for his policy leadership will look primarily to but one segment of his party. To this extent a portion, but not all, of his party serves him as an instrument of policy control.

The success of a President in achieving his foreign or domestic programs is closely related to his ability to win and maintain the support of the coalition that elected him to office. The nationwide success of his party is in large part dependent upon the quality of his leadership as President and the support his programs receive within the electorate. A highly popular President is a distinct asset to party candidates at other levels. Party fortunes in general tend to rise and fall with the success of the President. Thus, congressmen of his party have a significant stake in maximizing the favorable image of the President. They are interested in responding to presidential wishes and policies that will improve their chances of electoral success. This is not to say that all congressmen or local party leaders will respond favorably. A congressman or governor from the deep South will not normally be expected to support White House proposals for civil rights legislation since such support may mean his own defeat at the polls in the next election. Similarly a representative of an agriculturally dominated constituency may be hostile or indifferent to presidential programs for urban development, especially when his constituents oppose such programs.

A President is not without partisan controls of his own. As party leader he dispenses patronage and political favors of all kinds. A reluctant congressman of *either* party often supports presidential measures in return for a new post office in his district, the appointment of a candidate he has recommended to a federal job, or a flood-control project in his state. By threatening to withhold his support of a congressman on his party's ticket, a popular President can win concessions that no other kind of sanction or persuasive measures could induce.

As a result of the nationalization of party politics in the past two or

[16] Frank Munger and James Blackhurst, "Factionalism in the National Conventions, 1940–1964: An Analysis of Ideological Consistency in State Delegation Voting," *The Journal of Politics*, XXVII, No. 2 (May, 1965), 375–94.

three decades, the President's position as party leader has been enhanced. Local party leaders are less free to oppose presidential leadership since the Presidency shapes and represents the party program and the party's image more than ever before. Associated with nationalization is a technique frequently being used now — the appeal to the public-at-large. Having access to mass communication, the President can appeal on short notice to the public and can mobilize opinion in behalf of his program, thereby bringing pressure upon members of both parties in Congress. Thus, presidential leadership can counteract the localism of legislators and the recalcitrance of local party leaders and organization. Franklin D. Roosevelt employed the famous "Fireside Chats" to generate public support for his programs. By utilizing the first person plural in his radio messages ("We cannot fail"; "our plan") Roosevelt was to build a close relationship with the people; a relationship that could not be ignored by congressmen and local party officials. Factors that have contributed to the nationalization of party politics and presidential leadership have led some people to believe that the "personalism" of the Presidency may be a threat to party organization at the local levels. As Lester Seligman puts it, "Interest groups, ardent amateurs in political clubs, and public-relations experts are tending to fill the vacuum of political leadership and organization." [17] A president may not be able to develop a party appeal or retain party support within the electorate. Dwight D. Eisenhower was never able to transfer his own great personal popularity to support of other Republican candidates, a fact indicated by Democratic congressional majorities during six of the eight years of the Eisenhower administrations.

The President retains yet another means of exercising party leadership. The Cabinet and top staff of the President are largely drawn from the groups that are instrumental in winning the nomination and election for him. Therefore, the people around the President are part of what might be called the "presidential party," a group that helps to shape and execute their chief's program. All Presidents since Franklin Roosevelt (although the same was true to some extent in earlier administrations) have brought to the White House a group of advisers who were generally identified as the nucleus of the presidential party. Members of Roosevelt's so-called "brain trust" occupied key positions in his administration and helped to formulate New Deal policy. Truman's "Fair Deal" program was also identified with men working closely with him; Eisenhower had a close association with his top advisor, Sherman Adams, and certain other members of the White House staff; John F. Kennedy took with him to

[17] Lester G. Seligman, "The Presidential Office and the President as Party Leader," in Johnson and Walker, op. cit., p. 191.

the White House a group of highly competent young men who had been associated with his campaign for the Presidency; and Lyndon B. Johnson has surrounded himself with advisers and Cabinet members sympathetic to his "Great Society" program.

The Executive Office of the President, created by executive order in 1939, now includes the White House Office, the Bureau of the Budget, the Council of Economic Advisors, the National Security Council, the Office of Emergency Planning, and the Office of Science and Technology. These units serve as major sources of presidential information and assistance in the formulation of policy for the presidential party. Staffed by presidential appointees chosen for their ability to contribute to presidential programs, they represent a level of policy-making substantially removed from the influence of interests that operate in the legislative branch. In short, the interests which enjoy access to these agencies are often those which most closely represent the center of the presidential party.

But our discussion of political nationalization and the growth of presidential controls should not obscure the fact that American parties are still basically fragmented in organization and leadership. They are national parties only when they elect a President or organize the houses of Congress. A President is limited in the extent to which he can provide direction and demand support within his own party. The fact that congressmen of the President's party frequently refuse to support his legislative programs is clear evidence that dominance of the party organization is not the pattern. The role of the President in the American system is an ambiguous one. The Presidency as the symbol of national unity places demands on the executive to represent a constituency of all the people, yet as leader of his party he is also expected to pursue partisan goals. To achieve a major part of his programs, a President must depend upon the votes of opposition party members in Congress. To appear as an extreme partisan is to run the grave risk of solidifying the opposition and defeating his program. In pursuing partisan ends, he is expected to refrain from putting too much pressure on his own party's congressmen and recognize that congressional constituency interests must sometimes be given preference to presidential demands.

The President, in short, must balance the interests of major groups that make demands upon him. He must satisfy interests both as a party leader and President of all the people. In this pursuit, he can neither appear as an opportunist who seeks goals without considering all the people nor can he create an image of indifference to partisan demands. A President does command great resources in pursuing his goals, but the decentralized and diverse nature of the American party system and the

President's need to retain the support of the coalition of voter groups that put him into office clearly limit their use.

PRESIDENTIAL PRESSURES
AND POLICY LEADERSHIP

THE PRESIDENT AND POLICY PRESSURE

The President is always aware of the varied and conflicting demands made upon him, yet these must be filtered through his own goals and his own image of the office. Richard Neustadt has long been an adviser to presidents as well as a student of presidential politics. He identifies five major constituencies of the modern Presidency: the administrative bureaucracy, Congress, fellow partisans, the general citizenry, and foreign groups. Each makes different claims upon the President's time, energy, and influence. Each depends upon him for benefits but does not always support him in exchange. This divergence between constituency demands and supports flows from the fact that the President views his obligations in a totally different light than the interests that depend upon him do. His constituents rely upon him but do not feel obligated to him. His bureaucratic clients have their own responsibilities and concerns to deal with daily. Congressional allies have their own constituencies to represent. His partisan friends have narrower demands than the President can normally give into without compromise. Community leaders may turn for aid to places other than Washington. And, as Neustadt concludes, "private groups that seek him out are not compelled to govern," and "friends abroad are not compelled to run in our elections." [18]

It falls to each President to define for himself the role he will play in our sprawling, diversified political community. In building support for policy that reflects his own goals, he gradually moves closer to some constituents than others. His personal assessment of *his* incumbency yields selective attention and inattention to consideration of community conflicts. Many of the pressures he encounters are of his own making to the extent that, in defining his role, he chooses the major areas of conflict from which demands will come.

A President's conception of what he ought to do and what he can do is in part dependent upon his concept of the office itself. Professor Corwin, in saying that the history of the Presidency is "a history of aggrandizement," points to the development of the office under five major personalities: Jackson, Lincoln, Wilson, and the two Roosevelts. These men all possessed a keen sense of history, circumstances, and timing; conse-

---

[18] Neustadt, *op. cit.*, p. 8.

quently, they were able to act successfully in the achievement of their goals. According to Corwin, each had a clear concept of what he deemed should be the role of the President in the American community. Theodore Roosevelt articulated a theory of presidential powers that we use today in describing the "strong" Presidency. Roosevelt termed it the "residuum of powers" theory: [19]

> I insisted upon the theory that the executive power was limited only by specific restrictions and prohibitions appearing in the Constitution or imposed by the Congress under its Constitutional powers. My view was that every executive officer, and above all, every executive officer in high position, was a steward of the people bound actively and affirmatively to do all he could for the people, and not content himself with the negative merit of keeping his talents undamaged in a napkin. . . . I did not care a rap for the mere form and show of power; I cared immensely for the use that could be made of the substance.

One of the most severe critics of Roosevelt's stewardship perspective was his successor, William Howard Taft. For Taft, any powers exercised by the President had to be traced to some specific authority granted either in the Constitution or by statute. "There is no undefined residuum of power which he can exercise because it seems to him to be in the public interest . . . an undefined residuum of power . . . is an unsafe doctrine." [20] Taft reviewed Roosevelt's concept of stewardship as an attack upon limited government. He felt it would be especially dangerous under emergency conditions when the temptation to use arbitrary action would be greatest.

President Hoover's approach was more in harmony with strict constitutional edict. He was committed to the preservation of the Constitution in its full letter as well as spirit. Although he modified his views toward the end of his term, Hoover's style reflected a strong moral and legal commitment to constitutional government buttressed by an equally strong belief in "American individualism." He expressed the belief that the executive must not encroach on "the independence of the legislative army," and he confessed to having "little taste for forcing Congressional action or engaging in battles of criticism." [21] Although he exercised the

---

[19] Theodore Roosevelt, *An Autobiography* (New York: Charles Scribner's Sons, 1946), p. 35.

[20] William Howard Taft, *Our Chief Magistrate and His Powers* (New York: Columbia University Press, 1916), pp. 139–40, 140–45; see also Norman J. Small, *Some Presidential Interpretations of the Presidency* (Baltimore: The Johns Hopkins Press, 1932); Arthur Bernon Tourtellet, *The Presidents on the Presidency* (Garden City, N.Y.: Doubleday & Co., 1964).

[21] Herbert C. Hoover, *Memoirs, the Cabinet and the Presidency, 1920–1933* (New York: The Macmillan Co., 1952), p. 217.

veto, he generally disapproved of its use in defeating congressional will or in forcing legislative action into desired channels; rather, the veto was to be used to protect the fundamentals of the Constitution.

The contrast between Hoover's perspective and that of Franklin D. Roosevelt is striking. Roosevelt believed that a President must be "alert and sensitive to change." He forcefully used the prerogatives and prestige of the Presidency to lead the nation to what he conceived as desired ends. Roosevelt's biographers have generally agreed that F. D. R. thoroughly enjoyed the exercise of leadership and that he viewed his role in highly personal terms. As Richard Neustadt puts it, "He saw the job of being President as being F. D. R. He wanted mastery, projected that desire on the office and fulfilled it there with every sign of feeling he had come into his own." [22]

Of the four Presidents since Franklin Roosevelt all have generally recognized the key role the President must play in national leadership. There have been, however, notable differences in their leadership style and their likes and dislikes in exercising presidential powers. President Eisenhower displayed what Nelson Polsby has called a "passive presidency." His administration was characterized by "withdrawal from partisan politics, a dislike of rough and tumble, a preference for decision-making at the staff level. . . ." [23] For his predecessor, Harry S. Truman, the Presidency was viewed as a challenge and a test of man's capacity for making choices and providing leadership. Truman likened the Presidency to "riding a tiger." In fulfilling the office, a man "has to keep on riding or be swallowed." He "either is constantly on top of events, or, if he hesitates, events will soon be on top of him." [24] President Kennedy brought to the White House a firm conviction that the presidency is the focal point of the political system. He cited Lincoln, Jackson, Wilson, Truman, and both Roosevelts as models of what the presidency should be. As President, Kennedy exercised firm control over staff operations and generally followed a policy of persuasion rather than pressure in his dealings with Congress. Lyndon B. Johnson's service as Senate majority leader provided him with a background of skills and experience that he has readily utilized as President. A strong advocate of an active presidency, Johnson has succeeded in achieving passage of substantial portions of his legislative program. His early invitation "Come, let us reason together," represented an appeal to all groups to participate in furthering the goals of the "Great Society." The quest for a general consensus led to an emphasis on

[22] Neustadt, op. cit., p. 162.
[23] Nelson W. Polsby, Congress and the Presidency (Englewood Cliffs, N.J.: Prentice-Hall, 1964), pp. 20–21.
[24] Harry S. Truman, Years of Trial and Hope (Memoirs, Vol. II; Garden City, N.Y.: Doubleday & Co., 1956), p. 1.

a highly personalized presidency in which competing interests are balanced in order to achieve widest possible support for Johnson policies.

Professor Louis Koenig has constructed three "models" or styles of presidential behavior. The first of these, the "Literalist," includes those Presidents (such as Madison, Buchanan, Taft, Hoover, and to some extent, Eisenhower) who define their powers in accordance with constitutional edict, are conscious of the constitutional prerogatives and role of Congress, and display little desire to change existing social policy. In contrast, Koenig describes a group of "Strong" Presidents: Washington, Lincoln, Jackson, Wilson, and the two Roosevelts. They give broad interpretations to presidential authority, are willing to break existing precedents regarding prerogatives and limitations, and generally expound Theodore Roosevelt's stewardship theory. Strong Presidents are usually the product of times of crises. Koenig's third type, the "Middle" group, occupy a position somewhere between the other types. Koenig asserts that the Presidency of the 1960's must be of the strong variety. "The great, if not the foremost, task of American politics is to convert the strong Presidency, which has appeared only intermittently, into an assured and constant feature of our government." [25]

The record of American Presidents since 1933 indicates that no occupant of the White House can escape the demands of circumstances. Events since World War II have made crises part of the "normal" pattern of events. Where crisis prevails, a President must act. To an extent he can rely on the customs established by predecessors. And he can utilize the authority conferred upon him by the Constitution and by congressional statute. In the end, however, how effective he is as President will depend upon the man himself — especially his ability to perceive the realities and demands of presidential power and to use the resources available to him. The nature and limit of his machinery are discussed below.

THE PRESIDENT
AND POLICY CHOICE

Despite the great powers of the office, no President can monopolize the policy process. As the preceding sections have emphasized, the Presidency encompasses a variety of roles, each of which is conditioned by other elements within the system. His style of leadership and his policy choices depend upon the circumstances of constitutional fragmentation, social pluralism, personal relationships, and the diverse and dispersed nature of the two-party system. Overarching these factors is the President's view of his role.

[25] Koenig, *op. cit.*, pp. 13–15.

Whether a President is thrust into policy conflict by force of circumstance or whether he deliberately selects particular disputes that require his leadership, he is confronted by a variety of choices. Theodore C. Sorenson, Special Counsel to President Kennedy, in assessing presidential influence in policy-making, observed, "Any President, in short, must always be setting priorities and measuring costs." [26] The choices available to him are limited by the type and extent of the resources he can command in relation to the interests in conflict. An effective President will be aware of the resources he has available at any particular time. Some matters will provide a greater opportunity for mobility and a larger number of alternatives than will others. The decisions that he finally makes will be based on the available data and the basically immeasurable factors of intuition, hunches, and sheer conviction that one is "right" and others "wrong."

The President does represent all the people and must be sensitive to demands that reach the White House from all sectors of the electorate. He must balance as best he can the demands of a pluralistic constituency. Business, labor, agriculture, regional interests, minority groups, occupational groups — all seek access to the President. A policy alternative acceptable to one interest will be viewed as anathema to another. The same groups will, however, also seek access to Congress and often to the courts. The institutional composition, procedures, and traditions of these branches are in many important respects different from the executive branch (and from each other). Groups with limited access to the President may be in a much better position in relation to Congress or court, a variable that will certainly affect the policy process. Where, for example, the President may view flood control and reclamation primarily as an issue of national-conservation policy, congressmen may perceive it more in terms of an appropriations issue or as a matter of high salience to agricultural water-users in their constituencies. Courts might deal with the same matter in terms of a legal controversy over the water rights of states in the federal system. In shaping his policy goals and winning their acceptance, the President to varying degrees must take factors such as these into account. The process by which issues reach the President, the knowledge he acquires of them, and the sources he relies upon in acquiring such knowledge are of acute importance in his policy choices.

Policy Issues and Policy Choice. Presidential response can sometimes mean the success or failure of the goals of any pressure group. Although few groups have direct access to the President, pressure leaders are often invited to visit with the President for purposes of airing views on issues,

[26] Theodore C. Sorenson, *Decision-Making in the White House* (New York: Columbia University Press, 1963), p. 28.

soliciting support for presidential programs, or bringing the weight of the Presidency in support or opposition to group programs. The presentation of pressure goals and demands is more often accomplished through means other than direct communications with the President. The President listens carefully to congressmen, especially those who occupy key positions in legislative policy-making. Through a congressman, an interest may have its view effectively represented. Within the administrative branch, interests may have a particular spokesman. A Cabinet officer or a member of the President's staff may hold views that parallel those of a pressure group. Thus, that interest will have a significant voice at the highest levels of executive decision-making. Party leaders plead the cause of special interests supporting the party. A President must pay some heed to the party organization that he employs to win reelection. The press is another channel through which issues can be articulated and communicated to the President. A President sometimes finds himself unable to avoid dealing with an issue that has been publicized widely. President Johnson, despite signs that he was reluctant to discuss the issue, was forced to clarify American policy in Viet Nam when the press gave wide-scale coverage to criticisms of administration policy.

Within the President's own circle of advisers and within the bureaucracy, conflicts arise that force the President to decide between the interests represented. State and Treasury Departments sometimes are in fundamental disagreement on the proper approach to world trade; the Defense Department and the Secretary of State may see matters affecting foreign policy quite differently; and the Agriculture Department may view farm-subsidy programs from an entirely different perspective than the Bureau of the Budget. These kinds of conflicts extend far beyond the boundaries of the administrative hierarchy. They represent interest groups at many levels, and they reflect the clash of personalities in the President's own administrative family. The President is ultimately confronted with the necessity of bridging the conflicts.

Some Presidents go out of their way to generate clashes between close advisers in order to obtain all points of view prior to making a policy choice. Franklin Roosevelt delighted in stirring up the strong convictions of a very diverse group of policy subordinates. President Truman made it a practice to seek out opinions of staff members prior to making a decision. Dwight Eisenhower was more prone to demand that agreement be reached on a policy recommendation before it reached him; he could then exercise the option of acceptance or rejection. Again, disagreement marked the deliberative sessions of President Kennedy's advisers. Finally, President Johnson has been widely heralded for his capacity to forge a working consensus from basically incompatible interests voiced by members of his personal staff, Cabinet members, congressional leaders, and pressure-group leaders.

Some decisions are self-generating. The President cannot avoid nominating Supreme Court justices, Cabinet officers, and other officials. Similarly the preparations and presentation of the Budget and the State of the Union addresses are mattters fixed by Constitution and statute. Most decisions are not linked to this kind of inescapable timetable. Some, such as the need to respond quickly to the presence of Soviet missile bases in Cuba in 1962, demand immediate action. Others, such as the question of American policy in Viet Nam, are debated over long periods of time both within and outside the Executive branch before decisions are reached or policies altered. As the Presidency has grown in prestige, prerogatives, and stature, more and more conflicts have gravitated toward that office. The President finds it increasingly difficult to exercise free choice in selecting those conflicts that he personally will attend to.

Policy Access and Policy Choice. When Woodrow Wilson was incapacitated by a stroke, Mrs. Wilson, seeking to insulate her husband from as much strain upon his health as possible, served as the final judge in deciding who could see the President. The President's wife denied that by overseeing his appointments calendar she was running the country; yet, in effect such screening controlled access to presidential deliberations. People permitted to see the President and to offer advice were in a crucial position to influence presidential decisions.

From this example we see how the communications reaching the President have significant bearing on his policy choices. The Presidency as an institution is composed of a vast array of agencies, offices, bureaus, special advisers, and committees available to the Chief Executive. Individual Presidents have utilized available sources of information in substantially different ways. We will better understand presidential leadership if we examine such sources and then view the practices of recent Presidents in utilizing the executive organization.

The Cabinet developed as an extra-constitutional body to "consult" with the President. Some Presidents have viewed it as an important policy-making body; others have utilized it as a means of gathering information through reports, discussions, and debate of major issues. A few Presidents have treated it as little more than a collective meeting of department heads in which pleasantries are exchanged and, at the same time, public expectations that the Cabinet should meet to consider pressing matters are satisfied. The common view of the Cabinet as "the board of directors" of the nation or the President's major source of advice on policy formulation is inconsistent with its actual role during the great part of this century. Richard F. Fenno takes the position that the Cabinet cannot be considered as simply an "ornamental antique" but its function falls short of its image as a high-powered unit that assists the President. He stresses that the Cabinet fails to coordinate relations between the executive departments. Nor is it an effective forum for "well-informed, well-organized discussion of policy alternatives." Its principal uses include advising the President and serving as a sounding board for a variety of interest responses.[27]

Department heads that make up the Cabinet are appointed for a variety of reasons. A need to balance the representation of a diversity of interests and thereby win broad public support is a major consideration in many appointments. President Kennedy named Douglas Dillon, a highly respected Republican businessman who had served in the Eisenhower administration, as Secretary of the Treasury. Robert C. Weaver, appointed by President Johnson to head the new Department of Housing and Urban Development, was the first Negro appointed to a Cabinet post. Dillon's appointment encouraged confidence in Kennedy's fiscal policies and Weaver's appointment received wide support among civil rights groups. Including such considerations in his choice of Cabinet members also provides a President with a variety of views when making decisions. Other factors, including administrative experience, personal relationships (appointing close friends or those in whom he has great confidence), or prior legislative experience may influence a President's selection of Cabinet members.

The fact that the choice of a department head may be dictated by considerations having little or nothing to do with personal confidence in the man as a potential adviser tends to operate against the Cabinet as a major formulator of policy. Secondly, each member of the Cabinet heads a major department. His interests are directed to those of his own department and to the clientele (bureaucratic, congressional and private) it represents and to which it is largely responsible. Those circumstances of particularism and departmentalism diminish the Cabinet's function as a collective body with collective responsibility.

Past Presidents have rarely relied heavily upon the Cabinet as a collegium for advice and counsel in matters of major importance. Individual Cabinet members may be personally influential in the President's policy decisions. More often, the nature of the selection process and the exclusive concerns of Cabinet members have led Presidents to rely more heavily for advice on people personally chosen for such support. Presi-

[27] Richard F. Fenno, Jr., *The President's Cabinet* (Cambridge, Mass.: Harvard University Press, 1959); see also Herman Finer, *The Presidency: Crisis and Regeneration* (Chicago: The University of Chicago Press, 1960), and Wilfred E. Binkley, *The Man in the White House* (Revised Colophon ed.; New York: Harper & Row, Publishers, 1964).

dent Jackson drew advice and counsel from a small group of people who had helped him win the Presidency. Those close advisers reportedly entered the White House through the kitchen door and earned the sobriquet "Kitchen Cabinet." All Presidents have had "kitchen cabinets," although their composition and use have differed with the particular needs of the man in the White House. Franklin Roosevelt gathered around him a small group of men headed by Harry Hopkins. President Truman confided closely in men chosen for their personal loyalty to him and for their knowledge of political affairs. President Eisenhower relied very heavily on Sherman Adams, officially titled Assistant to the President but called by critics "Assistant President." President Kennedy's "kitchen cabinet" consisted of a group of young advisers drawn from the White House staff. Some (Theodore Sorenson, Pierre Salinger, Lawrence F. O'Brien, Kenneth O'Donnell) represented the core of the group of men instrumental in Kennedy's campaign for nomination and election as President. Kennedy relied for advice and counsel upon these men rather than his Cabinet.

Apart from the Cabinet, a total of about twenty-five hundred people — most of whom are specialists of one kind or another — comprise the President's staff. Of these, his personal staff in the White House Office are the "eyes and ears" of the Chief Executive. The Press Secretary, the Appointment Secretary, and staff members assigned for liaison with members of Congress have rather clearly defined duties. The remainder serve in whatever capacity the President desires. Chosen for their loyalty to the President as well as their ability to perform essential services, the White House staff assists the President in gathering information; "reading" the sentiments of congressmen, bureaucrats, and the public; and serving as instruments of presidential leadership. Since the establishment of the White House Office in 1939, journalists have paid increased attention to the men around the President — specifically, to how the President uses these men and how much responsibility he delegates to individual members. Sometimes a President relies heavily upon a particular aide. Woodrow Wilson maintained an especially close relationship with Colonel Edward M. House, who represented the President in important domestic and foreign assignments. Franklin D. Roosevelt had great confidence in Harry Hopkins whose liberal social and economic views became the object of severe criticism by members of both political parties. Such associations serve to highlight a President's dilemma in maintaining the line between using his staff as an *aid* and delegating to it the authority to *make* policy choices. The ultimate boundary must be guarded by the President.

One of the major agencies within the Executive Office is the Bureau of the Budget. Through it the President may command rather than bargain or persuade; he can cajole and threaten as well as plead and sell. Created in 1921, the Bureau was initially located in the Treasury Department. Its purpose was to provide an "executive budget"; that is, to bring under presidential control the formulation of a single budget reflecting the over-all requests of all executive departments and agencies. It was only after 1939 that the Bureau began to serve as a major device for initiating presidential policy. In that year Congress transferred it to the Executive Office, and it has subsequently become a major arm of presidential leadership and control. Appointed by the President (Senate consent to the nominee is not required), the Director of the Bureau is directly responsible for (1) formulating the budget by reviewing departmental appropriations requests and controlling the rate of expenditures after Congress has passed on appropriations; (2) clearing executive-agency requests for legislation to see that they conform to the President's program before they are submitted to Congress; (3) studying and recommending changes in the organization and management of executive agencies; and (4) reviewing and improving (in conjunction with the Treasury Department and the General Accounting Office) financial-management practices.

The way in which a President chooses to utilize the Bureau will determine its position and functions in policy-making. The actions and policies pursued by the Bureau sometimes provide a gauge to the intent of the President; for example, Franklin D. Roosevelt's Director of the Budget was instrumental in developing presidential leadership and initiative. Under President Eisenhower, the Bureau took on the image of an agency concerned more with administrative functions than exerting presidential leadership. Kennedy's Directors of the Budget, David E. Bell and Kermit Gorden, enjoyed relations with the President similar to Roosevelt's Director.

As a device for coordinating administrative interests and programs, the Bureau's review of budget requests is invaluable. Such review can be used to cut into the semi-autonomous policy coalitions that form about executive bureaus and congressional committees. Congressional leaders are ever mindful of this threat and periodically seek to reveal Bureau attempts to "strangle" the initiative and discretion of executive policy formulators. Eisenhower's efforts to coordinate the various military services through budgetary controls proved ineffective when Congress appropriated to the separate services more money than the President had requested. A competition between President and Congress, in which each branch attempts to make the executive agencies dependent upon it alone, may result. The upshot is that such agencies may grow independent of both by playing one against the other.

The President and Vice-President. Historically the Vice-President has often been viewed as a superfluous figure. Constitutionally he is given the job of presiding over the Senate, a position of far less significance than the role of the Speaker of the House of Representatives. The Constitution also designates him as successor in the event of the death, removal, or resignation of the President, or the President's inability to discharge his duties. During the past three or four decades, however, the office of the Vice-Presidency has received increasing respect.

In practice, the Vice-Presidency early became a victim of the American party system. Prior to adoption of the Twelfth Amendment in 1804, the candidate winning the second highest number of electoral votes became Vice-President. After 1804, when electors were required to choose a President and Vice-President separately, the position of the Vice-Presidency was reduced to a means of "balancing" the party ticket. Vice-Presidential candidates were selected less for their potential as occupiers of the highest office than for their usefulness in winning sectional or factional support for the presidential candidate. As a result, the office lost any standing it might have had under other circumstances, a development attested to by the unimpressive caliber of a great many Vice-Presidents. Not until 1841, when Martin Van Buren was elected President, did a Vice-President move to the Presidency by election. Perhaps symbolic of the status of the office prior to recent years is President Truman's testimony that he was unaware of the existence of the atomic bomb when he succeeded Roosevelt to the Presidency in April, 1945.[28]

In the modern era, the sudden death of President Roosevelt in 1944, the heart attack suffered by President Eisenhower in 1955, and the assassination of President Kennedy in 1963 made the American public acutely aware of the possibility of the Vice-President assuming the Presidency. In recent years, Congress has been under strong pressure to provide a procedural basis for succession to the presidency in the event of his incapacity. President Eisenhower had a written agreement with his Vice-President that provided for the Vice-President to assume the duties of the President if he were incapacitated. President Kennedy had a similar agreement with his Vice-President. Some experts suggested this as a better method than reliance on statutes that might be too rigid when applied to specific cases. On the other hand, the problems that would confront the nation (and, more particularly, the Vice-President) in the event of a mentally-unbalanced President or a President completely un-

---

[28] Harry S. Truman, *Memoirs,* Vol. 1, Year of Decisions (Garden City, N.Y.: Doubleday & Co., 1955), pp. 10–11.

able to respond would not be met with the agreement device. Notwithstanding an existing agreement, a Vice-President may be risking serious consequences, including political suicide or at worst impeachment, by assuming the duties of the President under circumstances where doubt was present as to the extent or nature of the President's incapacity. In 1965 Congress submitted to the states the Twenty-fifth Amendment (ratified in 1967) which established procedures for determining presidential incapacity and for allowing the Vice-President to act as President during the interim. Under this amendment the President is also empowered to name — subject to approval by a majority vote in both houses of Congress — a Vice-President if that office becomes vacant.

Another factor that has enhanced the public esteem of the Vice-President is the role that occupants have played in the administrations of recent Presidents. Eisenhower sent Vice-President Nixon on important foreign-policy missions, and Nixon served the President in domestic matters as well. Lyndon Johnson was appointed chairman of the President's Committee on Equal Employment Opportunity, a position that increased his contacts with Negro interests and enhanced his political image with minority groups. Vice-President Humphrey has also served in a number of important roles. In large part, the importance of the Vice-Presidency will depend upon the will of the President. If he is unwilling to utilize the potential services of the Vice-President, there is little the Vice-President can do to develop his importance in decision-making processes. Adoption of the Twenty-Second Amendment which limits a President to two terms in office, may buoy up the political aspirations of the Vice-President, since he becomes, by virtue of his office, a potential candidate for President. Yet the extent a President is willing to use the services of the Vice-President will have significant bearing upon the latter's chances to capture his party's nomination when the President's eligibility has expired. Further, any benefit along these lines accrues to a second-term Vice-President (provided, of course, the President is reelected), and the possibility of a President choosing another running mate after the first term reduces the Vice-President's ability to develop his own image outside the shadow of the President. In fact, a Vice-President may not be able to maintain an image within the party and among the electorate independent of that of the President. Vice-President Humphrey, long identified with the liberal wing of his party, came under severe criticism from liberals over his support of President Johnson's Viet Nam policies. Yet it would be very difficult, and probably impossible, for a Vice-President to oppose administration policies even if he felt strong opposition. The Vice-Presidency is still largely an instrument of the Presidency despite the impressive caliber of recent occupants of the office.

PRESIDENTIAL LEADERSHIP

The President's power is of great magnitude. Originally constituted authority has proved flexible enough to permit vast expansion of action within the prescribed framework. Factors producing that expansion include the continuing growth of a sense of community, an environment of enduring political crises, a gradual nationalization of politics, the emergence of widely shared popular expectations that the President is *the* leader of America, formal delegations of authority, and ever broadening notions held by Presidents of their responsibilities in the twentieth century.

But the President also "wears many chains from which he cannot escape." The same forces that shape the power of the modern Presidency also restrict its exercise. The President is as much bound by constitutional and policy traditions as liberated by them. His constitutional jurisdictions in administrative, military, state, foreign, legislative, and partisan affairs not only overlap but sometimes collide. This incompatibility restricts his capacity to regulate social conflict. He often "muddles through" by increments like other officials. Given the limitations, a President may find it better to bridge disagreements, exploit selected controversies, and even avoid rather than reconcile opposing forces. Some aspects of the Presidency dictate that it is better to put off until tomorrow what *must* be left undone today.

But circumstances are such that not all conflicts can be postponed, circumvented, or exploited. Some must be met head on, and terms of policy must be fixed to deal with them. The President is then forced to accept an environment of restrictions and do what he can within it. Thus, as a leader in making policy, the President must persuade because he can seldom command, must bargain because he cannot coerce.

President Truman once said, "I sit here all day trying to persuade people to do the things that they ought to have sense enough to do without my persuading them. . . . That's all the powers of the President amount to. . . ." President Johnson's invitation to congressmen to "come reason together" reflects a similar emphasis on bargaining and persuasion as the preferred, perhaps the only, methods of exerting presidential policy leadership. What a President wants and what he is capable of achieving are parts of that "discontinuous continuum" (see p. 281) linking citizens and officials. His achievements will depend largely upon his appraisal of when and how he should use his position. There is no formula or clear-cut criteria for presidential leadership that fits all situations. Despite its shell of constitutional tradition, the Presidency is largely an institution whose occupant must "play it by ear."

The Presidency will continue to grow in importance as a fundamental institution of the American political community. The complexity and impersonalism characteristic of contemporary America lead community members to focus their anxieties and aspirations on the President. Some have expressed fears that the modern Presidency heralds an end to our most sacred governing principles — separation of powers, checks and balances, and federalism. From what has been said in this and the preceding chapter, it seems unlikely that presidential leadership will have such an impact for some time to come. Moreover, even if the President does dominate policy leadership, policies must be adopted before they become the law of the land. In the next chapter we shall explore the relation of policy adoption to the processes of formulation and leadership already discussed.

BIBLIOGRAPHICAL NOTE

The Presidency covers virtually all aspects of American politics. Histories of the United States and day-to-day commentaries by journalists are two prime sources of knowledge of the institution in America. The following books are a few of the great number of additional sources on various aspects of the office of President.

There are excellent general treatments of the Presidency. The following are in paperback editions. Edward S. Corwin, *The President: Office and Powers*, 4th edition (New York: New York University Press, 1957) is a classic and thoroughly documented treatment of the office in its constitutional setting; Harold Laski, *The American Presidency* (New York: Grosset & Dunlap, 1940) is a famous Englishman's views of the place of the Presidency in the American system; Clinton Rossiter, *The American Presidency*, 2nd edition (Harvest Book; New York: Harcourt, Brace & Co., 1960) illustrates the growth of presidential powers and describes the multiple roles of modern Presidents; and Richard Neustadt, *Presidential Power* (New York: John Wiley & Sons, Inc., Science Editions, Inc., 1960) defines and illustrates the bargaining context in which presidential power can be utilized. Wilfred Binkley, *President and Congress* (New York: Vintage Books, 1947) is among the most distinguished histories of the Presidency.

The importance and role of presidential advisors are treated in Louis W. Koenig, *The Invisible Presidency* (New York: Henry Holt & Co., 1960). A brief but perceptive and sympathetic view of presidential power and responsibilities by a close presidential advisor is Theodore Sorenson, *Decision-Making in the White House* (New York: Columbia University Press, 1963). Available in paperback: Richard Fenno's *The President's Cabinet* (New York: Vintage Books, 1959) analyzes cabinets and their role from Presidents Wilson to Eisenhower. Sidney Hyman (ed.), *The Office of the American Presidency*, in the *Annals of the American Academy of Political and Social Science* (Vol. 307,

September, 1956) covers a wide variety of aspects of the Presidency ranging from the broadly theoretical to interpretive comments in specific areas. An excellent book of readings, Donald B. Johnson and Jack L. Walker, *The Dynamics of the American Presidency* (New York: John Wiley & Sons, 1964) contains material and commentary on specific aspects of the changing presidential role. Lauren L. Henry, *Presidential Transitions* (Washington, D.C.: The Brookings Institution, 1960) treats the important area of changes in personnel from one administration to the next. Ruth C. Silva, *Presidential Succession* (Ann Arbor: University of Michigan Press, 1951) covers the history and interpretation of provisions pertaining to the inability or death of incumbent presidents. Irving G. Williams, *The American Vice-Presidency: New Look* (New York: Random House, 1954) perceptively views the changing role and the importance of the Vice-Presidency. It is available in paperback.

The changing relationship of the President to courts and to Congress provides a major example of informal constitutional change. In addition to the general works cited earlier, the more specific facets of this relationship are dealt with in the following works. Arthur B. Tourtellet, *The Presidents on the Presidency* (Garden City, N.Y.: Doubleday & Co., 1964) provides perspective on how incumbents have differed in their views as to their constitutional powers and leadership role; Lawrence H. Chamberlain, *The President, Congress and Legislation* (New York: Columbia University Press, 1956) reveals the presidential role as chief legislator; Glendon A. Schubert, Jr., *The Presidency in the Courts* (Minneapolis: University of Minnesota Press, 1957) shows and analyzes the ability of the judiciary to restrain presidential power; J. Malcolm Smith and Cornelius P. Cotter, *Powers of the President During Crises* (Washington: Public Affairs Press, 1960) discusses an especially relevant area for the contemporary era.

There are many excellent autobiographies, biographies, and other works on particular presidents and their administrations. Those listed below are representative of the best work in this area. Available in paperback editions are: Marquis James, *Andrew Jackson: Portrait of a President* (New York: Universal Library, 1937); John M. Blum, *The Republican Roosevelt* (New York: Atheneum, 1954); Robert E. Sherwood, *Roosevelt and Hopkins: An Intimate History* (New York: Universal Library, 1948). In hardback editions are: Theodore Roosevelt, *Autobiography* (New York: Charles Scribner's Sons, 1946); Harry S. Truman, *Memoirs*, 2 vols. (New York: Doubleday & Co., 1955); Henry F. Pringle, *The Life and Times of William Howard Taft* (New York: Farrar & Rinehart, 1939); James MacGregor Burns, *Roosevelt: The Lion and the Fox* (New York: Harcourt, Brace, & World, 1956); Theodore Sorenson, *Kennedy* (New York: Harper & Row, 1965); and William S. White, *The Professional: Lyndon B. Johnson* (Boston: Houghton Mifflin, 1964).

CHAPTER
THIRTEEN

Policy Adoption

At some point in the process of negotiating final policy in a liberal democracy, there is a need for an overt public demonstration of the acceptability and desirability of decisions. In popular democracy that support is engendered through the vote of all political participants in the community. But in a republic the legitimacy of public policy is obscured by the fact that those who obey the law take no active part in formulating it. If they are bound at all, it is through the actions of popularly chosen representatives who consent to the desirability of policies in the name of community members. It is this act of accepting the final terms of negotiated policy on behalf of the community and thereby rendering the policy legitimate that we label policy adoption.

CONGRESS AND PUBLIC POLICY

Traditionally we have come to view legislative bodies as the places of final reckoning in matters of policy-making. One of the long-term effects of the American Revolution was a continuing popular suspicion of executive authority. In the era of the Articles of Confederation both state and central authority (what there was of it) was lodged in legislative bodies. Under both the Virginia Plan and the New Jersey Plan for constitutional

353

revision in 1789, the heart of the governing process was a national congress with sweeping jurisdiction. Despite the gradual domination of presidential leadership in this century, the Congress of the United States continues to occupy a pivotal position in the making of public policy and to serve as a continuing challenge to presidential policy formulation.

Although Congress adopts policy, it is not the sole locale of this activity. In American government there are relatively few cases in which the President, administrative bureaucracy, or courts are given sole jurisdiction for policy adoption. The working principle of checks and balances projects each governing institution into the affairs of others. We cite here a few examples that illustrate the overlapping nature of policy adoption. Although two-thirds of the U.S. Senate must agree to final adoption of treaties with other nations, the President may negotiate executive "agreements" or "compacts" without congressional approval. Since in the modern era, however, Congress must appropriate the funds necessary to carry out presidential agreements, it has been able to maintain some control over such agreements. But even here there is a vast difference between obtaining a simple majority (one more than half of those voting) in both houses of Congress and achieving two-thirds agreement in one. A treaty requires the approval of two-thirds of Senators voting on the measure; thus, a relatively small minority can block its implementation. Appropriations bills, on the other hand, require action of both houses but a simple majority vote reduces the opportunity for veto by the minority. The result is to place the President in a stronger position in foreign policy adoption. Moreover, in recent decades Congress occasionally has delegated to the President the authority to adopt final policy within broad limits placed by Congress. For example, under reciprocal trade-agreements legislation, the President (more specifically, his administrative subordinates) negotiates reductions in tariffs with foreign nations. Thus, Congress has not only shifted some of its authority to adopt policy to the President but has also relieved itself of many of the pressures formerly brought upon congressmen by groups seeking favorable trade arrangements and price protections.

Administrative agencies also adopt policies in final form. This is especially true of regulatory agencies that are given the authority to formulate, adopt, apply, and interpret policies governing the behavior of specific economic interests (see Chapter Fourteen). Courts are also policy adopters. The Supreme Court, in declaring a legislative act unconstitutional (as it did in many instances prior to 1940, but less so today) has challenged Congress' function of rendering policy legitimate. In so doing, it has reinforced the legitimate position and claims of other institutions in the policy process. In other instances, it has placed the final seal of approval on policies adopted by Congress, as it did in upholding the legitimacy of the provisions of the 1964 Civil Rights Act, which provided for equality of opportunity for service in public restaurants, cafeterias, etc.

In addition to adopting policy, Congress often formulates policy. Hence, policy activities of congressmen really amount to both *adoption* and *modification* of policy proposals. The legislative process is an intricate and often bewildering series of relationships, procedures, and circumstances that are difficult to unravel. Yet there are broad patterns of activity that tend to recur. Institutional arrangements generally fix the boundaries within which decisions are made. Moreover, there are a multitude of informal relationships, less easily identified, but of major importance to the process of policy adoption. By exploring the general contours of the legislative process, we can get some idea of the factors that shape the policy choices of congressmen and the forces that contribute to congressional perspectives and pressures.

PATTERNS OF CONGRESSIONAL PERSPECTIVE

The policy view from Capitol Hill is every bit as varied as it is from the other end of Pennsylvania Avenue – the White House. There are 535 different outlooks on what the individual congressman should do for his constituency, for the American community, and for himself. Congressional perspectives filter the more salient policy pressures that reach the legislator. Those perspectives are molded by several factors: the bases of congressional representation, the boundaries of constitutional authority, the nature of congressional partisanship, the energy of congressional leadership, the form of congressional organization, and the procedures by which policies are adopted. In conjunction with the modes of policy pressure and formulation discussed earlier, each operates to shape patterns of policy adoption in American government.

CONTOURS OF CONGRESSIONAL REPRESENTATION

The legislative branch, as the most "representative" branch within the American constitutional structure, is probably the major institutional symbol of the democratic creed. The slogan of the American colonists, "No taxation without representation," was symbolic of a more basic conviction: the people must not only be represented but must be permitted to participate in the selection of those who would represent them. The Framers of the Constitution provided for an executive removed from direct control of the people and a judiciary given independence and insulation from the majority. Although one of its Houses was to be selected only indirectly by the people (senators were chosen by state legislatures) and was based on area rather than population, the national legislature was nevertheless designed to reflect the "will of the people" to a greater extent than either of the other two branches. It was only after the Seventeenth Amendment was ratified that senators were subject to direct election by the people.

What exactly is meant by congressional representation? Generally a congressman "represents" a constituency to the extent that he is delegated the authority to speak for that constituency in the adoption of policies and to make binding commitments for it. The problem lies in defining "fair" representation. The perspective one may take in arriving at a definition will depend, of course, upon the Constitution, pertinent statutes, and social backgrounds of representatives. It may also depend upon a personal definition of what it is that a representative *ought* to represent.

The Bases of Congressional Representation. No method for apportioning representatives is neutral. Some interests will be advantaged and others disadvantaged by any arrangement. Although a two-house legislature (bicameral) is not an essential feature of a federal system it is part of the institutional arrangements through which the federal principle was incorporated into the Constitution. The federal bargain struck at Philadelphia in 1787 provided for representation of states in the Senate and representation based on population in the House of Representatives. This system of representation and the bicameral arrangement have significantly shaped the patterns of congressional policy adoption.

The Constitution requires that each state have equal representation in the Senate notwithstanding the size of its population. This produces striking patterns. Alaska, with a population in 1960 of about 250,000, is given the same representation as California and New York. The combined population in 1960 of the states of Alaska, Delaware, Idaho, Nevada, Vermont, and Wyoming was roughly equal to the population of Kansas. Yet Kansas (not a populous state) has two senators, and the other six states combined have twelve. The federal principle also is reflected in the composition of the House of Representatives. Congress fixes by statute the size of the House (currently set at 435 members) and also distributes seats to each state on the basis of population. Each state must be granted at least one representative notwithstanding its population, a requirement that tends to distort accurate apportionment. Using the example cited above, in 1960 the six states whose population was roughly equal to the population of Kansas elected seven representatives to Kansas' five.

Bicameralism works with federalism in shaping formal representation patterns. Since senators are elected by statewide popular vote, they normally respond to a wider spectrum of interests than a member of the

House would. The representative from an Illinois district that is primarily rural and agricultural deals with a constituency different from that of an Illinois senator, who must concern himself with Chicago voters as well as those of rural areas. Under these circumstances, the perspective on issues among representatives and senators will be different.

Not only are the constituencies of senators more heterogeneous than those of House members, but there is evidence to indicate that senators support "liberal" measures to a greater extent. Lewis A. Froman, Jr., compared House and Senate constituencies on the basis of population factors usually associated with liberal and conservative policy stands; per cent of non-white constituents, per cent urban dwellers, and per cent owner-occupied dwelling units.[1] Where the per cent of non-white and the per cent urban were higher than the state averages, and where the per cent owner-occupied dwelling units was *lower,* the district was classified as liberal. Since senators are elected by the entire state, the state averages on these characteristics would be the senator's constituency. Froman found that there were more House districts within the conservative classification; that is, more were below the state averages on the first two criteria and above on the third. His evidence also demonstrated that senators supported liberal legislation more than House members. Liberalism was defined in terms of ten major proposals in President Kennedy's domestic welfare program in 1961. Included were bills in such areas as civil rights, aid to education, minimum wage, social security, housing, unemployment, and aid to depressed areas. Although the Senate did not support all ten proposals to a greater extent than the House, Froman found that the Senate was generally more liberal on these measures.

Social Backgrounds of Congressmen and the Representative Pattern. The preponderance of congressmen from certain occupational and social-class groupings also raises questions as to the representative nature of Congress. Legally, any person meeting the age, residency, and citizenship requirements under Article I of the Constitution is eligible to serve. In fact, eligibility is considerably more limited. Viewed in terms of their social and occupational backgrounds, congressmen "speak mainly in the idiom and accents of the middle and upper classes."[2] They are better educated than the average American. A majority are of professional, business, and farming occupational groups; lawyers, for example, constitute about 1 per cent of the labor force yet occupy one-fourth to one-half of legislative seats. The average age of all Americans is ten to twenty years

[1] Lewis A. Froman, Jr., *Congressmen and their Constituencies* (Chicago: Rand McNally & Co., 1963), pp. 71–84.
[2] William J. Keefe and Morris S. Ogul, *The American Legislative Process* (Englewood Cliffs, N.J.: Prentice-Hall, 1964), p. 126.

lower than that of representatives and senators. Negroes constitute more than 10 per cent of the population, yet only six of their number served in Congress in 1965. Elected in 1966, Edward W. Brooke of Massachusetts became the first Negro senator in almost one hundred years. In 1959, 36 per cent of church members were Catholic, yet only 19 per cent of congressmen were of that faith. Despite their proportion of the total electorate, only ten women served in the House and two in the Senate in 1966.[3]

The statistics cited above suggest that there are certain characteristics generally necessary for success in seeking legislative office. "Both the local party and the constituency tend to select representatives who reflect the dominant social values in the district. . . . Recruiters must find a candidate whose social affiliations enable him to win the confidence and support of his neighbors."[4] In some areas of the nation, candidate recruitment and selection reflect the heavy concentration of particular religious, racial, or minority groups. For example, in large Northern urban areas with heavy concentrations of Negroes or Catholics, successful candidates for House seats are drawn from these minority groups. Although senatorial constituencies are large, and thus include a larger number and variety of social groups, these factors may still apply. It is considerably more likely, for example, that a Catholic will be elected in Massachusetts than in Mississippi where the population is predominantly Protestant. As the franchise is effectively extended to areas in the South, more Negro candidates are likely to be recruited and elected.

Important to an understanding of the representative system is the extent to which occupational interests affect or determine legislative policy-making. A recent study on the relation of the legal profession and policy-making in four state legislatures found no evidence to support the belief that lawyers are more conservative than other occupational groups.[5] On the other hand, Donald R. Matthews found that on fifteen major issues in the Eighty-first Congress a number of occupational, religious, and sectional groups showed greater unity in roll-call votes than Republicans and Democrats. Yet Matthews cautioned that such studies "indicate only correlation, not cause and effect."[6]

In some cases, the fact that some groups are underrepresented may

[3] On the implications of the lack of representativeness in Congress see the Report of the Twenty-sixth American Assembly, The Congress and America's Future (New York: The American Assembly, 1964).

[4] Herbert Jacob and Kenneth N. Vines (ed.), Politics in the American States (Boston: Little, Brown & Co., 1965), p. 166.

[5] Heinz Eulau and John D. Sprague, Lawyers in Politics (New York: Bobbs-Merrill Co., 1964), p. 26.

[6] Donald R. Matthews, The Social Background of Political Decision-Makers (New York: Doubleday & Co., 1954), pp. 40–41.

mean that certain interests are not heard. Southern Negroes have had little access to those who represent their district or state. As a national group, Negroes have been vastly underrepresented in numbers in both houses of Congress, a factor which contributed to their seeking redress of grievances through the judicial and executive branches.

Yet the fact that some occupational groups are overrepresented in relation to their numbers does not mean that access is denied to other occupational interests. Where overrepresentation exists, some benefits may result; but until more systematic studies are made regarding the relationship between occupational and social backgrounds and legislative behavior, conclusions must be very cautiously drawn. Congress is sensitive to demands of many groups despite the fact that its membership fails to reflect an accurate cross-section of the national population. Considering, for example, the amount and scope of social and economic legislation supported by, and beneficial to, underrepresented socio-economic groups in the system, it seems rather obvious that these groups have access to the legislative policy-makers.

Legislative Apportionment: The Key to Power. Since 1930, by action of Congress, the 435 seats in the House have been automatically redistributed among the states on the basis of the decennial census. The drawings of congressional districts within states, or redrawing them in the event of gain or loss of congressional representation is a task of state legislatures. A state legislature can affect the basis of representation in two major respects: *malapportionment* can produce inequities in district populations; *gerrymandering* maximizes the electoral strength of the legislative majority and minimizes that of the minority party.

In 1963 Andrew Hacker found that 41 per cent of congressional districts were inequitably drawn.[7] Hacker's standard of equitable representation was obtained by determining the average number of people that ideally should comprise each state's congressional districts if apportioned in direct proportion to population. He then computed the extent to which districts varied from this norm. A variation of 15 per cent from this average, either up or down, was considered equitable; districts outside this range were termed inequitable. Projecting population changes and present trends to the Ninety-second Congress (1971–72), Hacker predicted that by that date 63 per cent of congressional districts would be classified as inequitable. In 1964 the U.S. Supreme Court ruled in *Wesberry* v. *Sanders* that when wide discrepancies in number of persons contained in each congressional district existed, the equal protection clause of the Fourteenth Amendment was violated. The impact of this decision

---

[7] Andrew Hacker, *Congressional Districting: The Issue of Equal Representation* (Washington, D.C.: The Brookings Institution, 1963), p. 104.

can be measured by noting statistics compiled by the *Congressional Quarterly*.[8] Between the *Wesberry* decision and May, 1966, twenty-seven states — containing 258 House districts — had redistricted either under direct court order or as the result of the Supreme Court's action. Six other states, containing 79 congressional districts, were expected to redistrict by 1968. In 1965 the House of Representatives approved a bill requiring that congressional districts may not deviate more than 15 per cent from the average district population in each state, but the full Senate took no action on the bill in either 1965 or 1966. Only two of the twenty-seven states which have redistricted since 1964 would fail to meet the standard set by the House proposal.

Considering these developments, Hacker's predictions will most probably not be realized. Thus far, federal courts have varied in their acceptance or rejection of deviations in the size of districts. In three states where federal courts have themselves redistricted as a result of failure of the state legislature to set equitable standards, maximum population variations between districts approved have ranged from about 8 per cent in Arizona to about 3 per cent in Montana.

As a result of malapportionment over the past three or four decades, suburban, and to a lesser extent urban, sectors of America have been underrepresented. Rural districts are generally smaller in population and often are drawn so as to make the district "safe" for the incumbent congressmen. Although the Supreme Court in the *Wesberry* decision outlawed excessively malapportioned districts, state legislative majorities can distinctly aid the majority party within the state without creating wide discrepancies in the population of districts. Gerrymandering, a practice which can be traced back to the Eighteenth Century, is the drawing of district lines by the majority party in the state legislature so as to maximize the advantage of the majority party. Another device, the *silent* gerrymander, achieves the same end by failing to redraw congressional districts (provided the state's representation in the House has not been increased or reduced) despite major shifts of population within the state.

What are the effects of these practices on the legislative process? Evidence is scattered and incomplete yet by no means lacking. James M. Burns points out, "The basis of the congressional system is the one-party district, as established and protected by the state legislatures."[9] About one-half of the 435 House seats are consistently held by the same party, and another one-fourth rarely change from one party to the other. Most

---

[8] *Congressional Quarterly Weekly Report*, XXIV (April 15, 1966), 812–14.
[9] James M. Burns, *The Deadlock of Democracy* (Englewood Cliffs, N.J.: Prentice-Hall, 1963), p. 241.

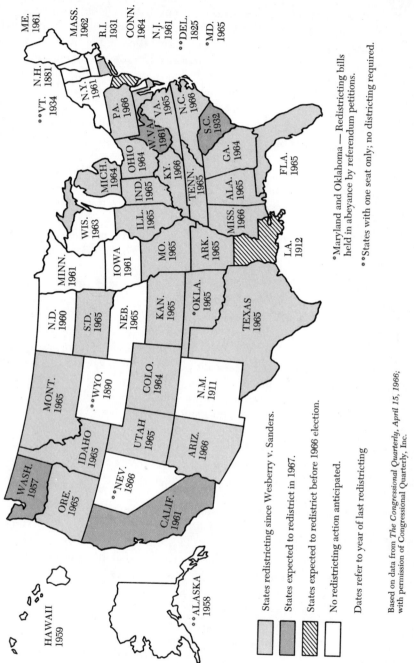

CONGRESSIONAL REDISTRICTING: STATUS IN THE 50 STATES

ME.
1961

MASS.
1962

R.I.
1931

CONN.
1964

N.J.
1961

°°DEL.
1825

°MD.
1965

°°VT.
1934

N.H.
1881

N.Y.
1961

PA.
1966

W.VA. VA.
1961 1965

N.C.
1966

S.C.
1932

OHIO
1964

IND.
1965

KY.
1966

GA.
1964

MICH.
1964

TENN.
1965

ALA.
1965

FLA.
1965

ILL.
1965

MO.
1965

MISS.
1966

ARK.
1965

LA.
1912

WIS.
1963

IOWA
1961

MINN.
1961

N.D.
1960

S.D.
1965

NEB.
1965

KAN.
1965

°OKLA.
1965

TEXAS
1965

MONT.
1965

°°WYO.
1890

COLO.
1964

N.M.
1911

IDAHO
1965

UTAH
1965

ARIZ.
1966

WASH.
1957

ORE.
1965

°°NEV.
1866

CALIF.
1961

HAWAII
1959

°°ALASKA
1958

°Maryland and Oklahoma — Redistricting bills
held in abeyance by referendum petitions.

°°States with one seat only; no districting required.

States redistricting since Wesberry v. Sanders.

States expected to redistrict in 1967.

States expected to redistrict before 1966 election.

No redistricting action anticipated.

Dates refer to year of last redistricting

Based on data from The Congressional Quarterly, April 15, 1966;
with permission of Congressional Quarterly, Inc.

one-party districts are located in rural areas of the Democratic South and the Republican Northeast and Midwest. Since incumbent congressmen from one-party districts are reelected with little, and in many instances no, opposition, they tend to build seniority in Congress. Seniority is the major factor in acquiring committee chairmanships. Thus, key positions are monopolized by congressmen who represent rurally based interests.

Where urban-based interests are denied an equitable access to Congress, the tendency has been to look to the President for representation. The Presidency has become the spokesman for urban voters, a development due partly to the fact that urban voters constitute the vast bulk of the presidential constituency. Rurally biased representation also affects genuine competition between the two parties: rurally based congressmen, despite their party affiliation, often adopt positions more consistent with rural interests than the party leadership in Congress. The "presidential party" (largely based upon urban interests) is often frustrated by congressmen in key positions (for example, committee chairmanships) whose views are more representative of rural voters.

It should be recalled, however, that in 1789 there were few common interests that transcended all areas. The mercantile interests that had to be served, for example, were those primarily from New York, Baltimore, Philadelphia, or some other area. But in the modern era locally based interests ally themselves and cross the boundaries of congressional districts. The result is that large-scale pressure organizations are interested in community-wide legislation beyond the more parochial interests and activities of the local district. Arthur Bentley accurately gauged the impact of this social transformation long ago: "What we have therefore is a collection of congressmen and senators, coming from locality groups, which in comparison with the powerful interest groups that function through Congress, are of a formal nature, answering more as a technical means of election than a real embodiment of the strong existing lines of pressure." [10]

The Perspective of Congressional Representation. When confronted during a campaign with the charge that he had consistently voted against the legislative program of President Eisenhower, a midwestern Republican senator justified his position on grounds that he voted the way "his people" felt about the issues in question, in spite of contrary views that the "national interest" or "party welfare" was being sacrificed. In this instance, the legislator viewed himself as an agent of his constituency rather than a presidential ally.

What interests ought a congressman to represent? A classic answer to this question was offered by Edmund Burke who, following his election

[10] Arthur Bentley, *The Process of Government* (Bloomington, Ind.: The Principia Press, Inc., 1949), p. 369.

to the House of Commons from Bristol constituency, told his constituents: "Parliament is a *deliberative* assembly of *one* nation, with one interest, that of the whole — where not local purpose, not local prejudices, ought to guide, but the general good, resulting from the general reason of the whole. You choose a member, indeed; but when you have chosen him, he is not a member of Bristol, but he is a member of Parliament." [11] Burke's refusal to sacrifice his personal judgment for the demands of his constituents has been echoed by many legislators. Behind this stance lies the assertion that constituents may not know the facts or otherwise may fail to understand them. Under these conditions the representative better "represents" them, despite the fact that his view may be clearly at odds with what the people in his district say they want. In contrast to the Burkean emphasis on conscience and independent judgment is the view that the constituents should be given what they want. All congressmen are sensitive to the ultimate decision of the voters. Failure to take into account constituency views may result in defeat at the polls.

There is relatively little empirical data in the literature of political science on the relationship between legislators and their constituents. How does a congressman acquire his knowledge of constituency views? Is the congressman's vote on legislative matters determined more by his own preferences or those of the people he represents? Warren E. Miller and Donald Stokes attempted to compare the votes of 116 members of the House of Representatives with the views of their constituents.[12] Constituency opinion was learned by interviewing constituents within a district on three policy issues: civil rights, American involvement in foreign affairs, and social welfare legislation. The extent to which the representative and constituents were aware of each other's stands on these matters was also measured.

Miller and Stokes concluded from their findings that representatives were influenced by constituency attitudes in civil rights and social welfare matters (especially the former), but district opinion had little bearing on how they voted on foreign-policy matters. On the question of awareness, the authors found: "The Representative has very imperfect information about the issue preferences of his constituency, and the constituency's awareness of the policy stands of the Representative is ordinarily slight." Despite the lack of a high degree of awareness among both congressmen and constituents, representatives were not free to vote as they pleased. The majority of congressmen *assume* their record is crucial to their re-election. Also, while only a small number of constituents may be aware

[11] Edmund Burke, *Works* (Boston: Little, Brown & Co., 1886), II, 95–96.
[12] Warren E. Miller and Donald E. Stokes, "Constituency Influence in Congress," *The American Political Science Review*, LVII (March, 1963), 45–56; Charles L. Clapp, *The Congressman: His Work as He Sees It* (Washington, D.C. : The Brookings Institution, 1963), pp. 50–103.

of their congressman's record, many are able to acquire a general impression of his positions. Finally, freedom of action is further limited if a congressman deliberately avoids taking a stand that will arouse voter awareness. Some congressmen avoid action that will lose votes even though inaction will not win votes either.

Lewis A. Dexter's study of the relationship between the policy stands of the representative and the views of his constituents led him to the following assertion: "The fact is that the Congressman represents his image of the district or of his constituents (or fails to represent his, or her, image of them)." [13] Dexter's findings — based on 650 interviews with congressmen, administrators, and leaders of interest groups — emphasized the difficulty of knowing what constituents' views are on an issue. What a congressman hears is affected by the source of his information, his understanding of the facts, and how he views his job and his constituency. "The notion of the congressmen representing 'the' district at least needs restatement," says Dexter, "*in terms of a particular congressman who represents what he hears from the district as he interprets it.*" What he hears is usually the views of those close to him and those who agree with him, and he tends to filter what he hears through his own biases of what policy ought to be.

The elected legislator comes to Congress with attitudes and relationships that he cannot cast aside. His social background, group associations, and convictions affect the manner and tone of his constituency relationships, his relations with colleagues, and his attitudes toward the political community itself. His membership in the House or Senate adds another dimension to already existing group associations. These memberships overlap. Some pressure groups, for example, are given special access if a large number of congressmen are affiliated with the group. Since one-third to one-half of the members of Congress are members of the American Legion, the access of that organization is considerably enhanced. Similarly the United States Chamber of Commerce enjoys access to Congress as a result of having a large number of its members in that body.

The environment in which legislative policy is made includes expectations as well as affiliations that provide advantages or disadvantages to exclusive interests. Among these expectations are behavioral norms set by the public at large and also by the legislative body itself. A congressman is expected to observe standards of conduct held by the American public. These include avoiding relationships and associations (at least openly) that raise questions about his honesty or ability to weigh evidence

---

[13] Lewis Anthony Dexter, "The Representative and His District," in Robert L. Peabody and Nelson W. Polsby (ed.), *New Perspectives On The House of Representatives* (Chicago: Rand McNally & Co., 1963), pp. 3–29.

impartially, defending orderly procedures so that the opposition gets its day in court, and observing generally accepted norms of personal behavior outside the legislative halls.

Legislative membership also carries with it the expectation that the informal standards of behavior established by the legislative body itself will be observed. In the words of Professor David B. Truman, Congress "has its standards and conventions, its largely unwritten system of obligations and privileges. . . . The neophyte must conform, at least in some measure, if he hopes to make effective use of his position."[14] If a member of the House of Representatives (especially a freshman legislator) fails to "go along" with the customs of the House, he will usually be unable to accomplish his goals. These "folkways" are of even greater importance in the Senate where they apply to participation in debate, the need to specialize in a particular area of legislative interests, rules of courtesy, loyalty to the Senate, and serving an "apprenticeship" period before assuming full status in the Senate. Although there are nonconformists and "mavericks" (they are usually found among senators with liberal dispositions, presidential aspirants, and ex-governors) most senators conform to these folkways.[15] In a television interview in July, 1965, Senate Minority Leader Everett M. Dirksen observed that Senate folkways and practices had frustrated and broken some freshmen senators who came to the Senate as recognized potential leaders. Senator Robert M. Kennedy, a major national figure before his election to the Senate, waited six months before delivering a major address on the floor of the Senate. Even then, some of his colleagues thought he had spoken too soon for a freshman senator.

This atmosphere of the so-called Senate "Establishment" or "Club" also conditions perspectives of Senatorial representation. William S. White distinguishes between those senators who belong to the "inner" club and those who belong to the "outer" club. The latter group consists of all senators, while the "inner" club is composed primarily of Southern Democrats and senators of both parties from other areas of the nation. Members of this inner group, says White, "express consciously or unconsciously, the deepest instincts and prejudices of 'the Senate type.'"[16] No explicit qualifications for membership exist, but it is this core that is sometimes perceived as "running" the Senate through its control of im-

[14] David B. Truman, *The Governmental Process* (New York: Alfred A. Knopf, 1955), p. 344.

[15] For a full discussion of Senate conventions and their operation see Donald R. Matthews, "The Folkways of the United States Senate: Conformity to Group Norms and Legislative Effectiveness," *The American Political Science Review,* LIII (December, 1959), 1064–89.

[16] William S. White, *The Citadel: The Story of the U.S. Senate* (New York: Harper & Bros., 1956), Chap. VII.

portant party posts, committee chairmanships, and legislative leadership. In 1963 Senator Joseph Clark charged that an "Establishment" controlled the Senate. This elite, which he characterized as "the antithesis of democracy," is composed largely of political conservatives from the Democratic South and Republican conservative senators. By virtue of having acquired seniority status, this group effectively manages the majority of committee chairmanships and other important posts.[17] Whether such control is quite as stringent as Clark charges is open to question, yet senatorial perspectives are in some instances shaped by the belief that such control does exist. Those senators who support the position of Senator Clark will view their relationship to the legislative process from a different perspective than will the "Establishment." Also, interests which seek access to decision-making processes must take into account the norms and expectations of legislators. "In a stable political system the competing demands of organized interest groups are meaningless unless they are viewed in the context of these limiting and defining norms."[18]

In sum, what any senator or representative can accomplish will be the product of a great number of things, but these would certainly include his personal views of what a representative ought to do; the way he views the characteristics and desires of his constituents; the extent to which he observes the customs of the house in which he serves; and the position he occupies by virtue of seniority, party (majority or minority), or status (committee memberships or party post). In the larger sense, representation of interests is obviously affected by the basis of apportionment of congressmen. Federalism as it is reflected in the bicameral arrangement; the practice of gerrymandering; the malapportionment of House districts, clearly obstruct some interests and enhance others. The American political community is one of multiple access. Congress is one major institutional mechanism legitimatizing the compromises that emerge from the struggle between interests within the political system. Legislators also ratify compromises reached among official and nonofficial interests operating within other governmental agencies as well as the legislature. In so doing, Congress helps shape the nature of those compromises.

CONTOURS OF CONSTITUTED CONGRESSIONAL
AUTHORITY AND STRUCTURE

Article I of the Constitution provides for a broad scope of legislative jurisdiction and authority. Discretion to raise and support an Army and Navy, tax and spend for the general welfare, borrow money, regulate commerce, coin money, establish courts, declare war, establish post

17 Joseph S. Clark *et. al.*, *The Senate Establishment* (American Century Series; New York: Hill and Wang, 1963).
18 Truman, *op. cit.*, p. 351.

offices, and govern the capital district, provide the broad basis for legislation. Article I, Section 8 — the "necessary and proper" clause — laid the basis for the implied-powers doctrine voiced by John Marshall in *McCulloch* v. *Maryland.* In Chapter Four we also noted the interpretation of legislative prerogative under this doctrine has advanced the extension of national legislative authority into virtually every major area of community affairs.

The power of Congress is nevertheless limited in a number of ways by the working principle of balanced government.[19] The presidential veto and judicial review are major potential limitations on congressional authority. So, too, the separation-of-powers doctrine prohibits legislative encroachment on the jurisdiction of the other two branches. The separation principle also limits the extent to which Congress may delegate to administrative or judicial agencies matters which are "legislative" in nature. Congress itself restrains actions of the other two branches. Treaties, major appointments of the President, and all appointments to the federal courts must be approved by the Senate. The authority to impeach resides with the House of Representatives, and impeachment trials are conducted by the Senate. Through its ability to investigate and appropriate funds, Congress possesses the legal means to check and supervise the operations of both coordinate branches.

Four other responsibilities complete this general listing of constitutional provisions for legislative authority. First, by a two-thirds vote of both houses, Congress may propose constitutional amendments. Second, new states are admitted to the Union by legislative action. Third, the power to investigate and hold hearings enables Congress to educate and inform the public (as well as itself) on social and economic problems and other matters of public importance. Finally, Congress performs an elective function. In the event that no candidate wins a majority of electoral votes, the House selects the President and the Senate selects the Vice-President.

To say that Congress adopts policies implies that proposals are initiated elsewhere. In fact, most major legislation is generated by administrative officials, interest groups, parties, policy clusters, and by the President. Congress is the arena in which struggles over the appropriateness of public policy take place. Congressmen are faced with the pressures and counterpressures related to proposed policy choices. The bargain of 1787 that produced a bicameral legislature sewed into the policy process a tension that has never truly been relieved despite the emergence of partisanship, presidential coordination and policy coalitions.

That tension marks the policy process is illustrated by recalling the

---

[19] For specific constitutional restraints see Article I, Section 9 of the Constitution of the United States.

nature of Senate and House constituencies. We noted that the larger, more heterogeneous constituency of a senator, coupled with direct election since 1913, has tended to produce a different legislative perspective for a senator than for a member of the House of Representatives. Both chambers must concur in the passage of legislation. As a result, a "conservative" House can block (largely through its committee system) legislation passed by the more "liberal" Senate. Yet differences between the Houses on the liberal-conservative spectrum should not be over-emphasized. On some matters, such as civil rights legislation, procedural rules of the Senate (for example, the filibuster, discussed on page 385) have permitted the Senate to block legislation already passed by the House. House procedural rules are stricter than those in the Senate, a factor that enables House leadership to control the agenda and procedures in that body. To some degree, party organization is stronger in the House, a difference attributable in part to the greater degree of independence demanded by senators. Moreover, the six-year term of senators, as compared to the two-year term of House members, tends to provide senators with a greater degree of flexibility in making policy choices. Where elections are further removed in time, a senator is less conscious of the hazards of opposing constituency wishes.

With the exception of special Senate prerogatives in foreign affairs (for example, approval of treaties) and presidential appointments, and the constitutional requirement that all revenue bills must originate in the House, the legal authority of both branches is much the same. In terms of overall procedures and organization — with some significant exceptions — the two houses also operate in much the same fashion. Both place great emphasis and prestige on committee and leadership selection through seniority. Finally, the smaller size of the Senate enhances the public awareness and prestige of the individual senator as compared to a representative. Rarely, if at all, do senators aspire to membership in the House. Representatives, on the other hand, frequently seek the greater prestige (and longer term) that accompanies a Senate seat. Yet those members of the House who hold significant positions of leadership and control seldom seek a Senate position. Influence in the legislative process is not necessarily dependent upon which house of Congress a member serves in. His legislative perspective and importance are governed far more by the position he holds in the congressional organization of the House of Representatives or the Senate.

CONTOURS OF PARTISAN
CONGRESSIONAL ORGANIZATION

As discussed earlier, uneven distribution of access to congressional policy-makers is conditioned in part by legal factors of apportionment and constitutional structure. Policy access is also a function of the internal organization of each house in the bicameral legislative body. The partisan character of that internal organization is of particular importance. Where partisan control rests in the hands of a clearly identified individual or group, there are means for disciplining members of Congress and thereby both commanding and persuading them to convert party programs into public policy. But if party influence is scattered among a number of individuals who are not held responsible for their actions, the individual legislator is more likely to operate from autonomous bases of support. If this is the case, social interests can facilitate unobstructed access to legislative policy-making by negotiating mutually beneficial exchanges of support between themselves and congressmen.

Between the 1964 and 1966 parliamentary elections in Great Britain, the Labour party held a three-vote majority in the House of Commons. Although it had difficulties maintaining control with such a slim margin, it successfully fought off repeated threats from the Conservatives. One key to understanding the British arrangement is party discipline. A member of Parliament is expected by his party and constituents to support partisan positions on issues designated by party leaders as crucial.

Biennial congressional elections produce a majority party and a minority, yet virtually the only occasion in the American Congress when all Republicans vote in opposition to all Democrats is at the beginning of each session. The first item of business in each chamber is to "organize": to select the Speaker of the House, the President *pro tempore* of the Senate, majority and minority floor leaders, and to name the members of the standing committees. Not unexpectedly, the candidates offered by the majority party are elected. Once the key posts are safely in the hands of the majority party, partisan behavior takes on an image of two highly fragmented groups, and, as Bertram Gross has characterized it, "in the great majority of legislative struggles the major parties are observers on the side lines." [20]

Although Gross's evaluation is to some extent an overstatement of the character of party cohesion in Congress, we have already noted the parochial nature of the American party system in Chapter Nine; in this chapter we have talked about the localized nature of congressional constituencies as compared to the presidential constituency. In his widely discussed and debated book, *The Deadlock of Democracy*, James MacGregor Burns has argued that for all practical purposes there is a "four party" system in the United States: presidential Democrats, presidential Republicans, congressional Democrats, and congressional Republicans. The four groups form a liberal-conservative continuum, as determined

[20] Bertram M. Gross, *The Legislative Struggle* (New York: McGraw-Hill Book Co., 1953), p. 67.

by policy stands on domestic and international matters. Both presidential parties are more liberal than the congressional parties, and liberal Republicans and Democrats in Congress belong to the "presidential" parties. The situation, argues Burns, is one in which the conservatives (the congressional party) control Congress and the liberals control the White House. As a result, national policy-making suffers from a lack of "leadership, vigor, speed, and effective and comprehensive national action." [21]

There is sharp disagreement over Burns' typology of the American party structure, but there is no doubt that partisan organization in Congress mirrors the fragmented nature of the national parties. The extent of internal partisan cleavages is evidenced in a number of ways. First, the power of party leadership is more dependent upon personal skills than it is upon formal powers. Direct commands are rare; persuasion is common. Although both parties in Senate and House provide for a formal party caucus, these meet infrequently and rarely attempt to bind their members. Lyndon Johnson, a very effective majority leader during his tenure in the Senate, made the following comment regarding the powers of the majority leaders: "The only real power available to the leader is the power of persuasion. There is no patronage; no power to discipline; no authority to fire Senators like a President can fire his members of Cabinet." [22] This does not mean that party leaders have no means to discourage recalcitrant members. A Speaker, for example, has favors and benefits to dispense, and members are reluctant to disappoint or defy his expectations. Coercion is relatively rare; such an exchange of support is more often in the form of a conjectural bargaining for "good will."

Secondly, the majority party is fragmented. Its ability to formulate a program and guide it through Congress is seriously impaired by the fact that key points in the legislative process are frequently occupied by congressmen jealous of their prerogatives and responsible neither to leadership in Congress nor influential party spokesmen outside Congress. To weld together a partisan coalition of Congressmen in semi-independent positions such as presiding officer, floor leader, committee chairmen, and members of the Rules committee is extremely difficult. Further, party leaders cannot and will not insist on a legislator's support when constituency preferences run contrary to the party's position.

It must also be recognized that many of those who exercise significant influence on legislative decision-making are not members of Congress.

---

[21] Burns, *op. cit.*, p. 266.

[22] See the article entitled "Leadership: An Interview with Senator Lyndon Johnson," *U.S. News and World Report,* June 27, 1960, p. 90; also quoted in Keefe and Ogul, *op. cit.*, p. 262.

Included would be the President, spokesmen for administrative agencies, and pressure-group leaders. Some congressmen are highly sensitive to the claims made upon them by the influential groups within their district, while others will respond to the counterpressures of opposing clienteles. A Democratic congressman from a rural district of the South is seldom impressed with demands by party spokesmen for support of the liberal proposals of a Democratic President. As Arthur Bentley remarked in his analysis of the government process, advantages in access are more likely to go to the group that can accentuate and exploit the local preoccupations of legislators.[23]

Finally, one of the generally accepted norms of the legislative process is that steam-roller tactics are not acceptable rules of the game. Congressional majority leadership is expected to refrain from using any methods that prevent the minority from being heard. The Senate filibuster and the operation of the House Rules Committee (to be discussed below) are the two major procedural techniques that enable the minority effectively to block majority programs.

Party policy in Great Britain is made by the party leader in consultation with his advisers and party members in Parliament are expected to vote the party position. Divisions on policy do exist within the parties but these occur within the leadership ranks and are rarely evident within the rank and file in Parliament.[24] Party government in Congress on anything approaching the British model is precluded, whether or not it may be deemed desirable. Parochial interests control the nominations. National party platforms, which appeal to broad national groupings that elect Presidents, are often at direct odds with the kind of appeal a congressional candidate believes will win an election for him. A rural congressman from western Kansas is not likely to win nomination or election by supporting national party programs that reflect urban-based interests. Although sectionalism plays a smaller role than it once did in electing Presidents, the operation of sectional interests in Congress is still a crucial factor in the fragmentation of the majority party. Congressmen, in short, often support exclusive interests rather than more inclusive partisan programs, a condition which obviates a formal majority party organization commanded by its leadership.

Party influence on legislative behavior is, nevertheless, evident in a number of important ways. The parties organize the legislature, select the party leaders, carry on the legislative business, and keep the public informed of the issues before Congress. All of these are crucial roles. To

[23] Bentley, *op. cit.*, pp. 368–72.
[24] Richard Rose, *Politics in England* (Boston: Little, Brown & Co., 1964), pp. 155–56.

what extent, however, does party affiliation determine the voting behavior of congressmen?

Analyses of congressional voting patterns consistently show that constituency influences operate to reduce party cohesion. Table 13-1 indicates two traditional voting alignments that operate against party unity. North-South Democratic splits occur frequently. In the nine sessions included in the table (1957–1965) these two wings of the party differed on roll-call votes from 21 per cent (1962) to 40 per cent (1960) of the time. In addition, a coalition (generally conservative in nature) of Republicans and Democrats consistently opposed northern Democrats in sessions from 1958 to 1964. The number of roll calls in both houses classified as "coalition" votes ranged from 28 per cent in 1961 to 14 per cent in 1962. While this includes a minority of all roll calls, when the coalition operated, it got its way most of the time. Percentage of coalition victories ranged from a high of 89 per cent in the 1957 session to 33 per cent in 1965.

TABLE 13-1

Constituency Influences and Party Cohesion — 1957–1965

	REPUBLICAN-DEMOCRATIC "CONSERVATIVE COALITION" (PER CENT)*	PERCENTAGE OF COALITION VICTORIES	NORTH-SOUTH DEMOCRATIC SPLITS (PER CENT)
1957	14	89	31
1958	18	79	29
1959	17	71	27
1960	22	58	40
1961	28	55	33
1962	14	62	21
1963	17	50	24
1964	15	51	24
1965	24	33	35

* (Roll-call votes in which bi-partisan coalition or Democratic split was evident in both houses)
Data for this table drawn from: *Congressional Quarterly Almanac*, XV (1959), p. 141; *Congressional Quarterly Weekly Report*, XVIII (Sept. 30, 1960), pp. 1625–26; XXIII (Nov. 26, 1965), p. 2402.

Party pressures also operate in determining the outcome of roll-call votes, but more frequently in a political system like Great Britain's than in the United States. As far back as 1901, A. Lawrence Lowell, in his book *The Influence of Party Upon Legislation in England and America*, reported that party affiliation in the British House of Commons was far more influential than the party role in Congress. Lowell's test of party influence was based on roll-call votes. A "party vote" was one in which 90 per cent of one party voted in opposition to 90 per cent of the other party. In 1951 another political scientist, Julius Turner, compared the British and American legislatures again by using, with some modifications, Lowell's test. Although Turner found that only 17.1 per cent of all roll-call votes in the House between 1921 and 1948 could be classified as party votes, he concluded that "party pressure seems to be more effective than any other pressure on congressional voting, and is discernible on nearly nine-tenths of the roll calls examined." [25] ("Discernible" party voting is, of course, not the same as the "party vote" defined above.)

Cleavages within the Democratic or Republican parties are usually traced to constituency influences. Cohesion within the parties is a function of party pressures that operate on congressmen. Where constituency influences and party pressures diverge, the congressman is "cross-pressured" and may desert the party position. Yet constituency influences cannot be viewed solely as forces leading to fragmentation of party unity. To the contrary, there is evidence that the constituency factor also supports and accounts for party unity. Turner's study found that Democratic congressmen representing northern metropolitan districts with significant numbers of foreign-born voters tended to vote more consistently with the party majority. Republicans from midwestern rural areas with comparatively small numbers of foreign-born also displayed a high degree of unity and tended to vote the party position more frequently.[26] More recent studies have confirmed Turner's findings. Lewis A. Froman's examination of party support of President Kennedy's domestic policy programs (which were classified as "liberal" measures) revealed that Democratic congressmen who voted the Kennedy program came from urban districts with lower percentages of owner-occupied dwellings, more non-white voters, and higher population. Republicans who opposed the Kennedy programs tended to represent districts with higher numbers of owner-occupied housing, lower population, and fewer urban and non-white voters. Since a larger number of northern Democrats are elected from constituencies with "liberal" characteristics, and Republicans tend to represent a larger number of "conservative" constituencies, Froman's findings support the hypothesis that constituency characteristics reinforce party unity as well as account for the fragmentation of party unity on congressional roll calls.[27]

These findings imply that if there were a majority of congressional districts with pronounced conservative or liberal characteristics, party

[25] Julius Turner, *Party and Constituency: Pressures on Congress* (Baltimore: The Johns Hopkins Press, 1951), p. 23.

[26] *Ibid.*, p. 110.

[27] Froman, *op. cit.*, pp. 90–95; see also V. O. Key, Jr., *Politics, Parties, and Pressure Groups* (New York: Thomas Y. Crowell, 1958), pp. 736–37.

unity would be enhanced since constituency and party pressures would tend to coincide with each other. Constituency characteristics are not, however, so uniform: it is the existing variations in these characteristics that operate to limit party unity.

Despite the appearance of interparty coalitions and other constituency-based deviations within party ranks, there is some evidence to indicate that we may be moving in the direction of greater party integration in congressional voting. In his analysis of roll-call votes in the Eighty-first Congress (1949–51), David B. Truman found that "despite differences within the parties, a clear tendency toward partisanship in both House and Senate . . . distinguished most members of the majority parties from most of those in the minority." [28] Issues of a regional nature did reveal a voting pattern of interparty sectional coalition reported above. But on questions of a non-regional variety, particularly those involving support of the President's program, congressional parties tended to divide *as parties* rather than as coalitions of economic, regional, ethnic, or other interests. Moreover, Truman found that intraparty consensus within state delegations developed primarily on issues over which the party had split or those of such minor significance or purely local importance that the congressman could choose to vote as he pleased.[29]

The relationship between party affiliation and congressional voting is but one important factor in the policy-adoption process. Sectionalism, constituency differences, the intensity of group demands, legislative norms and customs, personal attitudes, reciprocal relations with administrative officials, and the segmentation of congressional leadership all contribute to limiting any trend toward partisan integration within Congress. Party cohesion is also, however, enhanced and supported by the similarity of constituencies.

CONTOURS OF CONGRESSIONAL LEADERSHIP

As indicated previously, the majority party in each house controls the selection of legislative officers, and each party chooses its own leaders. The presiding officer in the House, the Speaker, is certainly more pivotal in policy adoption than either of his counterparts in the Senate, the Vice-President or President *pro tempore*. Gradually developed during the nineteenth century, the prerogatives of the Speaker at the turn of the century were so great as to insure him personal control over the proceedings and much of the policy-making in the House. Before 1910 the Speaker appointed all standing committees and their chairmen, possessed

---

[28] David B. Truman, *The Congressional Party* (New York: John Wiley & Sons, 1959), p. 280.
[29] *Ibid.*, pp. 249–61.

unlimited discretion to recognize members in debate on the floor of the House, and served as chairman of the powerful House Rules Committee. In the so-called "revolution of 1910" a group of progressive-minded members "deposed" Speaker Joseph G. Cannon by severely restricting the authority of the Speaker. Speakers since Cannon have regained a great deal of influence. They must, however, share policy functions with others (for example, standing committee chairmen), a development that has fragmented House policy formulation, leadership, and responsibility. Under present rules the Speaker refers bills to committees, appoints special and conference committees, and rules on matters of procedure. The Speaker's discretion is, however, not so narrowly confined. Former Speaker Joseph Martin once said about his power during his four years as Speaker: "No Republican went on an important committee without my approval." [30]

Once chosen by his party, a Speaker is unlikely to lose his post unless the minority party in the House becomes the majority and puts its own candidate in the position. When this occurs, the Speaker normally reverts to the position of minority leader of his party. Since 1930 there has been a Republican Speaker for only four years: 1947–49 and 1953–55. In 1959 Republican Joseph Martin, who had served for twenty years as floor leader or Speaker, lost his position to Representative Halleck of Indiana.

The major partisan spokesmen in both houses are the majority and minority floor leaders. Chosen by respective party caucuses, they have little formal authority but exercise persuasive influence in the legislature. The major function of the House majority leader is to work in conjunction with the Speaker, the minority leader, and the Rules Committee in the House to set the schedule for debate. His role as chief strategist and tactician is an important one. Knowledge of procedure and parliamentary skill are valuable assets. David Truman describes the role of the floor leader as a "middleman in the sense of a broker." [31] He must not become identified with an extreme position within his party or he jeopardizes his leadership role. The difficulties of gaining cooperation and of communicating with the rest of the party leadership are rendered impossible by dogmatic affiliations.

Majority and minority leaders also serve as partisan spokesmen to the press and the public. The joint radio and television appearances of Republican minority leaders Senator Everett M. Dirksen and Representative Charles Halleck during a half decade were dubbed the "Ev and Charlie" show. Many Republicans viewed these appearances as harmful

[30] Joseph W. Martin, Jr., *My Fifty Years in Politics* (New York: McGraw-Hill Book Co., 1960), p. 181.
[31] Truman, *The Congressional Party,* pp. 106–16.

to the image of the Republicans in Congress. They did provide a forum through which congressional partisans could offset the demands and publicity of Republican presidential aspirants serving as governors, ambassadors, or in other official capacities.

The ability of a floor leader to combine parliamentary skill, persuasion, ties with the administration (if he is of the President's party), and good personal relationships with his party's members determine his effectiveness as a leader. In the Senate the majority leader occupies a crucial legislative role; in the House he is next to the Speaker in importance. In the absence of a strong party organization, and given the fragmented nature of congressional leadership, the majority and minority leaders must build their strength and influence from other sources.

In addition to the floor leaders, each of the parties selects a whip or assistant floor leader. The function of the whip is to keep the members informed of the weekly legislative schedule and to see that members are present for important votes on the floor. Party whips cannot command members to follow the party position. Their role is confined to persuading members to do so and communicating partisan strategy and position on particular measures.

Legislative leadership alone cannot produce highly unified and disciplined parties. In Great Britain, the Prime Minister and his Cabinet exercise the initiative and command the resources necessary to effective leadership. In the United States, the President, although his leadership is more one of bargaining than command, exercises this vital role of legislative party leadership. His role in this respect is, however, primarily in relationship to his own party, especially the party leaders. Where the opposition party controls the legislature or is the legislative minority, leadership tends to flounder and party disunity is more evident. This disunity and lack of leadership seriously hurts the minority party's "functioning as an 'alternative government,' [and] is a defect in the party system that merits more attention than the absence of tight party lines on many roll-call votes." [32]

CONTOURS OF CONVENTIONAL CONGRESSIONAL
ORGANIZATION AND PROCEDURE

Congressional procedures are a function of the interplay between legislative organization, tradition, leadership, and interests. Procedural habits, customs, and conventions in turn affect interest access, a congressman's independence in policy choice, and congressional policy adoption.

The Committee System. The work of Congress is done mainly in com-

[32] Allan P. Sindler, *Political Parties in the United States* (New York: St. Martin's Press, 1966), p. 86.

mittees, of which there are four general types. *Special* or *select* committees are created to perform a specific task (usually an investigation). They are appointed by the Speaker of the House and by the President of the Senate and are dissolved when their task is completed. A *joint* committee is composed of members of both houses appointed by the presiding officer in each branch. They are usually concerned with investigations (e.g. Joint Committee on the Organization of Congress), research, or the housekeeping activities of Congress (e.g. Congressional Library). Some joint committees are of great importance. Probably the most important and powerful of this type is the Joint Committee on Atomic Energy. A *conference* committee, consisting of members of both houses appointed by the presiding officers, irons out differences in Senate and House passed versions of the same bill. The role of conference committees is discussed later in this chapter. *Standing* committees, the workhorses of Congress, are by far the most important. They are permanently provided for by House or Senate rules.

The Standing Committees of Congress. In *Congressional Government*, written in 1885, Woodrow Wilson described the American political process as "government by the Standing Committees of Congress." He argued that the fate of all legislation lay in the hands of these "little legislatures." [33] Although Congress has changed other aspects of its leadership structure and procedure since 1885, the role of standing committees remains basically unchanged. Their functions are virtually those of Congress itself. Their number has varied through time; there are now twenty in the House and sixteen in the Senate. Some are of major importance (Appropriations, Ways and Means, Agriculture, Foreign Relations); others are comparatively insignificant. Membership on major committees is coveted by senators and representatives, but service on others (House Administration, Government Operations, District of Columbia) is deemed less prestigious. Every legislative matter is covered by one or more of the standing committees in each house, and the adoption of every bill lies largely in the hands of committee members.

The complexity and technical nature of legislation, as well as the sheer volume of bills introduced during each session of Congress, dictates the necessity of an orderly and efficient procedure for considering legislative business. To expedite business, each standing committee can create subcommittees to handle particular matters within the jurisdiction of the full

[33] Woodrow Wilson, *Congressional Government* (New York: Meridian Books, 1956 [originally published in 1885]); for other commentaries on the committee system see David N. Farnsworth, *The Senate Committee on Foreign Relations* (Urbana: The University of Illinois Press, 1961); Neil MacNeil, *Forge of Democracy* (New York: David McKay Co., 1963), pp. 148–74; James A. Robinson, *The House Rules Committee* (Indianapolis: The Bobbs-Merrill Co., 1963).

committee. While this practice facilitates a necessary division of labor, it also means a further splintering of legislative leadership and conflict. It is common for the full committee to accept sub-committee recommendations. Considerable discretion and power lies, therefore, in the hands of sub-committees, especially their chairmen. The effect is the existence of little legislatures within little legislatures and interest groups cultivate the favor of powerful sub-committee chairmen and members. Stephen K. Bailey describes the successful sub-committee chairman as "one who can refrain from antagonizing the full-committee chairman who appoints him, at the same time that he maintains enough autonomy to be cultivated directly by other congressmen, by constituents or group interests, and by the President." [34]

After a bill is introduced it is referred to one of the standing committees which may recommend it for adoption with only minor changes; may virtually rewrite the proposal; or may kill it by majority vote against it. If a House committee refuses to report a bill to the floor, a discharge petition signed by a majority of the House membership (218) can force the bill out of committee. The discharge method is rarely employed, but party leaders may threaten to use it in order to speed up committee action and pressure a report on the proposed legislation.

Proposed legislation must go through the committee stage in both House and Senate. In examining legislation, a committee (or sub-committee) may hold hearings; and on major bills sponsored by the administration or major interest groups, hearings will be held. Committees also act as investigative bodies. In pursuing this function, they may request or subpoena witnesses to testify and look into the operations of agencies in the executive branch. The operations and hearings of the House Committee on Un-American Activities (and its sub-committees) has long been a focal point for controversy — judicial, legislative, and public — over how much authority Congress has to investigate matters of political belief. More recently, hearings by the Senate Committee on Foreign Relations in review of Viet Nam policies prompted wide public interest and some criticism of committee members who were highly critical of administration policies.

The vital role of standing committees in the legislative process focuses interest group attention on the method of selection of committee members, the role of the chairman, and the jurisdiction of the committees (the decision as to which committee a bill is to be referred). Once an interest group establishes access by any means, it exerts pressure to protect its advantages — to retain the particular procedural arrangement that

[34] Stephen K. Bailey, *The New Congress* (New York: St. Martin's Press, 1966), p. 57.

yields access. Such procedural customs as the seniority rule, the filibuster, senatorial courtesy, and control of the legislative calendar may give access to one group in preference to another. To illustrate the point: the fact that Senator James Eastland of Mississippi is chairman of the Senate Judiciary Committee (when Democrats control the Senate) which handles civil rights bills gives opponents of such legislation considerable advantage. In 1963, proponents of civil rights legislation managed to by-pass Eastland's committee (which has never voluntarily released a civil rights bill) by an arrangement which assigned part of the proposed civil rights bill to the Senate Commerce Committee. Under Chairman Warren G. Magnuson of Washington, the committee held hearings and favorably reported to the Senate a bill concerning non-discriminatory access to places of public accommodation.

Assignment of Members to Standing Committees. The majority party in each of the two houses fills a majority of seats on all committees, a practice intended to insure partisan control. Traditionally the minority party is represented on each committee in rough proportion to its numerical strength; however, on some of the major committees, such as Appropriations, where the majority party wants to assure its control, the majority may assign a disproportion of seats to its own members. Since the passage of the Legislative Reorganization Act in 1946, each senator is limited to two standing committee assignments and each representative to membership on one standing committee.

Technically, the full House and Senate approve assignment of members to various committees; actually, each party determines the assignments of its partisans. Democrats in the House are assigned by the Committee-on-Committees, a body composed of all Democrats on the Ways and Means Committee, the Speaker, and the floor leader. Members of Ways and Means are selected by the party caucus which is composed of all party members in the House and meets at the opening of each session to elect party officers. House Republican assignments are made by a Committee-on-Committees appointed by the floor leader (or Speaker, when Republicans are the majority party). In the Senate, Republican committee positions are filled by a Committee-on-Committees appointed by the chairman of the Republican conference; for Democrats, the floor leader selects a Steering Committee to handle assignments.

Under present rules a member who has served on a committee — provided that he has been successfully re-elected — has a strong claim to continue on the committee. Also, if a party shifts from majority to minority status through election defeats, some members will lose their seats on important committees. Since membership on the Ways and Means Committee of the House, which handles tax legislation, is a highly sought-after assignment, the seniority rule tends to perpetuate its membership.

As indicated above, service on a committee usually insures reappointment. Seniority does not, however, have much to do with transfers to other standing committees and has nothing to do with assignment of freshmen congressmen. Nicholas A. Master's study of the assignment of new members to House standing committees found that placement on the three major committees — Appropriations, Rules, and Ways and Means — is based on three principal factors. 1) A candidate must be "responsible," that is, "one whose ability, attitudes, and relationships with his colleagues serves to enhance the prestige and importance of the House of Representatives." 2) Members chosen represent districts in which their re-election is probable thus permitting a high degree of flexibility (as against having to take uncompromising positions) in controversial matters. Only members who have served three or more terms are likely to meet this criterion for appointment. 3) Members chosen satisfy the need for geographical balance on the committee. Assignments to other House standing committees are based on such factors as the desire to place each party member on a committee that will help to win his re-election (this is the most important consideration); interest group support, professional background, and the geographical area the member represents.[35]

In the Senate, the Democratic Steering Committee and the Republican Committee-on-Committees have in recent years departed from the traditional custom that freshmen senators be given only minor committee assignments. Under previous practices only senators with previous service (seniority) were eligible for major committee positions such as Foreign Relations, Armed Services, and Appropriations. In 1953, Senator Lyndon Johnson used his influence as majority leader to place freshmen members on major committees, thus modifying the seniority principle in making assignments.

Although the major committees in the Senate do not reflect geographical or ideological balance, regional considerations are taken into account in filling vacancies. Normally, a vacancy is filled with a member from the same state that the departing member had represented.

The composition of some standing committees — Agriculture, Labor, Interior, and Insular Affairs, Judiciary — clearly reflects the interests of particular groups: congressmen from farm states control the Agriculture committees; Interior and Insular Affairs are dominated by western Senators; Labor committees are heavily seeded with congressmen from urban

[35] Nicholas A. Masters, "Committee Assignments in the House of Representatives," *The American Political Science Review*, LV (June, 1961), 345–57.

and industrial states; and lawyers dominate the Judiciary committees in both houses. Pressure groups are vitally interested in which committee is given jurisdiction over legislation because of the membership proclivities of various committees. The standing committee that has jurisdiction over a particular bill will hold hearings and report on that bill. A bill may be referred to a House or Senate committee whose membership is sympathetic to the legislation or to a committee that is hostile or divided. Although jurisdictional disputes are not common, they can affect group access. In 1948, for example, a bill for repeal of the federal tax on oleomargarine was taken out of the House Committee on Agriculture by discharge petition and subsequently passed in the House. After it reached the Senate, a dispute over committee jurisdiction arose between the Finance Committee, which claimed the bill was a tax measure, and the Agricultural Committee, which called it an agricultural matter. The latter committee was hostile to the legislation. The President *pro tempore* referred the bill to Agriculture. The action was, however, successfully challenged on the floor of the Senate. Had it stayed in the Agriculture Committee, no one doubted that the bill would have been killed.

The operation of the seniority rule is most apparent and of crucial significance in the selection of standing-committee chairmen. A chairman's power and influence extends to the control of committee agenda, the appointment of committee staff (the administrative specialists who serve the committee), the choosing of subcommittee chairmen and members, the decision as to whether hearings on the bill will be held, and the right to represent the committee on the floor. It is his responsibility to handle the bill once it reaches the floor. Chairmen have traditionally exercised the "pocket veto" or "pigeon hole" technique, a device that is usually effective, that precludes full committee consideration or hearings on policies.

The committee member of the majority party with longest uninterrupted service on the committee is automatically awarded the chairmanship. The member of the minority party with the longest continuous service is the ranking minority member and becomes chairman when his party gains a majority of the membership. To gain seniority, a senator or representative must be able to win reelection time after time, a task made considerably easier for those in states and districts dominated by one party. Congressmen rarely survive for extended periods the ups and downs of elections in marginal states and districts. As a result the majority of committee chairmanships are controlled by congressmen from a minority of states and from particular regions. To illustrate: Between the Eightieth and Eighty-fifth Congresses (1947–57), Southern Democrats controlled 53 per cent of chairmanships in the Senate and 62 per cent in the House. Midwestern Republicans held 53 per cent of these positions in the House and 66 per cent of those in the Senate during the years when their party was the majority. The Midwest and the South are traditionally the source of many "safe" districts.

In addition to the assertion that it favors one-party areas and conservative interests there are other criticisms of the use of the seniority rule in the selection of chairmen. It produces irresponsible partisans by placing policy choice in the hands of committee chairmen who are largely free from the control of party leadership. It also often elevates to positions of great importance men whose only claim to the position is the fact that they have served longer on the committee than any other member of their party; this practice tends to subordinate ability and competence to age, a practice neither desirable nor defensible. Moreover, it makes removal of a chairman extremely difficult, if not impossible. A chairman stands in the position of being able to block party legislative programs, including those of the President. Under these circumstances, the minority can effectively frustrate majority wishes. Supporters of the seniority principle argue that 1) committee chairmen *are* usually men of competence and great experience who understand the special problems and possess the technical "know-how" of the legislative process; 2) it is the most rational and efficient way to select chairmen since it eliminates continuous struggle for the control of key positions and thus enables committees to accomplish their purpose of expediting legislation.

Whatever the pros and cons of the present practice, it is obvious that the basis for selection of both members and chairmen of standing committees clearly affects the ability of groups to influence policy choices. It also contributes to the diffusion of leadership and control of the process of legislation, enabling groups to develop mechanisms for protecting interests.

Standing Committees at Work. The crucial work of standing committees takes place in the secrecy of executive (closed) sessions. It is here that much bargaining among interests takes place. Of course, groups must gain access to the committees long before actual decisions are made within executive session, or else they stand little chance of influencing the outcome of committee deliberations. Yet all major committees spend many hours holding public hearings, supposedly to hear from all interested parties. What purpose do hearings serve if the real decisions are made outside the confines of the open public hearing?

David Truman lists three major functions of public hearings.[36] First, and probably of least importance, interests can present committees with

---

[36] Truman, *The Governmental Process*, pp. 372–77.

information in support of their position. Second, groups are given a propaganda channel, a medium through which they can inform the public of their stand on public issues. The image of a group before the public can to some extent be enhanced or injured by the treatment accorded group leaders by the committee. A committee member may, for example, ask questions in a way which will reveal a group in its most favorable light or in a manner which presents a less favorable image of the group and its position. Third, committee hearings serve a "safety valve" or symbolic function. The opportunity to testify eases group conflict and also helps to satisfy a recalcitrant faction within the organization itself.

The House Rules Committee. The most crucial standing committee in either house of Congress is the House Rules Committee. Once a bill has been reported from committee, it is placed on one of five House calendars: the Union, House, Consent, Private, or Discharge calendar. Theoretically each bill placed on one of the calendars is considered in turn. Those reported first will be considered first. Bills reported from two committees (Appropriations and Ways and Means) are exceptions. They may be considered at any time as "privileged motions." The normal procedure is that the Rules Committee determines (by recommending special rules) not only the order in which bills are considered but often whether they will be considered by the full House at all. The Committee channels the flow of legislation to the floor by determining limits on debate, fixing the number and kind of amendments that may be offered and forcing changes and concessions in legislation before permitting it to reach the floor.

Clearly the Rules Committee possesses jurisdiction not accorded to any other standing committee in Congress. The only formal limits on the exercise of its authority are the discharge petition (rarely successful) and Calendar Wednesday, a procedure that permits standing committees to call up bills which have been blocked by the Rules Committee. Calendar Wednesday is a cumbersome and ineffective device for coordinating the conflicting interests represented by the Rules Committee and standing committees.

From the late 1930's to the early 1960's the Rules Committee was dominated by a coalition of Republicans and Southern Democrats. It successfully blocked legislation supported by the White House and often by a majority of the House membership. In the Eighty-sixth Congress a combination of four Republicans and two southern Democrats obstructed rather than channeled legislation dealing with public housing, civil rights, and school construction. The committee was deadlocked six to six between conflicting interests. Under House rules ties are not considered as affirmative action. Early in the Eighty-seventh Congress

(1961), a resolution which enlarged membership on the committee from twelve to fifteen and was backed by President Kennedy and Speaker Rayburn, was approved by a narrow 217 to 212 vote of the House. Two-thirds of the southern Democrats and all but twenty-five of House Republicans voted against this "packing" proposal, a vote which clearly revealed the stakes in the contest for legislative leadership. Two "liberal" Democrats and one "conservative" Republican were added to the committee. This addition broke the deadlock; the committee was now able to vote eight to seven in favor of presidential proposals.

In 1965 the House approved two changes in House rules which substantially weakened the authority of the Rules Committee to delay or block legislation. One was the 21-day rule (abandoned in 1967) permitting the introduction by a committee chairman (or committee member) of a bill which had been before the Rules Committee for twenty-one days without having been given a rule permitting consideration by the full House. Secondly, the committee's power to block or delay sending a bill to conference committee was considerably weakened. Under the new rule a majority vote of the House can send a bill to conference.

The Rules Committee remains, nevertheless, a powerful force in the House. Its clearing-house function can block and delay rather than propose. In this way it can afford special access to certain groups in the House: it can frustrate and block the majority from achieving its goals, and veto groups can force negotiation and compromise.

Floor Consideration and Final Passage of Bills. Once a bill reaches the floor of the House debate is rigidly controlled by time limits and other procedural rules. The size of the House demands orderly rules of consideration and debate, demands which are met through the functions of the Rules Committee. The whole House may choose to name itself as a special committee for discussion of a particular proposal. It does this by entering the "Committee of the Whole." Under this procedure proposals may be debated without members being subjected to all of the formal rules of parliamentary procedure. In this way, important decisions and compromises can be reached that could not be so easily negotiated under more rigid conditions.

Due to its much smaller size, the Senate does not need the restrictive schedules and controls of the House. Control of floor debate rests with the majority leader and (in a limited sense) the policy committee of the majority party. Party policy committees (each party in the Senate has one) consist of the party leaders and are theoretically responsible for guiding their party's legislative program. In practice, the policy committee exercises little effective leadership and the majority leader largely determines the agenda of the Senate.

The majority leader does not, however, have power to limit debate. Once a senator has the floor, he may talk as long as he pleases and he may yield the floor to whom he chooses. If there are a sufficient number of senators, they may succeed in talking a bill to death. This practice — the *filibuster* — is a device by which Senate proceedings are delayed in order to prevent a vote on a bill. Once he has the floor a member (except for insignificant limitations) may talk about anything he pleases; cook books, folk remedies, and other irrelevant material have been read to the Senate during filibusters. The filibuster has long been a weapon of the minority position on legislation and has been successful on many occasions in the past.

Debate can be limited only by the invocation of *cloture,* otherwise known as Rule 22 of the Senate. When at least sixteen members sign a petition for a cloture motion, cloture is voted upon two calendar days later. A two-thirds vote of Senators present ends the filibuster since cloture limits each senator to speak no more than one hour on the proposed bill. Cloture has been successful only six times in the history of the Senate. In recent years the filibuster has been a major weapon of southerners in opposition to civil rights measures and sometimes the mere threat of a filibuster has discouraged attempts at passage of such legislation. It has also been used in the past by other interests. In 1962, for example, cloture was invoked to bring to an end a filibuster that opposed private development of communication satellites (Telestar). Unlimited harangues can be combatted through other means, such as using round-the-clock sessions to physically exhaust filibusterers or by taking advantage of procedural mistakes. Unlimited debate is a vital weapon against partisan leadership. Like the Rules Committee in the House, it represents another *defensive* mechanism of minority interests against majority preferences. It serves to reinforce the tradition of policy incrementation by confining policy changes and additions to measures which reflect the accommodation of minority interests.

When House and Senate pass a legislative proposal, but disagree as to particular features, an *ad hoc* joint committee, called a *conference* committee, is created. Members are appointed by the presiding officers of each branch, but are usually drawn from the two standing committees that handled the bill on the floor. Each house may instruct its conference members. Although procedural rules prohibit conference committees from making major changes in the legislation, these instructions and limits are not followed. Bertram M. Gross has described the role of the conference committee as "committee power in its most concentrated form." [37] The influence of pressure groups, both private and official, would be

[37] Gross, *op. cit.,* p. 317.

expected to be great at this level of the legislative process. Decisions are made in executive (closed) session only, and the two houses have the option of accepting or not accepting the conference report without change. Under these conditions pressure groups have another opportunity to veto action or regain what has been lost in committee or on the floor.

CONGRESS AND POLICY ADOPTION

Decentralization pervades the legislative process. Certain features of Congress contribute to fragmentation of policy decision: A bicameral arrangement reflects the built-in parochial quality of federalism; a scheme of direct representation grants distinct advantages to particular interests via the single-member district, malapportionment, and gerrymandering; partisan organization reinforces localized and segmental control over policy adoption; legislative procedures facilitate multiple points of committee decision through which exclusive interests (official and nonofficial) can block, delay, frustrate, and sometimes force legislative policy. The consequences for the policy process are the same as those encountered elsewhere: limited presidential coordination, partisan ineffectiveness, negotiated decisions, difficulty in fixing policy responsibility, and policy by incrementation.

A somewhat overlooked ramification of legislative decentralization is the freedom of choice it affords the average congressman. On the surface fragmentation provides perfect conditions for pressure groups to dictate policy. We might expect legislators to be mere pawns of exclusive interests. Yet this is not always so. Congressmen cannot perceive, let alone respond to, all pressures. The factors we have discussed shape each legislator's perspective. That perspective filters out the pressures he does not want to bear, admits those that support him in his labor, and colors others. In short, "things interior to the Congressman's mind largely determine what events he will perceive as external pressure on him." The legislator thus "unconsciously chooses which pressures to recognize." [38]

Pressure groups succeed not because they apply such great force that a congressional leader must comply but rather because they create a "perspective compatibility" between legislator and group leaders. A congressman whose constituency is predominantly agricultural does not have to be "pressured" by agrarian groups. A compatibility of goals already exists. Under these circumstances, a legislator tends to view as "sound" or "in the public interest" group stands that parallel or support his own.

[38] Raymond A. Bauer, Ithiel de Sola Pool, and Lewis Anthony Dexter, *American Business and Public Policy* (New York: Atherton Press, 1963), p. 416; see also John C. Wahlke *et. al., The Legislative System* (New York: John Wiley & Sons, 1962).

But what is sound to one policy official may be "capitulation" when viewed from the perspective of other groups with conflicting aims. Pressure organizations naturally seek legislators on whom they can rely for support. Where perspective compatibility exists and the congressman occupies a key position (such as committee chairman), the group is in a good position to advance its claims.

But the policy independence of the congressman is not easily translated into policy independence for Congress. Committee chairmen, for example, are important allies with administrative and pressure leaders in negotiating party coalitions; yet Congress is not thereby coordinated with President and bureaucracy in initiating public policy. As a formal institution, Congress legislates less than it ratifies, formulates less than it adopts, and leads less than it responds. If legitimate policies are to be made for the community, congressional majorities must be mobilized behind proposals. But the proposals are normally initiated elsewhere.

The growth of government as a regulator of human relations is both a major fact and an issue of the modern era. The stakes involved are crucial to the survival of liberal democracy. In surrendering to the executive conflicts that it could not resolve, Congress delegated much of its policy leadership. It also altered its function of representing conflict as well. We hear little about a "congressional program" to meet modern demands, but much is written about the variable success of the "President's program." The so-called deadlock and impasse between the two branches has long been a source of concern for students of government. The success with which President Lyndon Johnson first channeled proposals through Congress does not detract from that concern. Suggestions for reforming congressional procedures by eliminating committee obstruction and tightening partisan leadership have been generated in the belief that Congress is a negative institution that can amend and veto but cannot exercise creative intelligence. Critics suggest that Congress can no longer "represent" if it serves as either obstacle or tool of presidential leadership.

As the focus of leadership in the American political system has turned more and more toward the President, observers continue to point out the dangers of fragmented parties in Congress and the decline of congressional initiative in policy-making.[39] The programs pursued by party leaders in Congress, whether of the minority or the majority, are heavily influenced by presidential initiative, prestige, and prerogatives. A representative or senator must consider the demands of both his constituency and the leadership of his party. This chapter has shown that legislative voting behavior is primarily influenced by party ties, but many other

[39] See, for example, James A. Robinson, *Decision-Making in Congress* (Washington: American Enterprise Institute, 1965).

variables must be taken into account in evaluating congressional policy choices. A congressman must be loyal to party, constituency, and interest groups. Under these conditions, as David Truman has pointed out, congressional leadership must define and balance many interests in the making of policy so that the individual legislator sees more advantage than risk in supporting his party's position. The power of congressional leadership is, then, "informal, personal, interstitial . . . the influence of the principal leaders depends heavily upon their recurrently improvising effective combinations among fragments of power of the most varied sorts." [40] The style of leadership in congressional policy formulation is, then, bargaining and persuasion, not command.

One student of legislative politics, Theodore Lowi, has suggested that in the future Congress may serve *as a place where the needs of the bureaucracy are continually being balanced against the prevailing special interests* in the community." [41] This brings us to another institution in the American political system — the administrative bureaucracy. In the next chapter we shall examine its function in the policy process — policy application.

BIBLIOGRAPHICAL NOTE

The literature on legislative policy-making is large and steadily growing. Here we suggest only a small portion of this literature, concentrating on works available in paperback.

There are a number of excellent introductory works and general treatments of the legislative process. George B. Galloway, *The Legislative Process in Congress* (New York: Thomas Y. Crowell Co., 1953) is a standard work in the field. Two recent texts incorporate a wide variety and amount of literature on the legislative process: William J. Keefe and Morris S. Ogul, *The American Legislative Process* (Englewood Cliffs, N.J.: Prentice-Hall, 1964); and Malcolm E. Jewell and Samuel C. Patterson, *The Legislative Process in the United States* (New York: Random House, 1966). The latter contains an excellent bibliography. David B. Truman, *The Governmental Process* (New York: Alfred A. Knopf, 1953) has had significant influence on research in the legislative process. Daniel M. Berman, *In Congress Assembled* (New York: Macmillan Co., 1954), emphasizes the formal organization and structure of Congress. In paperback edition, Bertram M. Gross, *The Legislative Struggle* (New York: McGraw-Hill Book Co., 1953) views Congress from the perspective of the struggle between interest groups.

[40] Truman, *The Congressional Party*, p. 294.

[41] Theodore J. Lowi (ed.), *Legislative Politics, U.S.A.*, Second Ed. (Boston: Little, Brown and Co., 1965), p. xix.

Increasing attention has been given to analyzing legislatures as social systems. The social backgrounds of legislative decision-makers and the legislators' perceptions of their roles are analyzed in the following works, all available in paperback editions: Donald R. Matthews, *The Social Background of Political Decision-Makers* (New York: Random House, 1954) is a seminal work in this area; Heinz Eulau and John D. Sprague, *Lawyers in Politics* (Indianapolis: Bobbs-Merrill Co., 1964) is one of the best studies of the relationship of the legal profession to the legislative process; Charles L. Clapp, *The Congressman: His Work as He Sees It* (New York: Doubleday & Co., 1963) is based on round-table discussions with and between representatives; Donald R. Matthews, *U.S. Senators and Their World* (Chapel Hill: University of North Carolina Press, 1960) combines the interview technique with statistical data; and James D. Barber's *The Lawmakers* (New Haven, Yale University Press, 1965) is an informative work in the area of social background of legislators.

Among the growing body of literature on legislative procedures and relationships, the following comprise a varied but representative sample. An excellent paperback readings book is Robert L. Peabody and Nelson W. Polsby, *New Perspectives on the House of Representatives* (Chicago: Rand McNally & Co., 1963). A useful technique in illustrating the complex nature of legislative decision-making is the case-study approach. Stephen K. Bailey's *Congress Makes a Law* (New York: Random House, 1950) views the process through description of the passage of the Employment Act of 1946; a paperback edition, Daniel M. Berman, *A Bill Becomes a Law: Congress Enacts Civil Rights Legislation*, 2d edition (New York: Macmillan Co., 1966) explains how procedures are crucial in legislative policy-making. The role of parties and congressional constituencies in congressional behavior is the subject of Julius Turner's influential study, *Party and Constituency: Pressures on Congress* (Baltimore: The Johns Hopkins Press, 1951). Lewis A. Froman, Jr., *Congressmen and Their Constituencies* (Chicago: Rand McNally & Co., 1963) is an excellent source on this subject, as is David B. Truman's *The Congressional Party* (New York: John Wiley & Sons, 1959). Available in paperback edition, Stephen K. Bailey's *The New Congress* (New York: St. Martin's Press, 1966) argues that Congress is now more influenced by presidential and party influences than by parochial constituency demands. Congressional-presidential relationships in policy-making are analyzed in Louis M. Koenig, *Congress and the President* (Chicago: Scott, Foresman, & Co., 1965) and Joseph P. Harris, *Congressional Control of Administration* (New York: Doubleday & Co., 1964). Both are in paperback editions. The influence of and problems created by lobbying activity are treated in Lester W. Milbrath's systematic study, *The Washington Lobbyists* (Chicago: Rand McNally, 1963).

The role and function of congressional committees are treated in many of the works cited above. Fuller understanding can be obtained by in-depth studies of particular committees. David N. Farnsworth's *The Senate Committee on Foreign Relations* (Urbana: University of Illinois Press, 1961), and James A. Robinson, *The House Rules Committee* (Indianapolis: The Bobbs-Merrill Co., 1963) are both in paperback editions. A massive and important recent work in this area is Richard F. Fenno, Jr., *The Power of the Purse: Appropriations Politics in Congress* (Boston: Little, Brown & Company, 1966).

Interest in the basis and importance of legislative apportionment has been recently stimulated by decisions of the Warren Court. Alfred de Grazia's *Public and Republic: Political Representation in America* (New York: Alfred A. Knopf, 1951) is an excellent basis to develop a theoretical perspective on the subject. Two recent paperback works treat the legal and political basis of the current debate: Gordon E. Baker, *The Reapportionment Revolution* (New York: Random House, 1965) and Glendon Schubert, *Reapportionment* (New York: Charles Scribner's Sons, 1965). The latter is a useful introductory study for those interested in developing their own analysis of this important question.

Congress-Court relations are treated in C. Herman Pritchett, *Congress Versus the Supreme Court* (Minneapolis: University of Minnesota Press, 1961) and Walter F. Murphy, *Congress and the Court* (Chicago: University of Chicago Press, 1962). The latter book provides a good historical perspective on clashes between the two branches. A related area, congressional powers of investigation, is dealt with in Alan Barth's critical study of the excesses of congressional investigations, *Government by Investigation* (New York: The Viking Press, 1955), and in Robert K. Carr's more balanced *The House Committee on Un-American Activities* (Ithaca: Cornell University Press, 1952).

The growing influence of the President and the great complexity of modern society has led to increased attention in reforming the machinery and procedures of Congress. Joseph S. Clark's *Congress: The Sapless Branch* (New York: Harper and Row, 1964) represents a plea for reform from a liberal Democratic senator. Two other paperback studies provide the views of academicians on the subject: Alfred de Grazia *et al., Congress: The First Branch of Government* (New York: Doubleday & Co., 1967) is a series of essays on the major aspects of legislative policy-making which together argue the relationship of the need for reform and the maintenance of democracy; and David B. Truman (ed.), *The Congress and America's Future*, American Assembly Series (Englewood Cliffs, N.J.: Prentice-Hall, 1964).

CHAPTER
FOURTEEN

Policy Application

In the classic pattern of separation of powers, governing authority is divided into executive, legislative, and judicial jurisdictions. Although the Constitution of the United States follows that design closely, Articles I and II provide the basis for complication of the classic arrangement. Article I grants Congress authority to create administrative agencies. Article II authorizes the President to appoint a variety of public officials to include "all other officers of the United States whose appointments are not herein otherwise provided for, and which shall be established by law." Aside from these provisions and a passing reference to "heads of departments," there is no other hint of the future development of a modern administrative bureaucracy. Today the federal government alone employs one of every twenty-six people in a total work force of approximately 65 million. The tripartite division has been superseded by the addition of a fourth governing "power." Some call the bureaucracy the "fourth branch of American government," an allusion not only to the great impact that administrative policy application has upon every citizen but also to the problem of control of the bureaucracy by the three constituted branches.

391

ADMINISTRATIVE BUREAUCRACY
AND POLICY APPLICATION

"Everywhere," wrote the noted sociologist Max Weber, "the modern state is undergoing bureaucratization." Weber viewed society as evolving initially from a nonspecialized mass in which the leader was believed to possess charismatic appeal. The quest for a stable foundation for the exercise of authority led to the gradual development of more routinized and systematic forms of organization. The modern pattern of policy application is based upon a highly rationalized, legalistic, and technical foundation. Weber termed it "bureaucracy": a type of organization developing out of the technological revolution and its accompanying demands for specialization.[1]

Americans do not view bureaucracy in such abstract terms. To the man on the street, the word often connotes "red tape"; yet there is no question that without an administrative bureaucracy modern government would function with considerable difficulty. The increasing complexity of technology and learning in the twentieth century has given rise to the era of the specialist and the expert in every field imaginable. Views toward bureaucracy are colored by our relations and experience with it. To a businessman required to file elaborate reports regarding income or social security taxes deducted from employee paychecks, bureaucracy may represent an inflexible, coercive force wrapped in red tape; but to the widow who, through the aid of a government administrator, discovers that she is eligible for social security benefits, bureaucracy is viewed in a more favorable light.

THE NATURE OF POLICY APPLICATION

The will of the community is reflected in public policies. If these policies are to be binding, there must be some way of assuring compliance to the rules and regulations. In the narrowest sense policy application comprises those activities that enforce compliance. But like the other phases of the policy process with which it overlaps — policy formulation and adoption — policy application is not limited to its distinguishing function.

Determining Goals and Procedures. In the American polity the administrative bureaucracy is the primary institution for applying policy. In performing this function, the bureaucracy must first determine community goals and then decide on the proper procedures for pursuing them. As in the other stages of the policy process, conflict is inevitable.

[1] H. H. Gerth and C. Wright Mills (eds.), *From Max Weber: Essays in Sociology* (New York: Oxford University Press, 1946), p. 232.

We have already seen that the stream of policy does not flow smoothly from leadership formulation to adoption to application to adjudication. Administrative bureaucrats are members of policy coalitions that enter each phase of the policy process. As partners in policy decision, they share in the establishment of community goals. They advance both the desires of their organizations as well as the specific group interests they represent in policy-making. They do not merely enforce the choices made by legislative leaders; they engage in negotiation of alliances that result in policy formulation. The notion that laws are made by legislatures through "politics" but that such politics is absent in the application of these laws by the administration is an unrealistic one.

Moreover, the policy goals articulated by political leaders, as fixed by policy coalitions and accepted by legislative leaders, are generally broad in their definition. Discretion is left to the bureaucracy as to what specific community aims should be within the framework of policies drawn by Congress and President. Some bureaucratic leaders like to distinguish between the *programs* that they administer and the *policies* produced by executive-legislative relations. Although administrative programs differ from general policy goals, they are nevertheless extensions of policy decisions; the policies on which programs are based provide considerable opportunities for administrative choice. Each such choice is an act of policy-making in its own right and directly affects the distribution of advantages and disadvantages between conflicting interests.

To the extent that they share in the determination of community goals, administrators are interested participants in the resolution of social conflict. They must also coordinate and rationalize human energies in the pursuit of agreed community values. Dwight Waldo has characterized this phase of administrative activity as "cooperative human effort with a high degree of rationality." Attaining community goals involves both the *organization* ("the structure of authoritative *and* habitual personal inter-relations") and *management* ("action intended to achieve rational co-operation").[2]

Thus we see that policy application is a complex process. First, in determining goals, bureaucratic leaders join with partisan appointees of the President, congressional leaders, and pressure-group leaders to formulate public policy. Here the bureaucrat is a resolver of conflicts involving both his organization and broader community interests. The administrator must then determine workable procedures for reaching community goals. In performing this task, he must accommodate and coordinate diverse interests within his own department, agency, or bureau.

[2] Dwight Waldo, *The Study of Public Administration* (Garden City, N.Y.: Doubleday & Co., 1955), pp. 11–12.

Characteristics of Policy Application. Patterns of policy application are shaped by two characteristics of the American political community. First, despite efforts to assure hierarchical controls and the style of command, both the authoritative structure of the Constitution and the habitual conventions of extra-constitutional procedures contribute to a highly decentralized administrative organization. As a consequence, bargaining rather than command characterizes policy application, particularly when bureaucratic leaders are able to construct autonomous bases of support with legislators and regulated pressure groups rather than remain dependent upon administrative superiors for favors. A second feature of the American political community — the policy tradition of incrementation (see Chapter Eleven) — tends to obstruct efforts of the administration to secure rational cooperation. The ends of administrative rationality often are defeated when it is necessary to compare each change in policy *and* program with the preceding policy decision. Administrative action is seldom planned on the basis of assessing the most efficient means of securing clear-cut policy goals. More often the procedure is one of "muddling through" by following piecemeal, but workable, solutions to immediate policy problems regardless of long-range impact.

FORMS AND TECHNIQUES OF POLICY APPLICATION

Forms of Policy Application. There are several recognized methods by which administrators apply policy. One of the most common is enforcement of existing statutes. Although the bulk of law enforcement occurs in state and local communities, there are innumerable federal statutes that must be applied under the jurisdiction of the national community. These include laws dealing with income taxes, corporate taxes, narcotics, voting rights, monopolies, kidnapping, and civil rights. When the Department of Justice detects offenders and apprehends, arraigns, and prosecutes violators, it is in effect applying policy. In recent years, for example, its Federal Bureau of Investigation and Civil Rights Division have been particularly concerned with violations of federal statutes dealing with voting rights.

Another form of policy application is through administrative adjudication. Administrators are charged with the task of adjudicating conflicts that arise between individuals or organizations that dispute the legitimacy of agency rules, regulations, and procedures. The dispute is settled, in effect, by administrative trial; rights of appeal to the courts are protected. The primary example of such adjudicative agencies are the independent regulatory agencies such as the Interstate Commerce Commission, the Federal Trade Commission, and the Federal Communications Commission.

Many statutes creating administrative agencies merely outline what the agency can and cannot do. In the absence of legislative direction, the agency itself must make specific rules and regulations. Freight rates for railways are established under jurisdiction of the Interstate Commerce Commission. Criteria for what constitutes "pure foods" are established by the Food and Drug Administration. Thus, administrators, in the process of applying policy, often make policy.

Techniques of Policy Application. One technique of applying policy is through the use of publicity. Some agencies have only limited authority to coerce offenders of agency regulations; therefore, they publicly expose the group involved in hopes of preventing further encroachments on the public interest. The Federal Trade Commission, for example, by publicly disclosing purported frauds, supplements its authority to take to court industries that engage in false and misleading advertising. If bad publicity threatens the industrial image, the businesses involved cease offensive activities.

Contact with the community through field offices is another technique of policy application. A number of federal agencies maintain regional and local offices, an organizational feature that brings the agencies directly into contact with a community-wide clientele. Such contact, by identifying local interests with wider organizational goals, sometimes serves as a means to generate wider support for the work of the agency. The Post Office department, for example, often speaks to local communities through the local postmaster.

It should be kept in mind that policy application, whatever its direction or techniques, requires administrators to make choices. When and if to prosecute, when and what to publicize, when and how to seek local cooperation — all are decisions that must be reached. How they are reached is determined in large measure by the administrator's perspective as a policy-maker, our next topic for discussion.

ADMINISTRATIVE PERSPECTIVE AND POLICY APPLICATION

Wrapped up in administrative policy formulation, organization, and management are rules, practices, and customs that shape perspectives of individual bureaucrats as they go about making policy choices. The work of any administrative agency is governed in part by the particular considerations that entered into the creation of the agency and the delegation of authority and responsibility to it. Administrative perspective is also conditioned by the fact that bureaucratic leaders operate within the framework of a large-scale organizational structure formally centralized in character. In addition, certain practices common to all administrative agencies — the recruitment, hiring, and promotion of agency personnel — modify the outlook of the administrator. Budgeting practices are also crucial to administrative policy-making. Moreover, there may be several areas of policy choice within which the administrative leader possesses customary discretion: what policies are appropriate to a given situation, when they should be applied, and with what intensity they should be applied (with flexibility or rigidity). There are areas of judgment regarding what information to secure prior to policy choice and what information to distribute. This involves communication within the organization and between the agency and its bases of support and opposition among the general public. In this section we consider the relation of a few of these features to bureaucratic behavior.

ORIGINS AND STRUCTURE
OF POLICY APPLICATION

Bureaucratic Origins and Growth. Constitutionally, the creation of an administrative agency is primarily a function of the legislature. Once established, agencies become separate units in the distribution of rewards or punishments within the political community. Even in applying spelled-out legislative directions, an agency must exhibit some discretion of its own. A law enforcement agency, such as the Federal Bureau of Investigation, must decide whether or not evidence is sufficient to arrest a person who has committed an action defined as criminal by statute. The agency may also have to consider who the violator is and possible repercussions if he is prosecuted. Legislative policy-making is usually not marked by a great deal of detail but rather by declarations of intent and general directives. The policy details become the province of the agency charged with administering the statute.

Legislation reflects the demands of interests that have sought the aid of government in achieving goals and purposes. Prior to this century the role of federal activity in community life was minimized. A constantly expanding frontier, where land was easily acquired and towns sparsely populated and generally isolated, generated a spirit of self-reliance, which looked with suspicion upon community-wide policies. Government was largely limited to a policing operation. Politics and economics were considered separate spheres, each independent of the other. This spirit, coupled with the rise of *laissez-faire* social and economic theories, kept government largely out of areas of economic and social legislation until late in the nineteenth century. Government intervention occurred first at the state level as agricultural groups, such as the Granger movement in the Middle West, began to agitate for regulation of railroads and other economic reforms. Initially "the new public administration was in a sense the unwanted child of a nation bent on the wild pursuit of material gain." [3] Gradually, as the nation experienced the impact of its industrial revolution, with its accompanying social and economic maladjustments, a strong movement formed to introduce federal action. The new federal agencies created by Congress after the turn of the century reflected the demands of emergent interests. These agencies were justified as attempts to control "private interests" whose activities were disapproved. The political culture provided a brake on private governing. Interests that fought the creation of agencies looked upon government's new regulatory role as "interference" with free enterprise.

In creating administrative agencies, Congress declared public policy; but it did so in broad terms. The technical nature of the tasks assigned to the new agencies made detailed direction not only undesirable but also impossible. As a result, congressional directives for the administration of public policy stated that agencies act in a "just" and "reasonable" fashion and in the "public interest" in fulfilling their responsibilities. Thus, much of the burden of reconciling group conflict was shifted from Congress to the administrative bureaucracy. It was not long until conflicts themselves were delegated to administrative policy-makers. Soon pressure groups affected by the activities of the new agencies sought to influence the policy choices of administrators. Sometimes they sought to protect the status quo; at other times they endeavored to advance new proposals. Administrative agencies became focal points for policy dispute and decision.

The Structure of Administration. One student of public administration has defined "organization" as "merely the means of dividing work." [4] In many ways government is itself an organization of people, and the performance of its function requires a division of work. A glance at an organizational chart of any major federal agency — not to mention the entire federal government (see chart, Chapter Eleven) — reveals the size and complexity of the formal division of federal administration. Generally speaking, the administrative branch is organized on the basis of functions performed and type of agency. The basic pattern is hierarchical: authority and responsibility (that is, the chain of command) are based upon superior-subordinate relations. At the top of this hierarchy, and in formal command of the entire administrative structure (except as discussed below), is the President, the "chief administrator." Immediately below the

---

[3] John A. Vieg, "The Growth of Public Administration," in Fritz Morstein-Marx (ed.), *Elements of Public Administration* (New York: Prentice-Hall, 1946), p. 14.
[4] Paul H. Appleby, *Policy and Administration* (University, Ala.: University of Alabama Press, 1949), p. 67.

President are the *executive departments* headed by secretaries who are also members of the presidential Cabinet. These include the Departments of State; Treasury; Defense; Justice; Post Office; Interior; Agriculture; Commerce; Labor; Health, Education, and Welfare; Housing and Urban Development; and Transportation. Each department is formally divided on a hierarchical basis into bureaus, divisions, sections and even desks. In many of these departments, subagencies operate autonomously; and the department itself coordinates administration to a minimal degree. For example: the Federal Bureau of Investigation in the Department of Justice or the Office of Education in the Department of Health, Education, and Welfare are only nominally administered from the center of the hierarchy. Attempts to coordinate often produce a form of corporate conflict between semiautonomous agencies and administrative superiors. This problem is encountered in efforts to "unify" the Departments of Army, Air Force, and Navy within the Department of Defense.

In addition to the departments there are a number of *independent executive agencies*. Generally designated as "independent" because they are not within a departmental organization, many of these agencies are still under presidential control. The Veterans Administration, for example, is responsible formally to the President in the chain of command, but its head does not carry Cabinet rank. Other examples are the Selective Service System, the Atomic Energy Commission, the Tariff Commission, the Civil Service Commission, and the United States Information Agency.

A number of independent agencies are free of presidential control. These are the so-called "quasi-legislative" or "quasi-judicial" agencies that exercise authority not purely executive in nature. They are the *independent regulatory agencies*. The authority of the Federal Communications Commission to issue licenses to radio and television stations, or to refuse to renew such licenses for violation of regulations set up by the Commission, illustrates the legislative and judicial nature of the independent commission. A body of members appointed by the President heads each commission; members can be removed only for causes specified by Congress. The independence of these commissions was protected by a Supreme Court decision in 1935 which held that these "quasi" agencies perform functions legislative and judicial in nature and that their members could not be removed by the President. The Interstate Commerce Commission, the National Labor Relations Board, the Federal Trade Commission, the Federal Power Commission, the Securities and Exchange Commission, and the Civil Aeronautics Board are all independent of presidential control.[5]

A fourth major type of administrative agency is the *oversight*, or

5 *Humphrey's Executor (Rathbun)* v. *United States* (1935) 295 U.S. 602.

service, agency, which serves other agencies of government. The General Services Administration is the purchasing agent, storage agency, documents clerk, and builder and maintainer of federal offices. The Bureau of the Budget is the major arm of the President in fiscal control and budgetary management. The General Accounting Office operates as the congressional "watchdog" of executive expenditures through its auditing functions.

Finally there is a fifth type of agency: the *government corporation.* Organized much like private businesses, government corporations — such as the Federal Deposit Insurance Corporation or the Tennessee Valley Authority — were created to carry out primarily economic operations not provided for by private enterprise. At present there are corporations that extend credit for farmers, produce electric power, insure bank deposits, provide loans for home buyers, and operate terminal and port facilities. Until 1945 these agencies were generally independent of budgetary and fiscal controls exercised over other government departments, but in 1945 Congress removed much of their fiscal independence.

Agencies are created by Congress with different purposes in mind. Some provide a voice for particular sets of stable community interests; these may be called *clientele agencies.* The creation of the Department of Agriculture in 1862 granted recognition to the agrarian interest and was designed to render special assistance to, and promote the welfare of, farm groupings. Two department-level agencies of this type were added during the early part of this century: Commerce in 1903 and Labor in 1913. While many federal agencies perform functions and services that aid particular interests (occupational, social, economic, and geographical), these three departments are more closely associated with a particular clientele than any other. The Department of Agriculture employs about seventeen thousand people who do research in animal and plant diseases, development of better crop yields, insect control, and other types of study aimed at improving the lot of the farmer. In addition, it supplies information — especially through its nationwide network of county extension agents — on hundreds of subjects of interest to the agricultural sector of the economy. Programs in soil conservation, rural electrification, and rehabilitation of tenant farmers are also major services performed to aid agricultural interests. The Department of Commerce has long been considered the "businessman's department" and Labor the "workingman's department" since both perform services and conduct programs aimed at the welfare of these groups. Other clientele agencies perform tasks directly associated with the needs and interests of more particular segments of the population. The Veterans Administration administers programs that dispense about 5 billion dollars per year in benefits to veterans.

Government corporations, which also are created to provide a voice for particular interests, may also be considered clientele agencies.

Some agencies may better be designated as *functional* in their nature. They are not created to serve a particular clientele but to perform a necessary governmental purpose. The Department of Treasury or Department of State are examples. Other agencies are *areal* in nature: they perform their functions and serve clienteles in a specific locale or region. Local draft boards of the Selective Service System are cases in point. Board members have considerable discretion in selecting individuals for military duty.

In the sense that all administrative agencies serve particular groups or draw support from special groups in planning programs, all are clientele agencies. Identification with a particular interest or interests can enhance the position of the agency; but, as the following two examples illustrate, it may also be highly detrimental.

The Tennessee Valley Authority, a government corporation, was established by Congress in 1933 for the purpose of developing the water, electric power, and agricultural resources of a vast multi-state region. Early in its history the TVA decided on a grass-roots approach in performing its administrative and policy-making functions. Local and state governments, as well as private interests within the area, became the instruments for carrying out the mission of the agency. This course was chosen as a more efficient and democratic method than directing the valley's resources from a central agency. Although grass-roots democracy proved highly successful, it also resulted in what Philip Selznick termed "informal cooptation" by the clientele groups within the valley. Selznick defines this process as "unacknowledged absorption of nucleuses of power into the administrative structure of an organization which makes possible the elimination or appeasement of potential sources of opposition." Further, "the organization commits itself to avenues of activity and lines of policy enforced by the character of the coopted elements." [6] As a result of its close association with local groups, TVA was forced, in order to retain the support of these groups, to alter some of its goals. TVA has, however, also managed to develop strong support outside the valley area for its general programs and has successfully defended its position against groups (for example, private power companies) who view their interests as adversely affected by the activities of TVA.

An illustration of an agency jeopardized by too close an association with a clientele group is afforded by the Interstate Commerce Commission's close association with railroad interests. Samuel P. Huntington has

[6] Philip Selznick, *TVA and the Grass Roots* (Berkeley: University of California Press, 1953), p. 217.

shown that historically (the agency was created in 1887) the Commission has followed policies that in many respects parallel the position of the railroad industry.[7] Railroad interests have yielded strong support for the agency against attacks on reorganization proposals stemming from private interests, the President, or Congress. As new developments and changes in the transportation industry occurred, the Commission failed to exercise leadership and has become, like the railroads, "a defender of the status quo." Because the commission has retained its association with the rather narrow interests of the railroad industry, it has lost support both within the executive branch and among pressure groups outside government.

Without access to administrative agencies, groups are clearly disadvantaged. The American Cotton Manufactures Institute, for example, has been generally unsuccessful in its campaign to prevent importation of Japanese textiles because decisions on trade agreements and restrictions have been the province of the Department of State. Textile interests have considerably less access to this agency than to the Department of Agriculture, where a clientele relationship is much more likely to exist.

If an agency has been established with the expressed purpose of reducing and controlling the advantages of a particular interest, then the legislation that created it is likely to be highly controversial. The agency is born as an unwanted child of the interest it must govern; moreover, it is likely to face congressional opposition for some time to come in requests for appropriations, more authority, and adequate personnel. The National Labor Relations Board, for example, created under the Wagner Act of 1935 to regulate labor-management relations, has been subject to periodic attacks from employers and congressmen who are unfriendly toward its existence or who charge that the Board follows pro-labor policies in handling disputes between management and labor interests.

The conditions under which an administrative agency is created have direct bearing on how well it can fulfill its purposes. If the agency originates in an atmosphere of muted conflict, then access to the agency by relevant social interests is likely to be clearly demarcated. But if the agency was born in an effort to compromise seriously hostile interests, then the agency itself turns into a battleground on which the unresolved conflict is fought. Generally pressure groups that were strong enough to effect the creation of an administrative agency will be strong enough to support it. But if the agency or its programs developed out of the President's or a congressman's ability to articulate *unorganized interests,* policy application may suffer once presidential or congressional leadership has faded. Then the organized interests that lost the battle for policy

[7] Samuel P. Huntington, "The Marasmus of the ICC: The Commission, the Railroads and the Public Interest," *Yale Law Review* (April, 1952), pp. 467–508.

leadership and adoption may win the war over policy-making by "capturing" the administrative agency designed to implement policies against these very same organized interests. Manipulation and abuse in the sale of securities prior to the 1929 stock market crash resulted in the creation of the Securities and Exchange Commission in 1933. Although the SEC has been granted strong authority to regulate securities transactions, the agency has relied on what is called "cooperative regulation," an arrangement under which the securities exchanges have largely been permitted to police themselves. This arrangement represents a built-in special access of the interests whose activities the SEC was created to regulate.

Professor David Truman points out that if the terms of the "legislative mandate" are ambiguous, there is an increased likelihood that organized interests — and not the administrator — can control access to policy application.[8] Legislation granting formal power to an administrator may reflect compromises dictated by competing interests. The administrator inherits conflicts postponed but not resolved by the legislative process. His task is to adjust the interests of competing groups; if he interprets his mandate so as to antagonize any of these interests he risks attack and the agency may be unable to perform its tasks. This underscores the point made earlier about pressure performance being conditioned in part by the pattern of policy. To survive, the bureaucratic leader may be forced to enter into informal agreements with the social interests he purportedly is to control. Thus, reciprocal relations between administrative and pressure leaders are fostered, and administrators may become mere pawns in the hands of pressure leaders rather than regulators.

Two conclusions can be drawn about the politics of administrative organization. First, although Congress adopts policies, implementation of these policies is left to the bureaucracy. Through bargaining within the two houses and between the two houses and the executive branch, Congress forges broad public policy. The application of these policies is the task of the bureaucracy; it is one which shifts the resolution of interest conflict from the legislative to the administrative arm of government. Policy-making, then, is further fragmented into a host of governmental agencies, each of which is the focal point for interest groups seeking accommodation of demands that may or may not have been met at the legislative level. Second, it is a vast oversimplification to view policy application as organized on a pyramidal structure controlled and supervised at the top by the President. Administrative agencies are in some cases statutorily independent of presidential control; but the actions of any agency are also shaped by pressures emanating from Congress, the

8 David B. Truman, *The Governmental Process* (New York: Alfred A. Knopf, 1953), pp. 443–44.

courts, private interests, and within the agency itself. Size alone militates against executive dominance of even that part of the bureaucracy over which the President legally has direct control. The problems of control over a constantly expanding "fourth branch" have led to three major reviews of the administrative branch in the last thirty years: President Franklin D. Roosevelt's Committee on Administrative Management (Brownlow Committee) in 1937; the Truman-appointed Hoover Commission, which reported in 1949; and a second Hoover Commission, which reported in 1955. All emphasized the "integrative principle" of organization, which suggests a hierarchical arrangement wherein a central superior supervises a relatively small number of subordinates (usually set at three to fifteen) and within which there should be clear lines of authority and responsibility. The first Hoover Commission recommended that there should be a "clear line of authority reaching down through every step of the organization and no subordinate should have authority independent from that of his superior." [9] But any attempt at administrative reorganization, as rational and wise as it may appear, is itself the focus of interest conflict, since interests (including agencies themselves) will frequently support or oppose change depending upon whether they stand to gain or lose by it.

ORGANIZATIONAL BEHAVIOR

As suggested above, an administrator's perspective is shaped partially by the type of agency in which he serves and the conditions surrounding its creation and development. But like his fellow administrators in other agencies, the bureaucrat is a member of a vast apparatus of political action. Modern bureaucracy is distinguished from other forms of organized policy-making; each feature of the modern bureaucracy influences the organizational behavior and policy choices of administrative officials.

Regularized Official Relationships. The rationale underlying the organization of bureaucratic activity is the attempt to regularize the relationships between policy officials. Preference is accorded to action occurring within a reasonably stable and predictable environment. The universe of chance occurrences, accidents, and the unexpected is gradually pared down to manageable proportions by a variety of techniques; formal prescriptions of what administrators should or should not do are codified; routine procedures are established for handling interest appeals, office communications, and public information; organizational charts are neatly arranged in order to remove as much ambiguity as possible from superior-subordinate relations.

---

[9] The Commission on the Organization of the Executive Branch of the Government, *General Management of the Executive Branch* (Washington, D.C.: Government Printing Office, 1949), p. 34.

An example of attempts to standardize policy activities can be found in the Federal Power Commission. The *Rules of Practice and Procedure,* under which this regulatory agency operates, comprise more than sixty pages of small print. Buried in these pages are precise prescriptions of what can be expected of commission personnel under any and all circumstances. Such matters are covered as who may file petitions before the commission, the operation of pre-hearing conferences and hearings before the commission, the procedures for issuing subpoenas, methods for taking depositions, etc. Indeed there is even a detailed description of the official seal of the commission: "a shield upon the breast of the eagle displaying a belt of lightning sinister-wise complemented by two gas flames representing the Commission's regulatory authority in the fields of electric energy and gas." [10]

Organizational Hierarchy and Control. Another feature of bureaucratic organization is its large size. Relations are largely impersonal, a feature that tends to intimidate many an individual making a plea before a bureaucratic agency. For the administrator dealing directly with a group, such impersonality within the organization permits him to refuse interest demands by citing an anonymous "they" who forbid action or a set of "rules" that limits discretion. Coordination of the far-flung impersonal apparatus is achieved through a hierarchical structuring of relations. Details of such structuring vary from agency to agency. One, for example, may strive for unity of command whereby a single official is ultimately responsible for all policy decisions; another may operate with a plural executive or set of officials sharing responsibility for decisions. Some agencies strive to centralize decision-making, as does the Department of Defense. Others, such as the Selective Service System, decentralize responsibility: the discretion for drafting and deferment is left to the draftee's "neighbors" on the local board.

A position within the hierarchical structure of an organization carries with it a certain status; one is superior to some and subordinate to others. Each status carries with it certain rights and duties. The administrator's perspective is naturally affected by his understanding of the prerogatives associated with command or obedience. Victor A. Thompson points to a few of the features that distinguish the "boss" from his underlings: he has final say on policy measures subject to no appeal; he may have absolute discretion in decisions affecting employee goals, including matters of raises and promotions; he possesses certain coercive tools that style his decisions as commands; and he can monopolize organizational communi-

[10] Federal Power Commission, *Rules of Practice and Procedure* (Washington, D.C.: Government Printing Office, 1958), p. 2.

cations both internally and with the public at large.[11] The status of the subordinate is threatened by both the chief and the continuing possibility of congressional investigation or cutbacks of personnel. Robert Presthus, in his study of the impact of organizational activity on American life, has termed this characteristic as "status anxiety," a condition in which the underling is never really secure in his position. His policy perspective is shaped by attempts to make his organizational surroundings more congenial to his personal interests.[12]

The "ideal" of hierarchical control may contribute to the development of oligarchical control within an agency. As a means of enhancing this status and protecting their positions from adverse action by superiors, bureau chiefs may tend to develop arrangements by which the superior-subordinate relationship is modified. Because of special skills or knowledge, strong public support, alliances with influential congressmen, or long career service bureau chiefs may enjoy a status that insulates them from control by superiors in the organization. Agency control may, then, lie in the hands of administrators officially subordinate to their superior but actually exercising a large degree of autonomy in making decisions. With its widespread public and congressional support, the Federal Bureau of Investigation in the Department of Justice under J. Edgar Hoover certainly enjoys special status. The Chief of the Forest Service in the Department of Agriculture and the Army Corps of Engineers occupy similar status.

Such relationships may not only produce oligarchical control but they also raise problems regarding the compatibility of bureaucratic and democratic theory. The liberal-democratic tradition insists on the "rights" of subordinates in the hierarchical organization (for example, personal dignity and advancement on merit), yet these rights may conflict with hierarchical theory. In essence, "the doctrines of democracy and liberalism which underlie our state have made almost no impact upon our bureaucratic organizations," a condition which leads to oligarchical control within agencies in attempts to protect subordinate rights in the face of the "actual power of hierarchies." [13]

Task Specialization and Professionalism. Bureaucratic organization is also differentiated by the degree of specialization of task within the department, agency, and bureau. The division of work is such that specific duties are routinized in order that "any fool can do it." Individuals are trained to task performance by adjusting to the modicum of standard

[11] Victor A. Thompson, *Modern Organization* (New York: Alfred A. Knopf, 1963), pp. 60–66.

[12] Robert Presthus, *The Organizational Society* (New York: Alfred A. Knopf, 1962).

[13] Thompson, *op. cit.*, p. 65.

operating procedures. Trained personnel may be moved in and out of slots without detriment to organizational goals. Administrative perspective is conditioned in part by this division of labor. Each bureaucrat's outlook on policy application is influenced by how he defines his role in the organization. To the extent that his duties are performed through routine rather than reflection, his view of personal discretion in policy affairs, his concept of organizational goals, and ultimately his notion of community interest will be affected. For example, an administrator who holds a narrow view of his discretionary authority will be less accessible to interests seeking to change his point of view. Where he holds a broader view of his discretion interest groups are more likely to be successful.

Not only are tasks specialized within bureaucratic organizations, but individuals also become specialists in particular matters within the broader specialization. For example: an individual employed by the Federal Home Loan Bank Board for twenty years can hardly avoid developing some degree of specialized competence in handling the special problems under that agency's jurisdiction. Subject-matter specialization, as well as task specialization, characterizes large-scale organizational life. But administrators are also specialized in another way. They become members in a single fraternity; that is, they are all government employees. With the exception of partisan appointees, most come through the ranks of civil service. They are professional administrators who make a career out of policy application. A professional outlook colors their conceptions of important policy values to be pursued; a professional *esprit* bands them together as career civil servants who are on the "inside" of policy-making and whose tenure as policy officials transcends that of partisan appointees, pressure-group leaders, and the sporadic awareness of a normally unconcerned community. Professionalism tends to set bureaucratic policy-makers apart from congressmen, judges, or the President. It also tends to set them apart from superiors who may be efficient administrators but less knowledgeable than their subordinates in matters involving specific areas of agency jurisdiction, or who may be political appointees unfamiliar with the specialized tasks of the professional in his department or bureau.

The amateur finds it increasingly difficult to deal with the problems and functions of modern government. Professionalism is the mark of modern administration, a trend that carries risks, as well as advantages, for the public. The risks involved have been classified by one student of administration, Emmette S. Redford, as "inertness, separation, and specialization." Inertness is prevalent when bureaucrats become "sluggish, self-satisfied, and interested in the survival of their existing habits and thought patterns." Adaptation to changing times and circumstances may be slow and individual initiative stifled. The second danger, separation, arises when a bureaucrat becomes so self-centered that he loses contact with lay opinion or develops a suspicion and distrust of outside forces. Specialization, which Redford sees as the "most persistent cause of separateness and the greatest danger of bureaucracy," produces administrators who fail to take a balanced view of situations and also creates problems in coordinating highly specialized personnel and agencies into a unified, coherent organization. "Each functional organization develops its own self-centered attitudes," a tendency that produces close ties with private clientele groups and with key committees and individuals in Congress in order to protect its status within the administrative structure.[14]

The characteristics of organizational behavior in the modern bureaucracy contribute to an administrative perspective that differs from others we have examined in discussing patterns of conflict resolution. But these same features are also the sources of conflict between organizational interests within an administrative department, agency, or bureau.

Victor Thompson's study of modern organizations underscores the point that much of internal bureaucratic conflict springs from a "disagreement over the reality of interdependence."[15] Administrators have different perspectives on how much they must depend upon one another in order to attain policy goals. Such disagreement flows in part from a refusal to accept new administrative specialties as legitimate in policy application. For example, it took some time before the computer specialist was admitted to the ranks of public administration; despite organizational disputes, he now occupies positions of high status in such agencies as the Internal Revenue Service, the Bureau of Census, and the Social Security Administration.

The major source of organizational conflict lies in the differing perspectives on policy application taken by the specialist in a particular area and the individual in a particular hierarchical niche. The former tends toward innovation of goals and procedures in continuing adjustment to changing problems and technology. The latter is oriented toward the status quo and is concerned with consolidating existing tasks and interests before pushing on to something new. There is a built-in tension in modern bureaucratic organizations. Efforts to produce rational organization and management result in differentiation of policy roles; these roles in turn contribute to divergent policy perspectives, values, and interests. Out of this differentiation comes intraorganizational conflict. Resolution of conflicts is complicated by the fact that either conflicts are never really recog-

[14] Emmette S. Redford, *Ideal and Practice in Public Administration* (Birmingham: The University of Alabama Press, 1958), pp. 63–67.
[15] Thompson, *op. cit.*, pp. 108–10.

nized as existent or, if recognized, are not accepted as legitimate. Conflicts are deemed abnormal. Efforts to resolve them are directed at formal reorganization of authority; but simple reorganization with new lines of command, new changes in staff and line functions, and modifications in organizational charts do not get to the source of the disputes. Hence, administrators look outside the organization for support of their positions within the bureaucracy. Informal policy alliances with partisan appointees, members of Congress, and pressure-group leaders are formed. External bargaining supplants internal resolution of organizational conflict.

ADMINISTRATIVE BEHAVIOR

The aim of administrative bureaucracy is rationality in both organization and management. But the behavior of the administrator is only in part conscious and reflective. Administrative behavior also includes activities that are conditioned and reactive. An administrator may provide clearly reasoned explanations for choices, but his real motives may remain clouded. His decisions reflect a continuing interplay between values and facts, between ends that are sought and the means for their achievement.[16] We noted in Chapter Eleven that the two are seldom easily separated in policy behavior.

A brief illustration should help to clarify the relation between ends sought and means used. A prison warden, in dealing with a recalcitrant inmate, is faced with a number of choices. Should the goal of prison administration be to rehabilitate prisoners so that they can ultimately assume the role of useful citizens? Or is the overriding end the maintenance of security within the prison? The choice of means in dealing with the recalcitrant prisoner will be significantly affected by which end value is chosen. There may, of course, be other value choices, and the means to achieve the goal or goals will be multiple. A particular choice is dependent not only upon the goals sought but also upon the course of action taken to realize them.

Certain *value premises* recur frequently in making bureaucratic decisions. Among these are the desire for efficiency, the quest for standards of fair play, achievement of the objectives of the organization, and the personal values of the bureaucrat. Efficiency, for example, is calculated in terms of the comparative "costs" of alternative courses of action. If two courses of action will achieve the same results, choice is determined by which costs less. The term "cost" includes general social cost of which money is one, but not necessarily the major, consideration. Or if two

---

[16] Herbert A. Simon, Donald W. Smithburg, and Victor A. Thompson, *Public Administration* (New York: Alfred A. Knopf, 1959), Chap. 3.

courses of action are equal in cost, then the action that produces the greater results will be chosen.

Fair play emphasizes fairness in dealing with individuals, including matters such as proper procedures ("due process") and equitable treatment of people in the application of rules. The activities of regulatory agencies, for example, would be premised upon the achievement of fair and equitable treatment of all interests subject to regulation.

Organization objectives are based on an organization's conception of which interests are to be served and which values are to be achieved in its operations. There may also be a close connection between the ability of an organization to survive and the objectives it seeks. Recalling the case of TVA, service to particular interests in the valley area was not only an early objective but became virtually a necessity if the agency was to retain major support for survival.

Finally, an individual may seek goals contrary to those of the organization, which may in fact pose a threat to the survival of the organization itself. The drive for higher wages and more prestige may, for example, lead an employee to ignore organizational values for purposes of achieving his own. On the other hand, some personal values may be utilized by the organization for the achievement of its own goals, efficiency, or fair play. High wages, prestige, or a feeling of participation and importance induce employees to accept goals desired by the organization.

The *background of the individual* — his education, formal training, economic class, religion, family life, and ethnic group — also shapes administrative behavior. Attitudes, knowledge, personality, and character are brought by the administrator into the organization. Further, all members are subject to the behavioral norms or mores of society. Thus, "beatnik" behavior by employees of an agency administering a government-sponsored youth program would most probably not be tolerated.

Administrative behavior is also affected by *social* and *personal relations* maintained both within and outside the organization. A clash of personalities within an organization can have direct bearing on the choice made by an employee. So, too, can the friendships and relations he makes with fellow employees. An employee tends to become involved with the purposes and goals of an organization and to develop agency loyalty. The development of high morale and avoidance of friction and uncooperative behavior are major concerns of those who seek to define standards of personnel administration. But it should be kept in mind that an individual's attitudes are also influenced by the professional, occupational, and other associations he holds outside the organization. For example, an attorney in the Department of Justice's Civil Rights Division, who also holds membership in the American Civil Liberties Union, is subject to having his attitudes on a particular civil rights question influenced by such association.

The Department of Agriculture has always had a large number of administrators whose training reflects the rural background of agricultural interests. Government service offers an attractive career for graduates trained in such areas as agricultural economics, soil conservation, or veterinary medicine. The Veterans Administration includes a high number of American Legion members in key positions. Also the growing emphasis on expertise and specialization brings increasing numbers of administrators with professional group memberships into the federal service. Although such relationships do not by themselves establish preferential access for certain groups, they help mold attitudes favorable to those groups in which the bureaucrat holds membership.[17]

ADMINISTRATIVE PRESSURES AND POLICY APPLICATION

The view from the bureaucrat's desk is a function of the factors mentioned thus far; but what he sees also depends on the pressures brought to bear upon him. The major sources of pressure are the Congress, the President, and both partisan and pressure leaders. Since group pressures have been dealt with in this and preceding chapters and since partisan pressures on administration are channeled primarily through the Presidency, we shall limit our discussion here to the controls of Congress and President over administrative action.

CONGRESS AND ADMINISTRATIVE BUREAUCRACY

Although the Constitution grants legislative jurisdiction to Congress, the bulk of federal law is not found in the *Statutes at Large* but in the *Federal Register,* the official publication of rules, regulations, executive orders, and directions of the bureaucracy. The reasons for the growth of administrative policy-making have been outlined previously. Generally speaking, the responsibility of Congress to make law cannot be exercised adequately without delegation of authority to the administrative branch. As working principles, separation of powers and checks and balances are not serious obstacles to administrative participation in policy-making. Separation of powers means that the *whole* function of one branch may not be exercised by another. By *blending* the functions of the three branches, the Constitution provides the basis for control of each over the

---

[17] See Francis E. Rourke (ed.), *Bureaucratic Power in National Politics* (Boston: Little, Brown and Co., 1965), *passim,* for other factors involved in bureaucratic behavior.

other. On the basis of this theory, Congress possesses authority to exercise control over the administrative branch. Article I grants to Congress the discretion to create administrative agencies, to advise and consent (or withhold consent) to presidential appointments of officials, and to exercise the "power of the purse."

Implicit in such delegations are other powers. The right to investigate the operations of the executive is derived from the authority to make laws. Authority to reorganize the structure of the administrative branch is implied from congressional discretion to authorize new programs and new departments. So, too, is the capacity to create agencies outside the control of the Chief Executive, such as independent regulatory agencies and government corporations. Congress has from its beginnings prescribed the organization of the executive branch, shaped the functions of government through appropriations, launched investigations of executive-branch practices and policies, and provided regulations regarding federal employees. Each of these congressional controls over administration is a subject of major importance in itself. Here we illustrate the scope of congressional control in one particular area: the civil service.

Congress and the Civil Service. Prior to the passage of the Pendleton Act in 1883, federal employment reflected the operation of the "spoils system" under which the incoming President replaced federal employees with personnel of his choice. Appointments largely depended upon partisan services rendered rather than qualifications for the position. The Pendleton Act inaugurated the *merit system* under which personnel were appointed on the basis of demonstrated ability, such as by examination, and retained their employment despite party change in the executive. By 1932 the merit system had been extended to cover 80 per cent of federal employees; but, as a result of exemptions covering new agencies and activities of the New Deal, this figure dropped to about 60 per cent by 1936. Through a series of executive orders issued by President Roosevelt in 1938 and also through congressional action in 1940, the percentage of federal employees under the merit system was raised to 95 per cent.

Congressional activity in the area of personnel administration prior to 1933 was relatively slight. Since then, however, over fifteen hundred statutes have been enacted covering a wide range of subjects. These include (1) regulations relating to the merit system and exemptions from it; (2) statutes relating to the administration and organization of the personnel system; (3) matters related to retirement, pay scales and other benefits; (4) veterans preferences and employee rights and conduct; and (5) other controls and limits imposed through riders to appropriations bills.[18]

[18] Joseph P. Harris, *Congressional Control of Administration* (Washington, D.C.: The Brookings Institution, 1964), p. 167.

Controversy over congressional activity has centered not on the question of whether the legislative branch has authority to enact such measures (which it does) but rather upon the desirability and wisdom of such control. Students of public administration generally agree that broad personnel policy (for example, retirement, salary schedule, organization, public employee organizations, and employee participation in party activities), is the province of Congress, but detailed rules and regulations should be left to the President and the Civil Service Commission.

The controversy over the relation of the Civil Service Commission to the President is really one concerning congressional control over personnel administration. The commission, created by the Pendleton Act, is charged with the overall administration of recruitment, classification, and placement of federal employees. Until 1956 its members were appointed and dismissed by the President. Congress in 1956 provided that members be given six-year overlapping terms, an action clearly aimed at making the commission less dependent upon the President. The President has, however, continued to exercise control over the commission. In 1960 a proposal to bring personnel administration more directly under the President and to reduce the authority of the commission failed to get to the floor of the Senate. The measure received strong support from the National Civil Service League and other interests which argued that the President should control personnel administration in carrying out his administrative responsibilities. In opposition stood representatives of public employee unions and veterans' organizations who feared that the legislation would affect their rights and benefits.[19] Basically the controversy was over whether the President was to be given control of personnel administration or the commission was to be considered an agent of the legislature. This dispute directly involved interest groups who benefited, or at least believed they would benefit, from arrangements under which congressional control could be more easily exercised.

By giving preference to veterans in federal employment, Congress again exercised control over the civil service. The practice of granting veterans special treatment in securing public employment dates back to 1865 when Union Army veterans who had been disabled by war were given preference by legislative action. The Veterans Preference Act of 1944 granted a wide variety of exemptions from existing merit regulations. Naturally, groups who support the strengthening of the merit system express concern over such legislation. Congress, however, has been responsive to veterans organizations, such as the American Legion, that have sought special considerations for veterans.

Congressional control over personnel administration has been exercised

19 *Ibid.*, pp. 35–36, 173–74.

in a number of other respects. In 1950 Congressman Whitten succeeded in winning approval of a rider to an appropriations measure that, among other things, fixed the number of permanent employees of certain departments and agencies at no more than the total number employed as of September 1, 1950. Professor Joseph Harris has commented that "no other rider illustrates so well the difficulties and unfortunate effects that flow from detailed legislative limitations and restrictions on personnel, however laudable their objectives." [20]

Congressional controls over personnel have sharply increased in recent decades. Because it was concerned about the loyalty of federal employees during and after World War II, Congress enacted legislation and sought presidential executive "Loyalty Orders" that required investigation of federal civilian employees. In addition to these measures, the power to confirm appointments, to limit staff by statutory restrictions on personnel, and to intervene by other means reveal the continuing struggle between Congress and President over control of the bureaucracy.

Congressional Supervision. In addition to the formal controls Congress has over the administrative branch, there are informal controls stemming from the relations between executive officials and individual legislators. In committee hearings, for example, legislators have the opportunity to ask questions and make statements. The attitudes revealed by these questions and statements must be taken into account by the administrator. Since major decisions are made in standing committees and are only infrequently rejected by the whole body, both administrators and interest groups will be aware of their importance. Moreover, congressional hearings can be used as a sounding board for administrators in a struggle against coordination by the President, pressures of private groups, and other administrative agencies.

One aspect of congressional-administrative relations that represents an important, if not formal, means of control is the role congressmen play as administrative "lobbyists" for their constituents. A telephone call or visit to an agency by a representative or senator in behalf of a constituent or interest group may be crucial in an administrator's choice of action. This will be of special importance if the legislator is in a key position (for example, a committee or subcommittee chairman, or an appropriations-committee member) to assist or block an agency's program or organizational goals. Whether the legislator is running an insignificant "errand" for a single constituent or representing major interest groups in his constituency, his inquiries and efforts are usually given special attention. An administrator will seek to avoid antagonizing a legislator; and, although

[20] *Ibid.*, p. 195.

he may not comply with demands, he will often make a serious effort to conciliate them.

Appropriations are of special importance in informal processes of control. Agencies need money to operate, but appropriations bills may be so constructed as to threaten the survival of the agencies themselves. In 1946, for example, a House Appropriations Subcommittee, which was hostile to the operation of the Grazing Service in the Department of Agriculture, cut the service's appropriation by almost half of what it had been. The result was that the Grazing Service had to curtail the number of its employees. The director of the agency was relieved of his duties. The agency was caught between the demands of its clientele — the users of federal grazing lands — who wanted low grazing fees and had access to the Senate Committee on Interior, and a hostile House subcommittee representing interests that demanded increased fees.[21]

Sometimes pressure groups and administrators, recognizing the powers of congressional committees, obtain advance clearance of policies that vary from the position of the committee. We noted the frequency of close relations between agencies and influential members of a committee, especially the chairman. Such a relationship existed during World War II between Representative Carl Vinson of Georgia, Chairman of the House Naval Affairs Committee, and the Navy Department. Because of Vinson's extensive knowledge of naval affairs — developed during more than twenty years of service on the committee — and his key role as chairman, the Navy Department frequently consulted with him. After the war and following the unification of the armed services, Vinson became Chairman of the House Armed Services Committee, a position that enabled him to develop much the same relation with the Army and Air Force that he held with the Navy.[22]

It is possible to distinguish between two types of legislative activity in relation to the administrative bureaucracy: legislative "control" and legislative "oversight." The first refers to actions that precede administrative activity. Included under control are instructions from the legislature regarding agency practices or consideration of administrative proposals for approval or veto. Legislative oversight takes place *after* administrative action has occurred. Action of this type includes committee reports criticizing the operation of an agency, full-scale investigation of a particular policy or the operations of an agency, or the cutting of appropriations to indicate disapproval of agency actions.[23]

[21] Phillip C. Foss, "The Grazing Fee Dilemma," *Inter-University Case Program* (University, Ala.: University of Alabama Press, 1957).

[22] Truman, *op. cit.*, pp. 423–24.

[23] Harris, *op. cit.*, pp. 9, 88–89.

Although administrative departments and agencies cannot ignore the legislature, the nature of the legislative process limits the ability of Congress to control the bureaucracy. The fragmented nature of congressional decision, the bicameral system, and the difficulties of party leadership all facilitate the dispersion of decision-making. For example, congressional control over appropriations is divided among an appropriations committee in each house. Both operate through an extensive subcommittee system. Often the members of these subcommittees represent interests vitally concerned with maintaining or increasing the budgets of the agencies under review; budgets of agencies that lack support of key clientele groups are often cut by a subcommittee.

Another serious limitation on the ability of Congress to control or oversee the administrative branch is the highly technical and complex nature of the federal budget itself. Although individual congressmen are experts in certain areas of administrative activity and retain professional staffs of experts, the acquisition of intimate knowledge regarding the activities of one department — not to mention the entire executive structure — is virtually impossible. Often there is no choice but to accept the word of the executive branch that requests funds or suggests that new or expanded functions of agencies are needed. The defense budget, which usually comprises about 69 per cent of the total budget, is based upon an appraisal of needs and information that may or may not be available to Congress. No congressman likes to be in the position of opposing expenditures that are declared essential to "national security" by military and civilian spokesmen of the President.

Even where Congress does attempt to force its will upon the administration, on major policy matters it may not succeed. For example: in 1962 Secretary of Defense Robert McNamara, with the approval of President Kennedy, proposed drastic cuts in appropriations for production of the RS-70 supersonic bomber.[24] The administration argued that bombers were technologically obsolete and that money should be spent on missile production. Opposition to the proposal came from the House Armed Services Committee, led by Chairman Carl Vinson, and from military and private interest groups. The Air Force wanted a buildup of the manned bomber program; and business interests, such as North American Aviation (who would build the RS-70), also fought the proposed policy change. Through the support of Representative George Mahon, chairman of the House Subcommittee on Defense Appropriations, the administration won, and RS-70 appropriations were drastically cut. The Senate did not, however, support McNamara's position and appropriated 491 million dollars for

[24] The following account is based on the description found in Peter Woll, *American Bureaucracy* (New York: W. W. Norton & Co., 1963), pp. 125–29.

the program, as against the 223 million dollars authorized by the House. In conference a figure of 362 million dollars was agreed upon. It was known, however, that Secretary McNamara had made a tacit agreement with House conferees that he would not spend the entire amount appropriated, thus making fruitless the Senate attempts to keep the RS-70 program alive. In this instance the administration was able to overcome strong congressional opposition to its policy proposals by taking advantage of the fragmented nature of the policy-making process in Congress. The "power of the purse" is clearly a less valuable instrument in some instances than might be supposed.

These factors highlight the inability of Congress to exercise a high degree of control or oversight over the bureaucracy. To say that Congress can *review* the administration is not to say that it can effectively regulate it. As the most representative branch in the system, its claim — both constitutionally and "democratically" — to have a voice in the policies and operations of the administrative branch can hardly be contested. How it should exercise its legitimate role in this regard is, however, a matter for debate. Whether Congress is equipped in available time and information or organization and procedures to do more than deal in broad policy areas is questionable.

THE PRESIDENT AND ADMINISTRATIVE BUREAUCRACY

A traditional struggle has existed between the executive and legislative branches, a struggle built into the system by the separation-of-powers and checks-and-balances mechanisms. As Chapter Twelve has suggested, the President is the most powerful single officer in the American political system. The congressional role in policy-making is shifting toward one of veto over executive proposals and away from policy initiation of its own. An increasing tendency to look to the President for policy leadership and initiation has paralleled this trend. Yet to what extent is the administrative branch itself controlled by the "Chief Administrator?"

Agencies exercising quasi-legislative and quasi-judicial functions are largely independent of presidential control, at least to the extent that their members are not subject to the removal powers of the President. Assuming an incumbency of eight years, however, the President will have an opportunity to select a majority of the membership of most such commissions. Government corporations occupy a similar status.

The President can seldom exercise supervision and direction over the entire administrative structure even if he possesses the formal authority to do so. He must deal with those matters he considers of greatest importance, thus leaving a sizable portion of the bureaucracy free to operate at the discretion of its administrators. Where discretion is greater, the ability of pressure groups to influence policy is enhanced, especially where the clientele of an agency is made up of one or a few major interests. If administrators resist such pressures, the group may seek its goals through legislative channels where access may be equally great or greater. Even where a department head or bureau chief is loyal to the President, he may be put in a position where he must weigh the effects of supporting his chief or risking the wrath of clientele groups with strong access to the legislature. Under circumstances where executive control is loose or absent, responsibility and control is fragmented among agencies in the administrative branch, a factor which makes it easier for interested groups to pressure administrators.

Even when a President does take personal interest in a dispute within the executive branch, he may be powerless to get his way. The classic example of this circumstance — although there are other less publicized instances — is that between the President and the Army Corps of Engineers. By statute the corps is placed within the Department of Army, but in fact it views its position as being responsible to Congress.[25] Originally designed to handle federal flood control and harbor projects, the corps began in the 1930's to expand its activities to reclamation, power production, irrigation, and other areas. It soon came into conflict with the Bureau of Reclamation in the Department of Interior, a controversy that brought President Roosevelt, and later President Truman, to intervene in behalf of the Bureau. Despite presidential directives and policy statements to congressional committees handling water projects, the corps used its close association with Congress to resist these directives. Although formally the corps is part of the Defense Department and thus subject to control by the Commander in Chief, Congress considers it responsible to Congress, not to the President. The fact that corps projects are of special interest to congressmen and their constituencies explains the inability of the President to develop a coordinated water-resources and flood-control policy. The clientele of the corps — congressmen and local interests — in this instance have exerted more pressure than the President.

Administrative agencies have a "survival interest" of their own. To survive, their functions must be politically accepted, and there must be "adequate consensus to permit administration."[26] To achieve such acceptance and consensus, attention must be given to interests concerned with the functions of a particular agency. Often a relatively small number of interests support an agency. When an agency is strongly backed by the

[25] Arthur A. Maass, "Congress and Water Resources," *The American Political Science Review*, XXXXIV (September, 1950), 576–93.

[26] Norton E. Long, *The Polity* (Chicago: Rand McNally & Co., 1962), p. 53.

interests it serves, it tends to support those interests and may become a captive of them. By comparison, the presidential constituency is much larger in scope. He must represent a larger public interest and make policies and decisions that accommodate a more diversified clientele. The compromises and considerations necessary in pursuing presidential goals are likely to differ from those negotiated in administrative agencies. A bureau in the Department of Commerce with a business clientele may reject presidential bids for coordination if it feels that its survival would be threatened by loss of business support. The Presidency is not the only source of bureaucratic vitality. Despite his grant of constitutional authority, the President finds it difficult to unravel the tangled threads of agency-clientele and agency-legislative-clientele relations.

POPULAR CONTROL AND POLICY APPLICATION

Liberal democracy leans heavily on the assertion that policy-makers must be responsible to the governed. That administrators make public policy is axiomatic. Modern bureaucracy poses two major problems. First, there is the quest for administrative efficiency, a concern of both democratic and non-democratic systems. Such factors as the recruitment and retention of competent public servants; maximum utilization of economic and human resources; and the effective management of large-scale organizations, are of prime concern to management experts. Secondly, there is the problem of keeping the bureaucracy responsible to the citizens in a democratic system.[27] Our discussion here is limited to the second of these two concerns.

Until about the time of the New Deal in the 1930's, Americans were generally more concerned with bringing a greater degree of professionalism into public service than they were with the power of the bureaucracy. The reforms of the latter nineteenth century, which emphasized merit and expertise as the basis for government employment, paved the way toward the elimination of the spoils system in the federal service. More recently, greater attention has been focused on the role of the public administrator in policy-making as well as the extent to which this role is related to the whole political system.

The bureaucracy, claims Peter Woll, "is deeply involved in the formulation of public policy and is not in many instances controlled in any meaningful way by the elected organs of government."[28] That the bu-

[27] See, for example, Friedrich A. Hayek, *The Road to Serfdom* (Chicago: The University of Chicago Press, 1944); Ludwig von Mises, *Omnipotent Government* (New Haven: Yale University Press, 1944).

[28] Woll, *op. cit.*, pp. 25–26.

reaucracy possesses great power resources is unquestionably true; however, as this and preceding chapters have emphasized, there are two basic and related features of the American system — a pluralistic community and the fragmentation of policy-making authority. A multitude of interests seek to influence the decisions of government. Separation of powers and checks-and-balances principles prevent any single branch of government from controlling the policy process. Federalism also divides governing authority and contributes to the fragmentation of community power. Moreover, there is the possibility that an uncontrolled bureaucracy may be less of a danger than the prospect that the fragmented policy process may produce an administrative organization unable to operate effectively, if at all.

Does fragmentation of policy-making in a pluralistic community encourage development of an autonomous bureaucracy? Admittedly, there are several important factors that contribute to the development of a high degree of independence of agencies *within* the bureaucratic structure. These include close association between agencies and congressional committees, the support of agency programs and goals by clientele groups, the ability of an agency to mobilize clientele and employee support in achieving the goals, the possession of technical and specialized knowledge by agency personnel, and lobbying of Congress by the bureaucracy. Congress has enacted statutory restrictions on administrative lobbying, and the President exercises a degree of control over such activities through the Bureau of the Budget; nevertheless, the practice continues and will undoubtedly do so in the future.[29]

Despite these factors, separation of powers is still applicable as a controlling mechanism. The bureaucracy should not be viewed as a monolithic force in contrast to a fragmented legislative branch and a President unable to halt administrative encroachments. The President *can* demand action from the agencies under his control, and he does so. The courts *can* rule against administrative action, and they do so. Congress *can* legislate changes and impose restrictions, and it does so. Further, competition within and between agencies is not uncommon, a result in part of diversified agency clientele and the competitive nature of personnel within the organizations. Competition fosters a pluralistic basis of decision-making similar to legislative and executive decision-making patterns; thus it provides a further barrier against bureaucratic autonomy.

In the very pluralistic and fragmented nature of policy-making in the American system may lie a problem more pressing than the danger of an

---

[29] See J. Leiper Freeman, "The Bureaucracy in Pressure Politics," *The Annals of the American Academy of Political and Social Science*, CCCXIX (September, 1958), 11–19.

irresponsible bureaucracy. Interests have multiple opportunities to block the implementation of rational goals. Inter-agency interests in resisting presidential directives (as in the case of the Corps of Engineers) can, in alliance with congressional committees or powerful congressmen, block compliance. Congressmen wielding the threat of investigation or loss of appropriations can prevent agency action or force action desired by special interests. Powerful private interests, allied in efforts to achieve ends inconsistent with general policy, can effectively veto unwelcomed agency proposals.

Pressure does not, however, flow in one direction only. Interests seeking one end are opposed by competing interests. An interest's access to one committee or one house of Congress (for example, the grazing interests) is balanced by opposing groups' access to other points in the legislative branch. Executive branch agencies seeking to block presidential policy are opposed by other agencies supporting the policy. Moreover, the setting or implementation of policy may be frustrated or blocked by interests within an agency.

In facing the pressures exerted by competing forces, an administrator may choose not to act, or his choice may represent the point of least resistance. In sum, the dangers of an arbitrary, manipulative, and irresponsible bureaucracy are probably less real than a bureaucracy immobilized by fragmented policy areas.

Any attempt to deal with the problem of controlling bureaucracy in a democratic system that is cast in terms of bureaucracy *versus* democracy is highly questionable. It distorts and misconceives the nature of policy-making in a pluralistic system. So long as the bureaucracy cannot insulate its policy-making processes from outside influences — either formal or informal — it cannot become autocratic. Interests in competition, with varying degrees of access to the sources of power within and outside the administrative structure, assure the injection of multiple outside influences. In this respect, there is a clear parallel between the fragmentation in legislative and administrative policy-making. Perhaps the greater problem lies in balancing the democratic need for wide public access to the bureaucracy with the need for autonomy adequate to the task of providing efficient management and leadership in a highly complex democratic polity.

Bibliographical Note

The study of public administration during the past two decades has increasingly concentrated on the bureaucracy as an instrument in policy-making. There are a number of good introductory texts available: Leonard D. White, *Introduction to the Study of Public Administration* (New York: Macmillan Co., 1955) is an influential traditional approach to public administration; Herbert A. Simon, Donald W. Smithburg, and Victor A. Thompson, *Public Administration* (New York: Alfred A. Knopf, Inc., 1950) is the first text to introduce behavioral concepts into the study of administration; Fritz Morstein-Marx, ed., *Elements of Public Administration* (Englewood Cliffs, N.J.: Prentice-Hall, 1961). For shorter introductory treatments in paperback form see Dwight Waldo, *The Study of Public Administration* (Garden City, N.Y.: Doubleday and Co., 1955); Peter Woll, *American Bureaucracy* (New York: W. W. Norton, 1963); and John J. Carson and Joseph P. Harris, *Public Administration in Modern Society* (New York: McGraw-Hill Book Co., 1963).

An outstanding history of the growth and role of American bureaucracy from 1789 to 1901 is found in the following volumes written by Leonard D. White: *The Federalists* (1958); *The Jeffersonians* (1951); *The Jacksonians* (1954); and *The Republican Era* (1958). All have been published by the Macmillan Company, New York; Paul Van Riper, *History of the United States Civil Service* (New York: Harper & Row, 1958) is an excellent study of federal personnel policies from an historical perspective.

Those interested in examining various approaches to the study of public administration will benefit from Dwight Waldo, *The Administrative State: A Study of the Political Theory of American Public Administration* (New York: The Ronald Press, 1948). For a comparative study of bureaucracy see Fritz Morstein-Marx, *The Administrative State* (Chicago: University of Chicago Press, 1957); and Robert K. Merton *et al.* (eds.), *Reader in Bureaucracy* (New York: The Free Press of Glencoe, 1960).

Students who seek to gain an overview of the role of bureaucracy in policy-making have a wide range of books from which to choose. The following are all available in paperback editions: Peter M. Blau, *The Dynamics of Bureaucracy* (Chicago: University of Chicago Press, 1956) explores the nature of bureaucracy in a democratic society; another work by Blau, *Bureaucracy in Modern Society* (New York: Random House, 1956) is a brief and general treatment of the theory and practice of bureaucracy; Robert Presthus, *The Organizational Society* (New York: Alfred A. Knopf, 1962) is a highly readable and scholarly exploration of bureaucracy at all levels of modern American society; Ludwig von Mises, *Bureaucracy* (New Haven: Yale University Press, 1962) presents a view of the bureaucratic phenomenon from the perspective of a widely-known conservative. Francis E. Rourke, *Bureaucratic Power in National Politics* (Boston: Little, Brown, & Co., 1964) is an excellent source of readings on various aspects of the politics of bureaucratic relationships. A recent paperback edition, Charles E. Jacob, *Policy and Bureaucracy* (Princeton, N.J.: D. Van Nostrand Co., 1966) discusses bureaucracy as a concept and treats the politics of administrative decision-making in a pluralistic system.

Close examination of specific areas of bureaucratic behavior and policy-making are necessary in developing a more sophisticated approach to the administrative role in American politics. Philip Selznick, *Leadership in Admin-*

istration (New York: Harper and Row, 1957) presents a sociologist's view of the role of bureaucracy; Herbert H. Simon, *Administrative Behavior,* 2nd edition (New York: Macmillan Co., 1957) presents a scholarly discussion of communications, informal organization, ethics, and motivational patterns of administration; Victor Thompson, *Modern Organization* (New York: Alfred A. Knopf, 1963) describes bureaucracy as a system of human behavior; a paperback edition, Samuel Krislov and Lloyd D. Musalf, *The Politics of Regulation: A Reader* (Boston: Houghton Mifflin Co., 1964) explores the growth and importance of the independent regulatory commissions; H. Emmerick, *Essays on Federal Reorganization* (University, Ala.: U. of Alabama Press, 1950) views administrative reorganization as a continuous process; J. Leiper Freeman, *The Political Process: Executive Bureau–Legislative Committee Relations* (New York: Random House, 1955) covers a vitally important area in the initiation and formulation of public policy; in paperback edition, Aaron Wildavsky's *The Politics of the Budgetary Process* (Boston: Little, Brown and Company, 1964) is almost essential reading in gaining an appreciation of the relation of the budget process to public policy; for a highly respected private interest group's recommendation on how to improve the budgetary process within the context of the formulation and coordination of national goals, see Committee for Economic Development, *Budgeting for National Objectives* (New York, 1966); Chapter Ten of Harmon Ziegler's, *Interest Groups in American Society* (Englewood Cliffs, N.J.: Prentice-Hall, 1964) explores the agency-clientele relationship and overall patterns of conflict representation and resolution within the administrative structure.

The problems, implicit and explicit, of bureaucracy's relationship to democratic and constitutional values are treated in a large body of literature. Paul Appleby, *Big Democracy* (New York: Alfred A. Knopf, 1945) presents the views of a former public official who argues the importance and responsibilities of the public executive. Charles Hyneman, *Bureaucracy in a Democracy* (New York: Harper & Bros., 1950) deals with executive-legislative relations and sets up basic requirements for establishing a responsible bureaucracy. E. Pendleton Herring, *Public Administration and the Public Interest* (New York: McGraw-Hill Book Co., 1936) is a perceptive study relevant to the politics of conflict representation in a bureaucratic framework. Roscoe C. Martin, ed., *Public Administration and Democracy: Essays in Honor of Paul H. Appleby* (Syracuse: Syracuse University Press, 1965) contains essays by leading scholars in the field of administration. Finally, the debate over bureaucratic social and economic planning and its relation to democratic values is illustrated in two commentaries, both available in paperback edition: Frederick A. Hayek, *The Road to Serfdom* (Chicago: University of Chicago Press, 1944) sees social planning as destructive of political and economic freedom; for a specific reply to Hayek's views, see Herman Finer, *Road to Reaction* (Boston: Little, Brown and Company, 1945).

CHAPTER
FIFTEEN

Policy Adjudication

In the early months of 1960, attempts by Negroes and whites to integrate segregated lunch counters occurred all over the South and in many border and northern states. The strategy was generally the same — Negroes denied service at lunch counters reserved for whites refused to leave but remained peaceful in their conduct. About 4000 of the demonstrators were arrested and charged with disturbing the peace, trespassing on private property, or disobeying police orders. Three of these cases, in which the state of Louisiana had obtained a conviction for disturbing the peace, reached the Supreme Court of the United States in late 1960. None of the demonstrators involved in the three cases — which were consolidated into a single case, *Garner et. al.* v. *Louisiana* — carried placards, made any verbal protest against segregated lunch counters, or resisted arrest. They had simply refused to move from the white counter when asked to do so.[1]

The right of a state to enforce statutes to protect the public peace and order was not at issue. Convictions in the three cases were challenged on grounds that no evidence existed that the defendants had actually disturbed the peace, as that offense was defined under Louisiana law.

[1] For a complete account of the origins and growth of the legal questions involved in the sit-in cases see Lucius J. Barker and Twiley W. Barker, Jr., *Freedoms, Courts, Politics: Studies in Civil Liberties* (Englewood Cliffs, N.J.: Prentice-Hall, 1965), pp. 202–29.

Also at issue was something larger than a conviction for breach of the peace. The social climate that underlay the custom of segregated public eating accommodations was also at stake.

In December, 1961 a unanimous Supreme Court overturned the three convictions. The Garner decision struck down the convictions on grounds that the defendant's rights under the due process clause of the Fourteenth Amendment had been violated. Louisiana had violated their rights by convicting them without evidence that they had disturbed the peace "either by outward conduct or by passive conduct likely to cause a public disturbance." By so ruling, the Court avoided meeting head-on the constitutional question as to whether a state can enforce a socially-based policy of segregation in privately-owned restaurants. In other words, are privately owned eating establishments sufficiently "affected with a public interest" so that government authority may not be used to enforce privately-set segregation patterns? In the Civil Rights Act of 1964 Congress declared such segregation illegal, but although this legislation provided a statutory basis to guide the judiciary, it did not remove the controversy. The Constitution and congressional statutes must be interpreted within the confines of the arena of conflict arising out of the changing social patterns of the 1960's.

In the Garner case, as in any legal controversy, the judiciary was asked to decide a dispute between competing parties. The sit-in demonstrations involved a major area of social dispute. The Constitution does not provide a categorical statement as to the legality or illegality of racially segregated lunch counters. Within this area of uncertainty the Supreme Court sought a solution to the controversy. As a result of broad constitutional language the limits of its discretion were broad. In most judicial controversies, however, community norms are more clearly and concisely defined. For example, criminal statutes and the law governing contractural relationships are generally clearer. But whatever the controversy, judges do exercise some discretion in deciding (or not deciding) "the law." Where their discretion is broad they can make broad public policy.

THE CONTEXT OF JUDICIAL POLICY-MAKING

Resolution (or attempts at resolution) of dispute takes place within a judicial framework marked by elements that clearly distinguish the judicial process from other units in the policy process. Yet the judicial process is also affected by some of the same broad features that demarcate the general context of policy representation and resolution in the American political system. Under the distinguishing features of the judicial branch we will discuss the constitutional authority (jurisdiction) of courts, their organization, and the selection of judges. Under the broad features that characterize our political system we include the way in which the principles of federalism, separation of powers, and checks and balances affect judicial policy-making.

JUDICIAL JURISDICTION AND ORGANIZATION

Federalism subjects Americans to a dual pattern of courts — state and federal. Each exercises authority in its own sphere. The Constitution speaks only of federal jurisdiction; that is, it assigns only to federal courts the authority to hear certain types of cases. The jurisdiction of state courts is fixed primarily by the constitution and laws of each state, all subject to the supremacy of the national Constitution.

Article III does not require that disputes included in federal jurisdiction be resolved solely by federal courts. *Exclusive* federal jurisdiction is granted only over certain matters such as admiralty, federal criminal, patent, and bankruptcy cases. In all other areas under Article III state and federal courts exercise *concurrent* authority. This means that cases may be heard in either federal or state courts. State courts are bound by the "supremacy clause" (Article VI) of the Constitution, which preserves the ultimate authority of federal law if two jurisdictions are in conflict. There are many areas, however, where both federal and state laws operate on an individual. A single act may violate both federal and state law; the accused is subject to trial in *both* federal and state courts.[2]

State courts in some areas have *exclusive* jurisdiction of their own. A violator of a state law may under certain conditions raise a federal issue, but the case must *originally* be heard in a state court. A person convicted of a crime in a state court may appeal to a federal court on grounds that procedures in his trial violated constitutional rights. The vast majority of cases heard and decided in American courts originate and are finally disposed of at the state-court level.

Unable to resolve the dispute over creating a complete and separate system of federal courts or allowing state courts (subject to review by a federal Supreme Court) to decide federal cases, the constitutional framers left it to Congress. Article III provided for a Supreme Court and granted Congress authority to establish lower federal courts. The Judiciary Act of 1789 decided the unanswered question; it established a Supreme Court of one chief justice and five associate justices and provided for thirteen federal district courts. Three circuit courts were created, each consisting of any two justices of the Supreme Court and the district judge in the district a case was heard. In 1891 Congress

---

[2] *Bartkus* v. *Illinois* 359 U.S. 121 (1959); *Abbate* v. *United States* 359 U.S. 187 (1959).

amended this arrangement by introducing a separate system of ten circuit courts of appeals. The number of justices on the Supreme Court has varied from five in 1801 to as many as ten in 1863, but has remained at nine since 1869. Three other courts (Customs and Patent Appeals, Customs Court, and the Court of Claims) complete the listing of constitutional courts.

All courts established under Article III are *constitutional* courts, as distinguished from *legislative* courts created by Congress under authority drawn from other clauses in the Constitution. Thus the United States Tax Court is a legislative court established under congressional authority to lay and collect taxes. The Court of Military Appeals and the system of territorial courts derive their existence from authority of Congress to regulate the land and naval forces and acquire and govern territories. Since legislative courts are not created under Article III, Congress does not have to adhere to requirements that judges be given life terms nor is it limited by restrictions concerning salary and removal of federal judges.

Federal courts exercise *original* or *appellate* jurisdiction, or both. Original jurisdiction refers to the level of court at which cases are first heard and decided; a court exercising appellate jurisdiction is authorized to hear appeals on cases decided at lower-court levels. Article III requires that the Supreme Court exercise original jurisdiction "in all cases affecting ambassadors, other public minister and consuls, and those in which a State shall be a party . . .". Except for this requirement, Congress may assign original or appellate jurisdiction to district and circuit courts as it sees fit. District courts exercise only original jurisdiction, ranging from criminal jury trials to review and enforcement of federal administrative-agency orders.

Most federal cases are decided at the district-court level. In 1966 alone over 100,000 cases began in district courts. At least one district court exists in each of the fifty states and one in the District of Columbia, Puerto Rico, Guam, the Canal Zone, and the Virgin Islands. Although at least one judge is assigned to each district, many of the district courts have more than one. The southern district of New York (located in New York City) has 23 judges. In 1966 there were 289 district judges. Almost half of all cases are filed in the twelve district courts located in the larger metropolitan areas. Normally one district judge presides over a case. Law requires a three-judge panel to hear certain types of disputes, the most important being those in which the court is asked to issue an injunction against the enforcement of federal or state statutes on grounds of unconstitutionality.

U.S. courts of appeals consist of ten circuit courts and one District of Columbia circuit court; each court ranges in size from three to nine

FIGURE 15-1
The Federal Court Structure

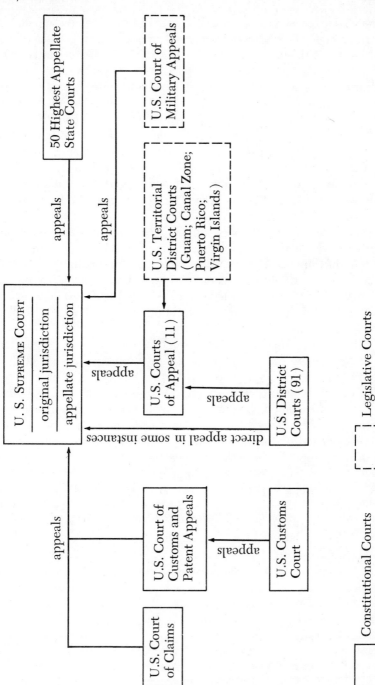

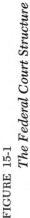

members. Jurisdiction of circuit courts is almost totally appellate. About 95 per cent of roughly six thousand appeals each year are finally disposed of at this level. Appeals may bypass the circuit courts only under the following circumstances: (1) decisions by three-judge panels at the district court level where a statute or administrative order has been challenged as unconstitutional; (2) where Congress has authorized direct appeal to the Supreme Court; (3) where it can be shown that a case is of such great public importance that immediate settlement is necessary.

The only court specifically mentioned in the Constitution — the Supreme Court — exercises both original and appellate jurisdiction. Cases falling under the first category are far less significant in the Court's work. Between 1789 and 1959 the Court rendered only 123 decisions under its original jurisdiction.

Cases heard and decided on authority of the Supreme Court's appellate jurisdiction (which may be withdrawn by Congress) have made the Supreme Court a vastly important formulator of policy. Appeals reach the Court on the basis of a *writ of certiorari,* a *writ of appeal,* or by *certification.* Certification is very rarely used and covers cases in which lower federal courts request instruction on questions of law. A *writ of certiorari* is an order issued by the Supreme Court to a lower federal court directing that the records of a case be sent to the higher court for review. Under procedural rules of the Supreme Court, at least four justices must vote to issue the writ. About 90 per cent of all cases reach the Court through this procedure, but the vast majority of petitions for the writ are denied. Hence, courts of appeal are usually courts of last resort.

The second of the two routes by which a case reaches the Supreme Court on appeal — the *writ of appeal* — is granted by statute. Congress has directed that a case may be appealed to the Court under any of the following circumstances: (1) if a state court declares a federal statute or treaty unconstitutional; (2) if a state court, in the face of a challenge that a state statute conflicts with the federal Constitution, law, or treaty, upholds the statute; (3) if a U.S. district court declares a congressional statute unconstitutional in a suit to which the United States is a party; (4) if a federal district court issues an injunction against enforcement of a state statute; and (5) if a U.S. court of appeals declares a state statute void as contrary to federal law or treaty. Technically the losing party has the right of appeal in such instances. In practice, however, the Supreme Court may refuse to hear an appeal on grounds that a "substantial federal question" does not exist. In a typical term (the Court normally meets each year from October to the end of June) over 50 per cent of appeals based on statutory "rights" are dismissed.

Article III of the Constitution restricts federal jurisdiction to certain "cases" and "controversies." There are two general categories: controversies involving "federal questions" and those relating to the "parties in dispute." A federal question arises when the subject matter of the dispute includes (1) cases under or involving the Constitution or federal laws and treaties; or (2) cases under admiralty and maritime laws. Cases over which federal jurisdiction may be exercised because of the parties to the dispute include controversies (1) to which the United States is a party; (2) between two or more states; (3) between citizens of different states (known as diversity of citizenship); (4) between a state or its citizens and foreign states or their citizens or subjects; (5) between citizens of the same state who claim land under titles granted by different states; and (6) involving ambassadors, ministers, and consuls of a foreign state.

In addition to constitutional restrictions on kinds of cases federal courts may hear, the Supreme Court has imposed its own restrictions. These fall under two general categories: (1) there must be an actual controversy involved; and (2) cases involving a "political question" will not be decided. The Supreme Court also traditionally refuses to render advisory opinions on constitutional questions; thus, a law must actually be tested before the federal courts will rule on its constitutionality.[3]

There are exceptions to the rules. In 1936, for example, the Supreme Court permitted the president of a coal company to bring suit against his own company and its officers to prevent their compliance with a federal regulatory statute that the president claimed was unconstitutional. Usually, however, the Supreme Court will hear only existing controversies. In *Poe* v. *Ullman* (1961), the Court refused to rule on a case brought by a doctor and his patients. The plaintiffs wished to challenge a Connecticut statute that banned the use of contraceptives and giving medical advice regarding their use. Connecticut had not attempted to enforce the 1889 statute against any of the plaintiffs; nevertheless, they sought a court order declaring the statute in violation of the Fourteenth Amendment. In the *Ullman* case the Supreme Court refused to rule on the issue in the absence of an actual prosecution for violation of the law; the Court felt that no actual case in controversy existed.

The Supreme Court may use the doctrine of "political question" to refuse to decide a controversy if the issue is one that the Court feels it cannot resolve. In short, the Court decrees that certain conflicts be left to the "political" branches; namely, Congress and the President. There is no precise definition of a political question. The rule was employed as early as 1849 when the Supreme Court refused to decide which of two govern-

---

[3] For a specific statement of these court-imposed rules see the concurring opinion of Mr. Justice Brandeis in *Ashwander* v. *TVA* 297 U.S. 288 (1936).

ments (both of which claimed legitimacy) was the lawful government of
Rhode Island. The question, said the Court, was "political"; therefore, it
must be decided by Congress and the executive. Subsequently the Court
has refused to decide when a constitutional amendment has been legally
ratified, what constitutes a "republican form of government" under the
"guarantee" clause of the Constitution, the dates of duration of a war,
questions involving the conduct of foreign relations, and matters relating
to the status of Indian tribes.[4]

In a real sense all questions decided by the Court are "political." Attempts to define the doctrine of political questions are difficult, if not
impossible. As John P. Roche has put it, the term "can be expanded or
contracted in accordian-like fashion to meet the exigencies of the
times . . . for at root the logic that supports it is circular: political questions are matters not soluble by the judicial process; matters not soluble
by the judicial process are political questions. As an early dictionary
explained, violins are small cellos, and cellos are large violins."[5] Conflicts
are sometimes passed from branch to branch when no one is willing to
resolve them.

JUDICIAL SELECTION

The perspectives of judges are shaped both by their backgrounds and the
process of judicial selection. Of the ninety-six justices who have sat on the
Supreme Court, the vast majority have been selected by Presidents more
interested in their "ideological partisanship" — that is, their positions on
the major socio-economic issues of the day — than their qualities as legal
scholars or prior experience on the bench. Although Presidents have
usually appointed members of their own party, they have tended to
choose those who are believed to be in ideological accord with presidential views. A growing sensitivity among political scientists to the impact of judicial selection on judicial behavior has spawned a number of
interesting studies of the whole process. Professor John R. Schmidhauser
summed up the politics of the selection process as follows: "The choice of
Supreme Court members has generally reflected the catholic political and
ideological considerations of a national constituency, rather than those of
region, state, or congressional district."[6]

It is not surprising that interest groups are vitally concerned with the

[4] *Coleman* v. *Miller* 307 U.S. 433 (1939); *Pacific States Telephone and Telegraph
Co.* v. *Oregon* 223 U.S. 118 (1939); *Ludecke* v. *Watkins* 335 U.S. 160 (1948); *The
Cherokee Nation* v. *Georgia* 5 Pet. 1 (1831).

[5] John P. Roche, "Judicial Self-Restraint," *The American Political Science Review,*
XLIX (September, 1955), 762–72.

[6] John R. Schmidhauser, *The Supreme Court* (New York: Holt, Rinehart & Winston, 1960), pp. 24–25.

choice of a nominee to the Court. Since few *major* issues fail to reach the Court, attitudes of the candidates for appointment are crucial to groups who stand to win or lose by the decisions of the justices. As Schmidhauser suggests, the nomination of Attorney General Tom Clark to the Court in 1949 by President Truman was strongly opposed by liberal groups and strongly supported by the American Bar Association, which looked kindly upon Clark's ideological conservatism. The ABA has sought, with some success, to serve as a consulting group in the appointment of judges by the President. In 1956, for example, President Eisenhower directed that the opinion of the ABA's Committee on the Federal Judiciary be obtained before he submitted the nomination of Justice Brennan to the Senate. However, President Kennedy's appointment of Justice Goldberg was made without seeking the Committee's opinions. The ABA has consistently urged the President to appoint judges who demonstrate qualities of intelligence, legal scholarship, and honesty rather than make "political" appointments. Nevertheless, the ABA's stands on socio-economic policies over the years have indicated a strong conservative bias. In this respect, the organization is no different from other groups that seek to influence judicial policy-making by urging appointment of justices with views similar to their own. That the ABA represents the legal profession, however, lends an aura of prestige to its views that is not usually accorded to other pressuring interests.

A variety of official and nonofficial leaders participate in the process of judicial selection. The Constitution vests primary responsibility for selection of Supreme Court justices in the President. Although Congress could probably delegate responsibility for appointment of lower federal judges to other officials, it has not done so. A central figure in court appointments is the Attorney General of the United States. His influence in selection at all levels of the federal judiciary is often determinative. In effect it is the Deputy Attorney General who screens nominees for appointments. His decisions often remove otherwise acceptable candidates from further consideration. Joel B. Grossman, in his study of judicial selection, summarizes the early stages of the process: "With the exception of those few nominations that are likely to become major public issues, recruiting judges is essentially a staff operation in the name of the Attorney General — and ultimately in the name of the President." [7]

In filling positions on district courts, the President must contend with the constitutional prescription that judicial appointments be made with the advice and consent of the Senate. He must comply with the custom of "senatorial courtesy," whereby a senator of the President's party may

[7] Joel B. Grossman, *Lawyers and Judges* (New York: John Wiley & Sons, 1965), p. 26.

block confirmation of appointees to district-court positions located in his home state. Moreover, senators may sponsor candidates for judicial appointments and must be consulted on prospective nominations. Finally, in hearings of the Judiciary Committee, whose members are attuned to objections from pressure groups, other senators, and the legal profession, the Senate can exert pressure against an appointment. For this reason Presidents sometimes make "recess" appointments when the Senate is not in session. Thus, when the Senate reconvenes and the Judiciary Committee does meet to pass on the nomination, it must in effect remove a judge from office if it wishes to reject his appointment. This is normally a high price to pay for exerting pressure on the President. On the whole, the President has become the dominant figure in the selection process.

There is nothing necessarily sinister in efforts to influence the choice of court appointees. In a political community in which the judiciary, especially the Supreme Court, exerts profound influence on policy, the absence of pressure would be surprising. Federal-court appointments have from Washington's Administration onward reflected partisan considerations. This is most evident in appointments to lower federal courts, especially the district courts. Senators have traditionally considered such appointments as falling within their prerogative.[8] Out of 920 persons appointed to the federal district bench from 1908 to 1960 (Presidents Taft through Eisenhower), 811 (88 per cent) were of the same party as the President making the appointment.[9] Of all confirmed appointments to the Supreme Court, only three have gone to candidates not of the President's party.

The relation between the basis of selection of federal judges and their performance on the bench is not clear-cut. Justice Frankfurter argued that donning a judicial robe changes the man and that attempts to link the social background and ideological bias of the appointee to his performance on the bench is "shallow talk." "The fact is," Frankfurter said, "that on the whole judges do lay aside private views in discharging their judicial functions." [10] Distinctions between "private views" and "judicial objectivity" are difficult to draw. No one can enter inside a justice's mind to read the factors influencing his decisions. Attempts to explain a particular justice's decision simply on grounds of political and social background are highly risky and often dubious. Presidents have sometimes been disappointed in justices they appointed when the actions of the

[8] *Ibid.*, p. 27.

[9] Statistics compiled from Hearings before Subcommittee 5 of the House Judiciary Committee on Bills to Provide for the Appointment of Additional Circuit and District Judges, 87th Congress, March 1 and 2, 1961, pp. 402–3.

[10] *Public Utilities Commission* v. *Pollak* 343 U.S. 451 (1952).

justice have run counter to the views of the administration in power. More often than not, however, appointments have justified presidential expectations. Appointees who were considered politically "liberal" or "conservative" when nominated usually supported these positions as members of the court. Professor Schmidhauser's analysis of the political and social backgrounds of justices of the Supreme Court concluded that insofar as the Court guards the American conscience, "it is essentially the conscience of the American upper-middle class sharpened by the imperative of individual social responsibility and political activism, and conditioned by the conservative impact of legal training and professional legal attitudes and associations." [11]

THE JUDICIARY, FEDERALISM, AND SEPARATION OF POWERS

The federal principle, as it operates in the organization of the American judiciary, has produced a dual system of state and federal courts. Each state has its own hierarchy of courts. At the national level the judicial structure reflects the geographical pattern of federalism in the sense that judicial districts generally follow state boundaries and the circuit-court system divides the nation into ten geographical units or circuits. At the apex of the federal-court system is the Supreme Court, which also exercises a degree of supervision over state courts through the "supremacy clause" of the Constitution. This clause empowers the Court to declare state actions void on grounds of conflict with the "supreme law of the land" — the Constitution, valid acts of Congress, and treaties of the United States.

Professor Walter F. Murphy has termed this hierarchical system "the judicial bureaucracy," and he points out that "what may appear to be a neat, hierarchical system often turns out on close examination to be a confused congeries of mutual controls. . . ." [12] As the President, in dealing with the administrative bureaucracy, is unable to simply issue commands and get compliance, so too the Supreme Court is limited in its ability to render a decision and expect easy or immediate compliance by lower federal or state courts. Fifty states, each with its own hierarchy of courts, create a situation in which the mandates of the Court may be ignored or interpreted so as to avoid compliance. To illustrate: of 175 cases reversed by the Supreme Court and returned to state courts for action during the period between 1941 and 1951, 46 were relitigated at

[11] Schmidhauser, *op. cit.*, p. 59.
[12] Walter F. Murphy, *Elements of Judicial Strategy* (Chicago: The University of Chicago Press, 1964), p. 91.

the state level. In almost half of these the "winner at the Supreme Court level lost his victory in the state court." [13]

Further, compliance by lower federal courts with Supreme Court decisions is by no means assured. In its decision in *Brown* v. *Board of Education* in 1954, a unanimous Supreme Court found that racial segregation of public schools violated the "equal protection" clause of the Fourteenth Amendment. Because of the great impact of the decision, and the widely varied local conditions (and, perhaps, to provide a "cooling-off" period), the Court postponed consideration of how its decisions should be implemented. It invited all participants to submit arguments on what type of orders should be issued. One year later the Court ordered "full compliance" and "with all deliberate speed." The task of implementing these orders fell to the federal-district and circuit-court judges in whose jurisdictions public school segregation was the normal pattern. In 1964 the United States Commission on Civil Rights reported that slightly more than 9 per cent of Negro public school pupils in southern and border states were enrolled in desegregated schools; only 1.2 per cent of the Negro student population were enrolled in desegregated schools in the eleven former Confederate states.[14] Professor Peltason has written the story of the forty-eight district judges and ten circuit judges in the South whose courts became the focal point for litigation following the 1954 decision.[15] Peltason stressed the social environment in which these judges had to operate. A district judge is a resident of the area he serves and as such he tends to reflect the prejudices, social values, and background of his community. He is exposed to these local pressures even though he is responsible for applying law that reflects the values of a national constituency. The result is that district judges will sometimes bow to local pressures by choosing an alternative that escapes the "spirit," if not the "letter," of the law. In this case, district judges may have ordered the school board to desegregate but used vague language regarding the time and manner of implementation. "Federal judges," writes Peltason, "do not live in a vacuum. Whatever the formal doctrine may be, community attitudes have been a crucial if unmentionable factor." [16]

Despite a formal hierarchy of federal courts and despite the "supremacy" of federal law as interpreted by the Supreme Court, the federal pattern of judicial organization injects a significant degree of pluralism

[13] See "Evasion of Supreme Court Mandates in Cases Remanded to State Courts since 1941," *Harvard Law Review*, LXVII (1954), 1251–59.

[14] 1964 Staff Report, United States Commission on Civil Rights, *Public Education,* Washington, D.C.: Government Printing Office, October, 1964, pp. 290–91.

[15] J. W. Peltason, *Fifty-eight Lonely Men* (New York: Harcourt, Brace & World, 1961).

[16] *Ibid.,* p. 132.

into judicial policy-making. The power of higher federal courts to reverse decisions does, of course, provide a major element of control over the actions of lower federal and state supreme courts. Also statutory means by which the judicial branch can supervise the activities of federal district judges exist. In 1939 Congress created in each of the ten circuit courts of appeals a judicial council, consisting of the circuit judges, with authority to "make`all necessary orders for the effective and expeditious administration of the business of the courts within its circuit." The judicial-council device for disciplining federal district judges has not, however, operated effectively. It is thought that such discipline may interfere with judicial independence. District judges are entitled to reach decisions without fearing that they may be punished for what they conclude.[17]

Finally, it must be recognized that executive and legislative prerogatives may limit what the courts can command. Alexander Hamilton recognized that the judiciary could be the weakest element in the governing process, for its effectiveness depended upon the support of Congress and President. He wrote in the Federalist, No. 78: "In a government in which [departments] are separated from each other, the judiciary, from the nature of its functions, will always be the least dangerous." It has "neither FORCE nor WILL, but merely judgment, and must ultimately depend upon the aid of the executive arm even for the efficacy of its judgments." A recent appraisal of the history of executive-judicial relations held that "the thread connecting court decisions with executive enforcement has often been thin." [18] Although the strong commitment to the "rule of law" and the prestige of the Supreme Court exert pressure for compliance with judicial decisions, presidential support for decisions must also emanate from other sources. If those pressures are not forthcoming from groups, Congress, popular opinion, or somewhere, a President may be tempted to ignore a court ruling. Presidents sometimes heed the apocryphal remarks of President Jackson concerning a particularly unwelcomed Supreme Court verdict: "John Marshall has made his decision, now let him enforce it." Lincoln bitterly criticized the Court for its decision in *Dred Scott* v. *Sanford;* Franklin D. Roosevelt reportedly was prepared to disobey a prospective Court ruling invalidating his decision to go off the gold standard; President Truman might have retained operation of the steel mills in 1952 despite the Court's decision in *Youngstown Sheet and Tube* v. *Sawyer* that declared his seizure of the mills was unconstitu-

[17] "Judicial Performance in the Fifth Circuit," *Yale Law Journal,* LXXIII (1963), 90–133.
[18] Walter F. Murphy and C. Herman Pritchett (eds.), *Courts, Judges, and Politics* (New York: Random House, 1961), p. 549.

tional; and President Eisenhower belatedly came to the support of district courts in the Little Rock desegregation crises of 1957. The possibility of presidential truculence and constitutional crises are potential restraints on judicial decision.

Congress also maintains some control over the judiciary. Its formal controls are extensive, including authority to alter or abolish jurisdiction of federal courts (excepting the Supreme Court's original jurisdiction), to control the purse strings (raise judges' salaries and provide funds for operating the federal court system), to increase or decrease the number of judges, to remove judges by the impeachment process, to confirm judicial appointments (Senate only), and to determine the time that the Supreme Court will sit. These will be discussed in detail later in this chapter. Here we cite them to emphasize the fact that policy adjudication is constitutionally assigned to the courts but that the principles of separation of powers and checks and balances reinforce the pluralism of judicial decision-making that is built in through the federal system.

DIMENSIONS OF JUDICIAL POLICY-MAKING: THE SUPREME COURT

One of the major functions of the courts is to enforce community norms. Ranging from the community's desire to control littering of the highways to preserving fundamental values upon which the political system is based, norms are found in statutes, community traditions articulated by judges (common law), and the Constitution itself. In enforcing existing norms, courts may create new ones known as precedents, which govern future cases. The application and creation of norms may involve relatively few individuals and groups or they may affect large numbers of people and major groups within the polity.

To some extent all courts make policy, but the opportunity to make policy at the appellate court level is greater since these tribunals handle legal controversies usually wider in scope and involving less clearly defined constitutional or statutory norms. A lawsuit is the medium through which issues formally enter the judicial arena. As such, the conflict is defined in terms of specific facts and specific legal issues. In this sense, judicial authority can be viewed as more structured, less ambiguous, and more limited than legislative or executive authority. Legal arguments in the form of briefs addressed to the issue at hand, procedural and jurisdictional rules, and the formal atmosphere of the courtroom distinguish policy adjudication from other levels of the policy process. In another sense these same features, plus the generally accepted myth that judges be impartial in their behavior and judgments, tend to obscure the actual role of the judiciary in conflict resolution. The public usually views the judge as a decision-maker who applies a more or less fixed set of rules to particular cases and whose decisions are, therefore, uninfluenced by forces outside the courtroom. Judicial rule-making is, however, the product of many interacting forces such as the immediate parties to a suit and other interested parties who may become involved; the strategies employed by both sides; legal precedents which apply to the issues at hand; existing public opinion on the questions raised by a legal controversy; changing social patterns that may affect the willingness of involved interests to accept the judicial decision; and the personal values and biases of the judge(s). This is not to say that every legal decision will involve such highly complex factors — most will not. Disposition of many controversies will be "routine" (for example, a suit to collect unpaid grocery bills) compared to controversies such as those over reapportionment of state legislatures or the constitutionality of legislation regulating business activities.

Parties involved in a judicial controversy — including the judges themselves — seek to achieve favorable resolution of the dispute by utilizing whatever resources they can command within the framework of the judicial arena. In this sense, bargaining takes place within the judicial realm since resolution will often depend upon accommodation of several interests. In this section we concentrate on the U.S. Supreme Court as a major policy-maker in the resolution of social conflict. Our concern is less with the substance of particular policy choices than the form and arena from which these decisions emerge.

JUDICIAL PERSPECTIVE AND POLICY CHOICE

The sources of judicial power neither began with *Marbury* v. *Madison* nor have they been sustained solely by subsequent Court reaffirmations of judicial review or its right to serve as "umpire of the federal system." Judicial power is rooted in popular expectations, ideological and political traditions, and also in the ability of the Court to respond to a changing political environment.

The judicial branch was designed as the instrument through which "rule of law" was to be realized. Granting federal judges life terms and protecting their salaries from reduction by congressional majorities helped insulate them from the demands of popular majorities. Consistent with their bargain to retain balance among three separate branches, the Framers left to Congress the authority to increase the number of judges, to determine the jurisdiction of the various federal courts (except for the Supreme Court's original jurisdiction) it created, and to remove judges by impeachment. The President was granted authority to appoint all federal judges, subject to the "advice and consent" of the Senate. Taken together, these tools were to serve the popularly elected branches in balancing the activities of the "non-democratic" judiciary. Beyond these limitations the Constitution is silent. If the judicial branch was designed to be the ultimate determiner of the powers of Congress and of the executive by exercising judicial review and to serve as the arbiter of relations between states and the national polity, the Constitution does not provide the absolute proof.

The history of the Supreme Court has been a continuing effort to develop and maintain its role within the ideological and constitutional framework of the community. According to Edward S. Corwin that environment was imprinted with twin doctrines of American constitutional law. On the one hand, says Corwin, Americans accepted the Lockean concept that individual rights were superior to any other legal claims. On the other, the doctrine of legislative supremacy, as argued by the great English jurist Blackstone, was also adopted by the American colonies. But, continues Corwin, the Constitution of 1787 avoided the contradictions inherent in this dualism — limited government and legislative supremacy — through incorporation of two basic propositions. First, the written constitution incorporated the Bill of Rights and other protections of individual freedoms; therefore, the doctrine of legislative supremacy did not become dominant. The concept of a "higher law" was a new kind of validity, "the validity of a *statute emanating from the sovereign people.*" Ordinary legislative authority was subordinated to a higher lawmaking body, the people speaking through the Constitution. Secondly, protection of the basic rights of the governed against legislative encroachment depended upon enforcement of these rights by a non-legislative authority — the courts. Judicial review made it possible for the courts to exercise this function: "Invested with statutory form and implemented by judicial review, higher law, as with renewed youth, entered upon one of the great periods of its history. . . ." [19]

As interpreters of higher law in face of congressional and presidential actions, judges represent the embodiment of the rule of law. Marshall's decision in *Marbury* v. *Madison* emphasized the responsibility of justices to uphold the Constitution against legislative actions. In the event of conflict between a law and the Constitution, said Marshall, "the court must determine which of these conflicting rules governs the case: this is the very essence of judicial duty."

Enforcement and acceptance of court-made policy depends upon the cooperation of the other two branches. But the Court is not helpless.

[19] Edward S. Corwin, *The "Higher Law" Background of American Constitutional Law* (Ithaca: Cornell University Press, 1955).

Public acceptance of its actions rests to a significant extent upon the notion that judges are non-political, or above political conflict, unlike Congress or the President. Judge Jerome Frank has criticized the "cult of the robe" as a symbol of judicial conservatism: "The desire to thwart democracy by means of the courts." [20] Although judicial decisions — especially those of the Supreme Court — often engender bitterness or outrage, for the most part they are accepted as law. This perspective has also assisted the Court in bridging the gap between the legitimacy bestowed on popularly chosen leaders and the legitimacy claimed by a nonrepresentative branch of government.

Another factor that enhances the position of judges in policy adjudication and stems in large part from popular expectations is the insistence that judges be insulated from all influences other than considerations of the "law." To write a letter or pay a personal visit to a judge urging him to adopt a particular view in his decision in a lawsuit would be considered outside the bounds of judicial propriety. Constitutional provisions giving federal judges life tenure and protecting them against reduction of their salaries are legal manifestations of a deeper commitment to the insulation of the administration of justice from popular pressure.

If popular attitudes and expectations operate to enhance the status of judges, the same expectations limit the extent of judicial choice between policy alternatives. A fundamental principle of English and American jurisprudence is that decisions on law handed down by the highest court having jurisdiction must be followed in similar cases in the future. Legally known as the *rule of stare decisis* ("stand by the things decided"), this principle lays the foundation for stability and general predictability of the law. Developed over the centuries, *stare decisis* is part of the "rules of the game" that govern the decisions of courts; as such, it represents a procedural-institutional limitation.

Courts are expected to exhibit consistency and certainty in policy formulation, yet justices do not always follow precedent for several reasons: (1) changing conditions demand changing law; (2) constitutional law in America has a relatively short history compared to other areas of law and is not as steeped in precedent; and (3) there are always conflicting precedents that judges may choose between in decision-making. Moreover, the behavior of judges may be more strongly motivated by considerations other than the rule of *stare decisis*. Current research illustrates that judges are motivated as much or more by attitudes toward the type of issue raised by a case as they are by the larger "constitutional

---

[20] Jerome P. Frank, *Courts on Trial: Myth and Reality in American Justice* (Princeton: Princeton University Press, 1949), pp. 254–55.

question."[21] A group of judges may, for example, consistently support civil liberties claims even though such support may contradict existing precedent ("law") in the civil liberties area.

Courts are not free to overturn precedent at will. Justices on the Supreme Court often recognize outmoded erroneous precedents. They are free to state their disagreement with the traditional ruling; but the precedent itself must be dealt with openly, not ignored. C. Herman Pritchett and Alan F. Westin summarized this restraint on a justice: "He has free choice, but only among limited alternatives and only after he has satisfied himself that he has met the obligations of consistency and respect for settled principles which his responsibility to the Court imposes upon him."[22]

The American public expects the use of judicial discretion in deciding what the "law" is. Coexisting with this expectation is insistence on objectivity and certainty in law. The public in turn exercises restraint and permissiveness in its criticism of judicial choice. Billboards that boldly proclaimed a campaign to "Impeach Earl Warren" shocked most Americans. Despite disagreement with the substance of Court decisions, the prestige and status of the Court as guardian of the Constitution limits the extent to which such criticism is generally accepted. Similarly the public image of the function of the Court imposes limits on proposals for judicial "reform." On the other hand, the Court itself must be sensitive to policy goals expressed by the other two branches of government and the public. The necessity of such understanding and restraint is clearly illustrated by the Supreme Court's reaction to the New Deal during the 1930's.

From 1870 until the 1930's the Supreme Court was forced to deal with the question of the extent to which the Constitution permitted governmental regulation of property and other individual rights (such as the right of contract) in order to relieve social and economic maladjustments arising from an altered environment. Prior to the New Deal the Court had regularly barred state and national regulatory statutes so that by the mid-1930's it was clear, as Robert G. McCloskey has remarked, that the Court looked upon itself as the "protector" of "all the 'common callings' (the grocer, the dairy-man, the butcher) from the peril of public rate control . . ."[23] The economic depression of the 1930's was the turning point for profound, long-developing changes in the attitudes of Americans

[21] See, for example, S. Sidney Ulmer, "The Analysis of Behavior Patterns on the United States Supreme Court," *The Journal of Politics*, XXII (November, 1960), 629–53.

[22] C. Herman Pritchett and Alan F. Westin. *The Third Branch of Government* (New York: Harcourt, Brace & World, 1963), p. 17.

[23] Robert G. McCloskey, *The American Supreme Court* (Chicago: The University of Chicago Press, 1960), p. 166.

toward political, social, and economic life. Franklin D. Roosevelt's New Deal was a visible response to this change. Acting under its commerce and taxing powers, Congress enacted laws establishing economic controls and social welfare programs, such as a compulsory social security program and minimum-wage and maximum-hour statutes. Between 1933 and 1937 the Supreme Court negated major legislative programs, decisions that threatened to "repeal" the entire New Deal program.[24]

The landslide reelection of Roosevelt in 1936, coupled with large Democratic majorities in Congress, was taken by many to be a sign of public approval of the New Deal. To circumvent the Supreme Court, Roosevelt proposed a plan (as noted in Chapter Nine) that would have permitted the appointment of one additional justice for every judge who had served for at least ten years and had failed to retire at age seventy. Six of the nine members of the Court met both qualifications. The proposal would also have affected some twenty-five federal judges at the circuit and district-court levels. What F.D.R. and his supporters termed "reorganization" was dubbed "court packing" by opponents who insisted that the proposal constituted "tampering" with the judicial function and represented action outside the "rules of the game." That Congress possessed constitutional authority to enact the reorganization plan was not the basic issue. "Political tampering" was the argument that led the Senate to reject the proposal and "save" a Supreme Court that a few months before had been labeled "reactionary." "No issue," wrote Walter Lippmann, "so great or so deep has been raised in America since secession."[25]

Defeat of court reorganization did not, however, eliminate a Supreme Court majority adamantly against new social and economic programs. Further maneuvers became unnecessary, however, when Justice Owen Roberts switched sides on the question of the constitutionality of New Deal proposals, turning what had been a five-to-four majority against these measures into a favorable majority. Beginning with *West Coast Hotel Co.* v. *Parrish* (1937), which upheld a Washington state minimum-wage law, the Court approved statutes that probably would have been scuttled earlier. Robert H. Jackson, then Attorney General and later a Supreme Court Justice, commented: "This paradoxical outcome is accounted for by the recognition on the part of some justices — belated but vigorous — of the validity of the complaints against their course of

[24] See *Panama Refining Co.* v. *Ryan* 293 U.S. 388 (1935); *United States* v. *Butler* 297 U.S. 1 (1936); *Carter* v. *Carter Coal Co.* 298 U.S. 238 (1936); *Railroad Retirement Board* v. *Alton R.R.* 295 U.S. 330 (1935); *Schecter Poultry Corp.* v. *United States* 295 U.S. 495 (1935); and *Morehead* v. *Tipaldo* 298 U.S. 587 (1936).

[25] Alpheus T. Mason, "Harlan Fiske Stone and FDR's Court Plan," *Yale Law Review*, LXI (1952), 796.

decision. They subdued the rebellion against their constitutional dogma by joining it." [26]

Jackson's evaluation suggests that there is more to adjudication than mere mechanical reading of the Constitution. A judge wears regal robes, but they do not insulate him from the conflict of overlapping interests that all public officials represent, resolve, and rejuvenate.

Judicial choices involve political perspectives, pressures, and restraints; yet judicial leadership is vitally different from that of President, congressmen, and administrators. Conventional factors that guide the outlook of all politicians, such as the setting of political attitudes, the framework of constituted authority, leadership selection, organization, and jurisdiction, are not the only factors that shape court perspectives. Judges act within a context of judicial traditions and expectations that affect their view from the bench. The collegial nature of the Supreme Court also shapes their choices. Judicial bargaining is reflected in the nature of and limits upon group access and also in the decisions made by the court. These factors are reviewed in the following sections.

THE GROUP BASIS OF JUDICIAL ACTION

In a real sense litigation represents a campaign. Cases that reach the Supreme Court reflect the carefully planned efforts of interested parties to achieve policy goals through legal victory. As indicated earlier, certain forms of judicial lobbying are considered outside the scope of accepted behavior. There are, however, a variety of ways by which groups gain access to judicial policy-making.

The legal brief is the most important instrument used by lawyers to plead their cause. The use of a special type of brief — amicus curiae, or "friend of the court" — enables groups not directly involved in litigation but with a vested interest in the case to present their position before the Court. Under Supreme Court rules amicus briefs may be filed with consent of both parties to a suit or, if consent is denied, by consent of the Court itself. Generally the Supreme Court will permit an amicus brief to be filed if a group can show ancillary interest in the case and offers arguments that may otherwise not be presented. About forty are filed each year. In 1962 six amicus briefs were filed for Engel v. Vitale, a case that banned the use of a state-sponsored, nondenominational public school prayer. Three briefs in opposition to the New York state prayer represented views of the American Ethical Union, the American Jewish Committee, and the Synagogue Council of America — the latter two representing most of the Jewish community in the United States. The New

[26] Robert H. Jackson, The Struggle for Judicial Supremacy (New York: Alfred A. Knopf, 1941), p. vi.

York State Board of Regents, a group of parents whose children attended New York public schools, and a joint brief of the attorneys general of twenty-two states represented interests in support of the use of the prayer.

Clement Vose has written that "organizations — identifiable by letterhead — often link broad interests in society to individual parties of interests in Supreme Court cases. . . . Perhaps the most direct and open participation has been by organizations which have been obliged to protect their own rights and privileges." [27] Certainly the most widely known organization that has used litigation effectively to achieve its ends is the National Association for the Advancement of Colored People. As a major group representing Negroes in this century, the NAACP includes some seventeen hundred state and local units in its organizational structure. In 1953 it numbered 535,000 members within its ranks.[28] With few exceptions, the cause of racial equality prior to the 1940's received little support from the executive and legislative branches of the national government. The NAACP turned to legal tactics in an effort to win its goals. Lawsuits during this century that won protection of rights in the areas of housing, transportation, voting, procedural safeguards, service on juries, and education were primarily the result of *test cases* initiated by the NAACP. The organization supplied financial resources and legal talent necessary for victory in the courts.

Of importance in the organization's efforts to bring an end to the practice of racial segregation has been the procedural device of the *class action*. A class action, as defined in the *Federal Rules of Civil Procedure*, permits a group of people to bring suit in the names of persons "constituting a class" so as to insure "the adequate representation of all" before the courts. The class action is especially appropriate for civil rights cases because it permits large numbers of people within a given jurisdiction to appeal without individually requiring them to seek redress of grievances. For example, cases challenging so-called de facto segregation in public schools have been filed in behalf of both the parties bringing the suit and all others similarly situated.[29] De facto segregation refers to racial segregation resulting from such practices as gerrymandered school boundaries; adherence to a traditional "neighborhood school" policy in cities where

[27] Clement E. Vose, "Litigation as a Form of Pressure Group Activity," *The Annals of the American Academy of Political and Social Science*, CCCXIX (September, 1958), 20–31.

[28] John A. Morsell, "The National Association for the Advancement of Colored People and its Strategy," *The Annals of the American Academy of Political and Social Science*, CCCLVII (January, 1965), 97–101.

[29] *Bell v. School City of Gary Indiana* 324 F. 2D 209 (1963); *Taylor v. Board of Education of New Rochelle* 82 Sup. Ct. 382 (1961).

Negroes are heavily concentrated in particular areas; or manipulating school transfer policies so as to achieve racially segregated schools. A class suit can encompass all children attending public schools with a total or almost total Negro enrollment.

While the class action has been utilized largely by civil rights interests, the test case device has also been utilized by economic groups — labor unions, agricultural groups, corporations, etc. Samuel Krislov observes: "The good test case is also one that has the proper emotional, non-legal overtones." [30] A case involving charges of obscenity against a literary classic stands a better chance of eliciting popular support against censorship than a novel of dubious literary value filled with lurid passages.[31]

Finally government — federal, state, and local — may itself be a litigant. The U.S. Department of Justice is involved, either as a party or by filing an amicus brief, in about half the cases heard each year by the Supreme Court.[32]

Group efforts to influence judicial decisions are also reflected in legal periodicals. Chester A. Newland has written that "periodical writing plays a leading part in the shaping of our law. . . . Although objections to judicial reliance on legal periodicals and related sources have erupted in Congress and the press . . . such writing has generally been accepted now for several years as a central part of the judicial process." [33] Newland raises the ethical question of the propriety of publishing commentaries on issues not yet decided by the highest courts. The increasing practice of citing opinions expressed in legal periodicals in writing court decisions does not establish a direct influence on judicial choice but illustrates another access channel through which interests "lobby" courts.

These devices considerably expand the scope of conflict representation. They also provide a broader and more democratic basis for judicial reconciliation of potentially explosive conflict. Judges are formally made aware of the views of widely varied groups. Such group resources in litigation inject new variables into the process of judicial policy-making. The

[30] Samuel Krislov, *The Supreme Court in the Policy Process* (New York: The Macmillan Co., 1965), p. 45.

[31] In 1966, for example, the Supreme Court upheld the conviction of Edward Mishkin, a publisher and retailer of sado-masochistic paperbacks. Virtually no support for Mishkin existed among civil libertarians and intellectuals. On the same day the Court reversed a Massachusetts ban on the Eighteenth-Century novel, *Fanny Hill*. In the latter case a large number of individuals and civil liberties groups strongly opposed the banning of the novel. See *Memoirs* v. *Massachusetts* (1966); *Mishkin* v. *New York* (1966).

[32] Krislov, *op. cit.*, p. 48.

[33] Chester A. Newland, "The Supreme Court and Legal Writing: Learned Journals as Vehicles of an Anti-antitrust Lobby?" *Georgetown Law Journal*, XLVIII (Fall, 1959), pp. 105–43, and reprinted in Robert Scigliano (ed.), *The Courts* (Boston: Little, Brown and Co., 1962), pp. 170–76.

judiciary's traditional insulation from the political arena resulting from such institutional arrangements as non-popular selection, life tenure, and nonpartisanship may in effect be altered.

CONFLICT AND CHOICE WITHIN THE COURT

The business of the Supreme Court takes place within a highly formal atmosphere of procedural rules and judicial protocol. Court sessions and deliberations are marked by pageantry, formal procedures, and an atmosphere of dignity. This atmosphere reflects and reinforces public expectations that the judicial process will be devoid of the political compromises and group struggles characteristic of the legislative and executive processes. Yet, as Professor Murphy has pointed out, "judges who wish to see their policy choices become operative cannot always escape the necessity of negotiation or resort to devious stratagems." [34] We have already discussed the external forces that shape Court perspectives; here we deal with internal procedures and relations that affect their actions.

The Court, by utilizing its power to hear or not hear an appeal, determines the cases it will rule on. About one hundred cases per year reach the formal decision stage. While each decision determines a "winner" and a "loser" in terms of the specific parties to the dispute, the division of opinion among the justices and the reasoning behind these opinions have implications that go beyond the simple winner-loser-dichotomy. Unanimous opinions are handed down in only about one in four cases. *Concurring* opinions – those that agree with the opinion of the majority but on different grounds – and *dissenting* opinions – the views of the minority – are frequently expressed.[35] Any justice may write, or join his fellow justices in a concurring or a dissenting opinion.

What do opinions mean, and how much can be inferred from their reading? Traditional approaches to the Court have closely examined opinions for what they reveal about the development of the law, the philosophy of the Court, the views of individual justices, and the role of the Court vis-à-vis other branches of government. This approach is both fruitful and necessary. More recently, effort has been made to develop more sophisticated tools of analysis that explain more fully the behavior of the justices.[36] As stated earlier no one can enter the mind of a justice, and existing tools of analysis are not adequate for drawing cause-and-effect relationships to explain judicial behavior. Furthermore, the Court

---

[34] Murphy, *op. cit.*, p. 209.

[35] Decisions are sometimes made on the basis of a tie vote, a result that can occur where all nine justices do not participate in the case. The effect of a tie is to uphold the lower-court decision, but no formal opinion is written.

[36] See, for example, Glendon Schubert (ed.), *Judicial Behavior: A Reader in Theory and Research* (Chicago: Rand McNally & Co., 1964).

as an institution is more private and therefore is less accessible than other areas of government. For example, Court norms prohibit justices from publicly criticizing decisions with which they have formally disagreed. Also personal antagonisms among the justices are usually not aired in public, even though they may be known to exist. Nonmembers of the Court cannot sit in on the *conference*, a meeting held at least once a week during the Court's term (October to June). In conference — which is formal in both procedure and protocol (justices are seated around the table in order of seniority, and the chief justice always speaks first) — the business of the Court takes place. Cases are discussed, appeals considered and passed upon, formal votes are taken, and justices are assigned the task of writing opinions.

The interaction of personalities, goals, and backgrounds of each of the justices has been the subject of an increasing amount of research. If his position on an issue is to prevail, a justice must win the support of at least four of his fellow justices in order to gain a majority of votes. The history of the Court reveals that some justices have possessed greater ability to persuade and influence. Although some of these justices have failed to convince a majority of their colleagues, their positions have become majority policy in subsequent Courts. As a classic example, the lone dissenting opinion of Justice Harlan against the Court's "separate but equal" doctrine in racial segregation (*Plessy* v. *Ferguson,* 1897) became the unanimous opinion in *Brown* v. *Topeka* in 1954.

Where the Court is seriously divided on an issue or where opinion of the court reflects ambiguity within the majority, there is greater expectation that losing interests will attempt to exploit this division or uncertainty with further litigation. Moreover, the Court's status as an enforcing agent and legitimatizer of public norms and policy decisions of other branches may be weakened by narrow majorities or ambiguous opinions. Under these conditions, severe public criticism is invited. The unanimous opinion in *Brown* v. *Topeka* and subsequent unanimity in segregation cases have lent strong authority to Court-made policy. In contrast, frequent five-to-four decisions in cases involving the procedural rights ("due process") of accused persons under the Fifth and Fourteenth Amendments have not only produced severe criticism of the Court but also great uncertainty among public prosecutors as to what standards the Court requires.[37]

To prevent the effects of division and ambiguity and thus enhance the Court's capacity to resolve conflict, informal efforts may be made to ac-

[37] See, for example, *Escobedo* v. *Illinois* 378 U.S. 476 (1964) (right to counsel); *Gideon* v. *Wainwright* 372 U.S. 335 (1963) (right to counsel); *Townsend* v. *Sain* 372 U.S. 293 (1963) (forced confession by use of "truth serum"); *Malloy* v. *Hogan* 378 U.S. 1 (1964) (applying Fifth Amendment ban on compulsory self-incrimination against the states via the "due process" clause of the Fourteenth Amendment).

commodate differing views and present a more unified front to the public. Efforts to produce a unified and productive Court involve Court leadership. The status and authority of the chief justice enhances his capacity to exercise this role. He presides over sessions of the Court and the conference. When in the majority, he assigns the writing of the opinion of the Court to one of the justices in the majority or he may write the opinion himself. (Writing of the minority opinion is assigned by the senior justice in the minority). The chief justice is responsible for administration of the Court's docket of cases and controls the timetable of the conference.

David Danelski has utilized a concept of dual leadership — task leadership and social leadership -- to evaluate leadership within the Court.[38] Highly esteemed by his colleagues, but reserved in his personal relations, the task leader clearly and forcefully presents his views in conference, leads the discussion, and provides guidance on difficult questions. The social leader, usually possessing a warm and responsive personality, concentrates on the "emotional needs of his associates by affirming their value as individuals and as Court members." His efforts are primarily aimed at unity and cohesion within the Court. More frequently the chief justice will exercise task or social leadership but not both types. He will share the dual leadership with one of his associates. In Danelski's opinion, Chief Justice Charles Evans Hughes exercised both roles; his successor, Harlan F. Stone, neither. The leadership abilities of the chief justice will depend upon many factors, including his personality, his view of his role, and the personalities of other members of the Court. Strong chief justices, such as Marshall, Taft, and Hughes, have succeeded in maintaining a sense of unity and cohesion in the face of both serious inner-court differences over policy areas and strong personalities that have conflicted with the Court. Others have failed. "The chief justiceship supplies numerous opportunities to exert influence; it offers no guaranty that the incumbent can utilize these opportunities to achieve his policy goals." [39]

The appearance of voting blocs within the Court lends support to the assertion that policy leadership is shared. Bloc-voting analysis has shown that "liberal-conservative" divisions on civil liberties issues occur with regularity.[40] Study of voting patterns provides both knowledge of the

[38] David Danelski, "The Influence of the Chief Justice in the Decisional Process of the Supreme Court," in Walter F. Murphy and C. Herman Pritchett (eds.), *Courts, Judges, and Politics* (New York: Random House, 1961), pp. 497–508.

[39] Murphy, *op. cit.*, p. 89.

[40] See, for example, C. Herman Pritchett, *Civil Liberties and the Vinson Court* (Chicago: University of Chicago Press, 1954), Chap. 9; S. Sidney Ulmer, "The Analysis of Behavior Patterns in the United States Supreme Court," *The Journal of Politics*, XXII (November, 1960), 629–53.

behavior of individual justices and a basis for predicting areas of controversy that will probably divide the Court in the future. They do not, however, provide explanations of *why* individuals behave as they do nor do they establish certainty in predicting the outcome of judicial disputes. They do increase our understanding of judicial behavior. Finally such studies, and also those relating to internal Court relationships, illustrate again the existence of a bargaining situation within the Court. Decisions, in short, result from attempts to accommodate a wide variety of interests both within and outside the judicial structure.

THE SUPREME COURT AND PUBLIC POLICY

Aside from the restriction that Congress cannot alter the original jurisdiction of the Supreme Court, there are no significant limits placed by the Constitution on congressional restraint of the judiciary. Yet, despite frequent criticisms of Supreme Court decisions by members of Congress, few formal prerogatives have been used to curb Court activities. Not until 1868 did Congress revoke the Supreme Court's appellate jurisdiction. In the bitter atmosphere of post-Civil War Reconstruction, a Radical Republican Congress withdrew (over a presidential veto) Court jurisdiction to decide a case already argued. An 1867 statute which had granted the jurisdiction was repealed. In *Ex Parte McCardle* (1869) the Supreme Court refused to decide the case on grounds that Article III of the Constitution granted Congress authority to remove the Court's appellate jurisdiction.

In the two major periods of congressional dissatisfaction with Supreme Court policy adjudication since the turn of the century, no action removing the Court's jurisdiction has been approved. President Roosevelt's threat against the Court in the 1930's, for example, took another form. Since the early 1950's the Court under Chief Justice Earl Warren has been a subject of criticism. Interests have charged that the Court has gone "too far" in several areas: civil rights and liberties (through invalidation of school segregation, limitations on the scope of federal loyalty-security programs, protection of personal rights under due process, protection against self-incrimination, etc.), legislative apportionment (particularly the decision that the principle of "one man, one vote" must prevail in portioning both houses of state legislatures), and religious freedom (cases involving invalidation of state supported public school prayers).[41]

---

[41] See *Brown v. Board of Education* 347 U.S. 483 (1954); *Watkins v. United States* 354 U.S. 178 (1957), in which the Court ruled that questions asked by congressional investigating committees not pertinent to the purpose of the investigation did not have

Criticism of the Court has generated more heat than fire. The school desegregation decision of 1954 produced the "Southern Manifesto" of 1956, a document signed by nineteen southern senators and seventy-seven representatives labeling the decision "unwarranted" and charging the Court with exercising a "clear abuse of judicial power." In an unusual action in 1958, the Conference of State Chief Justices formally criticized U.S. Supreme Court decisions concerning federal-state relations. The chief justices commented that the Court "too often has tended to adopt the role of policy-maker without proper judicial restraint" and should refrain from "the exercise of essentially legislative powers." [42]

Congressional dismay at Court actions took another form in an unsuccessful proposal to withdraw appellate jurisdiction of the Supreme Court in certain areas of national security. The sponsor of the bill argued that it was necessary action to deal with "the self-evident fact that we had a runaway Supreme Court." [43] Finally congressional reaction to Court reapportionment decisions was even more threatening. The House in 1964 approved a measure to strip federal courts of jurisdiction in state reapportionment cases. The bill did not pass the Senate, but a substitute motion sponsored jointly by Democratic majority leader Mike Mansfield and Republican minority leader Everett Dirksen appeared as an amendment to foreign-aid legislation. The proposal would have deferred execution of court-ordered reapportionment of state legislatures until Congress could submit a constitutional amendment to the states which, if ratified, would override the "one man, one vote" principle in upper houses of state legislatures. The proposal for a reapportionment moratorium engendered a filibuster that was terminated when Congress resolved that the Supreme Court should not disrupt forthcoming state legislative elec-

---

to be answered by a witness; in *Cole* v. *Young* 351 U.S. 536 (1956) and *Service* v. *Dulles* 354 U.S. 363 (1957) the Court limited the scope of certain provisions of the federal loyalty-security program. A 1956 decision, *Pennsylvania* v. *Nelson* 350 U.S. 497 (1956) invalidated Pennsylvania's anti-subversive activities statute on grounds that the federal government had preempted this area of national security by the Smith Act of 1940 and other statutes. Another 1956 decision, *Slochower* v. *Board of Education* 350 U.S. 551 (1956) held that a Brooklyn College professor could not be fired on grounds that he had invoked the Fifth Amendment privilege against self-incrimination before a congressional investigating committee. Finally, in *Schware* v. *Board of Bar Examiners of New Mexico* 353 U.S. 232 (1957), the Court ruled that New Mexico could not withhold admission to the bar on grounds that Schware was not of "good moral character" because he was an admitted member of the Communist Party from 1932 to 1940. A unanimous Court pointed out that the Communist Party during this period was a "lawful political party with candidates on the ballot in most States." Further, the state could not properly infer that membership during this time established the participation of Schware in illegal conduct.

[42] *Report of the Committee on Federal-State Relationships as Affected by Judicial Decisions*, August 23, 1958; reprinted in Scigliano, *op. cit.*, pp. 456–63.

[43] *Congressional Record*, CIV, 85th Congress, 2nd Session (1958), 18635.

tions by requiring prior reapportionment. The resolution did not affect Court appellate jurisdiction.

Senator Dirksen continued to seek a constitutional amendment in the next Congress. This device is rarely successful. Where the Court bases decisions upon interpretations of a clause of the Constitution (as in segregation and reapportionment cases), only amendment or subsequent alteration of the decision by the Court can reverse the result. Most decisions of the Court are not, however, based upon such explicit grounds; statutory interpretation comprises the bulk of policy adjudication. If statutory interpretation is the basis for decision, Congress may nullify the verdict by changing the law or passing new legislation. Where Congressional sentiment is mixed regarding the issue created by a Supreme Court decision, decisions are rarely overruled by statutory means. Professor Pritchett's analysis of twenty-one instances of congressional reversal between 1945 and 1957 revealed that most decisions provoke mixed congressional reaction and are successfully reversed only under special circumstances, such as an intense, nationwide lobbying campaign.[44]

President and Congress are not without means to check the judicial branch, yet our discussion has shown that the Court has suffered little in the way of direct interference or retribution from these branches during the twentieth century. Pritchett's analysis of congressional attempts to curb the Court's jurisdiction during the 1950's concluded with the following observation: One could well argue that congressional authority under the Constitution to control appellate jurisdiction "has in effect now been repealed by the passage of time and by the recognition that exercise of such power would be in the truest sense subversive of the American tradition of an independent judiciary." [45]

Debate over both the historical function of courts and what their role *ought* to be is sometimes cast as one between proponents of judicial "activism" and "self-restraint." The former include those who view the role of the judge as a shaper of constitutional meaning in order to promote "proper" social and political goals. An activist considers the values of objectivity or personal noninvolvement of lesser importance than the need to mold constitutional clauses into desirable form. He regards the judiciary as an ultimate arbiter of disputes between legislative declarations and the claimed rights of individuals or groups. In contrast, the advocate of judicial "self-restraint" emphasizes the court's duty not to intervene in policy matters unless such course is demonstrated as clearly necessary. Maintaining a constitutional balance between governing

[44] C. Herman Pritchett, *Congress Versus the Supreme Court* (Minneapolis: University of Minnesota Press, 1961).
[45] *Ibid.*, p. 122.

branches is considered more important than achieving particular social or personal values of judicial leadership. Without denying that judicial policy-making is unavoidable, this view prefers to keep it to a minimum.

Prior to 1937 the Supreme Court regularly interpreted economic rights under the Constitution as barring state and national regulatory statutes. In this instance an "activist" Court refused to accept the so-called "reasonable man" test, a doctrine which argued that courts ought not to nullify legislative policy unless a "reasonable man" could conclude that the legislature had not acted on rational grounds.

Activism in economic matters ended with the formation of the Roosevelt Court in the 1930's. It exists, however, in other areas. Justice Stone's "preferred position" argument laid down in the 1930's gave First Amendment freedoms a special position not accorded to other clauses of the Constitution (see Chapter Three). Under Stone's test, legislative action qualifying these freedoms should be more thoroughly examined than other types of legislation. Justices have sharply differed over considering some liberties superior ("preferred") to others. Justice Hugo L. Black, among the staunchest supporters of judicial activism in First Amendment controversies, urged that the Bill of Rights contains "absolutes" in the sense that government "was denied all power to do some things *under any and all circumstances. . . .*" [46]

Until his retirement in 1962, the major antagonist of the activist position was Justice Felix Frankfurter. Frankfurter's view was clearly expressed in his dissenting opinion to a decision that held that a West Virginia law requiring all public school children to salute the flag (*West Virginia Board of Education* v. *Barnette,* 1943) was a violation of the First and Fourteenth Amendments. A member of the Jehovah's Witnesses, a religious sect which looks upon such practices as worshipping false idols, attacked the law as a violation of religious freedom protected by the First Amendment. Dissenting from the majority view that a state may not invade "the sphere of intellect and spirit" by imposing such a requirement, Frankfurter argued that the judiciary should bow to legislative judgment. West Virginia's legislature, said Frankfurter, required the compulsory flag salute on the wholly reasonable grounds that the practice would promote patriotism and loyalty.

Where once property rights occupied a preferred position in the minds of the majority, the areas of religious freedom, criminal law, legislative reapportionment, and racial justice now seem to hold a special place in the hierarchy of constitutional values. Circuit Judge J. Skelley Wright, a proponent of the activist position in these areas, holds the view that "the

[46] Hugo L. Black, "The Bill of Rights and the Federal Government," in Edmond Cahn (ed.), *The Great Rights* (New York: The Macmillan Co., 1963), p. 45.

courts can act as the collective conscience of a sovereign people." [47] At bottom, popular assessments of the role of the courts as either conscience or reflector — the two are quite different — of American values depends to a great extent on agreement or disagreement with particular decisions. The debate over the proper role of courts certainly hinges on broader considerations than being on the winning or losing side of a decision; yet what was "judicial usurpation" yesterday may, under changed circumstances, become "sound law" today.

Neither constitutional restraints nor self-restraints can guarantee that policy adjudication will always be conducted in the tradition of liberal democracy. Judicial review is, of course, a central feature of American constitutional democracy. But as we pointed out in Part One, there is no assurance that liberal and constitutional democracy will always be compatible. To what extent *can* the Supreme Court impose its own policy preferences over those of legislative majorities?

Congressional efforts in this century have not restrained judicial activity in particular areas; many would argue that the Supreme Court has also failed to restrain itself. Yet we know that courts are not free to do anything they want; certainly the Supreme Court has succeeded in blocking congressional majorities for only relatively short periods of time. Congress and President have not restrained the courts; neither have the courts permanently checked the other two branches. What accounts for this? The answer may lie in the nature of majorities in pluralist America.

Majorities are coalitions of interests that elect presidents, articulate opinion, and govern the policy process. Americans normally look to the partisan process for the generation of majorities. The activity of the Supreme Court has been related to the effectiveness or lack of effectiveness of such majorities. Wallace Mendelson argues that where a high degree of cohesion within dominant partisan alliances has prevailed, courts have not been successful in determining national policy.[48] According to Mendelson's data, between 1790 and 1864 the Supreme Court declared only two congressional measures unconstitutional — in *Marbury* v. *Madison* and *Dred Scott* v. *Sanford*. From 1865 to 1937 the Court used the veto in seventy-six instances. According to Mendelson, the substantial increase in judicial review was largely due to the clash between businessmen, grain farmers, and laborers — the interests constituting the dominant Republican coalition — which left the Court free to exercise a veto without united opposition. In the conflict within the coalition, business emerged

[47] J. Skelley Wright, "The Role of the Courts: Conscience of a Sovereign People," *The Reporter*, XXIX, (Sept. 26, 1963), 27.

[48] Wallace Mendelson, "Judicial Review and Party Politics," *Vanderbilt Law Review*, XII (1959), 447–57.

victorious, not by legislative victories, but through the Supreme Court's exercise of the judicial veto over legislative economic policy. The pro-business, *laissez-faire* orientation of the Court was maintained until the New Deal coalition reclaimed the dominant role as national policy-maker. Since 1937 the Court has exercised restraint in cases dealing with economic legislation. Mendelson concludes that "judicial 'legislation' apparently feeds on defects in the political structure."

Stuart Nagel has also examined the relationship between judicial review and party politics.[49] Utilizing the Lowell-Turner method for determining differences between the parties (see Chapter Thirteen), Nagel found that the period of highest incidence of judicial review (1865–1936) was also a period during which strong differences existed between the two major parties. That is, the percentage of party-oriented votes in Congress was higher during this period than during periods when the occurrence of judicial review was less. Although Nagel's findings deal with differences between the two parties — whereas Mendelson concentrates on differences within the dominant Republican alliance — his findings tend to qualify Mendelson's emphasis on intra-party differences as an explanation of a high incidence of judicial review. Nagel does, however, find some important relationships between the American party system and judicial review: (1) Judicial review has increased during periods when one party controls Congress and a majority of the justices on the Court are of the other party (as determined by their party affiliation at the time of their appointment). (2) There is a high correlation between Democratic party control of all three branches of government and a low incidence of judicial review. Historically, Republican party platforms have shown a more favorable attitude toward the Court's exercise of judicial review. Democrats, on the other hand, have more frequently (for example, in 1908, 1924, and 1936) favored constitutional amendment as a device to get around Court decisions. Since 1936, however, the pattern has been reversed. (3) In a total of eighty-six instances of judicial review from 1789 to 1960, Democrats on the Court tended to support an activist position (i.e., for court intervention) in the sixteen cases striking down legislatively imposed restraints on civil liberties, and tended to exercise restraint (i.e., against court intervention) in fifty cases dealing with governmental regulation or taxation. In contrast, Republicans on the Court have shown more restraint in civil liberties matters and a greater degree of activism in tax and regulatory matters. The remaining fifteen cases involved neither civil liberties nor tax and regulatory statutes and no pattern of partisan support was evident.

[49] Stuart S. Nagel, "Political Parties and Judicial Review in American History," *The Journal of Public Law*, XI (1962), 328–40.

Weaknesses in the party system occur primarily during periods when the old dominant alliance is breaking up and giving way to a new coalition. Since these periods of transition are relatively short-lived, the judiciary cannot control community policy whenever it wishes. Seen from this perspective, Professor Robert Dahl holds that the common assumption that the Supreme Court protects minorities against national majorities is not supportable. The Court can delay, but not permanently block, a law-making majority. In fact, the history of its role is basically one of legitimating the policy of the dominant national alliance. Yet, says Dahl, the Court is more than simply an "agent" of the alliance. It is an essential part of political leadership and possesses "bases of power of its own, the most important of which is the unique legitimacy attributed to its interpretation of the Constitution." Thus, at its best, "the Court operates to confer legitimacy, not simply on the particular and parochial policies of the dominant political alliance, but upon the basic patterns of behavior required for the operation of a democracy." [50]

Debate over the role of the Supreme Court in a democratic system sometimes overlooks the fact that the Court's function is largely a negative one. It can order reapportionment of a state legislature or the end of segregated public schools only by ruling that existing state practices violate positive constitutional provisions. What is more, the Court cannot initiate or propose alternative public policies. Yet of the three branches of government, only the Supreme Court "articulates the character of the constitutional system and indicates the nature of its unity." [51] Fragmented congressional leadership in policy adoption and presidential difficulties in bringing unity to the administrative branch are familiar patterns in policy-making. In contrast, Americans are quite accustomed to viewing judicial policy-making in terms of *the* decisions of the Supreme Court; that is, they tend to ignore or remain unaware of divisions within the Court.

The judiciary serves to legitimate policy formulated by administrators, congressmen, and pressure leaders; moreover, it symbolizes the protective shield of those practices and procedures that make democracy operable — political and individual rights and freedoms. At the same time, the inherent ambivalency in liberal ideology — the emphasis upon both individual rights and majority rule — is mirrored in American attitudes toward the proper role of the Supreme Court. Is the Court to be an instrument of the majority or is its role more properly one of checking the

---

[50] Robert A. Dahl, "Decision-making in a Democracy: The Supreme Court as a National Policy-Maker," *The Journal of Public Law*, VI (1957), 279–95.

[51] Carl Brent Swisher, *The Supreme Court in Modern Role* (New York: New York University Press, 1965), p. 70.

majority? The answer given is often dependent upon which side of a controversy the Court supports. The role of the judiciary in accommodating conflict is not easily assessed. Courts cannot be isolated from the other major components of the decision-making processes. Their role, properly understood, conditions, and is conditioned by, these components.

BIBLIOGRAPHICAL NOTE

Until recent years literature on the judiciary was largely confined to judicial history and examination of substantive issues (case law). Current research and writing heavily emphasizes factors which place the courts, especially the U.S. Supreme Court, in a political setting. Essential to an appreciation of this approach, however, is an understanding of the historical background and knowledge of case law in substantive areas. The standard history of the Supreme Court is Charles Warren, *The Supreme Court in United States History,* 3 vols. (Boston: Little, Brown and Company, 1922–1923). A recent paperback outlining the development of the constitutional system is Arthur N. Holcombe, *Securing the Blessings of Liberty* (Chicago: Scott, Foresman & Co., 1964). There are several textbooks which emphasize the case-law approach. Among these are Rocco J. Tresolini, *American Constitutional Law,* 2nd edition (New York: Macmillan Co., 1965) and Alpheus T. Mason and William M. Beaney, *American Constitutional Law,* 3rd edition (Englewood Cliffs, N.J.: Prentice-Hall, 1964). A paperback work by Tresolini, *Constitutional Decisions in American Government* (New York: Macmillan Co., 1965) contains some of the most important decisions of the Supreme Court. The following paperbacks combine historical outlines of the development of constitutional law with analysis of major areas of controversy: Carl Brent Swisher, *The Growth of Constitutional Power in the United States* (Chicago: University of Chicago Press, 1946) treats the Court from Marshall onward; Alpheus T. Mason, *The Supreme Court From Taft to Warren* (New York: W. W. Norton & Co., 1958) examines major substantive issues within the context of debate over the proper function of courts in the American system; Robert G. McCloskey (ed.), *Essays in Constitutional Law* (New York: Vintage Books, 1957) contains commentary on broad substantive questions such as federalism, economic rights, and church and state by leading authorities in the field. A short hardbound volume, Thomas Reed Powell's *Vagaries and Varieties in Constitutional Interpretation* (New York: Columbia University Press, 1956) is a series of witty and brilliant lectures on the content and direction of constitutional doctrine in various areas.

The procedures and structures of the judiciary are treated in a number of books. Paperback works at the undergraduate level include Henry J. Abraham, *The Judicial Process* (New York: Oxford University Press, 1962) which also discusses the nature of law and provides some comparison of the American and other judicial systems; Delmar Karlen, *The Citizen in Court: Litigant, Witness, Juror, Judge* (New York: Holt, Rinehart & Winston, 1964) is the work of a lawyer writing for a lay audience; C. Gordon Post, *An Introduction to the Law* (Englewood Cliffs, N.J.: Prentice-Hall, 1963); and Loren P. Beth, *Politics, the*

Constitution, and the Supreme Court (Evanston, Ill.: Row, Peterson & Co., 1962). State courts are also discussed in these works. For a description which views the judicial process in a major state from the perspective of the actors in it, see Beverly Blair Cook, *The Judicial Process* (Belmont, Calif.: Dickenson, 1967).

Behavioral and systems approaches to the judicial branch are incorporated in many recent works. Among the foremost representatives of the behavioral frame of reference is Glendon Schubert. His *Constitutional Politics* (New York: Holt, Rinehart & Winston, 1960) is a sophisticated undergraduate text which focuses upon how and why the Supreme Court makes certain decisions. He has also edited *Judicial Behavior: A Reader in Theory and Research* (Chicago: Rand McNally & Co., 1964), a comprehensive cross-cultural approach which discusses the relationship between the study of judicial behavior and other disciplines such as traditional public law and history. Schubert's recent paperback *Judicial Policy-Making* (Chicago: Scott, Foresman & Co., 1965) is an application, at the introductory level, of systems theory to the judicial function. Other paperback editions at the introductory level which represent contemporary behavioral approaches to the study of the judicial process are: Herbert Jacob, *Justice in America* (Boston: Little, Brown and Company, 1965); Samuel Krislov, *The Supreme Court in the Political Process* (New York: Macmillan Co., 1965) is especially useful in understanding internal relationships and processes of the Supreme Court; Robert Scigliano, *The Courts: A Reader in the Judicial Process* (Boston: Little, Brown and Company, 1962) provides a broad spectrum of various approaches to understanding the judiciary in action; and Jack Peltason, *Federal Courts in the Political Process* (New York: Random House, 1956) analyzes the federal judicial system from the point of view of interest group theory. A hardbound edition, Walter F. Murphy, *Elements of Judicial Strategy* (Chicago: University of Chicago Press, 1964) views the role and functions of judicial policy-making within the context of the policy-oriented judge.

The politics of judicial selection and the social background of Supreme Court justices are discussed in John R. Schmidhauser, *The Supreme Court: Its Politics, Personalities, and Procedures* (New York: Holt, Rinehart & Winston, 1961). Also available in paperback, David J. Danelski, *A Supreme Court Justice is Appointed* (New York: Random House, 1964) is an engaging account of the nomination of a Supreme Court justice and provides valuable insights into the nominating process in general. Joel B. Grossman, *Lawyers and Judges: The ABA and the Politics of Judicial Selection* (New York: John Wiley & Sons, 1965) offers a close view of the role of the bar in federal judicial appointments. The relationship of interest group activity to judicial policy-making is discussed in Clement Vose, "Litigation as a Form of Pressure Group Activity" in *The Annals of the American Academy of Political and Social Science*, Vol. 319, (Sept. 1958); in Vose's *Caucasians Only* (Berkeley: University of California Press, 1959); and, in more general terms, in David B. Truman, *The Governmental Process* (New York: Alfred A. Knopf, 1953).

Empirical measurement of judicial behavior has become progressively more sophisticated. A seminal work in the area of measuring judicial attitudes is C. Herman Pritchett's *The Roosevelt Court* (New York, Macmillan Co., 1948), which studies the 1937–1947 period on the basis of voting records of individual justices. Pritchett's *Civil Liberties and the Vinson Court* (Chicago: University of Chicago Press, 1954) also applied the bloc voting analysis device. Quantitative measurement of judicial decision-making is the subject of Glendon Schubert's *Quantitative Analysis of Judicial Behavior* (Glencoe, Ill.: Free Press, 1959), especially Chapter Four, and Schubert's *Constitutional Politics,* cited above.

Debate over judicial activism versus self-restraint has been widely discussed. It is inextricably involved with the larger question of the relationship of judicial review and the democratic system. A classic study in this area is Edward S. Corwin's *The Doctrine of Judicial Review* (Princeton: Princeton University Press, 1914). Charles S. Hyneman, *The Supreme Court on Trial* (New York: Atherton Press, 1963) analyzes the Court's position as a policy-maker and supports the concept of judicial restraint in viewing legislative policies. The following are all available in paperback editions: Alexander M. Bickel, *The Least Dangerous Branch* (Indianapolis: Bobbs-Merrill Co., Inc., 1962) argues that the role and function of the Supreme Court is consistent with the theory and practice of democracy; Robert H. Jackson, *The Supreme Court in the American System of Government* (New York: Harper & Row, 1955) is a brief, but insightful view of the Court and its relationship to democratic government by a former justice; Alan F. Westin (ed.), *The Supreme Court: Views from Inside* (New York: Norton, 1961) presents the views of some of the justices on this important matter.

Judicial biography is an excellent source for gaining insight into the workings of the Court. Among the many outstanding biographies of justices, are the following: Charles Fairman, *Mr. Justice Miller and the Supreme Court 1862–1890* (Cambridge: Harvard University Press, 1939); Merlo J. Pusey, *Charles Evans Hughes,* 2 vols. (New York: Macmillan Co., 1951); Alpheus T. Mason, *Harlan Fiske Stone: Pillar of the Law* (New York: Viking Press, 1956); and Arthur J. Beveridge, *The Life of John Marshall* (Boston: Houghton Mifflin Co., 1919). A paperback, Allison Dunham and Philip B. Kurland (eds.), revised and enlarged edition, *Mr. Justice* (Chicago: University of Chicago Press, 1964) contains twelve biographical studies by leading judicial biographers.

The Pluralistic
Aspiration:
A Concluding Note

The capacity of a political community to manage conflict and build consensus on the legitimacy of public policy decisions is clearly related to the degree that interests can articulate and achieve representation of their demands. The personal, social, and politico-constitutional manifestations of American pluralism have been demarcated in this book. Bargaining, the product of the pluralist community, is the common denominator in achieving conflict regulation and maintaining consensual norms. Patterns such as the relationship between democratic ideals and practice, the party system and political choice, the legislative process and group access, administrative policy-making, and the role of the judiciary in conflict resolution have revealed the basis and nature of the bargaining process. Bargaining styles demonstrate the existence of uneven resources and varying skills of the participants. The formation of policy clusters are the result of a combination of rule by minorities and by concurrent majorities. Under these conditions responsibility for public policy is difficult to fix and the ideals of larger and rationally-arrived-at community goals tend to become lost in the compromises forced by the bargaining process.

458

Finally, we have shown that group leaders, in their efforts to conserve their bargaining resources for use in matters of concern to the groups they represent, tend to avoid those issues outside their particular bargaining arena.

In conjunction with bargaining we have emphasized the pattern of policy-making by increment. A variety of interests operating on widely diffused centers of power conditions the polity to gradual and limited changes in public policy. Traumatic reversals of existing policy or revolutionary new departures seldom characterize American political patterns. Emphasis is on continuing adjustment of interest demands within the constitutional bargaining arrangements. Policy by increments operates to reinforce the status quo rather than as a catalyst in introducing new demands of new interests or in adjusting serious conflicts which may arise outside existing group relationships. That is, interests which have achieved special access or reached a *modus vivendi* with competing interests within the centers of policy-making tend to protect their status rather than risk an altered decision-making environment through the introduction of new interests.

That the pluralist framework of conflict regulation includes many diversified interests in policy-making is obviously consistent with democratic theory. However, emphasis on this point may obscure the fact that there are distortions within the pluralist pattern that, potentially at least, force adjustments in standard political patterns in efforts to continue peaceful accommodation of community disputes. For example, it was suggested at the close of Part Two that selectivity in political communication frequently distorts representational patterns to the point that serious social cleavages are masked. Some remain unnoticed or ignored by policy officials until they explode to the forefront of public attention as a result of circumvention of normal patterns of conflict representation. Sit-in demonstrations, protest marches for equality in public housing or minimum wages, and similar activities by civil rights groups, Mexican-American farm laborers, and opponents of sundry community policies may be viewed as a reaction to failure in achieving satisfactory representation of minority group demands within the normal institutional arrangement.

Such attempts to adjust conflict representation to the interests of dispossessed minorities are not new. In the nineteenth century and opening decades of the twentieth both agrarians and organized labor also struggled to achieve demands by resorting to techniques outside the scope of conventional patterns of communication and bargaining. It is a mark of the flexibility of the American polity that it adjusted then to the forces that were shaping a new community such that today the demands of organized labor, business interests, and agrarian groups are reflected in the incremental changes struck through policy bargaining. In similar fashion today, and in the future, other interests striving to be heard and declared legitimate members of the political community will work both within and outside the political processes described in previous chapters. As they do they will help remold the ever-changing patterns of conflict regulation that characterize the American polity and, in the doing, modify the personal, social, and politico-constitutional forces that define the American community.

Institutional and procedural arrangements in any political community distribute advantages and disadvantages unevenly among social interests. We are not suggesting that the American governing institutions must or can be blindly impartial in their relationships to interests within the polity. Nor could it be validly argued that America is ruled by a dominant elite or elites capable of achieving private ends irrespective of competing demands within the polity. The pluralistic nature of interest access and the diffusion of power within the community clearly argue the viability of wide-spread democratic participation and procedures in the making of public policy. But the pluralism inherent in the democratic creed, and manifested in American attitudinal, social, and political patterns, requires continuing readjustment and accommodation of changing group relationships within the polity. Indeed it is essential if Americans are to realize the substantive aim of liberal democracy — human dignity — *and* the procedural goal of community viability through representation and resolution of social conflict. The twin ideals of individual perfectability and collective stability depend in large measure upon political patterns that permit the absorption of emergent, diversified interests into the existing governing scheme. This is the working meaning of the pluralist aspiration in the politics of liberal democracy.

APPENDIX

The Constitution
of the United States

WE THE PEOPLE of the United States, in Order to form a more perfect Union, establish Justice, insure domestic Tranquility, provide for the common defence, promote the general Welfare, and secure the Blessings of Liberty to ourselves and our Posterity, do ordain and establish this CONSTITUTION for the United States of America.

Article I

SECTION 1. All legislative Powers herein granted shall be vested in a Congress of the United States, which shall consist of a Senate and House of Representatives.

SECTION 2. (1) The House of Representatives shall be composed of Members chosen every second Year by the People of the several States, and the Electors in each State shall have the Qualifications requisite for Electors of the most numerous Branch of the State Legislature.

(2) No Person shall be a Representative who shall not have attained to the Age of twenty-five Years, and been seven Years a Citizen of the United States, and who shall not, when elected, be an Inhabitant of that State in which he shall be chosen.

(3) [Representatives and direct Taxes [1] shall be apportioned among the

[1] The Sixteenth Amendment replaced this with respect to income taxes.

461

several States which may be included within this Union, according to their respective Numbers, which shall be determined by adding to the whole Number of free Persons, including those bound to Service for a Term of Years, and excluding Indians not taxed, three fifths of all other Persons.] [2] The actual Enumeration shall be made within three Years after the first Meeting of the Congress of the United States, and within every subsequent Term of ten Years, in such Manner as they shall by Law direct. The Number of Representatives shall not exceed one for every thirty Thousand, but each State shall have at Least one Representative; and until such enumeration shall be made, the State of New Hampshire shall be entitled to choose three, Massachusetts eight, Rhode-Island and Providence Plantations one, Connecticut five, New-York six, New Jersey four, Pennsylvania eight, Delaware one, Maryland six, Virginia ten, North Carolina five, South Carolina five, and Georgia three.

(4) When vacancies happen in the Representation from any State, the Executive Authority thereof shall issue Writs of Election to fill such Vacancies.

(5) The House of Representatives shall choose their Speaker and other Officers; and shall have the sole Power of Impeachment.

SECTION 3. (1) The Senate of the United States shall be composed of two Senators from each State, [chosen by the Legislature] [3] thereof, for six Years; and each Senator shall have one Vote.

(2) Immediately after they shall be assembled in Consequence of the first Election, they shall be divided as equally as may be into three Classes. The Seats of the Senators of the first Class shall be vacated at the Expiration of the second Year, of the second Class at the Expiration of the fourth Year, and of the third Class at the Expiration of the sixth Year, so that one-third may be chosen every second Year; [and if Vacancies happen by Resignation, or otherwise, during the Recess of the Legislature of any State, the Executive thereof may make temporary Appointments until the next Meeting of the Legislature, which shall then fill such Vacancies] [4]

(3) No person shall be a Senator who shall not have attained to the Age of thirty Years, and been nine Years a Citizen of the United States, and who shall not, when elected, be an Inhabitant of that State for which he shall be chosen.

(4) The Vice President of the United States shall be President of the Senate, but shall have no Vote, unless they be equally divided.

(5) The Senate shall choose their other Officers, and also a President pro tempore, in the absence of the Vice President, or when he shall exercise the Office of President of the United States.

(6) The Senate shall have the sole Power to try all Impeachments. When sitting for that Purpose, they shall be on Oath or Affirmation. When the President of the United States is tried, the Chief Justice shall preside: And no Person shall be convicted without the Concurrence of two thirds of the Members present.

(7) Judgment in Cases of Impeachment shall not extend further than to removal from Office, and disqualification to hold and enjoy any Office of honor, Trust or Profit under the United States: but the Party convicted shall neverthe-

[2] Repealed by the Fourteenth Amendment.
[3] Repealed by the Seventeenth Amendment, Section 1.
[4] Changed by the Seventeenth Amendment.

less be liable and subject to Indictment, Trial, Judgment and Punishment according to Law.

SECTION 4. (1) The Times, Places and Manner of holding Elections for Senators and Representatives, shall be prescribed in each State by the Legislature thereof; but the Congress may at any time by Law make or alter such Regulations, except as to the Places of Choosing Senators.

(2) The Congress shall assemble at least once in every Year, and such Meeting shall [be on the first Monday in December,] ⁵ unless they shall by Law appoint a different Day.

SECTION 5. (1) Each House shall be the Judge of the Elections, Returns and Qualifications of its own Members, and a Majority of each shall constitute a Quorum to do Business; but a smaller number may adjourn from day to day, and may be authorized to compel the Attendance of absent Members, in such Manner, and under such Penalties as each House may provide.

(2) Each House may determine the Rules of its Proceedings, punish its Members for disorderly Behavior, and, with the Concurrence of two thirds, expel a Member.

(3) Each House shall keep a Journal of its Proceedings, and from time to time publish the same, excepting such Parts as may in their Judgment require Secrecy; and the Yeas and Nays of the Members of either House on any question shall, at the Desire of one fifth of those Present, be entered on the Journal.

(4) Neither House, during the Session of Congress, shall, without the Consent of the other, adjourn for more than three days, nor to any other Place than that in which the two Houses shall be sitting.

SECTION 6. (1) The Senators and Representatives shall receive a Compensation for their Services, to be ascertained by Law, and paid out of the Treasury of the United States. They shall in all Cases, except Treason, Felony and Breach of the Peace, be privileged from Arrest during their Attendance at the Session of their respective Houses, and in going to and returning from the same; and for any Speech or Debate in either House, they shall not be questioned in any other Place.

(2) No Senator or Representative shall, during the Time for which he was elected, be appointed to any civil Office under the Authority of the United States, which shall have been created, or the Emoluments whereof shall have been increased during such time; and no Person holding any Office under the United States, shall be a Member of either House during his Continuance in Office.

SECTION 7. (1) All Bills for raising Revenue shall originate in the House of Representatives; but the Senate may propose or concur with Amendments as on other Bills.

(2) Every Bill which shall have passed the House of Representatives and the Senate, shall, before it become a Law, be presented to the President of the United States; If he approve he shall sign it, but if not he shall return it, with his Objections to that House in which it shall have originated, who shall enter the Objections at large on their Journal, and proceed to reconsider it. If after such Reconsideration two thirds of that House shall agree to pass the Bill, it shall be

⁵ Changed by the Twentieth Amendment, Section 2.

sent, together with the Objections, to the other House, by which it shall likewise be reconsidered, and if approved by two thirds of that House, it shall become a Law. But in all such Cases the Votes of both Houses shall be determined by Yeas and Nays, and the Names of the Persons voting for and against the Bill shall be entered on the Journal of each House respectively. If any Bill shall not be returned by the President within ten Days (Sundays excepted) after it shall have been presented to him, the Same shall be a Law, in like Manner as if he had signed it, unless the Congress by their Adjournment prevent its Return, in which Case it shall not be a Law.

(3) Every Order, Resolution, or Vote to which the Concurrence of the Senate and House of Representatives may be necessary (except on a question of Adjournment) shall be presented to the President of the United States; and before the Same shall take Effect, shall be approved by him, or being disapproved by him, shall be repassed by two thirds of the Senate and House of Representatives, according to the Rules and Limitations prescribed in the Case of a Bill.

SECTION 8. (1) The Congress shall have Power To lay and collect Taxes, Duties, Imposts and Excises, to pay the Debts and provide for the common Defence and general Welfare of the United States; but all Duties, Imposts and Excises shall be uniform throughout the United States;

(2) To borrow money on the credit of the United States;

(3) To regulate Commerce with foreign Nations, and among the several States, and with the Indian Tribes;

(4) To establish an uniform Rule of Naturalization, and uniform Laws on the subject of Bankruptcies throughout the United States;

(5) To coin Money, regulate the Value thereof, and of foreign Coin, and fix the Standard of Weights and Measures;

(6) To provide for the Punishment of counterfeiting the Securities and current Coin of the United States;

(7) To establish Post Office and post Roads;

(8) To promote the Progress of Science and useful Arts, by securing for limited Times to Authors and Inventors the exclusive Right to their respective Writings and Discoveries;

(9) To constitute Tribunals inferior to the supreme Court;

(10) To define and punish Piracies and Felonies committed on the high Seas, and Offenses against the Law of Nations;

(11) To declare War, grant Letters of Marque and Reprisal, and make Rules concerning Captures on Land and Water;

(12) To raise and support Armies, but no Appropriation of Money to that Use shall be for a longer Term than two Years;

(13) To provide and maintain a Navy;

(14) To make Rules for the Government and Regulation of the land and naval Forces;

(15) To provide for calling forth the Militia to execute the Laws of the Union, suppress Insurrections and repel Invasions;

(16) To provide for organizing, arming, and disciplining the Militia, and for governing such Part of them as may be employed in the Service of the United

States, reserving to the States respectively, the Appointment of the Officers, and the Authority of training the Militia according to the discipline prescribed by Congress;

(17) To exercise exclusive Legislation in all Cases whatsoever, over such District (not exceeding ten Miles square) as may, by Cession of particular States, and the acceptance of Congress, become the Seat of the Government of the United States, and to exercise like Authority over all Places purchased by the Consent of the Legislature of the State in which the Same shall be, for the Erection of Forts, Magazines, Arsenals, dock-Yards, and other needful Buildings; — And

(18) To make all Laws which shall be necessary and proper for carrying into Execution the foregoing Powers, and all other Powers vested by this Constitution in the Government of the United States, or in any Department or Officer thereof.

SECTION 9. (1) The Migration or Importation of such Persons as any of the States now existing shall think proper to admit, shall not be prohibited by the Congress prior to the Year one thousand eight hundred and eight, but a tax or duty may be imposed on such Importation, not exceeding ten dollars for each Person.

(2) The privilege of the Writ of Habeas Corpus shall not be suspended, unless when in Cases of Rebellion or Invasion the public Safety may require it.

(3) No Bill of Attainder or ex post facto Law shall be passed.

(4) No capitation, or other direct, Tax shall be laid, unless in Proportion to the Census or Enumeration herein before directed to be taken.[6]

(5) No Tax or Duty shall be laid on Articles exported from any State.

(6) No Preference shall be given by any Regulation of Commerce or Revenue to the Ports of one State over those of another: nor shall Vessels bound to, or from, one State, be obliged to enter, clear, or pay Duties in another.

(7) No Money shall be drawn from the Treasury, but in Consequence of Appropriations made by Law; and a regular Statement and Account of the Receipts and Expenditures of all public Money shall be published from time to time.

(8) No Title of Nobility shall be granted by the United States: And no Person holding any Office of Profit or Trust under them, shall, without the Consent of the Congress, accept of any present, Emolument, Office, or Title, of any kind whatever, from any King, Prince, or foreign State.

SECTION 10. (1) No State shall enter into any Treaty, Alliance, or Confederation; grant Letters of Marque and Reprisal; coin Money; emit Bills of Credit; make any Thing but gold and silver Coin a Tender in Payment of Debts; pass any Bill of Attainder, ex post facto Law, or Law impairing the Obligation of Contracts, or grant any Title of Nobility.

(2) No State shall, without the Consent of the Congress, lay any Imposts or Duties on Imports or Exports, except what may be absolutely necessary for executing its inspection Laws: and the net Produce of all Duties and Imposts, laid by any State on Imports or Exports, shall be for the Use of the Treasury of the United States; and all such Laws shall be subject to the Revision and Control of the Congress.

[6] Changed by the Sixteenth Amendment.

(3) No State shall, without the Consent of Congress, lay any duty of Tonnage, keep Troops, or Ships of War in time of Peace, enter into any Agreement or Compact with another State, or with a foreign Power, or engage in War, unless actually invaded, or in such imminent Danger as will not admit of delay.

Article II

SECTION 1. (1) The executive Power shall be vested in a President of the United States of America. He shall hold his Office during the Term of four Years, and, together with the Vice-President, chosen for the same Term, be elected, as follows

(2) Each State shall appoint, in such Manner as the Legislature thereof may direct, a Number of Electors, equal to the whole Number of Senators and Representatives to which the State may be entitled in the Congress: but no Senator or Representative, or Person holding an Office of Trust or Profit under the United States, shall be appointed an Elector.

[The Electors shall meet in their respective States, and vote by Ballot for two persons, of whom one at least shall not be an Inhabitant of the same State with themselves. And they shall make a List of all the Persons voted for, and of the Number of Votes for each; which List they shall sign and certify, and transmit sealed to the Seat of the Government of the United States, directed to the President of the Senate. The President of the Senate shall, in the Presence of the Senate and House of Representatives, open all the Certificates, and the Votes shall then be counted. The Person having the greatest Number of Votes shall be the President, if such Number be a Majority of the whole Number of Electors appointed; and if there be more than one who have such Majority, and have an equal Number of Votes, then the House of Representatives shall immediately choose by Ballot one of them for President; and if no Person have a Majority, then from the five highest on the List the said House shall in like Manner choose the President. But in choosing the President, the Votes shall be taken by States, the Representation from each State having one Vote; A quorum for this Purpose shall consist of a Member or Members from two-thirds of the States, and a Majority of all the States shall be necessary to a Choice. In every Case, after the Choice of the President, the Person having the greatest Number of Votes of the Electors shall be the Vice President. But if there should remain two or more who have equal Votes, the Senate shall choose from them by Ballot the Vice-President.] [7]

(3) The Congress may determine the Time of choosing the Electors, and the Day on which they shall give their Votes; which Day shall be the same throughout the United States.

(4) No person except a natural born Citizen, or a Citizen of the United States, at the time of the Adoption of this Constitution, shall be eligible to the Office of President; neither shall any Person be eligible to that Office who shall not have attained to the Age of thirty-five Years, and been fourteen Years a Resident within the United States.

[7] This paragraph was superseded in 1804 by the Twelfth Amendment.

(5) In case of the Removal of the President from Office, or of his Death, Resignation, or Inability to discharge the Powers and Duties of the said Office, the same shall devolve on the Vice President, and the Congress may by Law provide for the Case of Removal, Death, Resignation or Inability, both of the President and Vice President, declaring what Officer shall then act as President, and such Officer shall act accordingly, until the Disability be removed, or a President shall be elected.

(6) The President shall, at stated Times, receive for his Services, a Compensation, which shall neither be increased nor diminished during the Period for which he shall have been elected, and he shall not receive within that Period any other Emolument from the United States, or any of them.

(7) Before he enter on the Execution of his Office, he shall take the following Oath or Affirmation: — "I do solemnly swear (or affirm) that I will faithfully execute the Office of President of the United States, and will to the best of my Ability, preserve, protect and defend the Constitution of the United States."

SECTION 2. (1) The President shall be Commander in Chief of the Army and Navy of the United States, and of the Militia of the several States, when called into the actual Service of the United States; he may require the Opinion in writing, of the principal Officer in each of the executive Departments, upon any subject relating to the Duties of their respective Offices, and he shall have Power to Grant Reprieves and Pardons for Offenses against the United States, except in Cases of Impeachment.

(2) He shall have Power, by and with the Advice and Consent of the Senate, to make Treaties, provided two-thirds of the Senators present concur; and he shall nominate, and by and with the Advice and Consent of the Senate, shall appoint Ambassadors, other public Ministers and Consuls, Judges of the supreme Court, and all other Officers of the United States, whose Appointments are not herein otherwise provided for, and which shall be established by Law: but the Congress may by Law vest the Appointment of such inferior Officers, as they think proper, in the President alone, in the Courts of Law, or in the Heads of Departments.

(3) The President shall have Power to fill up all Vacancies that may happen during the Recess of the Senate, by granting Commissions which shall expire at the End of their next Session.

SECTION 3. He shall from time to time give to the Congress Information of the State of the Union, and recommend to their Consideration such Measures as he shall judge necessary and expedient; he may, on extraordinary Occasions, convene both Houses, or either of them, and in Case of Disagreement between them, with Respect to the Time of Adjournment, he may adjourn them to such Time as he shall think proper; he shall receive Ambassadors and other public Ministers; he shall take Care that the Laws be faithfully executed, and shall Commission all the Officers of the United States.

SECTION 4. The President, Vice President and all civil Officers of the United States, shall be removed from Office on Impeachment for, and Conviction of, Treason, Bribery, or other high Crimes and Misdemeanors.

Article III

SECTION 1. The judicial Power of the United States, shall be vested in one supreme Court, and in such inferior Courts as the Congress may from time to time ordain and establish. The Judges, both of the supreme and inferior Courts, shall hold their Offices during good Behavior, and shall, at stated Times, receive for their Services a Compensation which shall not be diminished during their Continuance in Office.

SECTION 2. (1) The judicial Power shall extend to all Cases, in Law and Equity, arising under this Constitution, the Laws of the United States, and Treaties made, or which shall be made, under their Authority; — to all Cases affecting Ambassadors, other public Ministers and Consuls; — to all Cases of admiralty and maritime Jurisdiction; — to Controversies to which the United States shall be a Party; — to Controversies between two or more States; — [between a State and Citizens of another State]; [8] — between Citizens of different States; — between Citizens of the same State claiming Lands under Grants of different States, and [between a State, or the Citizens thereof, and foreign States, Citizens or Subjects.] [9]

(2) In all Cases affecting Ambassadors, other public Ministers and Consuls, and those in which a State shall be Party, the supreme Court shall have original Jurisdiction. In all the other Cases before mentioned, the supreme Court shall have appellate Jurisdiction, both as to Law and Fact, with such Exceptions, and under such Regulations as the Congress shall make.

(3) The trial of all Crimes, except in Cases of Impeachment, shall be by Jury; and such Trial shall be held in the State where the said Crimes shall have been committed; but when not committed within any State, the Trial shall be at such Place or Places as the Congress may by Law have directed.

SECTION 3. (1) Treason against the United States, shall consist only in levying War against them, or in adhering to their Enemies, giving them Aid and Comfort. No Person shall be convicted of Treason unless on the Testimony of two Witnesses to the same overt Act, or on Confession in open Court.

(2) The Congress shall have power to declare the Punishment of Treason, but no Attainder of Treason shall work Corruption of Blood, or Forfeiture except during the Life of the Person attainted.

Article IV

SECTION 1. Full Faith and Credit shall be given in each State to the public Acts, Records, and judicial Proceedings of every other State. And the Congress may by general Laws prescribe the Manner in which such Acts, Records and Proceedings shall be proved, and the Effect thereof.

SECTION 2. (1) The Citizens of each State shall be entitled to all Privileges and Immunities of Citizens in the several States.

(2) A Person charged in any State with Treason, Felony, or other Crime, who shall flee from Justice, and be found in another State, shall on demand of the

---

[8] Restricted by the Eleventh Amendment.
[9] Restricted by the Eleventh Amendment.

executive Authority of the State from which he fled, be delivered up, to be removed to the State having Jurisdiction of the Crime.

(3) [No Person held to Service or Labor in one State, under the Laws thereof, escaping into another, shall, in Consequence of any Law or Regulation therein, be discharged from such Service or Labor, but shall be delivered up on Claim of the Party to whom such Service or Labor may be due.] [10]

SECTION 3. (1) New States may be admitted by the Congress into this Union; but no new State shall be formed or erected within the Jurisdiction of any other State; nor any State be formed by the Junction of two or more States, or parts of States, without the Consent of the Legislatures of the States concerned as well as of the Congress.

(2) The Congress shall have Power to dispose of and make all needful Rules and Regulations respecting the Territory or other Property belonging to the United States; and nothing in this Constitution shall be so construed as to Prejudice any Claims of the United States, or of any particular State.

SECTION 4. The United States shall guarantee to every State in this Union a Republican Form of Government, and shall protect each of them against Invasion; and on Application of the Legislature, or of the Executive (when the Legislature cannot be convened) against domestic Violence.

Article V

The Congress, whenever two-thirds of both Houses shall deem it necessary, shall propose Amendments to this Constitution, or, on the Application of the Legislatures of two-thirds of the several States, shall call a Convention for proposing Amendments, which, in either Case, shall be valid to all Intents and Purposes, as part of this Constitution, when ratified by the Legislatures of three-fourths of the several States, or by Conventions in three-fourths thereof, as the one or the other Mode of Ratification may be proposed by the Congress; Provided that no Amendment which may be made prior to the Year One thousand eight hundred and eight shall in any Manner affect the first and fourth Clauses in the Ninth Section of the first Article; and that no State, without its Consent, shall be deprived of its equal Suffrage in the Senate.

Article VI

(1) All Debts contracted and Engagements entered into, before the Adoption of this Constitution, shall be as valid against the United States under this Constitution, as under the Confederation.

(2) This Constitution, and the Laws of the United States which shall be made in Pursuance thereof; and all Treaties made, or which shall be made, under the Authority of the United States, shall be the supreme Law of the Land; and the Judges in every State shall be bound thereby, any Thing in the Constitution or Laws of any State to the Contrary notwithstanding.

(3) The Senators and Representatives before mentioned, and the Members of the several State Legislatures, and all executive and judicial Officers, both of

[10] This paragraph has been superseded by the Thirteenth Amendment.

the United States and of the several States, shall be bound by Oath or Affirmation, to support this Constitution; but no religious Test shall ever be required as a Qualification to any Office or public Trust under the United States.

Article VII

The Ratification of the Conventions of nine States, shall be sufficient for the Establishment of this Constitution between the States so ratifying the Same.

DONE in Convention by the Unanimous Consent of the States present the Seventeenth Day of September in the Year of our Lord one thousand seven hundred and Eighty seven and of the Independence of the United States of America the Twelfth. In Witness whereof We have hereunto subscribed our Names.

Go WASHINGTON
Presidt and deputy from Virginia

ARTICLES IN ADDITION TO, AND AMENDMENT OF, THE CONSTITUTION OF
THE UNITED STATES OF AMERICA, PROPOSED BY CONGRESS, AND RATIFIED
BY THE LEGISLATURES OF THE SEVERAL STATES, PURSUANT TO THE FIFTH
ARTICLE OF THE ORIGINAL CONSTITUTION.

Amendment I [11]

Congress shall make no law respecting an establishment of religion, or prohibiting the free exercise thereof; or abridging the freedom of speech, or of the press; or the right of the people peaceably to assemble, and to petition the Government for a redress of grievances.

Amendment II

A well regulated Militia, being necessary to the security of a free State, the right of the people to keep and bear Arms, shall not be infringed.

Amendment III

No Soldier shall, in time of peace be quartered in any house, without the consent of the Owner, nor in time of war, but in a manner to be prescribed by law.

Amendment IV

The right of the people to be secure in their persons, houses, papers, and effects, against unreasonable searches and seizures, shall not be violated, and no Warrants shall issue, but upon probable cause, supported by Oath or affirmation, and particularly describing the place to be searched, and the persons or things to be seized.

Amendment V

No person shall be held to answer for a capital, or otherwise infamous crime, unless on a presentment or indictment of a Grand Jury, except in cases arising in the land or naval forces, or in the Militia, when in actual service in time of

[11] The first ten amendments were adopted in 1791.

War or public danger; nor shall any person be subject for the same offence to be twice put in jeopardy of life or limb; nor shall be compelled in any criminal case to be a witness against himself, nor be deprived of life, liberty, or property, without due process of law; nor shall private property be taken for public use, without just compensation.

Amendment VI

In all criminal prosecutions, the accused shall enjoy the right to a speedy and public trial, by an impartial jury of the State and district wherein the crime shall have been committed, which district shall have been previously ascertained by law, and to be informed of the nature and cause of the accusation; to be confronted with the witnesses against him; to have compulsory process for obtaining witnesses in his favor, and to have the Assistance of Counsel for his defence.

Amendment VII

In suits at common law, where the value in controversy shall exceed twenty dollars, the right of trial by jury shall be preserved, and no fact tried by a jury, shall be otherwise reexamined in any Court of the United States, than according to the rules of the common law.

Amendment VIII

Excessive bail shall not be required, nor excessive fines imposed, nor cruel and unusual punishments inflicted.

Amendment IX

The enumeration in the Constitution, of certain rights, shall not be construed to deny or disparage others retained by the people.

Amendment X

The powers not delegated to the United States by the Constitution, nor prohibited by it to the States, are reserved to the States respectively, or to the people.

Amendment XI [12]

The Judicial power of the United States shall not be construed to extend to any suit in law or equity, commenced or prosecuted against one of the United States by Citizens of another State, or by Citizens or Subjects of any Foreign State.

Amendment XII [13]

The Electors shall meet in their respective states and vote by ballot for President and Vice-President, one of whom, at least, shall not be an inhabitant of the same state with themselves; they shall name in their ballots the person voted for as President, and in distinct ballots the person voted for as Vice-President, and they shall make distinct lists of all persons voted for as President, and of all persons voted for as Vice-President, and of the number of votes for each, which lists they shall sign and certify, and transmit sealed to the seat of

[12] Adopted in 1798.
[13] Adopted in 1804.

the government of the United States, directed to the President of the Senate; — The President of the Senate shall, in presence of the Senate and House of Representatives, open all the certificates and the votes shall then be counted; — The person having the greatest number of votes for President, shall be the President, if such number be a majority of the whole number of Electors appointed; and if no person have such majority, then from the persons having the highest numbers not exceeding three on the list of those voted for as President, the House of Representatives shall choose immediately, by ballot, the President. But in choosing the President, the votes shall be taken by states, the representation from each state having one vote; a quorum for this purpose shall consist of a member or members from two-thirds of the states, and a majority of all the states shall be necessary to a choice. [And if the House of Representatives shall not choose a President whenever the right of choice shall devolve upon them, before the fourth day of March next following, then the Vice-President shall act as President, as in the case of the death or other constitutional disability of the President.] [14] — The person having the greatest number of votes as Vice-President, shall be the Vice-President, if such number be a majority of the whole number of Electors appointed, and if no person have a majority, then from the two highest numbers on the list, the Senate shall choose the Vice-President; a quorum for the purpose shall consist of two-thirds of the whole number of Senators, and a majority of the whole number shall be necessary to a choice. But no person constitutionally ineligible to the office of President shall be eligible to that of Vice-President of the United States.

Amendment XIII [15]

SECTION 1. Neither slavery nor involuntary servitude, except as a punishment for crime whereof the party shall have been duly convicted, shall exist within the United States, or any place subject to their jurisdiction.

SECTION 2. Congress shall have power to enforce this article by appropriate legislation.

Amendment XIV [16]

SECTION 1. All persons born or naturalized in the United States, and subject to the jurisdiction thereof, are citizens of the United States and of the State wherein they reside. No state shall make or enforce any law which shall abridge the privileges or immunities of citizens of the United States; nor shall any State deprive any person of life, liberty, or property, without due process of law; nor deny to any person within its jurisdiction the equal protection of the laws.

SECTION 2. Representatives shall be apportioned among the several States according to their respective numbers, counting the whole number of persons in each State, excluding Indians not taxed. But when the right to vote at any election for the choice of electors for President and Vice-President of the United States, Representatives in Congress, the Executive and Judicial officers of a State, or the members of the Legislature thereof, is denied to any of the male inhabitants of such State, being twenty-one years of age, and citizens of the

[14] Superseded by the Twentieth Amendment, Section 3.
[15] Adopted in 1865.
[16] Adopted in 1868.

United States, or in any way abridged, except for participation in rebellion, or other crime, the basis of representation therein shall be reduced in the proportion which the number of such male citizens shall bear to the whole number of male citizens twenty-one years of age in such State.

SECTION 3. No person shall be a Senator or Representative in Congress, or elector of President and Vice-President, or hold any office, civil or military, under the United States, or under any State, who, having previously taken an oath, as a member of Congress, or as an officer of the United States, or as a member of any State legislature, or as an executive or judicial officer of any State, to support the Constitution of the United States, shall have engaged in insurrection or rebellion against the same, or given aid or comfort to the enemies thereof. But Congress may by a vote of two-thirds of each House, remove such disability.

SECTION 4. The validity of the public debt of the United States, authorized by law, including debts incurred for payment of pensions and bounties for services in suppressing insurrection or rebellion, shall not be questioned. But neither the United States nor any State shall assume or pay any debt or obligation incurred in aid of insurrection or rebellion against the United States, or any claim for the loss or emancipation of any slave; but all such debts, obligations and claims shall be held illegal and void.

SECTION 5. The Congress shall have power to enforce, by appropriate legislation, the provisions of this article.

Amendment XV [17]

SECTION 1. The right of citizens of the United States to vote shall not be denied or abridged by the United States or by any State on account of race, color, or previous condition of servitude —

SECTION 2. The Congress shall have power to enforce this article by appropriate legislation.

Amendment XVI [18]

The Congress shall have power to lay and collect taxes on incomes, from whatever source derived, without apportionment among the several States, and without regard to any census or enumeration.

Amendment XVII [19]

The Senate of the United States shall be composed of two Senators from each State, elected by the people thereof, for six years; and each Senator shall have one vote. The electors in each State shall have the qualifications requisite for electors of the most numerous branch of the State legislatures.

When vacancies happen in the representation of any State in the Senate, the executive authority of such State shall issue writs of election to fill such vacancies: *Provided,* That the legislature of any State may empower the executive thereof to make temporary appointments until the people fill the vacancies by election as the legislature may direct.

[17] Adopted in 1870.
[18] Adopted in 1913.
[19] Adopted in 1913.

This amendment shall not be so construed as to affect the election or term of any Senator chosen before it becomes valid as part of the Constitution.

Amendment XVIII [20]

SECTION 1. After one year from the ratification of this article the manufacture, sale, or transportation of intoxicating liquors within, the importation thereof into, or the exportation thereof from the United States and all territory subject to the jurisdiction thereof for beverage purposes is hereby prohibited.

SECTION 2. The Congress and the several States shall have concurrent power to enforce this article by appropriate legislation.

SECTION 3. This article shall be inoperative unless it shall have been ratified as an amendment to the Constitution by the legislatures of the several States, as provided in the Constitution, within seven years from the date of the submission hereof to the States by the Congress.

Amendment XIX [21]

The right of citizens of the United States to vote shall not be denied or abridged by the United States or by any State on account of sex.

Congress shall have power to enforce this article by appropriate legislation.

Amendment XX [22]

SECTION 1. The terms of the President and Vice President shall end at noon on the 20th day of January, and the terms of Senators and Representatives at noon on the 3d day of January, of the years in which such terms would have ended if this article had not been ratified; and the terms of their successors shall then begin.

SECTION 2. The Congress shall assemble at least once in every year, and such meeting shall begin at noon on the 3d day of January, unless they shall by law appoint a different day.

SECTION 3. If, at the time fixed for the beginning of the term of the President, the President elect shall have died, the Vice President elect shall become President. If a President shall not have been chosen before the time fixed for the beginning of his term, or if the President elect shall have failed to qualify, then the Vice President elect shall act as President until a President shall have qualified; and the Congress may by law provide for the case wherein neither a President elect nor a Vice President elect shall have qualified, declaring who shall then act as President, or the manner in which one who is to act shall be selected, and such person shall act accordingly until a President or Vice President shall have qualified.

SECTION 4. The Congress may by law provide for the case of the death of any of the persons from whom the House of Representatives may choose a President whenever the right of choice shall have devolved upon them, and for the case of the death of any of the persons from whom the Senate may choose a Vice President whenever the right of choice shall have devolved upon them.

[20] Adopted in 1919. Repealed by Section 1 of the Twenty-first Amendment.
[21] Adopted in 1920.
[22] Adopted in 1933.

SECTION 5. Sections 1 and 2 shall take effect on the 15th day of October following the ratification of this article.

SECTION 6. This article shall be inoperative unless it shall have been ratified as an amendment to the Constitution by the legislatures of three-fourths of the several States within seven years from the date of its submission.

Amendment XXI [23]

SECTION 1. The eighteenth article of amendment to the Constitution of the United States is hereby repealed.

SECTION 2. The transportation or importation into any State, Territory, or possession of the United States for delivery or use therein of intoxicating liquors, in violation of the laws thereof, is hereby prohibited.

SECTION 3. This article shall be inoperative unless it shall have been ratified as an amendment to the Constitution by conventions in the several States, as provided in the Constitution, within seven years from the date of the submission hereof to the States by the Congress.

Amendment XXII [24]

SECTION 1. No person shall be elected to the office of the President more than twice, and no person who has held the office of President, or acted as President, for more than two years of a term to which some other person was elected President shall be elected to the office of the President more than once. But this Article shall not apply to any person holding the office of President when this Article was proposed by the Congress, and shall not prevent any person who may be holding the office of President, or acting as President, during the term within which this Article becomes operative from holding the office of President or acting as President during the remainder of such term.

SECTION 2. This article shall be inoperative unless it shall have been ratified as an amendment to the Constitution by the legislatures of three-fourths of the several States within seven years from the date of its submission to the States by the Congress.

Amendment XXIII [25]

SECTION 1. The District constituting the seat of Government of the United States shall appoint in such manner as the Congress may direct:

A number of electors of President and Vice President equal to the whole number of Senators and Representatives in Congress to which the District would be entitled if it were a State, but in no event more than the least populous State; they shall be in addition to those appointed by the States, but they shall be considered, for the purposes of the election of President and Vice President, to be electors appointed by a State; and they shall meet in the District and perform such duties as provided by the twelfth article of amendment.

SECTION 2. The Congress shall have power to enforce this article by appropriate legislation.

[23] Adopted in 1933.
[24] Adopted in 1951.
[25] Adopted in 1961.

Amendment XXIV [26]

SECTION 1. The right of citizens of the United States to vote in any primary or other election for President or Vice President, for electors for President or Vice President, or for Senator or Representative in Congress, shall not be denied or abridged by the United States or any state by reasons of failure to pay any poll tax or other tax.

SECTION 2. The Congress shall have power to enforce this article by appropriate legislation.

Amendment XXV [27]

SECTION 1. In case of the removal of the President from office or of his death or resignation, the Vice President shall become President.

SECTION 2. Whenever there is a vacancy in the office of the Vice President, the President shall nominate a Vice President who shall take office upon confirmation by a majority vote of both Houses of Congress.

SECTION 3. Whenever the President transmits to the President pro tempore of the Senate and the Speaker of the House of Representatives his written declaration that he is unable to discharge the powers and duties of his office, and until he transmits to them a written declaration to the contrary, such powers and duties shall be discharged by the Vice President as Acting President.

SECTION 4. Whenever the Vice President and a majority of either the principal officers of the executive departments or of such other body as Congress may by law provide, transmit to the President pro tempore of the Senate and the Speaker of the House of Representatives their written declaration that the President is unable to discharge the powers and duties of his office, the Vice President shall immediately assume the powers and duties of the office as Acting President.

Thereafter, when the President transmits to the President pro tempore of the Senate and the Speaker of the House of Representatives his written declaration that no inability exists, he shall resume the powers and duties of his office unless the Vice President and a majority of either the principal officers of the executive departments or of such other body as Congress may by law provide, transmit within four days to the President pro tempore of the Senate and the Speaker of the House of Representatives their written declaration that the President is unable to discharge the powers and duties of his office. Thereupon Congress shall decide the issue, assembling within forty-eight hours for that purpose if not in session. If the Congress, within twenty-one days after receipt of the latter written declaration, or, if Congress is not in session, within twenty-one days after Congress is required to assemble, determines by two-thirds vote of both Houses that the President is unable to discharge the powers and duties of his office, the Vice President shall continue to discharge the same as Acting President; otherwise, the President shall resume the powers and duties of his office.

[26] Adopted in 1964.
[27] Adopted in 1967.

Index

477